FREEDOM

FREEDOM

VOLUME I:
FREEDOM IN THE MAKING
OF WESTERN CULTURE

ORLANDO
PATTERSON

BasicBooks
A Division of HarperCollins*Publishers*

Library of Congress Cataloging-in-Publication Data
Patterson, Orlando, 1940–
    Freedom / Orlando Patterson.
      p. cm.
    Includes bibliographical references and index.
    Contents: v. 1. Freedom in the making of western culture.
    ISBN 0-465-02535-8 (vol. 1)
    1. Liberty. I. Title.
JC585.P32 1991
323.44--dc20   90-55593
                                                         CIP

For the Unfree of the World

Greeks were born to rule barbarians, Mother, not barbarians
To rule Greeks. They are slaves by nature; we have freedom
in our blood.

—Euripides, *Iphigenia in Aulis*, 1400–1

Suffer us to go back whence we came; suffer us to be freed at last
from these fetters that are fastened to us and weigh us down.

—Epictetus, *Discourses*, 1.IX

For freedom Christ has set us free; stand fast therefore, and do not
submit again to a yoke of slavery.

—*Galatians*, 5.1

CONTENTS

Preface   ix
Introduction: The Meaning of Freedom   1

Part One
The Stillbirth of Freedom in the Non-Western World

1 Primitive Beginnings   9
2 For the Creation of Eyes: Why Freedom Failed in the
  Non-Western World   20

Part Two
The Greek Construction of Freedom

3 The Greek Origins of Freedom   47
4 The Emergence of Slave Society and Civic Freedom   64
5 The Persian Wars and the Creation of Organic
  (Sovereignal) Freedom   82
6 Slavery, Empire, and the Periclean Fusion   95
7 A Woman's Song: The Female Force and the Ideology
  of Freedom in Greek Tragedy and Society   106
8 Fission and Diffusion: Class and the Elements
  of Freedom in the Late Fifth Century and Beyond   133
9 The Outer Intellectual Response   146

10 The Turn to Inner Freedom   165
11 The Intellectual Response in the Hellenistic and
     Early Roman World   181

Part Three
Rome and the Universalization of Freedom

12 Freedom and Class Conflict in Republican Rome   203
13 The Triumph of the Roman Freedman: Personal Liberty
     among the Urban Masses of the Early Empire   227
14 The Augustan Compromise: Sovereignal Freedom
     in Defense of Personal Liberty   258
15 Freedom, Stoicism, and the Roman Mind   264

Part Four
Christianity and the Institutionalization of Freedom

16 Jesus and the Jesus Movement   293
17 Between Jesus and Paul   304
18 Paul and His World: A Community of Urban Freedmen   316
19 Paul and the Freedom of Mankind   325

Part Five
The Medieval Reconstruction of Freedom

20 Freedom and Servitude in the Middle Ages   347
21 Medieval Renditions of the Chord of Freedom   363
22 Freedom in the Religious and Secular Thought
     of the Middle Ages   376

Coda   402
Notes   407
Index   471

PREFACE

No one would deny that today freedom stands unchallenged as the supreme value of the Western world. Philosophers debate its nature and meaning endlessly; it is the catchword of every politician, the secular gospel of our economic, "free enterprise" system, and the foundation of all our cultural activities. It is also the central value of Christianity: being redeemed, being freed by, and in, Christ, is the ultimate goal of all Christians. It is the one value that many people seem prepared to die for, certainly by their words, and often by their actions. During the long nightmare of the Cold War, leaders of the West had even divided the world into two great camps, the free world and the unfree, and repeatedly declared, with dreadful sincerity, that they were prepared to risk a nuclear holocaust in order to defend this sacred ideal we call freedom.

Today we are living through another explosive diffusion of this ideal. The extraordinary developments in Eastern Europe herald only the latest and most dramatic phase of the commitment of peoples all over the world to freedom. Since the Second World War, scores of countries all over the Third World and the Far East have embraced the value and sometimes lived by it. There is now hardly a country whose leaders, however dubiously, do not claim that they are pursuing the ideal. The very hypocrisy and absurdity of many of these claims attest to the enormous power of this ideal. People may sin against freedom, but no one dares deny its virtue.

This book examines how freedom became such a powerful value, and how such an extraordinary commitment to it came about. To those who hold that freedom is a natural concept, something that all human beings, simply by being human, would naturally want, my objective must seem strange. Yet, there is nothing at all self-evident in the idea or, more properly, the high esteem in which we in the West hold freedom. For most of human history, and for nearly all of the non-Western world prior to Western contact, freedom was, and for many still remains, anything but an obvious or desirable goal. Other values and ideals were, or are, of far greater importance to them—values such as the pursuit of glory, honor, and power for oneself or one's family and clan, nationalism and imperial grandeur, militarism and valor in warfare, filial piety, the harmony of heaven and earth, the spreading of the "true faith," nirvana, hedonism, altruism, justice, equality, material progress—the list is endless. But almost never, outside the context of Western culture and its influence, has it included freedom.

Indeed, non-Western peoples have thought so little about freedom that most human languages did not even possess a word for the concept before contact with the West. Japan is typical. The current Japanese word for freedom only acquired this meaning during the nineteenth century with the opening of the country to the West. Even then, however, Meiji translators had great difficulty finding an equivalent term to denote this weird Western concept. Significantly, the word they chose to designate the concept of freedom, *jiyu*, previously had as its primary meaning "licentiousness." Much the same holds for Korea, where the term—borrowed from the Chinese—was used for the first time in the nineteenth century under linguistic pressure from Western intruders. Even where an indigenous, pre-Western term roughly equivalent to some aspect of our notion of freedom existed, as in China, it was typically used in the pejorative sense of license, very occasionally in the slightly less negative sense of existing by oneself (hardly a virtue in China), and rarely in the vaguely positive aesthetic or Confucian sense of avoidance of egotistical evils. In general, the term was hardly used. Even so, China was exceptional among non-Western societies in recognizing a need at all for this odd, seemingly unnecessary concept.

So strong is our commitment to this value, however, and so insistent our claim that this commitment is natural, that we have assumed that something is wrong with the rest of the world and with the majority of human history during which no one ever thought it necessary to express and cherish freedom as an ideal. Our political scientists, oblivious to the way we have inverted history and social reality, repeatedly write learned treatises explaining why the rest of the world and history have not embraced freedom.

As a result of the inverted parochialism of our civilization, we have posed the problem the wrong way around. Like Aristophanes' frogs we have not only assumed that it is natural for all creatures to croak, but are puzzled when others are not gladdened by our sound. In fact, it is not the rest of the world that needs explaining for its lack of commitment to freedom, and all works of social science and history that attempt to do so are hopelessly misguided; rather it is the West that must be scrutinized and explained for its peculiar commitment to this value.

But once we pose the problem in this way, we are immediately faced with an extraordinary intellectual paradox. Western civilization, by taking its most important ideal and core value for granted, has failed to ask the most important question about it, namely, How and why did freedom emerge, develop, and become institutionalized as our civilization's preeminent ideal? Since valuing freedom is not a part of the human condition, not something we are born with, we must inquire not only into the reasons for the West's extraordinary devotion to it but into the circumstances under which it was first invented or socially constructed.

From what has been said, it should already be clear that this book is not another history of the idea of freedom; and most certainly it is not a philosophical study of what it is, or should be. Rather, it is a historical sociology of our most important cultural value. My aim is to understand how ordinary and influential persons socially constructed freedom as a value, and why they remained so profoundly committed to it. In the course of this inquiry I naturally examine what the value meant to them. Because the philosophical mind has been so attuned to the value, however, it is necessary to understand what philosophers have had to say on the subject, but only insofar as their views have influenced the valorization, understanding, and institutionalization of the value.

To be more specific, this work attempts to answer four questions. First, how and why was freedom initially constructed as a social value? Second, how and why, after having been invented, did it emerge as the supreme value distinct from any number of other important values? Third, why did this rise to cultural supremacy happen only in the Western world, and for so many centuries remain confined to this civilization? Finally, having achieved preeminence, what forces maintained its status as the core value of Western civilization throughout the course of its history?

A few important attempts have been made to answer the first and second of these questions, but all such efforts have left fundamental questions unanswered. I will return to these works shortly. No extant work has ever satisfactorily answered the third and fourth questions. There are remarkably few general histories of freedom, and those few amount merely to a record of the ideal in different periods without any serious attempt to explain why the commitment persisted throughout the millennia of Western history. When we have explained how a cultural pattern emerged, we still have to account for the reasons for its persistence. A given value complex or behavioral pattern emerges as a result of a specific configuration of historical factors. Once present, however, additional forces account for its institutionalization, and these, in turn, vary from one period to the next. The earlier a core value emerged, the greater the need to explain its continuity since it is usually the case that human values change over time. The most stunning characteristic of the history of freedom is its continuity. Freedom, we will see, emerged as a supreme value over the course of the sixth and fifth centuries B.C., at the very dawn of Western civilization. Typically, historians and political scientists who attempt to explain freedom address the problem of origins in ancient Greece, then make a spectacular leap to the sixteenth and seventeenth centuries, where the story is picked up again with the rise of the modern world. A vast chasm of continuity, two millennia wide, is simply left unexplained. Such a procedure is not simply unsatisfactory; it is absurd.

Most serious students of the history of freedom, while recognizing the problem, have ultimately evaded its demands, and instead have concentrated on specific periods in the development of freedom. The great majority of works have concentrated on the modern history of the subject; the historiography is enormous, dealing with both the modern West in general and specific countries. There is thus a serious limit to the explanatory force of nearly all of these works: they either neglect the previous history of freedom, or, worse, they assume that the ancient, and especially the medieval, experience of freedom has little or nothing to do with its modern history. Thus, in his "Two Concepts of Liberty," possibly the most widely read modern essay on the subject, Isaiah Berlin claims that personal liberty "is comparatively modern. There seems to be scarcely any discussion of individual liberty as a conscious political ideal (as opposed to its actual practice) in the ancient world."

Nothing could be further from the truth. Indeed, one of my major objectives will be to show that in all respects our modern conceptions of, and intense commitment to, freedom were fully established in the ancient world, and that a pattern of continuity links the ancient to the modern expression and experience of the value. There has been no lacuna in the Western idealization of freedom, certainly not in the medieval world where, contrary to the common view, commitment to the ideal, including the notion of negative, personal freedom, was as great as it had been in the ancient past and as it is today. No understanding of the modern history of freedom is possible without a complete appreciation of the fact that freedom has been the core value of Western culture *throughout* its history. Attempting to understand the nature and history of freedom while neglecting its premodern past is as absurd as an attempt to understand Christianity in the absence of any knowledge of Christ, Paul, the Apostles, or the early and medieval history of the religion.

The basic argument of this work is that freedom was generated from the experience of slavery. People came to value freedom, to construct it as a powerful shared vision of life, as a result of their experience of, and response to, slavery or its recombinant form, serfdom, in their roles as masters, slaves, and nonslaves. This basic insight has long been recognized by philosophers, though usually only in passing, and by several important scholars. The pathbreaking comparative work of David Brion Davis, and later that of his Yale colleague, Edmund Morgan, on early Virginia, demonstrated the enormous importance of slavery in the social and intellectual reconstruction and reconfiguration of freedom in the *modern* West. In *The Problem of Slavery in Western Culture*, Davis's problem was to explain why, after taking slavery for granted since the beginning of its history, the West, in a remarkably short period of time during the late eighteenth century, redefined slavery as the greatest of evils, a moral and socioeconomic scourge that had to be exterminated. In this work and later works, he brilliantly demonstrated the latent ideological significance of the antislavery movement: the promotion of personal liberty, not the emancipation of black slaves, was the powerful cultural subtext of the movement.

Originally, the problem I had set out to explore was the sociohistorical significance of that taken-for-granted tradition of slavery in the West. Armed with the weapons of the historical sociologist, I had gone in search of a man-killing wolf called slavery; to my dismay I kept finding the tracks of a lamb called freedom. A lamb that stared back at me, on our first furtive encounters in the foothills of the Western past, with strange, uninnocent eyes. Was I to believe that slavery was a lamb in wolf's clothing? Not with my past. And so I changed my quarry. Finding the sociohistorical roots of freedom, understanding its nature in time and context, became my goal, and remained so for these past eight years. What I found is reported in this work.

Almost every historian of ancient Greece has had something to say about the origins and development of some aspect of freedom, and there are numerous specialist works on the subject, to many of which I am greatly indebted. Nearly all of these works, however, confine themselves to only one aspect of the rise of freedom in ancient Greece (by which is usually meant Athens), namely, democracy, and are concerned with a narration, or analysis, of *how* the institutions of the democratic city-state developed. The remarkable characteristic of ancient Athens, however, is that all the fundamental elements of secular freedom that were to dominate the Western consciousness developed simultaneously there over the course of the sixth and fifth centuries B.C. Only three students of the subject have emphasized the role of slavery in explaining both how and *why* this remarkable social construction took place when and where it did. They are the late Anglo-American Cambridge scholar Sir Moses Finley; the German historian of ancient thought Max Pohlenz; and the Swiss-American philologist and historian of ancient Greece and Rome Kurt Raaflaub, presently at Brown University.

Of the three, Finley's ideas are the best known, and the most misunderstood. While Finley emphasized the fact that there was an important *association* between slavery and freedom in all its aspects in ancient Athens, his views on the *genetic and causal* historical relationship between the two ran diametrically opposite to those of Pohlenz and Raaflaub and of my own. His argument ran as follows: first, freedom emerged as a result of a peculiar configuration of historical circumstances in the late seventh and early sixth centuries B.C.; this then stimulated the unprecedented rise of large-scale slavery; and this, in turn, became the socioeconomic foundation or "basis" for the civilization in which classical democracy flourished. Thus, while large-scale slavery was a structural precondition for classical freedom, it was the latter that historically triggered the former. He explicitly rejected the thesis that is central to this work, and to that of Pohlenz and Raaflaub: that the very idea and valuation of freedom was generated by the existence and growth of slavery.

We are left, then, with Pohlenz and Raaflaub as the only two scholars who have previously explored the role of slavery as the decisive factor explaining the social invention and nature of freedom in ancient Athens. I am indebted to these two scholars, especially Pohlenz, whose work, ironically, is almost never cited by Anglo-American scholars concerned with the origins of freedom. While I have examined the primary materials myself and, as will be seen, drawn radically different conclusions from theirs on many important aspects of the subject, their insights and powerful philological analyses were indispensable to me. Indeed, while I arrived independently at the hypothesis that it was slavery that generated freedom in the course of my earlier studies of slavery, I doubt that I would have had the nerve to enter the academic field of the ancient sources had I not the assurance that these two distinguished classicists were already "on my side," so to speak.

Nonetheless, it is important to indicate at the outset the two most critical respects in which I differ from these and all previous scholars who have explored the problem of the origins of freedom in the ancient world. First, there is my wholly unanticipated discovery that women played a decisive role in the Western social invention of *personal* freedom. I now find it extraordinary that this fact had not been previously established. What is more, women continued to play a critical role in the history of this element of freedom, continuously reconstructing a distinctively feminine version of the value after men had embraced and refigured it in its now more familiar negative form.

My second major departure from Pohlenz, Raaflaub, and others who emphasize the role of slavery in the construction of Greek freedom originated in unease with one aspect of their comparative methodology. If it is indeed true that freedom emerged in the ancient West as a direct result of the social dialectics of slavery, then one fundamental question has been left begging. We know that slavery was a nearly universal institution, and was certainly well established in the advanced civilizations that long preceded the rise of classical Greece. Why, then, did freedom not emerge as a major core value in these societies? Clearly, a heavy burden of negative proof rests on all who argue this thesis. An analysis of the Greek data is obviously *necessary* to make the case for the Greek origins of the value, but it cannot be *sufficient* even for the Greek case. We are required to examine the non-Greek experience of slavery in order to show why, in spite of the existence of slavery, freedom did not emerge in these societies, especially those in the ancient Near East which were not only as advanced as the ancient Greek city-states but, as Martin Bernal has recently reminded us in *Black Athena*, the source of many of Greece's most important innovations. Hence, the work opens with an attempt to answer just this question. It is, I believe, the first attempt to examine the failure, or "stillbirth," of freedom in the non-Greek world, with a view to demonstrating the sufficiency of the argument that freedom, as a core value, was first socially constructed in ancient Athens.

Having explained the origins and rise to prominence of the value of freedom in the Greek world, I next had to show how it became not simply a Greek but a Western-wide value. Here the Roman world was the decisive factor. My argument is not a simple diffusionist one. That Greece greatly influenced later Western history no one doubts; what is rarely explained is how it did so, and why. It is not enough simply to point to contact, or even a willingness on the part of the Romans to embrace Greek ideas and attitudes. We know, in fact, that there were many things the Greeks cherished that the Romans either neglected or despised. The Romans adopted later Greek comedy but neglected tragic drama; they admired Greek philosophy, but Latin scholarship never produced an original philosopher. We will see that freedom triumphed in the Roman world both because there was a massive independent redevelopment of the condition that originally generated freedom—large-scale slavery—and because of the cultural influence of Greek views on freedom. Thus, there was both continuity and reconstruction; diffusion as well as adaptation and refiguration. Because Rome dominated the Western world, freedom was spread to all corners of that world, in both the elite and the personal version embraced and celebrated by the urban masses of Rome.

It was in imperial Rome, too, that the third great development in the history of freedom took place: the rise of Christianity. The same class of people who dominated the Roman economy and popular culture and made of freedom a secular mass value were the ones who transformed the rustic Jewish sect into a world religion. In the process, they refashioned the original religion of Jesus into their own image, making it the first, and only, world religion that placed freedom—spiritual freedom, redemption—at the very center of its theology. In this way, freedom was to be enshrined on the consciousness of all Western peoples; wherever Christianity took root, it garnered converts not only to salvation in Christ but to the ideal of freedom. As long as Christianity survived, so, at least in spiritual form, would the deep Western commitment to the ideal of freedom.

In this respect, the significance of the Middle Ages lies in the fact that it was dominated not only by the religion of freedom but by the spread first of slavery, then of the recombinant slavery we call serfdom, to nearly all corners of Europe. In medieval slavery and serfdom we trace, once again, the reconstruction of the chord of freedom even as it resounded from the overarching spiritual culture of the civilization. By the end of the Middle Ages, Europe had been not only formed as a cultural unity but, in the process of its creation, infused, body and soul, with the value of freedom. Here we end our story. The modern history of freedom, to be taken up in a later, shorter work, is merely a long series of footnotes to the great civilizational text that was already complete, and almost fully edited, by the end of the Middle Ages.

* * *

One incurs many debts writing a book. I must single out three scholars who were of great help. First, I wish to thank my dear friend Professor Heinz Heinen, chair of the Department of Ancient History at the University of Trier in West Germany. As my host on two visits to his department, one of them sponsored by the Mainz Academy of Science and Literature, he went well beyond the call of duty in his weekly one-on-one seminars with me, during which I learned a great deal about both the ancient world and medieval Germany, as well as gaining the insider's approach to their study.

Professor Valerie Warrior very carefully scrutinized an earlier version of the chapters dealing with ancient Greece and Rome, graciously lending me all the skills of her philological training and the wisdom of her scholarship on ancient Greece and Rome. She alone knows the number of academic pitfalls and mines I was gently steered away from in my often too eager efforts to make sociological sense of the ancient texts. Finally, I am extremely indebted to my colleague Professor Thomas Bisson, who kindly read an earlier version of the chapters dealing with the Middle Ages. His cogent criticisms had me returning to the stacks, leading to a better understanding of the world he knows so well. Needless to say, I am solely responsible for the final version of this work, which was not seen in its entirety by any of the scholars before going to press. Any error of a factual or bibliographic nature is entirely my own; and the same goes for whatever is lacking in the soundness of the argument.

The basic premise of this work was first given a public hearing at the Legal Theory Workshop of Yale University in the fall of 1983. That was a bracing, wonderful experience for me. One cannot imagine a better way to test the viability of one's ideas than to expose them to two long hours of nonstop questioning from some of the nation's finest minds in legal, historical, and social analyses. Having survived that gauntlet, I decided that the book I had in mind was well worth writing.

During the 1988–89 academic year, I was a Phi Beta Kappa visiting professor, and had the opportunity to present earlier versions of this work to historians, classicists, and sociologists at universities around the country. I received many useful criticisms and suggestions from the many fine scholars I met on these visits. I want to express special thanks to the classicists, historians, and sociologists at the University of California, Santa Cruz, Rice University, Kalamazoo College, Middlebury College, and Union College in New York.

My wife, Dr. Nerys Wyn Patterson of the Department of Celtic Languages and Literatures at Harvard, taught me not only all I ever need to know about slavery, kinship, clientship, and the position of women in medieval Ireland and Britain, but a good deal about Dark Age Europe generally. As a fellow historical sociologist, she patiently listened to, and offered valuable criticisms of, my ideas at both their half-baked and fully developed stages.

Professor Eiko Ikegami, now of Yale University, generously translated an important Japanese work on freedom for me, and was very helpful in my attempt to understand what did not happen in Japan; and Drs. Sook-Jong Lee and Hou-keun Song, then graduate students in my department, kindly assisted me in my work on premodern Korea and China. Finally, I wish to thank Ms. Sandra Leonard and Ms. Kara Blackman for their skillful help in preparing various versions of the manuscript.

FREEDOM

INTRODUCTION:

The Meaning of Freedom

Freedom, like love and beauty, is one of those values better experienced than defined. On the verge of waging one of the bloodiest civil wars of all time in its defense, Abraham Lincoln complained that he knew of no good definition of freedom. The situation is hardly different today, in spite of a vast literature on the subject. As Lawrence Crocker recently observed, "While there is overwhelming agreement on the value of liberty . . . there is a great deal of disagreement on what liberty is," and it is "this fact that explains how it is possible for the most violently opposed of political parties to pay homage to the 'same' ideal."[1] One is tempted to pronounce the effort futile, even at times to support the skeptical view that nothing useful can ever come of rational reflection on the subject.[2] Yet, as Leonard Krieger remarked, if one plans to explore the subject, "the initial problem is posed by the necessity of finding a working definition of essential terms that will function as a criterion of relevance without stacking the cards a priori."[3] This introduction aims at such a working definition, inevitably anticipating issues to be discussed at greater length in later chapters.

Common usage offers little help. Nearly everyone in the Western world worships freedom and will declare herself willing to die for it. Like all intensely held beliefs, it is assumed to be so self-evident that there is no need for explicitness. Clarity on something so charged and sacrosanct might even by undesirable, for the virtue of a vague idea is that everyone can safely read his or her own meaning into it.

We have, however, a strong tendency in Western culture to rationalize our values, to explain them, and to demonstrate their internal coherence. The more important the value, the greater the effort. We even write treatises on love. Almost from the moment freedom first entered the stream of Western history, a struggle began to redefine it philosophically, to embrace and refine it apart from its vulgar base, and to render it coherent and acceptable to thinking people and their audience. The result has been not one but two interacting histories of freedom. There is the history of freedom as ordinary men and women have understood it—vague, to be sure, yet intensely held, a value learned in struggle, fear, and hope. Paralleling this has been the history of people's efforts to define "true freedom," to arrive at the essence of what freedom really is, if only we thought about it logically, or moralized correctly. Invariably, freedom came to be defined as what the thinker in question most favored, whether it was truth, god, the world soul, property, or communism. Indeed, very soon after it was fully formed in classical Greece, freedom, as we will see, was being defined as the very opposite of what any sane, ordinary person on the streets of classical Athens, or in the market, assembly, or palaestra, would have imagined it to be.

No other value or ideal in the West carries such a heavy intellectual burden—one impossible to discard or neglect. The very obsession of the philosophical mind with the idea is itself the best index of its general importance. And this involvement, in turn, reinforced the common idealization of the value. Further, it was not long before ratiocination on the subject came to influence how ordinary people thought and felt about freedom. This is why, in spite of our sympathy for Robert MacIver's complaint that, with respect to liberty, "the greatest sinners against reason have been the reasoners, the philosophers, and high priests,"[4] we must nonetheless consider the views of these intellectual sinners.

This philosophical concern has a good and a bad side. It means that we have a record of how the idea fared through the ages, not only among philosophers but among the generality of ordinary women and men. But in this very advantage we face our biggest problem: that most of what we know about the common person's view of the subject comes from writers who despised what ordinary people thought about it. Our best evidence that freedom had become a mass value in late-fifth-century Greece, for example, is the relentless condemnation of popular conceptions of the value by the Greek elite thinkers.[5]

However, as we shall see, this dialectic between the thought of ordinary men and women and that of the intellectual elite was itself the outcome of a more basic interplay of thought and social action. In answering the question of how freedom became a value to the ordinary person in the first place, we arrive at this more fundamental process. I will show, in later chapters, that freedom was socially constructed—not discovered, for it was an invented value, however "startling" this might seem to some[6]—in a specific pair of struggles generated by slavery. One of these inhered in the master-slave relationship itself; the other arose from the confrontation between slaveholders and slaves, on the one hand, and slaveholders and other free persons, on the other.

But all that is to come. We must still say, in a preliminary way, what freedom is, without unduly "stacking the card a priori." Freedom, I will show, is a tripartite value. Behind the term's numerous shades of meaning are three ideas, closely related historically, sociologically, and conceptually, which may be called personal, sovereignal, and civic freedoms. The musical metaphor of a chordal triad is very useful in understanding the term and its constituent elements or notes, and I will be employing it frequently in this work. We think in chordal terms when we speak generally of "our freedom," meaning a gestalt, a harmonious whole which is its own special value. This is the main reason why social scientists, especially opinion pollsters, have such a devil of a time getting the public meaning of freedom statistically right. Within the context of the chord, however, we may want to emphasize one or another element of our expression. Further, the different elements also exist independently. People can, and often do, play them separately, and this also makes for easier observation and analysis.

Personal freedom, at its most elementary, gives a person the sense that one, on the one hand, is not being coerced or restrained by another person in doing something desired and, on the other hand, the conviction that one can do as one pleases within the limits of other person's desire to do the same. Both aspects, negative and positive, lie and have always lain at the heart of the common, and common-sense, conception, whatever philosophers may think. Isaiah Berlin's celebrated attempt to distinguish between the positive and negative aspects of this value has not held up to philosophical scrutiny, and was always a nonstarter sociologically, especially his attempt to confine it to a purely negative meaning.[7] As Bertrand Russell clearly saw, "the absence of obstacles to the realization of desires" implies, in both logical and practical sociological terms, "the attainment of a condition for the satisfaction of our impulses."[8]

The second note of freedom which emerged in the West at about the same time as personal freedom is what I will call sovereignal freedom. This is simply the power to act as one pleases, regardless of the wishes of others, as distinct from personal freedom, which is the capacity to do as one pleases, *insofar as one can*. Russell observed that while everyone desires freedom for the satisfaction of his own impulses, these impulses are often in conflict among individuals (and, we might add, within individuals, but this is another matter). This is so for two reasons: first, because people frequently desire more than their fair share and, second, because "most human beings . . . desire to control not only their own lives but also the lives of others."[9] Russell, as a philosopher attempting to define what freedom really is, or should be, dismisses such impulses from the domain of freedom. But this is precisely where sociology and history differ from philosophy. It may, indeed, be illogical and immoral to desire for oneself the absence of obstacles, only to be able to restrain others, but, as this work will demonstrate, it is a sociohistorical fact that human beings have always sought to do just that, and have frequently succeeded in doing so. What is more, they have, until quite recently, found no problem calling such constraint on others "freedom." The idea that there is something wrong with this is one of the peculiar products of Enlightenment rationalism. The sovereignally free person has the power to restrict the freedom of others or to empower others with the capacity to do as they please with others beneath them. This conception of freedom is always relative. At one extreme stands the person who is absolutely free with respect to another, namely the slavemaster or absolute ruler or god; at the other extreme is the person who has no freedom with respect to another, namely, the slave in relation to his master. Between the two are all other human beings with more or less power or freedom, with respect to others.

Civic freedom is the capacity of adult members of a community to participate in its life and governance. A person feels free, in this sense, to the degree that he or she belongs to the community of birth, has a recognized place in it, and is involved in some way in the way it is governed. The existence of civic freedom implies a political community of some sort, with clearly defined rights and obligations for every citizen. It does not necessarily imply a complete political democracy; full adult suffrage is a peculiarly modern variant of it. In ancient Athens, where democracy was first constructed, it was, as will be seen, an exclusive male club, closed to female citizens and all resident aliens. And in republican Rome it was even more restricted, being confined to male aristocrats.

Participative politics is a necessary but not sufficient condition for civic freedom. In comparative terms, many non-Western societies, especially those tribal proto-democracies described by political anthropologists, exhibited some form of participation, at least among all senior male members of the community. What is unique to the West is the combination of civic participation and organized polities. In other parts of the world, whenever centralized states emerged, the price paid for this more complex form of political organization was the loss of adult (male) participation in the decision-making process. The unique achievement of Athens was neither its participative politics nor its centralized city-based polity but its being the first political entity in which the two processes coexisted. It is in this happy conjunction (for men) that all that was necessary and sufficient for democracy was attained. Explaining how large-scale slavery not only made possible but directly fashioned what resulted from this political configuration will be another task of this work.

These, then, are the three constitutive elements of the uniquely Western chord of freedom. The manner in which the chord has been played in the music of Western time is itself a complex and fascinating story. I will show that hardly had the triad been constructed than people began to reconceptualize it on different levels—the physical or outer, the inner or philosophical, and the spiritual or religious. And I will demonstrate, further, that on all levels there have been important changes, over time, in the way in which the chord has been played in the Western consciousness, such changes coming from the relative emphasis given one or another of the three elements or notes of freedom. Even today, Western societies vary in their choice of the fundamental note of the triad. Switzerland, Sweden, and America all cherish freedom as their supreme value, but consider how discordant the triads of these cultures sound when played too closely together to the mind's ear. From the moment of their chordal fusion in classical Greece, a tension has always existed among personal, civic, and sovereignal freedoms. Yet, however stridently and disharmoniously one of them has played at the expense of the others, all three have remained a vital part of the Western consciousness. We will see how that tension, existing within an unbroken though often fragile unity, had its roots in the paradoxical source of the value itself: the social death that was human slavery.

PART ONE

The Stillbirth of Freedom in the Non-Western World

CHAPTER 1

Primitive Beginnings

Who were the first persons to get the unusual idea that being free was not only a value to be cherished but the most important thing that someone could possess? The answer, in a word: slaves. Freedom began its career as a social value in the desperate yearning of the slave to negate what, for him or her, and for nonslaves, was a peculiarly inhuman condition. Now, in stating this I am proposing nothing new. Many historians and philosophers have already noted that freedom started as a special legal status. As Bernard Bosanquet correctly observed, "It will not lead us far wrong if we assume that the value we put upon liberty and its erection into something like an ideal comes from the contrast with slavery." This contrast, he correctly insists, "we may take as the practical starting point in the notion of freedom."[1]

What has not been recognized, however, is the critical fact that the idea of freedom has never been divorced from this, its primordial, servile source. Failure to recognize this springs from too great an emphasis on the legal aspects of the status first called freedom. When a person was enslaved or freed, however, much more was going on than the simple creation of a new legal status. To understand this requires a better knowledge of the condition called slavery.

Slavery is the permanent, violent, and personal domination of natally alienated and generally dishonored persons.[2] It is, first, a form of personal domination. One individual is under the direct power of another or his agent. In practice, this usually entails the power of life and death over the slave. Second, the slave is always an excommunicated person. He, more often she, does not belong to the legitimate social or moral community; he has no independent social existence; he exists only through, and for, the master; he is, in other words, natally alienated. As Aristotle observed, "The slave is not only the slave of his master; he also belongs entirely to him, [and has no life or being other than that of so belonging]."[3] Third, the slave is in a perpetual condition of dishonor. What is more, the master and, as we shall see, his group parasitically gain honor in degrading the slave.

Slavery, however, has never existed in a social vacuum. Like all enduring social relationships, it has existed only with the support of the community, and its peculiar interpersonal qualities and symbolic meanings have inevitably been institutionalized. A slave relationship, in short, requires at least the tacit support of those not directly involved with it, and it calls into being a slave culture, however rudimentary. As Plato saw, all too clearly, the master's power was nothing in isolation from fellow members of his community. And it has been shown, elsewhere, that the peculiar symbolic conceptions of the slave and the slave relationship were meaningful only when these conceptions were shared by all members of the community.[4] What are these shared cultural conceptions of slavery?

In all societies the three constitutive features of the slave condition add up to a generalized conception of slavery as a state of social death. The slave is always conceived of as someone, or the descendant of someone, who should have died, typically as a result of defeat in war, but also as a result of poverty. His physical life was spared, or as Hobbes put it, "his life and corporall Libertie given him, on condition to be Subject to the Victor, . . . subject of him that took him; because he had no other way to preserve himself."[5] Few writers have more bluntly stated this nearly universal way of rationalizing and symbolically expressing the condition of slavery than Locke: "having, by his own fault, forfeited his own Life, by some Act that deserves Death; he, to whom he has forfeited it, may (when he has him in his Power) delay to take it, and make use of him to his own Service, and he does him no injury by it."[6]

Slavery posed at least two fundamental problems wherever it existed. One of these was more social or communal; the other, interpersonal. In the solving of these two problems, the value of freedom was born. The two problems are actually aspects of each other and should not be too rigidly separated. We do so only for the sake of clarity and exposition.

The interpersonal problem was that of getting the slave to serve the master diligently. Actually the problem developed later than the social dilemma, for the simple reason that the demands of the master were not great in the most primitive societies where we find the relationship. Rarely, in these cases, did the master rely on his slaves for economic purposes. What the master wanted was honor and deference. The slave was a living embodiment of his prowess in warfare. It did not take much to achieve this satisfaction. The slave merely had to exist and behave himself. In most such societies, the slave was well looked after, sometimes even pampered, by the master. Only later, when more complex demands were to be made on the slave, did personal motivation become a problem.

What became problematic from the moment a slave was introduced into a society, however primitive it might have been, was the communal acceptance of the slave and of the slave relation. How does a society, any society, come to terms with the idea of socially dead persons in its midst? Why would a community, in the first place, permit such a bizarre relationship? Clearly, there must have been something in the relationship which served the interests of the community, some compensating factor. The simpler, the smaller, and the more primitive the community, the greater would have been the need for such compensations. There were few distinctions of rank or personal power in such communities, so no prospective master or group of masters was powerful enough to impose its will on the rest of the community. As Michael Mann, synthesizing a long tradition of political anthropology, has recently pointed out, all precivilized societies were hostile to the accumulation of personal power; power, where it existed, was collective and "almost totally confined to the use of 'authority' on behalf of the collectivity."[7]

Further, because the earliest societies were small, tightly knit groups, three or two slaves, or even one would have made quite an impact on the entire group. Everyone was alive to the presence of strangers in such societies, and that precisely was the condition of the slave, a permanent stranger, a kinless soul in their midst. In evolutionary terms, then, the social problem of slavery preceded its interpersonal problem. Hence its resolution, and the kind of freedom it intimated, comes before all others.

The comparative, ethnohistorical evidence on slavery among hunter-gatherers and primitive agriculturalists is quite rich, making it possible to understand how the dilemma was resolved in these societies and what it implies for our story. Slaveholding and trading existed among the earliest and most primitive of peoples. The archaeological evidence reveals that slaves were among the first items of trade within, and between, the primitive Germans and Celts, and the institution was an established part of life, though never of major significance, in primitive

China, Japan, and the prehistoric Near East. Among preliterate tribal peoples of the nineteenth and twentieth centuries, the relation was institutionalized and hereditary in nearly 30 percent of all cases observed by anthropologists, and at least incipient in another 15 percent of the cases. The conventional view that hunters and gatherers never kept slaves, because they lacked the resources to do so, is incorrect; a small but significant minority of these groups did so, and while their numbers were usually small, there are on record several cases of slave populations approaching 10 to 15 percent of the gatherers, most notably the Indians of the northwest coast of North America.[8]

Whatever their numbers, slaves were rarely of any economic significance among hunters and gatherers. Their cultural and social roles, however, were sometimes important, and in a handful of cases on record, one of which we will examine shortly, the slave loomed large in the cultural life of the tribe. In all these societies, the slave was mainly a shared social good. While every slave had a master, the master's gains were often secondary and, in all cases, heavily dependent upon the community's interest in the slave.

The pre-European Cherokees, studied by Theda Perdue, were typical of slaveholding hunter-gatherers and primitive agriculturalists. Most prisoners of war were killed, though some were occasionally adopted as full members of the victor's clan. In a few cases, however, captives were reduced to genuine enslavement. These were the *atsi nahsa'i*, people without clan membership and, as such, "without any rights, even the right to live," and over whom the master had absolute power. Slaves served no real economic purpose in this redistributive subsistence economy, although they were assigned servile or female work. They were entirely excluded from participation in the social life of the community. The slave, like the bear, Perdue tells us, "was an anomaly because he had a human form but could not lead a normal human existence," and she suggests that it was precisely because they were anomalies that the Cherokees kept them. The Cherokees used the abnormal status of the slave as a way of strengthening their system of classification. Further, the deviant and outsider condition of the slave helped to establish Cherokee identity, "not by proclaiming what they are, or the norm, but by carefully defining what they are not." The kinless, clanless, socially dead slave negatively defined all that it meant to be socially alive and an active member of one's clan.[9] It is most significant that this earliest role of the slave, and of slavery, was a communal and social one. There is, as yet, no hint of individual freedom. Once a man was enslaved, he could not return to his own tribe, nor could he be promoted to the status of a full member of his captor's

society. The stain of slavery was indelible. Social death was like physical death: once dead, you remained dead.

While individual freedom was not possible, or even conceivable, in
these societies, the social definitions which slavery generated sometimes allowed for the possibility of something even more innovative.
We see this happening among those few societies of this type in which
there was an unusual ritual preoccupation with the slave, to the point
where it became the dominant focus of the entire culture, although at
any given time no more than two or three slaves may have been
around. The most fascinating case on record of this development
involved the Tupinamba of pre-European South America.

The Tupinamba belonged to the large group of Tupi-Guarani–speaking
peoples who, when discovered by the Europeans in the sixteenth century, occupied the eastern coastal strip of Brazil from the mouth of the
Amazon to Cananéa, located in the south of what is now São Paulo.[10]
The Tupinamba proper were the northernmost of this group of tribes.
When the Europeans arrived, they were just coming to the end of their
migrations into the coastal region and were perpetually at war with
the Tapuya peoples they had displaced. Their economy was a combination of farming, hunting, and gathering. Slash-and-burn techniques
were used to grow manioc and, to a lesser degree, maize. All the plant-
ing and harvesting was done by women, as was the gathering of the
highly favored tanajuras ants. There was also extensive fishing, especially of oysters. Hunting was carried out by men, either individually
or in small groups, the main game being certain ratlike rodents, although occasionally larger game, such as jaguars, were taken. There
was little domestication of animals, and none of any real economic
significance. It was hardly necessary. Food, including protein, was
abundant, and the Tupinamba nicely fit Marshal Sahlins's model of
Stone Age affluence.[11]

The Tupinamba lived in villages of between four hundred and sixteen hundred persons, in huge thatched houses holding between one
and two hundred persons, located around a central communal plaza.
Special parts of these houses were set aside for the heads of extended
families, their relatives, and their slaves. The villages were built on the
summits of hills for protection and were well defended. Any outsider
in such a community was highly visible and the object of constant
curiosity and watchfulness.

Since material wants were no problem, and since women were doing
most of the work, men had a lot of time on their hands. When men in
traditional—some may say, in all—societies had more time than they
knew what to do with, they invariably played, and made war, the two

tending to converge. The Tupinamba were a classic case in point. Warfare was the pivotal institution among them. According to Alfred Métraux, ''Rank was determined by war prowess (capture and ceremonial
execution of prisoners), magic power, oratorical gifts, and wealth.''[12]
The taking of captives was the major objective of warfare. The captive,
as the enemy within, provided for the extension of war and vengeance
against the enemy. The high point of social life and cultural play was
the ritualistic slaughter of the captives. Such slaves, then, played a
critical role in Tupinamba life and culture, even though few in numbers.

Of slaves, Métraux writes, ''Though, with few exceptions, all prisoners, male or female, were eventually eaten, they were kept long
enough in the community to be considered a special class within *Tupinamba* society. Possession of a prisoner was an envied privilege. One
who enjoyed it did not hesitate to make the greatest sacrifices to keep
his charge happy and in good health.''[13] Wives were found for the
slaves, sometimes from among the slaveholder's own kinsmen. The
children of male slaves, and those of female slaves by male slaves,
remained slaves. After they were captured and brought home, there
were elaborate rituals of enslavement in which the slave was incorporated into the group as an internal enemy. The slaves lived and worked
with their captors as junior kinsmen, although they felt the constant
threat of being slaughtered at any time. While generally well treated,
the slaves were objects of the usual combination of fear and contempt.
At any time they could become the target of the most violent insults
and abuses from nonslaves. The main symbol of slavery was a rope
tied around the neck of the slave, which sometimes was ''a symbolical
necklace strung with as many beads as he had months to live until his
execution.''[14]

Slaves had to respect their masters. Deferential behavior included
entering the owner's quarters through special areas. Indeed, the only
purpose the slave served for the individual master was to enhance his
sense of honor and to reinforce his sense of manly dignity.[15] In keeping
with the tradition of violence toward the external and internal enemy,
the Tupinamba had a highly developed timocratic character. Courage,
military prowess, and personal discipline alternating with the most
extreme expressions of brutality and rage against the enemy, both
without and within, were the highest virtues. An observer remarked,

Great stress was put on the smoothness of manners and gentleness, any
outburst of anger being looked on with abhorrence. People shunned the
company of temperamental persons. If an Indian felt incapable of con-

trolling his feelings, he warned those present, who immediately tried
to calm him down. When a serious quarrel broke out in a village, the
individuals involved went to the extreme of burning their own houses,
challenging their adversaries to do likewise. . . .

Blood revenge was a sacred duty.[16]

Considerable emphasis was also placed on proper etiquette and hospitality. If this all sounds highly familiar, it is only because there is
indeed an honorific complex which anthropologists, especially those
who work on the Mediterranean, have shown to exhibit striking similarities across levels, and regions, of human cultures. Slavery often,
though obviously not always, plays a pivotal role in supporting this
timocratic complex. The Tupinamba, the ancient Greeks and Romans,
and the southerners of the United States, so markedly different in time,
place, and levels of sociocultural development, nonetheless reveal the
remarkable tenacity of this culture-character complex.[17]

In a brilliant analysis, Florestan Fernandes, the Brazilian social an-
thropologist, has shown how warfare, slavery, religion, and human
sacrifice were all intimately related in Tupinamba culture.[18] The artic-
ulating cultural concept was vengeance. On the surface, vengeance
was important as the justification for war against the external enemy
and the cannibalistic slaughter of the slave. But the notion of vengeance also became a means of appeasement of, and solidarity with,
the ancestors, especially those who had been killed in warfare, and the
mythical founders of the community. Warfare—both external, in clashes
with the enemy, and internal, in the sacrifice of the slave—established
solidarity with the ancestors and the gods and reinforced communal
solidarity and strength.

The sacrificial murder and eating of the slave was undertaken with
considerable ritual. According to Fernandes, six kinds of rituals were
involved. First, rites of segregation. Because the slave had earlier been
incorporated by the rites of enslavement as a part of the community,
in it, though never a member of it, it was necessary before his sacrifice
to exclude him once again. Between exclusion and the actual sacrifice,
the slave was a masterless, uncontrolled person in their midst and
therefore, in this condition of intense liminality, a moral danger to the
community and greatly to be feared. The rites of segregation were
quickly followed by rites of inculcation in which the slave and his tribe
of origin were accused and reviled. This was followed by rites of preparation for sacrifice, usually the day before the execution. Then came
rites of symbolic escape and recapture, in which the slave was taunted
with the possibility of freedom. In cat-and-mouse fashion, he was de-

liberately allowed to escape and, just at the point when he thought he had regained his freedom and his life, was retaken with much abuse. Next came the rites of vengeance and, finally, the gruesome rites of slaughter. This complex of rites was followed by the cannibalistic feast, which also had its own elaborate rules and taboos, especially for the slaveholder, who had done the killing. After this came the final rites of purification.

We can now summarize and relate all this to the question of the origins of freedom. Slavery, on the level of personal domination, existed in all its essentials among the Tupinamba. There was the individualized domination of the slave by his captor, the slave's powerlessness, and his social death. Slaves were of little direct material value to their masters or to the community, but were vital in enhancing the honor, manhood, and dignities of the slaveholder. There was little need to motivate the slave. It was enough to treat him well, which was hardly a problem in this abundant Stone Age society.

Note, however, that the slave desperately desired his freedom. Throughout the years of his enslavement, he made frequent attempts to escape, the certainty of his eventual slaughter no doubt reinforcing this desire. The master and the other members of his community also recognized the slave's desperate yearning for escape and freedom. They actually taunted him with it. Neither, however, had any interest in supporting the slave's desire. Quite the contrary.

Thus the desire for personal freedom existed, but it could not become a value. It was known both by the slave and by his captors, who not only saw it in the slave's anguish but also deeply mourned the living and the dead among them who had been captured and slaughtered, and eaten, by the slave's natal tribe. They too must have tried to escape. So the desire for and the idea of personal freedom at its most basic and biological level were known by all. But it could not be actualized. For a desire to become value, there must be present the consent of the community. At the very least, the slave's master must have had to find some value in it. Among the Tupinamba, as among nearly all hunter-gatherers who held slaves and among many neolithic peoples, neither masters nor other members of the community had any motivation or interest in instituting freedom. Hence there was no social reaction, no fusion of slave's yearning, master's interest, and community's consent, which together, and together only, transformed desire and idea into enduring social value. That had to await further developments.

Now, while the master had no interest in supporting the slave's yearning for personal freedom, he did have a strong interest in being his benefactor. Until the day of his sacrifice, the good master did all he could to care for and protect his slave. He fed him well. He even found him a wife from among his kinfolk. There are many accounts of these wives' becoming very attached to their doomed husbands, some of them making pathetic attempts to help them escape. The master expected the slave to reciprocate his good treatment by honoring him. Thus we find, even in this most primitive situation, the rudiments of sovereignal freedom, the experience of freedom as the exercise of power. We will see how, in more complex social formations, that benevolence would fuse with the master's interest in freeing the slave, to create elementary personal freedom. But not yet. Not until the master had good reason to conspire with the slave's brute instinct to be free would desire become value and, in the process, give birth to personal freedom.

Nonetheless, as we have seen, there was one critical respect in which the community did become involved with the slave. Indeed, it was obsessed with him. The slaveholder's community participated in the relationship both in recognizing the slaveholder's claim to honor and prestige and in helping to control and recapture the slave. They all shared in the collective honor of the defeated enemy. And, most important of all, the keeping and sacrificing of slaves was a critical part of the dominant constellation of values that made Tupinamba life meaningful. Slavery, by bringing warfare home, made possible both the continuous exercise of vengeance and its most dramatic ritual expression. The slave became a kind of cultural money, a medium of social and ritual exchange, and a living expression of the value of freedom, and of the enormous risk of losing it in warfare. In the process of defining the enemy, the Tupinamba defined themselves, in social and in supernatural terms. Thus slavery made possible both group definition and group solidarity. The ritual slaughter of the slave brought together all who were not directly involved in the relation of slavery, even as it intensified the ties of solidarity between slaveholder and nonslaveholders. In short, slavery formed the basis of the most important civic act, the most intense form of participation.

At the heart of this civic experience must have been the consciousness of a negation, of a not-being which was the sheer joy, the intense exhilaration of not being the sacrificed slave. And in eating his body, and in drinking his blood, the Tupinamba experienced both personally and together the ultimate act of sanctification and communal solidarity—the consumption of the hated other, the not-being, the not-I, the

Them-object that made Us possible. By the literal consuming of the enemy, the enemy within the body social became the enemy within the real body. Thus the individual and the community became one.

And what was that one? A free one, of course, constantly alive to the idea of that freedom by being partly made up of the being that was not free. Incipient or proto-civic freedom, then, is found in the most primitive of social formations having slavery. To be sure, its creation was not yet complete. It still had to be given a name, to be intellectually purified, and to be morally transvalued, and that had to await the creation both of more complex polities and of more intellectually self-conscious peoples. And as we suggested earlier, its configuration with the other two freedoms was to give it a chordal quality wholly unknown among the Tupinamba. Even so, in the use of the slave as an object of communal solidarity, as a mode of defining the community, and at the same time defining it as not-slaves, and as a means of forging individual and collective consciousness around the negation, not-slave, the Tupinamba exhibited one of the most necessary elements of participatory or civic freedom.

Necessary, but not sufficient. For civic freedom also required the existence of a politically centralized community with governmental institutions. And that decisive development human beings resisted for a very long time, as Mann has so forcefully reminded us.[19] We will see later how slavery, when inserted on a large scale into such advanced polities, became a revolutionary force engendering civic freedom. What the Tupinamba case illustrates, however, is the primitive mechanism that underlay the propensity of slavery to generate such a revolution: its immediate stimulation of a bond of love among the nonslaves vis-à-vis the bonded slave—and it is no accident that we express solidarity in the language of the shackled—for it is its obverse, the hated enemy within, that defined, even in the absence of war, the political boundaries of the group: the primordial outsider who defined internally the nature of belonging and the privileges of membership of a social group. We are bonded together in love, because others are bonded to us in hate.

Before the slave came into being, the Tupinamba could define the boundaries of their group only by going to war and risking death. With slavery—with even one solitary slave—all the social and political functions of war were institutionalized, realized without risks, and given ritual expression.

But slavery did more. Unlike war, it began to identify, for the first time in human history, the community with something new, a new value, that being not-slave, not constrained, not socially dead—in other words, at least implicitly, socially free. This, primitive warfare by itself could not have done, for as we have seen, the norm was to slaughter the men and either kill or completely absorb the women. We may call what the Tupinamba experienced proto-civic freedom, the first experience of freedom as a socially valued good.

Nonetheless, it was a historical dead end. Nothing emerged directly from it. More advanced agricultural societies had to reinvent freedom as a social value. It took a long period of social time for this to happen. When it did, however, slavery, as we will see, was once again its handmaiden. Before coming to this reinvention, let us see why it did not happen in other societies, more developed than that of the Tupinamba, and with far higher levels of slavery.

CHAPTER 2

For the Creation of Eyes: Why Freedom Failed in the Non-Western World

I have suggested that freedom as a value was generated by, and socially constructed out of, the interaction among master, slave, and native nonslaves. Elsewhere, I have demonstrated that slavery was a nearly universal institution.[1] It should follow that the value of freedom was constructed everywhere. Yet, we know that this was not so. Indeed, one of the major objectives of this work is to show that freedom was a peculiarly Western value and ideal. How is the discrepancy explained?

Simply, by noting that while the idea of freedom was certainly engendered wherever slavery existed, it never came to term. People everywhere, except in the ancient West, resisted its gestation and institutionalization. This chapter will show why. It will be seen that resisting the promotion of freedom as value was the natural thing to do for most human societies, in much the same way that the long resistance to the concentration of power was natural for most human societies for most of human history. What is unusual is the institutionalization and idealization of this value, given its degraded, servile source. It is the ancient West that needs explanation. Because we are of the West and share its central value, we have turned the history of human societies around, and ethocentrically assumed that it is the rest of humankind, in its failure to embrace freedom, that needs explaining. To undo such preconceptions is another aim of the present chapter.

1. SLAVERY AND THE CONCEPTIONS
OF FREEDOM IN PRELITERATE CULTURES

As societies became more settled, more agricultural or pastoral, the captured enemy often became increasingly useful to his master or the person assigned personal control over him. The reasons for keeping slaves also became more complex and varied. Honorific factors remained important, as did ritual factors such as the sacrificial murder of slaves, spectacularly so in ancient China, where hundreds were buried alive with their deceased emperor masters, and in ancient Carthage, where large-scale economic uses of slaves went along with the mass ritual sacrifice of hundreds of them on special religious occasions.[2] Of increasing though never prime importance, too, was the economic use of slaves, either to supplement household labor or to generate surplus on specially assigned tenancies. In many societies, slaves were also used for military and bureaucratic or executive purposes. Female slaves, the majority in most premodern slaveholding societies, were valued as much for their reproductive as for their productive roles, especially in regions of low population density such as western Africa.

For the slaveholder in settled small communities, then, one of the main objectives in keeping slaves now became the services which he could extract from them. In such situations the second major problem of slavery asserted itself—that of motivating the slave to serve the master well. The greater the number of slaves owned, and the greater the dependence of the master on these slaves for his own status and material well-being and power, the greater became the need to find some way of motivating his slaves. But increased numbers of slaves created an even bigger problem for the slave owner: the need to placate the nonslaveholding members of his community. It is in the search for a solution to these two sets of problems that slaveholder, slave, and "freeman" began to discover, or stumble upon, aspects of the value of freedom. The outcome in these societies, however, is not what we had expected. Human societies had a difficult labor, giving birth to freedom.

The obvious solution to the problem of motivating the slave was, we know from hindsight, to hold out the promise of release from slavery. Nonetheless, the evidence is clear that in no premodern society outside of the West was personal freedom seriously entertained. It would be going too far to say that it was never conceived. A slave is a dead man. A man desperate for life. In desperation men and women conceive of anything. And anything, even the sociological impossibility of going it alone—a stranger, an outcast and runaway, a rebel, a bandit—might sometimes, must sometimes, have crossed the mind of the socially dead slave. And we know it to be true of all these societies that the rare slave did seek to actualize the impossible.

Nearly all slaves in premodern societies, however, dreamed of something more practical—to become again legitimate members of society, to be socially born again, in their next to wildest dreams, to be reborn in their native community, but in their more pragmatic dreams, to be reborn in the community of their enslavement. This last, for a small minority of them, was now possible. Possible because the master had reason to entertain it, and sometimes had the means to persuade the freeborn to accept it.

Sometimes. For the transition was always resisted by the freeborn, who had every reason to resent the intrusion of such formerly dead, utterly kinless persons into their midst. The freedman was no longer a slave, but it is important to note that what he had achieved with the release from slavery was not personal freedom; nor was he necessarily a freeman or citizen of his master's community. As Bosanquet nicely puts it, "A man may be a long way more than a slave and yet a long way less than a citizen."[3] It was very rare in the history of human servitude for the ex-slave to become immediately a freeman. It almost never happened in the slaveholding societies of the non-Western world. What Ignatious Gelb wrote of ancient Mesopotamia remained true of all non-Western societies throughout history, and of a good part of the history of Western slavery: "that the manumitted or freed individual remained in some state of dependency on their old master's household."[4] In these societies, that further transition to fully free status took at least a couple of generations. "To make them round" again, as the Toradja of the Central Celebes expressed it, took much time, deep rituals, and the exchange of many gifts. First, they were only "half round"; and so they remained for the rest of their lives. It was no easy matter this, the creation even of a half-free person. For people knew immediately that not just a radically new category of persons was being created but a profoundly new kind of value. They also say, the people of the Central Celebes, that the ritual and social change invoked in making this new thing was "for the creation of eyes."[5]

The creation of eyes, then, would be possible only where the freeborn benefited. We have already seen from our discussion of the Tupinamba that these benefits accrued even where no release from slavery was possible for the slave. That is, the mere existence of slavery created, among the nonslaves, a sense of civic pride, of solidarity, and of participation, identified with the mere fact of not being a slave. That happened, however, only where slavery and the ritual slaughter of the slave were central cultural preoccupations. But, as we argued above, precisely this cultural focusing on the slave was lost as societies became more complex and settled. So just when the master needed some such cultural compensation to justify not simply the holding but the release of some of his slaves, it was lost. This value thus had to be re-created or revived. One way or another, the creation of the freedman had to be complemented and compensated for, by the re-creation or intensification of the value of social or proto-civic freedom. Further, it had to await the construction of some social space for such a category of persons. Let us examine how this was done in those parts of the non-Western world where we find significant levels of slavery.

In precolonial African societies slavery was widespread and the release from slavery not uncommon. But as Igor Kopytoff and Suzanne Miers have shown, the antithesis of slavery in these societies was never freedom in the Western sense (by which they mean personal freedom). What the ambitious slave sought, and what the self-interested master offered, was the reduction of the slave's marginality and his partial resocialization in the master's community. Not autonomy or isolation, which was neither possible nor desired, but "new bonds must be created, in the integrative sense of 'bonding' him to the new society."[6] Ultimately, what the ex-slave wanted was "the condition of the complete insider, of the man born into the society as a full-fledged citizen. But the insider in most traditional societies of Africa was not an autonomous individual. His full citizenship derived from belonging to a kin group, usually corporate, which was the fundamental social, legal, political, and ritual protective unit."[7]

This condition of belonging, of participating, of being protected by the community, constituted the ideal nonslave condition not only in Africa but, as we shall see, in nearly all traditional societies. Personal freedom had no place in such societies. Indeed, such a condition amounted to social suicide and, very likely, physical death. In many respects it was a condition worse than slavery, even though, as we said earlier, a few slaves were desperate enough to try it. Something else was needed, some radically new social development, before this possibility could become anything more than the crazed musing of a desperate slave.

In order to come to a deeper understanding of the values which were actually possible in settled, kin-based agricultural societies, let us sharpen our focus on two pre-European slaveholding societies, the Imbangala of Angola and the Toradja of the Central Celebes, both reflect-

ing the full range of slavery in such societies, measured in terms of
the numbers and uses of slaves.

2. MAVALA AND JIMBANZA: FREEDMEN
AND KINSMEN IN AN AFRICAN CULTURE

What distinguished the slaves, or *abika*, among the Imbangala was the
fact that they did not have a wide network of affiliation, of persons on
whom to depend. Rather, as Joseph C. Miller, the authority on this
society, tells us, the slaves were exclusively dependent on one person,
their master, "who, in turn, was accountable to no social or political
authority that might act in their behalf. By definition, slaves lacked the
kinsmen who were constantly available to [others] for assistance in
avenging injustices, borrowing wealth, offering solace, or arranging for
a spouse."[8] In this situation, the idea of personal freedom made no
sense, even though the desire to be liberated from the condition of
slavery certainly did. That liberation, however, was found not in any
freedom from someone, since no one had or wanted that, but in involvement with, and closer bondage to, a wider network of persons.
Miller sums up the situation well:

> The slave/free dichotomy, familiar to Western heirs of the Enlightenment,
> would not appear so obvious to the Imbangala, since in Kasanje all status
> was seen as involuntary and no individual considered himself free in any
> sense close to Western theoretical notions of freedom. Everyone lived
> subordinated to the collective needs of his or her lineage, subordinated
> to the character of the name he or she assumed, subordinated to the
> ideally absolute authority of the king . . . all obediently suffered fates
> determined for them by the gods.[9]

While I am in general agreement with Miller's insistence that the Western slave-free dichotomy is not relevant to an understanding of the
African situation, I must at this point emphasize one crucial difference
between my own position and his, as well as that of Miers and Kopytoff. To the extent that these authors mean by the Western idea of
freedom only personal freedom, we are in complete agreement.
However, as I indicated in the Introduction, and will demonstrate in
the remaining chapters of this work, it is a serious error to claim that
the Western idea and value of freedom involve only the notion of personal liberty. That is one of the great myths of modern political and
economic theory which I hope to correct here. Western freedom is

unique in many respects—in the component of personal liberty, in the extraordinary emphasis placed on it, and in its trinitarian configuration. However, one of the three elements of freedom, the sovereignal, did emerge in the non-Western world, and there were clear precursors of civic freedom, both, as in the West, developing under the influence of slavery. But neither ever became a dominant or even a socially important value. To demonstrate this important point, we can do no better than to return to Miller's own, excellent ethnography of the Imbangala.

Now, the Imbangala are a fascinating group of people, bundling enormous social complexity on a primitive technological base, as only traditional Africans seemed capable of doing. In the latter half of the nineteenth century, when we come upon them, they were emerging from a long period of subjection to the despotic slave-trading state of Kasanje, the rulers of which had wreaked havoc on the peoples of the Lui-Kwango valley from the early part of the seventeenth century. Vast numbers of people had been brought into the region by the kings, and even more had been sold out to the Europeans. With the collapse of the centralized kingdom, many local petty kingdoms under provincial Kasanje rulers had appeared. In the face of all this, the indigenous Imbangala held on to, and even reinforced, their central social institution. This was the *ngundu,* the exogamous, matrilineal descent group. They considered this group "vital to their lives" since it determined their social and economic position and level of protection, as well as their access to the gods. Hence they evaluated these groups "at the very center of human existence, even seeing humanness itself as an attribute of membership in the descent group."[10]

A slave was a person without a lineage and, as such, someone whose very humanness was permanently in question. Numerous slaves, along with other, nonslave aliens, had been brought into the region by the Kasanje rulers, eventually outnumbering the indigenous Imbangala. Thus the native Imbangala found themselves in the middle of a hierarchical kingdom. Above them was the conquering group, which not only enriched itself by selling slaves abroad but used slaves as a praetorian guard to prevent native rebellion. Soon, however, the native Imbangala were procuring slaves themselves, and these they incorporated by creating a special class of lowly statuses bearing special relation to their own lineages. The Kasanje rulers had a different system of organization and were outside the lineage framework which the natives took to be so central to their existence.

The Imbangala's ideological response to this situation is interesting, for, as Miller tells us, it has parallels in other parts of the world, including Europe: they came to identify kings and slaves alike as belonging to the same category of outsiders. This made sociological sense, since the kings constantly struggled to undermine the central social position of the lineages, using their slave retainers to do so. The Imbangala fought back with their own slave recruits and by fiercely holding on to their traditional lineage system. "The abika thus served as the pawns that simultaneously maintained the political balance between kings and lineages in Kasanje and provided the plentiful slave exports for which Kasanje became justifiably infamous."[11]

In this situation, it is clear, some means of motivating the slaves was called for. The release from slavery, by both the kings and the lineage leaders, was the answer. A special category of freedmen called *mavala* was created for those locally born slaves whose skills and loyalty were highly desired. These *mavala* were important, not only in the struggles between the lineage and the kings but also in resolving a chronic intralineage problem peculiar to all matrilineal systems, that between a man's own matrilineage and that of his father. That is, the children of a man and his slave remained in the man's own retinue and did not belong to that of his wife, as was true of his own children. These *mavala* were certainly not full members of the lineage. Indeed, they were hardly even half members, since one became a member of a lineage only through the mother; and they had blood links only to one line. At the same time, they were no longer slaves. Rather, they were grateful and loyal supporters of the person who had released them from the socially dead condition of slavery.

Now, whatever the name the Imbangala might have given this relationship, the thing it described closely resembles what I have called sovereignal freedom. For the freedmen, it was a set of rights and capacities given by a slave owner to his slave which results in his release from a condition of complete social isolation and nonbeing, into one which, while not the same as that of a full member or citizen, at least allows for the possibility of his descendants' becoming full citizens over time; it also gave the freedman certain powers vis-à-vis native Imbangala. In return, the ex-slave offered further loyal service, deference, and loyalty; in other words, as a retainer he reinforced the honor and absolute sovereignal freedom of the ex-master. It was only in this and the slave relation that a person could freely exercise such absolute power.

Miller's ethnography makes it perfectly clear that "freeborn," or *jimbanza*, members of the community strongly resented the *mavala*. Indeed, he goes so far as to speak of "structural tensions" between *abika* (slaves), *mavala* (freedmen), and *jimbanza* (full members); this is understandable when it is considered that many favored *mavala* became more prosperous than *jimbanza* kinsmen, that is to say, had more liberties, in the prescriptive sense, than the latter did. The *jimbanza*, however, did gain from the presence of both slaves and *mavala*. In the first place, all slaves and freedmen had to pay special deference to *jimbanza*, no matter how wealthy the former and how poor the latter. I find it hard to believe that such a state of affairs did not imprint upon the consciousness of *jimbanza* the fact that not being a slave meant something valuable, regardless of what may have been the nature of dependency among such nonslaves.

It was in this way that among the Imbangala—as presumably among all tribal groups with significant numbers of slaves and freedmen—a wholly new category of persons was created, namely, that of the *freeman*. Note that no such category existed among the Tupinamba, or among other groups where the slave was only of ritual significance, however great that cultural role. The social category of freeman can exist only in contradistinction to the established social categories of slaves and freedmen.

Second, we find a strong sense of collective pride among the *jimbanza* vis-à-vis all slaves, *mavala*, and even the kings with whom they identified the slaves. All were outsiders. There can be no outsiders without insiders. And since what characterized all of these outsiders was their slaveness, the kings themselves included, the intense focus on the human-defining lineage must have been identified with the condition of not being the slave outsider. This is quite consistent with the fact, emphasized by Miller, that the Imbangala did not have a slave-free dichotomy in the Western sense, for we have seen that by Western freedom Miller meant only personal freedom. The Imbangala, however, did think in starkly dichotomized terms, as Miller himself attests, for he closes his analysis of the effects of slavery on the relations between states and lineages by stating, ''The state/lineage dichotomy in Kasanje was therefore also an alliance of outsiders, chiefs and abika or yijiko [another category of slaves], against the jimbanza of the lineages.''[12] It is in the face of just such a dichotomous social construction that people come to value their solidarity, and their civic participation, not only as something expressive of great social import but, substantively, as something that is the negative social essence: not-slave.

But note, immediately, two important aspects of this valuation. First, it is in no sense civic freedom and does not even hint at anything approaching democracy. Indeed, it is not even the proto-civic freedom of the more primitive Tupinamba. And this is so although the Imbangala had a centralized polity and a moderately developed system of governance. That polity, however, focused on a monarch and a ruling elite who were themselves considered outsiders. Far from seeking to establish solidarity with its elite vis-à-vis the slaves and freedmen, the Imbangala identified the ruling group and the slaves and freedmen as outsiders. The insider freeman was the native, but the native freeman did not constitute the civic community. The civic group, in turn, had no need or inclination to establish any bond with the native freeman versus the slaves and freedmen. Instead, it used its own slaves and freedmen to aid in the exclusion of the native group from the civic decision-making process.

The second important aspect of the native Imbangala's valuation of their freeman status is that it was just that—the valuation of a *status*, not of a principle or ideal; nor was it associated, in itself, with anything dynamic or creative in their social life. Being a free person was a mere passive aspect of something far more important, the real center of life, namely, belonging to the lineage. Thus, while every Imbangala would acknowledge with some pride that he or she was not a slave or a freedman, none, if asked to name the things that constituted human-ness, the things that were vital to their existence as active and engaged members of their community, would dream of mentioning freedom.

In fact, the only people in Imbangala society who would truly have valued freedom as something to strive for would have been the de-spised slaves seeking to become *mavala*, and once they achieved their release from slavery they ceased immediately to value its negation. No one in his or her right mind in Imbangala society desired personal liberty, least of all the *mavala*. What the freedman sought, instead, were the prescriptive liberties of sovereignal freedom and the enhancement of his patron's, and protector's, sovereignal power or freedom over his remaining slaves.

3. *KABOSENJA* AND SLAVE: THE FREE WHO ARE "GREAT" IN THE SOUTH PACIFIC

With all this in mind, let us now turn to the Toradja of the Central Celebes.[13] This remote group of tribes presents us with a valuable ex-perimental situation, in that here we find a people who were remark-ably similar in most sociocultural respects, except in one critical area. One group (the To Lage, To Onda'e, To Palande, and To Pada) had a large slave population organized into a clearly demarcated slave stand-ing, while the other group either had only a few slaves, who were not socially important and not reduced to a special standing, or had no slaves at all (for example, the To Pebato and To Wingkemposo). They permit us, then, to explore the effects of slavery on the construction of notions of freedom among a tribal people, as well as to examine the effects of a proportionately large slave population on a tribal, non-Western society.

These were classic tribal societies with little development of private property. All land and important movable property, including slaves, were collectively owned, though their usufruct was usually assigned to particular members of the family. As in Africa, we find a basic division between bought or captured slaves and those born in the family. Hereditary slaves were generally well treated, were assigned family land on which to set up their own households, and were permitted to marry. Favored slaves could even achieve a measure of prosperity above the average for free persons. Bought slaves had a more precarious existence. They could be resold and were the sources of ritual sacrifice either at the death of the head of the family or on other occasions requiring such sacrifice. Whether they were bought or homebred, however, a sharp social cleavage existed between free and slave persons. The latter had no role whatever in the political or social life of the village and, however well treated, were regarded with contempt.

Slavery had a profound effect upon the attitudes of the tribes with a slave standing, in some of which the proportion ran to over 50 percent. In the first place, it introduced a basic class division where none had previously existed, that between slaves and freeborn persons. What is even more remarkable, from our point of view, is the terminology used to describe the standing of the free. The term for the free was *kabosenja*. It literally meant "the great" and originally referred only to the house fathers or heads of families, as a collectivity when they met in council, or more simply to the village chief. Among those tribes with a slave standing, however, in sharp contrast to those without such a standing, one of the first things inquired of a person was whether he or she belonged to the *kabosenja*, "the great, the prominent, that is to say, the free, in contrast to the slaves."[14] N. Adriani and Albert C. Kruyt, the main ethnographers of the group, examine at length the effect of this status assimilation among the free and of social distancing from the slaves: "The great distance between the masters and their slaves was shown in daily life by the great respect that the latter showed their lords. A slave should not use the eating utensils of one of his masters, not eat before his master and help himself, take nothing from his master's *sirih* bag."[15]

Although the slave was under the direct control of the household head, because he or she was technically owned by the entire kin group, such deference was demanded by all members of the family, which meant all nonslave members of the community, since every family owned slaves. For all free Toradja among the slaveholding tribes, "it was therefore a matter of assuming a commanding attitude with regard to the slave. Through this, striking an attitude had become second nature to them."[16] Slaves were stereotyped as lowly and degraded, and they apparently lived out the slavish role expected of them. "Because of all this," the ethnographers found, "slaves are often rude, and *ada mbatoea* 'slave manners' is tantamount to 'improper behavior.' "[17]

By contrasting slaveholding with nonslaveholding tribes, Adriani and Kruyt were further able to isolate the effects on the character and public life of the former. Politics was conducted in a more authoritarian manner among the slave tribes, and there was a greater tendency toward centralization of decision making among them, a clear departure from the original, primitive communism witnessed in the tribes without a slave standing.

> First, this influence appears in the communistic social life. Formerly a chief among the To Lage (to take this tribe as representative of the slaveholding ones) would no more have ordered something that went beyond the adat than would a Pebato chief; the members of his own group would have turned away from him and would have gone to found a village on their own. But the manner in which a Lage chief handles matters *testifies to a feeling of power that has developed through mastery over his slaves, but from which the free in the society also feel the influence.*[18]

Younger members of the community, as a result of their mastery over slaves, became more authoritarian and at the same time more inclined to obey their superiors. In general, the ethnographers were impressed by what seemed like a more civilized manner in the generality of free persons. "Mindful of keeping their prestige high with regard to their slaves," the To Lage "made a more civilized impression on the foreigner than did the To Pebato who, not knowing this pressure, behaved more as they are, let themselves go more."[19]

In spiritual life, the large presence of a socially dead group of people led to greater skepticism about religious matters and to more reflectiveness. Power, they discovered, came not only from dead ancestors but in this life from mastery over their slaves. Religious behavior took on a greater element of "display" and "splendor," as if to impress the ever-observing, but excluded, slaves with their cultural superiority.

Slavery also generated cynicism and skepticism in another, more familiar way: freemen sexually exploited slave women and routinely denied paternity. At the same time, "the licentiousness of many female slaves made the free woman more prudish."[20]

In economic life, slavery also had an important effect, one we will return to when we come to examine the development of freedom in Western societies. The free among the slaveholding groups dressed better, had sounder houses, and imported more articles of trade than did their nonslaveholding neighbors. They also developed a contempt for manual agricultural work, leaving most of it to their slaves.

There was very little opportunity for mobility out of slavery in these societies. If a master had a child by a slave and chose to marry her, the child could be declared free after elaborate purification rites by the master. But such marriages were rare and negatively sanctioned, and the offspring always suffered some stigma. Free women who consorted with slaves were killed, along with the offending slave: "For the Toradja it was just as preposterous that a slave could be made free as that, for instance, a woman could be declared to be a man; it would have brought about a disturbance in the order of nature."[21]

There are several lessons to be learned from the case of the Toradja. First, having a large number of slaves was not sufficient to create a large-scale slave society. Genuine slave societies existed only where slaves were structurally constitutive, that is, were used to transform the preexisting social structure in some way, often economically, but, *pace* all Marxist students of slavery, often politically or militarily. The slaveholding Toradja had a higher proportion of slaves than did most states of the antebellum South or the large-scale slave systems of ancient Greece and Rome, but their slaves were passively articulated in their social systems, and the institution was in no way sociologically generative.

Second, because of this passive articulation, slaveholders were under no pressure to motivate their slaves, so the institution did not generate any willingness or desire on their part to cultivate the value of freedom. Nor was there any social space for a freedman standing in these societies. To make a slave "whole" again was so culturally and socially difficult that only a precious few ever experienced this transition.

Further, because all Toradja in the groups with slave standings owned slaves, either individually or collectively, there was no disgruntled group of nonslaveholding freemen to be placated. Thus, while there was a sense of pride in not being a slave, in being of the free standing, this was not generative of any compensating participative politics. If anything, slavery made the slaveholding Toradja more authoritarian in their civic culture. There was, however, an important difference from the African case, examined earlier. The pride the Toradja felt in being free did go beyond a mere passive enjoyment of a status. Freedom did become something of an ideal here, if not the *central* one; it would certainly have been listed among the important things in life by the typical free Toradja.

The freedom celebrated, however, had nothing to do with personal liberty or civic equality. Rather, it was the freedom to exercise complete power over another person and group, to do with them as one pleased. In other words, pure sovereignal freedom was the element of the value generated by the large number of slaves in their midst.

We can now make an important qualification to Michael Mann's recently stated generalization, to which we referred earlier. Mann correctly observed that people in precivilized societies were strongly egalitarian and that all attempts on the part of persons with authority to translate such collective power into personal, direct power were successfully resisted: "If the authority figures become overmighty, they are deposed. If they have acquired resources such that they cannot be deposed, the people turn their backs on them, find other authorities, or decentralize into smaller familial settlements."[22] All very true, but with one critical exception. That exception was the relation of slavery. This was the one, and only, situation in which authority figures in such societies could indeed become overmighty, could exercise absolute power over another. Indeed, it was in order to make this possible, to enjoy the delights of total personal power, that slaves were acquired in such societies, given that they were usually of little economic use and often a drain on resources. Precisely because the slave was considered socially dead, and emphatically one who did not belong, he could be freely and totally dominated. Slavery, then, while from its inception suggesting both the desire for the removal of constraint and the possibility or the freedom of absolute personal power, could generate only the latter in precivilized societies.

However, there remained a major limitation. The enjoyment of this absolute freedom to dominate another—incipient sovereignal freedom—was wholly confined to the domination of slaves. The master dared not extend it to nonslave persons; indeed, following the egalitarian principle, he was often forced to share this absolute freedom to dominate with other freemen in his kin group. Men no doubt enjoyed this incipient form of sovereignal freedom, as they would come to enjoy it even more in more civilized societies. But it could never become an ideal value. Its confinement to slaves would alone have smeared it;

and the chronic egalitarian bias of these societies would have cast a veil of suspicion around it, even as men enjoyed it. Sovereignal freedom of this sort was real, and desired, but it remained an obscenity, the psychosocial version of raping the virgins of the enemy.

4. CONTAINED POWER AND THE DAWN OF SOVEREIGNAL FREEDOM IN ARCHAIC POLITIES

Centralized polities first arose, as we know, thousands of years ago in the Near East. The institution of slavery existed in all of them almost from the moment they emerged. It is now generally accepted, however, that in none of them did large-scale slavery develop. Indeed, it was rare for slaves to be used in any productive activities. This has surprised many, and for a long time Marxist scholars indeed thought they had found large-scale slavery in many of these societies.[23] What else could have happened to the vast numbers of prisoners of war known to have been taken in the endless campaigns that checker the history of these earliest of civilized communities? Gelb and others have shown, however, that few of these mass imprisonments resulted in slavery. Instead, whole tribes and peoples were transported from their homelands and resettled elsewhere, or else were used as king's bodyguards, mercenaries, or ordinary soldiers or placed in the service of the temple.[24]

The best-known case in point is that of the Israelites. Their bondage, if that is the proper term for their sojourn in Egypt, was a collective one, and not slavery as we normally understand the institution. Quite apart from the fact that there is no extrabiblical reference to their flight from Egypt, the nature of the exodus is proof enough that the Israelites could not have been individually enslaved in Egypt, and this is borne out by what we know of Egyptian and related ancient Near Eastern slavery.[25] In all likelihood, the Israelites in Egypt were a subject population which had originally either gone there voluntarily or been transferred there forcefully, or perhaps both, then subjected to certain labor demands such as the corvée. The Egyptian term *Apiru* (the Akkadian *Hapiru*), if it is indeed connected to the term *ibri* (Hebrew), would reinforce this speculation, for it denotes a low-status group of foreign origin.[26] There were numerous such groups all over the ancient Near East, almost none of which were slaves. Because Israel's bondage was collective, so was its liberation. Its epic history, in which its Egyptian sojourn was retrospectively reinterpreted as slavery, has no special part in the history of individual freedom. Even though the ancient

Israelites, like all the neighboring peoples, kept slaves, these were
never present in significant numbers, even when state slaves are taken
into account. Further, manumission was rare for those who were of
foreign origin, which was the great majority.[27] Freedom, in fact, was
never a central value among the ancient Israelites and Jews. "The conception of freedom," as Alfred North Whitehead rightly observed,
"never entered into the point of view of the Jehovah of the prophets."[28] What the Egyptian sojourn taught the Israelites was a lasting
sense of ethnic identity, a yearning for home, and a passion for justice,
including justice for the stranger: "You shall not oppress a stranger;
you know the heart of a stranger, for you were strangers in the land
of Egypt."[29]

What genuine slavery existed in the ancient Near Eastern societies
was mainly of the personal and household kind, although in various
periods temple slaves did perform important economic tasks. Significantly, it was precisely slaves of the temple who were never manumitted. There is no evidence that a freedman class ever existed in any
of these ancient civilizations. The notion of the free person never became anything more than a minor legal category. Gelb, summing up
a lifetime of research on the subject, felt obliged to revise his earlier
view of Mesopotamia, in which he had distinguished between an upper, free class; semifree serfs; and chattel slaves. He came finally "to
doubt the validity of the criterion of freedom in class differentiation"—
indeed, to question the use of the class concept altogether. Instead, he
wrote,

> there was never a strong social cleavage in Mesopotamia as there was
> between the free and the unfree in Classical Greece and Rome, or be-
> tween the different castes in the Indic system. In the economic sense, we
> may very well distinguish not three, but two classes, the master class and
> the rest of the population. The latter could include all the dependent
> labor, composed not only of serfs and slaves, but also of the so-called free
> peasantry and craftsmen, who, while theoretically free and independent,
> sooner or later became dependent on the large landowners for water,
> draft animals, plows, seed grain, and other means of production.[30]

Nearly all Western scholars and post-Stalinist Soviet scholars now concur with this position.

The legal evidence clearly indicates that slaves could be manumitted
and that running away was sufficiently important a problem to justify
harsh, and repeatedly enacted, laws against persons harboring them.
The desire for personal freedom, then, was as much a fact of life as

slavery. One of the earliest manumission contracts on record is extremely revealing in this regard. It comes from the first dynasty of Babylon, and concerns a slave who used the traditional legal method of entering into a daughtership with her owner, agreeing to support her for the rest of her life. When the owner died, the slave became free. The document reads, "As long as E, her mother, lives, she [the adopted slave girl] shall support her; and E, her mother, will have been called away by her god, she shall be cleansed, she shall belong to herself, *all her desires will have been attained.*"[31] There is evidence, too, that masters sometimes used the carrot of manumission to motivate their slaves.

So the desire for freedom existed. However, the evidence is equally conclusive that personal freedom never became a value *of any importance* in any of these societies. It is remarkable that, although the laws made provision for manumission, there is "a conspicuous absence of manumission documents" in the hundreds of business records which have survived from ancient and neo-Babylonian times.[32] Isaac Mendelsohn's explanation was that the poorer slaves lacked the means to purchase their freedom, while the rich slaves were too valuable to be freed.[33] The problem here is that Mendelsohn himself had observed that slaves were sometimes motivated to work hard with the promise of manumission. And the same argument could have been used with respect to classical Greece and Rome, where, we know, high rates of manumission prevailed. It would seem that an additional factor explaining the extraordinary absence of records on manumission was the unwillingness of wealthy slaves to be manumitted. They did not want freedom, because there was no social space for the ambitious freedman, and it was not a valued state; indeed, being free involved a loss of status and power.

Bernard J. Siegel, in his monograph on slavery during the Third Dynasty of Ur, concludes that "there was very little difference between the poor man and the slave. Often the latter must have fared much better than the former."[34] It made no sense for a rich slave to become free, because, in a real sense, no one of any significance was, or desired to be, free. The only slaves who sought freedom were the downtrodden bondsmen of ordinary persons who wanted their freedom as a means of improving their material condition. These, however, were despised people, frequently prostitutes. They alone desired personal freedom, and by virtue of that fact, personal freedom, while it existed, was a despised value.

What Max Weber observed of Egypt was generally true of all ancient Near Eastern societies—that relations of personal dependence, and in-

stitutions based on retainers, affected all areas of society. The "prevailing rule would be 'no man without a master,' for the man without
a protector was helpless. Hence the entire population of Egypt was
organized in a hierarchy of clientages."[35] Such a system was actually
800quite consistent with—indeed, could even ensure—moderately equal
justice for all, as T. G. H. James has shown in his study of imperial
Egypt.[36] Many Egyptians made it an ideal to "give bread to the hun-
gry, water to the thirsty, clothing to the naked, a ferryboat to the boat-
less," an ideal which, as Eugene Cruz-Uribe has suggested, was done
in imitation of Isis as a protector goddess.[37] To belong, to be bonded,
was to be protected, by one's patrons and one's gods. To be personally
free was to be deprived of this vital support.

Nothing better illustrates the manner in which the idea of being set
free was evaluated in the ancient Near East than the old Egyptian word
for emancipating someone from slavery. First, there was no specific
word for this experience, which immediately suggests that it could
hardly have been a common or desired occurrence. More important,
however, was the term used to connote emancipation. It was the word
nmh, which literally meant "to be orphaned."[38] This, of course, was
consistent with the practice of ex-slaves giving themselves up for adoption by their former owners. Clearly, the idea of being released from
obligation, far from being a desired state, was equated with one of the
saddest conditions known to human beings, that of being deprived of
one's parents.

Personal freedom was a despised value, and there was hardly a trace
of civic freedom during the historic period. Thorkild Jacobsen argues
that in prehistoric Mesopotamia, as in primitive Europe and Africa,
there existed a kind of "primitive democracy" in the small, loosely
organized, unspecialized communities of the region. Popular assemblies composed of adult male heads of families seem to have played a
significant role in running the public affairs of their communities. These
assemblies, however, were the first of the old institutions to disappear
with the rise of the centralized states and monarchies. All over the
ancient world autocracy was the price of civilized, centralized governments. "The political development in early historical times seems to
lie under the spell of one controlling idea: concentration of political
power in as few hands as possible."[39]

Nonetheless, there is reason to believe that the idea of freedom as
total personal power did develop in these societies. Slavery liberated
the elite from all traditional constraints on personal power in their
relations with their slaves. These constraints, however, remained powerful in the distinctive pattern of clientship which dominated relation-

ships between persons. One detects, nonetheless, a tendency toward breaking out of these constraints. Ultimately, only the most powerful person could achieve this. From very early on, we find the idea expressed that all who serve the ruler were "slaves of the king." What is one to make of this notion?

It is too simple to say that it was merely a respectful mode of expressing deference. It was partly that, in that the upper-class courtiers and others who proudly declared themselves "slaves of the king" were far from being literal slaves. At the same time, it was true that the ruler often had absolute power in these early states. Weber observed of this linguistic pattern that "it reflects the essential characteristic of a liturgy-state: every individual is bound to the function assigned him within the social system, and therefore every individual is in principle unfree."[40] The correlate of this "absence of personal freedom" was, as Henri Frankfort comments, "the king's absolute power." Hence the expression "slave of the king" was really a way of designating the absolute mastery, the total freedom to do as he pleased, which only the ruler possessed. This sovereignal freedom the king used to fulfill "an indispensable function: his personal power appears as the integrating factor of the body politic."[41] It was a privilege to submit to such an all-powerful person. Pharaoh's power was divine; "his authority was founded not in the social, but in the cosmic order."[42] The king, by his divine quality, integrated the state with the powers of nature. For the ordinary Egyptians, this was enough to justify all restraint on their behavior. Indeed, it is anachronistic to think of them, even metaphorically, as sacrificing "all freedom in order to acquire this certainty of harmony with the gods."[43] The question never crossed their minds. Pharaoh was the source of truth, justice, and order.

Among the elite, however, it was different. Slavery established an extreme form of personal intimacy through total submission. The good slave was one who completely lost his identity in the master, became one with him, his mere surrogate. Since pharaoh was one with the gods, so were they, by being one with him, surrogates of the divine. What pharaoh said of his relation with the god, Re, they, as his slaves, could say of their relation with him: "I have made bright the truth (Maat) which he (Re) loves. I know that he lives by it. . . . It is my bread [too]; I too eat of its brightness. I am a likeness from his (Re's) limbs, one with him."[44]

Slavery in this kind of liturgy state, then, became the model of the ideal relationship. It was generative of the absolute freedom which resided in the absolute power of the divine monarch. It was not dialectical. None but the most degraded wished to be relieved of it. It created an ideal not in its sublation but in its imitation. Since only the king-god was free, the only freedom worth having was that which came vicariously in enslavement to him, unless one could replicate this godlike experience with another, a replication possible only with slaves.

For most of the history of the ancient Near East, this idea of freedom as total power remained implicit, expressed only in the positive value attached to the notion of being slave to the king. There was, however, one spectacular exception to this, one moment in which the idea of freedom as total power broke through to intellectual and religious expression. I refer to the heretic pharaoh Amenhotep IV, who reigned in Egypt during the fourteenth century B.C. and is best known as Akhnaton.

All sorts of speculative assertions have been made about Akhnaton, so let me hasten to state that it is not my aim here to add to the romantic folklore about him as the great isolated precursor of personal freedom, the tragic humanist a thousand years before his time, or, as J. H. Breasted grandly put it in a much quoted phrase, "the first individual in History."[45] Recent studies have given us a corrected, and far different, portrait of this favorite "great man" of romantic history.[46] Even so, once allowance has been made for these earlier exaggerations, an important core of truth remains in the romantic conception of Akhnaton.

A conspicuously ugly man, neglected by his father and outshone by his siblings, he ascended the throne of Egypt at the height of its imperial glory. A poor administrator and judge of men, he left the running of his vast empire largely to others, choosing to concentrate on religious reform, although, as F. J. Giles has warned, the letters from the period suggest that historians might have exaggerated Akhnaton's neglect of his empire.[47] In doing so, Akhnaton created cultural havoc, declaring the complex traditional religion, with its rich mythology, anathema and replacing it with the worship of the solar disk. The traditional claim that this idiosyncratic imposition of exclusive sun worship constituted an early form of monotheism is highly questionable. Religion, more than any other institution, is a shared experience, never a one-man show. Great religious innovators, however exalted their charisma, have always worked with, and through, legions of devoted followers. Akhnaton was no prophet; those who followed him did so out of fear or self-interest, not out of devotion or genuine belief. Both Giles and Donald B. Redford are of the opinion that Akhnaton was crazy; this, I might add, does not rule out the possibility that he was religiously inspired. Since the Egyptian king was always considered god incarnate, what was new with Akhnaton, in Giles's opinion, was the fact that he might "have taken this idea literally where other more stable monarchs took it figuratively. In other words, he identified himself with the Aton whose high priest he became at the beginning of his reign, considering himself Egypt's paramount god, and attempted to destroy the worship of all the gods except those connected with Aton (that is, himself)."[48] As someone who grew up in the tropics, I find it easy to sympathize with Redford's view that only a crazy tyrant would create a religion which required ceremonies and official audiences to be held in an ovenlike, open-air temple, under the heat of the noon sun. Apparently Akhnaton's Assyrian neighbors felt the same way.[49]

And yet, it remains ironically true that Akhnaton holds a special place in the history of freedom. Not personal, individual freedom, as it is traditionally imagined, but what we are calling sovereignal freedom. In this regard, Redford's final judgment on the man is worth citing in full:

> For all that can be said in his favor, Akhenaten in spirit remains to the end totalitarian. The right of an individual freely to choose was wholly foreign to him. He was the champion of a universal, celestial power who demanded universal submission, claimed universal truth, and from whom no further revelation could be expected. I cannot conceive a more tiresome regime under which to be fated to live.[50]

In their understandable desire to debunk the myth of Akhnaton, the great forerunner of personal freedom and independence, both Giles and Redford fail to emphasize something equally important in the rich body of materials they present us—that what this extraordinary palace revolution entailed was the conscious celebration of total power as total freedom. Hence, it is no accident that Akhnaton was something of an artist and poet and that he reigned during a period of imperial supremacy when an unusual number of genuine slaves were brought into Egypt and employed in all areas of court life. (The frontispiece of Redford's book is a decoration on the dais of Queen Nefertiti showing three bound female slaves, two of them black and one blond.) Redford expresses his displeasure at the "refined sloth" that undermines the superficially beautiful Amarna reliefs, and goes on to suggest that the same was true of the way of life which Akhnaton held up as an ideal. The two are not unconnected.

What Akhnaton did, or attempted to do, was to break through the one barrier that came between him and the freedom which only a single, universal god could claim. That barrier was Egyptian polytheism and its entrenched body of priests. In the heavenly world, as on earth, a plurality of gods ensured a counterbalancing of divine powers. As imperial monarch, Akhnaton ruled supreme in this world; but he was still not totally free, for he still had the gods and their priests to contend with. So by abolishing all other gods, and replacing them with one god, the solar disk, and by then identifying himself with it, Akhnaton achieved the absolute freedom of total sovereignty, both in heaven and on earth.

Alfred North Whitehead was among those who rightly recognize Akhnaton's revolution as a quest for total freedom, but he was of the view that "Akhnaton, having exercised his freedom, evidently had no conception of freedom as such."[51] In this Whitehead was clearly wrong. A close examination of Akhnaton's iconography and the beautiful hymns to the sun-god which he, in all likelihood, composed himself leaves us in no doubt that he was quite conscious of the intellectual implications of his heresy and knew it to be a pursuit of absolute freedom. Thus he permitted only a few, carefully selected icons traditionally associated with the solar cult, and, as Redford observes, he was "doing so consciously" in order to undercut the role of magicians and craftsmen in determining the sun-god's earthly image: "Pointedly the king alludes to the Disc as 'the one who built himself by himself, with his [own] hands—no craftsman, knows him!' "[52] From as early as the First Intermediate Period, Egyptian "commoners of repute" (literally, "the excellent little men" of their times) had used the expression "to act with one's own arm" as a metaphor of independence. John A. Wilson held that by the Twelfth Dynasty it had gone out of use among ordinary people but, ironically, had been adopted by the pharaohs to describe themselves: "the claim of individualism and independence became a boast of overriding authority."[53] It is this claim to total authority which Akhnaton now took to its logical extreme. As absolute ruler of the universe, the sun disk had to be treated with supine reverence. The sun disk was identified with Akhnaton's father and in this way became "the hypostasis of divine kingship, a pale reflection of his own on earth, projected heavenward."[54] What Akhnaton sought, and very nearly achieved, was something all advocates of sovereignal freedom were to yearn for, with less success, throughout the ages: "He was the Disc's image on earth, and for that reason occupied the central position in the whole system. Since he only was the one that knew his father's mind and will, he alone could interpret that will for all mankind."[55] A. R. David has more recently suggested that Akhnaton's heresy was not so much a revolution as a culmination of ideas and beliefs already under way during the Eighteenth Dynasty.[56]

It was a terrible development of previously existing themes, perhaps, but we cannot deny its originality. This was not the invention of monotheism, as was earlier thought, for precursors of monotheism had existed long before, and were to linger long after, Akhnaton's experiment crumbled.[57]

Akhnaton does, however, have a role in the history of freedom. In an important sense, romantic historians of the nineteenth and early twentieth centuries were right in their claim that this was the first individual in history. For Akhnaton is the prototype of the European romantic hero, the man who alone is free and in his freedom ensures the glory of others whose freedom exists in mere submission. The idea had long existed in Egypt that security was best found in submission to the pharaoh. As a nobleman advised his children some 350 years before Akhnaton, "Worship King (Amen-em-het III), living forever, within your bodies and associate with his majesty in your hearts."[58] With Akhnaton such worship amounted to total surrender:

> To the king, my lord, my pantheon, my Sun-god, say: Thus Yapahu, thy servant, the dirt (under) thy two feet. At the feet of the king, my lord, my pantheon, my sun-god, seven times, I fall. Everything which the king, my lord, said to me I have heard most attentively. . . . Now I have heard the sweet breath of the king, and it goes out to me, and my heart is very serene.[59]

Akhnaton was the first person to identify such total power over others as a supreme form of freedom, and to give it intellectual expression.

Later, in the religions of the Near East, the idea that only the gods were free would become commonplace. And both the Hellenistic Greeks and the Romans, as well as the Christian fathers, would find the idea extremely attractive. It is important to remember that it had its first explicit, intellectual—if not ethical—expression in the power lust of an ugly, artistic tyrant.

5. CONCLUSION

Let us summarize what we have learned from these case studies. First, we have seen that some notion of freedom existed wherever slavery was found. To have a notion of something, however, or even for a segment of the population to want it, is not to make a value of it. A value emerges, is socially constructed, only when a critical mass of persons, or a powerful minority, shares it and, by persistently behaving in accordance with it, makes it normative. Slaves, by themselves, could never have their aspirations institutionalized, being despised nonmembers of their masters' communities.

Second, in the non-Western world, or in preclassical Europe, personal freedom was nowhere actualized, not even where slaves were released from their condition in less than insignificant numbers. I was quite surprised by this finding, because my initial hypothesis had been that personal, negative freedom would have been the first to emerge out of the simple, desperate yearning of the slave to negate his or her condition. But the comparative data soon exposed what was wrong with this view. No slave, except the most degraded, such as prostitutes and robbers, wanted personal freedom where no nonslave found it worthwhile. That was like jumping from a slave ship into a shark-filled ocean. Only where the possibility existed for the isolated individual to fend for himself economically, and to survive the hostility of the freeman socially and culturally, could the slave begin even to think about his freedom as the absence of personal restraint and as doing as he pleased. No such social space ever existed before the rise of slavery in ancient Greece.

Third, while the slave may have been the first to yearn for freedom of this kind, it was not he, or she, but the nonslave who first actually experienced freedom or, more properly, free status as a value. For the slave becoming free entailed the act of emancipation, always a complicated cultural process. For the nonslave becoming free simply entailed an awareness of a not-being or, as we shall see in the case of Homeric and Hesiodic Greece, of being aware of the possibility, the terror, of becoming a slave. To contemplate the social death of the slave was to conceive of one's existence in a wholly new light, as the cherished condition of not being socially dead, not being kinless, not being bereft of one's household and tribal gods. Who in his, or her, right mind would ever have thought of anything so crazy until the perverse reality of slavery came into the world?

Even so, we have also learned that valuing the status of being a freeman did not necessarily entail valuing freedom as an ideal to be *actively* pursued. And it was a far cry from identifying it with the right to participate in the running of one's community. The freeman in simple and archaic society valued his free status, but not his freedom. The free group was a mere collective status; it never became a positively active group; it failed to achieve that transition into the thing Sartre called a "fused group."[60] It had no aim, no being-in-the-world other than not being slave, and some marginal pride in that non-nonentity. Free status never became civic freedom. The closest that simple or archaic society came to such a breakthrough was, ironically, in the most primitive case of the ritual and cannibalistic concentration on the slave; and that, as we have seen, was an evolutionary sink.

One element of freedom did, however, emerge in the slaveholding societies of the non-Western world and pre-Greek Europe—what we have called sovereignal freedom. Indeed, in perhaps the majority of cases where slaves were of no economic or political or ritual value, the only reason for keeping them was to experience the freedom of total power over another person or group of persons. We have emphasized that, in spite of the authoritarian nature of most human societies, this kind of sovereignal freedom to do utterly as one pleased with another simply did not normally exist. People sought to be bonded, to belong in some way to authoritative others, or the groups they represented or led, and, as we have seen, it was just such bonds that the person released from slavery in such societies sought immediately to establish. But such bonds always existed within the context of a network of countervailing powers. No one could do with another as he pleased, precisely because others had a vested interest in him or her. A woman may have belonged to her husband, but she also belonged to her lineage or clan. A father may, in theory, have had the right to kill his child, but in practice he had better have had a good reason for so wantonly depriving the group of a valued member. Being at the nexus of an elaborate system of cross-cutting bonds and allegiances both constrained and protected the individual and, we might add, gave his or her life meaning. Big men, lineage heads, paramount chiefs and kings, even divine ones, were also constrained, if not by ties of kinship, by their relations to the gods and to the priests and shamans who interpreted the ways of the gods.

This constraint on power, however, should not be identified with freedom. Michael Mann has repeatedly warned that "it is important to liberate ourselves from modern notions of society," a dictum he follows admirably in his discussion of power. And yet, ironically, Mann falls prey to just such an anachronism when talking about freedom, when, for instance, in reference to the constraints on power in simple societies, he asserts, "First, the people have possessed freedoms. They have rarely given away powers to elites that they could not recover. . . ."[61] The second statement is as correct as the first is wrong. People shunned absolute power in these societies, yes; but its alternative was almost never the embrace of anything approaching the value we know as personal freedom, or rights.

What Sahlins wrote of paramount chiefs and *romage* heads in traditional Polynesia holds for all societies at this level of development,

namely, that their position "in the social hierarchy is reflected in beliefs in their divine descent, in their *mana* and tabu elaborations, in the
ornateness of their life-crisis rites, and the like."[62] These beliefs and
tabus, under the ever-watchful eyes of the priests or shamans, were
even more powerful constraints on the exercise of absolute power than
the kinship nexus of ordinary mortals. In ancient Mexico, as in ancient
Mesopotamia, "power remained multicentric."[63] This was true even
of the divine pharaohs, for, as Weber correctly observed, "every attempt of the pharaohs to free themselves from the power of the priests
was thwarted."[64] The attempt to escape from just these constraints was
precisely what made Akhnaton's project so audacious and historically
precocious.

In resisting despotic power and the possibility of sovereignal freedom, people sought for themselves not personal freedom or freedoms
but submission to controlled, countervailing authority, the tight protective bondage of the kin-based group. The very fact that this authority was ultimately constrained, that power was multicentric, was what
made obedience a "prime virtue." What Thorkild Jacobsen said of
Mesopotamia was true of all archaic societies—that "the 'good life' was
the 'obedient life' " and that the "individual stood at the center of
ever wider circles of authority which delimited his freedom of action.[65]

It was slavery, and slavery alone, which made it possible to enjoy a
certain kind of freedom, though once men learned its perverse delights
their effort to extend it to other relations of inequality became cease-
less. For most of human history, and in nearly all parts of the non-
Western world, such attempts failed.

How, why, and when did those conditions emerge that made
possible the institutionalized valuation of personal and civic freedoms?
How did these two elements of freedom fuse with the sovereignal
freedom of the master to create the chordal triad that constituted the
supreme general value we call freedom? How could a triad of values
with so degraded a sociological pedigree, and so manifestly dangerous
in its propensities, come to conquer the culture and consciousness of
a people, any people, and, even more incredibly, the civilization that
later came to dominate all the peoples of the world? To these questions
we now turn.

PART TWO

The Greek Construction of Freedom

CHAPTER 3

The Greek Origins of Freedom

1. THE SIGNIFICANCE OF GREECE
IN THE HISTORY OF FREEDOM

Between the end of the seventh and the early fourth century B.C., five great revolutions took place in ancient Athens that were to transform the history of the West and, by extension, that of the world.

One was economic: the creation of a complex preindustrial economy of independent family farms and large peri-urban estates, centered on an export-oriented mining and urban craft economy, occupationally dominated by slave and ex-slave labor.

The second was social and of a twofold nature. On the one side, there emerged for the first time in human history a relatively large slave population which sustained the aristocratic, and a good part of the nonfarm, population of a society. On the other side, we find, also for the first time, the majority of a population entirely emancipated from ties of economic and social dependency on its ruling class.

The third revolution was political: quite simply, the invention of the democratic state in Athens engaging the full participation of all adult male members of the political community.

A profound change in human thought marked the fourth revolution: the discovery of rationality as an end in itself and, by this means, the generation of secular philosophy and the social and moral sciences.

The fifth of these revolutions was the social construction of freedom as a central value, in the course of which we find the creation of per-

sonal freedom and its unique configuration with the other two forms
of freedom in a triadic value that was to remain preeminent in the
Western system of values.

All five revolutions were intimately related. They were so much of
a piece that it is impossible to imagine the emergence of one without
the others. Yet, though all were inextricably linked, one of these developments formed the base for the other four: that foundation being
large-scale slavery. The origins of Western culture and its most cherished ideal, freedom, were founded, we will see, not upon a rock of
human virtue but upon the degraded time fill of man's vilest inhu-
manity to man.

2. EARLY GREEK SLAVERY AND FREEDOM

Freedom in early Greece will be considered in the light of four periods:
the period of *palatine centralism*, essentially Mycenaean Greece from
1400 to 1200; the period of *decentralized tribalism*, roughly that between
the collapse of the palatine states to the end of the ninth century; the
period of *rudimentary state formation*, approximately the late ninth and
eighth centuries; and the period of *aristocratic resurgence*, which roughly
coincides with the late eighth and seventh centuries.

In all essential structural terms, Mycenaean Greece was similar to
the contemporary states of the ancient Near East.[1] It was a cluster of
small states in which a rural population was dominated by a heavily
fortified palace. These separate states were politically highly centralized and hierarchical, but were apparently more decentralized economically, the rural communities being semiautonomous, though obliged
to support the palace population and the warrior aristocracy. The king
or *wanax* stood above three distinct classes—the priest bureaucracy, the
warrior aristocracy, and the farmers.

A fourth class, the slaves, seems to have been an important economic category in the service of the palace, but while they were important for the palatine elite, it seems a reasonable guess that they
were in all likelihood not a major economic force.

That Mycenaean Greece was deeply involved with warfare and foreign trade and that a significant proportion of the slaves, many of
whom must have been war captives, were slaves of the gods are highly
suggestive. It appears that slaves performed a wide variety of tasks
and were permitted the usufruct of land. Interestingly, unions between slaves and nonslaves, especially between slave men and ''free''

women, were "relatively common," and slaves seem to have associated equally with the nonslave population in religious worship.[2]

While it seems reasonable to suppose that slaves could be released from their condition, the distinction between freedom and slavery was not the important one in this society. What was critical, rather, was a person's relation to the palace. The vast majority of persons were in a condition of dependency to the ruling class. No one either sought or was able to escape this dependency; rather, people strove to improve their position in the tight pecking order that existed. In all these respects, the system was very much like that in the contemporary ancient Near East, discussed in the preceding chapter.

The sudden collapse of the Mycenaean kingdoms ushered in one of the great regressions in human history. Literacy, centralized political organization, trading, and the elaborate architectural heritage of the previous millennia were all lost, as the Greek world sank to the neolithic condition of small-scale tribal communities, employing the most primitive technology. Not everything was lost, however, though the issues of vestigial continuities is problematic.[3] One scholar who, while not underestimating the changes, nonetheless makes an imaginative case for at least one crucial continuity is Jean-Pierre Vernant. He argues that the semi-independent, rural communities under their basileus—originally the village head—continued to exist on their own, under the wings of the now independent aristocrats. There was a shift from the palace to the agora, the market center of the local community. He traces the Greek city-state to this shift of social focus. There might be something in this, but it is highly speculative.[4]

Greece during the period of decentralized tribalism—so-called dark-age Greece—was a thoroughly primitive society.[5] It had mainly a grazing economy with a meat-based diet. Politically we find a large number of autonomous kin-based units in which a royal clan formed the nexus of the social order. Increasingly the royal clan seems to have become the first among equals with respect to the aristocratic clans, and while kingship persisted until well into the ninth century, by that time the authority of the basileus, who was really no more than a local chief, had been largely usurped by other aristocratic clansmen. Here, as in all such systems, it is dangerous to speak of class distinctions. As A. M. Snodgrass has observed, "Even such apparently clear-cut issues as those of freedom, serfdom and slavery, or the ownership of the land, may have been far from straightforward in contemporary eyes."[6] We must certainly agree with V. A. Desborough that there is no evidence whatever for the existence of a warrior class: "it is, in fact, most unlikely, as most of the communities were simply far too small for such a separate class to exist."[7] Vertical kinship divisions were far more important. There was little or no room for slavery in these dirt-poor communities, where almost everyone lived in mud huts and tended sheep and cattle, although it is not being suggested that poverty is any obstacle to slavery. At the very most, "a few slaves no doubt remained in the possession of the better off,"[8] but they were of little economic significance.

When we move to the period of rudimentary state formation (the Greece Homer was really writing about, about 750 B.C., although he thought or suggested that he was writing about the period of palatine centralism), several developments immediately impress us. In material culture we find the beginnings of a shift away from a livestock-based economy to arable farming. It was a slow process. As late as 700 B.C. "Greeks still needed exhortation on elementary instruction in arable farming."[9] Closely related to this shift was a rapid increase in population. Land hunger in the grazing economy may have initiated the changeover to arable farming, which then had a dramatic effect on fertility, leading to a surge in population. So, in Malthusian fashion, the land hunger may have then returned. It was probably the main reason for the colonization movements which began in the latter part of the eighth century. While of major importance culturally, the emigration had little effect on population growth.[10]

In the nonmaterial areas of culture, we find the emergence of a stratified society with a rudimentary state system. Enough surplus was being generated to support a dominant class in modest style. The three-class society that emerged consisted of the ruling aristocracy or chieftains; the *demos*, described by F. M. Heichelheim as the "mass of small free landowning peasants who had approximately equal shares of land after regulated field grass economy had been given up for good and the tribal area had been finally distributed"; and the *thetai*, "free people who owned no land, and were instead traders, craftsmen, agricultural laborers, and the personal servants of the upper class, a group which fluctuated between wide extremes."[11]

Below this group were the slaves, still small in number but no longer a wholly insignificant group. Indeed, it is not unreasonable to assume that their ranks were modestly growing in light of the increasing militarism of the aristocratic clans during this period. Finley's interpretation of slavery in the world of Odysseus is still generally accepted:

Slaves existed in number; they were property, disposable at will. More precisely, there were *slave women*, for wars and raids were the main source of supply, and there was little ground, economic or moral, for sparing the lives of the defeated men. The heroes as a rule killed the males and carried off the females, regardless of rank.[12]

The slave women were used as household help in the *oikos* and as concubines. Because status was determined by the father, and not the mother, slave children were constantly assimilated into the nonslave group; given the relative infrequency of male slaves, this meant that slaves would have been recruited largely from outside.

The rudimentary state structure was physically represented in the growing tendency of townlike habitations to emerge as the aristocrats built their homes around the basileus' abode. At the same time, this encirclement of the basileus' domain reflected, perhaps in more than symbolic terms, the aristocracy's growing encroachment on the authority of the chieftain. Increasingly, the latter lost his powers as the aristocrats became more and more independent, leading, for example, their own war parties in raids on other societies. Closely related to this was the growth of a strongly agonistic spirit among the aristocrats. *Arche*, as Vernant observes, was no longer the exclusive property of the king.[13] More and more, collective problems had to be brought to the market square. There was a gradual but decisive shift from the basileus' domain to the agora. Among the aristocrats the dominant value was honor and the critical distinction was that between those who were worthy and those who were not. It was naturally assumed that birth was the main determinant of this quality. Freedom and slavery were not matters that even entered into the domain of values, largely because slavery was not a risk of warfare: men either escaped after defeat or were killed.

While slavery was not of any structural significance, its cultural and psychological impact was increasingly important. Indeed, there was one important category of persons to whom enslavement and, antithetically, freedom were critical—namely, women. Freedom began its long journey in the Western consciousness as a woman's value. It was women who first lived in terror of enslavement, and hence it was women who first came to value its absence, both those who were never captured but lived in dread of it and, even more, those who were captured and lived in hope of being redeemed or, at the very least, being released from their social death and placed among their captors in that new condition which existentially their whole being had come to yearn for.

Even though one of the most memorable of the nonheroic characters of the *Odyssey*, the slave Eumaios, is male, nearly all of Homer's references to slavery are to women, and all but one of his references to freedom involved women. The famous scene in which Odysseus, in disguise, meets and converses with his faithful old slave is as significant for what is not said as for what is said. At no time does Eumaios yearn for his freedom or express any regret at its loss. He is the model of the faithful slave. He does indeed make a celebrated comment on the effect of enslavement: "Zeus, of the wide brows takes away one half of the virtue from a man, once the day of slavery closes upon him."[14]

The context in which the remark is made, however, must be emphasized. Eumaios is referring to Odysseus' dying dog, Argos, which, he claims, has been neglected both by the women of Odysseus' household and by the household slaves. Of the latter, he complains that they "are no longer willing to do their rightful duties" when "their masters are no longer about to make them work." It is not freedom, then, which constitutes half of a man's virtue but men's "willingness to do their rightful duties." Eumaios' enslavement has not prompted him to make any existential discovery of freedom. He is still thoroughly wedded to the dominant value of his own former aristocratic class, having been the son of a king before his capture, and to the aristocrat to whom he is enslaved.

Contrast this now with Homer's references to freedom, all of them appearing in the *Iliad* (there is no reference with the root *eleuther* in the *Odyssey)*. Three of the four significant references to freedom express the fear that was omnipresent in times of war—the loss of freedom of the women in the city. In these three references the same formulaic term is used, namely, the loss of "the day of liberty" (*eleutheron hemar*). The *day* of liberty implies the *night* of compulsion or slavery. Night has power even over the gods[15] and is the most potent symbol of compulsion in archaic Greek poetry. We know from Hesiod that it was not only the mother of sleep and its brother, death,[16] but also, significantly, the mother of day.[17] Hidden in this earliest reference to freedom, then, is a powerful symbolic statement of its origin in the social death that is slavery.

Let us look briefly at the references to freedom. Achilles taunts Aeneas with the memory of how he chased him into Lyrnessos, stormed the place, and "took the day of liberty away from their women and led them as spoil," even though Aeneas got away.[18] Hector, just before killing Patroklus, shouted triumphantly,

> Patroklos, you thought perhaps of devastating our city, of stripping from the Trojan women the day of their liberty and dragging them off in ships to the beloved land of your fathers. Fool! When in front of them the

running horses of Hector strained with their swift feet into the fighting, and I with my own spear am conspicuous among the fighting Trojans, I who beat from them the day of necessity.[19]

But it is in Hector's concern for the fate of his wife, Andromache, that we find one of the most revealing passages on the subject of freedom. In what is perhaps the tenderest passage of the *Iliad*, Hector responds to the fears for his life by his wife, who pleads that she does not want to be a widow. He says that he understands her concerns, that it is not the men of the city he is worried about, should the Greeks win the war, since they will all be killed, but rather:

> . . . the thought of you, when some bronze-armored Achaian leads you off, taking away your day of liberty, in tears; and in Argos you must work at the loom of another, and carry water from the spring Messeis or Hypereia, all unwilling, but strong will be the necessity (*ananke*) upon you. . . . [20]

The cumulative effect of these passages is clear. Personal freedom was a matter of concern in early Greece. Slavery, the day of necessity, was dreaded, and freedom was deeply valued. It was real not only in the constant threat of slavery but also in the actual experience and negation of slavery. The word *ananke*, meaning necessity, or being under compulsion, is used twenty-two times in the *Iliad*, always in a strongly negative manner. In Homer's world we are already far removed from the Mesopotamian ideal of the "good life" as the "obedient life," and it is remarkable that this horror of necessity, of forced obedience, applies as much to women as to men. Only women, however, could recover from its experience.

For one thing, women were sometimes ransomed. The obvious fact should not be neglected that the Trojan War was fought over a woman. While Helen might have wantonly gone off with Paris, as far as the Greeks were concerned, Paris' abuse of his host's hospitality was equivalent to the kidnapping and enslavement of his host's wife. For another, slave women were sometimes married and absorbed into their master's household. This is implied in the reality that the children of slave women by their masters became the accepted progeny of their fathers.

The female origin of freedom is reinforced by another important fact about women in all primitive and archaic societies. It was women who usually moved to their husband's household. Further, where we find many small autonomous warring societies, women were invariably used as pawns and as a means of cementing alliances between these societies in much the same way that they were the means of securing alliances and harmony between feuding or potentially feuding clans within the same society. Thus, in earliest times it was not movement from their families, or even from their societies, that women dreaded, for from infancy they would have been reared for just that. Separation from home was then, as it remains today, a male anxiety. What women and the men of their families dreaded was the forced removal of women, the dishonor to their person and their family, and the absence of any recognized place for them, or their children, in the society of their masters, as the exchange between Hektor and Andromache illustrates. Enslavement was the social death of forced illegitimacy. Once a man suffered such a death, he might as well be physically dead, since there was no prospect of his regaining his honor, not in these earliest kinds of honorific societies. Indeed, as Gregory Nagy makes wonderfully clear, death for the epic Greek hero was not something reluctantly chosen as the lesser of two evils but something actively struggled for in order to gain the glory and honor that were "unfailing," immortal. It is for this reason that Achilles refuses to go back home and die a quiet old age, choosing to stay and fight in Troy and die young; in this way he becomes the epic hero, "destined for immortality in the form of a cultural institution that is predicated on the natural process of death." The greatest of heroes must die.[21]

Women, however, were not caught in this honorific trap. Since they were not expected to be able to defend themselves, they suffered no irreparable loss of honor in their submission and could, indeed, be the symbol of the heroes' honor, dramatically illustrated in the opening chapter of the *Iliad* by the myth of Chryseis, Agamemnon's honor gift, and Briseis, Achilles' slave concubine, and the quarrel between the two men over Briseis. Hence with them the possibility of the restoration of their status as legitimate members of their master's or their own former community existed.

In other words, gender expectations in early Greece made freedom a possibility for women, even as they closed it off to men. It was something for which women could yearn both openly and, like the chorus of slave women in Aeschylus' *Libation Bearers*, in their secret heart, in ways not open to Eumaios, the male swineherd. It was simply not possible for a swineherd to become a prince again. Indeed, for the best of the Achaeans, it was not possible to go home again. Paradoxically, because women had less to lose, they had more to hope for. In that hope, and in its realization, was born the Western valuation of personal freedom.

I am therefore in complete disagreement with Yvon Garlan's view that *freedom* in Homeric Greece referred not to a personal condition of the nonslave population but to the collective independence of a city, "freedom of the state rather than freedom in the state."[22] What could be more personal than the fear of rape and captivity? What could be more cruelly individualistic an experience than the lonely terror of actually experiencing it? And what could more forcefully impress upon the individual consciousness the value of freedom than to be released from this condition?

What Garlan, rather surprisingly in these times, fails to note is that freedom in Homeric society was not a personal or individualistic value *for men*. Another classicist, Kurt Raaflaub, has correctly emphasized that reflection on freedom did not enter into the consciousness of men in Homeric society, since for them death was the only honorable alternative to failure in war. Men fought for status, family, and life, not for freedom. He goes on to observe that women, however, could lose their freedom and obviously dreaded this possibility. But then, inexplicably, Raaflaub asserts that this terrible fear of enslavement among women caused no development of any consciousness of freedom in these societies.[23] I entirely disagree with this conclusion, and will demonstrate why in this and a later chapter. For now, it is enough to note, however embarrassingly obvious the fact, that women have always constituted slightly more than half the human species. If a value was of enormous importance to them, then it must have been an important human value, however irrelevant to their honor-crazed warrior men.

When Homeric men used the term *freedom*, they meant the collective honor of the community, self-sufficiency and independence. It is in this sense that the noble Hector uses the term in his man-to-man talk with his brother Paris. He defends his brother's honor in battle, but feels obliged to express his concern about "the shameful things" being spoken of his (Paris') valor by his fellow Trojans who are undergoing "hard fighting" for his sake. But like a good older brother he ends his speech on the bright side:

> Let us go now; some day hereafter we will make all right
> with the immortal gods in the sky, if Zeus ever grant it,
> setting up to them in our houses the wine-bowl of liberty
> after we have driven out of Troy the strong-greaved Achaians.[24]

Someday, not long thereafter, this whole male view of freedom was to change.

Moving to the fourth of our periods, Greece of the late eighth and seventh centuries, we find a striking combination of factors leading to certain basic changes in the structure of the society. Though this is the period of aristocratic dominance and exploitation, it is also a period of considerable mobility, both physical and social.

A natural economy still prevails, but population growth is now in full swing, in no way abated by the colonization movements. Land hunger increases among the peasants and reaches the point where, on the one hand, a substantial number of lower-class persons become landless and, on the other land, the poorer elements among them become increasingly indebted to the aristocrats. Hesiod's world, Boeotia of about 700 B.C., was one of unremitting toil, though not one that was desperately poor. It was an extreme case of the peasant-based society characterized by a "pugnacious assertion of the self-sufficiency of the individual household."[25] Nearly all land was now held in private property and could be sold on the market. Of crucial significance at this point was the introduction of coinage, sometime during the seventh century B.C., although it would not be until the second half of the seventh and the sixth century that the money economy began to transform, in a vital way, the pattern of trade and the structure of production.[26] Recent studies suggest that in its earliest Greek uses, money was not primarily a medium of exchange (although Athens may have been an exception) but a means of storing value, of defining established norms, and "a civic emblem."[27] An early effect of the introduction of money, however, would have been to facilitate the growth of credit and debt as well as the accumulation of property in land. Hesiod complained bitterly about the rapacious aristocrats, in spite of his respect for law and order.

It is important not to exaggerate. This was not a two-class society of rich and poor; rather, it was one in which substantial numbers of the more marginal smallholders were declining into debt serfdom even while the more prosperous were improving their lot. A distinction must be made between the debt-ridden peasants and the landless *hektemoroi*, who were essentially sharecroppers "who worked land on terms of a fixed rent of one sixth the crop."[28] The aristocrats and nouveaux riches used the distress of these indebted people to secure a flexible labor force (rather than to earn interest, as Finley rightly insists).

Another significant development during the course of the seventh century added to the increasing complexity of the class structure. This was the growth in importance of the hoplite phalanx, which now shifted the fortunes of war in favor of the infantry. It was no longer the heavily armed aristocrat with his prohibitively expensive armor who decided the outcome of battle but the disciplined, swift-moving phalanx. The horse gave way to the ambitious small farmer.[29] More wars and more successes in them meant, of course, more prisoners of war and, therefore, slaves. Furthermore, the increasing role of the peasant in warfare meant that for the first time the prosperous small farmer could hope to own one or two slaves.

To summarize, it is a reasonable speculation that there were six distinct classes of people in Greece at this time. First, there was the class of the dominant and increasingly wealthy aristocrats. Second came the upwardly mobile nonaristocratic farmers who had benefited from the hoplite revolution and were included in the expanded assembly. Third, there was the plurality of hardworking, barely coping farmers still able to hold on to their independence. It was to this group that Hesiod belonged, and his anxieties and resentments are typical of this group of small farmers. He lives in dread of falling into the desperately declining classes just below him. Only grinding work and prudence prevent his downfall. But he is hanging on, and commentators too easily place him in the group which, but for the grace of the gods, he clearly feels he would fall into. Note, however, that he is prosperous enough to own a few slaves and to hire landless laborers, possibly on a sharecropping basis. Hesiod also resents the classes above him. Again, commentators place heavy emphasis on his resentment of the bribe-swallowing princes. But it strikes me that it is the injustice of that section of the lords which meted out unfair judgment in return for bribes which Hesiod rails against, rather than the class as a whole. One gets the strong impression that he is as resentful of another class between his own and the lords. These would be the idle gossipers and high livers, the people who had time for "brawls and gatherings," who already had "plenty of this [grain] and then incite brawls and strife over another man's possession."[30] These sound very much like the men who had made it through the hoplite phalanx, the wrong-doers who, in league with the aristocrats, had won "the court decisions." So successful have they been that Hesiod, in one of his whiniest outbursts, forgets about the justice he extolled and declares, "As matters stand, may neither I nor my son be just men in this world, because it is a bad thing to be just if wrongdoers win the court decision."[31] And while this is an unwarranted speculation, I suspect that Perses, the brother to whom the work is addressed, belongs to this successful class against whom Hesiod self-righteously rails.

Below Hesiod's class of coping small farmers were the sharecroppers and debt bondsmen. The former could easily become the latter, as could the more precarious but still independent farmers. It was the growth of debt bondage which was the most serious social problem

during this period. The bondsmen provided most of the labor force of
the aristocrats, supplemented by the sharecroppers. They were more
critical for the aristocrats than the sharecroppers were, however, not
only because of their greater numbers but because of the greater flexibility of their labor, a flexibility required to produce the new crops the
aristocrats were increasingly interested in.

Finally, there were the slaves who, by now, must have been a significant and growing element. We have seen that they supplemented
the labor force of the small and upwardly mobile farmers. The aristocrats would no doubt have used them in their households as personal
servants. However, we know from the comparative data on servitude
that an aristocratic class always prefers to exploit the members of its
own society where it can get away with it. The start-up costs of imported slave labor are much greater; and their supervision also imposes added administrative costs when used in large numbers, costs
relatively insignificant for the small farmer who labored side by side
with his two or three slaves, as Hesiod did.

It was the aristocrats who were the driving force in all these new
developments, especially the massive growth of debt bondage in Athens. What had taken place was the emergence of new tastes among
them. Their consumption patterns were being increasingly influenced
by their oriental neighbors, with whom their contact, both military and
pacific, grew daily. To get the luxury goods they needed and to live
the new, grander styles of life they coveted, they had to resort either
to plunder, always an inefficient and disruptive means, or to the production of goods which they could use to exchange for the foreign
products they wanted. As C. G. Starr has pointed out, the seventh
century saw the "creation of consciously aristocratic patterns" corresponding to "new modes of artistic and poetic thought."[32] A more
urbane way of life, a more centralized and exploitative political structure which was nonetheless expanded to include the more ambitious
and successful farmers and foot soldiers, a change in the underlying
economic base to a more diversified and specialized economy in both
the agricultural and the nonfarm sectors, and a ruthless exploitation of
the new class of landless laborers and debt bondsmen was the new
order of the day.

This was not a social order generative of the value of freedom. First,
it should be noted that although the absolute, and possibly even the
relative, number of slaves had increased, the proportion of the population in dread of enslavement, and hence antithetically conscious of
freedom, had significantly declined. This was so because female slav-

ery, and its threat, had decreased as a result of the more settled nature of life and of the greater success of Greek soldiers in warfare, both in assault against others and in defense of their own communities. It is this very success which accounts for the greater number of prisoners of war and, hence, of slaves. External trade, too, would have facilitated the importation of slaves. And the new demand for slave labor, even by small farmers, meant a shift of preference toward male slaves. What we may infer, then, is a slow masculation of the experience of slavery, but one not yet expressed in any masculation of the expression of freedom. There was still no social space for freedmen in Hesiod's world; and the radical response of Greek freeborn persons to the intrusion of slavery had to await developments during the sixth century, when we find not simply a significant increase in the slave population but, of even greater importance, a marked change in their uses and their structural impact of the Athenian economy.

The continued indifference of males to the value of freedom is most strikingly revealed in the absence of any reference to freedom, or any related term, in most of the archaic writers. Hesiod never once uses the term, in spite of his many references to slaves. This absence is extraordinary, given the numerous occasions on which a recourse to the value of freedom would seem opportune. Instead, Hesiod's central values are the virtue of work and the divinity of justice: "man must sweat to attain virtue"[33] and "Justice is a maiden and daughter of Zeus" whose "noble title" is respected by all the gods.[34] We may see this as the rustic little man's response to what must have been the dominant values of the dominant classes: the pursuit of honor and glory in warfare and athletic events.

The most prestigious clans, which had united to form the ruling classes, had by the early seventh century either completely gotten rid of the chieftains or so hedged in their power that they were little more than figureheads. In doing so, they emphasized the value of equality, although, of course, equality was only for the worthy. Originally, the aristocratic clans, in their struggle against the basileis, established the principle that those who shared in the fighting shared in the power. Naturally, this had to be extended to those who fought in the hoplite phalanx, especially during the late seventh century.[35] But this was as far as the principle of equality could be taken. Equality, in fact, meant complete mobility and liberation for the aristocrats, limited mobility for the new merchants and hoplite soldiers, and considerable inequality for the majority. This combination of the rise of equality as a value among the dominant classes, and the growth of mobility for a few, and the rise of mass inequality may seem sociologically paradoxical, even impossible. In truth, it is the norm during times of social change: exactly the same situation exists today in the new Third World states of Africa, Asia, and Latin America.

At the same time, freedom, to judge from the existent literary sources, meant nothing to the newly dominant classes. If they thought about it at all, they would have regarded it with contempt. The view that a warrior chose death over slavery still prevailed. The growing number of male slaves, men who had resigned themselves to life and slavery over honor, was living proof of not only the dishonor of their choice but the contemptible nature of the thing they, the slaves, unsuccessfully yearned for—their freedom.

And what of women? While the risk of enslavement may have abated for freeborn Greek women by Hesiod's time, there is no reason to believe that women's freedom consciousness declined. Quite the contrary. As we will argue in a later chapter, women were closely associated with slaves, and empathized with them. Further, we know, and indeed will show in later chapters, that once a group acquires the value of freedom, it does not easily abandon it, even when the dreaded experience that originally generated it has abated. A positive valuation of freedom would surely have persisted among the women of Hesiod's day, at any rate among a good number of them. And the best evidence of such persistence is found in Hesiod's notorious misogyny.

How else can we explain it? Nothing in Homer prepares us for Hesiod's contempt for women.[36] The man is as obsessed with the evils of women as he is with the virtue of work and the injustice of his betters. It is not just his explanation of all evil in terms of the temptation of women which is striking, since this is clearly a borrowing from the neighboring Near East. It is his utterly gratuitous nastiness about women that shocks. The gift of evil which the gods sent to men as punishment for Prometheus' stealing of fire was no pretty weak Eve through whom Satan easily worked but a woman with "stinging desire and limb-gnawing passion" having "the mind of a bitch and a thievish nature," the ultimate scourge for toiling men.[37] Hesiod expresses all the most fundamental male fears about women. He warns his brother "not to be deceived by a woman who wags her tail as she chatters sweetly with a greedy eye on your possessions. You trust a thief when you trust a woman. Men should also marry a girl from the neighborhood whom they should check out carefully so that their bride "will not be the neighborhood joke."[38]

Some historians of ancient Greece have found nothing unusual in such expressions of misogyny, considering it typical of male attitudes in the premodern world. This will not do. As Linda S. Sussman rightly comments, "The literary expression of sexism is a phenomenon that requires an explanation."[39] Many have concluded from all this that Hesiod's world was a "fiercely patriarchal" one. I have drawn just the opposite conclusion. In fiercely patriarchal societies men cease to be obsessed with women harming them; women are so thoroughly under control that they no longer preoccupy men, except when they seek to marry, procreate, and satisfy their sexual appetites.

It is not so in Hesiod's world. He is mightily disturbed by women and obviously fears them, but I cannot agree with Sussman that he has depicted women as "total non-person[s]."[40] That is what patriarchs, wholly secure in the control of women, do. Marylin B. Arthur gets closer to the heart of the matter when she emphasizes Hesiod's ambivalence. He recognizes the positive aspects of women which make them useful, even essential for men, especially in producing male heirs and working in the household, but he "regards as negative those qualities which involved open or secret assertiveness of her own will."[41] Arthur is on the right track, but she presents a too balanced picture of Hesiod's ambivalence. His vehemently negative attitude far outweighed his grudgingly conceded positive view of women. Something more complex was at work.

What we get is a picture of chronic male insecurity about the nature and status of women. Women are clearly out of their place. They are greedy and promiscuous. They incite in Hesiod chronic castration anxieties. How else can we explain the bizarre obsession with pissing in the right places? Granted that there may have been legitimate ritualistic concerns behind the admonition not to "piss as you stand and face the sun" or into springs, it is nonetheless difficult to resist a Freudian explanation of the following advice to his brother:

> Do not piss either off or on the road while you walk.
> The devout and wise man squats for this act,
> Or does it against the sturdy wall of some yard.[42]

Squat! What a revealing piece of advice from a misogynist! It is not only the gods whom Hesiod fears to offend in his advice to his grown brother to act like a woman when pissing by the roadside. The man who fears deeply identifies with what he conceives of as the aggressor—indeed, feels protected in behaving like him, or her. It is likely that this idea was peculiar to Hesiod in his own community.[43]

What I am suggesting then, is that Hesiod's world may well have been the first, brief moment of female liberation in Western history, or at least one in which women asserted themselves. This would be consistent with the prevailing mobility I mentioned earlier. And it is equally consistent with the one other piece of hard evidence we have on gender relations from the early seventh century, a poem in which a young man tries to seduce a girl, in the course of which she first resists, suggesting that he try his luck with another beautiful young woman "who is eager . . . young and delicate."[44] He persists, telling her that the other woman is something of a nymphomaniac who cannot get "enough, a man-woman who knows no measure." After hinting that he will be careful not to get her pregnant, by withdrawing before ejaculation, she willingly agrees. They both then thoroughly enjoy themselves, she "trembling like a fawn," he putting "ashore at [her] garden's grass" before he "sent his white force aside, touching her blonde hair." Such a scene is simply inconceivable in fifth-century Athens. It is significant that the woman was not a noblewoman but an ordinary person. If she was typical—and there is no reason to believe she was not—then, when viewed in the light of Hesiod's obsessive misogyny, and that of other writers of the period,[45] it suggests a period of female assertiveness.

This all makes sense in terms of my argument that in the previous centuries freedom was a female preoccupation. Moreover, this liberated behavior was not confined to Hesiod's class. W. K. Lacey thinks that the women of the aristocratic families "enjoyed considerable freedom."[46] This perhaps overstates the case, though only slightly. I find it significant that the liberation of Greek art from the rigid, geometric abstraction of Homeric times culminated, in its archaic phase, not so much in the *kouros*, the naked standing youth, but in the *kore*, the draped girl, whose depiction, according to Denys Haynes, anticipated, more than any other artistic creation during this period, the extraordinary vitality of the succeeding period.[47] This development is revealing enough by itself, especially when it is contrasted with what later became the quintessential Greek artistic ideal—the young male nude figure. If there is any plausibility to Haynes's argument that the liberation of Greek art reflected the growth of the idea of freedom, the artistic evidence is doubly supportive.

In these experiments in spatial and anatomical representation we may recognize a new visual language expressing a new view of life. Man's conviction of his dependence on powers outside himself, of which . . . archaic convention is the visual symbol, is beginning to yield in Greece to a revolutionary conception of human freedom symbolized by the illusion of organic movement in space. We have reached the threshold of classical art.[48]

And, alas, we have also reached the threshold of man's tolerance for the freedom woman had constructed. Hesiod leaves us in no doubt about what the typical man of Greece thought of this behavior. Women were not only asserting freedom as a value but acting freely; and men abhorred it. "The two best days in a woman's life," wrote the sixth-century poet Hipponax, "are when someone marries her and when he carries her dead body to the grave."[49] The same forces that were paving the way for the male discovery, and appropriation, of freedom as a value were also laying the groundwork for the nearly complete subjection of women. By the end of the sixth century, it would indeed be true that only what men thought mattered, or so it seemed on the surface. The reality was far more complex.

CHAPTER 4

The Emergence of Slave Society and Civic Freedom

Enormous class tensions broke out in many parts of Greece, including Athens, toward the end of the seventh century B.C. The evidence is sparse; indeed, we have no data whatsoever on the period of transition itself. Nonetheless, from what we know of the end result, it is a reasonable extrapolation that a fundamental upheaval took place between Hesiod's time and Solon's. The *Theognidea*, or that authentic part written by Theognis of Megara, makes it clear that the tensions were not confined to Athens. G. E. M. de Ste. Croix is not far wrong in his claim that in these poems "we see bitter class struggle with a vengeance."[1] In the case of Athens, it was to avert social and economic disaster that Solon was called upon to reform the system. However, one critical question remains unanswered about the social upheaval which made the reforms necessary. Why did it take place?

The typical response is to point to the iniquities of Hesiod's time and assume, correctly, that these must have gotten much worse in the succeeding period. To a historical sociologist, however, this begs the question. History presents us with too vast a catalog of oppressed rural classes who never revolt, certainly never to the point of prompting a massive socioeconomic reform, to leave us satisfied with immiseration as an explanation. One need go no further than Sparta to make the point that oppression, while necessary, hardly suffices to explain the extraordinary developments in Athens at the close of the seventh century. Unfortunately, the available evidence does not provide us with anything approaching sufficiency, so we are obliged to speculate.

I suggest that three crucial factors were at play, and they are already broadly hinted at in Hesiod. One, the most important, was the rise of the new class of persons made possible by the hoplite revolution in warfare, the group against which the conservative aristocrat Theognis railed, in the case of his home city of Megara. It was noted earlier that the more prosperous members of this new group were quickly embraced by the aristocrats and were as eager to act as their allies in return for inclusion in the assembly and the economic perquisites that went with their new status. The presence of this class added fuel to the already desperate situation, making it explosive in two ways. First, their very success demonstrated that the aristocracy was not invincible and not the exclusive holder of power. Second, precisely because they came from the nonaristocratic, perhaps in some cases even the oppressed, classes, their presence reinforced the sense of resentment. I am saying, in short, that relative deprivation may have been one critical additional factor explaining the revolt. This is consistent with what we know about servile revolts elsewhere. It is when the oppressed see elements of their own group succeeding and hobnobbing with the powerful that they are most emboldened to revolt, partly because of what the successful demonstrate is possible, partly out of resentment and envy, but also, let it not be forgotten, partly because bolder and more radical elements among the successful would assume leadership in the revolt against the oppressors.

A second critical factor may have been the introduction and spread of literacy, making possible the codification of laws, starting with Draco from the middle of the seventh century. These early laws may have been "written in blood,"[2] as Demades remarked, but they were still laws. And laws, however oppressive, do set limits. Thus the aristocrats really made a strategic class error in codifying the customs of Athens, since they thereby established a measure by which all later judgments could be assessed. Hesiod, who apparently preceded this codification, had nothing to appeal to in his resentment of the "bribe-swallowing" aristocrats. Not long after him his fellow sufferers did. Here I find Vernant's speculations most illuminating. He sees during the late eighth and seventh centuries a rise in the power of speech over other instruments of power. The art of politics became increasingly the management of language, a tendency strongly reinforced by the introduction and spread of literacy. Thus what he calls a "double impulse toward democratization and disclosure" took place. "Greek culture took form by opening to an ever-widening circle—and finally to the entire demos—access to the spiritual world reserved initially for an aristocracy of priests and warriors."[3] This broadening involved a radical transformation: "Knowledge, values, and mental techniques, in becoming elements of common culture, were themselves brought to public view and submitted to criticism and controversy.''[4] In this regard, I might add, perhaps the most remarkable thing about Hesiod's work is the status of the author himself: a disgruntled modest-sized farmer found the time and the literacy to educate his brother and his community on the nature of the gods and on justice, in the process throwing in his own two bits on contemporary injustices. This is amazing: such literary productions would excite wonder even today if written by any of the millions of counterparts to Hesiod in Latin America or Asia. What all this signaled, then, was the end of scribal literature and the growth of rational standards common to all, reflected not only in the codification of the laws but in the citywide generalization of religious cults and ''the transformation of secret wisdom into a body of public truths''.[5]

A third critical factor would have been slavery itself. We have suggested that the numbers, and even the proportion, of slaves had increased during Hesiod's time. We have also argued, however, that there was greater security within Greece itself and a decline in the dread fear of slavery. It was more equity that men yearned for in Hesiod's time. However, something happened sometime between Hesiod's day and the last decades of the seventh century which thoroughly outraged the oppressed masses and may well have been the spark that threatened to blow the whole system apart. That threatening spark, I want to suggest, was the reduction to genuine slavery of Greek debtors who defaulted and, even worse, the new practice of selling Greek debt bondsmen into foreign slavery. Given Hesiod's propensity to catalog the evils of his time, we can be as certain as it is possible to be, when drawing on this kind of negative evidence, that had the practice of sale abroad existed, Hesiod would have cried foul about it. He never mentions such a practice, so we may reasonably conclude that it did not exist in his time. Yet, one of Solon's most unusual reforms was the buying back of Athenians who had been sold into slavery. Clearly, this had been a new development, the one that broke the camel's back. Clearly, too, there must have been very strong pressure to undo the practice, reinforcing our view that this and slavery at home were the key precipitating factors in the threatened revolt. Strong pressure, we are certain, because we know from our comparative study of slavery that buying slaves back from foreign lands is a nearly impossible thing to do. That it was even attempted was extraordinary enough; that Solon apparently succeeded in the effort is very nearly incredible.[6]

Now, while Solon's abolition of all debts in the famous *seisachtheia*, or discharge of burdens, and of all forms of debt bondage and enslavement for debt was an extraordinary reform by any standard, it is important to realize that it was not intended as a revolution from above.[7] As Plutarch makes clear, the condition of the lower groups, especially those who had fallen into the *hektemors'* status, was certainly stabilized, but their land hunger continued, and while some elements of the upper classes may have temporarily suffered, on the whole it seems that the reforms worked in favor of the aristocrats and their new commercial allies. While of lasting social, legal, and political importance, the reforms brought only temporary material benefit to the mass of rural Athenians. There is general agreement with Heichelheim's view that, with the possible exception of the Periclean age, little general material improvement in the standard of living of the mass of Greek people occurred in the long period of antiquity.[8] Whatever the intent of the reforms, and however disappointing the long-term material consequences for the mass of Athenian small farmers, the unintended economic and political consequences for Athens were indeed revolutionary.

What the reforms set in train was an enormous labor crisis and a radical, though *sectoral,* reorganization of the Athenian economy. Like all peoples recently emancipated from dependent labor, the Greeks developed a deep loathing for any form of labor for others. Actually, the Greek attitude to manual labor was a complex issue which deserves closer scrutiny since it was so pivotal in the emergence and perpetuation of slavery on a large scale. The general impression one gets from the later classical sources is that the Greeks despised all forms of manual work. However, as Rudolfo Mondolfo has pointed out, this became true only after the fifth century. Pre-Socratic Greece had a healthy respect for agricultural labor and "recognized the threefold value of labor: economic, moral and intellectual."[9] By the fifth century, though, a growing contempt for all forms of labor is clearly discernible. M. I. Finley has pointed out that the Greeks made an important distinction between manual labor, as such, and independent labor.[10] It was lack of independence that they despised rather than manual work. I think, however, that this distinction holds only until about the middle of the fifth century, after which a general contempt for all manual labor, independent or not, developed in the *urban* areas under the impact of its burgeoning slave economy.[11] I will return to this matter in a later chapter.

In Solon's time, however, the all-important distinction was that between independent and dependent work. People prized working their own plots, and continued to do so, in the agricultural sector, throughout the ages of Greek antiquity. Like the ex-slaves of the West Indies immediately after emancipation, they were induced to work for others only by the threat of starvation, especially with the dread times of debt bondage and sale abroad still fresh in their minds. The members of the ruling class and their hoplite allies suddenly found themselves without a work force, and it was this labor crisis that precipitated the turn to large-scale imported slave labor.[12]

The turn to slavery, however, had its origins not only in a crisis in the supply of labor but in a preexisting demand for it. Finley has stressed the new needs of the elite in generating the demand crisis: "Without a sufficient cash-income the Athenian elites could not have acquired the necessities for even their relatively low life-style, for their indispensable weaponry, or for the taxes which paid for public works, public festivals and public cults."[13] The essence of Finley's argument is that these needs, when combined with the crisis in the supply of labor, led to the adoption of large-scale slavery. I am in complete agreement with the argument as far as it goes, but I suspect that one piece is still missing. Finley focuses on labor needs and supply. But something else was afoot, which requires us to focus more on the production end of the Athenian economy at the end of the seventh century.

There is reason to believe that by the start of the sixth century the intensification of the changeover to olives, figs, and viticulture was no longer optional but essential, not only to meet the need of the aristocrats for imports but also because of declining marginal productivity in grain agriculture. The problem, I am suggesting, ran far deeper than the unfulfilled tastes of the elite. There existed in Athens the ancient version of what economists of the Third World would today call a structural adjustment problem, brought about not only by the rising expectations of the elite but by the declining productivity of the mass of producers. The orthodox view is that by the early sixth century Athens was having difficulty meeting its grain demands, although this view has recently been challenged by Peter Garnsey. Thus, it was obliged to move, on the one hand, into craft industrial and commercial activities, including seafaring, and military exploits as well as mercenary activities and, on the other hand, into agricultural products in which it had a comparative advantage. More land, too, including what was formerly marginal, had to be brought into production. This had the effect of deforesting the countryside. As Jules Toutain pointed out long ago, all over the Greek world "there was an insatiable demand for wood, for building the expanding towns, for shipbuilding to facilitate the expanding trade and for carpentry."[14] As the land was cleared to facilitate these activities, it was planted out, not in grain, but into the new fruit groves—the direct ancient counterpart to a modern underdeveloped economy which shifts from locally consumed cereal production to commercial crops aimed at the export market. This argument, it should be emphasized, does not need to make the assumption that there was a massive increase in population growth during the sixth century.[15]

None of this is meant, for a moment, to deny the traditional explanatory emphasis on the crisis in the labor supply brought on by the *seisachtheia*. This production crisis, however, may well explain an otherwise puzzling aspect of the reforms—the equanimity with which the ruling class accepted them. Classicists even take it for granted that the dominant classes actually initiated the reforms, bringing in Solon for the purpose. As a comparative sociologist, I find this quite improbable. Ruling classes simply do not behave this way, no matter how much in their interests the final outcome. More plausible is the view that the reforms were congruent with their already existing inclination to change the economic bases of their own wealth, a change we should not confuse with the entire economy, which continued to be dominated by small, now-independent farmers. This, plus their recognition that dependent local labor was unsuitable for such a transformation, would have inclined them toward imported slave labor and would have muted their resentment of the reforms.

We know from the comparative data on slavery that the kind of transformation being introduced at that time was highly congruent with slavery.[16] Fruit farmers often require heavy capital expenditure, and there is a long wait before returns. Olives have to be irrigated; vines are notoriously labor-intensive. Such crops can be introduced only very slowly over a period of generations by small farmers. Furthermore, fruit production is notoriously sensitive to calamities, especially war. A grain-growing peasant whose fields are destroyed by the enemy can bounce back in a year; a fruit producer whose olive trees may have taken fifteen years before yielding a profit will have been wiped out if this was his only source of support. The changeover to fruit production on even a moderate scale, then, is not something for the small independent farmer to rush into; he can wisely invest only a part of his land in such crops, and only over several generations. If such crops are introduced on a significant scale, this will be done by the elite, which means that the labor of others will be required.[17] In the absence of native labor, only one kind of labor was available at that time, imported slave labor. On this I wholly concur with de Ste. Croix that in light of "the poor supply of free, hired labor, the easy availability of

slaves, their cheapness,'' and their greater flexibility, ''slavery increased the surplus in the hands of the propertied class to an extent
which could not otherwise have been achieved.''[18] Thus a peculiar convergence of factors explains the extraordinary turn to slavery from the
first half of the sixth century B.C. It was the joint occurrence of all three
factors—the preexisting demand for more flexible foreign labor, the
sudden loss of the traditional source of labor, and the crisis in productivity—that was peculiar to Athens and explains its extraordinary development of the slave economy. To these we should add another
factor, which Garlan considers essential: ''these developments were
favored by a powerful surge in both the military and the commercial
sectors, a development that made it possible for the Greeks gradually
to acquire a position of hegemony vis-à-vis a 'barbarian' world over-
flowing with human livestock.''[19]

Of course, once the process was under way, all three factors reinforced each other. Slavery would have intensified the small Athenian
farmer's loathing for any form of labor for others, a distaste already
well developed from its association with debt bondage. In the absence
of improved agricultural techniques of grain production, any withdrawal of land from grain would have worsened the problem of grain
supply; the small farmer was increasingly reduced to the status of a
self-sufficient, subsistence producer.[20] Thus the elite would have become increasingly dependent on slave-grown, commercial fruit crops
to meet both their foreign-exchange needs and those of the growing
local urban market, and on their slave-manned home farms and urban
households to meet their own food and artisanal needs.

Let me make my own position clear, especially in light of a recent
study by Ellen Meiksins Wood which sharply criticizes various interpretations of the rise of slavery during the sixth century. It is not my
position that slaves ever became the majority of the productive force
in ancient Athens. Most producers throughout Greek antiquity remained in agriculture, and the vast majority of the rural producers
remained free persons in Greece. I wholly agree with Wood that one
of the decisive features of ancient Athens was the free citizen workers'
independence from control by their own elite. Nor am I saying that a
''slave mode of production'' emerged in Greece. There is no such
thing, as I have pointed out elsewhere.[21] What did emerge in Greece
over the course of the sixth and fifth centuries, however, was what
may be called a large-scale slave system or, more simply, a slave society. While the numbers of slaves are always substantial in such a
society, they need not be, indeed rarely are, the majority. Thus to deny

the existence of such a society by arguing about the relative size of the slave population, as Wood and many classical historians, among them Chester G. Starr and A. H. M. Jones, have done, is to miss the point.[22] As Carl Degler pointed out long ago in his criticism of Starr, "the really significant question about the place of slavery in antiquity is not 'Did slaves do most of the work?' but 'What role did they play in the economic process?' "[23]

What emerged in the course of the sixth and fifth centuries was, first, a sectoralized economy with a "modernizing" farm sector dominated by slave labor, upon which the elite increasingly depended.[24] This does not exclude the existence of other forms of surplus extraction, such as rent, or other forms of labor exploitation, such as hired labor, although it should be emphasized that hired labor came increasingly from the pool of rented slaves. Nor does it exclude the possibility, argued strongly by Michael H. Jameson, that slaves became an important supplementary work force for the small, independent farmer in the traditional sector; however, while I am sympathetic to Jameson's position, it is not required by the sectoral modernization model of Athenian economic change I am presenting here.[25] The vast majority of the population remained independent smallholders in the traditional sector, with little real change in their economic condition until the last decades of the fourth century.[26]

Second, the sectoralization of the economy led increasingly to the growth of a "modern" urban sector concentrating on the production of craft goods by slaves, freedmen, and resident aliens as well as citizens and, especially from the early fifth century, to a greatly expanded mining sector almost wholly dominated by slaves. The modern sector made possible the urban civilization and all its manifold cultural achievements. It supported both the aristocratic elite, which continued to gain its wealth mainly from their slave-farmed land and which had dual residence in both city and country, and an urban-based middle class of metics and citizens. The slave-based sector, it must be emphasized, also included the freedman class, which was directly generated by the institution of slavery; another reason why simply relying on counts of slaves is likely to be misleading. Even so, the generally accepted proportion of slaves in the population of Athens during the late fifth century is in no way out of line, in terms of the comparative data on large-scale slave societies.[27] Indeed, the consensus estimate that one in three adults was a slave is almost identical with the estimates of the American South, at the height of the antebellum slave system. Furthermore, as Degler cogently observed, less than a quarter of all southerners owned any slaves and less than 3 percent of all slaveholders owned lots of more than fifty, yet no one ever questions whether the antebellum South was a large-scale slave society.[28]

However, this economic configuration had societywide social and cultural implications for all Athenians (in much the same way that antebellum southern slave society had major consequences for the 75 percent of all southerners who owned no slaves), which is why we use the term *slave society*, rather than slave economy. The first implication was that the modern sector was not divorced from the traditional rural sector. Athens was simply too small a society for that to happen. There was structural articulation, mainly because the elite used their slave-based wealth to control and transform the society. Second, the mere mass of slaves in such a small society also had direct effects on the class of smallholders whether or not they owned slaves. The smallholders not only used slaves as an optional supplementary force when they could afford it but, as I will argue shortly, had strong views about the intrusion of these aliens into their midst, as they did about the extraordinary structural changes taking place in what we have called the modern sector. And third, there were the vital cultural and psychological effects, the most important of which was the promotion of freedom consciousness. This whole process was fraught with conflict, especially between the independent small farmers in the traditional economic sector (whether or not they used slaves) and the slaveholding elite and middle classes in the modern rural and urban sector. It was out of this conflict that democracy emerged.

The sixth century saw a continual struggle on the part of the Attic lower classes to expand the limited gains achieved through the Solonan reforms. Their repeated demand was for a redistribution of land. They did not succeed in achieving any significant economic redistribution. However, the Pisistratids responded to their claims with certain social and legal reforms which emphasized the collective solidarity of all free persons, but met the economic crisis only in a stopgap way. This tradition began with Solon himself, who did not redistribute wealth but, in addition to the legal reforms mentioned earlier, introduced certain jural and religious reforms which have led many to view him as the initiator of the jural-political process which culminated in the fully developed democracy instituted in the reforms of Ephialtes. Accompanying these jural reforms were religious ones. Indeed, it is the main argument of James H. Oliver that the Greek invention and promotion of the value of freedom always had a religious basis. In a felicitous passage, Oliver sums up the achievements of Solon as follows:

What did Solon do to the Athenian assemblies? Solon re-established the union of all citizens by rejecting the theory that only men of property were entitled to sit in the Assembly. . . . As he guaranteed to the *thetes* their place in the Assembly, he gave his action a religious basis by founding a sanctuary of Aphrodite Pandemos. With this dedication Solon called for mutual affection, a union of hearts within the community, a love for each other and for the city, and thereby he created a social ideal not only for Athens but for all Greece and eventually for the whole Mediterranean.[29]

I can accept all of this, even the ringing Grecophilic rhetoric. What Oliver never attempts to answer, however, is the question immediately posed by his encomium: Why did the Athenian ruling class end up inviting its formerly semi-enslaved masses to such a communal love fest? I said earlier that the threat of revolt brought on by the reduction of native Greek farmers to domestic and foreign slavery is what initiated the process. What consolidated and intensified it was the enslavement of non-Greeks in the Attic homeland, within the context of the continued struggle of the Athenian small farmers for greater economic equality.

Plutarch, citing Theophrastus, tells us that Peisistratus "devised the law against unemployment, which made the city more peaceful and the countryside more productive."[30] This sounds for all the world like the make-work, special employment projects of modern Third World governments, desperately staving off lower-class rebellion. The Greek tyrants, however, were smarter, in that they actively pursued programs aimed at enhancing social solidarity. The building program of the Peisistratids, by increasing the social capital of the state, was also a form of indirect redistribution, although the emphasis was clearly on social solidarity and the centralization of the state. This is most clearly seen in the religious reforms of Peisistratus. His glorification of the cult of Athena reinforced the role of the state cult.[31] At the same time, the more primitive aspects of Athena's divine attributes were removed, and replaced by an emphasis on the three dimensions of her divinity which would appeal directly to the three major classes of men in Athens: Athena the armed goddess and champion of the aristocratic warrior ethic; Athena the goddess of handicrafts, protector of the new commercial groups; and Athena the goddess to whom the olive tree was sacred, with immediate appeal to the agricultural sector, but especially that segment involved with the most modern and progressive area of Greek farming. As Walter Burkert has pointed out, "what unites these divergent spheres of competence is not an elemental force, but the force of civilization."[32]

This appeal to collective solidarity would have been facilitated by slavery in several ways. First, the wealth of the Peisistratids and other tyrants was based on mining and trade, two activities heavily dependent on slave labor. Second, the intrusion of slaves into the Athenian body politic would have created resentment on the part of the average Athenian. The religious reforms then attempted to kill two birds with one stone. On the one hand, they muted resentment over the growing number of slaves by emphasizing the value of being a freeborn Athenian. On the other, they displaced resentment over the refusal of the upper classes to grant meaningful redistribution by offering a sharing of collective goods.

These reforms, however, did not remove the desire for greater equality on the part of the mass of freeborn Greeks. If anything, they stimulated the need for more such reforms. "The *tyrannis*," as Victor Ehrenberg has observed, "was the necessary and creative antecedent of democracy."[33] If political equality was the price the elite was going to pay for its growing wealth and increase in the size of the slave population, much more than collective religious participation and the juridical reforms introduced by Solon would be demanded. Those demands came to a head during the last decades of the sixth century and culminated in the reforms of Cleisthenes.

There is no need here to get into the intricacies of these reforms. Their broad outline is well established, and they still dazzle the sociological imagination.[34] What Cleisthenes did, in effect, was to shift the focus of social and political life from kinship to locality, from an emphasis on the *genos* and the phratry to one on the deme. It is an established fact of historical anthropology that such a shift is always conducive to, and indeed generative of, both a centralization of state functions and an equalization of political participation.[35]

In his excellent recent study on the subject, Robin Osborne has nicely summed up the Athenian experience in this transition:

> To be a member of a genos or a phratry was to set oneself apart from some or most of one's geographic associates, while to be a demesman was normal, expected, and meant joining them. The deme as an essential basis of democracy was founded upon the principle of equality, and it was active in all those areas of life where men could plausibly by claimed to be equal; the genos and phratry upheld privilege and inequality, and where the importance of blood ties or the physical variations involved in growing up were paramount, there these exclusive groups were supreme.[36]

The deme, then, became the basis of the new participatory democracy. It was the deme that determined who was and was not a citizen. And the demarche, who was popularly elected, became a key figure not only in local politics but in the central government. Further, the demes selected the *bouleutai*, the people who served on the boule, the council of five hundred, which, under the direction of a subcommittee of *prutaneis* ("presidents"), acted as a kind of steering committee for the *ekklēsia*, or general assembly, which was open to all.

It is a common mistake, however, to conclude from all this that a direct democracy had emerged. Osborne has persuasively questioned the current orthodoxy on this matter. In the first place, bouleutic service was very demanding. It required nearly permanent residence in the *astu*, the city, during the year of service, and only the more prosperous small farmers could afford this. Even so, it was not at this level that the limitations were greatest, since persons closer to the city could perhaps manage the task, and indeed Osborne has marshaled the available data to show a clear geographical bias in attendance at civic meetings.[37] More important, the executive branch of the Athenian government remained firmly in the hands of the aristocracy and the new wealthy elite. The reason for this was that serving in the central government required dual residence, one in the city and a base in the rural deme. And only the wealthy could meet both these conditions. Having a rural residence—manned invariably by slaves if one resided in the city—provided a source of income as well as legitimacy. Members of the upper class developed a certain ambivalence toward the countryside and the deme. They celebrated its virtues but disdained the more demeaning aspects of deme service, not to mention the dreariness of country life. By preserving the integrity of the deme and landownership as an essential precondition of political service, they effectively excluded urban freemen of modest means from the political directorate; but by concentrating centralized political life in the city, they effectively excluded most of those in the rural population who could not keep a permanent dual residence. What emerged during the first half of the fifth century, then, was a genuine democracy, but one in which the wealthy class was in control of executive power though it ruled in cooperation with the popularly elected *boule*. It was the absence of any sharp distinction between city and countryside, and "the absence of a recognizable division separating small and large landowners" (though in fact there was considerable variation in the number of land fragments owned), which explains the workings of this complex democratic process.[38] Osborne's final evaluation of the system is worth quoting in full, although it should not go unnoticed that it betrays the influence of the parliamentary democracy of his native Britain:

The deme was the essential link, forging strong bonds of service and obligation between men of various circles, and connecting the humble demesman to the network of well-to-do through which the main power flowed. Through the demes, what was in theory a direct democracy was in practice a subtle representational one.[39]

One other major development completed the process of democratization, this being the reforms of Ephialtes, who in 462–61 stripped the aristocratic Areopagus of its judicial powers in political cases and handed it over to the jury court, on which all male citizens were eligible to serve. As in all such developments, this critical change came only with great struggle, Ephialtes paying with his life the same year. In his magisterial study of the rise of democracy in Athens, Martin Ostwald has analyzed this process in terms of certain key constitutional changes which culminated in the fifth-century Athenian jury system, a system which, accordingly to Aristotle, was the basis of popular democracy in Athens. The process began with Solon's creation of a popularly elected court of appeal and his institution of the right of any citizen to bring charges against anyone who had committed an offense against the state. Through the changes he made in the council and the assembly, Cleisthenes added the right of the people to determine the legislative process. Then came the reforms of Ephialtes:

> by transferring jurisdiction in political cases from the Areopagus to popular organs, Ephialtes gave the *dēmos* an effective control over the executive offices that is tantamount to guardianship over the state; by extending to judicial proceedings the *isonomia* that Cleisthenes had given the people in legislative matters, he created popular sovereignty, which was justly called *dēmokratia*.[40]

Like Osborne, Ostwald is at pains to show that, even at the most extreme point of development of the Athenian democracy, its important leadership positions all remained in the hands of the propertied and aristocratic classes.[41] The political gains of the mass of male Athenian citizens were revolutionary, and historically unprecedented. For the first time in history, the majority of magistrates in a society was chosen by lot from among all male citizens; an elected council of five hundred supervised the magistrates and prepared the agenda of the assembly, which met some forty times each year and selected all the important military officers; a popular law court, chosen by lot, acted as a supreme court of last resort hearing private and public cases; and, after Pericles, people were actually paid for the performance of their political duties.[42]

All this emerged out of the struggle between the free small farmers and the landowning elite, a struggle in which renegade elements of the aristocracy—libeled as autocratic tyrants by their own class—offered their leadership to the mass of free, independent farmers. I agree with Ellen Meiksins Wood that the independence of the free citizens, not their leisure, was a critical factor in the development of Athenian democracy.[43] But I part company with her when she insists that this was the decisive factor. I can see no compelling reason why the mere fact of being economically independent should induce a population to demand political equality with its rulers. Indeed, what evidence exists suggests that what the mass of Greek farmers wanted was more economic redistribution, more land. In this they failed completely, as other such classes have failed throughout time. What they did get was political redistribution. I would be inclined to believe that this was a second-best demand made by the masses, if there were evidence of even one radical leader who had his roots in the rural smallholder class. The most astonishing—and revealing—thing about Athenian history is that there never existed such a person. The men who instituted the breakthroughs to democracy were nearly all aristocrats. Why did they take these radical steps? What really was going on? Singing paeans of praise to the independent rural farmers of Greece simply will not do. I could offer similar encomiums for the independent small farmers of Jamaica who, like their Athenian counterparts, steadfastly refused to work on the sugar plantations after the abolition of slavery. They too were proud, even aggressively proud, small farmers. They too wanted more land, and even fought a viciously repressed peasant war in their efforts to get it. For over a century it got them nowhere—not even to a parochial vote. The British colonial elite simply refused to play political or economic ball. Endless parallels to the Jamaican case could be found all over the world and throughout history. In sixth-century Athens, however, the rulers had played a serious, sometimes deadly game, with each other and with their free, rural masses. What resulted was the thing that came to be called democracy, in the fifth century B.C.

Slavery was the decisive factor in this development. As we have indicated before, it was both a precondition for and constitutive of the growth and nature of civic freedom. A comparison of the male creation of civic freedom with the way women constituted the idea and value of personal freedom will draw our attention to yet another distinction, that between what may be called the empathic and the contradistinctive modes of constitutively constructing freedom from slavery. Women, we have suggested, and will demonstrate at some length in

a later chapter, came to the value of personal freedom out of an inevitable empathy with the slave condition. When the average woman of
sixth- and even fifth-century Greece saw a slave and paused to reflect
on her or his condition, her musings must have run along the lines of
"There but for the grace of the gods go I." By empathizing with the
slave end of the master-slave relation, then, women became more conscious of freedom by the ever-present experience of powerlessness,
natal alienation, and dishonor, the three basic elements of all slavery
seen from the viewpoint of the slave; of the three, the most important
was the simple horror of total powerlessness. Women never asked
"What can I get out of this relationship? How can I leverage it into
some concession from the ruling class?" They never asked such questions, for the simple reason that it was pointless for them to do so.
Women were excluded from the public household.

Quite the contrary was true of the mass of male farmers during the
sixth and fifth centuries. Empathy was not the prevailing response of
men in the face of the large-scale introduction of slavery. Rather, it
was envy, envy of the master for his good fortune. And the entrenched
nature of envy and competition in Athenian culture is now sufficiently
established among scholars for me not to have to belabor this point.[44]
What impressed the average Greek male about slavery was not the
plight of the slave but the power and honor enhancement of the master. In the zero-sum approach to life which typified these men, rich
and poor alike, the recognition of the master's gain would immediately
have induced a sense of outrage about what was being lost to those
who were not benefiting from the large-scale introduction of slavery.
The answer came easily: what was being lost, or rather being threatened, was the integrity of the homeland. The slave's, and later the
metic's, alienness was emphasized because it was precisely on this
basis that the class of large-scale masters was most vulnerable and that
concessions could be wrung from it. Such concessions, I am saying,
took the form of growing civic freedom. The slave's alienness enhanced the value of the freeman's nativeness. And the master class,
in turn, paid for its desecration of the community with the intrusion
of slaves and other foreigners by making a special value of what it
shared with all who were neither slaves nor aliens. Citizenship, then,
had its crucible in the contradistinction with the non-native, the most
extreme case of which was the slave. The mass of Greek men never
lost sight of this valuable contradistinction. As we will see, nothing is
more fully supported by the available evidence on Athenian democracy than the close causal link between the value of citizenship and
the exclusion of the non-native. The slave, as the quintessential non-

native, was the focus of this culturally creative contradistinction. But it was extended to all foreign elements which the slave system encouraged—indeed, in the case of freedmen, generated. As David Whitehead, writing more of the end result of this process in the late fifth century, pointed out,

> Their preoccupation was with a single, all-embracing demarcation between citizen and metics, which reserved for themselves alone not only all political decisions but the eligibility (if not always the ability) to be permanent and honored shareholders in the social, economic and religious focus of the community, the soil of Attica.[45]

What is more, this emphasis remained wholly male. Athenian democracy, it cannot be too often stressed, was an exclusively male club. Indeed, as Pierre Vidal-Naquet has pointed out, the exclusion of the alien slave was conflated with that of women: "The Greek city in its classical form was marked by a double exclusion: the exclusion of women, which made it a 'men's club'; and the exclusion of slaves, which made it a 'citizens club.' "[46]

It is possible to trace the emergence of this process in the development of the Greek language, more particularly in the terms used for freedom, slavery, and citizenship, and to relate this to contemporary events. Two scholars have undertaken this task: Max Pohlenz, the first modern scholar to expose the central role of slavery in the development and nature of freedom[47]; and, more recently, Kurt Raaflaub, in a brilliant and painstaking study that is as culturally sensitive as it is philologically informed.[48] Both show how freedom began as a term confined to the private-individual realm, in other words, describing what I have called, simply, personal freedom.[49] In one of my few serious disagreements with Raaflaub, I have pointed out the significance of the overwhelmingly female reference of such terms, and will return to the subject in my discussion of the treatment of women and freedom in classical tragedy. The first significant change, after this, came with Solon in his writings on debt bondage. That he was dealing with fellow members of the community, struggling for a recognized place within it, made this the ideal situation for the stimulation of freedom consciousness, and this is faithfully reflected in his language. Men, for the first time, began to take freedom seriously. In doing so, however, they transferred it from the individual-personal domain of language to the public realm. There is clear philological evidence of a growth in the appreciation of the free status of the citizen with the growth of slavery and the resident alien population during the sixth century. Raaflaub finds a strong correlation between the development of the polis and the concept of citizenship, on the one hand, and a sharpened polarization between free and unfree, on the other.[50]

However, it was not only among the mass of Athenian citizens that freedom consciousness developed. Slavery had rendered the independence of the mass of native Greeks possible, not by making them a leisure or idle class, as was once naively thought,[51] but by making their independence tolerable to their former masters by providing them with an alternative, more flexible labor force. But in doing so, slavery had also made the ruling class independent of native free labor, a point that is rarely emphasized. In gaining their labor independence, the small Greek farmers had lost the leverage power of threatening to withdraw their labor in their struggle for greater equality. This is why they turned to renegade members of the aristocracy to help them in their continued struggle for a greater share of the expanding Athenian economic pie. As I argued earlier, what the tyrants gained for them was a greater share of the expanding civic and cultural-religious pie. They offered solidarity with the ruling class on the basis of a common ancestry in the soil of Attica, over against all non-natives, especially slaves. Apart from being a brilliant strategy for maintaining peace with the disgruntled and envious free natives, this strategy would certainly have had a second, equally important function, which no one has ever mentioned with respect to Athens but which is immediately apparent to any student of comparative slavery: it was a powerful means of controlling the growing slave population. Encouragement of hostility to the slave, and identification with the slaveholder class in a unified civic community—given powerful symbolic expression in the promotion of Athena—made not only good political but good economic sense, since it greatly reduced the supervisory costs of slavery. The proud, free citizen-farmer, jealous of any alien intruding on the civic community, would happily do that for the slaveholders.

Nonetheless, the encouragement of civic participation and a sense of contradistinctive identity with the elite alarmed the more traditional aristocrats, who now, for the first time, ceased to take their freedom for granted. A point to note here is one emphasized some time ago by Anthony Andrews: that during the course of the sixth century there was a permanent expansion of the Athenian elite. Many of the tyrants he persuasively argued, were supported by the richer section of the hoplite class in its conflict with the more traditional elements of the nobility.[52]

The philological and related cultural data examined by Pohlenz and by Raaflaub reveal how the internal threat of tyrannies, combined with the external threat of invasion—ever real throughout the late sixth and early fifth centuries—and the need to avoid both, led to what Raaflaub calls a "breakthrough" toward their own notion of freedom among the aristocrats. For the aristocrats, freedom meant power and political equality, *among their class equals*. As Pohlenz neatly stated it, "The concept was transferred from the private sphere when in the class struggles the victory of the other party was described as slavery, so that freedom came to be appreciated from the point of view of home politics," and not just external defeat.[53] For the masses, of course, it also meant equality, but *among class unequals*. The final resolution of intra-elite and interclass conflicts came with the extraordinary reforms of Cleisthenes, reforms made possible, according to Herodotus, only because Cleisthenes, who had been on the losing side in an intra-elite squabble, "took the people into his party," people whom he had "previously held in contempt."[54]

This is where the situation stood at the turn of the fifth century B.C. It was a tense moment in the history of freedom, in consciousness of it, and in the very language used to convey it. But it was a tension pregnant with enormous possibilities. Bringing the whole thing to fulfillment, the very birth pangs of freedom, so to speak, were the Persian Wars.

CHAPTER 5

The Persian Wars and the Creation of Organic (Sovereignal) Freedom

In the last chapter we examined the relationship between the growth of slave society and that of early democracy. It should be noted, however, that there was as yet no general name for this social revolution. The term *demokratia* was not commonly used until late in the fifth century B.C., and then in a perjorative way by the conservative writers who first tell us about it. More important, it was not yet called freedom, though that, of course, is what we know it to have been from the hindsight of history. As Max Pohlenz observed some time ago, ''A really major experience was still necessary, it would appear, before the concept of freedom and enslavement could become central in the thoughts and feelings of the natural community.''[1] There were two such major experiences, the first, and the most important for the history of freedom, being the Persian Wars. The second, to be examined later, was the Peloponnesian War.

Let us be absolutely clear about the point we are making. Freedom, as social value, was already well in existence by the end of the sixth century. We have attributed the invention of the element of personal freedom, the first to emerge, to women; and the invention of civic freedom to the male small farmer in his relations with the wealthy large-scale slaveholders. Before the Persian Wars, too, there existed a primitive precursor to the idea and value of the third element, namely, sovereignal freedom, in the Homeric notion of the free community, that is, one not in subjection to another, and in the transfer of that notion to the domestic scene, in the idea of not being beaten by another elite rival in the struggle for political power.

What we are now about to embark on is an examination, first, of the means by which the language of freedom became fully attached to these three values, whatever they may have been called and however conceived at the end of the sixth century, and, second, of the coming to full term of the value of sovereignal freedom. As we will see, the birth of sovereignal freedom as a fully developed element of the chordal triad was also the occasion for the imprinting of the language of freedom on the preexisting reality of the personal and civic elements as well as on the new element itself. The process by which this imprinting of the language of freedom on the Greek consciousness through the Persian Wars came about, however, was complex. Let us begin by exploring the underlying sociopolitical realities.

The most recent reviews of the evidence suggest that the Persian Wars were not "long enough or destructive enough . . . to produce serious social consequences in Greece," compared with, say, the effects of the Peloponnesian War or of the Punic Wars in Rome.[2] Even so, the Persian episode remains critical for our subject in two respects. First, there can be no doubt that it created for the first time a general male anxiety over the risk of enslavement. The experience of the Greeks in Asia made it clear to everyone that enslavement was one very real cost of war. The world of the early fifth century was far removed from the world of Odysseus, when victory, death, or escape was the overwhelming male experience of warfare. Persia was a relatively advanced empire with a well-developed demand for slaves and a well-established slave-trading system. The masculation of slave anxiety, then, was one crucial effect of the Persian Wars, and with it the antithetical zest for freedom. What men made of this anxiety and newfound zest, however, was different from what women had made of them, as we shall see shortly.

Second, we should be careful not to go too far in underplaying the direct effect of the Persian Wars on Greek social and economic life. The occupation of northern and central Greece and the evacuation of Attica twice during the wars did create social and economic havoc, especially with smaller farmers. These dislocations, the inevitable financial demands of a war economy, must have created openings for the new commercial classes, the very ones most dependent on slave labor. More important, the war worked to the advantage of Athens, not only politically but economically, in giving it access to, and later domination of, the Black Sea route, one that was critical for grain imports and that was, moreover, the most important slave-trading route in antiquity. The Persian Wars also greatly expanded the number of persons exposed to the superior life-style of the Persians, an exposure that had begun with the Persian conquest of the Greek cities of Asia Minor about 547 B.C.[3] Not only would the appetite of the dominant classes have been increased for the luxuries they already knew about, but so would that of the smaller hoplite soldiers, now much more numerous. The satisfaction of these appetites meant one thing: more slavery.

There was, however, yet another respect in which the Persian Wars were crucial in the history of Greek freedom. They led to a temporary political extension of the Hellenic sense of unity which had previously been culturally expressed merely in games and ritual, and they also brought to the level of political consciousness and rhetoric the ideas both of political freedom and of the link between this and other kinds of freedom. The wars were interpreted as wars of liberation. Greeks now began to celebrate their love of freedom as something that distinguished them from the Persians and other barbarians. As Pohlenz observed, the antithesis between Greeks and barbarians came to parallel that between Europe and Asia, and both in turn parallelled the antithesis between the slave and the free mentalities.[4] Kurt Raaflaub has more recently built on this initial insight to give us a rounded picture of the effects of the wars on the discourse of freedom. "The natural freedom of the Greeks vis-à-vis the oriental slave natures of the barbarians, the liberal state-form of the Greek polis vis-à-vis Persian despotism, all these considerations reached prominence in people's thought processes."[5] How, exactly, did this transformation come about?

What the Persian Wars did, first of all, was to provide a wonderful opening for a new, aristocratic reconception of freedom. Victory over the Persians was, after all, the most glorious expression of an old aristocratic value: *arete*—glory, manliness, and valor in warfare and athletics. In Homer's time it was called something else; now the ruling class sought to embrace the rapidly emerging value of freedom by identifying it with the wonderful victory over Persia. Thus freedom was in one fell swoop fused not only with the Hellenic spirit, long an aristocratic monopoly in the Olympic Games, but also with the glory of war and with political independence. From the aristocratic viewpoint this conception of freedom had nothing to do with personal liberty or democracy. Aristocrats were, of course, prepared to broaden it to include all those who had distinguished themselves in war, but not to deepen it to include the other two conceptions of freedom. Indeed, as many passages in Herodotus make clear, freedom for the victorious aristocrats and plutocrats meant the freedom to rule over others. Note, however, that even in this aristocratic conception the antithetical contrast with slavery was central. Thus, when Miltiades urged the polemarch Callimachus to cast his tie-breaking vote in favor of engaging the enemy at Marathon, he said, "It is now in your hands, Callimachus, . . . either to enslave Athens, or to make her free and to leave behind you for all future generations a memory more glorious than even Harmodius and Aristogeiton left."[6]

This language was typical.[7] Men died in battle, wrote the enormously influential Simonides, "to leave to their children their city prospering in freedom."[8] A native of the small island of Ceos, Simonides, who lived during this crucial transitional period (556–ca. 468 B.C.), became a devotee of the pan-Hellenic ideal and a confidant of some of its leading men. He was one of the first persons to speak of the Greek city as a teacher of civilization to men.[9] More than any other lyric poet, he celebrated the aristocratic ideal of the noble, beautiful death. There was, it is true, an unbroken tradition from Homer in praise of what the seventh-century Spartan poet Tyrtaeus called a "beautiful" death, falling for the fatherland. But Simonides was the first to join this theme with that of the freedom and glory of Greece: "If to die well be the chief part of virtue. Fortune granted this to us above all others; for striving to endure Hellas with freedom, we lie here possessed of praise that groweth not old."[10] It was not long before the causal chain was reversed. The Persian Wars were seen not as a struggle for survival which was later interpreted as a struggle for freedom, but from the beginning as a fight in which men died so "that Greece should never strip from their dead heads the crown of freedom."[11]

We can trace, too, in the odes of Pindar, the association of the new ideal of freedom with the traditional aristocratic virtues of war, good living, economic independence, and athletic prowess. The noble person leads "a life without labor," which is left to "others [who] support a burden not to be looked upon."[12] We know by now who those "others" mainly were. The noble person now has "wealth and the fortune to be wise as well," and the power over men and cities, a power which his "free heart displays."[13] Freedom joined to nobility can even overcome treachery. Anguished over the siding of his native Thebes with the Persian enemy, Pindar consoles himself with the thought that "even those things / Can be healed by men if freedom is with them."[14]

James H. Oliver has made a strong case for his thesis that these shifting meanings of the term *freedom* among the aristocrats always had powerful religious associations.[15] Nike—victory—is personified as a goddess and is often associated with the nearly miraculous triumph of the Greeks at the Battle of Marathon, one celebration of which is the

famous Darius Vase of the Naples museum in which the winged goddess awaits the order to fly at the knee of Zeus.[16] But her role in the
Greek aristocratic conception of freedom long predated the Persian
Wars. Nike was the first ally of Zeus in his struggle to establish his
own cosmos. By the late seventh and sixth centuries, she was associated with Zeus in his role as god of the free class within the Greek
populations: "The terms *hellenioi theoi* and *eleutherioi* arose when certain sanctuaries, either newly established or previously exclusive, were
opened to a wider circle in times of compromise or of community
peril."[17] Significantly, from very early on, "the antithesis of *eleutheroi*
was at first helots (or penestae) and slaves," as well as independent
non-Greeks. The Olympic Games gave athletic expression to this zest
for victory and provided a safe outlet for adventurous spirits: "That
was where the family's and his personal pretensions to special *arete*
could be justified." To maintain their prestige, all aristocratic families
had to have such victories. The nike of the aristocrat was interpreted
as an offering to the community's god, and in this way the aristocrats'
glory and right to rule, as defenders of the community's freedom and
civic constitution, were given religious legitimation: "Nike . . . sym-
bolizes, on the one hand, the patriotism and service of the aristocrat
to the civic community, and on the other hand, the reciprocal blessing
of the *hellenioi (eleutherioi) theoi* to civic communities. The little *nike* of
the individual and the big *Nike* of the god are both for the republic."[18]
If Oliver is correct, we should be careful not to go too far in our claims
concerning the cultural impact of the Persian Wars on the history of
freedom. Nonetheless, a fundamental shift in emphasis did come about
as a result of this conflict.

For the aristocrats, the word *free* shifted both in meaning and in
importance. From its sixth-century, domestic meaning of not being
dominated by tyrants, of being an equal part of the political oligarchy,
and of being defenders of the freedom and honor of the Hellenic civic
constitution, it was extended outward to mean, in its negative aspects,
not being enslaved by tyrannical foreigners, in the sense of liberation
from the threat of conquest. In its positive aspects, this meant, however, first a combining of the notion of the national liberation of the
Greek homeland with the traditional aristocratic virtues of honor, glory,
power, and freedom from vulgar work. Second, it meant a greatly
sharpened identification of the culture of the homeland with the culture of the free, in contrast with the culture of the barbarian. To be
free was thus to be Greek, to be noble, to be politically independent,
and to be invincible; to be non-Greek was to be a slave, fit only to be
ruled. The Olympic ideal or ethos was politicized, but was still kept as

an aristocratic ideal. This received expression in the erection of statues all over Greece, including Athens, to Zeus the Liberator. To commemorate the liberation of Hellas, the Eleutherian festival was established, convening every four years.[19] The aristocratic propaganda found expression in all areas, especially in Greek drama. For instance, the only extant Greek tragedy dealing with a contemporary historical event was Aeschylus' *The Persians*. John Herington observes that this departure from the conventional use of mythic sources was not as exceptional as it appears at first sight:

> The fact was that the great Persian invasion of 480–79 B.C. made a unique impact on the Greek imagination. Fifth-century Greek lyric poets, wall painters, and sculptors, who, like the tragedians, traditionally worked through mythology alone to express their visions of life, similarly made an exception for the Persian Wars, for these were felt at once to possess the same exemplary and universal quality as the myths inherited from the far past.[20]

The propaganda was aimed at all classes. Because nearly all freeborn Greeks had participated in the glorious victory over the Persians, all native Greeks could legitimately claim a part of that aristocratic heritage. The aristocrats were now prepared to democratize *arete*, the aristocratic ethos, as long as it was understood that they, more than anyone else, embodied its ideals and were therefore best qualified to rule. Indeed, their claim to have led the liberation of Greece was the ultimate proof of their right to rule. But that right to rule was something in which the poorest of freeborn Greeks could vicariously share with respect to all those who belonged to other states, especially barbarian states, and, more ominously, who were non-Greeks, wherever they might reside, including resident aliens. The freedom of the Greeks, then, the real freedom that existed, became an aristocratic invitation to share in the overlordship of all slave peoples, that is to say, all non-Greeks. In this development was born the Greek, and Western, conception of sovereignal freedom. It was still to be given full expression. So far it was largely an ideal constructed, in the heady experience of the Persian victory, from traditional aristocratic secular and religious values. In a later chapter we will see how the elite intellectuals of the late fifth and fourth centuries brought it to the full conception of organic freedom.

That was how the ruling class saw it. Was that the way the other groups of Athenians interpreted the Persian victory? The evidence is murky, but I am inclined to doubt it. As early as the first half of the seventh century, we find the lyric poet Archilochus (ca. 680–40 B.C.) expressing what looks like skepticism about the ideals and values of the heroic tradition. Consider the following:

> I don't like a great general, one walking legs astride,
> nice hair, shaved, proud of it.
> No, give me a little fellow, legs you can see between—
> that bowlegged!—standing firm on his feet, full of heart.[21]

With Archilochus we get an all too rare, not to mention intimate, glimpse into the thoughts and feelings of those robust, mobile foot soldiers whose unyielding courage and skill were the real engines of Greek military and political change. It is a tragedy of history that we are left so few records of what these men thought; we would love to know, for example, just what Archilochus meant when he expressed the desire "to get to know the rhythm that holds mankind."[22] Archilochus' scornful rejection of aristocratic *arete* and honorific excesses would almost certainly have persisted throughout the sixth century. With the Persian Wars we find an attempt by the aristocrats to persuade all classes of Greeks that they had been saved from slavery, and their freedom preserved, by the glorious exercise of the noble, free spirit of the aristocrats. The question is, Did the nonaristocratic Greeks surrender to this audacious aristocratic claim, or were there still stalwarts around with the temper of Archilochus?

The crucial literary evidence here consists of the early tragedies, especially Aeschylus'. If these tragedies tell us anything about our story, it is that advocates of all three versions of freedom freely staked their claims to the glory of the Persian victory. The transition from the aristocratic to the democratic appropriation of the idea of freedom is most dramatically seen in a comparison of Aeschylus' *The Persians*, first performed in 472, and *The Suppliant Maidens*, produced about a decade later. Both plays emphasize the differences between Greeks and barbarians. And both are very much concerned with the issue of freedom. There are, however, several profound thematic differences between them (quite apart from major stylistic differences, which need not concern us). Herington points out that in *The Persians* "the cosmos remains an intact, static unity," whereas with *The Suppliant Maidens* and the *Oresteia* "the ancient cosmos is riven asunder, and the ancient certainties are gone."[23] He attributes this change to the important political events that had taken place in the interval: "the violent struggle to replace the old constitution by the radical democracy" of Ephialtes and Pericles. Subsumed within this change, however, was another, fully reflected in the plays' thematic differences, to which I now want to draw attention. These plays differ not in the presence of concern with civic freedom in one and its absence in the other but rather in the kind of freedom that was being celebrated. *The Persians* celebrated the great victory over the Persians at Salamis. Persia had been defeated in its attempt "to yoke in servitude Hellas." And their battle cry had been:

> O Greek
> Sons, advance! Free your father's land,
> Free your sons, your wives the sanctuaries
> Of paternal gods, the sepulchers
> Of ancestors.[24]

In this play Aeschylus also explored just what that freedom meant, beyond the preservation of the fatherland. The chorus suggests one dimension: the freedom of people to speak their minds freely, "to bawl their liberty."[25] And, as if aware of the aristocratic extension of the glory of victory to their conception of manly virtue, Aeschylus explicitly states one of the morals of the victory in terms that could not have been missed by his aristocratic peers:

> Insolence (hybris), once blossoming, bears
> Its fruit, a tasseled field of doom, from which
> A weeping harvest's reaped, all tears.
> Behold the punishment of these! remember
> Greece and Athens! lest you disdain
> Your present fortune, and lust after more,
> Squandering great prosperity.
> Zeus is the chastener of overboastful
> Minds, a grievous corrector.[26]

Now, while this is certainly meant to be taken in the religious sense of a condemnation of overweening ambition in the face of the gods,[27] there can be little doubt that it also has a more directly political meaning. One can well imagine the ambivalence of a man like Pindar about such a passage. Two years before the play was produced, he had been reprimanded in Thebes for praising Athens too extravagantly, but even he must by then have begun to have second thoughts about Athens' imperial designs. At the same time, these lines questioned everything he stood for and celebrated in his odes.

When we move to *The Suppliant Maidens* and *The Eumenides* we find a marked transition from the theme of freedom as an outward-looking and elite value, as collective autonomy and aristocratic glory, to the

idea of freedom as an inward-looking, demotic value, the celebration
of participatory, though still limited, democracy. The good king Pelasgus tells the maidens seeking sanctuary from Egyptian tyranny and
enslavement that he is not free to make "promises" until he shares
"with all the citizens."[28] And he sharply rebukes the Egyptian herald
who has come to demand the maidens back. The people have voted
unanimously to offer sanctuary to the maidens, he informs them, and
their word is law, "announced by the tongue of freedom's voice."[29] It
is not clear, though, just how inclusively defined the citizens are.

There is one fascinating additional feature in *The Suppliant Maidens*
on which I have read no satisfactory commentary. This is the seemingly incongruous reference, near the end of the play, to the condition
of the resident alien. After the herald departs, the king turns to the
maidens and their fathers and makes a speech that sounds for all the
world like the resident alien's bill of rights, rights which we know
were, in practice, severely limited.[30] The extraordinary thing about this
passage is the response of the maidens, which is anything but gracious. They thank the king and then add, "Everyone's quick to blame
the alien. [*allothroos*; lit. "people who speak a different language"]
May it be for the best!" Now, granted that these maidens were not
meant to be an attractive bunch (in the lost sequel, forty-nine of them
massacre their Egyptian husbands on their wedding night!), this comment seems gratuitously ungrateful. Aeschylus, however, seems at
pains not to let us attribute the remark to the mean streak of the maidens, for in the next speech their gentle and more solicitous father offers
his daughters, as his most important counsel:

> Time becomes the touchstone of the alien
> [here "*metoikus*," metic, is used],
> Who bears the brunt of every evil tongue,
> The easy target of calumny.[31]

It cannot be an accident that in this earliest extant play to celebrate
civic freedom, there is a harping on the role and status of the alien. By
now, of course, this group would have grown considerably, largely as
a direct result of the expansion of the urban slave-based sector. In
Aeschylus' youth and middle age, that is, up to about the year 465,
the influence of slavery on the growth of the metic population would
have been mainly indirect; but during the last ten years or so of his
life the rate of growth of the metic population would have accelerated,
with increasing numbers coming from the ex-slave population. For the
freeborn Greek, however, the resident alien population would have

been grouped, along with the now-numerous slaves, as part of the growing alien sector, something toward which he was very ambivalent. He could see, by then, the value of both slaves and metics for the urban, not to mention the mining, economy. But he was also anxious to protect, even more, the privileges of his citizenship. As these privileges grew, that is, as democracy expanded, the value of being a freeborn Athenian was increased. It was further increased, the larger the number of persons excluded from it. Thus the alien population both enhanced and defined the value of citizenship. We find, then, a further intensification of one of the most entrenched aspects of the growth of civic freedom in Greece, its tendency toward exclusiveness even as it expanded within a clearly defined group. The deme, we have seen, shifted the basis of Athenian life toward the more inclusive principle of locality. But clear limits were imposed on that inclusiveness. To make membership worthwhile, the club must eventually become a closed group. This tendency toward exclusive inclusiveness, found at the very birth of civic freedom, was to remain with it right down to present times, as will be seen.

Martin Ostwald, in his interpretation of The Suppliant Maidens, argues that it is not only a recasting of the mythical story in support of a democratic constitution but also represents a conflict between the demands of traditional religion (the Danaids' appeal to the sacred right of sanctuary) and those of the security of the state (the risk of war entailed by the granting of the Danaids' request). The conflict is resolved by the state's assimilating religious policy as its own prerogative: "The democratic state has become the protector of religion."[32]

The concerns expressed about the resident alien in The Suppliant Maidens increased in the years immediately after the production of this play. In the light of what I said earlier, it should come as no surprise that in 450, the same year that saw the most generous expansion of democracy for free native Athenians—to the point where, for the first time in history, people were paid to perform their civic duties—we also find a further tightening up of the requirements of citizenship. From then on, both parents had to be citizens (not just the father, as previously) in order for a person to become a citizen. The high point of democracy was also the high point of its exclusiveness. The reasons for this law are complex and not fully understood, but Simon Hornblower is certainly right in his view that "part of the idea may have been a selfish desire to limit citizenship to as few people as possible, now that it brought greater material advantages."[33] Its immediate and long-term effect, writes Davies, was that it "made the Athenian citizen body into a closed group, inaccessible from outside, which it remained until the late third century B.C."[34]

Seven years before these developments, Aeschylus produced the *Oresteia* trilogy, the third of which marked at once the culmination of the grand spiritual themes of the series and Aeschylus' most direct commentary on contemporary internal political developments. The old nobleman poet seems to have adapted well to these radical changes; indeed, Aeschylus belongs to that small group of great Western intellectuals who grew more radical as they grew older, responding gracefully to the swift flow of history in their times, the most famous modern example being John Locke. The renowned speech in which Athena praises democracy is striking not only as a "charter myth"[35] of civic freedom now expanded to the entire adult, male, native Greek population but also for its exclusiveness and condemnation of "foul infusions":

> Here the reverence
> of citizens, their fear and kindred do-no-wrong
> shall hold by day and in the blessing of night alike
> all while the people do not muddy their own laws
> with foul infusions. But if bright water you stain
> with mud, you nevermore will find it fit to drink.
> No anarchy, no rule of a single master. Thus
> I advise my citizens to govern and to grace
> and not to cast fear utterly from your city.[36]

Classicists have long puzzled over the question of what group Aeschylus had in mind in his reference to foul infusions. Dodds suggested that the term refers to "the influx or infiltration of the lower class into the aristocratic Chamber."[37] I am not at all persuaded by this for it is inconsistent with Aeschylus' other references on this subject at this period.[38] It seems more likely that this is a reference to the alien population. The speech has a definitely chauvinistic tone, later contrasting Athens both with other Greek states which were not democratic, most notably Sparta (Pelops' land), and with barbarians. It is not insignificant that the barbarians referred to were the Scythians, who by then formed the most visible ethnic group among the slaves and ex-slaves: they were being introduced just about the time of the play's first production, in an extraordinary role as the policemen of Athens.[39] So, once again, we find an emphasis on exclusiveness in the very celebration of democratic inclusiveness.

The hostile reference to Sparta is very significant. The great celebration of freedom after the Persian Wars was very much a Panhellenic affair, one to which Sparta claimed as much right as, if not more than, Athens. As long as the freedom being celebrated was sovereignal freedom as defined above, Sparta had no problem with it. Indeed, throughout the sixth century it had taken leadership in both the internal and the external defense of the Greek aristocratic ideal of freedom. One of the most famous passages in Herodotus is the conversation between Demaratus, the dethroned king of Sparta, and the Persian king Xerxes, just before his invasion of Greece. Xerxes wanted an assessment of the Greek willingness to resist in the face of seemingly insurmountable force. "Poverty is my country's inheritance from of old," Demaratus said, "but valour she won for herself by wisdom and the strength of law. By her valour Greece now keeps both poverty and bondage at bay."[40] Xerxes wanted it explained how a country that idealized freedom could have strong, obedient soldiers, to which Demaratus answered, "They are free—yes—but not entirely free; for they have a master, and that master is Law, which they fear much more than their subjects fear you."[41] There are two things to note about this extraordinary exchange. The first is that it expresses, in its most perfect and idealized form, the sovereignal conception of freedom: aristocratic valor and wisdom committed to the external protection of the civic community from foreign bondage and to its internal liberty under the rule of law. The second, equally important fact is that Demaratus made a point of informing Xerxes that his remarks applied only to the Spartan group of Dorian Greeks.

Up to the end of the sixth century, the free population of Sparta was, in all likelihood, freer than that of any other Greek states, except perhaps Chios.[42] The slavelike helots there served the same cultural function of generating freedom consciousness that slaves had served in Chios and Athens. True, there were already signs of a divergent path being taken by Sparta, not only in its institution of helotage and militarism but in its legal system, especially the power of the ephors. But the really permanent deviation from Athens came with the Cleisthenean reforms. The Persian Wars papered over these differences, not only because of the common threat but also because the kind of freedom they intensified and celebrated was the Panhellenic aristocratic ideal, now transformed into the notion of sovereignal freedom.

After this, the differences rapidly became more than apparent. They were exacerbated by Athens' growing imperial pretensions, coupled with, indeed ideologically justified by, its claim to leadership of the Greek world on the grounds that it had saved Greece from barbarian slavery and had a superior experience and conception of freedom. But if Athens became the model of civic freedom, both in practice and in propaganda, it remained the apotheosis of sovereignal freedom in the real world, not least of all among the reactionary elite thinkers of late-fifth-century Athens, horrified by the course democracy had taken.

CHAPTER 6

Slavery, Empire, and the
Periclean Fusion

Before moving to the climactic point in the development of Greek freedom, we ought to step back and briefly examine the sociopolitical background during the momentous interval between the end of the Persian Wars and the outbreak of the Peloponnesian War. The massive expansion of silver mining in Laurium after 483 B.C. had an effect on slavery that was as direct as it was brutal. Almost all the miners were slaves, and their condition was the most pitiable and isolated in all antiquity.[1] Indeed, the system was so brutal that, paradoxically, it may have had little direct antithetical effect on the development of freedom. One way in which slavery made freedom possible was through the mechanism of manumission. Although manumission was theoretically possible, very few mining slaves in Laurium could ever realize their desperate hope for manumission.[2] The passion for freedom, however, was as intense among these miners as among their more favored urban counterparts, demonstrated by the fact that during the Peloponnesian War they staged the greatest mass escape of slaves in the whole of antiquity.[3] Nonetheless, the Laurium mines were crucial for their effect on the development of Athenian imperialism and its urban slave economy.

The wealth from these mines fostered the early-fifth-century surge in the growth of the plutocracy in the cities and provided the state with the venture capital not only to build a massive fleet for external domination but, along with the ensuing spoils of empire, to go on an ambitious building spree which greatly expanded urban growth and employment. Athenian imperialism, in turn, worked to the economic benefit of Athens and to the development of the radical phase of its democracy. "The interplay of these two forces—imperialism and democracy—was so great," writes John V. A. Fine, "that it is impossible at times to be sure of the cause and effect relationship, for, if imperialism influenced the growth of democracy, it is equally true that democracy fostered imperialism."[4] All perfectly true; but imperialism and democracy themselves were both inextricably tied up with, indeed, *initially* made possible by, the mining and urban slave sectors.

Internally, as both Finley and De Ste. Croix show,[5] the prosperity generated by slavery and empire not only created more opportunities for the class of propertied "new men" to enter the circle of the traditional ruling class but "satisfied the aspirations of the humbler Athenians."[6] The inflow of wealth from tribute and tax, the earnings and rent of the expropriated land from rebellious subject states, and the mass employment in the greatly swollen fleet (paid for mainly by the subject states) and dockyards benefited rich and poor urban Athenians alike. Finley thinks that the members of the urban lower half of the Athenian citizen body were the greatest beneficiaries, that indeed they gained "to an extent unknown in the Roman empire, or in modern empires."[7]

But the elite also profited handsomely, although to what extent remains uncertain. Prosperity therefore subdued class conflict at Athens but did not entirely do away with it. The struggle for the control of the state, which had resulted in the extraordinary creation of democracy—guaranteed in the jural reforms—continued, with renegade members of the old aristocracy, such as Pericles, and many from the class of new men, such as Cleon, providing leadership for the demos. Although these democratic leaders were despised and caricatured, especially those from the newly rich, and condemned as "demagogues," the democracy was tolerated because, as De Ste. Croix observes, "it was widely recognized to be an integral part of the foundation on which the empire rested."[8]

Finley emphasizes another gain which may have mattered more to the Athenian elite. Imperialism enhanced their lust for power and honor. In other words, it reinforced that conception of sovereignal freedom which had already been brought to a climax in the Persian Wars and the propaganda surrounding them. What, indeed, had happened was that the claim to superiority and the freedom that was the right to rule, which had originally been propagandized as the birthright of all Greeks, was now appropriated by the Athenians and turned against their fellow Greeks. The idea was expressed with imperious candor by the Athenian representative in the debates at Sparta which culminated in the declaration of war against the Athenians:

> We have done nothing extraordinary, nothing contrary to human practice, in accepting an empire when it was offered to us and then in refusing to give it up. Three very powerful motives prevent us from doing so—honor, fear and self-interest. And we were not the first to act in this way. It has always been a rule that the weak should be subject to the strong; besides we consider that we are worthy of our power.[9]

Finley, who cites this passage, might have added that this view of power and empire was one fully shared by all Athenian citizens, even if disproportionately so by the ruling class. The Athenian masses had eagerly embraced the invitation to democratize the aristocratic conception of freedom, while continuing to insist on the priority of civic freedom.

The Athenian system of civic freedom proved to be astonishingly stable. Between the reforms of 508–7 and the destruction of the democracy by the Macedonians in 322, there were only two brief periods of oligarchic rule—in 411 for four months and in 404–3—led by men from the wealthiest classes. De Ste. Croix has rightly described the Athenian demos' resistance to the second of these as "one of the most remarkable and fascinating episodes in Greek history."[10] It should be further noted that so strong was the commitment to democratic rule that when its conqueror Macedon fell to the Dardani in 230, Athens seceded and reestablished a democratic republic, an event celebrated by the creation of a new cult dedicated, significantly, not to Zeus any longer but to the Demos and the Graces. The days of war and imperialism were over. Freedom was now identified with love and graciousness, a development James Oliver finds "full of meaning for a student of the history of freedom."[11] This clearly implies that imperialism, as such, was not a prerequisite for the continuation of the democracy, even though it played a vital role in ensuring its survival during the critical period following its fruition in the reforms of Cleisthenes and Ephialtes. The distinction between those factors that bring a process into being and ensure its early institutionalization and those that account for its perpetuation is one of the most fundamental in historical sociology. It is a distinction, unfortunately, which is too often neglected.[12]

Slavery, unlike the empire, remained with Athens throughout the period of its independence, and beyond, supporting the elite and thereby obviating any need on its part to exploit the demos. What slavery continued to do for the mass of Athenian citizens—to repeat one of my main points—was less to provide them with an economic base (it may well have been an important economic supplement, but this is not required by my argument) than to keep their elite off their backs and to grudgingly reconcile it to the juridical system that was the foundation of the democracy. Nor should one overlook the wisdom of the reforms themselves, in explaining the longevity of the system. As Martin Ostwald has made clear, Ephialtes and his successors ''built sufficient safeguards into the system to prevent it from getting out of hand.''[13]

Perhaps one of the most effective of these safeguards, however, is something none of the reformers could have built into the constitution: the fact that the most important offices of the state remained in the hands of the rich and the aristocratic. And this remained so, astonishingly, even though they were filled by direct election. How do we explain the extraordinary willingness of the Athenian masses to let the ruling class rule, even though it was in their powers so easily to undo it? As Finley observed, ''The people claims *isegoria* [equal freedom of speech and the right to be heard in the Assembly, Council, and jury courts] but left its exercise to a few.''[14] The reason for this, he argues, is that the people were more interested in the decisions arrived at and ''were content with their power to direct those decisions through their power to select, dismiss and punish their political leaders.''[15] The insufficiency of the governmental machinery, the system of pay for holding political office, and the state pensions for war veterans all added to this willingness to let the rulers rule, Finley goes on, for it supported a conception of democratic freedom as a bundle of ''claims on the state, not merely the right not to be interfered with in the private sphere.''[16]

This is all correct and important, but it still does not get to the heart of the problem. Assuming that the mass of Athenians shared the strong competitive ethos of the culture, the love of glory, and the chance to rule, it is hard to understand why some elements of the ordinary people did not force the issue and offer themselves for leadership. For me there is one obvious answer: the strong sense of civic solidarity that existed between the masses and their rulers, which had been nurtured during the sixth century by the deliberate fostering of the idea of their common Greek freedom, vis-à-vis all slaves, freedmen and other aliens, was given renewed vigor by the Persian Wars, and following it, by the even greater growth of the servile, alien population. Finley once remarked, in a much-cited passage, that Greek slavery and freedom developed "hand in hand."[17] However, he meant this only in the preconditional sense. The relation between slavery and freedom, however, ran much deeper than that, as we have already emphasized. The demos accepted the rulership of the traditional ruling class because they saw its members as kinsmen, kith and kin against a world of unfree barbarians. It was slavery that created this conception of the world, one shared by rulers and demos alike.

The imperial period marked one critical phase, the historical high point, of this contradistinctive process. And at the height of this period something profoundly new happened in the history of freedom. All three elements of freedom were identified as part of a single, tightly interrelated process.

Two great Athenian colleagues, whose lives were coterminous with the rise of Athens as an imperial and urban slave power, have left us the most powerful statements of the nature and meaning of freedom in Athens at this critical moment in the history of freedom: Pericles and Sophocles. Both men represented the best of the two wings of the elite—Pericles from the traditional nobility, Sophocles the son of a wealthy arms manufacturer.[18] Both were deeply committed to the ideals and practice of the democratic state and devoted their lives to the service of its political and cultural life. Both were acutely conscious of the dangers of democracy, and of the tension between it and the other two elements of freedom, and came to terms with it in their own, very special ways. Pericles expressed this tension and its resolution in the funeral oration, the great civic stage of the classical drama of democracy. Sophocles explored the cultural chord in his dramas, but nowhere more so than in the work which the West has come to view with a reverence close to that reserved for Scriptures—the *Antigone*. In the remainder of this chapter, I will examine the stateman's conception of the nature and dynamics of the cultural chord, and what this conception meant for the history of freedom; at the end of the next chapter, I will step back about twelve years in time to 441 B.C., approximately when the *Antigone* was first produced, and briefly examine the poet's exploration of the chord.

In the funeral oration of Pericles, given at the end of the first year of the Second Peloponnesian War, we find the first clear statement of freedom as a chordal triad. For me, this is the key significance of the oration. Before this the three different elements of freedom stood apart, were indeed even seen by many as hostile to each other. What is more, the term *freedom* was applied only sporadically to the different elements. Now, for the first time in history, we find not only an unequivocal use of the word *freedom* in terms entirely comprehensible to a modern person but also its application to the three basic components of the value. The three elements are also now conceived of as a fusion generating a more generalized value. But the fusion is not static. There is a clear recognition of a tension within it. Before exploring the nature of that tension, let us briefly look at what the oration actually says.

The funeral oration provided an occasion both to praise the war dead and to celebrate the heritage which "their courage and their virtues" had made possible: "a free country."[19] This is freedom stated as a generalized, chordal value, used then exactly as it is used today when an American, an Englishman, or a Jamaican speaks of his native land as "a free country." In one sense, there was nothing new in this. What is historically unprecedented is Pericles' awareness that it is a composite of three related values. For he goes on to deconstruct this generalized idea into its three component parts.

First and foremost it meant civic freedom:

> Our constitution is called a democracy because power is in the hands not of a minority but of the whole people. When it is a question of settling private disputes, everyone is equal before the law; when it is a question of putting one person before another in positions of public responsibility, what counts is not membership of a particular class, but the actual ability which the man possesses. No one, so long as he has it in him to be of service to the state, is kept in political obscurity because of poverty.[20]

Second, this freedom also meant personal liberty, and there is no ambiguity on the subject in the oration. The words speak for themselves:

> And just as our political life is free and open, so is our day-to-day life in our relations with each other. We do not get into a state with our next-door neighbor if he enjoys himself in his own way, nor do we give him the kind of black looks which, though they do no real harm, still do hurt people's feelings.[21]

I cannot conceive of a better definition of personal freedom than this. And, as if to leave his audience in no doubt about his meaning, Pericles returns to the subject later in his speech in even more telling terms;

> . . . I declare that in my opinion each single one of our citizens, in all the manifold aspects of life, is able to show himself the rightful lord and owner of his own person [self-sufficient], and do this moreover, with exceptional grace and exceptional versatility[22] [i.e., without suspicion, like the Spartans].

Note how personal freedom is here defined in terms of an antithesis to slavery: the personally free person is one who is "owner of his own person [literally "body"]," in contrast to the slave, who is the only human creature that does not possess such self-ownership. Two millennia later, we will find John Locke defining personal freedom in identical terms.[23]

Finally, there is organic or aristocratic freedom. Pericles, an aristocrat of "majestic bearing" and a "nobility of utterance" that some rivals found "disdainful and arrogant,"[24] at first chooses his words carefully in praising this element of freedom. Early in the speech, he contrasts the Spartan version of *arete* with the Athenian: Spartan *arete* is based on autocracy, secrecy, and a restrictive educational system, in contrast with Athens'. The idea being conveyed is that there is a distinctive form of courage and manliness, one based not on fear but on openness, and one intimately linked to the other two elements of freedom.[25] The Athenian way is to meet danger "voluntarily, with an easy mind, instead of with a laborious training, with natural rather than with state-induced courage."[26] Pericles is also very careful to reject the organic version of sovereignal freedom earlier advocated by people such as Pindar. Contrast the citations from Pindar in the last chapter with the following:

> Our love of what is beautiful does not lead us to extravagance; our love of things of the mind does not make us soft. We regard wealth as something to be properly used, rather than as something to boast about. As for poverty, no one need be ashamed to admit it: the real shame is in not taking practical measures to escape from it.[27]

This statement is astonishingly similar to how an upper-class Whig statesman in mid-nineteenth-century Britain would go about defining what freedom meant. Where Pericles differs is in his advocacy of the other two elements of freedom, and in the care he takes to contrast this progressive conservative conception with its closely related autocratic version, which he identifies with the Spartan way. Pericles also appears, at first, to be placing this conception of freedom at the bottom of the triadic hierarchy. Indeed, he prefaces his detailed discussion of it with the remark "And now the most important of these words *has been* spoken. . . ." That is, having "sung the praises of our city"— namely, civic freedom and personal liberty—he will now go on to say a little something about the third element of freedom.

But a strange thing happens from this point onward. For one, having led his audience to expect a few carefully chosen words of praise for this new version of the aristocratic ideal, Pericles gives it, instead, the most expansive statement of the three conceptions. It is as if his head is at odds with his heart here. He tells the audience not only what it wants to hear but what his intellect tells him it ought to hear. This is the voice of Pericles the dissident aristocrat, the colleague of Ephialtes, who had abandoned his class's prejudices and declared himself in favor of the civic and personal freedom of the masses. But when he comes to say his word or two about sovereignal freedom, Pericles the born aristocrat seems to take over. He is more at ease. He cannot restrain his admiration for the value he was brought up to love. The "consummation which has overtaken these men," he says—men who we have already learned have "nobly fought and nobly died"— demonstrates "the meaning of manliness."[28] The war dead may have had their faults, but what should remain in our memory of them is, first, "their gallant conduct against the enemy in defence of their native land." Fair enough. But then he goes on to tell his audience that the task of repelling the enemy "was a risk most glorious, and they accepted it, willing to strike down the enemy and relinquish everything else. . . . In fighting, they thought it more honorable to stand their ground and suffer death than to give in and save their lives."[29] This is beginning to sound more like the traditional ethic, and it becomes positively aristocratic in the next, ringing phrase: "So they fled from the reproaches of men, abiding with life and limb the brunt of battle; and, in a small moment of time, the climax of their lives, a culmination of glory, not of fear, were swept away from us."[30] Pericles then goes on to account for the glory of Athens in terms of the actions of these men. Earlier in the speech he attributed the courage of the war dead to their free spirit and democratic social background. Now, in stark contrast, he attributes it to something else. What made Athens great was "men with a spirit of adventure, men who knew their duty, men who were ashamed to fall below a certain standard. They gave her their lives, to her and all of us, and for their own selves they won praises that never grow old. . . . Their glory remains eternal in men's minds."[31]

And the audience is taken back, almost to the Homeric ethos, when he declares that it was "good fortune—for men to end their lives with honor, as these have done, and for you honorably to lament them: their life was set to a measure where death and happiness went hand in hand."[32] At this point Pericles realizes that the aristocrat in him has completely taken over. He feels obliged to add immediately, "I know that it is difficult to convince you of this." Indeed. One can just imagine the thinly veiled expression of skepticism on many a poor face in the crowd. One recalls that biting piece of political sarcasm from Cassandra in response to the chorus's exhortation: "Woman, be sure your heart is brave; you can take much." Her reply: "None but the unhappy people ever hear such praise."[33] One recalls, too, Herodotus' account of the debacle at the Battle of Lade, during the Persian Wars, when the Ionian sailors, unimpressed by the aristocratic commander's rhetoric to his "fellow countrymen" that only through hard discipline would they be able "to defeat the Persians and keep [their] liberty," chose to abandon ship, saying they preferred the threat of the "slavery" they knew to that of the aristocratic liberty which might well be worse.[34] Was it this kind of skepticism among the poorer elements of the demos that Pericles had in mind when he made that odd remark? Or was he too persuaded by his own propaganda about the superior manliness of all Athenians to have entertained such thoughts? But if so, why should he, even for a moment, have thought it difficult to convince the audience of what he was then saying?

It is important to understand what has happened here. Pericles has isolated, and praised, all the three basic elements of freedom. He has seen how they form a unity, how each requires the other two. But he has clearly seen the tension in the triad. One of the three elements of freedom must form the fundamental note, and the speech seems to be a struggle aloud, an internal debate in the full glare of the Acropolis, and of history, over which element should dominate the harmony. The first half of the speech intellectually concedes the fundamentality of civic freedom; the second half expresses the true feeling of the ruler, that the triad of freedom should be dominated by the sovereignal element having its roots in the aristocratic ethos. Pericles remains wedded to important aspects of this tradition. There is some truth in Thucydides' encomium that he was the sort of aristocrat who "could respect the liberty of the people and at the same time hold them in check," although he goes against the weight of his own evidence when he adds that "in what was nominally a democracy, power was really in the hands of the first citizen."[35] There are two radically new dimensions to this old ideal. One is its democratization. What we have here is the expression of a fundamental principle of Athenian social life and change from the sixth century, the extension "downwards, to the rest of the descent-group, [of] the applicability and appropriateness of aristocratic life-styles and values."[36]

Nicole Loraux has recently pointed out that we find in the funeral oration the transformation of the idea of glory into a political concept.[37] By joining *arete* (glory) with military behavior, the city placed the oration in the hoplitic tradition. Its central theme is the notion of a fine death, and this is more demanding than the athletic prowess of the living, celebrated by the aristocrats. The city is placed above the individual, and the fine death becomes "the model of a civic choice that is both free and determined."[38] Loraux is struck more by Pericles' silences and ambiguities than by what he actually says. She notes that he speaks of government *for* the people, and that the idea of the masses engaging in actual government is suppressed throughout. She is persuasive in her contention that the funeral oration "draws widely on the repertoire of *arete* and makes an aristocratic democracy the very symbol of unity."[39]

In the funeral oration, most notably that of Pericles, a subtle ideological struggle is going on, a struggle in which the distinction between style and substance becomes critical. The substance of civic and personal freedom is expressed in terms of the aristocratic style of sovereignal freedom, and Loraux argues that style may well have triumphed over substance. The central paradox of political thought in classical Athens, she notes along with many others, is that, in the absence of a democratic way of speaking about democracy, the funeral oration became "an aristocratic eulogy" and discourse on democracy.[40] Perhaps.

It seems to me important, however, that another critical new dimension was being added to the discourse. This was the final renaming and reconception of *arete* as a form of freedom, one intimately related to the other three, but the one that should be dominant. Pericles leaves this abundantly clear: "Make up your minds," he says, "that happiness depends on being free, and freedom depends on being courageous."[41] Thus, at this most critical moment in the social construction of freedom, we find a mutual intellectual appropriation rather than a hegemonic triumph through mode of discourse: the masses have finally appropriated the aristocratic ethos; *arete*, the manly Greek virtue which alone is free, has been democratized and is accessible to all. Or so it seems. But the aristocratic ethos has also appropriated, in the process, the most valued ideal of the masses. From now on it is not only the common man who can sing of freedom in all its three meanings. The chordal triad of freedom has now become the common cultural property of all classes. From this point onward, and throughout the agonistic course of Western history, the struggle was no longer over whether there should be freedom or not, or even over whether one or other of the three notes in the chord should exist, but which note, which conception, should dominate the chord and which class should control its meaning.

And above all, which gender. In the last three chapters we have examined the masculinization of the value and ideal of freedom. In the course of that development, the people who had first constructed freedom as social value had gone through a terrible transformation in their status. None other than our man Pericles chose to close his oracular paean to freedom with "a word or two on the duties of women," aimed at the mourning war widows allowed to join the great civic assemblage of the city worshiping itself. What does the great man say? "Your great glory is not to be inferior to what God has made you, and the greatest glory of a woman is to be least talked about by men, *whether they are praising you or criticizing you.*"[42] Clearly, the primal struggle for the appropriation of freedom had to be fought with the people who had invented it. There is every reason to believe that women fought a mighty cultural war to maintain some control of that wisdom, that value, which they had "won from pain." We now turn to that struggle.

CHAPTER 7

A Woman's Song:
The Female Force and the
Ideology of Freedom in Greek
Tragedy and Society

The close correlation of three dramatic developments characterizes the historical sociology of Athens from the end of the aristocratic age to the decline of the polis: the rise of large-scale slavery, the growth of the idealization and the practice of all three elements of freedom, and the changing social condition of women. In this chapter I will examine the last of these developments, paying special attention to its relation to the ideal of freedom as expressed in the most important body of cultural evidence on the subject: Greek tragic drama.

1. THE SOCIAL CONDITION OF WOMEN
IN CLASSICAL ATHENS

The subject of the condition of women in classical Athens is highly controversial.[1] Nonetheless, it is generally agreed that all generalizations must take account of class, status, and regime differences. As slavery and democracy grew in Athens, upper-class and urban middle-class women from Athenian citizen families were increasingly confined to the household, and their lives no doubt became far more circumscribed. The only certain benefit that civilization brought was greater legal protection, and that was largely a by-product of the desire of their menfolk to protect their property.[2] Young women had almost no freedom of choice in selecting their husbands,[3] and while they could, in theory, initiate divorce proceedings, this was rare. Nothing better expressed the real intent of Athenian legal protection of women than the fact that men who violently raped women were punished less severely than those who seduced them, since the latter case entailed the corruption of the woman into a person who dared to exercise her freedom of choice.[4]

Women were married at an early age, nourished less than men, deprived of adult male and even free female company, restricted to unsanitary household conditions and household chores, and wholly excluded from political life—a general pattern of gender segregation which had major implications for the sexual and social life of males and females alike.[5] They also lived between five and ten years less than men, and female infanticide was not uncommon.[6] During the classic period, there were "no traces of literary activity among Athenian women."[7] Several scholars have emphasized that there was a close link between the condition of Athenian women and the growth of both democracy and slavery. The urban slave system made middle- and upper-class women largely redundant in the extra-household economy. It is significant that one of the earliest acts aimed at democratizing the Athenian polity—Solon's abolition of ostentatious funeral processions—restricted the participation of women in funerals.[8]

One should be careful, however, not to paint too bleak a picture. The above generalizations apply largely to middle- and upper-class women in urban areas. Rural women of modest means, of whom we know next to nothing, would in all likelihood have continued to play an important role on the farm. In the urban areas, poor women from Athenian citizen families did engage in the extra-household economy, especially petty trading. And noncitizen women—particularly freedwomen—participated in many areas of the economy and were quite "liberated," both in economic terms and in their relations with men. Many were traders, craftswomen, and innkeepers.[9] Their role as courtesans and prostitutes is well known, although this is admittedly ambiguous evidence for greater personal freedom. Regarding the middle and upper classes, it should be remembered that, however confined, women did manage what was the major part of their husband's property: his household.[10] Within the household, slaves would have been the main adult company of nearly all such women, and one can easily guess at the implications of this close association. In addition to their slaves, women had the company of their children, upon whom they would have exerted more than normal influence, in view of the father's absence from the household.[11]

Men were fully aware of this other world which women created for themselves, and expressed great ambiguity toward and insecurity about it, but this very ambiguity also implied "some movement toward the acceptance of women as full human beings'' and an expectation that women would in one way or another ''assert their claims'' as persons to be respected.[12] These ambiguities, insecurities, and expectations were all fully expressed in tragedy.

2. TRAGEDY AS CULTURAL EVIDENCE

It has frequently been observed that Greek tragedy presents us with a sociological and literary paradox: these dramas were written by authors living in a world of confined women, for an audience of males who seemed to hold women in contempt, yet they are overwhelmingly focused on strong female characters. How do we explain this? And to what degree can tragic drama be used as evidence for the condition of women or attitudes toward freedom in classical Greece?

This is not a false problem which can be dismissed with the observation that the Greek myths which the tragic dramatists were required to use referred to a supernatural world with no link to social reality, or that, insofar as it referred to any real social system, this was the Bronze Age world of the epic poets. We know that the dramatists departed from the traditional version of the myths precisely in their greater emphasis on the centrality and strength of their female characters. These dramas are clearly valuable evidence. But evidence for what?

Not, most certainly, for the social condition of fifth-century Athenian women. It is one thing to argue that the dramatists must have drawn on real women for their characters, which was surely true of Euripides, but quite another to draw conclusions about their social life on the basis of these characterizations, as H.D.F. Kitto and others have attempted.[13] But while nearly useless as evidence on social condition, classical drama is perhaps the perfect body of data for our understanding of fifth-century Athenian values and ideals concerning freedom and women. To be more specific, these dramas tell us a great deal about what men thought about women and freedom, and what they believed women thought about these subjects, much of which may well have been true.

The reason for this is simple. Greek drama was a kind of natural poll of fifth-century Athenian values and ideals; indeed, it was more accurate on such opinion than any randomly administered opinion poll might have been. Ordinary polls measure what Oliver Taplin, speaking of the nature of tragedy, calls the '' 'tragedies' of real life,'' which, ''unlike those of the stage, are often shapeless, sordid, capricious, meaningless."[14] And this is precisely why today we are often so dissatisfied with the facts these polls present us. In Greek drama we find a unique body of sociohistorical material in which dramas, skillfully selected for their expression of the most profound cultural and social ideals, by persons whom we would today call cultural experts, are preserved precisely because they have won the popular approval of the Athenian audience. These tragedies were certainly a means of eliciting and engaging "the emotional experience of [their] audience," as contemporaries like Gorgias, Plato, and others attest.[15] Equally important is the fact that the tragic poets, as Martha Nussbaum has pointed out, "were widely assumed to be the central ethical thinkers and teachers of Greece." They depict "values as plural and incommensurable" and embody "in both their content and their style a conception of human excellence." Whether these conceptions still have relevance to us is something for classical philosophers to ponder, as Nussbaum so skillfully and persuasively does.[16] To the historical sociologist of culture, however, their significance lies in the extraordinary access they give us to the deepest values and ideals, in all their intensity and contradictions, as they reflected and shaped the "collective fantasies" of the Athenian audience.[17] They not only expressed the society's most profound values and ideals but constantly questioned and conversed with them. Simon Goldhill has powerfully expressed this aspect of the genre, and what he has to say deserves to be cited in full:

> Indeed, the institution of tragedy seems to flourish precisely over the period in which the democratic city comes into being. As the city itself lives through the tensions of a changing society, tensions between the public and private life, between the old, traditional ways and the new requirements of the new political order, the tragedies produced in the city seem to draw on the vocabulary, issues, and power struggles of that developing civic language. Tragedy's moment, tragedy's force, is in the articulation of the struggles of the city's discourse.[18]

3. WOMEN, SLAVERY, AND PERSONAL FREEDOM IN GREEK TRAGEDY

Women, if we are to believe these tragedians, not only invented personal freedom but brought something special to its expression, beyond the primal desire for the removal of brute constraint, as the male slaves and freedpersons of the classical and later periods would come to define it. In all Greek drama, both tragic and comic, women stand powerfully, and exclusively, for personal independence, for the voice of individual conscience against personal and political tyranny, for universal and natural, as distinct from man-made, justice, and for the freedom to worship their gods and love whom they choose to love.[19]

It is significant that the tragic heroine is also often a slave: Cassandra in *Agamemnon*, the loyal Techmessa in Sophocles' *Ajax*, and, most powerfully, Euripides' Andromache and Hecuba. This is even more true of many of the minor female roles, but perhaps most important of all is the role of the female slave chorus in many of these dramas, especially the captive Trojan women in *Hecuba* and *Trojan Women*. It is from the chorus of *free* women in one of Aeschylus' earliest extant tragedies, *Seven against Thebes*, that we get one of the most frightening, and accurate, statements of what slavery and the dread fear of it meant to ancient Greek women.

> Pity it were that this city, so ancient,
> should be cast to the House of *Death*,
> a spear-booty, a slave,
> in crumbling ashes, *dishonorably*,
> sacked by an Achaean, with the God's consent;
> that its women be hazed away,
> *captives*, young and old,
> dragged by the hair, as horse by the mane,
> and their raiments torn about them.
> Emptied the city walls,
> as the captive spoil, with mingled cries,
> is led to its *doom*.
> This heavy fate is what I fear.
> It is a woeful thing for maidens unripe,
> before the marriage rites, to tread
> this bitter journey *from their homes*.
> I would say that the *dead*
> are better off than this.[20]

In Greek myth, Greek life, and Greek drama, we find not only that "servile power and female power are linked"[21] but also that the two are linked with the strong desire for, and dangers of, complete personal freedom. The women of Euripides' *Bacchae* are perhaps the best known in this regard, and will be examined in a later chapter. However, nearly all the women of tragedy, especially those who are slaves, express a powerful drive for personal freedom. Andromache remains defiant, boldly criticizes her jealous mistress for being "addicted to injustice," insists on sticking to her principles,[22] and dares Menelaus to kill her: "But not before you and your daughter [Hermione] feel the edge of my tongue."[23] The remarkable thing about Aeschylus' suppliant maidens is their aggressiveness in pursuit of their independence. They threaten not only suicide but sacrilege if they do not get their way. And they are in no doubt about what they want. It is to be removed from "the pride of men, pride well hated."[24]

Aeschylus' *Libation Bearers* is, above all, a play about the struggle for personal freedom and the price one must pay, the suffering, to achieve it. There are other meanings of this tragedy, to be sure, perhaps even more important ones. But the author explicitly draws our attention to the fact that this is one of the play's significant meanings. It is surely significant that all the characters, whatever their outward status, claim to be slaves or to have experienced slavery. Electra says of herself that she has "been sold" by her mother, is like someone kinless, and now is "what a slave is."[25] Orestes tells his mother before he kills her, "I was born of a free father. You sold me."[26] Most important, the chorus apparently shares with Electra the central roles in the play.

Now, the remarkable thing about the chorus is that it consists of slave women who have joined in a conspiracy to murder their master and mistress with the objective of achieving what they explicitly state to be freedom, both for their free or half-free coconspirators and, by implication, for themselves. Once we realize this, something else immediately becomes evident—namely, that everything the chorus says has a double meaning, one spoken by slaves revolting for another set of masters seeking vengeance and the return of their patrimony, the other spoken for themselves, as slaves hating their own condition and their masters, any masters.

In the very first scene, the disguised Orestes sees them coming with libations to the tomb of Agamemnon, and it is significant that although they enter with Electra he takes note of them only with the vivid description "women veiled in dignities of black."[27] And it is the chorus that next speaks, not Electra. Further, the first thing the women have to say concerns their condition of enslavement. Only later do we hear about Electra's agony. They hasten out of the house "hurt by the hard stroke of hands."[28] After setting the scene, they end with another lament on their condition:

> But as for me: gods have forced on my city
> *resisted fate*. From our father's houses
> they led us here, to take the lot of slaves.
> And mine it is to wrench my will, and consent
> to their commands, right or wrong,

> to *beat down my edged hate.*
> And yet under veils I weep
> the vanities that have killed
> my lord; and freeze with sorrow *in the secret heart.*[29]

That last sentence is one of the most loaded in all Greek drama, pregnant with a triple meaning. On one level they are simply mourning their cruel fate. And yet they claim to weep secretly for their murdered lord, Agamemnon, the very man who enslaved them. This, of course, is in earshot of Electra, with whom they will very shortly be joining in murderous conspiracy against their present masters, Clytaemestra and Aegisthus, but this is not the end of it. What exactly is it that's veiled? What sorrow lies hidden? Surely, it is the desperate longing for escape, freedom from their horrible social death. These are not loyal slaves stupidly aiding one pair of future masters against the present. They have already gone through one exchange of masters as a result of the murder of the former by the present. They are unlikely to go through it again, this time as coconspirators with no reward in sight. Aeschylus' Electra is far too shrewd a character not to know this. She says to them,

> We hold a common hatred in this house. Do not
> for fear of any, hide your thought inside your heart.
> The day of destiny waits for the free man as well
> as for the man enslaved beneath an alien hand.[30]

Indeed. But as if to hammer home the point that freedom, and freedom now, is what lies centrally on the mind of the chorus, there follows a dialogue in which Electra asks, "Whom of those closest to me can I call my friend?" to which the chorus responds, with brutal candor, "*Yourself first;* all who hate Aegisthus *after that.*"[31] And lest anyone misses the point, Electra spells it out: "You mean these prayers shall be for you, and for myself?"[32] But she has gone too far. The secret heart of the slave praying for freedom must be ever on guard. No free person can be trusted, not even a closely watched, lonely daughter psychotically bent on revenge for her murdered father. For the time being, Electra must settle for the cryptic response, uttered from behind the veil once more, "You see it now; but it is *you* whose thought this is."[33]

Once the plot is hatched and the slave chorus knows where it stands, the women can be more open. Their excitement grows as the plan to murder the usurpers progresses, and it is not long before we get the distinct feeling that there is a certain sweet tingle, a "love in hate" excitement in their expressions of fear, like that of thieves breaking out of a maximum-security prison who have just killed the guard. Aeschylus leaves us in no doubt that what excites them, what justifies their revolt, is the prize of freedom. What they need, they tell Electra, is "some man at arms who will set free the house, holding the Scythian bow backbent in his hands, a barbarous god of war spattering arrows of closing to slash, with sword hilted fast to his hand."[34] Once again there is a strong duality of meaning here. To Electra's ears this is simply a metonymical appeal to Ares, the god of war. But every member of Aeschylus' fifth-century audience would immediately have caught the second meaning, for the police force of classical Athens was made up exclusively of Scythian slave archers. It was a daring piece of irony for Aeschylus to have a group of slave women plotting murderous rebellion against their masters, literally praying for the slaves who kept the public house of Athens in order to set them free with a barbarous spatter of arrows. The attentive theatergoer would also have remembered Electra's first words to the chorus only a few minutes earlier. She had made her entry with the chorus, had stood silently, dramatically, during the *parodos*, before the tomb of Agamemnon which was center stage, young, innocent, yet in her very innocence disturbingly female, the embodiment of "the female force,"[35] capable of "innocent murder,"[36] a living womb, essential for life, set before its outward expression, a cavernous tomb (a man's house?) equally necessary for life. And her first words had been "Attendant women, who order our house . . ."

When, in the next instant, Electra discovers Orestes' lock of hair, the chorus squeals, "My heart is in a dance of fear." Maybe, but the women are also having the time of their wretched lives. As women and as slaves, they see men as standing most strongly for what they are up against. The struggle for freedom is the resistance of the female force against the brutal assault of men:

> The female force, the desperate
> love crams its resisted way
> on marriage and the dark embrace
> of brute beasts, of mortal men.[37]

The celebrated choral ode to Zeus, in which the chorus prays for Orestes' success in avenging the death of his father by killing his mother and her husband, is often taken by commentators as simply the traditional, and fading, Greek concept of justice through vengeance. But such an interpretation is meaningful only if we view the chorus in its role as attendants. A different light is cast on the ode when we view its members as slaves who have joined in a palace revolt for the sole purpose of gaining their freedom, and I do not see how we can avoid such an interpretation, since one of the most stunning expressions of freedom, as the antithesis of the dark tomb of slavery, lies at the very center of the prayer:

> And you, who keep, magnificent, the hallowed and huge
> cavern, o grant that the man's house lift up its head
> and look on the shining daylight
> and *liberty [eleutheria]* with eyes made
> glad with gazing out from the helm of darkness.[38]

The "huge cavern" is a reference to the inner sanctum of the temple of Apollo at Delphi, and it powerfully echoes both the outer womb of Agamemnon's tomb and the inner womb of women, fusing together the image of the female force. Hogan notes that Apollo and Hermes, referred to in the next stanza, "make a pair of sons of Zeus, one from light, the other for darkness, to guard the son of the house."[39] What is powerfully expressed in this unforgettable tripartite symbol is the tripartite chord of freedom: womb is generative personal freedom; Agamemnon's tomb is male force, freedom as deathly power; and Apollo's sanctuary is the Athenian temple of civic freedom. It is the female force, however, that generates the triad and remains its fundamental element. Freedom, the chorus tell us, is "a woman's song":

> Then at last we shall sing
> for deliverance of the house
> the woman's song that sets the wind
> fair, no thin drawn and grief
> struck wail, but this: "The ship sails fair."
> My way, *mine*, the advantage piles here, with wreck
> and ruin far from those I love.[40]

The women pray again to Zeus as Aegisthus is being murdered by Orestes. And once again, it is freedom that comes to their lips: ". . . our man will kindle a flame and light of liberty, win the domain and huge treasure of his fathers."[41] And when, moments later, he takes his mother inside to cut her down, they break out into a joyful celebration, first of justice, which is vengeance, but then, even more ringingly, of what that justice means:

> Raise up the high cry over our lordship's house
> won *free* of distress, *free* of its fortunes wasted
> by two stained murder,
> *free* of its mournful luck.[42]

Again the dual meaning; for if my reading is correct we must now ask, Whose distress are the women really talking about, whose wasted fortune, and whose mournful luck? When Orestes begins to suffer pangs of guilt over murdering his mother, they reassure him that what he did was well done because he "liberated *all* the Argive city" when he killed his mother and her husband.[43] But Orestes is not to be let off so easily. The furies, all women, set upon him. There is something almost detached about their advice to the tormented Orestes that he should go to Loxias, whose touch will set him free, and a note of contempt in their offhand "good luck to you then" as he exits, pursued by the furies.[44] Why should they care? He has served his purpose, a savior of sorts, they hope. Or, "shall I call it that, or death?"[45] The male force that was a necessary agent of their liberation must now pay his debt of social life to the female spirits of vengeance.

I began by saying that the chorus apparently shares pride of place with Electra in *The Libation Bearers.* That statement must be revised. Electra quietly vanishes halfway through this drama. And Orestes is a nearby faceless prop for achieving the goal of the real protagonist of the play. This is the chorus, the actual libation bearers. In this regard the drama goes back to the very roots of Greek tragedy, which, it is known, grew out of choral performance. Do we detect in this formal regression a suggestion that what obsessed this first actor, this first personality in the history of Greek drama, now transposed to the drama of Greek history, was a woman, a slave, threatening chaos with her demoniacal striving for personal freedom? For this is not primarily a play about vengeance at all. It is a play about a group of foreign slave women struggling against slavery in its literal form and in its sexual form of male force. It is a play about their mounting excitement and joy as they find a way out of their social death. It is a play about a slave rebellion. It is a woman's song about personal freedom at its most pristine moment.

In Sophocles' and Euripides' versions of the myth, Electra comes more into her own. Sophocles' Orestes knows of what he speaks when he wryly asks Electra to "consider that in women too there lives a warlike spirit. You have proof of it."[46] This is the most unsympathetic of the three portrayals of Electra, and there can be no doubt here that vengeance is the central motif, though it is condemned in the unat-

tractive portrait of the protagonist. Although there are important differences in Euripides' and Sophocles' interpretation of Electra's
character, one thing they have in common is the idea that allied to the
primitive blood vengeance she pursues is the experience of freedom.
This, indeed, is the moral given by the chorus in the very last utterance
of Sophocles' play:

> O race of Atreus, how many sufferings
> were yours before you came at last so hardly
> to *freedom [eleutheria]*, perfected by this day's deed.[47]

Here we have a fascinating variation on the theme, already well established in Aeschylus, that wisdom comes through suffering. For men,
that wisdom may be self-knowledge, or some deeper truth about the
human condition in the face of the gods. For women, that wisdom
means one thing, simple justice and personal freedom. It is in the
works of Euripides that this identification is most forcefully explored.
His Electra is little better than a slave and, indeed, considers herself
one. Her first words on hearing that Orestes has murdered Aegisthus
is a song of joy to freedom, the deep intimate sense of release that
comes with the realization that force has been met with force and that
justice has been done:

> O flame of day and sun's great chariot charged with light,
> O earth below and dark of night where I watched before,
> my eyes are clear now, I can unfold my sight to freedom
> [literally: "now my eye and its openings are free"],
> now that Aegisthus, who had killed my father, falls.[48]

This is an extremely complex passage, and in its symbolism lies the
whole meaning of the drama. The flame of day was one of the com-
monest symbols of freedom among the Greeks, going back to Homer's
stylized "day of freedom." We also know that the earth below was
the region of the forces of traditional justice and is closely associated
with the female principle. But darkness was also the antithesis of the
light of freedom, symbolic of slavery. Here, then, we have a subtle
and telling symbolic conflation of the forces of personal enslavement
and of primitive justice. The suffering of personal enslavement can
lead to justice, and when it does the prize is personal liberation, the
creation of eyes, as the primitive Toradja put it, the joy of personal
freedom. Moments later Electra makes the same point more simply,

and more brutally, as she turns to the dead body of Aegisthus and tells it of her deep yearnings "through·rising nights" to shout her feelings to his face—"if only I were liberated from my fears of old." Now at last she can do so. Finally, in the vicious verbal duel between Electra and her mother before the latter is taken off to have her throat slit, Clytemnestra lets slip a curious phrase that is deeply revealing. At the end of a spirited and most persuasive defense of her murder of Agamemnon, a defense significantly posed in terms of male-female conflict, she says to Electra, "Speak if you have need or reason. Fight me free: demonstrate how your father died without full justice."[49]

The symbolic use of light, and its conduit, the eyes—that exposed part of the human soul and brain[50]—for freedom, is found in all Greek literature, but especially in tragedy. Euripides' Electra's cry of satisfaction after vengeance was done is typical: "my eyes are clear now, I can unfold my sight to freedom."[51] Images of light, eyes, and blindness pervade the *Antigone*, reinforcing our conviction that it is the ultimate Greek exploration of freedom.[52] But it is in the *Hecuba* that the symbolic association of light and freedom, as well as its dangers, is most explicitly stated. Hecuba, once proud queen of Troy, is now reduced to the utter degradation of enslavement. There is hardly a reference to her which does not emphasize the fact, beginning with the anguished cry of her son's ghost.[53] Euripides, at the risk of authorial intrusion, has Coryphaeus remarking, "This is what it means to be a slave: to be abused and bear it, compelled by violence to suffer wrong."[54] Hecuba's slavery is explored in both its psychological and its outer aspects, with numerous references to psychic and physical "blows" as one horrible news about her slaughtered family follows closely on another. Over and over again Hecuba, or the chorus, uses the metaphor of social death to describe her condition. She has been left "to live, a slave in the light,"[55] she has "died long ago,"[56] has "died of sorrow while [she] was still alive";[57] the lament of the chorus is most powerful as Polyxena is taken away to be sacrificed by the Greeks:

> I live, but live a slave,
> forced to a foreign land,
> torn westward out of Asia
> to a marriage that is death.[58]

Change *Asia* to *Africa*, and you have the words to a great spiritual.

The association of the imagery of eyes, light, and freedom in gen-

erative contrast with the darkness of slavery and death is explicitly
given in the lament of Polyxena, Hecuba's daughter, as she prepares
to die nobly rather than face the ugly darkness of slavery:

> And now I am a slave
> It is that name of slave, so ugly, so strange,
> that makes me want to die. Or should I live
> to be knocked down to a bidder, sold to a master
> for cash? . . . Never.
> *With eyes still free, I now renounce the light*
> *and dedicate myself to death.*

The gouging out of eyes, then, must mean the destruction of a person's freedom, whether self-inflicted, as in *Oedipus Tyrannus*, where it
is also associated with blindness to truth and clarity,[59] or inflicted by
another, as happens, most terrifyingly, in the *Hecuba*. After she first
savagely gourges out the eyes of the man who had murdered her son—
uncreated his eyes, made him eternally unfree—her dread future is
foretold by her victim. She will be "changed to a dog, a bitch *with
blazing eyes*," attempt to climb the masthead of the ship taking her to
Hellas, fall, and drown at sea. Her grave will be called "Cynossema,
the bitch's grave, a landmark to sailors."[60] This prophecy is a complex,
gruesome image which fuses some of the most potent symbols of Athenian culture, and in which is summarized the whole meaning of the
play. The dog, as Martha Nussbaum points out, ranked low in Greek
animal symbolism. From Homeric times, to call someone a dog or
"dog-eyes" was a great insult, "one that lays particular stress on the
insulted person's selfishness and lack of regard for the community."[61]
But that is not all. Hecuba becomes a dog that drowns. Emily Vermeule,
in her exploration of Greek sea images, points out how the surface of the
sea held a special fascination, provoking "a kind of double vision," representing "the horizon between what they knew and what they imagined."[62] Fish, of course, were eaten by people; but they also ate people;
between the two species lies a brutal interdependence, one that sometimes elicited a grudging admiration from men: "the feelings of being at
home in the dark and vulnerable to the sun belong to the fish, as though
man's world and the sea's world were in mirror image, sometimes in-
imical, sometimes sympathetically linked, like men and gods."[63]

Dogs also had this dread interdependence with people, and we are
not surprised to find the images of fish and dogs being frequently
juxtaposed.[64] In Hecuba's end we find one such fusion. Immediately
implied in her metamorphosis is the most serious criticism that classi-

cal Greek thinkers could make of the value of personal freedom, its tendency toward license and selfishness, resulting in the eating of the polis—something to which we will return when we examine Plato and the elite thinkers of the late fifth and fourth centuries. As if to leave no doubt about this, Euripides makes her no ordinary dog but one with blazing eyes. How powerful a symbolic transformation this is! We cannot help recalling the young, still virginal Polyxena nobly going to her death with "eyes still free," and contrast this scene with that of her old and utterly degraded mother going to her death, also with eyes still free, but those of a blazing bitch. Those who eat the community will, in turn, be eaten. Personal freedom is at once the most desired of values and the most destructive. There is a foreshadowing of *The Bacchae* not only in Hecuba's character[65] but more directly in Polymestor's claim that his prophecy of her ghastly transformation was made known to him by none other than Dionysus.[66] Her grave, her tomb, becomes an omen for the ship of the democratic state, of what can happen if personal freedom, perverted by hate, vengeance, and selfishness, is not watched.[67] A man, a polis, who is not careful, who does not heed the tomb of the bitch at Cynossema, might end up either being eaten alive or, if he is lucky, like the friend of Archilochos, "slammed on the shore of Salmydessos, vomiting seaweed and chattering [his] teeth like a dog."[68]

But it would be unfair to suggest that Euripides leaves the matter in this one-sided way. As I said earlier, he wholly shared the classical Greek ambivalence toward personal freedom. The dog is not entirely without honor, even in Homer, as Odysseus' faithful hound Argos shows. In the generation after Euripides, Diogenes of Sinope embraced the abusive designation *kuon*, dog, as the name of his movement of philosophy, one which, as I will show in a later chapter, was the most extreme statement of personal freedom in the ancient world. Euripides may well have known Antisthenes, the man who most influenced Diogenes, and may have heard his view that the ultimate freedom came from total liberation from all material wants and desires.

Nor should we neglect the fact that the noblest and most admirable character in the *Hecuba* is the woman who came from her womb, Polyxena. It is not true that Polyxena goes to her death all innocence. Innocent girls know little of the value of freedom. Polyxena has had to face the degradation of impending slavery, and even though she remains a virgin, coming to terms with that social horror, that "ugliness," has been enough to rape her mind into a new consciousness, that being to see and know the special light of personal freedom from the dark shadows of enslavement falling upon her. If we fail to understand this, her characterization makes no sense; indeed, her nobility and strength seems too good to be true, becomes ridiculous. But she *has* lost her innocence. She has seen the creeping darkness of living death, the horror of her marriage with it. And from this evil she has discovered, has constructed all on her own, the one good that would succor her as she freely, gladly goes to her ritual murder: that she would die free. So, as she leaves us, she could turn to the frigid, ungrateful Odysseus, the very embodiment of free male, sovereignal force, and sing her swan song to freedom in a manner that we find thoroughly believable:

> Oh light of day!
> I still can cry the light
> in that little space of life I have to live
> before I die upon Achilles' tomb![69]

4. DECONSTRUCTING THE CHORD: PERICLES, SOPHOCLES, AND THE TWO TRAGEDIES OF THE *ANTIGONE*

Most classical historians would agree with Victor Ehrenberg that Pericles and Sophocles "are not only the greatest, but together also the most representative men of their state."[70] Yet, in spite of their friendship and deep respect for each other, and their common devotion to their city, they held profoundly differing conceptions of the nature of the social, intellectual, and spiritual life of Athens. This becomes immediately apparent when we take note of one vital missing element in Pericles' oration, and the meaning he gave to one important utterance.

It is astonishing that Pericles, in an oration for the war dead, a profoundly religious occasion, never once makes reference to the gods. And it is significant, further, that in referring to the "unwritten laws" of the city, he uses the term in the wholly sociological sense of strongly sanctioned conventions which, if broken, are punished not by the gods but by social disapproval.[71] Pericles was typical of the enlightened, pragmatic leaders of Athenian life and politics. For him the state and its laws were man-made achievements, a community held together by traditions and laws which were effective because people both respected and feared them. The gods had their parts, but they were either confined wholly to things religious or were merely a supplementary force, lending weight to tradition. Beyond that, the two realms remained separate.

It is Ehrenberg's view that, for Sophocles, such an attitude to life was terribly wrong. For him all laws were ultimately of divine origin: the city lived and had its being, and its greatness, in the very infusion of the divine into the secular. Failure to recognize this was the greatest of tragedies. Behind the many antitheses of the *Antigone* is one fundamental conflict: "Antigone believes in a divine order of the world; Creon relies on human laws and standards, whether of individual man or the State."[72] There is some truth in this, but where I part company with Ehrenberg is in his further claim that Antigone's world was also Sophocles'.

The plot of the *Antigone* is simple. Polyneices and Eteocles, sons of Oedipus by his own mother, have killed each other in a civil war, and Creon, now ruler of Thebes, has forbidden the burial of Polyneices, in accordance with state law. Antigone, their sister, defies the order, even after her sister, Ismene, has refused to join her. She is condemned by Creon, in spite of the pleas of his son, Haemon, who is betrothed to her. Creon changes his mind after being warned by the blind seer Teiresias that he has offended the gods by not burying the dead and by condemning Antigone to entombment alive, which confused the upper and lower worlds. He rushes to the tomb, only to find that Antigone has committed suicide, and to see his son kill himself over her body after angrily attempting patricide. He returns to his palace to find that his queen, Eurydice, has also killed herself, after hearing the news of her son's death. Utterly broken, Creon asks to be taken away, crying, "My fate has struck me down." This is a thoroughly death-soaked play, as many have noted. Quite apart from the bodies strewn on and off stage, there is the death obsession of Antigone. She is driven to near madness by her determination to bury her treacherous brother, and goes willingly to her living death among her dead ancestors as the price for doing right by her family and the dictates of the gods.

The play has been read on many levels, with the focus on one or more of its many binary images.[73] It is most commonly interpreted as a conflict between duties to the family and those owed to the newly emerged state, symbolized by Creon.[74] Most readers now reject, or downplay, the view of the drama made popular by Anouilh's *Antigone*, as a struggle between individual freedom against state repression. Ostwald, for example, sees its central theme more as a conflict between "the *nomos* [laws] of the state" and "the *nomima* [unwritten laws] administered by the family for its own members."[75] While it is certainly simplistic to read the play as a libertarian struggle, we will see shortly that a more sophisticated grasp of its meaning does indeed bring us right back to the question of human freedom.

Civilization is the culturing of self-consciousness. In tragic drama we find classical Greece at its most civilized and self-conscious moment. There is a profound exploration not only of people's place in the social and moral cosmos but of the place of language and "of man's place in language."[76] The *Antigone* is at once a tragic drama and a drama about tragedy, and any understanding of the former requires at least an awareness of the latter project. In the *Antigone* Sophocles discovers for himself, and for us, a second kind of tragedy, a second way in which men and women exist, against their will, both in and against their world. This second kind of tragedy, which contrasts with the traditional divine form, is mortal or social tragedy.

Divine tragedy is the classic encounter between people and the gods: men and women at the mercy of fate. Such tragedy is powerfully present in the *Antigone*. Antigone seems caught at every turn in cruel twists of fate. She is utterly loyal to the dictates of the gods and single-mindedly obeys their laws, at the risk of her own life, in burying her brother, convinced that the sameness of a common womb transcends the sameness of a common state. Yet the brother she so blindly serves is the product of a polluted womb, the son of his own grandmother, the seed of his own brother. Quite apart from his treachery against the state—to which she is recklessly oblivious—it would seem that piety to such an offspring is an insult to the gods. But there are numerous other ways in which her very attempt to avoid sin leads her to commit greater sin. It is her divine duty as the only betrothed member of her family to ensure its continuity by bearing children. Yet she sins against this sacred familial obligation by choosing death in a virgin state, caring not for the living but for the dead. She offends the gods above by choosing the gods below. She insults her sister. Her love destroys her betrothed, who is also very much a member of her family, being both her cousin, the son of her uncle, Creon, and her nephew, being her father-brother brother's son. As the chorus rightly comments: the woman is mad with a strange kind of love.[77] A love more with death, it would seem, both to us and to her, for she surrenders calmly to her "marriage" with death.[78] Whatever else we may conclude about Antigone, this much is clear: the woman is a sinner. Not, of course, in the Christian sense of knowingly committing evil, but precisely in the Greek sense of being condemned to doing that which she, and the gods themselves, most abhor. She commits the most egregious impieties in her most consciously pious endeavors. Like her siblings, she was condemned at the moment of her horribly incestuous conception. That is divine tragedy.

Creon too, has his share of divine tragedy, though on a far less spectacular scale. Quite apart from his refusal to bury the dead, he has caused his own son's and wife's death and destroyed his house. Even so, there is a fundamental difference between Creon's tragedy and Antigone's, brought into sharp relief by the very contrast between them. Whereas Antigone's impieties are the unwitting consequences of her attempt to do the right and the just, Creon is the agent of his own downfall. The chorus, on seeing him returning with his son's body, remarks, "His own hand brings / the witness of his crime / the doom he brought on himself."[79] Creon, it is true, cries in his sorrow, "It was a god who struck / who has weighed my head with disaster; he drove me to wild / strange ways."[80] But this sounds very much like a man momentarily trying to ease his grief by trying to pass the buck to the gods—similar, say, to a grief-stricken African-American who has just shot his woman in a lover's quarrel, crying, "It was the devil made me to it"—and he knows it, for not longer afterward, on receiving the final blow of his wife's suicide, he confronts himself squarely and says, "This is my guilt, *all* mine."[81] In this critical respect, Creon is a figure fundamentally different from Oedipus, in spite of their outward political similarities, which we should be careful not to overplay.[82]

It is difficult to become engaged with Creon as a tragic figure in the traditional, divine sense, precisely because he is so obviously the source of his downfall. This crisis of engagement is twofold. First, not only does his responsibility severely mute the tragic impact, but his punishment seems humanly unjust. The man was facing the worst possible kind of political crisis: a fratricidal civil war. His actions were hardly intemperate; further, he takes the people seriously, and it is gross literalism to judge him too exactly by the standards of the Periclean democratic state. He was not all that bad a person; he obviously loved his family, even if he was something of an emotional bumbler, and he did do something extraordinary when compared with other male tragic heroes, something which should elicit our admiration, not our contempt: he changed his mind. Second, the religious explanation offered by Teiresias for Creon's downfall sounds contrived. His refusal to bury the traitor Polyneices was consistent with divine law, and the business of confusing upper and lower worlds is too pat an explanation; it works conceptually, but does not engage us artistically or emotionally. There is not that sense of awesome incomprehension which divine tragedy elicits from us. This is so because Sophocles conceived of Creon as a tragic figure not in the divine sense but in another, new mode of the tragic.

I want to suggest that Creon's tragedy was mortal in that it emanated from the seemingly arbitrary punishment heaped upon him by the very world he had created and had unwittingly offended. I think Sophocles came to a radically new insight in this play: it was his recognition that the mortal social universe that people created had an autonomy and an unpredictability not different from that of the world of the gods. Mankind had created something wonderful in fifth-century civilization, yes, but it was something that it could no longer control. Sophocles' insight was the fundamental sociological one: that people by their collective actions construct a universe that works by its own laws and reason. This surely is what is meant by the lines near the end of the ode to mankind:

> Clever beyond all dreams
> the inventive craft that he has
> *which may drive him one time or another to well or ill.*[83]

This is exactly how the Greeks spoke of the supernatural forces of the divine order. Mankind's wonderful creation—civilization—has become another arbitrary universe with which mankind must contend. This is the nature of Creon's tragedy. He is a victim of the mortal, social universe whose written, man-made, but now autonomous, laws he serves with the same single-minded devotion with which Antigone serves the unwritten dictates of the divine cosmos. The planner has been destroyed by his well-intentioned, rational plans, in the same tragic way that Antigone has been destroyed by her own well-intentioned pieties. Creon ends up discovering, to his utter dismay, that his "planning was all unblest."[84]

Sophocles recognizes the autonomy, even the greatness, of this mortal social cosmos, but he sees deep flaws in its grandeur. He does not, however, take the simple-minded, reactionary position that the divine order is best. Like Goldhill, I cannot understand how any reading of the *Antigone*—or of any of the Theban plays, for that matter—could end up with such a conservative view of Sophocles.[85] For it is certainly true that Sophocles recognizes problems in the divine order and its dealings with mankind. As an enlightened man of his times, a citizen who loved and participated fully in the civic culture of his city (and a handsome cruiser who was no angel),[86] he too must have begun to lose patience with the gods and their reckless, tragic ways. When Oedipus repeatedly exclaims with mortal, though vain, defiance, "No I did not sin!" and later, "Before the law—before God—I am innocent!''[87] we can be sure that there is at least an echo of Sophocles' voice in that cry, and the voice of all thoughtful Athenians, even if they were only, like Sophocles, partially committed to the new Sophist learning. It was all in vain of course. In the end they all had to settle for the gift of poor Oedipus' ''beaten self,'' and the mocking crumbs of comfort offered by the gods for their divine beastliness: the pitiable freedom of choosing the moment of his death, and the blessing of his last hour and place of rest.[88]

Once we recognize that there are two domains of tragic conflict in this play, not only does Creon's tragedy (now seen as primarily mortal) make sense, but we begin to understand why it is simplistic to ask whether Antigone wins or loses, as so many have done. Antigone, we will see, both wins and loses; she is both tragic victim in the divine domain and tragic victor in the mortal domain. And she is mother of freedom as well as handmaiden of chaos and despair. There are two basic distinctions, which have Antigone in common: that between male (Creon) and female (Antigone) principles of social and civic life, on the other hand; and that between mortal life (Antigone) and divine life (the chthonic and Olympian gods), on the other. Divine tragedy occurs in the symbolic space between Antigone (that is, what she represents) and the gods; social tragedy occurs in the mortal space between Antigone and that which Creon represents. Antigone is utterly central: the play revolves around her as the figure who, by mediating between mankind and the gods and between male force and female force, distills and integrates all. Antigone is the archetypal woman who, as Charles Segal explains in a discussion of Euripides, defies the male Greek desire for definitional clarity. ''Her position between culture and nature . . . confuses the basic antinomies with which the Greeks demarcate the human, civilized world from the savage, chaotic, violent realm of the beats 'outside.' ''[89]

These symbolic forces are themselves of several kinds. Lacking the space here to discuss them at any length, I will mention only the four most important categories of symbolic antitheses. There is that category of antitheses which may be termed *biomorphic*[90] or *generative*, having to do with the rites of life, death, and renewal: death versus life, womb versus tomb, degeneration and decay versus liberation and growth. Second, there is the *sociomorphic* category of binary symbols, such as age (young-old), principle of social grouping (kin versus locality or, more specifically, phratry versus deme), master versus slave, free versus unfree. Third, there is the category of *technomorphic* oppositions such as city versus house, state versus people, written laws versus unwritten traditional laws, civic freedom versus civic exclusion. Finally, there is a category of *psychomorphic* symbolic oppositions, images representing antitheses such as those between reason and passion, obedience and defiance, discipline and license, hate and love, and freedom as power and control over others versus freedom as independence and the expression of love and devotion to all things held dear. I have summarized all this in the table below.

BINARY SYMBOLS	MALE (CREON)	FEMALE (ANTIGONE)	THE GODS
Psychomorphic Symbols	Reason Obedience Hate Freedom as power/control	Passion Defiance Love Freedom as release/friendship	Olympian Gods
Technomorphic Symbols	City State Written laws Order Freedom as civic participation	House People Unwritten laws Disorder Freedom as social participation	
Sociomorphic Symbols	Age Deme Master Native Social life Freedom as hierarchic integration	Youth Phratry Slave Alien Social death Freedom as belonging	
Biomorphic Symbols	Seed Tomb Head Above earth Dark-in-light Death-in-life Death as end	Womb Cave Body Below earth Light-in-dark Life-in-death Death as renewal	Chthonic Gods

(Between the MALE and FEMALE columns, vertical text: "Domain of Mortal/Social Tragedy"; between the FEMALE and THE GODS columns, vertical text: "Domain of Divine Tragedy")

Note that the four kinds of images are used in the two kinds of tragedy explored by Sophocles in the *Antigone*, although they may have radically different significations, depending on whether they refer to the divine or the mortal domains of tragedy. The most obvious case in point from the *Antigone* is the symbolism of death. In the mortal domain, death is usually evil, symbolic of darkness, slavery, isolation, and disorder. As Creon exclaimed in his grief, the unhappy man is "a breathing corpse."[91] However, in mankind's relation with the divine order, more specifically the chthonic realm, death is a positive, generative state. As Charles Segal has explained, Antigone's death obsession and eventual descent into the cave tomb to which she has been condemned by Creon is partly modeled on the Kore-Persephone myth, in which the maiden descends to the underworld, marries death, and, after a season of mourning and barrenness on earth, joyfully returns with the regenerative powers of spring.[92] The gods of the underworld are, for Antigone, the divinities who share their house with justice.[93] However, things go terribly wrong for Antigone because her devotion to the oneness of those from the same womb, which she places over loyalty to the oneness of the city—all perfectly correct in the cult of the dead—cannot overcome the original pollution of the womb from which she and Polyneices came. I will have little more to say about the divine order, mainly because, as I have noted earlier, there is no space for freedom here.

It is quite another matter on the mortal side of Antigone's fence. The fundamental opposition—what Victor Turner would call the "master symbol"[94]—is that between male and female. As the table shows, the four categories of images all coalesce into two opposing forces, which are repeatedly identified as male and female. Women "are subject to strong power," male force, which is identified with royal law.[95] Creon interprets Antigone's defiance not only as an attack on "established" law but as an assault on his very manhood: "I am no man and she the man instead / if she can have this conquest without pain."[96] Antigone, along with all women, is associated with treachery, "disorder" and "license."[97] She describes herself as someone who has been socially dead for a long time, in terms very similar to those used by other tragic heroines referring to their slave condition, and her repeated reference to her marriage with death must be understood, apart from its chthonic allusions, as a double reference to real and metaphoric death.[98] One could easily show how all the other antitheses in the table are either directly or indirectly derived from the primary gender antithesis, but we do not have the space to do so.[99]

Once we recognize the primacy of this gender conflict, it becomes obvious that, in the most profound sense, the play is in its mortal aspects a study in the nature and limits of freedom. Creon identifies his manhood with his sovereignal freedom and power, under which women are supposed to yield, and with the civic community and its laws, from which women are excluded. Antigone opposes both, advocating a different ideology of life and social order based precisely on their gender differences. As Segal notes, "The word *krate,* 'victory,' 'power,' repeatedly describes his sovereign power in the state (166, 173, for example). He sees Antigone, then, as a challenge to his most important values and his self-image."[100] Creon tells his son, "I must guard the men who yield to order / not let myself be beaten by a woman. . . . I won't be called weaker than womankind."[101] Against the state's written laws Antigone opposes the unwritten laws of kin-based tradition. This not only defies the patrilineal principle of Athens but flies in the face of the most important sociological basis of the democratic state: the Cleisthenian shift from kin-based phratry to localized deme.[102] Thus Antigone is forced, by her radically different conception of life, to choose freedom.

That Antigone's ideology refers to the traditional, kin-based ways and religion should not mislead us into discounting the radically innovative nature of her rebellion. Here defiance has a wholly negative aspect, a quite self-conscious delight in puncturing the balloon of male constraining power. When Ismene warns that she "craved what can't be done," she replies proudly, "And so, when strength runs out, I shall give over."[103] She is prepared to accept the consequences of her own actions, even if, as Ismene thinks, they are ill advised, as long as they are her "*own* ill-counselling."[104] It is precisely this pride in her defiance that has most rankled Creon, who finds her "an expert in insolence" who dares "to boast her doing, and to laugh in it."[105] In this self-conscious delight in the negative aspect of her assertion of personal freedom, we find the *slave* who happens to be a woman.

But Antigone is also a *woman* who happens to be a slave. It is this which leads her away from a purely negative conception of personal freedom to one that gives a positive content to this freedom, without her falling into the male trap of sublating it into positive freedom over others. She recognizes just this male, sovereignal freedom in Creon, and has the nerve to tell him so: "A king is fortunate in many ways," she says sarcastically, "and most, that he can act and speak at will." When Creon replies that the people do not think so, she lets him have it, loud and clear: "They see, and do not say. You have them cowed."[106] This is one feisty sister.

What is the positive aspect of freedom which the *woman*-slave discovers? It turns out to be exactly what every slave, if she or he seriously thought about the freedom they long for, would desire: the complete restoration of their natality. It cannot be too strongly emphasized that Antigone is a woman without any immediate male kin to protect her. The one man who should be doing so—her father's brother, Creon—is the very man who has enslaved her. What she wants is not just the release from his power but the restoration, the rebirth of her natality, her god-given, traditional claims as a human being. And with that restoration comes also the reciprocation of that love which, for a limbic, isolated female alien in a war-torn male world, is met only with the hatred of male force. "I cannot *share* in hatred, but in love," she tells Creon. Freedom is love. But not the love that seeks to dominate and own, that demands obedience, as Creon does from his own son.[107] Rather, it is the love that shares; and it is significant that this is the only instance in all extant Greek literature in which love is spoken of as something shared.

In a satisfying recent reading of the tragedy, Warren and Ann Lane have argued that in the *Antigone* Sophocles exposes—perhaps ironically, but it really doesn't matter—what may have been the most fatal flaw in Athenian democracy: its complete exclusion of women from its civic life. They point out that Antigone enters as a "political criminal" at the very climax of the great hymn to man's greatness, a juxtaposition so jarring it was surely meant to emphasize the ambiguity already evident in the celebration: "having sung the praises of civic 'man,' they are confronted with civic woman."[108] This exclusion is disastrous not only for women, as Antigone's agony demonstrates, but for men too, for they have lost touch with the three kinds of divinely inspired love, or philia, with which women, symbolized by Antigone, still infused their lives: "kinship, friendship and rootedness in city and homeland."[109] Martha Nussbaum suggests a less radical, but more nuanced, version of this thesis. Both Creon and Antigone have ruthlessly oversimplified their social worlds, allowing for no possibility of "conflicting obligations," and it is just this possibility which any humane, just society with a necessary plurality of values must allow for. The mortal or social tragedy of Antigone, then, is that of a world which comes crashing down because each part has too simple a vision of harmony, and so cannot tolerate the other, cannot see that "harmony . . . is not simplicity but the tension of distinct and separate beauties."[110] I find this interpretation attractive, but must emphasize that this tragic narrowness of vision is entirely the result of the male-imposed exclusion of women. We do not know what Antigone was like before she became "subject to strong power."[111] Perhaps she was a model of virginal pluralism; women tend to be. But we can never be sure, for by the time we meet her she has already become the female slave rebel, demoniacally obsessed with her freedom and the need for justice. Once that happens, a chasm emerges not only between her and Creon but, sadly, between her and the untransformed Ismene. And nothing can put her together again.

But, as in all Sophoclean tragedy, something is gained in the pain of its experience. We have seen how, at the end of his later play *Electra*, "freedom" is "won" by the house of Atreus "from all its suffering."[112] This too is what Antigone's deed "perfected." There was a golden time when she could take her rootedness and the love of her family for granted. At such a time, there was no need to valorize them. But her enslavement and her condition as a woman have forced her, in shame and isolation, to defy, to *make* a choice, and in the process to create something new: the energizing of these values, once so passively assumed, and their recruitment as the special object and content of the newly discovered and idealized capacity to choose. The celebrated dialogue between Antigone and Creon[113] has been described by George Steiner as "canonic in our western sense of individual and society," and I wholly share his suggestion that there is no "more intrinsically fascinating and consequential word-clash in any literature."[114] Antigone speaks not so much to Creon—for it is indeed a clash of words, not a real dialogue—but to all who, through their own pain and anguish, or that of their ancestors, have been forced to construct their own freedom and give it content. She speaks out of time, "out of eternity."[115] As rebel, woman, and slave—the ultimate male configuration of disorder—she comes to identify "right," "justice," and "law," unwritten, natural law, as the content of her personal freedom: "it is within the intensely energized terrain of values and application covered, bounded by these three terms, that the worlds of Creon and of Antigone clash."[116]

The symbolism of death and renewal, which in the domain of the divinities exposes the tragic fate of Antigone, in the mortal domain represents the triumph of the value she has discovered, constructed, and defends. Death makes a "living corpse" of Creon's male force, his enslaving sovereignal freedom. But in the mortal domain death for Antigone means the death of kinlessness, slavery, isolation, and lovelessness. Death is the double negation that leads to social rebirth, renatalization, reconnectedness. Like the archetypal slave among the primitive Callinago Caribs who were forced to mourn their own social death by cutting their hair in the style of mourners,[117] she too is one of those who, as Creon—most appropriately—observes, must "sing the dirge for their own death."[118] And willingly she sings, as she walks to the death that will undo her living social death:

O city of wealthy men.
I call upon Dirce's spring,
I call upon Thebe's grove in the armored plain,
to be my witnesses, how with no friend's mourning,
by what decree I go to the fresh-made prison-tomb.
Alive to the place of corpses, an alien still,
never at home with the living nor with the dead.[119]

She will not, of course, experience this freedom in this life. But she will regain her natality, her connectedness with her kinsmen from whom she has been torn, in the next. The tomb becomes a "marriage-chamber" from which she is led to her "own people." Every African-American, every West Indian, will be struck with awe by these lines, for it was one of the most passionately held beliefs in the mortuary practices of the New World slaves that death would restore them both to their freedom and to the African homeland from which they had been severed.[120] Antigone's "eloquent espousal of early death," writes Steiner, and he could just as accurately be writing of the vast number of West Indian slave rebels who committed individual and mass suicide in order to secure their freedom and hasten the return home, "is, at once, a defiance of the living, of those who set life above the eternities of moral law . . . and an assertion of personal freedom. To choose death freely, to choose it early, is to retain mastery and self-mastery in the face of the only phenomenon against which man knows no remedy."[121]

In the mortal domain of his tragedy, then, Sophocles has dazzlingly refigured the Persephone myth, making Antigone a sacrificial virgin figure to the cause of personal freedom, who for her "self-sufficiency"[122] is buried alive in the male womb that is Creon's civic tomb. She will find her freedom below; but her self-sacrifice makes personal freedom a value for us, energizes it with the demonic forces of her womanness and her passion. In the face of the gods, she dies a tragic, sterile death, a woman who has failed to regenerate—for that is the literal meaning of her name[123]—but in the face of men, she generates the monumental value of personal freedom and ennobles it with the weight of her love and her life. The chorus sings of her creation as she walks to the sacrificial tomb:

You went to the furthest verge
of daring, but there you found
the high foundation of justice, and fell.[124]

But she will never be forgotten. Antigone lives forever in the hearts of all women and men who cherish personal freedom, both in its defiantly negative and in its humanely positive aspects.

> God's child and god she was.
> We are born to death.
> Yet even in death you will have your fame,
> to have gone like a god to your fate,
> in living and dying alike.[125]

CHAPTER 8

Fission and Diffusion: Class and the Elements of Freedom in the Late Fifth Century and Beyond

The Peloponnesian War had a major impact on nearly all aspects of the socioeconomic and political life of Athens. The immediate economic and demographic effects were severe, although we should be careful to avoid exaggeration. The economy and the population had grown again by the early fourth century B.C., especially in Athens, although both entered another long secular decline during the last half of the century.[1] For us the important point to note is that those changes which the war brought about would have increased considerably the number of slaves. While there is little evidence of land accumulation, we know that there was enormous growth in craft manufacturing in Athens, based heavily on slave and metic labor. In the recovery from the war economy, the reliance on the silver mines would have been even greater, for by now Attica was wholly dependent on imports for its grain supplies.[2]

The war greatly increased the relative size of the urban population, although it should be noted that three-quarters of the Athenian population still owned some land at the end of the fifth century. The farmers, however, were devastated by the war, and throughout the fourth century we find a gradual increase in the economic insecurity of this sector. This economic impoverishment found its political expression in the decline in status, indeed in a retreat from the ideal, of the farmer-citizen. With the growth of the urban sector, there would have been greater dependence on the sector of the economy most in need of slave labor. At the start of the war, slaves constituted a third of the entire population and metics approximately one in every six Athenians. Still excluded from the city's political life, metics came increasingly to dominate its urban economic system. The growth of urban slavery, however, was accompanied by an even greater increase in the rate of manumission. We know from the comparative data on slavery that, as a society becomes more dependent on urban slaves and craftsmen, it has to increase its rate of manumission as the only effective way of motivating these more skilled slaves. The Greek evidence is consistent with this general finding.[3]

Thus a vital new thrust in the emergence of freedom as a mass value was set in motion. Slave masters now found it in their economic interest, as never before, to encourage their slaves' yearning for freedom. As the comedies of Aristophanes, written both during and after the Peloponnesian War, clearly demonstrate, slaves were not only everywhere and within the reach of all except the poorest of free Athenians but were held in as great contempt as they had ever been.[4] They were mere "human-footed stock," who, however, were found in almost all occupations since, unlike the modern New World, Athens saw no tendency toward occupational confinement. Because they dominated the skilled crafts, they had to be motivated to perform not only on their own but productively. One way of so motivating the slave was to allow him or her—the majority was still female—to work and live on their own. This paved the way toward manumission, since the hireling was in a better position to accumulate a *peculium*, that is, what was earned over and beyond what the master demanded. The *peculium* legally belonged to the master, as did everything the slave possessed, but the master with seeming generosity allowed the slave to save through superhuman effort. Thus, often near the end of the slave's working life, when he or she had managed to save the equivalent of the going replacement cost of a young slave, the *peculium* was handed over to the master as a redemption fee for his or her freedom. In the late fourth and third centuries, the system became even more elaborate, in that it was possible for the slave to make a down payment for his freedom, or to borrow the entire sum from a third party, procure his or her freedom immediately, and then pay it off later. The freedom thus procured, however, was often very conditional, in that freedmen were usually under contractual obligations to continue working for their former masters or mistresses.

In this system the master's gain was fourfold. The slave worked diligently all his life; the master received from the slave at the end of his period of service enough money to buy a brand-new slave; he was relieved of any responsibility to provide for the slave in his or her old age; and he now had a free retainer who was obliged to remain eternally grateful to him for granting him the privilege of buying his free-dom. The slave's gain was rarely material. The only thing he or she achieved was removal from the social death of slavery and the expe-rience of freedom: a pure, negative personal freedom which, by virtue of its very material insignificance, must have provoked in the freedman the most interesting speculation on the meaning of it all. Is it going too far to suggest that here is one source of the turn to inner freedom on the part of the *common man and woman* in the fourth century?

Freedom, of course, did not mean citizenship. The freed slave, in-stead, joined the metic group, and it is a reasonable speculation that freedmen were the main source of new metics after the fifth century.[5] Although freedmen were subject to an additional tax, their legal status was almost identical with the metics'. At the same time, however, social divisions were made within the metic class. It should not be forgotten that some of the most celebrated Greeks were metics, men such as Aristotle and Lysias, although there has been from antiquity a reluctance to call them that. For the freeborn Athenian the fundamen-tal distinction remained that between citizen and alien. As David Whitehead has pointed out, this basic distinction was reinforced, and muted, by various other vertical and horizontal divisions, but the evi-dence is unequivocal "that at best metoikos was an unattractive piece of nomenclature and at worst a ready-made jibe, a reminder of exclu-sion and ineradicable gulfs."[6] The principle of exclusive inclusiveness continued to inform the attitude of Athenian citizens throughout an-tiquity; indeed, it was intensified in response to the growth in numbers and economic significance of the metic group. For the poor Athenian citizen in the face of a wealthy metic, the distinction meant every-thing.[7]

While civic freedom remained the primary value for the Athenian citizens, this is not to say that they did not also value personal free-dom; rather, they placed it lower in the cultural chord. That, how-ever, was not how the freedman and other metics, not to mention the slaves, saw the matter. Since civic freedom was out of the question for them, it is understandable that personal freedom became the primary freedom in their conception of the triad. They, too, valued civic and organic freedom. The wealthier and more educated metics would have given anything for this status, and in a few rare cases unusual metics were so honored. But even such exceptional cases were resented. A telling instance of how reluctant Athenians were to grant civic freedom to metics is found in the proposal made in 403 by Thrasybulus to grant citizenship to the metics, including the wealthy and highly educated orator Lysias, who had fought with the democratic party to overthrow

the Thirty Tyrants. The proposal passed but was soon overturned by
Archinus on a technicality. Sixty years later Hyperides got himself into
serious trouble for his partially executed proposal to grant citizenship
to metics, and to release and arm the slaves during the emergency after
the defeat by Macedon.[8] And when his friend Lycurgus a few years
later prosecuted the cowardly Leocrates for betraying his duties as a
citizen by fleeing Athens during the emergency, he himself must have
been on the point of tears when he said,

> Many sufferings were being visited upon the city; every citizen had felt
> misfortune at its worst; but the sight which would most surely have stirred
> the onlooker and moved him to tears over the sorrows of Athens was to
> see the people vote that slaves should be released, that aliens should
> become Athenians and the disenfranchised regain their rights.[9]

Metics not only suffered numerous grievous legal disabilities but ran
the risk of enslavement, whatever their origins, if they exercised any
of the exclusive rights of citizens, such as owning land or marrying a
freeborn Athenian woman. All this meant, then, that personal freedom
loomed large in the consciousness of the metic, especially the freedman, not least of all because it was constantly under threat by an ever-
vigilant citizen population.

All but a disgruntled segment of the elite classes and status groups
of Athenians now valued freedom. It had become a truly universal
value, and this was as true of the slaves as of the free. But by the end
of the fifth and throughout the fourth century a critical sociological
development accompanied this universalization of the idea and value
of freedom. The three elements of freedom were ranked in the triad in
radically different ways by different groups of Athenian residents. For
the great generality of adult male citizens, the ordinary citizen on the
street, civic freedom followed either by personal or sovereignal freedom (depending on personal tastes and pretensions) was the order;
for the elite citizen who was not a die-hard oligarch, it was sovereignal
freedom followed by civic and, sometimes, personal freedom; and for
the slaves who longed for freedom, as well as for the freedmen and
other metics, the order was personal, and the dream (never to be realized in Athens, but certainly back in their native states, should they
ever return) civic and, sometimes, sovereignal freedom.

What we learn from Aristophanes and other writers of the period is
that while different groups most valued one or another of the three
elements of freedom, the element emphasized would also largely depend on the social context and on the most important status difference

between the interacting parties. For example, if a citizen was interacting with a metic, he would in general be inclined to put down the latter by emphasizing his civic freedom, especially if the metic was of non-Athenian but Greek origin, and most emphatically so if he was wealthy and of upper-class origins and sentiment. Upper-class metics like Lysias (ca. 459–ca. 380 B.C.) and Aristotle (384–322 B.C.) must have resigned themselves to such interactions. As Whitehead cogently observes, Aristotle viewed his status as one lacking in *timai*, the capacity to engage in political life, and a note of contempt characterized his writings on the subject, one which seemed to veer between "cool objectively [and] bitter irony."[10]

In his relations with, or reference to, slaves, the citizen normally emphasized his personal freedom, and the slave's slaveness, since his civic freedom was something so completely out of the question for the slave that even to mention it in such a context would be to tarnish the thing he most valued. Thus it is personal freedom which Praxagora has in mind when she gives, as her reason for wanting to close down all the brothels, the fact "that these freeborn ladies can enjoy the young men's attentions, instead of letting dolled-up slave girls snatch the pleasures of love from under their noses."[11] As we have seen, for women, personal freedom would have been doubly meaningful since civic freedom was denied them. This emphasis on personal freedom by free women is, as we would expect, particularly marked in the humorous war of the sexes portrayed in *Lysistrata*, where both Lysistrata and Stratyllis, on separate occasions, remind the men that they are free with the expression "I'm not a slave, you know."[12] And one of the most important attributes of personal freedom is spelled out by Isaeus when he reminds his audience that only slaves are subject to torture, "when it is necessary that some contested point should be cleared up" in a court case.[13]

In relations between citizens, on the other hand, a lot would depend on the relative class positions, gender, and even age of the interacting parties. A humorous case in point is the conversation in *The Clouds*, in which Pheidippides tells his father that if it was all right to be hit by him for his own good, it must be equally proper for him to bash the old man for the same reason, since "I'm a free man just like you."[14] It is significant that in *The Wasps*, Aristophanes' satire on civic freedom, the critic of radical democracy tells its supporter that he was being bamboozled by the demogogues, and adds, "You're a slave, without knowing it."[15] What this and numerous other examples indicate is that by this time the slave relation had become the dominant, indeed the only, idiom for the antithetical expression of all three elements of freedom. Even in fantasy it was not possible to get away from this metaphor.[16]

In the sociologically telling diatribe *The Constitution of Athens*, written during the last third of the fifth century, we get an excellent record of these developments from the viewpoint of an upper-class reactionary. He condemns the tendency of citizens to vote for a demagogue who leads not in the interests of the city as a whole, but to promote the selfish interests of his popular base of support. People know that "this man's ignorance, baseness and favor are more profitable than the good man's virtue, wisdom, and ill-will." What is interesting about the Old Oligarch's prose is that he calls the absence of civic freedom "slavery," as if this is the most natural possible way of putting the matter. That he is against democracy, and therefore for the political slavery of the masses, occasions no squeamishness on his part.

> For the people do not want a good government under which they them-
> selves are slaves; they want to be free and to rule. Bad government is of
> little concern to them. What *you* consider bad government is the very
> source of the people's strength and freedom. If it is good government
> you seek, you will first observe the cleverest men establishing the laws
> in their own interests. Then the good men will punish the bad; they will
> make policy for the city and not allow madmen to participate or to speak
> their minds or to meet in assembly. As a result of these excellent mea-
> sures the people would swiftly fall into slavery.[17]

As one would expect, the Old Oligarch speaks loathingly of the slaves and metics, among whom "there is the greatest uncontrolled wantonness." People had to be careful not to strike a slave, because slaves were so similar in dress and appearance to free Athenians that one might end up accidentally striking a free man, which was a serious offense. Nonetheless, so great was the demand for slaves and metics that even this old reactionary has to accept the need for them. What is more, he also recognizes the need to motivate the slaves by manu-mission in an urban economy highly dependent on their skills, mainly by means of permitting them to work and live on their own and paying the master an agreed-upon rent, the balance accruing to the slave's *peculium*. This seems to be the obvious interpretation of a corrupt passage which is otherwise senseless:

> For where there is a naval power, it is necessary from financial consid-
> erations to be slaves to the slaves in order to take a portion of their earn-
> ings, and it is then necessary to let them go free. And where there are

rich slaves it is no longer profitable in such a place for my slave to fear you.[18]

In attempting further to understand elite and middle-class conceptions and evaluations of freedom at this time, we will do best to turn to the "half-contemporary, half-legendary world"[19] of Euripides, especially that of his middle and later plays. Euripides' version of the Electra myth, produced in 413, offers us one of the most class-conscious passages in tragic drama. This is the episode in which the aristocratic Orestes meets the poor farmer whom Electra has been forced to marry. He laments that it is no longer possible to recognize goodness and worth in men when it is met, "since all our human heritage runs mongrel."[20] He has sometimes seen the descendants of noble families behave like cowards, "while minds of stature struggle trapped in starving bodies." The result is sociological confusion. There is no easy outward test by which "man [can] distinguish man." Wealth is useless since, as often as not, "that measure means poverty of mind." But it is silly to romanticize the poor, because "the pauper owns one thing, the sickness of his condition, a compelling teacher of evil." What about the traditional aristocratic criterion of courage in war? That's hardly practical anymore, because men have become so concerned with saving their own lives in battle that no one is able "to witness his companion's courage." One recognizes this at once as a society going through considerable social change, under the impact of the war. Euripides leaves us in no doubt where his sympathies lie, for in a passage that must have startled his Athenian audience, he delivers a "middle-class" solution (I simply cannot think of a better term, though I am fully aware of its anachronism) loud and clear:

> Can you not come to understand, you empty-minded,
> opinion-stuffed people, a man is judged by grace
> among his fellows, manners are nobility's touchstone?
> Such men of manners can control our cities best,
> and homes, but the well-born sportsman, long on
> muscle, short
> on brains, is only good for a statue in the park,
> not even sterner in the shocks of war than weaker
> men, *for courage is the gift of character.*[21]

This is a thoroughly perverse play, written by Euripides in a very complex mood, and it is risky trying to fathom just what he really thought. It is likely, as M. T. W. Arnheim has suggested, that Euripi-

des' main concern was with the absence of any standards for the judgment of character in his chaotic social world.²² Whatever Euripides'
views, there seems little doubt that the ideas expressed here were
widespread. What we find is not so much the democratization of the
aristocratic ethos as its embourgeoisement. It is as if we were in the
middle of a class reclamation of the aristocratic ethos—a reclamation
that also entails its transformation. The popular vulgarization of the
ethos, nobly but impractically suggested by Pericles, has already been
rejected. Here in the *Electra* its middle-class version is examined and
castigated. External criteria have ceased to be of much use in judging
moral worth. As R. B. Appleton noted, "Life has become too complex
for such simplicity."²³

Eight years later, in his last, unfinished play, the *Iphigenia in Aulis*,
written in palatine comfort at the court of King Archelaus of Macedon,
and in mutual disgust with his native Athens, we get the complete
aristocratic reclamation of their values, only now it is fully allied to,
and expressed in, the idiom of freedom and its antithesis, slavery.

Consider, first, the soliloquy of Agamemnon in which he reflects on
the problems of his aristocratic status:

> To be low-born, I see, has its advantages:
> A man can weep, and tell his sorrows to the world.
> A king endures sorrow no less; but the demand
> For dignity governs our life, and we are slaves
> To the masses. I am ashamed to weep; and equally
> I am ashamed not to weep, in such a depth of grief.²⁴

The idea of a leader being a slave to the masses is a novel one. It
could be taken to suggest a radical kind of democracy; but this is clearly
not what Euripides has in mind. Indeed, it is doubtful whether this is
even an affirmation of the moderate democracy which obliged Aeschylus' king Pelasgus to seek the approval of the people before granting
the suppliant maidens sanctuary. Sadly, one must conclude that this
passage is just what it seems to be, an affirmation of popular kingship
by a disillusioned democrat. And yet, the metaphor of slavery persists.
At the end of the fifth century, nothing could repress it, not even
disgust with civic freedom. Agamemnon seems to be obsessed with
this idea of his enslavement to duty. It is fascinating, however, how
the metaphor of slavery works in generating the organic version of
sovereignal freedom. Explaining to his daughter, Iphigenia, why he
has to kill her sacrificially, he says,

I am slave to Hellas; for her, whether I will or not,
I am bound to kill you. Against this I have no power.
So far as lies in you, child, and in me, to ensure
Hellas must be free, and her citizens must not
Have their wives stolen forcibly by Phrygians.[25]

In a way, this is the mirror image of personal freedom. In the latter, freedom is expressed in terms of the release from or absence of the restraint of slavery. With this organic version of sovereignal freedom, we have freedom being achieved for the masses through the enslavement of the king, an enslavement so cruel that it incurs also the sacrificial murder of his own daughter. We immediately recognize in this shades of that crowning glory of Euripides' genius, *The Bacchae*. A very old idea and a very new one are fused together. The theme of man's lack of freedom in the face of the gods, the tyranny of fate, harks back to the earliest Greek drama and beyond. Much of this remains, and in its most primitive form. Artemis' insistence on Iphigenia's blood as the price for allowing the Greek fleet to sail to Troy is not just incomprehensible in the normal way of the gods; it is utterly contradictory, since she is the goddess who is supposed to protect the young. However, what we now have is the added idea of the people of Hellas as another almighty force against which the king is powerless. But at least this force is comprehensible: to save the honor of Greek women in the future, Iphigenia must be sacrificed. Comprehensible, yes; but no less contradictory than the gods, because as Iphigenia and her mother indicate clearly in their arguments, it makes no sense whatever to send the entire force of Greece against Troy to avenge the honor of a woman, Helen, who went off with her lover Paris of her own free, if perverted, will. In the sacrifice of Iphigenia, however, we find a symbolic conflation of the two almighty spheres of incomprehension. The king stands between the two, the intermediary between the all-powerful gods and the all-powerful people. His enslavement, and the sacrifice of what is most dear to him, ensures the future freedom of the people. Here, in its most extreme and sublimely aristocratic form, is the idea of sovereignal freedom in its organic aspect. Freedom lies in the power of the king, who in his thralldom to the gods and man, and in his willingness to sacrifice all, integrates heaven and earth, rich and poor. Euripides the democrat has become the prophet of the return to kingship that, eight decades later, would overwhelm the Hellenistic world.

A far less exalted conception of freedom prevailed among the elites of the real world during the late fifth and fourth centuries. It always threatened the other two elements of freedom within their own states, and all freedoms in other polities. In essence it was the identification of freedom for oneself with the right to dominate others. The domestic version of this elite view was best expressed by the Old Oligarch, discussed earlier. The external version, with disastrous consequences for the ideal of Greek unity, is most notably expressed in Thucydides' own views, well summarized by Larsen: "States fight either to protect their own freedom or to secure domination over others."[26] This elite conception of freedom created the paradoxical situation in the Greek world in which, as Larsen nicely phrases it, "The chief obstacle to freedom was freedom itself."[27] He also shows that this attitude was as true of the elites in the smaller, lesser known Greek states as it was of those of Athens and Sparta.

These, then, were the three elements of freedom which we find fully developed by the last decades of the fifth century and the opening years of the fourth. The latter, as is well known, was marked by considerable class and economic conflicts and by a sharp turn to individualism. If the fifth century can be characterized as the century of civic freedom, in that this element was pervasive in the hegemonic group, the fourth century increasingly became the era of personal freedom. To be sure, those who were citizens continued to place civic freedom at the top of their scale of values, but with the decline of the political integrity of the polis, economic factors and personal advancement became uppermost in the minds of those who determined the economic life of the states and in not a few of those who controlled its political affairs.

By the middle of the fourth century, these conflicts had become matters of great concern. Wars, food crises verging on famine, economic depression, unemployment, proletarianization, and growing inequality marked the course of the fourth century down to the Alexandrian conquests.[28]

It is in the writings of Demosthenes that class and ideological tensions are most vividly preserved. Politics, he tells us, has become the path to riches, and individuals no longer place the state before themselves, but rather see the state as a means of promoting their own personal wealth.[29] He is only too aware of the oligarchic tendency to define freedom in terms of power over others, in other words, of the conflict between sovereignal and civic freedom. "The few," he writes, "can never be well disposed to the many, nor those who covet power to those who have chosen a life of equal privileges"[30] And he shrewdly comes to the realization that, in the final analysis, all forms of freedom rest on some power to defend them: "For I notice that all men have their rights conceded to them in proportion to the power at their disposal."[31]

Freedom as an ideal, both in its generalized form and in its competing elements, continued to grow and spread throughout the Greek world. When the Panhellenic chauvinist Isocrates wrote his address to Philip of Macedon urging him to unite all Greece in a war against the traditional enemy, Persia, he was convinced that the lure of freedom was so great, even to barbarians, that its promise would be enough to induce many of the satraps to join him against their king. No fourth-century passage more powerfully demonstrates just how far the idea and value of freedom had soared as the preeminent value of the Greek world than this: ". . . you will also induce many of the other satraps to throw off the King's power if you promise them 'freedom' and scatter broadcast over Asia that word which, when sown among the Hellenes, has broken up both our empire and that of the Lacedaemonians."[32]

Isocrates did not live long enough to see his wish come true. In any case, it was only half fulfilled. The value of freedom spread to the end of the world known to the Europeans with Alexander's conquests and the rise of the Hellenistic states. Mainland Greece, although it benefited economically from the conquests, remained as divided as ever. Warfare remained chronic, and as Rostovtzeff has shown, was fueled by the renewed prosperity of the late fourth and early third centuries.[33] A new factor however, was added to or, rather, intensified in this conflict. Already in the fifth century the pattern existed of the conservative elites appealing to Sparta for support against the civic freedom of their own lower-class citizens. This pernicious pattern continued with the decline of Sparta, as supporters of the organic view of sovereignal freedom turned to Macedon for assistance against their own people. It was certainly this kind of freedom that Isocrates had in mind in his address to Philip. This appeal to a dominant external power was usually made by the conservative elites, but defenders of civic freedom sometimes played the same game. In the fifth century Athens had been the champion of those who had sought to preserve, or restore, democracy, responding to such appeals with its own imperial interests in mind. There was a dearth of such external champions of civic freedom in fourth- and third-century Greece, but Philip V of Macedon was a notable exception. After coming to power in 221 B.C., he actively promoted class conflicts and donned the garb of the common man in promoting himself as the defender of civic freedom in Greece.[34] He may have been sincere; who knows? What we do know is, as Erich S. Gruen has recently reemphasized, "that declarations of 'freedom,' in one form or another, play a persistent role in international affairs through the whole of the Hellenistic era."[35]

Nonetheless, the situation was different in the Hellenistic kingdoms of the Seleucids and Ptolemies.[36] First, it should be noted that the mass of the native rural population was hardly affected by Greek values, and certainly not by the Greek passion for freedom, of whatever sort. These people continued to live as they had always done, as exploited peasants. The only thing that had changed for them was the ethnic identity of their exploiters. As Ernst Badian has cautioned, one must view all the talk, both ancient and modern, about Alexander the harmonizer of mankind with a heavy grain of salt.[37] In the cities of the Hellenistic world, however, especially Naucratis, Ptolemaïs, Philadelphia, and, above all, Alexandria, the Greek elite and the Hellenized Asians and North Africans sought, and achieved, the most freewheeling form of personal freedom the world had yet witnessed.[38] It was every man for himself in these bustling, cosmopolitan commercial centers. Urban slavery was widespread, overlaying the traditional forms of bonded labor, which remained largely untouched. Because slaves were employed largely in craft industries and services, manumission rates were extremely high, and in many occupations freedmen were preferred.[39] Ethnic Greeks enjoyed a fair measure of civic freedom. However, not only was this nothing compared with that in the democracies of the homeland, since the states were essentially despotic monarchies, but few ethnic Greeks placed civic freedom above the personal freedom that was the order of the day. The exceptions to this declining commitment to civic freedom occurred in the military settler colonies in Seleucid Asia, which somewhat resembled an ancient version of the white tribes of imperial Africa, though we do not know enough about them to say anything about how the democratic processes worked, if they worked at all.

With the coming of Rome, the Greek elites persisted in their old habit of turning to an exterior power for support against their own democratic masses. In much the same way that Macedon had used the rhetoric of freedom and brotherhood as a propaganda weapon in its imperial conquest of Asia, so now the Greeks were paid back in kind and fell victim to an ideological strategy they had perfected. Rome conquered one Greek state after another, pretending to protect its political freedom, which usually meant the sovereignal freedom of the elite. Usually, though not always. As John Briscoe has pointed out, correcting the simplistic consensus, "The result of Rome's victory was indeed to stem the tide of democracy and the ultimate victory belonged to the upper classes. But it would be wrong to infer that was Rome's object from the very beginning."[40]

But if the conquest by Rome meant the beginning of a steep decline in the relative status of civic freedom in the Greek world, it certainly implied no such thing for the value of freedom itself. For by this time this value had become preeminent in its generalized form throughout the Hellenistic world, and no power, not even Rome's, could remove it. Indeed, as we have already noted, Rome was shrewd enough to use a version of the freedom value in its own conquest. The tripartite and chordal quality of freedom was by now the common possession of all civilized Western peoples. Personal freedom was by now the element in the chord that dominated the popular, and middle-class, consciousness on the material level.

But by this time another critical development had come to fruition, one which was to ensure that freedom not only remained a dominant value in the Hellenized world but would soon triumph in the consciousness of the new conquering elite itself. This was the idea of inner and spiritual freedom. It was the culmination of a long ideological struggle, on the philosophical and spiritual levels, for the appropriation and redefinition of the very meaning of freedom. The struggle had commenced with the attempt to appropriate the value, on the outer level, by the elite Greek thinkers of the fifth and early fourth centuries. With this audacious intellectual project began the Western philosophy of freedom, a philosophical tradition which, throughout antiquity, was never divorced from the outer social struggles that continued to sustain freedom as a sociologically real value. It is to this ideological struggle that we now turn.

CHAPTER 9

The Outer Intellectual Response

We began this work by warning that this is not an intellectual history of freedom. What intellectuals thought will be considered only to the degree that these ideas influenced the development of the notion of freedom as a sociologically meaningful value. Ancient Greece marks one such case in point. From the middle of the fifth century B.C. down to the end of the second century of our era, intellectuals and their ideas were taken seriously by opinion molders and even by the ordinary man in the street in Greece, so much so that the professional purveyor of ideas sometimes ran grave risks, as Socrates' death bears witness.

Let me anticipate the main point of this and the next two chapters by pointing out that intellectuals made two kinds of responses to the construction and elevation of freedom in their societies: one external, the other internal. By the external response I mean the intellectuals' reflections on freedom as we have discussed it so far, freedom as men and women understood it, having direct meaning for their political and social lives. Up to the end of the fifth century, the dialogue, if one may so call it, was engaged essentially on this level, although, as we have seen, there were important precursors in tragic drama. At about the end of the century, and certainly by the early fourth century, however, there occurred a radical new turn in the discourse on freedom. While the intellectuals certainly continued to ponder ordinary, or external, freedom, a critical distinction (always implicit in the real, external construction of the value) was now made explicit and strongly emphasized: that between outer and inner freedom.

In a sense, this distinction was itself an assault on the ordinary, now outer, value of freedom, since it came to be held in near contempt by the intellectuals when compared with what now became really important, namely, inner freedom. Not that ordinary men and women necessarily accepted this intellectualist view of the matter. We have every reason to believe that the man on the Athenian streets—like his later Hellenistic and Roman counterparts—continued to value greatly the ordinary, outer freedom disdained by the intellectuals. We should not make the mistake of identifying the ideas we are about to discuss with the popular morality of the times. As K. J. Dover has demonstrated, "moral philosophy and popular morality are sharply contrasted in respect of reason and reflection," not to mention "idiosyncratic moralities."[1]

Whatever their mutual antagonisms, however, this was not a dialogue of the deaf, as it later became during periods such as the Middle Ages. Between the late fifth century and early Roman times, what intellectuals thought mattered more for the lives and ultimate thoughts and feelings of the ordinary person than it did at perhaps any other time in human history. Indeed, for the philosophers of the late fifth century, the popular interest in what they were up to was decidedly too great. As E. R. Dodds has shown, there was a strong popular reaction against the Sophist enlightenment toward the end of the century, leading to the most savage prosecution and sentences.[2]

There are two reasons for the importance of intellectuals during the fifth and fourth centuries. Intellectuals were taken seriously by many whom today we would not expect to show great interest in intellectual creations[3] and by leaders, often powerful ones. However such leaders may have distorted the ideas of their teachers, their interest meant that ideas indirectly influenced the lives of ordinary people to an unusual degree and were popularized at an extraordinary pace. It cannot have been unimportant that Alexander the Great had been a tutee of Aristotle, although it should immediately be noted that the idea with which we most associate Alexander, the unity of mankind (leaving aside, for the sake of the argument, the thorny question of the authenticity of these "extraordinary ideas"), is not what springs to mind when we think of Aristotle. Nonetheless, from the perspective of our own times, when the president of the world's most powerful nation makes a point of deleting his distinguished academic record at college from his publicized vita, Alexander's association with such "big" ideas, even if—or especially if—they were mainly propaganda, is indeed remarkable.

The second reason for the central role of ideas during this and the entire period of classical antiquity is perhaps the more important. And that is that the secular intellect had a more direct, even if often hostile, influence on religious movements and beliefs—of which this period is one of the most fertile in Western history—than it had at any other time. If theology is what most directly exercised the mind of ordinary men and women, the susceptibility of the new religions—most conspicuously of the greatest of them all, Christianity—to the ideas we are about to survey ensured that the intellectual had a powerful, though indirect and often delayed, impact on what ordinary people came to value. As De Ste. Croix has observed of the Christian era, "religion in those days was universally regarded as a matter of enormous importance" and the "niceties of doctrine could obsess very ordinary minds."[4] It was because they feared the effect of the new ideas on their religious beliefs—beliefs that were themselves going through an alarming regression to primitivism—that the common Athenians of the late fifth century turned so vehemently against the intellectuals among them.[5]

The shifting of levels in the history of freedom, then, was a critical development. All this has been well established, especially since Pohlenz's brilliant work on the subject.[6] Less well understood is the nature of the internal response on the part of the intellectuals. It will be the main burden of this and the following two chapters to argue that freedom as a tripartite value was lifted in its entirety to the level of the secular mind, the inner being, and later to the level of the spiritual or religious. That being the case, the tension inherent in the generalized value, between its three elements, remained. I will argue that a direct counterpart to the outer struggle was present on the inner level. The struggle over freedom, then, did not end with the intellectual shift of levels; it merely shifted to a new terrain. This is one of the most remarkable aspects of the history of freedom.

The first group of philosophers to have a popular impact on Greek thought and values, the Sophists, were preoccupied with the value and idea of freedom. As Erik A. Havelock observed, "liberalism was in the field first."[7] They could not help doing so, given the enormous significance freedom had acquired by the second half of the fifth century. The Sophists were very much men of the world, scholars who moved freely from one city-state to another to make their living by educating the youth and others on practical matters—on the art of political persuasion—and on philosophical, social, and ethical issues. Long before Socrates' trial and execution, Protagoras recognized the occupational hazards of his profession, especially among the conservative rulers of Greece. He should have been warier of Greece's conservative intellectuals. The Sophists, more than any other group of thinkers, have suffered from the distortions of the intellectual conservatives—

most notably, Plato and Aristotle—who informed succeeding ages about them.[8]

For us, the key point about the Sophists is that every single one of their major doctrines bears directly on the issue of freedom.[9] First and foremost was their humanistic individualism. It was they who finally humanized the Delphic injunction "Know thyself as a human being, and follow the god," by transforming it into a wholly secular precept best expressed in the celebrated *homo mensura* maxim of Protagoras: "Of all things the measure is man, of the things that are, that they are, and of the things that are not, that they are not." Implicit in this is a momentous shifting of the focus of thought from people in their relation with god, to people as the basis for all judgment about the world.[10] When we ally this epistemological leap to the Sophists' agnosticism, we find the ethical principle that individuals in their relations with each other become the focus of human reflection. Implicit in this development, too, is a bias toward relativism, one that becomes explicit when related to another basic distinction in Greek thought which the Sophists clarified—namely, that between *phusis*, or nature, and *nomos*, or convention and laws, what today we would call culture.[11] This sociological sensitivity to the distinction between nurture and nature was no doubt stimulated by their peripatetic life-style. A far more powerful reason for the sensitivity to *nomos* has been so well argued and demonstrated by Martin Ostwald that it is enough simply to summarize his findings. His philological analysis shows that the profound shift in the conception of, and attitude toward, *nomos*—defined as "a social norm accepted as valid and binding by those among whom it prevailed"—was directly related to the Cleisthenean democratic revolution. "Norms," he writes, "which before Cleisthenes were thought of as having existed from time immemorial, now came to be regarded as having been enacted and as being enforceable in a way similar to that in which statutes are decided upon by a legislative agency."[12] Receding, though never eliminated[13] from the conception of norms, were the qualities of timelessness and immutability, derived from the archaic view that they were engendered by the gods; replacing them was "the idea that human agents now became the authors, formulators, enactors, and enforcers of a *nomos* that could no longer be taken for granted as a perennial pattern of human existence."[14] The change was most marked among the intellectuals and leaders, but there is clear evidence of such developments in popular thinking, though in a more agglomerative way, since archaic patterns of thought, as Dover has shown, persisted alongside and sometimes contradicted the new.[15]

Here we have a beautiful example of the endless dialectic between

social processes, social thought, and intellectual reflection. The Cleisthenean revolution, we have seen, was the result of human struggle,
social reality on the ground, so to speak. An immediate outgrowth of
this is what may be called primal social thought, the mind's raw collective responses to struggle which find their most authentic phenomenal expression in language—in this case, in what Ostwald felicitously
calls "the language of rule and the language of practice," the syntax
and meaning of which the sociologically attuned philologist is peculiarly qualified to read. But no sooner does this language make its appearance than one group of native speakers begins to reflect on it and,
in the process, to change it: "Practice and theory," writes W. K. C.
Guthrie, "acted and reacted mutually on one another."[16] These most
sophisticated native speakers are the people we have come to call philosophers, and they first emerged as a distinctive, specialist group in
the history of the West—some would say, in all history, but I would
not be so bold—precisely at this moment. Sophist philosophy is the
pristine philosophy of the West, which is not at all to say that it was
not strongly influenced by non-Western modes of thought or by what
went before. Indeed, given the Ionian origins (southwest coastal region of Asia Minor, now Turkey) of many of their precursors, and the
ancient links between them and the Near East, we are inclined to agree
with Martin Bernal that there were strong non-Greek influences on
these developments.[17]

Western philosophy itself emerged as a part of the progress of the
struggle for freedom, often interpreted as a struggle for survival itself,
a product of its age which "assisted in [its] turn in crystallizing its
ideas."[18] It saw its first and central task as a profoundly committed
discourse with, and engagement in, that struggle. This is why no historical sociology of freedom is possible without a sociology of knowledge about it. But to understand this sociology, one must first
understand that knowledge. Let us return, then, to these first philosophers.

Relativism in philosophy and social life, humanism, and individualism—the basic ideas of the Sophists—all powerfully reinforced the
value of freedom, as they were to do again some twenty-three hundred
years later in the second European Enlightenment. But which element
of freedom? And how? The Sophists' doctrine moved in several directions, mainly because the relativism that informed much of their
thought was then, as always, a two-headed creature; and when it is
joined to the nature-culture distinction, it becomes positively hydra-
headed. Where a particular thinker ends up depends to a large extent
on how he or she interprets nature and its role. It is remarkable that

these first social theorists plunged straight into a set of sociological problems which are still very much with us today. Thus relativism can have the salutary effect of promoting tolerance toward cultures other than one's own, and this was certainly the approach of Antiphon, Hippias, and, most radically, Alcidamas. But it can also breed skepticism, even cynicism, about human values, as it did in people such as Gorgias.

When these differences are linked to different conceptions of nature, the resulting social doctrines tend to extremes, being either unrealistically revolutionary or dangerously tyrannical—indeed what, at the risk of anachronism, we would today call fascist. As Dodds has observed, the "grand question" for the Sophists in the face of conflict between law and human nature was this: "Is the social restraint which law imposes on nature a good thing or a bad thing?"[19]

Protagoras, rightly called "the first democratic political theorist in the history of the world,"[20] and his most loyal disciples had taught that all men were by nature equal and had held that good laws and justice required each other and were improvable; virtue could be taught and was not at the mercy of birth or nature.[21] Just as important, against the frivolous arguments of Socrates, Protagoras insisted that what he called "civic virtue as a whole," or political wisdom, was found in everyone and was an essential precondition for democracy. Thus, he praised the Athenian citizens for distinguishing civic virtue as a special quality shared by all: "when the subject of their counsel involves political wisdom, which must always follow the path of justice and moderation, they listen to everyman's opinion, for they think that everyone must share in this kind of virtue; otherwise the state could not exist."[22] We may therefore interpret Protagoras' ideas as the earliest and, during the fifth century, most influential intellectual defense of civic freedom. He and his followers "rationalize[d]" the social structure and democratic achievements of the age of Pericles.[23] In the process he developed a social philosophy which was the ancient antecedent of what sociologists today call symbolic interactionism. He believed that the social universe was a socially constructed order which emerged dialectically from the interactions of persons with each other and with the culture they inherited, this culture itself being the accumulated product of earlier interactions. While we are strongly influenced by these ongoing and inherited patterns of interactions, and are obliged to respect them, we are not passively determined by them. Instead, Protagoras uses the metaphor of the practitioner or craftsman to explain how the creative process, whereby we engage in the practical discourses of living in its totality, produces what he calls "civilized

and humane society." By practicing "the art of politics" we make ourselves "good citizens," and more generally, by engaging in the art of
living we teach each other virtue.[24] In her account of Protagoras' conception of the relation between the two realms of cosmos and community, Cynthia Farrar offers a textbook definition of symbolic
interaction:

> Order in these realms is to be understood not as transcendent, but as
> built up through interaction and stability, and interactions are to be seen
> as implicit in the world of change, the world of experience. Protagoras
> formulated a view of human knowledge which located the development
> of beliefs in the interaction of persons as they experience themselves in
> the world, and a view of human needs which suggested that all men must
> and can display civic qualities.[25]

On the moderate, pragmatic wing, there can be no doubt that the most
thoughtful was Democritus, who, as Farrar has splendidly demonstrated, developed an atomist ethic resting "on a concept of personal
autonomy not limited to those with superior social resources and privileges" and, more audaciously, also not necessarily requiring any special social or political order.[26] Man creates himself and his social order;
"the source of freedom and order" is relocated inside the individual.[27]

More conservative, but still very much in the defense of civic liberty,
is a possible pupil of Protagoras, the anonymous writer quoted by
Iamblichus, who condemns political instability on the grounds that it
disrupts trade and commerce and offers fertile ground for tyrants. He
cautions that the people, if they are to preserve their civic freedom,
must behave themselves properly and be ever respectful of the constituted laws of the democracy.[28] All the students of Protagoras followed
the master in one crucial respect: they reconciled the demands of the
individual for personal fulfillment with the needs of the polis, not only
by their audacious claim that the polis exists ultimately to meets these
needs but by their advocacy of a reductionist theory of the relation
between human nature and the prerequisites of society.[29]

But there was a more radical side to this "liberal temper" of the
Sophist movement, as Havelock calls it. This was the outright egalitarianism of men such as Hippias, who considered all fellow thinkers
his "kinsmen and family and fellow citizens—by nature, not by convention"—and whose individualism was so radical that it condemned
convention as "the tyrant of mankind" which "does much violence to
nature."[30] Even more radical in its thrust was the view of the fourth-
century Sophist and rhetorician Alcidamas that "God has left all men

free; Nature has made none a slave"—the closest the ancient world came to an outright critique of slavery.[31] Most people would perhaps not have taken it seriously as a proposal for social reform, so completely was slavery taken for granted, and in any case it is doubtful if Alcidamas would have himself seriously advocated such a change. Nonetheless, it is important not to go to the other extreme and underplay the antislavery sentiments of radical Sophists. Such sentiments are a logical radical development of the basic tenets of the movement.[32] With Antiphon that logic veers toward anarchy. An angry, humorless man, as Havelock notes, his "embittered criticism of the society of the city-state," including its institutions of marriage and the family, is wholly impractical and sometimes incoherent.[33]

The celebration of personal freedom is what the radical wing of the Sophist movement held in common: the removal of all constraints except those absolutely necessary, the denial of all man-made authority and of the enslavement to convention. As Dodds has remarked,

> It shows the same typical traits as the liberal thought of the eighteenth and nineteenth centuries: the same individualism, the same humanitarianism, the same secularism, the same confident arraignment of tradition at the bar of reason, the same robust faith in applied intelligence as the key to perpetual progress.[34]

And, we might add, the same antislavery sentiments. I have no doubt, either, that it did so for the same reasons: not just as an ethical imperative of its humanitarianism but as the inevitable way of defining antithetically, and expressing metaphorically, the idea and value of personal freedom.

But the Sophists' relativism and emphasis on nature could also go in quite the opposite direction. It may amaze some to know that exactly the same reactionary turn which this combination of tenets took during the nineteenth century had its precursor in the first movement of secular philosophy in the West. It is not for me to come to the defense of extreme statements of personal freedom, but Dodds surely misses the point when he asserts that it was this which "heralded" the civil wars and dictatorships of the "second *turannis*." The Sophists did not create personal freedom—intellectuals never create values, at any rate not values as monumentally important as personal freedom—but they brought it to the level of intellectual reflection, explicated it to the civilized consciousness, reinforced, if one likes, with the weight of reason what had already long been created out of the brutal social dialectics of master, slave, and freeman and had already been given expression in the symbolic discourse that springs directly from creative social conflict. Here we are concerned with what intellectuals came to discover long after the phoenix had risen from the ashes of slavery.

What determined the drift of the Sophists' thought was not the brutal logic of social conflict but the logical implications of their own first principles. As Farrar has wisely emphasized, Protagoras' theory "was a *theory*," though one offered by an outsider "as part of the process of socialization which he encountered at Athens" and which he hoped would help heal the wounds of social conflict.[35] When an egalitarian conception of nature is added to relativism and humanism, the equation generates a commitment to either civic or personal freedom. However, nature can just as easily be interpreted in an inegalitarian manner. When this is added to the other ingredients of relativism and humanism, the result is the celebration of the egomaniac, the hero. Note, however, that the ideal here is still freedom, only now the freedom of the community finds expression in the heroic character of the leader. This is really only the secularization of a religious idea that had been around for some time, namely, that only Zeus is free. The replacement of a god-centered theology by a man-centered philosophy had disastrous implications. Man is the measure of all things, but some men are by nature superior to others; some are by nature leaders, others by nature followers. Some are by nature free, others by nature slaves.

Similarly, culture, convention, and laws may be man-made, but this does not necessarily mean that we should respect them all as being of equal worth. To the contrary, some are inferior, others superior; some are free cultures, others slave cultures. What makes the superior better and free is, of course, the superiority of its people, and what makes for the superiority of the superior collectivity is the genius and natural superiority of its leaders. True freedom now becomes power; the more powerful the person, the freer he is. The freer a man is, the greater his right to rule over the less free. The unfree, or the less free, should also recognize that it is in their best interest, their true freedom, to be ruled by the more powerful. Here we have arrived at the intellectual reconstruction of sovereignal freedom. Sadly, this is what became the favored conception of freedom among the conservative intellectuals, those very ones who have had a disproportionate influence on the Western mind. There is, however, a crude and a refined version of it or, what may be the same thing, an early and a later stage of its development. Both also emerged from Sophist principles: it is a serious error to assume that the temper of the movement was exclusively liberal.

The cruder, earlier version found expression in the thought and actions of men such as Thrasymachus, Critias, Alcibiades, and Polus. They originate in the cynical rhetoricism of Gorgias, who advocated and taught "the power to convince by words." This power Gorgias identifies with freedom. It is "the greatest boon, for it brings freedom to mankind in general and to each man dominion over others in his own country."[36] Note the easy and complete use of the slave relationship, both metaphorically and literally, in this rhetorical version of sovereignal freedom. The power of persuasion makes the entire community free vis-à-vis other communities and so is to the benefit of all; but it is also to the benefit of the superior individual. And Gorgias not only calls this benefit "freedom"; he openly calls the condition of those who are so dominated "slavery": ". . . possessed of such power you will make the doctor, you will make the trainer your slave, and your businessman will prove to be making money, not for himself, but for another, for you can speak and persuade multitudes."[37] To the charge of amoralism from Socrates, Gorgias responds with an argument which we still hear daily from advocates of the right-to-bear-arms lobby. The teacher is not guilty, nor is the art evil, "but those who make improper use of it."

Callicles takes an important step forward in the more sophisticated expression of these views. He condemns the timidity of his teacher Gorgias and of pupils such as Polus for falling into Socrates' moral trap in admitting that the powerful man who does wrong is unhappy. This simply does not square with reality as he sees it; it is an "upside-down" view of the world. Nature and convention "are antagonistic to each other." The populace in a democracy has molded laws and convention in such a way that power over the many has been identified with injustice. If the naturally powerful man, then, takes democratically made laws seriously, he is bound to find himself in a state of self-contradiction.[38]

But in my view nature herself makes it plain that it is right for the better to have the advantage over the worse, the more able over the less. And both among all animals and in entire states and races of mankind it is plain that this is the case—that right is recognized to be the sovereignty and advantage of the stronger over the weaker. . . . We mold the best and strongest among ourselves, catching them young like lion cubs, and by spells and incantations we make slaves of them, saying that they must be content with equality and that this is what is right and fair. But if a man arises endowed with a nature sufficiently strong, he will, I believe, shake off all these controls, burst his fetters, and break loose. And trampling upon our scraps of paper, our spells and incantations, and all our unnatural conventions, he rises up and reveals himself our master who was once our slave, and there shines forth nature's true justice.[39]

I have quoted this passage at length because I think it is one of the most important in all of Plato's social writings, not only for the light it throws on the extremely conservative wing of Athenian Sophist thought but for what it reveals about the development of Plato's own social ethics and theory of freedom. First, let us agree with Ehrenberg about the outcome of ideas such as those propounded by Callicles. Unlike Dodds, he correctly sees this as the origin of the superman doctrine and its awful political consequences: "This law of nature is not the natural law of later times, rather the forerunner of Nietzsche's *Herrenmoral*, a law nevertheless, the law of unlimited individualism, the law lived by such men as Alcibiades, Lysander, and Critias."[40]

But what of Plato? Where, with his overwhelming later influence on the Western mind, does he—and his main pupil, Aristotle—stand in relation to the external intellectualization of freedom? The sane, moral views of Socrates dominate the early, aporetic dialogues. Whatever his disagreements with his Sophist teachers and associates, Socrates shared with them to the end of his life not only a humanism and commitment to the secularized precept "Know thyself" but a commitment to this-worldliness and, whatever his reservations, to the democratic polis. In the end he refused to go into exile to save his life. He had freely chosen the city, and agreed "in deed if not in word, to live [his] life as a citizen in obedience to [its laws]."[41] Socrates, it is safe to say, was a conservative advocate of civic freedom.

Not so his star pupil. Few scholars today would care to challenge the harsh and frequently cited judgment of R. H. S. Crossman: "Plato's philosophy is the most savage and most profound attack upon liberal ideas which history can show. It denies every axiom of 'progressive' thought and challenges all its fondest ideals. Equality, freedom, self-government—all are condemned as illusions which can be held only by idealists whose sympathies are stronger than their sense."[42] Indeed, some scholars, like Karl Popper, go even further and claim that Plato's political program, "far from being morally superior to totalitarianism, is fundamentally identical with it."[43]

How did Plato came to such an extremely hostile external view of freedom? I am in basic agreement with Popper that while Plato's class background and experience with war and a chaotic phase of Athenian democracy are important in explaining his political and ideological biases, more significant are his underlying essentialist epistemology and methods. There is no need for me to summarize Popper's argument here. I will focus, instead, on a distinction which Popper does not pay sufficient attention to, that mentioned earlier between external and internal views of freedom. In this chapter I concentrate on his external conception of freedom; in the next, on his even more important views on inner freedom.

Plato's middle period, to which the *Republic* belongs, is both more positive than the first in the search for basic principles and ideals of behavior and more removed from the world, indeed disdainful of it. We ought not to lose sight of the obvious fact that the *Republic*, in its sociological and political aspects, is a utopian tract and that this second phase is followed by a third, in which the elderly Plato tries to fashion a more sociologically realistic set of views.[44]

Early in the *Republic* a basic principle of inquiry is laid down which has immediate implications for any serious external conception of freedom, the view that, in our search for the nature of political and social justice, we "first look for its quality in states, and then only examine it also in the individual, looking for the likeness of the greater in the form of the less."[45] Such an approach is always dangerous for any but the sovereignal conception of freedom. God may no longer be the measure of all things; but no longer, either, are human beings. Rather, abstractions or forms are the measure of things human; and they dictate an intellectual progression in which we move from the forms to their collective approximations and then to real individuals.

The theory of society which Plato develops in the *Republic* may be described as an extreme form of naturalistic functionalism. Society is divided into a hierarchy of functions—leadership, protection, and labor—with their respective collectivities: leaders, guardians, and workers. Each group is selected according to its natural capacities for each of the three basic functions. Only the wise are fit to rule, and they will have the power to manipulate religion and education, to deceive, and to enact strict censorship of the arts and all forms of oral and written literature—in short, to "fitly lie on account of enemies or citizens for the benefit of the state."[46] The result will be a thoroughly harmonious and fully integrated state, one which exhibits the four cardinal virtues of wisdom, courage, discipline, and justice. Up to this point there has not been any mention of the word *freedom*. Plato has such a distaste for the concept that, at this stage in his intellectual development, he will not even try to appropriate it. Yet, as we will see, that is what he eventually condescends to do, and the ground is being paved here, for the utopian state we have just described is easily reinterpreted as the organically free state.

Before getting to this point, however, we find in the later pages of the *Republic* a discussion of democracies, which Plato judges the second-to-worst form of imperfect societies, ranking only above despotism in the scale of political degeneracy. Timocracy comes closest to the ideal form of the state. Plato clearly modeled it on Sparta, and its most salient features are "ambition and the competitive spirit." An honorific ethic and the quest for military glory and political power constitute the modal personality type of this kind of society. Democracy is dismissed with acerbic humor as "an agreeable, anarchic form of society, with plenty of variety, which treats all men as equal, whether they are equal or not."[47] In the course of discussing the democratic character, Plato condemns both civic and personal freedom. Indeed, the two are related in an interesting way, in that personal freedom is seen as the prevailing quality of persons who live in democratic societies; to put it another way, civic freedom is the dominant feature, the main "objective" of the democratic state, while personal freedom is the prevailing quality of the typical citizen in such a state. It is the excessive desire for the objective of democracy which is the cause of its downfall.

> "And what is this objective?"
> "Liberty," I replied, "for you may hear it said that this is best managed in a democratic city, and for this reason that is the only city in which a man of free spirit will care to live in."[48]

Mob rule, demagoguery, and a chronic tendency toward anarchy are the essential weaknesses of democracy; while the fundamental problem of personal liberty is its tendency to become personal license and selfishness. "A very good description of one who believes in liberty and equality" is the comment on the definition of "democratic man" as one who has "no order and restraint in his life" and who "reckons his way of living . . . pleasant, free and happy."[49]

In the final period of his life, Plato returns to a more realistic view of the world, and it is useful to follow the development of his ideas on freedom and governance at this stage. My basic point is that Plato returns—if that is the right term—to a view of freedom and society which is closely related to that of Callicles quoted at length above. The best state is one in which there prevails not the rule of law but the rule of the expert statesman: "the political ideal is not full authority for laws but rather full authority for a man who understands the art of kingship and has kingly ability."[50] This is the reactionary Sophist's rejection of law in favor of the skill, power, and vision of the natural-born leader. The skilled statesman is no longer the utopian philosopher, wise in all things, but one wise in the art of politics, which is compared to weaving. The statesman weaves together the basic characters of the "herds of free bipeds" into a single cloth, the state which embodies the one in the many and the many in the one. Those who cannot acquire virtue are banished; and those who lack nobility of character—who can be neither moderate nor courageous—are given over as slaves to the rest of the community. While the best state is one without laws, Plato allows that a second-best arrangement might be necessary, in which the true statesman becomes "the good and true lawgiver, who alone is able—for who else should possess the power—to forge [implant] by the wondrous inspiration of the kingly art this bond of true conviction" among the young elite.[51]

In what was perhaps his last work, the *Laws*, Plato finally attempts to specify what these laws should be like in the second-best state. The rule of law is grudgingly acknowledged. There is a retreat from the abstract forms of the *Republic*, and from the superman of the *Statesman*, as the measure of all things, back to god as the measure.[52] Further, while he still eschews democracy, it is striking that in this last work of sociology and political ethics Plato, for the first time, embraces the idea of freedom in its external meaning. "A community," he now claims, "should be at once free, sane, and at amity with itself, and . . . these are the ends a legislator must keep in view in his enactments."[53] The number of basic kinds of constitutions has been reduced to two: monarchy and democracy. All other kinds partake of these two strands, and elements of both are necessary in the second-best state which combines liberty, amity, and wisdom.[54]

Plato takes Persia as representing the most advanced type of monarchial society, and its decadence, from the good days of Cyrus, was explained in terms of a too "excessive curtailment of the liberty of the commons." In discussing why the opposite type, Athens, fell from the desirable state it had reached at the time of the Persian Wars, Plato offers what is, in effect, a historical sociology of freedom. Its decadence was due to "extravagant liberty of living," especially among the multitude. The mass of the people lacked any sense of fear generally, or respect for their betters, indeed had grown impudent from "a reckless excess of liberty."[55] What was needed was a willing submission to virtuous laws. Plato's ideal state for the real world, his idea of a mixed constitution, is autocracy, a system in which a virtuous autocrat, aided by wise elders and educated guardians, rules a mass of citizens whose only role is passive "conformity to the traditions embodied in the laws."[56]

It is perhaps unfair to call Plato's statement a program for totalitarianism, though the charge holds for most of his earlier writings. It certainly rejects democracy and personal liberty. However, we can interpret it as an advocacy of organic freedom, which is the ultimate Greek refinement of sovereignal freedom. Although Plato, in the later books of the *Laws*, drops the language of liberty, he clearly meant the final outcome to be seen as a fuller exposition of how a state which blends liberty, amity, and wisdom should be governed.

An organic, harmonious society, then, is his ideal. The basic problem of the state is anarchy, which "we should expel root and branch from the lives of mankind," an understandable obsession in any sensitive and intelligent person who has survived the horrors of the Peloponnesian War and the civil strife it engendered. But he goes overboard in stating the positive implications of this concern. Society is like an army at war in which "no man, and no woman, be ever suffered to live without an officer set over them."[57] Harmony will come not only from external coercion but by internal mind control in which everyone will have ingrained in his soul "the habit of never so much as thinking to do one single act apart from one's fellows, of making life, to the very uttermost, an unbroken consort, society, and community of all with all."[58] Plato was obviously aware of the extremity of his stand, as the occasional intrusions and gentle protests of his other characters indicate. But he clearly felt it to be necessary, in the light of his experience.

So have countless advocates of the organic version of sovereignal freedom for centuries after Plato. What is extraordinary about his statement is that it presents all that is best and appealing, and all that is worst, in any theory of organic freedom. The idea of the harmonious society which condemns selfishness and promotes the cardinal virtues, one led by a pious and wise autocrat with a strong conviction of his divine mission, has appealed to many leaders and followers down the ages of Western history; and it still does. And, as often as not, such a program has been labeled, rightly, as a form of freedom, though, wrongly, as the only and true form. However distasteful democrats and libertarians may find it, we cannot deny the idea or language of freedom to those who advocate its organic and sovereignal component, for it was conceived in the same dread embrace or fear of slavery and had its birth from the same social womb, its infancy in the same period and place, its initiation in the Western consciousness in the same historic ritual of the classical funeral oration, and its identity and expression forever fused with the other two elements with which it formed the chordal triad of freedom. And while history presents us with numerous horrible instances of attempts to implement societies based on organic sovereignal freedom as the fundamental note in the triad, it should also not be forgotten that for most of Western history it was indeed the dominant note. We may criticize Plato for the extremity and harshness of his program, but we should recognize the power of his sociological insights and the wisdom of his prophecy, though some may say that his prophecies were all too self-fulfilling.

Let us conclude our discussion of the external intellectual response to freedom with a consideration of Aristotle, whose views in this regard are largely elaborations of Plato's later writings. Like Plato, Aristotle is highly critical of the actual democratic Greek states in which he lived, though he gives us a valuable political sociology and history of them. Like his teacher, too, he expresses a preference for a mixed constitution of the best elements of oligarchy and democracy, one that is almost as elitist as Plato's but has a more "bourgeois" bias. In his critical analysis of what he called "democracies of the extreme type," which were "regarded as being peculiarly democratic," Aristotle leaves us in no doubt that in the "actual practice" of his day personal and civic freedom were considered integrally related:

> There are two conceptions which are generally held to be characteristic of democracy. One of them is the conception of the sovereignty of the majority; the other is that of the liberty of individuals. The democrat starts by assuming that justice consists in equality: he proceeds to identify equality with the sovereignty of the will of the masses; he ends with the view that "liberty and equality" consists in "doing what one likes." The result of such a view is that, in these extreme democracies, each man lives as he likes—or, as Euripides says, "For any end he chances to desire." This is a mean conception of liberty. To live by the rule of the constitution ought not to be regarded as slavery, but rather as salvation.[59]

Later on, Aristotle labels these two forms of liberty the "political" and the "civic."[60] He explicitly agrees with Plato in identifying excessive personal liberty with license[61] and claims that such liberty promotes license not only among slaves but among women and children and "ensures a large body of support" for demagogues.[62]

It has often been said that personal freedom is a peculiar product of the modern world, especially the peculiar version which emphasizes freedom against the state. It is one of the main burdens of this work to demonstrate the complete error of both these views. We have already fully established the first—that personal freedom is a major element of the ancient conception of freedom—and it is from no less an authority than Aristotle, the best sociologist of the ancient city-state, that we get an unequivocal statement of not just the existence but the popularity of the second, something that deeply disturbed him.

> Such a life [living as you like], the democrats argue, is the function of the free man, just as the function of slaves is *not* to live as they like. This is the second aim of democracy. Its issue is, ideally, *freedom from any interference of government*, and, failing that, such freedom as comes from the interchange of ruling and being ruled. It contributes, in this way, to a general system of liberty based on equality.[63]

Note that Aristotle, in reporting the common view of freedom in his day, correctly defines it as the man in the street would have done, as the opposite of the slave condition. The institution of slavery, as we have seen, was still flourishing during the fourth century, when Aristotle wrote. Indeed, it was during his time that manumission would have become a common, and necessary, part of the system of slavery as a way of motivating the large number of highly skilled urban slaves. Thus a high proportion of the metic population in his time would have been made up of the ex-slave population. However uneasy Aristotle may have felt about the matter, he having been a metic for nearly all his professional life, he clearly recognized the need to motivate slaves by means of both good treatment and the incentive of manumission.[64]

It has startled many, and no doubt been a source of some embarrassment for admirers of Aristotle, that his *Politics* opens with a long discussion of the household, beginning with an analysis of the essential role of slaves in the well-run basic unit of the state. I think far too much, in the way of moral judgment, has been made of Aristotle's comments on the institution. What he has left us is a first-rate sociology of it, written from the viewpoint of someone who, like nearly everyone else in his day, assumed that it was essential for economic and social life. He makes the case for a natural view of slavery; it is a very weak argument, and not only does one get the distinct impression that he is not persuaded by it himself, but it is often not clear whether he is merely reporting the views of others who defend slavery on natural grounds or presenting his own views; and he does present the opposing Sophist argument in a manner which, one suspects, would have appeared more attractive even to readers of his time.

Three final points may be added. What to a moralistic reader may seem a brutally insensitive position on slavery is actually a sociologically very accurate description of the master-slave relationship, for example, the statement that "the slave is a part of the master, in the sense of being a living but separate part of his body."[65] Second, we know from Aristotle's own words and deeds, especially the evidence of his will, that he was an extremely humane master, as masters went, freeing several of his slaves in his will and ensuring that others were not sold. Third, and perhaps most important in the light of our discussion later, although Aristotle talked more about real, external slavery than Plato did, his method of reasoning, and his ethical and political discourse, was not in any way as influenced by the institution as was Plato's. Ironically, as we will argue in the next chapter, Plato's thought was infused with the metaphor of slavery. Aristotle, on the other hand, repeatedly went out of his way to deny this subtle epistemological (or discursive) influence and seems to have deplored it in Plato, though he never said so outright.[66]

Aristotle was a middle-class democrat who believed that citizenship involves active participation in the state and, for this reason, should be restricted to those who are superior in goodness and wealth. The "good citizen must possess the knowledge and the capacity requisite for ruling as well as for being ruled."[67] However, unlike Plato, he makes a sharp distinction between rule over slaves and menials and rule of one's equals in the political process. For Aristotle, members of the middle class make the best citizens and dominate the best sort of states. He is suspicious of the rich and noble because they have a tendency toward violence and are unwilling to obey; he also rejects the poor, who tend toward roguery and "are far too mean and poor-spirited." The middle class "forms the mean" and exhibits that moderation which is always best. Its members listen to reason; they are comfortable and materially secure and do not envy others.

In his ethical works, Aristotle defines what the good life entails. It is a thoroughly bourgeois existence—"living well and doing well—" which is the equivalent of happiness. While essentially an activity of the soul in the pursuit of virtue, this activity requires a fair amount of secure property and a nice, leisurely environment.[68] Aristotle clearly identifies this life of virtuous moderation as a kind of freedom, for in the *Politics* he refers to, and summarizes, his discussion in his ethical work with the statement that "a truly happy life is a life of goodness lived in freedom from impediments."[69] He concludes with a virtual paean to his class:

> It follows that a state which is based on the middle class is bound to be the best constituted in respect of the elements [i.e., equals and peers] of which, on our view, a state is naturally composed. The middle classes [besides contributing, in this way, to the security of the state] enjoy a

greater security themselves than any other class. They do not, like the poor, covet the goods of others. . . . Neither plotting against others, nor plotted against themselves, they live in freedom from danger; and we may well approve the prayer of Phocylides:

> Many things are best for the middling:
> Fain would I be the state's middle class.[70]

Here, then, in the last great thinker of the classical Greek period, we find one of the best and most candid expressions of the bourgeois version of organic sovereignal freedom. There is a return to a pre-Cleisthenean conception of citizenship in which "the over-poor, the over-weak, the utterly ignoble" are excluded from the ideal democracy led not by the opposite extreme of "the over-handsome, the over-strong, the over-wealthy" but by personally free, civic-minded men of solid middle-class backgrounds such as Solon, Charondas, and Lycurgus, all of whom Aristotle insisted, against tradition, belonged to his own, virtuous class.[71]

CHAPTER 10

The Turn to Inner Freedom

1. BEFORE PLATO

Before Plato, there were well-established currents in Greek thought which tended toward an emphasis on the inner person. To some extent, the aristocratic emphasis on nobility of character, which, we have seen, culminated in the organic view of external freedom, already suggested some notion of a freedom which had to do more with the inner man than with outward circumstances. But it was only suggestive, for we have emphasized that this element of freedom, although it referred to character, was very much focused on the external world, on the exercise of power over others. Manliness, courage, glory, and honor were all in and of the world; they added up to a character complex that was nothing if not "other-directed." Something significantly new was needed to shift the focus of character inward.

One new element we have already mentioned. This was the secularization of the Delphic commandment "Know thyself." One can easily see how Socrates' exploration of the nature of virtue would blend easily with the traditional pursuit of *arete* on the part of his upper-class students, transforming the older aristocratic virtue into something more intellectually and morally advanced. Even so, it cannot be too greatly stressed that Socrates never departed from the Sophist concern with the external world. What he sought, through self-examination and probing dialogue, were the principles of justice, the nature of the good, so that people could live better lives. It was the unexamined *life* that was not worth living; not the unexamined *soul*, which became Plato's peculiar obsession.

Preoccupation with the nature-versus-convention distinction was also important, although it moved in two radically different ways. We examined in the last chapter its diverse external implications. But the distinction was just as explosive, and as varied, in its impact on conceptions of the inner person. If one saw nature and convention as hostile to each other, then one view of true freedom became the removal of the constraint of corrupting, man-made conventions on the natural person—or the domination of the conventional by the natural. However, the question still remained: What was the nature of the natural being that was either being released or asserting control? Answers varied. The one we know most about, and have come to associate with Greek culture, was the identification of the natural inner being with reason. But it is quite likely that this view of the matter is a distortion resulting from the fact that the extant evidence on classical Greece is heavily biased in favor of those who held this view. Another answer, and the one which may well have been the more popular, was the identification of the true nature of man with the irrational impulses.[1]

Another preoccupation of Greek life and thought also contributed to the ultimate focus on the inner life. This was the problem of fate, the complete absence of freedom in the face of the gods, and the utter tyranny of destiny. By the middle of the fifth century, however, many Sophists and some others had begun to question this complete surrender to fate in the traditional view of things.[2] Like their concern with outer freedom, their reflection on fate was the philosophical counterpart to the effects of the Cleisthenean democratic revolution on religious thinking. Religious norms, too, lose their immutability and timelessness and "are also infused with a human sanction analogous to the popular authority that sanctions the enactment of statutes."[3] In questioning the tyranny of fate, of course, Sophists posed in explicit terms the ultimate problem of freedom.

We can trace many of these developments in tragic drama. Against destiny and death no one can win. This is the dreadful truth revealed over and over in nearly all the works of Aeschylus. Mankind comes to dignity not in vainly defying this primal logic but in behaving nobly in full recognition of it. We already saw in an earlier chapter how this ordered cosmos had begun to crumble in *The Suppliant Maidens*. In *Prometheus Bound*, written near the end of Aeschylus' life, we find an even more extreme change: a rebellion against the sheer injustice of it all. It is a rebellion that occurs on many levels, each, as David Grene has pointed out, involving two basic principles in conflict: law and justice against tyranny; knowledge against force; intelligent man against the forces that would keep people in ignorance; humanity against god.[4] There is, however, one set of conflicting principles which must be emphasized: those involving inner and outer freedom. Prometheus' external condition is the ultimate symbol of enslavement: he is nailed to the rocks of hell in "fetters unbreakable of adamantine chain" for ten thousand years, at the will of his angry master, Zeus. And yet, in spite of his horrible outward suffering and indignity, his will remains unbroken. He has inner freedom, and this is precisely what those around him make a point of. The sympathetic chorus laments,

> You are stout of heart, unyielding
> to the bitterness of pain.
> You are free of tongue, too free.[5]

In the conversation between Prometheus and Hermes, the conflict between inner and outer freedom is most explicitly expressed. Prometheus addresses Hermes with contempt for his loyalty to Zeus, calling him "the lackey of the Gods." Because of his youth he thinks that "the tower in which [he] lives is free from sorrow." But Hermes is a fool for thinking only of his external freedom. "Be sure of this," Prometheus says to him, "when I set my misfortune against your slavery, I would not change." To which Hermes can give only the lame response "It is better, I suppose, to be a slave to this rock, than Zeus's trusted messenger." The answer, of course, is yes. Prometheus will never "crouch before your Gods." He talks to Hermes as he would address a slave, calling him insolent and childish.[6] What is more, the play makes clear the nature of that inner freedom. In addition to the strength of will to resist any enslavement of the soul, it is control over one's own mind and a refusal to be controlled by the minds of others. The real conflict, then, is that between the will of Zeus and that of Prometheus. The chorus says,

> . . . I shiver when I see you
> wasted with ten thousand pains,
> all because you did not tremble
> at the name of Zeus; *your mind*
> *was yours, not his,* and at its bidding
> you regarded mortal men
> too high, Prometheus.[7]

Prometheus' crime is twofold. Not only had he defied the will of Zeus, he had given mankind the capacity to do the same by giving them not merely knowledge and skill but also, by shrewdly making them ignorant of their fate, the power of hope. Prometheus is defiantly proud that he gave men "the use of their wits and made them masters of their minds." This mastery of mind now becomes the essence of true freedom. Freedom, then, is self-power. In this regard, it is most important to note that it is the direct inner counterpart to the external freedom of power in the sense of brute force which Zeus represents. In the opening dialogue of the play, Might tells the blacksmith Hephaestus, whose unwanted task it is to enchain Prometheus, that "only Zeus is free," a familiar Greek idea. By the end of the play, however, we learn that there is another kind of power which ensures freedom. On both levels, Aeschylus seems to be saying, freedom is power. What is more, he strongly suggests not only that inner power is superior but that in the end it may even lead to outer power. For in the end it is Prometheus who will triumph over Zeus, since the latter will have to come and beg him to reveal the knowledge of how to escape his downfall. Zeus "for all his pride of heart [will] be humble yet."[8]

These ideas are highly reminiscent of those of the philosopher Anaxagoras, (ca. 500–ca. 428 B.C.) whom Pericles had invited to live in Athens. His most original idea was that mind is the controlling force of the world: "All things which have life, both the greater and the less, are ruled by Mind. Mind took command of the universal revolution, so as to make (things) revolve at the outset."[9] This inner force was considered divine by him. But he also thought that it had an external dimension. His friend Pericles was seen as an agent of the divine mind power operating externally to control the brutal force of the political world. This was a thoroughly outrageous idea even in the fifth century. Anaxagoras was accused of impiety, saved by Pericles, and banished from Athens. It is interesting that until the Romantic revival of the play in the nineteenth century, Western audiences responded similarly to Aeschylus' *Prometheus Bound*. According to John Herington, Byzantine scribes considered the play's ideas "treason and blasphemy," and "to many subsequent Christian editors it was a cause for scandal, or at least suspicion."[10]

There are strong traces of these developments in Sophocles, especially in the last of the Theban plays, *Oedipus at Colonus*. It is perhaps noteworthy that, like Aeschylus' *Prometheus Bound*, this play came at the very end of Sophocles' long life, a time of deep soul-searching when the contrast between inner strength and outer frailty is most readily embraced. There are numerous reflections on the freedom of the will in this play. Oedipus, though frail, ugly, and physically wrecked, nonetheless remains morally defiant. He insists on his innocence. Since the gods ordained his horrible patricide and incest, he is guiltless. "Before the law—before God—I am innocent!"[11] Outwardly he is like a slave, ending up a stranger in a strange land. And yet, he has achieved inner freedom. The point is made explicitly by Theseus, who contrasts it with the outer freedom of the powerful:

> Angry men are liberal with threats
> And bluster generally. When the mind
> Is master of itself, threats are no matter.[12]

But Sophocles goes a step further than Aeschylus. Prometheus, for all his defiance, was forced to accept one ineradicable truth: no one, not even Zeus, can "escape what is fated"; and he too, with all his craft, is powerless against it: "Craft is weaker than necessity."[13] In the face of destiny there is no freedom, not even for the inwardly free. Sophocles begins to question this. Not only is Oedipus at Colonus able to defy outer enslavement with his inner freedom but, in the face of his fated death, he is able to assert a kind of freedom. He can choose where and how to die. "He lived his life," the chorus comes to realize. But his daughter, Antigone, tells them that he did more: "In this land among strangers he died where he chose to die."[14] The chorus concurs: "This his last hour was free and blessed." His heritage would be to bless and make free the spot on which he had, nobly, defiantly, though outwardly powerless, discovered the true meaning of freedom:

> I come to give you something, and the gift
> Is my own beaten self: no feast for the eyes;
> Yet in me a more lasting grace than beauty.[15]

Five centuries later another man, through a similar suffering, blessed the world with a similar gift: that of inner freedom. Indeed, the Christian universalization of this conception of inner freedom was fully anticipated by Euripides, who in his last two plays pulled together and took to their logical and emotional conclusion all that had been anticipated in earlier fifth-century drama and philosophical thought.

The remarkable thing about Euripides is the synthetic nature of his genius. We have already seen how he explored, on the outer level, all three versions of freedom. The other tragedians had done the same, but in looking inward they had isolated only one kind of inner freedom: freedom as inner power and control. Euripides, though making it clear which of the three he favored, presented with nearly clinical detachment all three versions of freedom on the inner level. Thus *Iphigenia in Aulis* achieves in her final moments the same kind of freedom on both the outer and the inner levels. Outwardly, her decision willingly to sacrifice her life gains for her an outer organic freedom achieved only rarely by women. She expresses the most organic, the most Greek male version of freedom in her assertion that Greeks alone have freedom in their blood and that they "were born to rule barbarians."[16] But then, in the same act, she also achieves the inner version of this freedom, in much the same way as Oedipus did at Colonus. She has defied the fear of death, asserted her freedom against it, and "made a virtue of necessity" by choosing to die. And she dies knowing that this most sublime of freedom-recruiting death will be a blessing to all Greece and that she, in turn, "will be blessed and celebrated as one who set Hellas free."[17]

Inner civic freedom is also expressed in this play. Indeed, the only point to the chorus's presence seems to be to give a running authorial commentary on this view of freedom. Fate may be inevitable, but it is sharply questioned: "when we meet it, it is evil."[18] It is to the inner world what tyranny is to the outer. Inner civic freedom is the harmony and sense of duty that comes with "the quest of virtue,"[19] a quest open to every free person and achievable for women through chastity, for men, with proper discipline, in much the same way that every male on the outer level can become a good citizen. It should be noted at once, though, that toward the end of his life Euripides nostalgically, and conservatively, returned to an early conception of democracy implicit in the archaic cosmologies, that being the idea of the state as a tightly knit community in pursuit of a common natural justice, in which duty is paramount.[20] And just as both Anaxagoras and Aeschylus thought that their version of inner freedom as power had consequences for the external world, so did Euripides with his conception of virtue as inner civic freedom. The quest for virtue, in men and women alike, he tells us, "exalts a city to greatness."

There is also the third inner counterpart to freedom: inner personal freedom. In the external world, as we have seen, this is the freedom symbolically expressed by "the female force" by all the tragedians. Aeschylus and Sophocles were unequivocal in their condemnation of extreme outer personal freedom. As Plato later concluded, no doubt partly influenced by them, it was tantamount to license and anarchy. Euripides, we have seen, was more ambivalent. He discerned the dangers of personal freedom, and his own preference was clearly for an ordered, disciplined civic freedom. But he also fully recognized not only its better aspects but the reasons why it so powerfully appealed to the common folk.

That ambivalence or, to put it more fairly, that recognition of the good and evil in personal freedom is fully transferred to the inner level when Euripides examines it in his last completed and greatest play, *The Bacchae*. Let there be no doubt about it: this play is wholly focused on the problem of personal freedom. *The Bacchae* is not so much a world turned upside down as a world turned inside out. It is a world in which the deep, dark forces that lie at the root of our souls are set free, turned loose upon the inner landscape. Women, the female force and the symbol of outer personal freedom, are here also the symbols of inner freedom, the nonrational and passionate in the soul of all persons. Pentheus, who stands for male force and for inner and outer control, comes to accept, too late, the fact that "women should not be mastered by brute strength." In order to witness the revels of the women, he must first dress in women's clothes and suffer the indignity of walking so clad through his own city. Dionysus, the youthful, long-haired incarnation of the god of freedom, has set them free. "I tremble to speak the words of freedom before the tyrant," says the leader of the chorus, whose members are Asian followers of Dion. "But let the truth be told: there is no god greater than Dionysus."[21] The chains fall from the arms of the imprisoned and enslaved women, and they go skipping off to the field to join the revels. Hair symbolism is one of many used to express the conflict between order and freedom, might and emancipation. Perseus cuts the holy curls from Dion's head, much as the policemen of Kingston used to cut the holy dreadlocks of imprisoned Rastafarians. The women let their hair fall loose as they joyfully cavort, exercising their "right to worship as [they] please."

All forms of inner and outer power and pride—freedom as power and arete—are condemned, for "he who hunts glory, he who tracks some boundless, superhuman dream, may lose his harvest here and now and garner death."[22] On the other hand, there is a celebration of the "doubly blessed night":

> whose simple wisdom shuns the thoughts
> of proud, uncommon men and all
> their god-encroaching dreams.
> But what the common people do,
> the things that simple men believe,
> I too believe and do.[23]

The freedom of the slave, the afflicted, the oppressed released from the power of the master finds its counterpart in the simple freedom of the soul released from the power of false, man-made wisdom, represented by fifth-century modernity and civilized inhibitions.

> Blessed is he who escapes a storm at sea,
> who comes home to his harbor.
> Blessed is he who emerges from under affliction.
> In various ways one man outraces another in the race
> for wealth and power.[24]

This is a play about two cities, an outer city ruled by Pentheus and an inner city ruled by Dionysus. Only when Pentheus has been possessed by the god does he "see two suns blazing in the heavens. And now two Thebes, two cities, and each with seven gates."[25] Once it is recognized that this play is an exploration of the inner city, using as a metaphor the struggle for freedom in the outer city, the old emphasis on the conflict between modernity, represented by Pentheus, and tradition, represented by Dionysus and the women, is seen as misplaced. This is emphatically not a play about the conflict between modernity and tradition: that is a modern obsession, if not quite an anachronism. Pentheus, who represents modernity in the outer city, comes to represent the conscious and the inhibited in the inner city, while the women, who represent tradition in the outer city, come to symbolize the passionate and nonrational in the inner city. In other words, signifier and signified on the outer level fuse to form a single, composite metaphor when transposed to the inner level. The distinction between law and nature is then integrated into this complex symbolic statement. The chorus of women makes the claim that there is no conflict between tradition and nature: "the law tradition makes is the law of nature."[26] What this means in the inner city is clear: inner personal freedom, the release from bondage of our most passionate selves, is what is most natural in us. Know thyself, yes. But what is knowledge? Not the knowledge of the philosophers but the knowledge which every ordinary, humble man possesses: knowledge of our deepest passions, which is gained only through release from the constraints of our repressive consciousness.

But there is a dark side to all this. Knowledge of our deepest nature may release forces which in the end destroy us and those we most love. This point is made with a symbolism that, in contrast with that of the rest of the play, is almost crude. Pentheus is torn apart by the women, led by his own mother, Agave, who in her possessive trance confuses him with a lion. She proudly displays her son's head on a stake, only to have her vision restored and to discover the horror of her deed. Her god does not spare her. Dionysus is merciless. The entire house of Pentheus is brought to ruin by this vengeful boy-god, including Agave, whose only crime was to have worshiped him.

If we have followed the symbolism of the play carefully, the punishment meted out to Agave by the lovingly cruel Dionysus, in addition to the horror of unwittingly butchering her son, comes as no surprise: it is exile and slavery. So the final meaning of the play comes down to this. The inner nature of people cannot be denied and must be made free. But that inner freedom can be as dangerous as too much personal freedom in the outer city. It unleashes forces which we cannot control and which, in the end, can come to enslave us even more than the conscious discipline from which we freed out natures.

One final point about Euripides. The inner person which he explores is the spiritual person, not the rationalistic. The spiritual, the religious, is thus identified with the most instinctive and nonrational, which is also the most natural, in humankind.

2. THE PLATONIC TRANSFORMATION

Plato's great achievement was to have taken all the preexisting strands of Greek thought regarding the idea of the inner person and welded them into a startlingly new synthesis, one from which the Western mind has never quite recovered. The two key ingredients in this epoch-making intellectual transformation were his theory of the soul and his theory of slavery—both literally, in political life, and metaphorically, in the inward life.

Plato's theory of the soul is developed from the Pythagorean mind-body view, with its mystical conception of a union of opposites. It goes well beyond Pythagoras' concept, however, in the critical role it came to play in resolving a key problem in Plato's metaphysics—namely, how do we come to know the nature of the forms, the ideals, which are the only truly real and really truthful beings? We come to know them by means of our soul's affinity for these forms. This affinity is in the nature of a force of love. The process of acquiring knowledge of the forms assumes the immortality of the soul, since this acquisition comes through the soul's remembering what it knew in a previous existence outside of the body.[27]

But what is the nature of the soul? Plato's analysis of it is based on a direct analogy from the nature of the state, and his external theory of slavery and freedom thus becomes critical for his cosmology and metapsychology. A preliminary version is found in one of the earlier dialogues, the *Phaedo*, in which Socrates' question "Is not the body like the mortal—meant to serve—and the soul like the immortal—meant to rule?" is answered in the affirmative.[28] In the *Republic*, however, we get a thorough treatment of the subject. Beginning with the assumption that "we are bound to admit that the qualities that characterize a state must also exist in the individuals that compose it," we move by analogy to a tripartite conception of the soul. There are the elements of reason, of courage or spirit, and of appetite or desire. The function of reason, like that of the philosopher king of the state, is to rule. The function of the spiritual element, like that of the guardians, is to obey reason and to act in concert with it to rule the third element, "which forms the greater part of each man's make-up." The appetite is directly analogous to the mass of slaves who make up the ideal state and whose function is to work and obey. The ideal condition of the soul exists when there is self-control, "when all these three elements are in harmonious agreement, when reason and its subordinates are all agreed that reason should rule and there is no dissension." True justice, the ultimate virtue, exists when each part does what it does best and is in harmony with the others.

> Justice therefore, we may say, is a principle of this kind; but its real concern is not with external actions, but with man's inward self. The just man will not allow the three elements which make up his inward self to trespass on each other's functions or interfere with each other, but, by keeping all three elements in tune, like the notes of a scale . . . will in the truest sense set his house in order, and be his own lord and master and at peace with himself. When he has bound these elements into a single, controlled and orderly whole, and also unified himself, he will be ready for any kind of action. . . . [29]

Just as in the external world there are different kinds of states, depending on which of the three elements is dominant, so in the human world there are three different kinds of individuals, "according to whether their motive is knowledge, success or gain; and each type, of course, has its appropriate pleasures." The worst kind of individual, then, is one in whom the base or slave element rules. This is internal tyranny and results in the entire soul's being in a state of slavery. This, incidentally, means the slavery of the tyrannous element itself. Plato insists that in the inner life, as in the outer, the different elements are at peace only when each performs its most appropriate task. The slave element is most at peace, most free, when it is ruled and is in a real state of slavery when it tries to rule. Thus the man who has been taken over by his base or slave element "will hardly be able to call his soul his own because the best elements in him will be enslaved and completely controlled by a minority of lower and lunatic impulses."[30] On the other hand, "the wise man speaks with authority when he prefers his own life" and in his wisdom will rank ambition, the spirited element (equivalent to the guardians of the upwardly mobile, competitive hoplite class), second and the material, greedy element, third. This subjective tendency of the inner life dominated by reason to prefer itself and order its inner world in this way is objectively the true and ideal state of affairs. This is so because only reason is "truly real" and "belongs to the realm of unchanging and eternal truth, exists in and shares its nature." That which "supplies the bodily needs is less true and less real than what supplies mental needs." In conclusion, "if the mind as a whole will follow the lead of its philosophic element, without internal division, each element will be rightly performing its own function, and in addition will enjoy its own particular pleasures, which are the best and truest available to it."[31]

The critical role of the idea of slavery in Plato's conception of the inner person should already have been obvious from all this. However, its importance is even greater than appears at first sight, and we are indebted to one of the most authoritative scholars of Plato's thought for bringing it to light. In a seminal paper Gregory Vlastos shows how the crucial role of real slavery in Plato's external political theory is directly carried over into his cosmology, to such an extent that the latter is unintelligible without constant reference to it. Plato sees slavery as a deficiency of reason. The slave "has *doxa* but no *logos*. He can have true belief, but cannot know the truth of his belief."[32] The slave can be persuaded, can be changed, which is the opposite of reason, which is eternal and unchangeable. Plato's conception of all government is identical with his view of the government of slaves. The masses are governed for their own good and are best when they obey. By "generalizing the government of slave by master" to all political relationships, Plato came to the view that democracy is unnatural, in sharp contrast to those theorists who saw democracy as the natural condition of political life. This approach is taken over directly to his cosmology. "Thus a scientific explanation of the shape and position of the earth must prove that it has that particular shape and position because these are 'best' for it."[33] Plato's otherwise puzzling theory of causation is also made intelligible by reference to the slave metaphor. He posits two kinds of causes: the primary cause, which is divine, and the secondary causes, which are "necessary, irrational, fortuitous and disorderly." How, Vlastos asks, can we make sense of the notion of "disorderly necessity," since to our way of thinking any notion of casual necessity must imply order? The self-contradiction is explained once we understand that Plato thinks of necessity not in mechanical terms but in terms of a "living instrument" much like a slave, and such an instrument has no inherent logic but rather is subject to external persuasion. Left to his own inherent being, the slave quickly creates disorder. The wise act, like the master, persuades necessity, imposes its will on it. Vlastos makes the insightful observation that Plato resorts to the slave metaphor at exactly the point in his intellectual development when he departs from the cosmology of earlier Greek thinkers, all of whom adhered—as we do today—to the notion of "rational and immanent necessity," the idea that nature has its own internal, inherent logic and that nothing occurs randomly. Greek science had indeed made the revolutionary breakthrough to the idea that motion and matter were one, obviating the anthropocentric need for a "first cause" to set matter in motion. Plato was outraged by this rejection of the idea of a divine mind controlling the movement of all things. He attacks Ionian physics on both philosophical and political grounds, "so that both the political and cosmological associations of slavery came into play in his polemics." The soul, Plato insists, generates all motions. It rules matter. And the soul's rule is the rule of god, since the former shares in the essence of the latter. "The link between religious cosmology and political religion is the slave-metaphor."[34] We shall see how vital this metaphorical use of slavery was to become in the later history of Western social thought, in general, and of reflections on freedom, in particular.

Let us conclude by drawing out the immediate implications that Plato's conception of that inner life and the role of slavery had for the history of freedom. Note, first of all, that while Plato's discussion of the inner life is suffused with the master-slave relationship, he himself rarely uses the term *freedom* to define his ideal state. Instead, he tends to employ the term *justice* or *virtue*. This was partly due to his utter contempt for the value of freedom as it was popularly understood in his time. In his external political theory, he does reluctantly come to recognize the idea of liberty and, as we have seen, to develop an organic theory of freedom. By analogy, then, the internal state of harmony in which reason rules the counterpart to the guardian and slave/serf elements (that is, spirit and appetite) is his inner counterpart to the organic freedom of the mixed constitution which he favors in the *Laws* and the *Statesman*.

There is no need, however, for us to second-guess Plato. One of his really important achievements was to shift the focus of nearly all major subsequent thinkers down to the eighteenth century toward the idea that the inner world is not only superior to the outer but is ultimately the only truly real world. Thus it was not long before men, many with substantive views quite different from Plato's, began to distinguish between ordinary, unreal freedom and the truly real freedom which invariably meant, first, inner freedom and, second, the version of inner freedom which they favored. Another of Plato's achievements was to provide later thinkers with a model of how their reflections on external freedom could be transferred to the internal world. Essentially, this always involved some division of the inner person, either in tripartite terms following Plato or, less elaborately, in dualistic terms between the base or the bodily and something else which stood in mastery over it. To the secular mind, that something else was often reason. To the religious mind, it naturally became the divine in mankind. To moralists it might be the good, as they interpreted it. Or, again following Plato, all dimensions of the superior inner master could be identified as one, a trinity, or what have you. And as often as not, that inner master was also identified with freedom.

Plato's most important intellectual bequest was, ironically, his least original. It was his complete internalization of the sociologically real understanding of freedom as the antithesis of slavery, and of the idea that freedom and slavery dialectically require each other, a Pythagorean union of opposites. The notion that freedom requires the existence of the fear of slavery was a commonplace in Greek thought by the time Plato was born. Indeed, the idea was already well established in the popular mind when Aeschylus celebrated it in *The Eumenides*, first performed in 458, by giving a place to the Furies in the democracy established by Athena, who advises her "citizens to govern and to grace, and not to cast fear utterly from the city. What man who fears nothing at all is ever righteous?"[35] By so completely infusing his own thoughts on the inner life with the metaphor of the master-slave relationship, Plato ensured that wherever his influence reigned, this primal generative role of the slave relation would come to dominate people's minds, including that of people who later lived in societies where slavery was either of minor significance or nonexistent. Now, if there is any truth in the celebrated commentary of Alfred North Whitehead that all subsequent Western thought must be read as mere extended footnotes to Plato, we can begin to understand the impact of his ideas on all later thought about freedom.

Even so, we should not get the impression that Plato's thought was the only important Greek influence on conceptions of inner freedom in antiquity. Plato was still a youth when Euripides died, and we have already seen that the latter, through the medium of poetry and drama, had formulated his own synthesis of ideas about the inner person and, what is more, had explored more explicitly than Plato the meaning of freedom in this inner life. Plato's distinctive contribution to the Greek doctrine of the soul was to make it the source of reason, and to imprint upon this conception the idea that reason is a master of the slave emotions.

A comparison of Plato and Euripides is a good way to end this chapter. While I cannot agree with Thomas G. Rosenmeyer that ideas are what count most in *The Bacchae*, I am intrigued by his suggestion that the play is "a forerunner of the Platonic dialogues" in that "the smiling god is another Socrates, bullying his listeners into a painful reconsideration of their thinking and their values."[36] *The Bacchae* also anticipates the inward turn of the dialogues, as well as the metaphorical transposition of the outward political experience of freedom and power in the city-state to the inner landscape of being. But here the similarities end. The reconsiderations forced upon their respective listeners lead in radically opposite directions. The inner life which Plato explored was essentially a philosophical one in which reason reigned supreme. Euripides turned to another dimension of the inner life, what may be called the spiritual. Now, while it is true that Plato identified the rule of reason with the rule of the divine, in this manner initiating a kind of philosophical religion, there is a fundamental difference in the thought of the two men in regard to how people came to know the inner person. For Plato, in the final analysis, it was through speculation; for Euripides it was through revelation. Herein lies the fundamental distinction between the religious and the philosophical, however infused with the divine the latter may be. As Richard Kroner has cogently distinguished it,

> The truth that speculation knows is scientific, i.e., theoretical, detached, demonstrative, impersonal; it is disengaged from the thinking subject, as an individual. The truth mediated by revelation, in contrast, is practical, committing, undemonstrable, personal—in short, religious; it is addressed to man as an individual.[37]

There is more to this distinction. It subsumes that between existence and essence. George Boas, in his study of rationalism in Greek philosophy, has noted that "for Plato essence is prior to existence, and its priority is in the field of conjecture. The distinction between knowledge and observation is ultimate."[38] What is more, the sphere or realm of reason not only is distinct from that of perception but is "neither in space nor in time."[39] For Euripides existence precedes essence, and its reality is very much rooted in this world, both the world of the senses outside of persons and the inner world of the passions. What Plato rejects as either unreal or in need of control for its own good, Euripides sees as that which struggles to be emancipated. For Euripides the problem is not to enslave this real, sensate inner self, since this is impossible; the problem is how to give it its freedom without risking spiritual implosion. Pentheus, who denies Aphrodite and irrationally refuses to acknowledge the mysterious and irrational in nature, is killed by Agave, "the primal love-object" under the sway of Dionysus, the mysterious god of the irrational, "nature deified."[40] But Agave's ecstasy also destroys her, for her *enthousiasmos* is that of the unaware, unwilling worshiper, unlike the willing non-ationality of the Asiatic chorus who worship and abandon themselves in full spiritual consciousness.

There is yet another difference between the two realms of the inner life which these men explored, and it goes back to the seminal Greek contrast between nomos, or law, and physics, or nature. Plato condemns the Sophist antithesis between law and nature because "nature itself," as Guthrie has summarized, "as the product of natural design, is the supreme embodiment of law and order."[41] Now, it is interesting that Euripides, too, comes to a similar rejection of the nature–traditional law antithesis. In *The Bacchae*, the chorus, to return to a passage touched on earlier, declares,

> Small, small is the cost
> to believe in this:
> whatever is god is strong;
> whatever long time has sanctioned,
> that is a law forever;
> the law tradition makes
> is the law of nature.[42]

Note, then, that although both men reconcile law and nature, the casual chains that link the two run in opposite directions. For Plato nature and law are one because nature is the product of law; for Euripides nature and law are one because law is the child of nature.

Finally, there is something startlingly different in both the nature of religious experience and in the way god and man approach each other in Euripides. Plato's rational god is an orderly, law-giving first cause, up toward which the soul moves, seeking to bask in its divine essence.

In late-fifth-century Athens, Dionysus was revived in a new form not simply as the god of wine and intoxicated ecstasy but as a god for whom frenzy, "intensified mental power," becomes an end in itself. And as Walter Burkert further tells us, ecstasy is achieved as a mass phenomenon spreading infectiously.[43]

But there is something else. This is a god who spreads across national boundaries—the chorus in *The Bacchae* is Asiatic—and across lines of class and gender, a horrible prospect in the Platonic scheme of things. Furthermore, it is important that the god searches for adherents. Dionysus comes down to man, is incarnated into the body of an effeminate youth; it is not the soul of man that reaches up to the exalted heights of the heavenly divine anymore. God comes to mankind and offers something in return for worship: that something is liberation. The freedom of the spirit from the constraints of mind in this world, and the freedom of the spirit from temporal enslavement: the freedom of an eternal "blessed afterlife."[44]

What this comparison all adds up to, then, is this. We began our analysis with an exploration of freedom in the outer, the material and political, world. At the start of this chapter we discovered a second realm of freedom: the inner realm of intellect. Now we have discovered a third. It too is found within mankind, but its realm is as different from the inner intellectual as both are from the external. This third realm of freedom is what we may call, simply, the spiritual. It shares with the intellectual an opposition to the external realm, but in every other respect it is different. For it is existential, the other essentialistic; it is revelatory, the other speculative; it is grounded in nature, the other in law; its seat is the passions, the other's reason; it is approached by god, while the other grasps; its goal is liberation, whereas the other seeks union; it is human, all too human, and most emphatically of this world and of this changing time, whereas the other disdains the worldly and, transcending space and time, vainly embraces a realm of eternal beings and certitudes that condemns time to an eternal return and humanity to an utter otherness.

CHAPTER 11

The Intellectual Response
in the Hellenistic and
Early Roman World

I. INTRODUCTION

"Aristotle and the classical *polis* died at about the same time," writes
M. I. Finley. "Henceforth the search for wisdom and moral existence
concentrated on the individual soul so completely that society could
be rejected as a secondary and accidental factor."[1] Aristotle's logic
and physics were to remain important, Finely adds, but not his politics, because the latter was regarded as too intellectually tied to
the politically decadent and irrelevant polis. And Plato survived
by being "depoliticized." His mysticism and his emphasis on the
soul were what appealed to both the secular and, later, the religious
minds concerned with salvation. " 'Know thyself' remained the motto,
but with implications which would have astonished Socrates, and perhaps appalled him." Let us explore further these appalling developments.

But note at once something that may appear paradoxical, especially
in the light of our opening quotation from Finley regarding the influence of Plato's conception of the soul. That influence was very peculiar
and was confined mainly to the Stoics, who admittedly formed the
most important of the three schools of thought—the other being Cynicism and Epicureanism—that dominated the Hellenistic world. It was
not only Plato's political ideas that were rejected but his epistemology
and cosmology. All the doctrines of the Hellenistic and early Roman
worlds were extremely materialistic and this-worldly. People became

concerned with the inner life, yes, but with that life as the senses
directly interpreted it and with that life in the here and now.

This may seem odd because we have come to identify the inner life
with other-worldliness (largely because of post-apostolic Christianity
and the influence of Platonism on it), but there is actually no necessary
relationship between the two. Indeed, from the viewpoint of the comparative sociology of secular and religious thought, the search for personal salvation, for inner security, is more often materialistic than
essentialistic or idealistic in orientation. All seekers were on an inward
pilgrimage to a shrine with the Delphic message "Know thyself," but
the means by which they arrived there varied. One thing they all had
in common, however, was their reliance on the slavery-into-freedom
metaphor as a virtual epistemological and methodological genie, to get
them to their destination. The continuing experience of real slavery,
joined now by the intellectual spell of the classical tradition of discourse so deeply fashioned by it, prolonged and intensified the mes-
meric hold of this metaphor on the consciousness of Europe. How they
used it offers the most fundamental clue to the differences between
the three major schools of thought that dominated the Hellenistic
world, and to show this is the objective of this chapter.

To do so, we must first return briefly to Socrates. The Hellenistic
thinkers may have reinterpreted Socrates in ways that would have
appalled him, but precisely for this reason a brief look at the Socratic
conception of the soul—as distinct from Plato's—is a good point of
departure for an examination of their thought.

2. THE SOCRATIC BACKGROUND

Socrates' method may be described as a form of *moral introspection*. For
him, self-knowledge entails an inward exploration of the soul in search
of excellence and virtue, as a guide to good living *here and now*. We
learn from the *Phaedo* that human beings are part body, part soul. The
soul is the invisible, invariable, and eternal part of the individual; and
the body, in which it is trapped during life, is the visible, mortal, and
variable part. Socrates employs the slave metaphor in a complex way
to explain the body-soul relationship. For the soul is, in one sense,
enslaved to the body during life, and this is true of everyone. Yet it
rules like a master that to which it is enslaved; at least this is true of
those who are good. The bad, those lacking in virtue, are those who
allow that which enslaves their soul, in the sense of confining it, also
to enslave their soul, in the sense of directing it. The distinction be-

tween being *confined* and being *directed* is crucial. Clearly, it makes sense only if we bear in mind the enormous importance of the idea of freedom as power, the capacity to direct someone or some circumstance. Thus the body's enslavement of the soul can be dismissed with contempt—a slavish kind of slavery offering no possibility of freedom to the master, since the master merely confines, not directs—and is overridden by the soul's divine enslavement of the body, divine because "it is the nature of the divine to rule and direct." Finally, only when the soul converses with itself, as one master to another, is it truly free or, rather, does it experience the superior form of freedom which is wisdom. And when the body dies, the soul is doubly freed. It is released from the base enslavement of the body and "if it carries with it no contamination of the body, because it has never willingly associated with it in life" but has shunned it and practices philosophy, which Socrates identifies with "practicing death," then its reward will be a place very much like itself "where happiness awaits it," and it spends the rest of eternity with god.[2] Souls which in this life are enslaved by the passions, on the other hand, will be weighed down by their contamination with the mortal at death and instead of going to the bliss of Hades will hover above tombs like ghosts, half corporeal, half spirit.

It is already clear from the *Phaedo* that inner personal freedom and autonomy are central to Socrates' thought, although one has to drag it out of Plato's text, given the latter's hostility to the idea of freedom. Fortunately, we have in Xenophon's *Memorabilia* independent evidence of this. There we learn of Socrates' remarking that "freedom is a noble and splendid possession both for individuals and communities."[3] Wisdom is identified with inner personal freedom. By means of self-control and disciplined introspection, this "greatest blessing" is achieved. Socrates also holds that self-control generates a capacity for abstinence which enhances pleasure when it is enjoyed. Outwardly, this is a trite idea, but in terms of inner freedom—in a discussion of which the passage comes—it may not be the stupid distortion of Socrates that commentators have claimed it is. What Socrates is saying, then, is not only that we enjoy our emotions more if they are mastered and disciplined by the soul but, more profoundly, that these impulses are not inherently bad but become so only when they are in control. There is nothing trite about all this. Indeed, it is the point of departure for Aristotle's own theory of ethics.[4] Nor is it a form of proto-puritanism; it may well be that the "puritanism" of the *Phaedo* was a Platonic intrusion.[5]

3. CYNICISM

The first and most outrageous development from Socrates' conception
of the soul and its complex mutual slave relation with the body was
Cynicism. The basic doctrine of Cynicism can be easily summarized: it
was totally committed to the idea and practice of complete personal
freedom on both the outer and the inner levels. Indeed, it is no exaggeration to say that Cynicism is the most extreme version of personal
freedom that the West has ever seen. If this is true, then our thesis
immediately suggests that it was dialectically involved with slavery in
an extreme way. And so it was: utterly. An extraordinary number of
the most prominent early Cynics and those who influenced them were
either slaves or intimately touched by slavery. Antisthenes was the son
of a Thracian ex-slave woman; Diogenes of Sinope, the founder of the
movement, was for most of his life an exile, banished from his own
society, though the old claim that he ended his days as a slave is now
doubted; Bion of Borysthenes, one of the most important founding
fathers of the movement, had been a slave, bought and used by his
master for homosexual purposes; and Menippus of Gadara had also
been a slave and may indeed have been born one.[6]

Antisthenes, a disciple of Socrates, took the latter's asceticism to its
extreme. It was he who said repeatedly, "I'd rather be mad than feel
pleasure."[7] Like Socrates, he saw philosophy as a way of conversing
with himself. What the wise man sought was complete self-sufficiency,
a virtuous and noble state of inner freedom which could be taught to
others. Where Antisthenes differed from Socrates is in his way of
teaching virtue to himself and to others. This he did by living a life of
minimal dependence on physical and social goods. Freedom meant as
complete an escape from such dependence as possible, a dependence
which he equated with slavery. The title of one of his lost works, we
are not surprised to learn, is "Of Freedom and Slavery."

It is now very doubtful whether Diogenes was ever a pupil of Antisthenes, but no one questions his great influence on Diogenes.[8] By
taking the Socratic asceticism of Antisthenes to its logical conclusion,
he developed what may be called a philosophy of *naturalistic introspection*, in contrast to Socrates' moral introspection. Indeed, whether true
or apocryphal, the claim that Plato used to say that Diogenes was Socrates gone mad makes a lot of sense. The Cynic method of living like
dogs—hence the name—was not, as some commentators like to call it,
a way of life. Diogenes' outrageous minimalism was not an end in
itself—as was more true of the Epicureans—but a means toward the
end of virtue, which was a sublime state of freedom in which he was

free of all external and internal bodily demands except those that were essential. All things, Diogenes held, belong to the gods, and because the wise are friends of the gods, they hold all things in common. He and his followers lived the homeless life of beggars, Diogenes himself residing in a tub.

The Cynics were not so much radicals as anticulturalists, because, unlike radicals, they had no political platform and disdained politics. They showed their contempt for the bourgeois way of life, in which people were enslaved to external material goods and cultural patterns, by practicing "shamelessness." Such a course of action would have been extraordinary in any society, but it was particularly effective as a statement of rejection of Greek society in view of the special role of honor and shame in ancient Greece.[9] They disdained not only philosophy generally, as a waste of time, but also the comfortable way of life—the "highminded" mean—which Aristotle so extolled.[10] Indeed, Aristotle's discussion of courage, the golden mean between fear and confidence, offers the perfect antithesis of what Diogenes stood for:

> There are some things which it is right and noble to fear, and which it is disgraceful not to fear, e.g. ignominy; for to fear ignominy is to be virtuous and modest, and not to fear it is to be shameless. A shameless person is sometimes called courageous by a figure of speech, as he possesses a certain similarity to a courageous person; for the courageous person is also fearless.[11]

Far from considering the courage of shamelessness as a figure of speech, Diogenes believed literally that it was the only true form of courage. As Diogenes Laërtius reported, "to fortune he could oppose courage, to convention nature, to passion reason."[12] The Cynics advocated extreme personal freedom both in its inner and—unlike the Stoics—in its outer forms. Through shamelessness, the Cynic achieved outer freedom, especially freedom from convention and cultural constraints. Because the emphasis was on cultural freedom, it was possible to experience external freedom while being in a condition of external *social* and political restraint. Diogenes' seemingly puzzling admiration for Sparta is explained by this critical distinction. The Spartans lived under great social and political constraint, but they were so culturally free that their women could practice their gymnastics naked in the open.

With his notorious sense of irony, Diogenes saw, millennia before Hegel, that in the domination of the slave the master exposes himself to a kind of slavery more real than that of his slave, because he ends up being dependent on him. On seeing a master whose shoes were being put on by his slave, Diogenes remarked disdainfully, ''You have not attained to full felicity, unless he wipes your nose as well; and that will come, when you have lost the use of your hands.''[13] Outer and inner freedom mutually reinforced each other. Diogenes was a complete materialist. The journey inward began from the outside and ultimately returned to it. The central dogma of Cynicism, the point at which it is most original, is its celebration of a freedom that crosses back and forth between the inner and the outer world, between the freedom of the flesh and the freedom of the mind, between the freedom of convention and the freedom of nature.

In the light of all this, we can now understand why Diogenes called Heracles his favorite god, ''asserting that the manner of life he lived was the same as that of Heracles when he preferred liberty to everything.'' Donald R. Dudley explains the choice of Heracles as the near ''patron saint'' of Cynicism in terms of the great hardships the god endured, but I find this unsatisfactory.[14] The Cynics were ascetics, not masochistic altruists. Though one of the most popular of Greek gods, Heracles was peculiar in a number of respects. First and foremost, he belongs to the category of beings who move easily between the heroic-chthonic and the Olympian spheres, between the world of the dead and the world of the gods. He is associated with wild animals, killing the most dangerous, and is frequently depicted fighting with lions. It was he who brought Cerberus, the hound of Hades, from the underworld, no doubt a point of special appeal to the dog-man, Diogenes. Though the greatest of Greek heroes, he is associated strongly with oriental motifs. He is eternally youthful, a compulsive cosmopolitan, wandering from place to place, with no home of his own. This powerful hero in the end not only meets a terrible death at the behest of a jealous woman but, as Burkert notes, ''he also contains his own antithesis. The glorious hero is also a slave, a woman, and a madman. The son of Zeus is no Zeus-honored king. . . . The extreme must turn into its opposite, impotence and self-destruction, in order to affirm itself again.''[15]

Whereas Socrates used verbal dialogue to get to the truth, Diogenes used the dialectics of self-dramatization and of myth. This dog-man of the Western world completely identified with his hero Heracles. Like him, he recognized and lived the principle of creative antithesis. In his shamelessness was his dignity, in his madness lay his sanity, in his homelessness he became, as he said, ''a citizen of the world,'' in his savagery, his life stripped bare to the bone, he laid bare what was most human for the world to see, his freedom, within and without.

After the drama of his life, no one would forget him or what he stood for. The story goes that when, one day, Plato styled him a dog, he replied to the reactionary aristocrat, "Quite true, for I come back again and again to those who have sold me."[16]

Cynicism had its strongest influence during the late fourth century, after which it appears to have declined as a direct influence. However, it continued to make an impact through its influence on Stoicism, within which it formed what Dudley calls "a left wing . . . throughout its history."[17] It did survive as an independent though minor movement throughout the Hellenistic period and has been shown to have greatly influenced Philo; its literary influence on Hellenistic literature was also not insignificant. Cynicism went through a revival in the first and second centuries A.D., partly as a result of interest in Stoicism; it greatly influenced the thought of Epictetus, as we will see, and had an undercurrent of influence in Christianity, one which persisted, in traces, through the Middle Ages.

4. EPICUREANISM

The second of the three major philosophical developments in the idea of freedom during the Hellenistic period was Epicureanism, which may be defined as a philosophy of hedonistic detachment. Much as I value the judgment of Max Pohlenz, I simply cannot agree with him that "the idea of inner freedom is not of central significance for Epicurus."[18] Materialism, as we already saw in our consideration of Cynicism, does not imply any disregard for the inner life. Rather, it refuses to make any rigid separation between the two. Mind and body, the outward and the inward, are different spheres or dimensions of nature. Epicurus did not claim that they were not different but, rather, emphasized their interconnectedness. "The mind and the spirit," wrote Lucretius, "are firmly interlinked and constitute a single nature," and he later added that "this same reasoning proves the nature of the mind and spirit to be corporeal."[19]

Epicurus, alone among the Hellenistic philosophers, took a more prudent—and, we think, more realistic—approach, in giving equal play to both the outward and the inward dimensions of freedom. Unlike Plato, Epicurus employed what may be called a cross-parallel approach to inner and outer freedom. There were outer constraints on outer freedom and inner constraints on inner freedom, but in addition there were outer constraints on inner freedom and inner constraints on outer freedom. This approach is far more consistent with the realities of human life. To take an extreme example, someone suffering from agora-phobia is as much constrained and unfree to walk outside as if he or she were being held prisoner inside by someone. Conversely, it is reasonable to consider outer constraints as serious impediments to inner freedom. Imprisonment and poverty make the attainment of peace of mind, or whatever one calls inner freedom, very difficult. This, in essence, is the commonsense approach to freedom advocated by Epicurus.

Everything we choose to do or to avoid, Epicurus held, is related to "the health of the body and the soul's freedom from disturbance, since this is the end belonging to the blessed life. For this is what we aim at in all our actions—to be free from pain and anxiety."[20] Pleasure is "the beginning and end of the blessed life," the true measure of all things. However, while all pleasures are inherently good, not all are choice worthy, and this is a central distinction for Epicurus. We choose to avoid some pleasures if in the long run they cause us greater discom-fort. Conversely, while all pain is inherently bad, we may sometimes choose to experience pain temporarily if the long-term outcome is a greater measure of comfort. In other words, "we have to make our judgment on all these points by a calculation and survey of advantages and disadvantages." Herein we find the clear antecedent to the Ben-thamite notion of a calculus of pleasure, and it should be noted at once that Utilitarianism is one of the few modern philosophies which have openly admitted their Epicurean origins.[21]

Epicurus' answer to the vulgar charge, already rampant in his own day, that he advocated license and merely "having a good time" is that the best pleasure for him is "sober reasoning which tracks down the causes of every choice and avoidance, and which banishes the opinions that beset souls with the greatest confusion." In all this, pru-dence is the best course and "the natural source of all the remaining virtues."[22]

Epicurus also played a critical role in the development of the idea of freedom because he was the first philosopher to take the freedom of the will seriously and to argue the case for a radically indeterminist ethic. Determinism was implicit in the atomism of Democritus, which he embraced. Determinism had apparently not bothered Democritus[23] and had not been a serious issue for Plato and Aristotle. For Epicurus, however, it became an issue precisely because freedom was the central value in his philosophy. He wanted to rid mankind of the fear not only of the gods but of fate, and he considered the latter an even greater terror than the former, "for it would be better to follow the mythology about gods than be a slave to the 'fate' of the natural philosophers:

the former at least hints at the hope of begging the gods off by means of worship, whereas the latter involves an inexorable necessity."[24]

Epicurus offered a variety of arguments in favor of free will, but they are too technical to be considered here at any length.[25] There is a purely logical defense which holds that the determinist is condemned to self-contradiction: "The man who says that all events are necessitated has no ground for criticizing the man who says that not all events are necessitated. For according to him this is a necessitated event."[26] There is, second, a psychological argument. People are born with the seeds or potential for a variety of developments. How we develop, what we make of ourselves, is at least partly "up to us." Closely related to this is Epicurus' metaphysical doctrine that the self is not reducible to the atoms that constitute a human being, since behavior is an emergent property with its own autonomous laws of motion, a view that is a remarkable precursor of both psychological and, by extension, socio-logical autonomism.

Epicurus' third argument in favor of free will is what may be called sociological pragmatism. If there were no freedom of will, morality as we understand it would be impossible, since we could hold no one responsible for his or her actions, and a world without morality is sociologically impossible. Whatever else the determinist holds, he at least lives by an indeterminist ethic. This argument is usually offered in pragmatic terms. But a more sophisticated version of it reverts to the logical critique of determinism. The determinist may respond to the argument of sociological pragmatism that people are compelled to think in indeterminist terms precisely because that is what makes the system work. To this Epicurus responded with the infinite-regress argument. The fact that morality is sociologically necessitated does not relieve the determinist of the charge of self-contradiction, for "this sort of account is self-refuting, and he can never prove that everything is of the kind called 'necessitated'; but he debates this very question on the assumption that his opponent is himself responsible for talking nonsense."[27] To this the determinist will further respond that he is compelled to behave in this manner, and will keep on making this defense on further being challenged, ad infinitum.

Epicurus' final argument for freedom may be called his naturalistic defense: in a nutshell, it is natural to be free. However, he explicitly excludes the kind of freedom exhibited by a caged animal from the domain of freedom, calling that spontaneity. Wild animals are always compelled to express their own spontaneous natures. It is precisely because only human beings are capable of emotional falsehood, of nonspontaneity, that the concept of purely human freedom becomes meaningful. Human freedom is distinct in being chosen freedom, and we are so free when we are most ourselves. Epicurus knew that civilization had become an obstacle to such real feelings of freedom—hence his critique of society. "We must liberate ourselves from the prison of routine business and politics," he argued. "Let nothing be done in your life which will bring you fear if it should be known to your neighbor."[28]

However, he was not an ascetic. He sought to peel away those conventions that made the return to spontaneity impossible. Chief among these civilized conventions was the chronic Greek competition for power and honor leading to "enmity, resentment and disparagement." These are things the wise man masters. Furthermore: "Once he has become wise, he no longer adopts the opposite character *and does not intentionally feign it either*; rather, he will be affected by feelings but without having his wisdom impeded."[29] A watchful passivity was his recommended stance toward politics.

Unlike the Cynics, Epicurus felt strongly that a crucial part of the return to our real, spontaneous, and humanly free selves involved a return with others of like mind. Hence his strong emphasis on friendship with kindred free spirits. Friendship is an intrinsically good value and is critically linked to human freedom; like all such values, it is ultimately based on pleasure. This does not exclude altruism, for, as Plutarch pointed out, Epicurus felt that it was "more pleasurable to confer a benefit than to receive one." The emphasis on friendship is tied to the central role of freedom in their ethics.

Of all the Hellenistic doctrines of freedom, that of Epicureanism is the one which most resonates with our modern conception of the value. During the millennia between its birth and the nineteenth century, it has been quietly influential even when shunned and condemned. More than any other Western theory of freedom, it has been distorted by friends and foes alike. Augustine's theory of freedom owes much to it, even though he would have been horrified by the thought; as late as the sixteenth century, Giordano Bruno was burnt as a heretic for advocating aspects of the Epicurean cosmology. It was not until the coming of Utilitarianism, the theory that has most shaped our modern view of freedom, that the influence of Epicureanism was openly acknowledged.

5. STOICISM

We come, finally, to Stoicism, whose doctrine of freedom had the greatest influence in the ancient world, especially the Roman world that followed. Zeno, the founder of Stoicism, was a student of the Cynic Crates, and any attempt at an understanding of the philosophy must begin with the reasons for Zeno's break with his former teacher. We can do no better than summarize John M. Rist's careful analysis of the key points of difference leading to the separation.[30] The break, it turns out, hinged on their differing conceptions of freedom, more specifically, on the way in which the slave metaphor was used in defining freedom. Like the Cynics, Zeno and his followers accepted, as the ultimate good, life according to virtue, which they identified with the complete freedom of the wise man. What, however, does virtue mean? What are virtuous acts? Diogenes had held to an extreme form of negative freedom. For him there were three kinds of acts: the vicious, the virtuous, and the indifferent. Virtuous acts, which were acts according to nature, he explained largely as acts which were not vicious, not enslaving. He never explained virtue in positive terms, nor did he explain why virtuous acts should be consistent with nature, because he did not have a theory of nature. The Cynics also insisted on the utter insignificance of indifferent acts such as masturbation and public defecation.

Zeno took up the challenge and attempted to provide positive answers where the Cynics gave merely negative ones, and to provide a theory of nature where the Cynics had none. In doing so, he went far beyond Cynicism, though never so far that his ideas were not, in principle, reconcilable with important aspects of it. Nonetheless, Zeno's Stoicism was more than a positive statement of Cynicism. Zeno found it impossible to practice shamelessness, and this points to a major difference between the two dogmas. Zeno felt that many actions which were not themselves moral—indifferent acts—could nevertheless promote morality. From this emerged the doctrine of appropriate things, those preferred because they were natural. The only alternative criterion for preferring certain acts was the will of the detached, negatively free, wise person which Cynicism advocated. Zeno was suspicious of this since will could easily be confused with whim. Harmony with nature was a better guide to preferred action—hence the importance of studying and understanding physics.

Nature, for the Stoics, means both external nature and inward human nature. The two are aspects of a single cosmos. "Monism and immanence," as Robert B. Todd emphasizes, "are the central ideas in

Stoic physical theory.''[31] What makes them one is the principle of reason, which acts externally through the laws of the universe, and internally through the human mind behaving wisely. This immediately takes us to a different conception of freedom, for whereas the Cynic emphasis was negative, obsessively reducing all constraints to the minimum, the Stoic emphasis now becomes not simply the minimal positivism implicit in all negative freedoms—the absence of constraint on my desire to masturbate publicly implies a minimally positive freedom to masturbate publicly if I so desire; though it is not to say that doing so is intrinsically good—but something new. That something new is what may be called intrinsically positive freedom, and to anyone who strongly believes in purely negative freedom, as the Cynics did, this is always a dangerous development, for these intrinsically positive freedoms entail a conception of freedom that identifies it with obedience to laws. That is precisely what Stoicism ended up doing. Virtue, true freedom, came to mean life according to the laws of nature, both human and universal, which is ''the right reason which pervades all things and is identified with Zeus.''[32] The happy man is he in whom ''all actions promote the harmony of the spirit dwelling in the individual man and the will of him who orders the universe.''[33]

In breaking with Cynicism, Zeno and his most important disciple, Chrysippus, went back also to the parallelistic conception of the relation between the inner and the outer world which we first found fully developed in Plato. The inner world was a microcosm of the outer, only now their unity was based on a thoroughgoing materialism instead of on a soul mediating between being and imperfect being. For Plato only the forms were really real; for Zeno and Chrysippus, only nature. All agreed that reality was identified with reason, although Stoicism came to lay much greater stress on this identity, seeing it as the divine principle. Everything done by the wise man was a manifestation of this divine principle acting in accordance with nature.[34] The Stoic god, as Todd very nicely puts it, ''is like a Platonic demiurge who does not however copy a pattern but brings himself as a pattern to the creation and structuring of the universe that directly embodies his identity.''[35] This, to be sure, is a more humane conception of people's relation to the ultimate and accounts for Stoic dignity and self-confidence in the cosmic scheme of things, but it conceals a fundamental contradiction. How do we reconcile this laudable dignity with the complete determinism implicit in the Stoic theory of god and nature? Zeno, like Plato, was not much bothered by this problem, though Chrysippus was to be preoccupied by it. I strongly suspect that the reason Zeno was not is that, like Plato's, his positive conception of freedom was an internal version of sovereignal, organic freedom.

In a complicated passage, Diogenes Laërtius lays bare Zeno's views on inner and outer slavery:

> They declare that he alone is free and bad men are slaves, freedom being power of independent action, whereas slavery is privation of the same: though indeed there is also a second form of slavery consisting of subordination, and a third which implies possession of the slave as well as his subordination; the correlative of such servitude being lordship; and this too is evil. Moreover, according to them not only are the wise free, they are also kings; kingship being irresponsible rule, which none but the wise can maintain.[36]

Two things, it seems to me, are being said here. First, there is inner freedom, which is the power to act independently, and inner slavery, which is the absence of such power. Second, there is outward slavery, which is external subordination, and correspondingly there is external lordship. This external lordship is an evil, but note that external slavery is not being condemned. In this regard an anecdote about Zeno is highly revealing of his views on both real and metaphysical slavery. Once, while he was whipping a slave for stealing, the slave pleaded that it was his fate to steal, to which Zeno replied, "Yes, and to be beaten too."[37] All that is being condemned is lordship by people who are not wise; the foolish master ends up being a slave to his power. The wise, however, have the right to rule; freedom is sovereignal power which only the wise can enjoy. This, in practical terms, is very close to Plato's conception of inner and outer slavery and freedom. Zeno, too, emphasizes duty and morality in a manner very similar to Plato's.[38] Passion and emotion are also "irrational and unnatural movements in the soul, or again, as impulse in excess," and the wise man must control them to the point of being "passionless."

Thus Zeno, for all his materialism, ends up with an organic conception of inner and outer freedom not dissimilar to Plato's. This situation changed with Chrysippus, who not only systematized Stoic philosophy but made the problem of free will and moral responsibility a matter of central concern. Chrysippus believes that nature is an eternal, unbroken causal chain. Fate is the law of universal causation and allows for no variation, no swerve. But he also believes in human freedom, that our actions are in our power. Chrysippus uses a variety of arguments to get around this basic problem, all in support of a fundamental distinction between causal determination (fate) and necessitation. One relies on the fact that all actions are complex and co-fated. It is a fallacy to argue that you will recover regardless of whether you call the doctor or not, since your recovery is fated because it is as fated that you should call the doctor to aid in your recovery as is the recovery itself.[39] Another approach is to distinguish between antecedent and primary or proximate causes. Fate is seen as antecedent or secondary cause, and over such causes we have no control. But there is a second category of causes—namely, primary or immediate causes, the impulses leading to an action—and these are in our power.

These arguments are not terribly persuasive. It is only when Chrysippus and later Stoics resort to a version of the free-slave metaphor that they get anywhere. The fundamental difference between Chrysippus and Zeno, a difference which also comes out in the free-will problem, is that Chrysippus takes over to the inner world, and to the philosophical plane, a universalist and more humane version of the outer, one which corresponds to the final maturation in the previous century of democracy in Athens as a form of civic freedom based on sovereignty of law.[40] Chrysippus emphasizes unity in the outer city, but he rejects the notion of the wise autocrat dispensing law, and in his politics speaks instead of the rule of law, which applies as much to the mighty as to the lowly. Thus he opens his book *On Law* as follows: "Law is king of all things human and divine. Law must preside over what is honorable and base, as ruler and as guide, and thus be the standard of right and wrong."[41]

In this harmonious cosmos, freedom comes through assent, not conformity, and Chrysippus is insistent on this critical difference. Because the principle of reason is within us as in the universe, it is in our nature to behave consistently with nature's laws. The wise person freely chooses the right course, and it is most natural for us so to choose. Fate or law acts through us, and because of this it acts with our assent, in much the same way that the laws of the harmonious democratic state are one with the intentions of the demos and are implemented with their assent.[42] But democratic unity and assent, however enlightened, still require a strong executive power, and the direct counterpart to this in Chrysippus' inner and world cosmos is the notion of the "commanding faculty," the executive coordinator or mind (*nous*) of the soul.[43]

The analogy suggests another Stoic argument in defense of freedom. The laws of the benign, organic democratic state are not only reasoned laws but laws originally generated by reasonable people. We live by laws; we assent to their implementation both because they are reasonable and because they were originally our creations or those of our ancestors, to whom we are linked in a community of memory. The same is true of the laws of the cosmos. Because we partake of the divine, we were present at the creation, so to speak; to put it differently, the ancestry of our reason links up with the original creation of reasoned laws in the same way that the organic citizen body linked up with its Cleistenean and Solonic ancestors. Thus we have made our fate by being one with reason, and we continue to exercise our democratic assent to the unity as the fate we made acts through us. Stobaeus tells us that in several of his books Chrysippus speaks of fate as "the rationale of the world" or "the rationale of providence's acts of government in the world."[44]

Thus from the old Greek idea that only Zeus is free we find an extension in Zeno to the still-conservative notion (strongly influenced by Plato) that only the wise and virtuous are free: that they form an inner aristocracy of the soul that admits of a basic division in the inner city between ruling reasons and ruled passions, and in the cosmos between the wise rulers and the foolish ruled. From this we move to the enlightened organicism of Chrysippus in which all citizens of the world soul are free in a civic democracy of mind and cosmos under the rule of law. For Chrysippus there is no part of the inner soul which does not partake of reason and which has to be controlled. What does not partake of reason has to be banished from the inner and world soul, not tyrannized into submission. Chrysippus, like Zeno, recognizes only one kind of inner freedom, that which comes from union with the power of reason. Freedom means *pneuma*, power, the fiery principle of the universe. It is no longer true that only Zeus is free; but it remains incontrovertibly true that the only freedom is union with the all-powerful reason of Zeus.

It is precisely in this respect that middle Stoa, which emerged in the second and first centuries B.C. of the Roman world, most significantly differs from early Stoa. Panaetius and Posidonius deviate from early Stoa in several respects. First, they return to a dualistic conception of the person. On the one hand, they see a contrast between nature and soul, the former being concerned with reproduction, nourishment, and growth and the latter with the inner processes of the mind. On the other hand, they hold that the soul is further divided into reason and impulse and, unlike Chrysippus, believe that impulse or the irrational cannot be eliminated but has to be controlled. Second, in its ethics the middle Stoa places far less stress on the reconciliation of the human soul with the cosmic soul, although it does not wholly abandon the idea. Rather, it emphasizes overwhelmingly an exploration of the inner soul of the person. People should live according to nature, they still hold, but the nature they have in mind is the propensities of human beings generally and individually. The return to dualism, then, had aspects of Cynic and Platonic dualism but differed radically in its this-worldliness, in this respect being more closely akin to Aristotelian views on the matter. The four virtues of wisdom, justice, manliness, and temperance were for Panaetius practical ideals focused on our actions rather than our motives.

Far more original was the development of these emphases by Posidonius, who, in contrast to early Stoa, distinguishes god from nature. He sees god as the active principle and nature as the world's body. The goal is still to live in accordance with reason, but now we find a striking new conception of inner freedom coming about as a result of the shift back to a dualistic conception of physics and psychology. As Rist explains, "Where the Old Stoa urged us to follow nature, Posidonius wants us to join in the organization of nature."[45] In other words, there is an internalization of the civic conception of freedom, but with the problem of disorderly personal freedom (or impulses) reinstated. The human soul is akin to but different from the world soul. Human reason remains, in the Stoic tradition, closely allied to cosmic reason and so can work with it. But the human soul differs from the world soul in having an irrational element, the source of all evil, that cannot be discarded but must be controlled, whereas there is no such evil in the world soul. The most noble task of the human being is "to join in God's work in ordering the physical world to the best of his ability." Such an internalization of civic freedom was inconceivable in early Stoa, because the principles of cooperation and participation imply differences between the elements of the whole, and no such differences were allowed in the highly monistic view of the inner and outer universe held by early Stoa. The microscopic human soul had no choice but to find its freedom in union with the organic power of the world soul with which it was one or nothing. The return to dualism changed all that.

Freedom, then is the *polis* of the mind, but one no longer under the rule of law, an inner *polis* of active participation in the world soul, the cosmos, assenting to its acts of government in the world. The person who does not understand and experience this cosmic city is a slave, an inwardly and cosmically dead outcast. Logos, understanding, is the cosmic equivalent of the exercise of civic freedom, and middle Stoa therefore places enormous emphasis on it. What Charlotte Stough observes, in her excellent paper on Stoic determinism and moral responsibility, is surely more true of middle than of early Stoa: "Understanding frees one from the compulsion of Nature. The person who comprehends the laws of external Nature as well as those of his own inner self will be able to approximate more closely the ideal human condition that the Stoics called freedom and contrasted with slavery."[46] And as she goes on to point out, while the concept of freedom is central in Stoic moral philosophy, it is a mistake to identify it, during the middle period, with Stoic notions of action and responsibility: "Both the ethical ideal of freedom as well as its opposed state of enslavement *presuppose* the concept of autonomous action."[47] Philosophical ignorance, inner slavery, is no excuse for external wrongdoing. The preoccupation with this distinction is a peculiarity of the middle period of Stoa. The emphatic monism of early Stoa would have obviated the need for such a distinction. In briefly turning to later Stoa, we find a deliberate conflation of the ideal of freedom with the notions of autonomy and responsibility.

With later Stoa, we are well into the Roman period in the history of freedom, and for this reason we will postpone a detailed consideration of it until later. For now, let us close our consideration of the Stoic tradition and, with it, of the Hellenistic intellectual response to freedom by noting that one idea dominates this last period: personal freedom explored on the level of the mind. The dualism found in Posidonius is taken to extreme lengths, and the whole point of philosophy becomes an examination of the emancipation of the soul from both its outer trappings and its inner constraints. In this pursuit the master-slave metaphor is used with a directness not witnessed since the time of Diogenes of Sinope.

In Philo (ca. 30 B.C.-A.D. 45) the transition is already complete, and it is hurled at us with the subtlety of a naked slave girl on an auction block:

> Slavery then is applied in one sense to bodies, in another to souls; bodies have men for masters, souls their vices and passions. The same is true of freedom; one freedom produces security of the body from men of superior strength, the other sets the mind at liberty from the domination of the passions. No one makes the first kind the subject of investigation.[48]

Actually, Philo uses the metaphor of personal freedom in an inconsistent manner. Sometimes he speaks of it in negative terms as the absence of compulsion: "the good man cannot be compelled or prevented: the good man, therefore, cannot be a slave."[49] At other times, however, he sounds almost Platonic in comparing inner freedom with the rule of law in the outer, well-regulated city: "Those in whom anger or desire or any other passion, or again any insidious vice holds sway, are entirely enslaved, while all whose life is regulated by law are free."[50] True freedom he identifies not only with wisdom and goodness but with nobility of character, which possesses "a kingly something" which circumstance cannot suppress, in contrast to the mean and slavish spirit of unfree men. The analogy becomes confused, however, by his natural theory of slavery, in which he speaks of slavish personalities and naturally free and noble personalities. For there is no good reason why a mean and slavish person cannot thoroughly control his passions; indeed, such persons are often only too much in control of their emotions. Conversely, an outwardly noble person who resists domination even when in chains may well be a libertine. The problem with Philo is his dispersive mode of argument: to make his point, he throws everything he can think of at the reader, regardless of coherence or consistency.

Three important conclusions, however, can be drawn from his writings. The first is that the overwhelming emphasis in Stoicism is now on the moral aspect of the inner person and that the essence of moral virtue is some version of inward personal freedom. Second, insofar as that view of inner personal freedom goes beyond a purely negative conception of the absence of inner constraint by the passions, its emphasis is on independence and autonomy, something which, as we saw above, middle Stoa kept distinct from the ideal of freedom. Philo is quite explicit in his opinion that "no two things are so closely akin as independence of action and freedom."[51]

A third thing to emerge from Philo is the enormous sociological significance of personal freedom in both its inward and its outward version in his day (he was born ca. 30 B.C.). Nothing better reveals this than his fascinating account of an audience's response to a play by Euripides in which freedom was praised, performed in Alexandria during the early years of our era:

> I saw the audience so carried away by enthusiasm that they stood upright to their full height and, raising their voices above the actors, burst into shout after shout of applause, combining praise of the maxim with praise of the poet, who glorified not only freedom for what it does, but even its name.[52]

Far more consistent and original in his use of the slave metaphor to express the idea of inner personal freedom was the ex-slave philosopher Epictetus. Whereas the early Stoics had made reason divine, Epictetus made freedom the divine value, identifying it with the highest moral virtue. The freedom of the will and the freedom of the inner person became one and the same with him. Metaphysical choice was reduced to moral choice, and both aim at one and the same thing: the complete autonomy of the person: "If you will you are free," Epictetus insisted; if you will, "everything will be in accordance with what is not merely your own will, but at the same time the will of God."[53] Using as his point of departure the dualistic break in the monist system introduced by middle Stoa, Epictetus returned to the Cynic roots of Stoicism and reclaimed its moral fervor. But in the process he healed the very breach that was his starting point. A unity was restored to the Stoic system, only now it was one firmly planted in this world and steadfastly focused on human beings, who became the center of the cosmos rather than an abstract principle such as *pneuma* or reason. It is a fitting irony in ancient Western history that Stoicism, the most advanced philosophy of the ancient world, the intellectual tradition that has most fashioned the Western notion of freedom in all its aspects, ended its career in the genius of a crippled ex-slave.

To conclude, then, the Stoa began in the Hellenistic world with a celebration of inner organic freedom, the universalized aristocracy of the mind in unison with the power of the cosmos. Middle Stoa shifted to an emphasis on the civic freedom of the mind, participating in the governance of the world soul, in stark—one is tempted to say, compensating—contrast to the decadence of the outer polis. And later Stoa—fashioned in a vast slave system that dwarfed those of classical Greece, an outer cosmos in which men and women found themselves isolated in a world empire far removed from the security of the polis or even from that of the Hellenistic ethnic enclave—moved to a celebration of personal freedom in what Epictetus called "the acropolis within us," one in which he could "sing hymns of praise to God" on the virtues of the self-sufficing soul.[54]

To the historical sociology of this world we must now turn our attention.

Rome and the Universalization of Freedom

CHAPTER 12

Freedom and Class Conflict in Republican Rome

With the emergence of Rome and, later, its large-scale slave system, freedom found an even more fertile social environment in which to take root and flourish in the West. And with Rome's triumph over the Mediterranean and northern Europe, the idea of freedom completed its conquest of the Western mind in both its secular and its spiritual aspects. The four chapters in this part examine the outward and the inward courses of this development.

Two broad periods may be distinguished in our survey of the development of freedom in republican Rome: that of the early republican era, from the end of the monarchy at about the end of the sixth century B.C. to 267 B.C., and that of the middle and late republic, from this point up to its collapse near the start of our era.

1. FREEDOM AND THE STRUGGLE OF THE ORDERS IN EARLY ROME

This complex formative period is characterized by three overlapping developments critical not only for the history of Rome itself but for our subject.[1] One is the so-called struggle of the orders, the prolonged class conflict between patricians and plebeians which occupied nearly the entire period, formally coming to the end of one phase in 287 B.C. The second development is the expansion of Rome into Italy, ending in the imposed confederation and Romanization of the entire peninsula. The most intensive phase of this development took place during the years between 340 and 266. And the third was the reorganization of Italian agriculture following the colonization of the peninsula.

Let us begin with a negative assertion. The struggle of the orders was not a struggle for freedom, although it had important indirect consequences for the history of freedom in Rome.[2] The removal of the monarchy may well have worsened the position of the plebeian classes, since it eliminated the one institution strong enough to protect the people from the rapacity of the aristocrats.[3] As in Hesiodic Greece, in Rome an exploitative aristocratic state emerged in which growing numbers of people faced debt and a shortage of land. Perhaps even more than in Greece, in Rome the impoverished faced not only debt bondage but real slavery. The cancellation of debts, and the demand for land redistribution, among the early republican Roman masses suggests a sociopolitical order quite similar to Greece's between Hesiod and Solon.[4] The Roman class struggle, however, took a different form, as did the solution eventually arrived at.

The Roman plebeians' means of resistance took the unusual form of withdrawal, or the threat of withdrawal, from the body politic—the *secessio* or political strike in which the masses not only rejected the leadership of the patricians but refused to fight their wars. As Jean-Claude Richard observes: "The plebs entered history in the guise of the foot soldiers who seceded in 494–93."[5] The Roman elite's solution to this extraordinary form of resistance through withdrawal had two closely intertwined features, one internal and the other external.

The internal solution was the complete co-optation of the leadership of the plebs. The patrician offer to share power and wives with the cream of the plebeian leadership in the 450s was eagerly accepted by the latter (ca. 443), the fusion of the two resulting in the Roman nobility of the middle to late republican era. The Hortensian Law of 287, in striking contrast to its surface appearance, marked not a triumphant leap toward democracy or civic freedom but a step in the opposite direction. So far from being "a victory for democracy," Arnold Toynbee wrote, "it had been a confirmation, on a broader and more solid basis, of the oligarchic regime under which the Roman people had been living."[6] The compromise that made the law possible, comments Raaflaub more recently, "ensured that tensions would continue between the new governing class (the patrician-plebeian nobility) and all those who did not share their wealth and power."[7]

Intra-elite rivalry now preoccupied the plebeian leadership, even though the underlying tension between the classes persisted. The tribunate, the political institution that had been instituted, probably in

471, to protect the interests of the plebeian masses, was distorted into a counterpoint to senatorial power, a basis for intense clique rivalry among the nobility, no more accessible to the mass of plebeian Romans than the Senate. Nonetheless, some concessions had to be made to the mass of Roman plebs. In addition to the necessity of allaying their severe economic plight, there was the external political need for a loyal reserve of manpower for the army.

The solution to the problem of how partly to meet the economic demands of the plebs without in any way adversely affecting its own interests came in the external activities of the Roman elite. The phase of the struggle between the plebeian elite and the patricians, culminating in the co-optation mentioned above, was accompanied by the political unification of the peninsula under Roman tutelage. There had been a seemingly endless series of wars with neighboring peoples of the peninsula. But up to about 340 B.C. Rome had been merely one player, though an increasingly important one, in a geopolitical peninsular system with numerous political units, many of which were evenly matched.

After the middle of the fourth century, however, the balance of power shifted heavily in Rome's favor, and during the three-quarters of a century preceding 266, it extended its political sway from the lower Tiber basin to the rest of the peninsula in a complex series of wars and alliances that devastated many areas of the peninsula. A substantial proportion of the land captured from the defeated Italian peoples was expropriated, amounting to about a fifth of the entire peninsula. This expropriated land was disposed of in several ways. Some of it was assimilated into Roman tribal territory, but most was colonized in a variety of ways, which we need not enter into here, and a good part was kept by the Roman state for use by its own citizens and some in the allied states. Roman plebeian farmers benefited from the distribution of this expropriated land.[8]

In this manner the Roman elite warded off all serious threats to its own wealth and power which lay implicit in the land hunger and indebtedness of the Roman masses. Basically, the defeated peoples of the peninsula paid the price. There were, of course, seeds of future conflict in this essentially short-term solution. The defeated peoples were precisely the ones who partly lost their autonomy. As long as they remained not fully integrated, their land could be expropriated by land-hungry Roman farmers. But to the degree that they became part of the expanding Roman state, they ceased to be outsiders and were transformed into another large disgruntled, landless segment.

Rome was not to reap the bitter harvest of this contradictory solution to its class problems until the period of the Social War (91–89 B.C.), when numerous other factors complicated and intensified the conflict.

The conquest and unification of the peninsula in a political mosaic of internally self-governing, semidependent, and wholly subjected subunits did bring some relief for a segment of the Roman plebs. But, perhaps even more important, it partly determined the peculiar political pattern that was to develop in Rome over the course of the next century and a half. The dispersal of the Roman plebeian population over a wide area of the peninsula meant that only the rich outside of Rome itself could participate in the political process, since political institutions remained concentrated in Rome. Furthermore, Roman citizens who took allotments in Latin colonies lost their citizenship outright. At the same time, by spreading the culture and language of Rome they "provided the instrument for the Romanization of Italy."[9]

The Roman elite also extended the principle of class co-optation in its dealings with the rest of Italy. There was a systematic enticement of the local ruling classes in the allied states, the ancient counterpart to what Latin-American sociologists call the comprador system, in reference to the alliance of metropolitan and local bourgeois elites in the process of underdevelopment. It involved an important shift away from the solidarity of all classes of Romans over against all other peoples of the peninsula, toward a class solidarity between the Roman elite and the elites of the other communities of the peninsula which had come under Roman tutelage. This cross-communal elite solidarity was greatly facilitated by the external adaptation of the *clientela* system, as E. Badian shows in his classic study on the subject.[10] The arrangement was mutually beneficial to all the elites of the peninsula, especially the Roman nobility. It lessened their dependence on their own masses, particularly in times of warfare; and it cannot be overemphasized that the main benefit to Rome, in many cases the only benefit, coming from its political hegemony was access to the military manpower of the conquered and allied communities.

For the local elites, Rome offered a powerful ally not only against potential external enemies but against their own masses, if they became assertive in their economic and political demands. At all times the Roman elite took a severely conservative stand in its intervention in the internal class problems of the allied and subjected communities. While external political autonomy was the price demanded by Rome in its rule over the peninsula, the price was made bearable to the local elites by two distinctly Roman practices.

One was the permission of an unusual level of local municipal autonomy. Roman indirect rule both encouraged and required administrative autonomy and local government along traditional city-state lines, even as it made the momentous historical leap into what Karl Christ has rightly called "a completely new form of organized rule," one which "succeeded in transcending the limitations of the ancient city-state, the polis, the self-governing community of free citizens."[11] This principle of indirect rule was to continue right through the period of the empire. As Peter Garnsey and Richard Saller have recently emphasized, Rome remained an "undergoverned" empire to the very end, and the "secret" of this government with minimal bureaucracy was the self-governing city in which the liturgical system, paid for by the local elites, effectively met the basic functions of government.[12]

The second incentive Rome offered in its embrace of the local elites was the promise of Roman citizenship. Rome's liberality in offering its citizenship to aliens and conquered peoples has frequently been remarked on. It was certainly unprecedented in world history and stands in stark contrast to the civic exclusiveness of the Greek world. This liberality began here in Rome's dealings with the local elites of the peninsula. "The liberal bestowal of Roman citizenship in its various forms was more than a diplomatic move," writes Alföldy. "It also laid the foundation for an increase in Roman manpower and thus for the unification of the peninsula within the framework of a state."[13] It was not only a means of exercising hegemony and co-optation but was made possible precisely because citizenship came to mean something quite different to the Romans.

The third overlapping development during this first phase of the republic is something that has only recently come to light, thanks largely to archaeological studies. I refer to the economic impact of the Roman conquest of the peninsula. The archaeologically based studies strongly suggest that while different categories of small-scale own-account freeholders must be distinguished, "it does seem that the unifying factors of personal freedom and of agricultural self-sufficiency of Rome's colonists spread a radical element through the Italian countryside."[14] The pattern of semiservile rural agriculture, found most conspicuously in regions such as Etruria, became a thing of the past. In spite of considerable variation in the size of holdings, the principle of the independent free farmer was diffused throughout Italy, thanks largely to the demonstration effect of the land-hungry Roman farmer-settlers.

How did these three overlapping patterns of change influence the development of freedom in Rome, if at all? First, let us take account of the nature of slavery during this period. Slavery had existed in Rome from earliest times. The laws of the Twelve Tables make two things clear. One is that genuine personal slavery had long been a well-established institution; indeed, M. I. Finley goes so far as to insist that Rome by the third century B.C. was not simply a slaveholding but a slave society.[15] The second is that debt bondage was also common and that debtors were harshly treated and could ultimately be reduced to real slavery if they defaulted on their debts. The demand for the cancellation of debts and the removal of the threat of enslavement, we have already pointed out, became the central grievances of the plebeians. The situation reached a crisis point during and after the Gallic catastrophe during the first half of the fourth century. The property of many people was destroyed. This was exacerbated by the huge ransom paid to the Gauls and by the financial burden of rebuilding the city. As one would expect, a disproportionate part of this financial burden fell on the plebs.

Many persons not only became debt bondsmen but were reduced to slavery and sold "across the Tiber," away from Rome, since, like most other peoples, the Romans shunned the presence of former citizens reduced to slavery in their midst. Early-fourth-century Rome's situation is therefore highly reminiscent of Greece's between Hesiod's time and the early sixth century when Athens faced a large-scale class revolt. There were some similarities in the solution as well. Various experiments were tried in an effort to alleviate the situation. The more cautious Roman elite attempted nothing like Solon's decisive law. Instead, the leaders it called on to solve the problem tinkered with various half-measures such as a partial reduction in the interest rate while the situation worsened. The available records leave us in no doubt that there was among the mass of plebs at this time great anxiety concerning the threat of *nexum*, or debt bondage, which always carried with it the even more terrifying prospect of real slavery.[16] Thus personal liberty, in the most literal sense of the removal of the threat of slavery, was closely tied to economic insecurity; while the two remained inextricably linked, it is significant that the final solution offered by the Roman elite first addressed the problem of freedom rather than that of economic equality. This is the celebrated Lex Poetelia Papiria (326 B.C.), which, Tenney Frank noted, "was long considered a partial Magna Carta of plebian rights."[17]

It seems reasonable to speculate that, in the years of long struggle leading up to the Lex Poetelia Papiria, the mass of lower-class plebs would have developed a strong feeling for, and commitment to, the value of personal freedom out of their anxiety about the very real risk of its loss. A similar situation prevailed in Athens, as we have seen, in the years leading up to the reforms of Solon. As in Greece, too, the removal of the threat of debt bondage and of real slavery may well have led to a decline in concern with personal liberty—decline, but never absence, for while the threat of enslavement as a result of poverty at home was removed, the possibility of enslavement in war was always a real one for the Roman farmer-soldier.

What of freeborn Roman women? The notion of an early period of Roman matriarchy has long been dismissed as a fabrication of nineteenth-century ethnohistory. Archaic Rome was a thoroughly patriarchial society. We are not able to speculate on the effects of the existence or threat of slavery on women's views of freedom because there is simply no relevant material. What can be reasonably asserted, however, is that in striking contrast with post-Solonian Athens, the growth of the state and slavery in Rome was correlated with a struggle for independence by women, resulting in a marked improvement in their status over the long run. Even Eva Cantarella, who paints a generally gloomy picture of the period under consideration, concedes that the extraordinary poisonings of many prominent men by their wives in 331 B.C. "indicate the definite existence of a problem."[18] The passage of laws forbidding women from drinking wine and dressing colorfully confirms the strength of male patriarchial values, but it also strongly suggests the existence of female resistance and independence.

"Female formidability" among the elite, as Judith P. Hallett has called it, existing in the midst of an outwardly patriarchal society, is one of the great paradoxes of elite Roman life, and its roots go back to early classical times.[19] Nor was this assertive pattern confined to elite women. The women who demonstrated for the repeal of the Oppian Law in 195, to move beyond the early republic, would hardly all have been from the patrician class; and even allowing for the exaggeration of the Roman annalists, it seems certain that hundreds of women from all classes were involved with the Bacchanalian scandal of 186 B.C.[20] The difference between Greece and Rome in this regard is almost certainly to be explained at least partly in terms of the radically different courses of development in the two slave systems.

Now, no comparison is more revealing for an understanding of the history of freedom in Greece and Rome than that between the crucial eight and a half decades spanning the reforms of Solon and Cleisthenes and the equally critical period of roughly eighty years between 338 B.C. and the outbreak of the First Punic War. In both Athens and Rome the demand for economic and some political equality—civic freedom— existed. And what Frank wrote of the Roman masses holds equally for the mass of hard-pressed Athenians, "that the fight for economic relief may have been basic and that the demand for political equality was raised largely in order to win the power by which to gain economic relief."[21] However, Rome at the passage of the Lex Poetelia Papiria in 326 was already fourteen years into its extraordinary sweep across the Italian peninsula, and its elite thus already possessed, in the captured territories, the resources partly to satisfy the economic needs of its disgruntled land-hungry farmers. (It could never fully satisfy these needs, not only because the powerful Romans and the state took too much for themselves but because of a catch-22 build into the allotment system to poor farmers and townspeople: they went disproportionately to younger sons, allowing them to marry earlier, or even to marry at all, which in turn led to rapid population increase among the poor).[22] It never faced a labor crisis of the Solonic sort; its turn to latifundia-type large-scale slavery was due to other factors and came long after its elite had learned to finesse and manipulate class conflict.

These differences in the *timing* of large-scale slavery (to say nothing of its differing structural location) and of the availability of resources to meet the economic demands of the masses are absolutely critical in explaining the differences in the history of freedom in the two states. In Rome, as we have noted, the demand for political equality was met by an alliance with the leadership of the plebs, culminating in the Hortensian Law of 287 B.C. And that marked the limits of civic freedom in Rome. From now on, until its termination two and a half centuries later with the founding of the principate, civic freedom meant political equality and participation *among different segments of the nobility*, an idea not dissimilar to the Athenian elite conception up to the end of the aristocratic era in the early sixth century—a conception that also allowed for the co-optation of the more upwardly mobile members of the hoplite class. When members of the Roman nobility spoke glowingly of their *libertas* and of the freedom of the republic, it was to this exclusively elite conception of civic freedom that they referred.

With the success of Rome in the wars in Italy later in the third and abroad in the second centuries, the leadership of the allies benefited in another very substantial way, demonstrated by Badian: through the foreign *negotia*, that is, commercial and financial activities abroad under the powerful protection and validation of Roman power. As Badian has commented, "Just as their lower classes were reconciled to the insecurity and inferiority of their position by their share in booty (regularly captured in large quantities, down to 146 B.C.), so these families were reconciled to their inferiority at home by their equality to Romans abroad and by the profits this brought them."[23]

The availability of conquered resources to the Roman elite and their absence in Athens is a crucial conditioning factor in any explanation of this vitally different outcome. But it cannot be the decisive explanatory factor, since history presents us with a vast catalog of elites without resources which did not become democracies and—most notably in the modern world—of richly endowed elites which did accept democracy. Clearly, the decisive difference was the presence of large-scale slavery in Athens and its absence in Rome during the crucial phase of the struggle of the orders, a struggle which, as De Ste. Croix has pointed out, "was *also* in a very real political sense a class struggle," in which fairly unified landowners were pitted against a more differentiated group resisting either political or economic exploitation.[24] When large-scale slavery came to Rome, the die of civic freedom as a "shadow-boxing" elite affair, in Toynbee's term, was already cast. If it was to have an impact on freedom, it would have to be on the other two notes of the chordal triad. It did. And to that story we now turn.

2. LIBERTAS IN THE MIDDLE AND LATE REPUBLIC

While the year 267 B.C. is a convenient and often-used point of transition in the republican history of Rome, two things should be emphasized at the start. One is that while intra-elite conflict was significantly attenuated, and would remain so for the next century and a third, social conflict did not cease, but acquired instead a more openly interclass quality. Second, the Punic Wars, while decisive in their impact on Rome, were nonetheless a sociopolitical extension, however dramatic, of previous developments in Roman society. As William V. Harris has pointed out, Rome had become a war-based social order, or more properly, its elite had come to depend heavily on war for the realization of its highest social, political, economic, and personal ideals: "The fixed pattern of annual warfare fulfilled such essential functions that it was not likely to be given up"; and when one adds to this, "the will to expand Roman power," full-scale war seemed a forgone conclusion once "the original aim of preventing Carthage from obtaining (or retaining) control over Messene had been achieved."[25]

The broad outline of developments during the period of the republic after the middle of the third century is reasonably well established, although specialists continue to dispute points of detail. The earlier phase, from about 266 B.C. to 133 B.C., was dominated externally by the Punic Wars and Rome's emergence as the major Mediterranean power and internally by the emergence of large-scale slavery and the consolidation of the patrician-plebeian nobility as a slaveholder class benefiting from both sets of changes. The second phase, that of the late republic, from about 133 B.C. to the establishment of the principate in 27 B.C., saw the intensification of the slave system, following a long period of chronic class conflict and civil wars. All these developments had radical implications for the history of slavery and its handmaiden freedom.

The Hannibalic wars brought devastation to large areas of the Italian countryside, delivered as much by Roman generals in their punitive and preemptive assaults on Italians who supported Hannibal as by the Carthaginians.[26] A series of interlocking forces was set in train which was to transform the Roman economy and its basic social system. Not only did the wars devastate major parts of Italy, especially the southeast, but they led to the confiscation of vast tracts of land from those who had collaborated with the enemy, especially in Campania, most of which fell to rich monopolists. Much of the confiscated land went in large consolidated tracts to members of the nobility and emerging equestrian class. The local population which did not lose its land was not displaced but was converted to rent payers, although the amount of surplus extracted from it was so exorbitantly high that it was soon impoverished.[27]

The Hannibalic wars offered a fateful solution to the problem they had created. Enormous numbers of persons had been taken captive in the wars, and they now provided the labor force which the landholders needed to exploit their newfound wealth. In bringing slave labor to southeastern Italy, the new landowners were introducing a radically new system of labor exploitation but nothing innovative in terms of the means of producing wealth. Pastoralism had always been important in this region, and the more efficient utilization of resources had already been largely accomplished in the earlier period of Romanization. The slave system continued to emphasize pastoralism; that is where the greatest profits were to be made. New, in economic terms, were the scale of the operation and the pattern of ownership. The consolidation of land and the use of slave labor allowed for a more effective utilization of transhumant pastoralism. Displaced peasants and imported slaves paid a high price in human suffering for this increase in productivity and individual wealth.

The wars in the eastern Mediterranean and Spain that followed the Hannibalic trauma were equally devastating in their socioeconomic impact. An unusually large proportion of the rural male population—as much as a half during the Second Punic War[28]—had been drawn off into the wars, with the result that large numbers of farms were neglected and abandoned. What is more, the experience of fighting for years on end in foreign lands, and exposure to more exciting ways of life, led men to lose touch with their homes and farms, resulting in the migration of many veterans to Rome. The introduction of increasing quantities of food from the captured lands would also have devastated the traditional cash crop subsector. In parts of southern Italy and Sicily, extensive cereal cultivation by slave labor replaced the free farmers who had abandoned their occupation for war, tribute, and the other rewards of empire or who were simply forced to become day laborers.[29]

Recent scholarship, most insistently that of Peter Garnsey, has cautioned us not to exaggerate the degree to which the free small farmer was removed from the scene.[30] That there was a radical change in the introduction of slave-based labor, no one questions. What is contested is the view that slaves completely or even overwhelmingly replaced free farmers and workers. Instead, the rural slave system that emerged—and it was a slave *system*—made use of both nonslave and slave labor. Free and tenant farmers were necessary for the slave economy (as they were in the U.S. South) not only in producing food for the slaves but in offering a supplementary work force during the peak seasons of labor demand, especially in the harvest.

Starting in the middle of the second century B.C., but especially after the confiscation following the Social War of the early first century, the third major feature in the development of the rural slave system took place. This was the rise of the classic plantation system focused on the villa. These large estates developed mainly in central Italy and are the ones with which we are most familiar from the descriptions of the Roman agrarian writers and manualists (and the modern archaeological evidence cautions us not to project this development back too far in the second century). They most closely resemble the modern slave plantation in their emphasis on specialized production for export to urban centers. The new products emphasized were wine, olives, and poultry. The villa was the residence of the partly absentee owner and was run in a highly organized way by a resident overseer, himself often a slave. It was here that the slaves were most brutally treated in antiquity—always, of course, excepting the Laurium and other mines. They were chained to their barracks at night and herded in gangs and whipped mercilessly during the day to extract maximum labor from them, the expectation being that if they survived for more than eight years, they would more than justify the initial cost of procuring them.

Paralleling these developments in the rural areas was an equally great transformation of the urban economy and society of Rome. The impact of slavery on the urban economy coincided with its effects on rural Italy. The two were intimately linked, but recent studies suggest that the political effects were greatest in the city. T. Gracchi's land bill was sparked by urban immiseration and unrest among the immigrants pushed off the land, as Henry Boren has argued,[31] although he is surely wrong in his extraordinary assertion that the Gracchi were trying to turn the clock back in seeking a rural solution. The Gracchi's problem was that they were too phenomenally ahead of their time in correctly identifying, and seeking to remedy, the rural source of the urban problem; all over the Third World today World Bank economists are belatedly urging leaders to do the same! Alas, these reforms had few positive long-term consequences for the small Roman farmer, and for the same reasons why they fail today: they were undermined by the actions of the large landowners. The allotments ceased in 118 B.C., three years after restrictions on their alienability were removed. With the push of foreclosure and economic instability and, later, the pull of service in the army as a result of Marius' recruitment drive, the drift to the city became a stampede.[32]

Rome, like Greece during the late sixth and fifth centuries B.C., had its urban economy transformed by slave and freed craftsmen, traders, and professionals. In the absence of easy international migration, slavery was the main means by which Rome recruited its technical and professional manpower, much as Greece had done previously.[33] Soon, all occupations except the military were dominated by slaves and ex-slaves. The Roman middle and upper classes gained enormously from this expansion of slavery. Not only were the manual and technical occupations dominated by slaves and ex-slaves, but so were domestic service, including the positions of accountants, clerks, and tutors. And as Badian has shown, they gained even more from the entrepreneurial opportunities generated by both the slave economy and the imperial plunder and tribute from the provinces, the two in turn themselves intimately linked.[34]

The urban slave system differed from its rural counterpart in one crucial respect. Manumission rates were high, whereas in the rural system very few slaves were ever freed. The reasons for the high manumission rate were the same as for those in Greece, and for all slave systems which rely on skilled slaves. Slaves could be motivated to work at skilled and demanding occupations only by the prospect of manumission.

However, additional factors in Rome magnified the manumission rate. First, it had a very long tradition of manumission, the direct result of its *clientela* system.[35] Second, there was the unusually strong distaste for all forms of trading and manufacturing on the part of the Romans generally and of the ruling elite in particular. Even more than in Greece, in Rome *governing* nobles were not permitted to sully their hands in many lucrative economic pursuits such as banking and trade. The most effective way of circumventing this self-imposed constraint was to allow one's slaves and freedmen to do it. The arrangement was beneficial to both master and slave. The competent slave enhanced his chances not only of becoming free but of accumulating considerable property. The master kept his honor while filling his pockets from the profits accrued to his dependents in the despised occupations. We must be very careful, however, in making general statements on this matter. Badian has shown that one of the main effects of the Gracchan reforms was to undermine the previous disdain for making money in nonfarm pursuits.[36] By the late second century, it was perfectly all right to do so, with one proviso: those making their wealth by the new nonfarm means should not engage in politics, especially not the wealthy tax farmers. However, by the last years of the republic, even this had begun to change, although there was still general disdain for the grosser forms of private enterprise. By that time, though, the pattern of employing one's slaves and freedmen as trusted managers of one's estates was well entrenched—indeed, could be described as the norm.

A purely legal factor also contributed to the high urban manumission rate. Roman law did not have, indeed explicitly excluded, the institution of agency. It was impossible to run a relatively complex economy, in which transactions often took place over vast distances, without some form of representation. The Roman solution, as Aaron Kirschenbaum has recently reemphasized, was the *familia*: sons, slaves, and freedmen became "a significant source of non-contractual agents." In this arrangement, the *peculium* became an important "instrument of agency" for the master, and by the same token, an instrument of freedom for the industrious slave.[37]

As a result of these developments, slaves and freedmen gradually replaced the freeborn in the urban industrial economy. By the first century A.D., the majority of artisans were freedmen. In fact, the great majority of the people of Rome were by this time slaves, freedmen, or freeborn persons of servile ancestry. Brunt has estimated that by the seventies B.C. the freeborn poor (neglecting whether or not their ancestors were slaves) constituted only a fifth of the free population.[38] The world had never witnessed anything like this before, nor would there ever be such a slave system again until the emergence of the

Caribbean slave societies in the late seventeenth century. "In conquering what they pleased to call the world," writes Brunt, "the Romans ruined a great part of the Italian people," while their upper classes grew fabulously wealthy. External and internal exploitation reinforced each other in the rise of Rome. The massive slave uprisings that shook the system between 135 and 71 B.C., the resistance of the provincials against the rapacity and brutality of Roman rule, the struggle of the Italians for economic relief and political equality culminating in the Social War of 91–89 B.C., were all intimately linked with the struggles within Roman society itself: between different elite factions, urban ruling class and dispossessed proletariat, impoverished peasants and large-scale, slave-based landowners. Behind the glamorous rhetoric of civilizational grandeur, which some Western historians still insist on propagandizing, lay a sordid tale of prodigious robbery by one of the most rapacious ruling classes that has ever existed. There had, of course, been ruling-class robbers using war and imperial expansion as a means of accumulation long before Rome. But "the Roman ruling class practiced it on the largest scale yet known; they robbed their subjects abroad so that they could better rob their fellow countrymen."[39]

Accompanying these fundamental structural changes were important developments in the political and cultural life of Rome. Imperial expansion and slavery, combined with an intensified use of the freedmen as clients, created a truly murderous political system. Even before the imperial wars of the late republic it was possible to detect an alarming growth in the *clientela* system as the newly wealthy members of the *ordo equester*, "craving for *gratia*, *auctoritas* and even *honores*," competed with each other for the size of their following.[40] Warfare, imperial expansion, and slavery, however, turned this into a vicious competition and acquisition of clients.

Beginning with Marius' fateful decision to abolish property qualifications in the recruitment of soldiers, army commanders increasingly relied on the practice of rewarding their soldiers by one means or another, most often through pillage but also out of their own pockets. In this way, soldiers became attached to their commanders rather than to the state, and many remained so even after they were demobilized. This was the first element in the development of the mass *clientela* system. It was, however, an enormously expensive undertaking for the patron. The wealth to support it came from two related sources. One was more warfare. Thus war bred more war to pay for itself and the growing *clientela* of the commander. More wars, in turn, increased the number of the patron's clients. The second source of wealth was, of course, slavery, both abroad and in Roman Italy itself. Most army commanders quickly translated the tribute and other rewards of war into slave latifundia, manned partly by captured prisoners or by slaves bought on the market.

But in so supporting their clients the army commanders were further undercutting the economic base of their freeborn followers, reinforcing the urbanization and economic marginalization of the lower classes. It was at this point that the system became murderous. The army commanders, conservatives and populists alike, increasingly paid off their clients with free food and straight bribes. In return they demanded the support of these clients in their vicious competition for power.

When this happened, the republic was on its way to disaster. All parties were debased by this corrupt system. In their struggle for *gloria*, *dignitas*, and power, the Roman elite resorted to every vile means it could think of, including lynching, arson, organized mob violence, and hired hit men. In the process the proletarians were also thoroughly debased, although, as we will see, not completely excluded from the political process. With the rural economy distorted by the slave latifundia, and the urban economy dominated by slaves and freedmen, the Roman proletarians became a redundant class economically, or at best a supplementary work force for the slave system. With unemployment rampant, they were easily bribed and bought off by the nobility, which did so with the enormous wealth pouring in from the conquered lands.

Civil war was the inevitable outcome of such a thoroughly perverted system. There was not only an "explosion" of traditional forms of competition, as Mary Beard and Michael Crawford have put it, but also an escalation of new forms of competition, exacerbated by the short tenure of political office.[41] Imperial tribute combined with the vast new wealth generated internally by the slave system meant that the value of prizes to be gained from competitive politics increased. So too, following the reforms of Sulla, did the number of competitors. However, while the stakes were vastly increased along with the number of players vying for them, the number of top prizes and positions actually declined. Roman politics increasingly became a winner-take-all game. The resort to violence and other illegitimate means was a foregone conclusion.

We should be careful, however, not to go so far in our *realpolitik* approach as to suggest that the republic was an inchoate system. In the first place, as Claude Nicolet has most recently emphasized, it was a *system* with its own internal coherence and political logic.[42] However hierarchical, oligarchical, plutocratic, corrupt, and just plain coercive the republic might have been—and it was all these things to an astonishing degree—a lively civic culture with its own political rules, its own grammar of politics, existed in Rome, and on a scale unknown elsewhere in the world until the rise of the modern state in Europe. Further, the system was highly inclusive, if hierarchical. It was ruled by a tiny group of elites—among whom alone was the notion of political equality meaningful—but it included vast numbers of people many of whom were no more than second- or third-generation Romans. Indeed, from a sociological point of view, it might be argued that hierarchy and total control were what allowed, what induced, the Roman elite to make its civic culture such an open one. It is easy to be cynical and say that the system was inclusive precisely because, to paraphrase Groucho Marx, any club so open was not worth joining. This was partly, perhaps largely, true, especially during the last tumultuous decade. But not entirely.

For several centuries a "dense" civic culture existed which, by means of the all-important census, placed vast numbers of individuals in a complex matrix of positions which determined their military, financial, and political activities, in a manner that for most crucial life events was not oppressive. The system was idealized as one working to the benefit of freely contracting individuals pursuing their own best interests. Reality was something else, but it depended on which reality one was talking about. The repressive aspects of the political system did not affect most people, for the reason already noted—the people who mattered enough to be repressed (and to have records left about their experiences) were also members of the exclusive ruling elite. And this is not to say that the ordinary citizen was not politically engaged; he was, as we will see. In his relations with administrators the ordinary citizen was likely to encounter outrageous corruption and coerciveness, but there were some safeguards, and, like the political apparatus, the administrative machinery was so rudimentary that the average citizen rarely had much occasion to get involved. Finally, there was the legal system, which advocated the rule of law and theoretical equality but which, too, was in practice riddled with privilege and the most egregious forms of corruption. Nonetheless, when all allowances were made for these realities, the legal system did provide an unusual measure of protection against arbitrary action in most areas of life. This complex civic culture could hardly be called a democracy, and no one at the time was naive enough to so describe it. But it was very much concerned with freedom, both as an ideal and in practice, as we will argue shortly.

When the assassinations and battles of the civil wars were over, the republic lay in ruins, and from its ashes emerged the principate of Augustus. It was an end which almost everyone welcomed, most of all the hard-pressed masses. Augustus brought peace—*otium*—and the price he demanded was civic freedom, or what was left of it among the upper classes. But if *libertas*, as the upper classes understood it, was well and truly dead, this does not mean that all forms of freedom died with it. Let us examine more closely what had happened.

3. *LIBERTAS* IN THE LATE REPUBLIC

The Latin word which most closely corresponds to the idea and value of freedom as we have so far understood it is *libertas*. By the late republican era the term was a common political catchword, as common as it had become in late-fifth-century Greece.[43] Several things should be borne in mind in any consideration of the Roman notion of freedom. The first is that the term *libertas* had many shades of meaning. The same person, and the same group of persons, used it in different senses. It also meant different things to different persons; and it most certainly varied in its meaning as one moves from the elite to the proletarian classes. All this is already familiar, for we saw the same thing happening in Greece, and, of course, we find much the same today. The question is whether there existed the same basic tripartite conception, the same chordal triad, as existed in Greece. We think so, and will return to this issue shortly.

The second point to bear in mind always is that for Rome, even more than for ancient Greece, our literary sources come almost exclusively from the upper classes. As Donald Earl cautions us in the early pages of his masterly study of Roman moral and political thought, we can speak in detail only of the upper classes.[44] This does not mean, however, that we know nothing about other classes in Rome. From the laws, inscriptions, and archaeological remains, as well as from the indirect remarks of the upper classes themselves, we can glean a fair amount of information about the views of the Roman masses. What we should always keep in mind is that class and status were decisive determinants of the conception of freedom which Romans held.

At first sight, the term *libertas* seems to have conveyed a bewildering variety of meanings to Romans who left literary statements on the subject. On this both C. Wirszubski and Jochen Bleicken, writing some two decades apart, are in basic agreement. Bleicken, for example, identifies about ten different uses of the term, including personal liberty, political will, control, political equality, and protection against municipal arbitrariness.[45] Wirszubski, writing at a time when the ideas of Isaiah Berlin were still very much in vogue, distinguishes between negative and positive aspects of the Roman usage.[46] Both correctly emphasize that the Romans, unlike the Greeks, developed no abstract theories or notions of freedom, in spite of the importance of the concept in ordinary life; this is hardly surprising, given the general distaste for abstract reflection exhibited in all their writings. What I do find most surprising is that both authors go out of their way to caution us against identifying modern notions of freedom with any of those held by the Romans. Surprising, because in their subsequent discussion of Roman usage both authors make it abundantly clear that the Romans indeed held a view of freedom remarkably like that of the Greeks before them, and like that which we hold today.

Behind the many shades of meaning, however, one finds the three basic elements of the triadic conception, plus the more general chordal meaning which refers to all three meanings taken together. No one seriously denies that the term *libertas* was often, perhaps most commonly, used in the sense of negative personal freedom, the right to do as one pleased without constraint from others or from the state. It may well have been the only meaning of the term in Roman law. In his magisterial study of Roman slave law, W. W. Buckland tells us that Justinian resolved "the hopeless task of defining liberty" by an adaptation from Florentinus: "Liberty is the natural capacity (*facultas*) of doing what we like, except what, by force of law, we are prevented from doing," and he adds that it "is presumed that a freeman can do any act in law: his incapacity must be proved." Just the opposite is true of the slave. Because the condition of slavery was well defined, a free person, in law, was simply "one who was not a slave," and Buckland is content to conclude, "we may leave the matter there."[47] Alas, we cannot; for while it is true that the Romans' most precise thoughts on freedom, like their views on slavery, were "developed by a succession of practical lawyers who were not great philosophers,"[48] it is most emphatically not true that ordinary and elite Romans did not have complex views on the subject of freedom. Nonetheless, as a starting point, it is well to remember that in their most respected way of thinking—the legal—Romans had a conception of liberty identical with that of a modern American lawyer.

In their use of the term to mean the expression of political will, of the power and control that inheres in the *auctoritas* of the powerful leader, we find versions of the sovereignal conception of freedom. And in their well-developed notions of equality before the law, as well as in the *elite* idea of political equality and the more general political notions surrounding the tribunate, especially during the period of the classical republic, the idea of civic freedom is clearly to be found. However, the important issue is which element of freedom was important for what group of people, and when. Did one of the three elements become dominant, and if so at what time?

The Roman nobility, we have seen, had a well-developed, if peculiarly elitist, conception of civic freedom. Though an important ideal, cherished by men such as Cicero, it is to be doubted whether it ranked at the top of their scale of values, even considered in its best (for them) pre-Gracchan form. Rather, it was one component of a broader complex of aristocratic values, the central focus of which was *virtus*. The quintessential quality of the strong-willed, self-controlled man, *virtus* was in its pristine aristocratic version realized in *gloria* and *fama*, and most frequently expressed in the personal qualities associated with *gravitas* and *dignitas*.[49] "Loyalty, trustworthiness, integrity, frugality and self-control complete the picture of the virtuous Roman," writes M. L. Clare, and these were often combined with the softer virtues associated with the notion of *humanitas*: pity, clemency, humanity, and kindness.[50] With the incorporation of the upwardly mobile plebeians, however, and the subsequent growth of competitive politics, *libertas* entered this value complex. The struggle of the orders had been, in its effects, mainly a struggle for *libertas* on the part of the plebeian leaders, who kept this ideal when they joined ranks of the nobility with the patrician class.

Libertas for them would have meant political equality, the right to participate in the running of an exclusive political system. In all this the Roman elite did not differ from its Greek counterpart. Where it parted company was in the degree of exclusiveness of the political club. As in the early republican era, *libertas* in the sense of civic freedom remained exclusively an ideal exercised by the nobility. Within this class the Romans were even more committed to civic equality than their Greek counterpart was. In order to ensure that as many upper-class members as possible participated, they rigidly limited the tenure of higher offices. Although the club was exclusively upper class, it was not entirely closed. Indeed, it was constantly in search of new talent, and recent studies have shown that the turnover was almost modern in its volume.[51] As Earl has observed, "Its attitude was one not of rigorous exclusion of outsiders but of carefully controlled inclusion,"[52] what modern British sociologists might call a system of sponsored mobility. But while the composition of the club changed, it ruthlessly excluded nonmembers from the operation of the political system. By this means, then, the value of civic freedom survived, but it did so outside the framework of democracy.

It should be noted that from a very early date the principle of popular election of magistrates had been established in the republican constitution, and in theory the right to vote was shared by all adult male citizens.[53] However, from an equally early time, the right to vote was made almost, though never entirely, meaningless by a series of enactments: voters had no say in who was nominated, and they had no control whatever over the magistrates they voted for, once the latter were elected. Further, even their capacity to vote was attenuated by the fact that plebeian clients were expected to vote for their patrons; and the long distances involved in going to vote in what was a huge country by ancient, even modern, standards effectively excluded most potential voters from the electoral process. As Finley has observed, "the formal devices designed to ensure tight elite control accumulated until they amounted to a veritable straightjacket."[54] An attempt was made to reform this system by the Gracchan initiative, which obliged the tribune to execute the will of the people and gave them the power to divest him of office if he did not. This was viewed as revolutionary by the conservative ruling elite, and so it would have been, had it been allowed to work properly. Superficially, it might seem that during the first century "the community's will and power of action, was more within the people's control than at any other time in Roman history," but as Nicolet has shown, a more careful look at the "juridical substratum" reveals a political process that was anything but democratic.[55]

In the late republic there was another important development of this peculiar commitment to civic freedom without democracy. The new men of the first century B.C., in their reinterpretation of the old aristocratic value system, completely dropped the old patrician emphasis on *ingenium*—birth or bloodline—as a source of virtue; instead, they broadened the notion of *virtus* to emphasize achievement through competition. A struggle now developed between two axial sets of values in the upper-class value complex: that between, on the one hand, *auctoritas* and *libertas* and, on the other, two versions of *libertas* itself. *Auctoritas* stressed the old ascriptively based aristocratic principle of authority and was embraced by the more reactionary element of the faction which became known as the Optimates. *Libertas*, on the other hand, became a political slogan which was claimed both by the more centrist elements of the conservative Optimates and by the radical faction of the elite, the so-called Populares.[56]

There was apparently much talk about the liberty of the Roman people by the leaders of the Populares, and the constitutional basis of their populism was the tribunate, an institution that had originally been developed as a basis of popular participation in politics but which, as we have seen, had been largely usurped by the patricio-plebeian upper classes after the Hortensian Law. In appealing to the tribunate, the Populares were in no way calling for any creation of mass democracy, not even the most radical of them, such as Caesar.[57] This is not to say that they were all cynically manipulating the masses. Caesar genuinely had the interests of the people at heart, even as he pursued his own. What Caesar did was to take the concept of liberty one step further. For him and his faction, following in the tradition of the Gracchi, it meant seeking the support of the masses and taking their interests into account in all major political acts, especially those likely to influence the people. It never meant taking the people, or their representatives, into the decision-making process. Caesar's conception of government could be called a plebicitary dictatorship. For him the liberty of the Roman people meant this form of government, and he was prepared to establish it even at the cost of undermining constituted authority.

In striking contrast with the Caesarean view of liberty was the more centrist Ciceronian view held, at least in theory, by the more moderate faction of the conservative elite.[58] Since this conception of liberty is the one which most influenced Roman legal thought, its importance went far beyond the conservative group who first fully articulated it in conjunction with their own interests. This view held in some suspicion the patrician notion of *auctoritas*. But while it was prepared to celebrate the value of freedom, *libertas* in its political aspect meant an elitist republican government in which competition for power was restricted to equal ruling-class members without any appeal to the masses, which was condemned as demagoguery. However, it also had individualistic aspects. One was an inclination to broaden it to include the notion of self-realization, which anyone could achieve if he had the right talent, energy, and character, a conception clearly congenial to the new men of the elite.

Another, equally important individualist emphasis among moderate Optimates was a respect for the rule of law and constituted authority in the relations of all Romans. In this regard, Cicero conceived of *libertas*, "that sweetest of all possessions," as restraint on the power of officials and powerful individuals in arbitrarily interfering with individual Romans; he accepted the notion of equality before the law in certain respects, while rejecting the idea of political equality.[59] All Roman citizens had certain basic rights, most notably that there should be no punishment without trial and conviction, enacted in the principle of *provocatio*, which in civilian life protected the life and person of the Roman citizen, the right of appeal, and the right to security of private property.[60]

So far this centrist elite view closely resembles modern notions of liberty. But there are some fundamental differences. One we have already noted, that *libertas* in no way implied political equality for all or the right to participate in government. It also differs from the modern view in that, while insisting that the state not arbitrarily interfere with the individual, it fully accepted the right and power of the state to interfere as long as it did so in a constitutional manner. Thus *libertas* meant "freedom from absolutism, and the enjoyment of personal liberties under the rule of law,"[61] but there was little of the modern liberal celebration of the individual in opposition to the state. Indeed, involvement with the state, a recognition of one's duties toward it and an acceptance of its power, was the obverse side of the state's recognition of the basic rights of the Roman citizen. As Wirszubski has noted,

> The Roman citizen sought to assert and safeguard his rights, not against the overriding authority of the state, or the tyranny of the majority—but against other citizens who were stronger than himself, or against the officers of the state who, in pursuit of his own private interests, might encroach upon his rights, abusing the power that had been entrusted to them.[62]

A third important difference with the modern notion of individual rights is the view that while there was equality before the law in certain basic respects, beyond these there was a recognition that some people had more rights than others and were to be treated differently in the legal process. According to Wirszubski, the "Roman conception of freedom, . . . includes equality before the law but not complete egalitarianism of rights; the essential thing is to have not equal rights, but enough rights on which to found freedom."[63] More recently, Peter Garnsey, in his definitive study of the workings of the Roman legal system, has shown how thoroughgoing was the principle of privilege in the treatment of people before the law.[64]

While the Ciceronian centrists spoke eloquently of freedom, it was the new populist style ushered in by the attempted reforms of the Gracchi, and culminating in the politics and thought of Caesar, that made *freedom* the major catchword of politics. The Populares, however, were prone to use highly unconstitutional means to obtain their objectives. In this regard, Caesar's critics and assassins were quite correct in accusing him of the political sin of *regnum*. In its dictatorial politics the behavior and thought of the Populares also showed little respect for legal rights, although they claimed to protect the personal freedom of the masses. A close examination of their behavior shows that their view of freedom was really wholly organic, but one which was complementary to personal freedom.

Caesar broadened his *clientela* to include all the Roman masses, in the same way that the *clientela* of the ancient kings had been the entire Roman people, or so it was thought. Legal safeguards of personal liberty were an irrelevance, since the masses were assured of their protection in their cliental bond with the great leader; and civic freedom was not merely unnecessary but dangerous, since it meant only the anarchic competition of elite factions for the power to exploit the masses. In the personality and power of the heroic popular leader, the *vindex libertatis*, rested the organic unity of the state, a unity that guaranteed the liberty of the Roman people.

This, then, was the position of liberty among the elite at the end of the Roman Republic. Earl is only partly correct in declaring these competing conceptions to be largely an elite propaganda affair making little difference to the actual experience of freedom among the masses.

> The only people who could claim such impairment were the political opponents of the faction which was at the moment in the enjoyment of power. For them and for their propaganda *libertas* had a peculiarly restricted sense. It stood for nothing more than the freedom to engage in the normal traffic of office and power, to manipulate the constitution to their own ends, to govern the Roman world according to their own desires and for their own profit. Caesar's *regnum*, hostile to *virtus*, impaired *libertas*. But the only liberty he impaired was that of his fellow nobles to amass prestige and power.[65]

Now, while all this is perfectly true, it would be going too far to claim that these views did not have some effect on the mass of people. They were, after all, deeply involved in the escalating chaos of the late republic. It mattered to them greatly what happened to those members of the elite they supported, however manipulative their leaders may have been. What their leaders said was taken to heart. As Nicolet has correctly pointed out, "the masses felt that the political game, though apparently confined to a very small group, was being played for stakes that concerned them directly."[66] Furthermore, they were thoroughly engaged in the political warfare. The struggle over liberty may have been an elite propaganda affair, but it was great, if murderous, spectacle, and the propaganda was as effective as a modern prime-time political broadcast. The obsessive talk about liberty among the elites and their use of it as a political catchword would, at the very least, have made it a central preoccupation among the masses. As in Athens during the late fifth and fourth centuries, in Rome at the end of the republic, freedom was on everybody's mind and lips. It had become, as Ronald Syme observed, the main political catchword for all political factions, and while the "*libertas* of the Roman aristocrat meant the rule of a class and the perpetuation of privilege, . . . *libertas* could not be monopolized by the oligarchy—or by any party in power."[67] Nor, we should add, could it be monopolized by the political class. If bread and material survival constituted one great collective concern of the masses, "the other great collective interest was freedom."[68]

But how exactly did the Roman masses interpret this political catchword? Did they simply imitate the various views expressed by competing elite demagogues, or did they reinterpret it in their own terms? More important, were there independent sources of influence on the conception of freedom held by the masses? The next chapter attempts to answer these questions.

The Triumph of the Roman Freedman: Personal Liberty among the Urban Masses of the Early Empire

A critical feature of our earlier argument concerned the timing of large-scale slavery and imperial expansion. What happened when large-scale slavery finally emerged? Why didn't the Roman masses force their elite to strike the same bargain that had been struck in Greece—the creation of an exclusive democratic club, even an all-male one, for all freeborn only?

The answer to these questions is complex.[1] First and foremost is the simple fact that large-scale slavery had a profoundly different impact on the social life and economy of Rome and Roman Italy. The traditional rural Greek economy had not been devastated by slavery, and the great majority of Greeks remained independent small farmers right down to the fourth century and beyond. Nor did warfare have the same chronic, long-term effect on Greece. In Roman Italy warfare, slavery, and imperial expansion wholly transformed the traditional communal structure. They alienated a substantial proportion of the freeborn from the land and from their communities. While I find the Marxist notion of a slave mode of production useless, there is one tenet of Marxist interpretation of ancient Rome with which I completely concur: that the fundamental conflict driving the system was that between the small- and large-scale landowners and certainly not that between the large proletariat and the equites. The mass democratic movement failed in Rome not, as Theodor Mommsen thought, because of the disloyalty of the proletarian base of the Gracchi and subsequent Populares leaders but because of the early desertion of the rural masses by their leaders who joined ranks with the patrician class against them.[2]

Even where freeborn Italians remained in the countryside, the presence of slavery created almost as strong a sense of alienation among them as among the slaves. Only this can explain the toleration of, and sometimes sympathy for, the robber bands of runaway slaves on the part of the rural free Romans, and the even more extraordinary fact that not a few freeborn Italians joined ranks with the rebellious slaves in the great servile revolts of the second and first centuries.[3] Indeed, so completely lacking was any sense of civic unity and responsibility in the latifundia-infested parts of southern Italy that "respectable aristocrats went around murdering and pillaging with the help of armed bands of [slave and freedmen] retainers."[4]

The idea of a civic bond makes sense only where people have some sense of community. By disrupting the traditional communities in both the rural and the urban areas, slavery undercut the drive toward a participatory civic order. Thus even though it remains true that non-slave labor did continue to make up a substantial, even major, part of the rural population of ancient Rome, too great an emphasis on the purely demographic fact is likely to miss the critical point: that free and slave alike were traumatized by the slave *system* and that the traditional rural communities were disrupted everywhere.

Second, there is the difference in scale, which we mentioned before but which warrants further discussion. In the absence of mass communication or highly developed systems of transportation, democracy is inversely related to scale. Rome had rapidly emerged as a Mediterranean power during the late republican era. Even the scale of Roman Italy was more modern than ancient. It was a very large state, an incredibly large one in ancient terms. With the machinery of politics concentrated in Rome, and with the ruling class determined to keep it that way, distance alone made the exercise of civic freedom an impossibility for most Romans.[5] The Roman system of voting by groups, had it been allowed to work, might well have gotten around some of the more serious geographical problems, but as Nicolet has shown, in this, as in nearly all other cases, the Roman elite was as adept at manipulating its admirably conceived procedures as at inventing them.[6] Finley is perhaps right that, despite the best of intentions, no voting procedure was available at the time to cope with the number of eligible voters.[7]

Third, there was the all-important demographic fact that, by the end of the republic and throughout the empire, the vast majority of Romans were of slave ancestry. Upper-class Romans were only too aware of this reality: "Segregate the freed," Tacitus wrote, "and you will only show how few free-born there are."[8] This was the most radical structural difference between Rome and Greece. Clearly, a proletariat of alien and slave ancestry would hardly be interested in establishing a democratic bond with its ruling class, when precisely one of the critical differences between the two classes was the native ancestry of one versus the alien ancestry of the other. Indeed, a closer consideration of this division reinforces our argument that democracy emerged as an exclusive civic bond among the native members of a slave society vis-à-vis those of alien ancestry. The Roman experience conformed to this principle, but with the striking difference that the only group of true natives left by the late republican period was the ruling class, and even it was being penetrated by second- and third-generation descendants of slaves—witness the great poet Horace. Like the *majority* of people in Athens, the native Romans, now a *minority*, utterly despised those of alien ancestry, who now constituted the majority. Historians of Rome have not sufficiently emphasized the fact of ancestry in their explanation of the ruling class's extraordinary contempt for the masses.

The reason why historians have failed to emphasize this fact is itself ironical. The failure is almost certainly due to the seeming generosity of the Roman elite in the granting of citizenship. This, we have already noted, was quite extraordinary. But its social meaning has been misinterpreted. Because citizenship became identified with democracy in Greece, and especially with an ethnically exclusive democracy, Roman liberality in granting it to non-Romans has been interpreted as an index of the absence of chauvinism among the Roman elite. The Romans themselves milked as much propaganda as they could from this apparently generous policy, frequently contrasting it with the Athenian exclusiveness. But the conclusion to be drawn from the liberality of the Romans in granting citizenship to aliens is not that they were more humane and inclusive but that mass democracy was anathema to them. As P.A. Brunt has observed, the policy worked only because the Roman system was undemocratic, or democratic only among a small segment of the population.[9] It was also, as contemporaries like Philip V of Macedon shrewdly observed, an extremely effective means of enlarging the size of the Roman state, and of recruiting fiercely loyal outsiders.[10]

Fourth, it was simply not true that the Roman masses did not strike a bargain with the elite. They did indeed demand and gain concessions. These were mainly economic; but they were also political. The pattern of material rewards of empire being shared with the plebs, which had already been established by the middle republic, continued with even greater force during the late republic and imperial periods. The free Athenian masses had demanded economic and political redistribution and had received only the latter, because that was all the elite could realistically give; they accepted it and called it freedom. The Roman masses had long given up any call for political redistribution and insisted instead on some economic redistribution of the wealth from the empire. They got it; and they also called it freedom. One of the many meanings of *libertas* was the political and economic security which the Populares of the late republic promised and partly delivered, and Augustus not only promised but fully made good. As Harold Mattingly noted, "One of the chief advantages of Libertas to our plain Roman was his share in the imperial largesses."[11]

Augustus, in seeking to legitimize his rule, went out of his way to meet his end of the implicit economic bargain. And his policy was followed by all subsequent emperors, right down to the crisis period of the mid-third century. The free Roman plebs formed a heavily subsidized class. Which is not to say that they were well off. Far from it. Welfare was expensive in late republican and in Imperial Rome, as it is today in neo-imperial America. The Roman freeborn plebs share certain striking characteristics with the Afro-Hispanic underclass of present-day America. They were a despised, ill-housed, unemployed minority in their own country, with sufficient political clout to wring enough economic concessions from the ruling class to stay just above the level of starvation, while remaining structurally irrelevant to the dominant modes of generating wealth, which in Rome's case was external tribute and large-scale internal production by slaves in both the rural and the urban areas. And like their modern counterpart, the members of the Roman urban underclass were also distracted by mass entertainments: circuses and blood sports being the ancient version of modern television and sports. It is all too easy, however, to condemn the Roman masses—as easy as it is to despise their modern counterparts.

The German classicist Karl Christ has summarized the long-established view of the urban plebs as a "systematically spoiled and corrupted"[12] class:

> The well-worn slogan *panem et circenses* gives the most telling description of the "common law" rights which more and more dominated the thoughts of the *plebs urbana* with all the privileges it still, even then, enjoyed. The distributions of grain and money were still carried out, even in the middle of the greatest crises. . . . At the beginning of the first century B.C. in Rome there were public games of the most varied kinds on a total of fifty-seven days in the year, whereas the calendar of the year A.D. 354 actually showed 177 games days.[13]

While the conventional view is largely true, it is possible to exaggerate the degree of political passivity and debasement of the Roman plebs. That they had no interest in participative democracy is correct. Indeed, they even feared it, for it was quite accurately identified with upper-class roguery as well as with civic and economic insecurity. They much preferred the rule of one man with whom they identified the state.[14]

Although the Roman plebs cared little for democracy, it is not entirely correct to say that they lacked interest in politics; and it is certainly false that they were not deeply involved with freedom. They had a clear understanding of the tripartite nature of freedom and of the inherent tension between the notes of this chordal value. After the horrible experience of the late republic, they realized that civic freedom as practiced by the ruling class was a clear threat to the personal freedom which they cherished. The implicit deal they made with Augustus, and subsequent emperors, was an acceptance of the organic version of sovereignal freedom which the emperors proclaimed, in return for the imperial support of personal freedom and security. This is precisely the note on which Nicolet ends his authoritative study of the ordinary Roman citizen: "*De facto* aristocracies were easily endured, personal power tolerated or even accepted, provided they upheld the autonomy of law; and the status of the citizen continued to be the indisposable and sufficient guarantee of this form of liberty."[15]

Since the plebs wrote no political tracts, how do we know this? From accounts of their behavior at public events, especially their violent collective acts, which speak far more eloquently than any words they may have written. As Ramsay MacMullen has cogently put it, "In the history of disorder, in fact, can be read more and more clearly the history of the *demos* itself, throughout the empire."[16] Theater and circus served political as well as entertainment ends. Emperors used the response of the crowd to test the political waters. Popular leaders were cheered, and unpopular ones booed in a pattern of ritual license which at times acquired the trappings of a political assembly and at other times escalated into political riots which now and then threatened the life of the emperor himself.[17]

In his classic study of the Roman mob, Brunt rightly upbraids "modern scholars who repeat ancient gibes that the doles corrupted the urban population," wondering whether they would "also condemn all modern measures of social welfare."[18] And he demonstrates how the Roman plebs used violence, and the threat of it, as the only rational means of achieving their social and economic objectives. But Brunt himself may have underestimated the degree to which the mob was interested in purely political objectives, and he falls in with conven-

tional opinion in overemphasizing the "volatility" and fickleness of
the plebs. Two incidents, cited by Brunt himself in his review of the
evidence, suggest otherwise.

One was the storming of the Senate by the mob in 67 B.C. in order
to ensure that Pompey received the command to clear the seas of pi-
rates, a command the Senate had been reluctant to give. Now, while
it is true that Pompey's subsequent success in clearing the seas had a
dramatic lowering effect on the price of corn, this was no simple political act. It reveals that the so-called mob could calculate a chain of
political events which would redound to its future economic well-being.
It seems, too, that the mob was as outraged by the intransigence and
dyed-in-the-wool conservatism of the Senate as it was kindled by its
own pressing need for cheaper food.

The second, and more telling, incident suggests a concern with civic
issues, as ends in themselves rather than as means to material survival.
It has to do with Cicero. It is one of the great misfortunes of Western
historiography that it has had to rely on this intellectually pretentious
and thoroughly heartless slumlord, "unreservedly fond of his own
glory,"[19] for information on one of the most vital periods of its classical
past. The plebs returned in kind his loathing of them. When he was
banished by their hero Clodius in 58 B.C., they not only burned his
mansion to the ground but then performed a symbolic act that speaks
volumes for their political engagement in general and for their view of
freedom in particular. On the ashes of Cicero's town house, they
erected a statue to Liberty. The idea of liberty they had in mind was
obviously not the liberty which Cicero mourned—namely, the elitist
civic freedom of the republic—but rather the minimal civil rights which
underlay personal freedom that Cicero, for all his pious cant about
being "slave to the laws that we might be free," had grossly violated
by executing Catiline's coconspirators without a trial. Significantly,
Catiline had been no great favorite of the urban plebs, his populist
base having been the disenfranchised peasants; indeed, they had earlier allowed themselves to be deceived by Cicero's rhetoric into believing that Catiline had planned to burn Rome down. This is not the
behavior of a debased class concerned only with economic survival.
The plebs certainly loathed Cicero because he was no friend, or advocate, of them; but they seem to have despised him even more because his conception of freedom was so at variance with their own. It
is perhaps not without significance that when Cicero fled his house
the one thing he took with him, if we are to believe Plutarch,[20] was his
prized statue of Minerva, the Italian goddess of arts and trades, later
identified with war and wisdom. Before leaving Rome, Cicero went to

the Capitol and dedicated it there with the inscription "To Minerva, Guardian of Rome." The republican elitist conception of freedom, as this most fervent defender of it openly and symbolically understood, depended on the exploitative monopoly of the means and rewards of warfare, knowledge, and trade.

Nor were the plebs as fickle or as "volatile" as even Brunt seems willing to admit. The Israeli classicist Z. Yavetz[21] has convincingly shown that the urban plebs remained loyal to men they liked, such as the Gracchi, Clodius, and Caesar. Nor did they necessarily like all those who tempted them with bread and circuses. Pompey, though he tried hard, never won their affection, in striking contrast to Caesar. Tiberius did all he could to win their adulation, yet they cheered when he died; they respected Augustus, loved Germanicus and Nero, but were either cool to or despised most of the Julio-Claudian emperors, even though all of them tried hard to win popular support. Why the difference? Greed and fickleness are too superficial an answer.

Yavetz found three striking factors underlying the plebs' attachment to or dislike of the leaders of Rome. One was their deep class hatred of the senatorial ranks. Related to this was their open rejection of the republican version of liberty, that is, elitist civic freedom, and their preference for a single powerful leader who could protect them from the violence and domination of the oligarchs.[22] They adored those emperors who humiliated the upper classes, as Caligula and Nero so outrageously did, compelling members of the senatorial class to abase themselves by appearing as gladiators and actors.

The second factor explaining their behavior was that they took Augustus' notion of *tribunicia potestas* seriously. This was one of the legal bases of his rule, his claim that he had restored the ancient power of the tribunate and, in the process, the rights of the Roman people. Contemporaries and modern historians alike have tended to sneer at this claim as sheer formalism on Augustus' part, and we shall return to the matter shortly. Yavetz is correct, however, in his insistence that for the Roman masses the *tribunicia potestas* was important. Though it was not an easy task for him, Augustus did work hard to legitimize his rule by acting, and appearing to act, on behalf of the people. This was no empty claim. He did reimpose the rule of law, which meant a recognition of the basic legal rights that safeguarded personal liberty, even as he abolished all forms of civic freedom. Surprisingly, Yavetz, while rightly emphasizing that "for the masses *libertas* had no appeal,"[23] neglects to point out that it was only *libertas* in the sense understood by the politically deposed elite which they despised and that, indeed, they warmly embraced the notion of *libertas* implicit in the *tribunicia potestas*—namely, that of the strong ruler who upheld the basic rights that underlay the personal liberty of the people.

The third factor explaining the behavior of the plebs was their well-developed notion of what the personality of the ideal leader should be like. Earlier we discussed the moral and personal ideals of the patrician aristocracy and of the new nobility. The masses, too, had their own conception of *virtus*, and there was a significant difference not only in what they rejected of the old virtues but in the configuration of virtues they favored. Their model ruler was one who provided for the basic material needs of his people; whose actions exhibited a respect for elementary justice; who shunned the old virtues of severity and *gravitas* and instead strove to be popular, which meant being something remarkably like the modern American idea of a "regular guy," a nice, compassionate man who was not puffed up and who, however brutal the reality of his politics, was capable of at least mouthing sentiments about a gentler, kinder sort of world, however he mouthed it in Latin. In short, someone willing to come down to their level and exhibit the quality that the senatorial class most despised: *levitas popularis.* "*Clementia, virtus, pietas, iustitia*, bestowed honour upon the Principate. *Liberalitas* was essential and this made it beloved by the people, but only when accompanied by what was termed *levitas popularis.*"[24] This view of the emperor was highly congruent with the masses' love of personal liberty, one component of which was the sense of being as good or as worthy as anyone else. When the mightiest man in the realm came down to their level, by demonstrating his *levitas popularis*, he was implicitly acknowledging the libertarian claim that while people might be unequal in power and wealth, as human beings they were all equal—a view, incidentally, that legal theorists of the time assumed to be a fundamental dictate of the law of nature.[25] Thus the *tribunicia potestas* and *levitas popularis* were mutually reinforcing, the former being the most important legal basis of the emperor's assumption of total power, with its historic obligation to defend the people and uphold their personal freedom, while the latter was the personal expression of that power. In the absence of any real constitutional safeguards against abuse of absolute power, the people had only the appearance and behavior of the man to go by. If he appeared and behaved in a trustworthy, caring manner, they could sleep more easily, knowing that he would protect their personal liberty from the abuse of corrupt or arbitrary magistrates.

Where did the masses' deep love of personal freedom come from? From the same source as that of their Athenian metic counterparts: the experience of slavery and disenslavement, either directly or indirectly, through their parents. There is really no need for us here to get into the thorny ongoing debate concerning the numbers or proportion of slaves manumitted, and whether it was true that the average Roman slave could expect to be free by early middle age. In comparative terms, there was actually nothing peculiar about the high manumission rate in Italy, especially Rome. *All* urban slave systems, both ancient and modern, exhibit high rates of manumission. This is as true of early Greece as of modern North Africa, the city-states of the Sahel, and the urban centers of Latin America. There is no known exception to this sociological law of slavery; it holds even for the one case of large-scale urban slavery in the non-Hispanic Caribbean, early-nineteenth-century Curaçao, situated in a sea of brutal plantation slave systems with extremely low rates of manumission.[26] The greater the reliance on slaves in the urban economy, especially skilled slaves, the higher the manumission rate, for the simple reason that this was the only effective means of motivating slaves to perform complex tasks.[27]

Additional factors, as we noted earlier, operated in Rome to make the rate even higher than normally expected; but for me the sociologically interesting question about Rome is not the one posed by Keith Hopkins—"why did the Romans manumit so many slaves?"[28] I am more interested in two other features that did indeed make the society peculiar. One was the willingness to grant freedmen citizenship, limited to be sure, but citizenship nonetheless—and, what is more, full citizenship to their descendants. This struck contemporary Greek observers as truly odd, as Thomas Wiedemann has recently reminded us,[29] and well it might. I know of no other case in the history of slavery, ancient or modern, which comes anywhere close to this situation. Other slave societies existed which manumitted an even higher proportion of slaves—those of the Tuareg of the Sahara and, in all likelihood, of the early-eighteenth-century Spanish Caribbean—but in all of them the ex-slave population, separated from the native freeborn by race and ethnicity, came to form a separate, dependent class approaching almost the status of a semicaste group with absolutely no pretensions to citizenship in the political community.

Rome's second peculiarity as a slave society flows from the first. Because freedmen became dependent citizens and their children full citizens, it was only a matter of time before the majority of citizens were descendants of freedmen. This was the situation by the late republican era and certainly by early imperial times. Stated in isolation, Tenney Frank's claim that nearly 90 percent of the Roman population was by the early empire of slave ancestry may seem unbelievable.[30] But it follows inevitably from simple demographic principles, especially when it is considered that while the slave population and the free population of slave ancestry were increasing rapidly, the population of native free ancestry was declining. All the evidence—literary, legal, archaeological, and epigraphic—points to one conclusion: that the Roman working class was what Beryl Rawson has called "a freedman proletariat."[31]

Thus, by the early empire, we find the sociologically bizarre situation in which a native population had been reduced to a small demographic minority by a population of servile ancestry; in which the vast majority of persons entitled to call themselves freeborn citizens were descended from slaves. This extraordinary sociodemographic reality plays a critical role in the history of freedom. For it meant that for the first time in history we find a society in which the great majority of free persons cherished the value of personal freedom in the most literal sense of liberation from enslavement. The evidence that they did so is abundant, coming from the most substantial source of data on Rome: namely, the large number of tomb inscriptions in which freedmen, and sometimes their masters on their behalf, celebrated the most important event in their life, an event that was to remain a source of pride to their descendants: the simple fact that they had been manumitted.[32]

When it was considered that this population resided at the center of a world empire, the importance of this development becomes even greater, for not only did all roads lead to Rome, but all important values held at the metropolitan center traveled out to the farthest corners of the Roman empire. One important way in which the high valuation of freedom was diffused is implicit in the status of freedmen in the conquered provinces. However much they may have been socially despised by the Roman aristocracy in Rome itself, all freedmen were ranked higher than all conquered freeborn provincials. Thus a man of provincial birth having "tasted Roman civilization at its fountain-head, albeit through slavery," was "better off than his countryman who was free-born but lived in an unprivileged part of the world."[33] The demonstration effect was not lost on the provinces. It was so great that, if we are to believe Petronius, some free persons may have willingly endured the temporary social death of slavery in order to experience later the sweet delights of being freed into Roman citizenship.[34]

In Rome itself the freedman's view of the world clearly became the dominant one among the mass of people, and was also highly influential among the elite. We have already noted that the freedmen completely dominated the economic life in Rome: their laissez-faire approach to life, their emphasis on competition, individualism, and personal drive became the norm for the economically productive population.

In the political life of the late republic, freedmen formed the majority of the urban tribes and were the main source of support for the Populares. They dominated the demonstrations and formed a majority of the *collegia* which were critical in the politics of the time.[35] But they were also influential among the Optimates, for not only did rich freedmen act as agents, confidants, and go-betweens for many of the conservative politicians, but in their roles as their wet nurses and nannies (the *nutrix*), pedagogues and courtesans, and confidants in league with them against the *senex*, or master of the household, they would have instilled many of their values in members of the upper classes during their most formative years. These relationships, especially that between slave tutor and adolescent master, are stock themes in Roman comedy of the late republic.[36] Stanley F. Bonner has persuasively shown that "apart from members of the family, it was the slave, or freedman, rather than the freeborn citizen, who did most to lay the foundations of education for Roman children."[37]

In religious life we find the same strong influence of freedmen. It is significant that even in the state cult, where their participation was confined by the establishment, their one important role was intimately concerned with the value they placed on freedom. It may seem paradoxical that the cult of the Lares was one of the traditional household cults of Rome which had gradually been assigned to the household slaves. Indeed, the term *Lar* was in early times applied to Aeneas as the ancestor of the Roman people.[38] The gods were also associated with the farm and the crossroads and, more generally, with boundaries, and, it has been suggested, with the human sacrifice of slaves.[39] The association attests not only to the antiquity of slavery in Rome but to the primitive practice of incorporating the slave as a fictive member of the household. Archetypally, the slave was a person who had been stripped of his natal kinship ties, and to be so deprived in any kin-based society was to be socially killed. Later the slave was reincorporated on the margin of society as a fictive kinsman in his master's household. He or she was forced to worship and accept as his or her own the most natal and ancestral spirits of the master: those of his dead ancestors.

Though socially dead, the slave retained the hope of rebirth into freedom. Here again the symbolic potency of the Lares cult speaks to the extraordinary sociological genius of the Romans, and also suggests that their emphasis on manumission may have been far more ancient than is normally allowed. One of the most important aspects of the Lares cult, as we have noted, was the gods' association with the cross-roads, symbolizing transition: "the oldest attested sphere of activity was at the boundary."[40] Originally, before it came to be associated with the slaves, the transition would have involved the most important of all rites of passage, that between life and death, the world of the living and that of the ancestors. The slave, as a socially dead person, existed in a permanent state of transition: socially dead, yet physically alive; an instrument, yet a vocal one; a two-legged beast, yet with a mind and soul; a physically separate being, yet no more than a living surrogate of the master. What more appropriate gods to worship than those of the crossroads? If in the worship of the Lares he was forced to look backward upon his deracination and incorporation into the ancestral spirit of another tribe, he was also encouraged to look the other way: at the possibility of his manumission, his rebirth into not only freedom but citizenship, the extraordinary prize it brought with it.

By the middle of the second century B.C. during the period of celebration of the Lares, slaves were allowed to give up the slavish mannerisms expected of them and act like freeborn persons, and "the cult leaders were also allowed for the duration to wear senatorial dress of purple-bordered toga, and like magistrates, were accompanied by two lictors."[41] In the late republican era, slaves increasingly looked in this direction. And so the Lares cult came to take on the association of life and freedom rather than death and loss of ancestry. More and more, this once most natal of Roman cults became appropriated by the freedman population as its own special cult. As this happened not only was the native population pushed aside but in the city of Rome, the slave, while still a slave, was relegated to minor roles.[42] Freedmen, in their desperate need not only to be free but to have a sense of belonging, took this cult as their very own.[43] Their masters, with astonishing social perspicacity, allowed them to do so.

With the establishment of the principate, this remarkable sociological episode in Roman religious life was taken one step further. Augustus, with quiet political genius, then linked the worship of the Lares with his own divinity and made it the special area of the state religion controlled by the freedmen. It is important to note that this was the only aspect of emperor worship sanctioned in Rome itself. The two traditional spirits of the Lares were joined with the *genius*, or living spirit, of the emperor to form a divine trinity, the Lares Augusti, and for the next two centuries the cult, under the direction of freedmen, became a vital part of Rome's state religion. By making the sevirate (the higher offices in the Lares state cult) "the highest object of a freedman's ambition," Augustus shrewdly joined all the energies and devotion of the most vital element of the population to his worship.[44] The highest achievement of freedom was the privilege of worshiping the emperor. Not so subtly suggested was the oriental and Delphic idea that the only true freedom came from enslavement to a god, a generous god who then, by not exercising this power of mastership, allowed effective freedom backed by his almighty power. We shall have more to say on this later when we consider the emperor's view of freedom.

Note the extraordinary symbolic power implicit in the divine trinity of the Lares Augusti and its close relationship with slavery and freedom. The traditional Lares, as we noted earlier, represented both the socially dead slave and the socially reborn freedman. Now standing above and fusing both was the living spirit of the benevolent father and savior, the kind master whose genius made possible the transition from one state to the next. Slave, master, and freedman were joined together in a single symbolic process of imperial salvation. What traditionally had merely been a few festive days of Saturnalian reversal now became a permanent possibility and a social reality. Most slaves could now look forward to the reality of freedom during their lives; and the ambitious freedman could look forward to the day when, if not he himself, his son could be a senator; already under Augustus Imperial Freedmen exercised extraordinary power. Surviving inscriptions leave us in no doubt that this was the interpretation of the Augustan Lares among the Greek-speaking devotees of the emperor, a view which would have been shared by the predominantly Greek-speaking successful freedmen of Rome who officiated at the rites of the Lares Augusti. One of them reads as follows:

> Immortal Nature, after Overwhelming Benefactions, has Bestowed on Men the Greatest Good of all. She has given the Emperor Augustus, who is not only the Father of his Country, Rome, Giver of Happiness to our Lives, but also the Fatherly God and Savior of all Mankind. It is He whose Providence has not only Fulfilled but even Surpassed the Prayers of all. For Land and Sea lie at Peace and the Cities bloom with the Flowers of Order, Concord and Prosperity.[45]

And for the slaves there was something too. They had the realistic hope not only of manumission and the dignity of serving in minor offices in the state cult but also of sanctuary while still slaves. For any slave who felt ill treated and wished to change his master could throw himself on the statue of the emperor and claim his divine *clementia*:

"Caesar was there to protect the rights of the underprivileged against injustice."[46]

Freedmen were also active in other native cults such as the Fortuna and Mens Bona, one which, not surprisingly, specialized in the promotion of careers. "In all these activities of freedmen," writes Susan Treggiari, "in priestly colleges, pagi and vici, and private trade or funerary colleges, one can surely see an urge to assert themselves in a society in which many of them were strangers."[47] A distinction must be made between these more "bourgeois" cults, to use Franz Bömer's term, and the cults more favored by the slaves and lower-class freedmen. Of these, the most important was undoubtedly the cult of Silvanus, which by late republican times was adhered to only by slaves and poor freedmen. There was never a state cult of Silvanus, so he was never seen as a ruling-class god. Silvanus was liked because he was a *rusticus*, poorly dressed and powerless. He was a god not of resistance but of resignation. Worship in the Silvanus cult was more individualistic, slaves were more in control, and the colleges (*collegia silvani*) were small congregations focused on different purposes such as gladiatorial contests and funerals.[48] Though the most popular one in imperial Rome, the cult of Silvanus was decidedly not the cult of the upwardly mobile freedman.

Freedmen were not content to worship only in the state and other native cults. They bombarded Rome with their own, foreign cults; or, perhaps more often, they converted in great numbers to the foreign cults of other strangers. Garnsey and Saller have pointed out that "Roman receptiveness to alien religions is a feature of the early and middle Republic and of no other period."[49] After that the Romans tended to be either hostile to new cults, especially when they seemed subversive, or grudgingly tolerated those they considered harmless.

The freedmen and their slave ancestors introduced nearly all the alien religions that came to dominate the spiritual life of the populace; eventually, it was one of these alien religions which was peculiarly their own, Christianity, that triumphed in the late Roman world. All of these so-called mystery religions bore the dominant value of the slave and the freedman: their emphasis on salvation and spiritual freedom.

One should be careful, however, not to simplify too much. Although the great majority of these mystery cults were religions of salvation, offering comfort and release from the travails of the real world, a few of them were religions of success and mobility. These, too, were dominated by freedmen. Indeed, it may be useful to distinguish between two kinds of cults, on the basis of the nature of their relationship to the real world. Following R. L. Gordon, we may speak of those, the majority, which were world denying and those which were world affirming.[50]

The typical religion of salvation was world denying. It promoted the spiritual and, often, the emotional freedom of the individual: the former in a projected afterlife and in the assertion of the superior reality of the spiritual life, the latter in orgiastic ritual. The classic case of such a cult was one of the earliest of these religions to invade Rome, the Dionysian mystery cult. A sanitized version of it may have existed in Rome several centuries before the sensational events of the early second century B.C. In typical Roman fashion it had been assimilated into the state religion; nonetheless, it is significant that even this early Romanized version known as the cult of Dionysus Liber was the patron of liberty.[51] The version of the cult which the Roman authorities ruthlessly repressed in 186 was the authentic Hellenistic version. The cult appealed to all those who "had been uprooted, ruined, or treated unkindly by life in some other way." This meant not only slaves but many less successful freedmen, uprooted peasants, and, significantly, women, especially freedwomen.[52]

If their experience in this life was painful, initiation into the Dionysiac mysteries gave them an assurance that, after death, they would enter into a blissful immortality. Meanwhile, even in the painful life in this world, entry into a Bacchic thiasos gave the outcast initiate something like a substitute for his former place in civil society. In the Dionysiac religious fraternity, secular distinctions of birth, rank, and wealth were transcended. Most attractive of all, the Bacchic ecstasy gave the devotee a license and an opportunity to retaliate against the society that, as he saw it, had treated him so badly.[53]

This retaliation was rarely political. Rather, it took the form of sexual license and unconventional behavior. For women this was particularly important, and there is every reason to believe that the sexual-liberation aspect of the cult is what most offended the Roman establishment. Otherwise it is impossible to explain why the Roman upper class was prepared to accept the cult of Magna Mater, one that was even more orgiastic, but dominated by men. Clearly, it was not sexual freedom that offended the Roman establishment—which by the later republic was to become one of the most licentious in the history of mankind—but the experience of such freedom by women and the lowly.

Much tamer was the slave and freedmen appropriation of the cult of Zeus Eleutherios, which had originally been assimilated by the Roman ruling class and made into a state cult. After 200 B.C., the god was stripped of his association with Greek national freedom and transformed into a god of personal freedom by the slaves and freedmen, many of them no doubt Greek slaves. A hybrid god, Jupiter Liber, was formed, his worship reaching a high point about A.D. 200, after which it declined and he became mainly a literary divinity.[54] Slaves and freedmen, but more the former, were also very keen on Fortuna, the goddess who would one day reverse everything.[55]

At the other extreme were those mystery religions which were not responses to deprivation but rather confirmations of success in the system. These tended to be world affirming, even if their theologies had notions of escape to a spiritual world. Such escape came as the ultimate confirmation or reward for earlier material and personal struggles and triumphs. Most important of all, instead of offering compensation or substitution for the real world, this other extreme of mystery religion offered a spiritual replication of it. The classic such mystery religion was Mithraism, which arrived in Rome in the second century A.D.—the last such cult from the East. By now, the situation was radically different from that of the early second century B.C. with its chaotic post-Hannibalic deprivations. Freedmen were preponderant in the economic life of Rome and its imperial administration; and the sons of freedmen constituted the majority of the centurion ranks of the army. Thus we are not surprised to learn that Mithraism was dominated by freedmen and the centurion classes in the army and that it was also the religion of choice among the imperial freedmen.

Mithraism was a kind of early Calvinism—the religion of the upwardly mobile and successful. Its organizational structure mirrored the hierarchical nature of Roman society, especially the army. Corresponding to the emperor was the father-leader of the cult, whose word was law. Below him was an elaborate system of grades, "which established the social and religious identity (within the cult) of every member, prescribed his ritual behavior, and set limits upon his access to complete purity and full knowledge."[56] Significantly, it was antifemale; alone among the mystery religions, it completely excluded women. At the same time, the religious values promoted by the cult reinforced those promoted by the Roman elite among the middle ranks of leadership: loyalty, honesty, cooperativeness, and identification with the master. The emphasis on fraternity was unusual. Bömer claims that no other ancient religion, except Christianity, used the term *brother* to describe coreligionists as frequently as members of the Mithras cult did.[57] These were the classic ideals of the highly motivated slave expecting his freedom and of the successful freedman in search of higher promotion. The success ethic of the cult was given religious expression in its theodicy of good fortune.

While Mithraism was very much concerned with freedom, its treatment of the value was fascinating and unique. This comes out clearly when we examine the central paradox of the cult: although it had a highly developed theodicy of success and good fortune and was very world affirming, it nonetheless, like all the other mystery religions, gave in its theology an equally central place to the idea of the soul's escape from the constraints of the physical world. Gordon has written,

> For some . . . Mithraism was closely concerned with the issue of power (and so of coercion). Yet attainment of power in the community involved, by its very nature, escape from the constraints of the world: the gratification of Fatherhood lay in the success of the flight as much as in the domination of his religious subordinates.[58]

Gordon does not satisfactorily explain this paradox. He tells us that, for the devotee, escape was "a serious, indeed desperate undertaking" and that it permitted a kind of denial of death. While this may be so, it does not explain why a cult of material success which reified the established social order should have been so concerned with the escape of the soul into the far stratosphere. It is all the more puzzling when it is considered that there is no hope of immortality in Mithraism.

What the theology of Mithraism tried to do was to conflate the slave's conception of personal freedom, as pure escape, with the successful freedman's assimilation of his master's view of sovereignal freedom as power and paternal integration. Note that most freedmen were not successful. The typical one would have been the proletarian man on the Roman street trying hard to make ends meet, or the petty trader or the craftsman just about coping with a life-style a cut above that of the rabble.[59] The typical freedman, then, remained close to his slave roots both literally—he may have had a spouse or kinsman still in slavery—and spiritually. Thus the slave ethos remained with him. He would have taken into freedom the passion for pure personal freedom which had motivated him all his life. It was this ordinary kind of freedman who dominated the popular consciousness of Rome and made personal freedom and independence the dominant value of the masses. Indeed, the Mithras cult seems to have held a special attraction for persons in what Bömer has described as "the shadowy zones between slave and free."[60]

But there was a minority of highly successful freedmen, those who achieved not only personal freedom but much of the power and wealth of their former masters—indeed, those who, like the imperial freedmen under Claudius, exercised power over some of the noblest of patrician Romans. Many of these would have continued to hold on to the value of personal liberty. But at the same time they would also naturally have identified with the master class's conception of sovereignal freedom as an organic force, not simply out of the desire to imitate but because they were now some of the greatest slaveholders themselves. Thus in the successful freedman master we find the union of the two versions of freedom generated by slavery. Mithraism became the favored religion of this class of men precisely because it brought together both conceptions of freedom and both value systems of Rome: that of freedom as power and organic integration under the wise father, and that of freedom as escape and of the denial of death, the death denied being not that of the body, as Gordon has surmised, but the social death of the slave.

Consistent with this interpretation is another important feature of Mithraism which remains otherwise unexplained: its strong emphasis on rebirth. Mithras' mythic struggle with, and slaughter of, the white bull made salvation and rebirth possible. This is the central charter myth of the cult. What more perfect myth for a class of liberated freedmen! Mithras' triumph had freed them from the death of slavery and led to their rebirth into freedom; and this freedom they now used to replicate his struggle, and to achieve their own triumph, expressed in success in the secular world and the position of father-leader, or some high grade, within the religious community.

In addition to their influence on the political and religious life of Rome, freedmen also critically influenced the secular values of Roman society, in both its low and its high culture. It is remarkable that modern historians of the freedmen have either distorted their secular influence or entirely missed what was certainly their most important contribution to the secular values of Rome. It is conventional to emphasize their materialism.[61] That the wealthy freedmen were materialistic and ostentatious, there can be no doubt. What is surprising about the historical commentary, however, is the slavish acceptance of the Roman upper class's contemptuous view of the freedmen. Surprising not only because it is such bad history but because it neglects the screamingly obvious: that the native Roman elite was arguably one of the most rapaciously materialistic and ostentatious in the entire history of ruling classes. It is the plutocratic elite which is the main source of Roman materialism.[62]

While Treggiari, in her fine study of the freedmen, does not make the mistake of attributing Roman ostentation to the group, she nonetheless fails to take into account the most important influence of the freedmen on Roman secular values, namely, the fact that they made the idea of personal freedom the dominant one among the Roman masses and also influenced the elite in adopting the inner version of this value. The evidence that they did so is overwhelming. As we have already noted, the inscriptions they erected constitute one of the most important bodies of evidence on Rome, and the single, all-important message of these inscriptions is that being freed, and experiencing personal freedom, is the most important thing in life. Further, it is striking that all freedmen, of all classes and political persuasions, shared this strongly held value.

First, consider the unfortunate Trimalchio, the subject of one of the great masterpieces of satiric literature.[63] The apotheosis of the *nouveau riche*, conceited, pretentious, and ostentatiously wealthy, Trimalchio is so delightfully vulgar that he is almost camp. But as we laugh with Petronius at Trimalchio's expense, we should be very careful not to miss what is perhaps the most striking thing about this rich buffoon: that he is not ashamed of his past, that the very first thing his astonished guests see as they enter his palace is indeed a mural depicting Trimalchio's life, from his being auctioned off as a slave to his entry into Rome, with long hair and holding Mercury's staff in his hand while being led by Minerva, and to his apprenticeship, promotion, and eventual ascent into heaven, raised by Mercury up by the chin, as Fortuna blows her horn and the three Fates twist their golden threads. When the laughter fades, one comes to the sudden realization that in no other slave society in the history of the world would a successful freedman paint such a mural. Unlike the freedmen of Greece before them, unlike the freedmen of Islam or the free blacks of the American South and Latin America centuries afterward, all of whom shunned the crushing memory of their enslavement and sought, wherever they could, to "pass" quietly into the free society, Trimalchio anticipates the gravestones of his less wealthy compatriots by celebrating his enslavement and his emancipation in the entry hall of his palace. It is as if he were shouting aloud that slavery was almost worth the suffering for what it made possible: freedom and opportunity in Rome. Indeed, that is precisely the view of one of the characters in the novel.

Let us now move from the freedman Trimalchio to a second-generation freedman, the poet Horace. In so doing, we not only shift back a couple of generations but seem to enter a wholly different world and move into the presence of someone who, both then and now, would be regarded as the very antithesis of Trimalchio. Horace was not just Rome's greatest and most popular poet before he died; he became the quintessence of the civilized Roman: a friend and protégé of the powerful Maecenas, admired by the emperor and his circle, Horace came to define all that was most prized in the Roman literary tradition. Indeed, his works were being used by Latin teachers as training manuals in the cultivation of young Roman nobles within a century after his death. What could such a person possibly have in common with the vulgar Trimalchio?

One thing only, but for both men, the most important thing in life: a paradoxical pride in their slave ancestry and in their liberation. Horace made no attempt to "pass." To the contrary, he revered his freedman father. One gets the distinct impression that the reverence for freedom was passed down from father to son like an heirloom. Horace was the least systematic, and the most occasional, of writers.[64] Nonetheless, on the subject of freedom and ancestry, he is sharply focused, unusually serious, and, in one case, so startlingly assertive that he is almost rude to his patron.

Horace's discussion of his gratitude to his father has been celebrated as one of the finest expressions of filial devotion in all literature. That may be so, but for me the fascinating and truly telling feature of the passage is Horace's insistence that he is not only not ashamed of his slave ancestry but indeed so proud of it, and so convinced that *its negation was a positive good*, in his father's and, by extension, his own life, that if he had had the power to choose his past, he would have chosen the one he had all over again, including, by implication, slavery. The passage deserves to be cited at length. I begin at the point where Horace, having attributed everything of merit in his character to his father's kindness and guidance, continues,

While I have sense, I will never regret such a father; Nor will I
Plead my defense like so many who mourn that it was not through any
Fault of their own that they missed having parents both famous and free-born.
My line of thought and my manner of speaking are wholly at odds with
Those people's. If, indeed, after attaining one age or another,
Nature's command were to live to that state of existence a second
Time, giving each of us freedom to choose other parents to suit our
Vanities, I would be perfectly happy with mine; I would not want
New ones entitled to escorts and chairs of authority. Vulgar judgements may
say I am "crazy," but "sane" will perhaps be what *you* would
Call my refusal to shoulder—unpracticed—a burden so dreary.[65]

Horace then goes on to spell out the burdens of a great pedigree, chief of which are the demands on personal freedom which living a haughty life-style made, and this he contrasts with his *modest* contentment, in which "three slaves suffice" him at supper. He concludes with the conviction that, because of his origins, he was able to "live a more pleasant existence/Than if [his] grandfather, father, and uncle had all served as quaestors."

Horace leaves us in no doubt that, of the vast range of subjects on which he so genially conversed, there was one—and one only—on which he was prepared to be serious to the point of abrasiveness. The seventh of his first collection of epistles stands out sharply from all the other verse letters. It is addressed to his extremely generous patron, Maecenas, and Horace suddenly departs from his inherently mellow, relaxed good humor and launches into a quite unprovoked defense of his freedom and independence in relation to the man whose only fault was to have supported him handsomely, but who, in so doing, threatened Horace with the one thing he dreaded most, his loss of independence, even the very hint of its possibility. In the inset parable of the fox who ate so much in the barn into which he had stolen that he could not get back through the hole whereby he had entered, Horace expresses his fear of losing his own freedom because of too much dependence on his patron and makes it clear that, should he become convinced that that was indeed so, he would immediately return everything his patron had given him. Between the vulgar murals of Trimalchio and the high poetry of Horace there is a nearly unbridgeable gulf of cultural form but, in one crucial respect, also an identical substance of meaning: slavery, by making freedom possible, creates the greatest possible value.

In the course of this discussion we have occasionally referred to the role of women in the institutionalization of personal freedom. Let us close by focusing on them. The triumph of personal liberty during the period we have covered was as much the work of freedwomen as freedmen. This should come as no surprise, for even in classical Athens the freedwoman enjoyed a considerable level of personal freedom. "It would probably be a safe guess," Moses Finley has written, "that women of the lower classes were more 'emancipated', more equal *de facto* if not in strict law, more widely accepted as persons in their own right than their richer, more bourgeois, or more aristocratic sisters." This is true of women in most urban societies, but especially so under conditions of large-scale slavery which, "alone—and specifically their experience, as females, while they were slaves—would have been enough to give them, and their men, a somewhat different attitude towards the accepted, traditional, upper-class values. Add economic necessity, slum conditions, the fact that their work was serious and not a pastime, and the rest follows."[66] Unfortunately, lower-class Roman women left no written records, so we can only guess how they felt about their condition and their freedom. We know from the evidence of writers from other classes, and from their tombstones, that childhood was short and grim,[67] and their life expectancy would in all likelihood have been lower than that of upper-class women.

We also know from the comparative data on slavery that for women everywhere slavery was, in a perverse way, also liberating.[68] For not only did it generate equally the love of personal liberty, but, by debasing both sexes indiscriminately it reduced both to a condition of gender equality. Men were emasculated and women defeminized, although not desexualized. The roles of father and husband were more vulnerable than that of mother, precisely because they were more socially determined. Hence under Roman law the mother, if a slave, determined the status of the child, in contrast with the children of free persons whose status was determined by the father.[69] Since the only recognized kinship tie was the uterine one, this meant that women always had a wider network of primary kinsmen on which to draw in their bid for emancipation. The bond between mothers and daughters was especially powerful in all slave societies, and Rome was no exception. One of the most moving epitaphs from this period, found in Reate, was written by a freedwoman for her daughter:

> Stop, traveler, and read what is written here. A mother was not allowed to enjoy her only daughter. Some god, I don't know which, begrudged her to me. Since I, her mother, was not allowed to dress her while she was still alive, I performed this task as was fitting after she died, when her time on earth was over. A mother has honored with this memorial the daughter whom she loved.[70]

Sexual ties were also likely to favor the manumission of women, both through their relations with male members of the master's family and freed or free male lovers outside the household, especially when it is considered that, in all likelihood, male slaves outnumbered females.[71] Finally, quite apart from sexual relations, gender tended to place the female slave in closer ties of intimacy with members of the master's household. Because free women spent most of their time in the household, and because further, status tended to be less severe an obstacle in relations between women than between men, close relations were more likely to develop between slave and free women. Such relations were also more likely between slave women and free men in the household, not only in the slave's role as concubine, but in her role as mother surrogate.

Upper-class Roman women were unusually reluctant to breast-feed their children; the result was that the nurse was usually a slave or *liberta*, and only occasionally a free woman of humble birth.[72] Keith Bradley has cautioned us not to romanticize the relationship between the *nutrix* and her nursling.[73] Agreed; especially when we read remarks like Cicero's that "it seems as if we drank in deception with our nurse's milk."[74] But when all is said and done, human beings will tend to behave humanly, especially when powerful impulses are set in motion, as they are in the primal act of suckling an infant, any infant, and being nursed by a woman, any woman. Cicero, as Bradley notes, was in a morbid mood when he wrote the passage cited above; it is perhaps of greater significance that, for all his hard-hearted conservatism, Cicero's relations with his slaves and freedmen were "as near ideal as could be expected."[75] True, we hear nothing of the female slaves, but that was because he never had reason to mention the humbler slaves in his letters. It is a serious mistake to assume that his devoted business manager, research assistant, and biographer, Tiro, was typical of the freedmen and freedwomen of Cicero's day, or even of Cicero's household.[76] While it was unusual for a Roman to pension off his old nurse with a small estate, as the Younger Pliny had done, Pliny's attitude toward the old woman was perhaps more the norm for upper-class Romans. In his letter to the man who had taken over the management of the estate for the old woman, he wrote: "You must remember that it is not trees and soil with which I have entrusted you (although I've done that too), but rather a gift that I had made, and that is as important to me who gave it as to her who received it, that it should be as profitable as possible."[77]

But what of the women of the upper classes? How free were they in this (personally) freest of premodern societies? It is hard to find a subject on which there is greater disagreement among historians of ancient Rome. Finley was firmly of the view that upper-class Roman women lived highly circumscribed lives: legal inferiors who were deliberately denied even a personal name because "women were not, or ought not to be, genuine individuals but only fractions of a family. Anonymous and passive fractions at that, for the virtues which were stressed were decorum, chastity, gracefulness, even temper and childbearing."[78] Jo-Ann Shelton has recently restated this view: "A woman had only a private life: she was somebody's daughter, somebody's wife, or somebody's mother." Women were valued only in the performance of these roles, were always under the guardianship of a man, and had to defer to men in all aspects of life. Their children could be exposed without their consent, and they lost custody upon divorce.[79]

While this was undoubtedly the male ideal, and in many respects the legal norm,[80] we find a radically different situation reflected both in the literature of the late republic and early principate, and in the behavior of the upper-class women. A great deal depends on what period one has in mind as the standard by which to measure the condition of upper-class Roman women; it is obviously anachronistic to use the status of modern Western middle-class women as one's yardstick. Compared with the condition of women in the early republic, in classical Greece and indeed, in any other period between the end of the second century A.D. and the early twentieth century except the late twelfth and thirteenth centuries, Roman upper-class women were, in fact, and to a considerable extent in law, the freest of all women. Fritz Schulz has called the classical law of marriage "the most imposing achievement of the Roman legal genius, a law founded on a purely humanistic idea of marriage as being a free and freely dissoluble union of two equal partners for life."[81] While the traditional institution in which the wife was *in manu mariti*—that is, under the complete legal control of her husband—persisted in theory and may have been practiced by a few couples, the norm by the late republic was the *sui iuris* or "free marriage" in which the wife was an independent legal personality. Under one of the most common legal forms of the traditional system of marriage, *coemptio*, the woman was sold, or sold herself, *nummo uno*, to her husband. This smacked of slavery; indeed, it was entirely modeled on the legal condition of children and slaves, and the fact that it was stated explicitly that the woman was sold, not as a slave but *matrimonii causa*, was little consolation. Women of the late republic rejected it precisely because it symbolically and legally reduced them to the status of slaves.[82]

Eva Cantarella speaks of a "new type of woman" appearing during the first century B.C., and goes on to show that important limitations had been placed on *patria potestas* by the end of the republic; that "rarely in history" had divorce been easier and, what is more remarkable, had women been given more equal rights in initiating divorce, and suffered fewer penalties for so doing: "The point here is that despite the undeniable double standard there was progress represented by the new configuration of marriage and the granting of new freedoms to women."[83] This radical change was best reflected in the dotal laws. While the husband, in theory, continued to have control over the woman's dowry, by Augustus' period severe constraints were placed on his capacity to alienate this property, and, of equal importance, the dowry reverted to the wife in the event of a divorce.[84] This and other changes led to a situation in which women made "full use of the law to end unhappy marriages and contract new ones. They practiced birth control and abortion, formed freely chosen amorous bonds, lived outside of matrimony, and enjoyed a new liberty that had been absolutely unthinkable—sexual freedom."[85] We know from the behavior of elite women that they greatly valued their freedom. Thus there was strong opposition to Augustus' moral and social legislation, even though its main purpose was more to maintain the hereditary legitimacy of the senatorial class than to limit divorces and strengthen the conjugal bond.[86] It is astonishing, even by modern feminist standards of political behavior, that upper-class women were so outraged by the laws controlling adultery, and their double standards. During Tiberius' reign several of them, as a form of protest, officially registered themselves with the aediles as prostitutes because the law excluded that category of women from prosecution.[87]

Further proof that times had indeed changed for women is found in the viciously misogynistic literature that accompanied these developments, most notably that of Juvenal. As we have seen in the case of Hesiod's world, men are only moved to write nasty things about women when women are quite obviously out of place.[88] In addition to the misogynistic literature, however, there existed, in the writings of the Roman elegists—writers such as Catullus, Tibullus, Propertius, and Ovid—what Judith Hallett has called a "counter-cultural feminism." These writers were opposed to the traditional ideal of the submissive woman and claimed that the changes, while seeming to improve the condition of women, were meant mainly to exploit them more effectively.[89]

While it is true that the changes in the condition of upper-class women benefited some men, it does not necessarily follow that women were made more vulnerable by these changes; there is more than a touch of cynicism in these elegists, and one is surprised to find Hallett taking them at their word. Hallett herself came to recognize this in her fascinating study of elite Roman women. There, she shows that the unusual importance of women in Roman social and political life was due to the structural centrality of the Roman upper-class family in the social and political life of Rome. Demographic, political, and legal changes created a situation in which women in their roles as mothers, older married sisters, aunts, and father's daughters achieved great emotional and social importance. Within the household this was achieved partly at the expense of the conjugal bond, which became tense and fragile, and was both the cause and effect of the high divorce rate.[90]

In the society at large, the main factor at play was the chronic male emphasis on patron-client relationships. The two most effective ways in which a powerful man could patronize, and control, a bright younger man on the make were to marry him off to his daughter or to adopt him, or, best of all, do both.[91] This lent great political importance to the role of father's daughter. When, to this, was added the strong emotional tie between the two—due partly to the weakness of the conjugal tie, and the competitive tension inherent in the father-son relationship—the conditions were ripe for the emergence of what Hallett calls "filiafocality." She writes that "elite Roman society accorded the role of father's daughter a strikingly positive image: bestowing attention and value upon individual daughters; culturally emphasizing and elaborating the daughter's role within the family."[92] She insists, further, that the importance of the father-daughter role did not derive from the more mature familial female roles such as mother and elder, married sister, but rather the opposite: the structural centrality of these roles, and hence of women in Roman society, resulted "from their initial valuation as their fathers' daughters."[93]

We have already seen that the growth of slavery had a direct effect on the liberation of the mass of lower-class women. The question we must now ask is whether the growth in slavery was in any way connected with the liberation of their elite counterpart. We think it was, and Hallett's study supports that position, but she fails to make the full connection.

We have observed that the daughter under the *potestas* of her father in traditional times preceding the late republic, and in preclassical law, was in a legal condition nearly identical with that of a child and "the status of a child in power was actually similar to that of a slave."[94] *Patria potestas*, "the fundamental institution of the Romans which shaped and directed their world-view or *Weltanschauung*," weighed most heavily on the daughter among free members of the traditional household.[95] She could be exposed as an infant, killed with legal impunity by the *pater familias*, sold into slavery, betrothed and symbolically sold against her will to a husband under whose power she then fell completely, being subjected to *manus mariti*. Sons, it is true, were also under the *potestas* of the father, but there were important differences. For one thing, the grown-up son could initiate claims on his own, and could be sued, though with some difficulty:

The daughter in power and the slave, however, were accorded no such recognition by the civil law. The daughter was probably altogether incapable of creating any primary contractual liabilities between herself and third parties, and a slave could certainly neither bind himself nor be a party in legal proceedings under civil law rules.[96]

Since women in traditional times were legally assimilated to the status of slaves, it follows that when they were liberated during the late republic they would be legally and socially assimilated to the status of freedpersons.

That is exactly what happened. The elite Roman woman acquired her freedom in much the same way as the freedperson, was so regarded by the person who freed her—her father—and in symbolic, psychological, and moral terms was treated in much the same way. In other words, the emancipation of the elite Roman woman was part and parcel of the triumph of the freedman and his ideal of personal freedom. The legal evidence draws us irresistibly to this conclusion.

First, consider the dotal laws. These, we have pointed out earlier, were the foundation of women's emancipation. It will be recalled that the peculium was the means by which most slaves won their freedom in Rome at this time, especially among the industrious slaves of the elite *familia*. It is remarkable that the legal-economic means by which the emancipation of women in free marriages was achieved was the payment of the dowry from the peculium of the *filiafamilias*—the bride herself. It is equally remarkable that the divorced husband was obliged to return this fund to her peculium: "thus both the act of constituting a dowry and the act of returning a dowry might have been accomplished through the peculium."[97]

In effect, the father gave his daughter the gift of freedom from both his own power and that of her husband. He made it legal in the same way that he did with the favored slave he manumitted. The slave's peculium legally belonged to the master, and allowing the slave to use it to buy his freedom meant that the master had given him the gift of the purchase money. The condition of both the freedman and the woman in a free marriage were often expressed in terms of each other. Both entered into a non-*potestas* relationship with the former master or father: "Similar to the wife in classical times, the manumitted slave was no longer tied to the *paterfamilias* by the bonds of *potestas*."[98] Both, being *sui iuris*, were legally free to do as they pleased; it was a basic rule of classical Roman law that "through a person *sui iuris* nothing can be acquired for us."[99]

However, as Kirschenbaum goes on to show, there really was no such thing as a free gift among the Romans.[100] Roman society was the classic exemplification of the Maussian theory of gift exchange: A gift establishes an obligation to reciprocate, and this reciprocation renews the obligation to give, initiating a new cycle of gift exchange in a system of "total prestation." In this way bonds of friendship are extended and intensified.[101] Thus Cicero fully anticipates Mauss when he wrote that

> men, too, are born for the sake of men that they may be able mutually to help one another; in this direction we ought to follow Nature as our guide to contribute to the general good by an interchange of acts of kindness, by giving and receiving, and thus by our skill, our industry and our talents to cement human society more closely together, man to man.[102]

We might add that the same may be true from father to daughter. This is clear not only from Cicero's own excessive preoccupation with his daughter,[103] but from what he writes later in the same work: "repaying a kindness already received takes priority over granting favours with the hope of future kindness; and requiring a favour takes precedence over initiating one."[104] I have shown elsewhere that manumission was symbolically reconfigured in exactly these terms in many societies, Rome being perhaps the most notable case.[105] The elite Roman father symbolically, and legally, refigured his relationship with his "freed" daughter in strikingly similar terms.

Scholars who argue that the elite woman was in a condition of subjection place great emphasis on the absence of individual names among them.[106] A different light is cast on this practice, however, now that the assimilation of the status of the woman in "free marriage" to that of freedperson is brought into focus. Like the manumitted slave, the "freed" daughter carried the name of her father. Thus, when the faithful Tiro was freed by Cicero, he became Marcus Tullius Marci libertus Tiro, meaning Marcus Tullius Tiro, freedman of Marcus Cicero. Similarly, unlike her brother who received his father's *nomen* and *cognomen* as well as an individual first name or *praenomen*, Cicero's daughter was known only by the female form of her father's family name or *nomen*, that is, Tullia.[107] So identical are these forms that in listing a woman's name it was proper to add *f(ilia)* to the genitive of the father's *praenomen* so as not to confuse her with a freedwoman.[108] We have no reason to doubt that women were as proud to be identified as the "freed" daughters of their fathers, as freedmen were to be known as the freedmen of their patrons. That the two developments were closely related, and indeed became models for each other, is supported by a seemingly puzzling historical fact. Women were normally assigned *praenomina* in early Rome; the practice of identifying them only by their father's name emerged late,[109] indeed precisely during the period of the rise of large-scale slavery, and with it, the massive enfranchisement of slaves. It is absurd to imagine that Roman men went out of their way to humiliate and dehumanize their women by depriving them of the right to have their own name at exactly the same period of time when they were busily enacting the most liberal marital and divorce laws in the history of mankind down to the early twentieth century. At the same time, no one has yet offered a satisfactory explanation for this seeming anomaly. Thus Hallett proposes that the practice implied "a symbolic pledge to his daughter's welfare on a father's part."[110] It is not at all clear, however, why such a pledge could not have been made to a child with its own individual name, which is exactly what fathers did for their sons. It is even less clear why the practice of giving girls individual names existed during the early period when the daughter's dependence on her father's pledge of support was far greater. The anomaly vanishes, however, with the explanation I propose. Modeled on the naming practice of enfranchised slaves, calling a woman only by the name of her father was meant to signal to the world that she was personally free, and that the author of her liberation was her proud and giving father, as proud as the generous patron of his devoted freedman.

As in the relationship between freedman and patron, the daughter was expected, in what had now become an extra-*potestas* relationship, to honor and repay his *beneficium* with a new *officium*, a service voluntarily rendered. Sometimes that service might mean the abandonment of her present husband for another man whose career her father wished to promote. There is no need to be squeamish in our judgment on such a reciprocation, as long as it was voluntary. In view of the fragility of the conjugal bond, it is likely that such requests were no great hardship and, indeed, may have been greeted eagerly by daughters bored with husbands going nowhere. In the "total prestation" system that was Roman political culture, a woman with a powerful father and an ambitious husband in her debt was a powerful person indeed.

Perhaps too powerful for the good of her freedom. Although largely excluded from the formal, outer trappings of power, the *virilia officia*, Roman women were able to wield real power precisely because, as Hallett brilliantly shows, such power was exercised within the structurally central domain of the household. Hence, unlike her Greek sisters before her and her late medieval counterparts that followed, elite Roman women were not forced by the pressures of male exclusion from the domain of sovereignal freedom to construct a compassionate, womanly version of personal freedom. As with their menfolk, personal freedom was quickly sublated to sovereignal power, and the results were, as often as not, equally unpleasant for the dominated. For all his bias, Sallust was perhaps not all wrong in his description of Sempronia's adventures as crimes "of masculine daring."[111] Women such as Servilia, the mother of Brutus and mistress of the man he assassinated; Mark Antony's wife, Fulvia; and the notorious Julio-Claudian women, all exercised the most ruthless form of sovereignal freedom. Ronald Syme has described the behavior of the twelve "princesses and court ladies" of the Julio-Claudian period as "a portentous story of ambition and crime, or folly and misfortune."[112] It is a tale equally portentous for the history of freedom. What does it mean that women, once given the chance, could so horribly have sublated their personal freedom into monsters of sovereignal power such as Agrippina? Her murderous reign through the husband she later poisoned was, according to Tacitus, "a stringent and masculine despotism," arrogant in public and with "no sort of immodesty at home, unless it conducted to power."[113] We can only hope that they were not typical of their class of women; they were certainly not typical of all Roman women who came to experience and enjoy their personal emancipation.

To conclude, then, in early imperial Rome personal freedom became the supreme value of the vast majority of the city that ruled civilized Europe, including its working and elite women. And what is more, the emperor, in whom supreme power was concentrated, reinforced this value even as he abolished civic freedom.

But what did Augustus hope to gain by wielding his awesome power in support of personal liberty? We have already stated our belief that his support for the expansion of personal freedom was genuine. Suetonius' frequently cited view that "to keep the people pure and unsullied by any taint of foreign or servile blood, he was most chary of conferring Roman citizenship and set a limit on manumission"[114] was tendentious racist nonsense, embraced for too long by reactionary historians of Rome.[115] As Kathleen Atkinson has persuasively demonstrated, had it been Augustus' policy to restrict manumission and repurify the Roman people—whatever that may have been—then these laws were in hopeless conflict with his marriage laws and, what is more important, had the opposite effect of what had been intended. The joint, long-term consequence of both sets of laws was to greatly increase the freed population of citizens,[116] and Augustus, whatever his moral failings, was neither a racist nor an incompetent legislator. His laws on marriage and manumission "indicate the systematic working out of the same general policy, which was to *encourage* the acquisition of Roman citizenship by the freedmen who would be likely to play a useful part in the general fabric of Roman society."[117]

But what exactly was Augustus' conception of his own freedom, and how was it related to the freedom of the populace? I will attempt to answer these questions in the next chapter.

The Augustan Compromise: Sovereignal Freedom in Defense of Personal Liberty

Augustus' support for the personal liberty of the masses was a political precondition for the promotion of his own version of *libertas*, namely, the Roman version of sovereignal freedom in its organic form. In Rome it was embedded in the imperial concept of *auctoritas*. Since this is the note that came to dominate the European chord of freedom for over fifteen hundred years, it is important that we look more closely at the views of the man who laid the secular groundwork for its later ascendancy.

Augustus' official autobiography, the *Res gestae divi Augusti*, may not have told the whole truth, but there can be no doubt that it told a part of it. It is therefore highly significant for the history of freedom that the very first sentence of the *Gestae* reads, ''At the age of nineteen on my own responsibility and at my own expense I raised an army, with which I successfully championed the liberty to the republic when it was oppressed by the tyranny of a faction.''[1] What did Augustus mean by the word *liberty* here? Obviously not the civic freedom of the Roman nobility. No one took seriously his claim to have restored the republic.

Augustus had as his ultimate model of freedom the patron-freedman relationship. Like the good master, he had used his power wisely, first to control and then to liberate the Roman people. It is important to understand that Augustus saw his interaction with the Roman people as something that moved between the two relationships of master (-slave) and liberator (-freedman). The best evidence for this comes from the propaganda imprinted on the coins issued over the long period of his rise to power and reign. In his authoritative study of the numismatic evidence, Michael Grant has shown that there were two basic periods in Augustus' political life, distinguished by two fundamentally different bases of rule.[2]

First, there was the period of his rise to power, in which his conception of the relationship would have been identical with that of his adoptive father, Caesar. The triumphant ruler during this period was *imperator*, which was unambiguous in its meaning: "Irrespective of salutations, it signified the Commander, i.e. the holder of a particularly important imperium."[3] Naked force, the control of the army, was the basis of the relationship between ruler and ruled during this period. The ruler might use his power wisely, of course, as Augustus certainly thought his adoptive father and he himself, during the triumvirate, had done. But, in the final analysis, his rule had no greater or lesser legitimacy than that of the slave master over his slave.

This is what Augustus sought to change, in 27 B.C., when he finally assumed complete and exclusive rule. From then until his death, the basis of his rule was *auctoritas*. The title of *imperator* disappeared from the coins after this date. "Government by military force had given way to government by personality and by advice." Grant further notes,

> Every office, every power, and every success—the constituents of *dignitas*—enhanced the inherited *auctoritas* of Augustus until it became his unique and personal attribute or characteristic, enabling him to act (in a way not permitted to mere men) without *potestas* or *imperium*. It was, in current political theory, the natural complement of *libertas*—it was the people's return to him for what he gave to them.[4]

The vehicle of auctoritas was the *tribunicia potestas*, and the coinage issued by Augustus repeatedly emphasized this constitutional link. Note, however, how directly all this reflects the duties and obligations of the patron-freedman relationship. Having freed the Roman people, Augustus felt that he had established a new relationship which replaced the *imperium* of the warlord and slave master, a relationship in which both parties—patron and freedman—had privileges and duties. It was his duty to protect and care for his people—the entire Roman people—and to guarantee their personal liberty in exactly the same way that the patron protected and cared for his ex-slaves: "The plebs of Rome," as Ronald Syme remarked, "was Caesar's inherited *clientela*."[5] This duty became the right of the liberated Roman people; the emperor's providence and justice guaranteed their security and liberty. What he gave them was not simply freedom "from the tyranny of a faction" but also freedom from fear and want. Hence he was especially proud to say, regarding a period of great scarcity of grain, that he "delivered the whole city from apprehension" at his own expense, and he boasted of the vast sums he had spent on the plebs as well as the gladiatorial games he had put on for them.[6]

It is a measure of Augustus' achievement that this conception of imperial duty—the obligation to provide for, and protect the liberty of, the public—persisted for several hundred years, through emperors good and bad. Mason Hammond agrees with Wirszubski that the imperial conception of the freedom which they protected was identical with that of the majority of Romans, namely, that it meant negative freedom and was directly derived from the idea of emancipation from slavery. It connoted "an existence ordered under law rather than under the arbitrary will of a master."[7] Hammond's important paper traces the struggle between this view of freedom held by emperor and plebs— that is, personal freedom—and the dethroned elite's conception of civic freedom, which persisted among the aristocracy and indeed remained a potential source of subversion up to Galba's reign.

In abandoning civic freedom, however, the emperors, especially those who had flirted with civic freedom before assuming power, all followed the tradition laid down by Augustus that it was their duty to preserve and protect the personal liberty of the Roman people. It is striking that in his propaganda Galba used as his symbol the pileus, which was the cap worn by the freed slave.[8] On assuming power, he returned to the Augustan, and Claudian, view that "public liberty, the security of the empire from arbitrary rule, was a responsibility and virtue of the prince."[9] Vespasian's propaganda leaves us in no doubt that the emperor's conception of the people's freedom was exactly that of a master who had liberated his slaves, for he uses the term *adserto* in reference to his relationship with the Roman people, a term normally used in defending an alleged slave's claim to freedom.[10] Galba's linking of the *princep*'s virtue with the people's freedom had an important implication, to which we will return shortly.

But first, let us examine the other side of the coin: what the people gave the prince in return for his protection of their liberty and security. Again, their responsibilities were exactly modeled on those of the freedman client. Eventually, it was not only the Roman plebs but all who lived in the Roman world who were his clients. "The army and the Roman people," Donald Earl has noted, "were the twin pillars of his power and his hold over them was personal and beyond the constitution."[11] They were to express their gratitude by supporting and enhancing his power. The people praised him and were loyal, he wrote, "on account of my courage, clemency, justice and piety," as a result of which he "excelled all in influence."[12] His power, he was claiming, ultimately rests on the grateful support of the people whose freedom he guaranteed. They reinforced each other. The more power the people gave him, the more power he had to defend their freedom. However, this power from below came not through the ballot box— that meant democracy, civic freedom, and chaos—but through the devotion and respect that his freedmen people showed him. And that personal devotion enhanced and legitimized his own imperial *dignitas*, that is, his claimed *auctoritas*. It is in this sense that I understand Michael Grant's assertion that the *tribunicia potestas* was the vehicle and constitutional basis of the emperor's *auctoritas*. Power and the ballot box—republican freedom—had been replaced by *auctoritas*, charismatic virtue, and the *obsequium* of the people. The term *obsequium* revolts us today, as it no doubt did the minority of Roman aristocrats. But for the vast majority of people in the Roman Empire it was a perfectly respectable word: the outward show of respect for the dignity and authority of the man who had liberated the freedman. In the end even Tacitus was forced to accept this common and imperial conception of freedom: that ultimately freedom for the ordinary man meant devotion and submission to the godlike prince. "The emotions of gratitude, of loyalty, and of worship were concentrated upon the ruler, who represented in his person the eternal might of Rome."[13]

In so promoting his *dignitas*, however, the Roman people gave their emperor something else—they gave him divinity, made him godlike. In other words, they promoted his special kind of freedom. When people said that only the gods were free, they clearly did not mean that they were not themselves free. Indeed, in the very same breath it was often also said that the only true freedom came from slavery to the god. The paradox dissolves once it is understood that two kinds of freedom are being referred to: the more negative freedom of the devotee—the freedom from the oppression of others and from fear and want—and the more positive or organic freedom of the god whose freedom rests in his total power, a power he uses for the good of all, including the guarantee of the personal freedom of ordinary mortals. That was the attitude of the ordinary Roman toward the divine emperor. Among his eastern subjects and among the mass of freedmen at Rome, he was literally a god; among freeborn Romans, he was something else, *divi filius*, an all-powerful prince whose *auctoritas* was almost godlike in its charisma and hardly less than divine in its secular power.

Like Augustus, all other Roman emperors directly linked the freedom of the people with their own imperial *dignitas*. Astute contemporary writers often interpreted Augustus' relation to the Roman body politic in explicitly organicist terms.[14] The emperors' exalted sense of freedom was really only the organic version of the sovereignal conception of *libertas* held by the ruling class. Both viewed freedom as the exercise of power over others. We agree with Yavetz that Augustus would have had no objection to a depiction of his principate "as absolute" and that "all he wanted to convey in the *Res Gestae* was the fact that his rule was not arbitrary, but founded on law."[15] When members of the ruling class complained about the destruction of their *libertas*, as Tacitus did for example, they were usually referring not to the loss of their civic freedom, but to the reduction of their own sovereignal freedom as a result of the enormous power of the emperors and the latters' tendency to use their absolute *libertas* on behalf of the masses. G. E. M. De Ste. Croix has cogently argued that when Tacitus complained about the destruction of liberty as a result of the intimidating presence of the Emperor Tiberius in the law court, what really bothered Tacitus was the fact that Tiberius was unjustly preventing them from exercising their freedom to be bribed and to pass unfair judgments on behalf of the powerful! This view was so taken for granted among the oligarchy that Tacitus, as one of its members, "felt no reason to conceal his deep conviction that the ability to exercise, *whether for good or ill*, the proper degree of patronage to which a great man's position in society entitled him was indeed an essential ingredient in *libertas*."[16] Many modern classicists and admirers of Tacitus are so embarrassed by this view of freedom that they have simply persisted in denying what the text makes perfectly clear. We know by now, however, that there was nothing unusual about Tacitus' view. It had long been the elite view of freedom throughout the ancient Mediterranean; indeed, as we saw in part one of this work, it is the one conception of freedom which had emerged and sporadically thrived in the non-Western world before the rise of the Greeks.

The emperors' exalted sense of freedom was also similar to earlier notions of organic freedom in that it resided in the quality of the inner man. The only difference now was that on this inner quality depended not a household or a city, not even a large state, but the whole Mediterranean world. Nerva directly linked justice, one of the supreme virtues of the emperor's character, with liberty, in his coinages. Two hundred years after Augustus issued his decree to Cyrene, whom he referred to as "all who are cared for by us," Severus Alexander sent an order to his governors in which he stated that he had "as much carefulness for the liberty of [his] subjects as for their goodwill and loyalty."[17]

The miracle of Rome was not that it fell eventually—and it is one of the bizarre aspects of European historiography that Rome's fall was for so long its major preoccupation—but that it lasted so long. And M. P. Charlesworth was certainly right in stating that it survived as long as it did "because the bond between ruler and ruled was one of goodwill and faith."[18] What happened when the bond was broken? Not the end of freedom but the uncoupled dominance of the sovereignal note of the chord.

It will be recalled that at the end of the fifth century B.C. there was an intellectual and spiritual response to, and attempted transformation of, the outward experience of freedom. Much the same thing happened in Rome. In our discussion of Roman religion, we saw elements of this response. In the secular and spiritual realms, however, two major responses dwarfed everything we have discussed so far: the dominance of Stoicism in the secular mind and, in its wake, the all-encompassing triumph of Christianity—the one a secular philosophy of freedom, the other mankind's only universal religion of freedom. It is to the secular of these two developments that we now turn.

CHAPTER 15

Freedom, Stoicism, and the Roman Mind

Stoicism's impact on the Roman upper class was complex. We know that the Romans were a pragmatic, unphilosophical people, and it is therefore tempting to dismiss Stoicism as just an upper-class fad, of no great import in the historical sociology of freedom. This would be a mistake. At the same time, though, we must take account of a subtle though fundamental difference both in the nature of Stoicism and in its impact on the Roman elite.

There were really two currents of upper-class Stoicism in Rome, but they were so closely intertwined that it is easy to neglect the difference between them. Both have their origin in the same historical source, the so-called middle Stoa. One current we may call reactionary Stoicism. It is most classically represented by M. Porcius Cato; indeed, it may be said to assume its Roman shape with him, is reflected in the thought of republican conservative centrists such as Cicero and others such as M. Terentius Varro (116-28 B.C.) and Sallust (86-35 B.C.), and acquires an almost fanatical tone in Porcia, Cato's daughter and the wife of M. Junius Brutus. This version of Stoicism was introduced to Rome starting in the early part of the second century B.C., mainly from Pergamum and Rhodes but also directly from Athens, the most important agents of diffusion being Panaetius of Rhodes (185-109 B.C.) and his successor Posidonius as well as Antiochus of Ascalon (d. 50 B.C.), who most directly influenced Cicero.

From these Greek sources a simplified version of the philosophy emerged in which it was reduced to an ethical creed wholly divorced from its original philosophical context. In this diluted form, it became the dominant educational force among the conservatives of the late republic and the principate. It appealed to the Roman elite less for what it taught them that was new than for the way it "was able to accommodate many traditional Roman attitudes about human excellence, and . . . also provided them with a theoretical basis in place of, or rather in addition to, custom and historical examples."[1]

Several factors stand out in explaining the appeal of this revised version of the philosophy. First, the elitist egalitarianism of middle Stoicism was the perfect intellectual match for the elitist republican. It will be recalled that Stoicism, in its most influential version, emphasized a kind of democracy of the soul. Reason, which was divine, ruled the cosmos. Human beings, as creatures of reason, shared in the cosmos. The wise man, by living according to nature, reconciled the divinity in himself with that of the cosmos. In this way he was free, since his conformity with the cosmos was exactly what he, in the exercise of his reason, would want to will. The idea of conformity to nature was obviously appealing to a conservative ruling class, especially one in the process of imperial expansion. Naturally, to the upper-class Roman mind, the Roman way was the way of reason.[2] The participative emphasis of Stoicism, the idea of man's sharing the direction of the cosmos with God, was also highly attractive to a very competitive ruling class which was strongly committed to the principle that each man have a turn at ruling for a short time.

Stoicism could also be easily adapted to the notion of an elitist conception of civic freedom. It made a rigid distinction between the wise and the ignorant: only the wise were free and good, and only the good and free were wise. Selectively read, Stoic writings provided an inner creed wholly in harmony with the outer political creed of the Roman republican elite. Zeno's extremely influential political treatise, *The Republic*, had claimed that "only virtuous people in the *Republic* [are] citizens, friends, relations and free," while the rest are "foes, enemies, slaves and estranged from one another."[3] By neglecting the radical aspects of Zeno's treatise and concentrating on this, the noble Roman found in Stoicism the perfect inner match for the elitist civic freedom practiced by his class. After condemning Athenian democracy, Cicero stated that, among "a free people," "the safety of the State depends upon the wisdom of its best men, especially since Nature has provided not only that those men who are superior in virtue and in spirit should rule the weaker, but also that the weaker should be willing to obey the stronger."[4]

The heavy emphasis on the inner man, and especially on the freedom of the soul in the face of external slavery, must be considered separately as another basis of appeal to the upper class. Its appeal was twofold. The inner man, interpreted to mean the character of the person, as distinct from his spiritual or intellectual being, was consistent with the traditional upper-class Roman stress on strength of character as the source of all good in the world. Further, the Stoic conception of fortitude and gravity, though originally an incidental aspect of a more profound Stoic theory of personality, in its simplified version seemed remarkably compatible with the old Roman virtues. In Cato's reading of the philosophy, the two became one. With Sallust we find this identification in its most vulgar form; he is typical of this group of Romans in that we sometimes find it hard to tell whether he is a Stoic or an Epicurean.[5]

Second, the inward emphasis of Stoicism also directly addressed what was later to become a pressing contemporary problem: the abolition of upper-class civic freedom by the *princeps*. The Roman elite saw this as a form of political slavery; indeed, this is precisely how it was described by those, such as Lucan and Persius, who dared to express themselves on the subject. Inner freedom, however, was possible in the face of outward slavery or the loss of republican civic freedom. In this it was subversive without being revolutionary, for "it sharpened the impulse and the courage to say what one felt, without supplying any specific political program."[6] It was also an effective form of consolation: for many upper-class Romans, Stoicism was very nearly a kind of religion. However, it was a religion which, as MacMullen has nicely put it, "made missionaries, but missionaries with very little more than the vague idea that men—*other* men—could be roused to revolution, or the emperor recalled to an antique virtue, by a great deal of defiance."[7]

By the period of the *princeps*, this current of Stoicism was thoroughly reactionary and, as Edward Arnold noted long ago, "was the common mould in which the educated youth of Rome were shaped in this period; it produced honest, diligent, and simple-minded men, exactly suited to be instruments of the great imperial bureaucracy."[8] All of them loathed the ordinary Romans and their love of personal freedom; and they despised even more the imperial compact between ordinary citizen and emperor. It was precisely these stolid upper-class Stoics whom popular emperors such as Nero liked to debase in order to curry favor with the masses. Acutely perceptive when it came to matters of his own political survival, Augustus saw clearly the social origin of this current of Stoicism: "The memory of Cato associated Stoic doctrines with republican views; vague idealizations of Brutus and Cassius suggested the glorification of tyrannicide."[9]

Persius was typical of upper-class Roman intellectuals who embraced a reactionary and mildly subversive version of Stoicism. Born in A.D. 34 to a wealthy equestrian family, he came at sixteen under the influence of the Stoic teacher Cornutus, a freedman of Seneca. Cornutus corrected his dissolute ways and led him to see how the sins of the flesh were a disease that had to be nipped in the bud.[10] In the best of the satires, the fifth, Persius, after thanking his teacher in mellifluous terms, launches into a discussion of the nature of inner slavery and freedom that must have been typical of the way the conservative Stoic saw things. He dismisses outer freedom in terms which not only identify it with license but betray his contempt for the real ex-slave with whom it is associated.

> We need freedom—not the sort which Jack acquires
> when he appears as John Smith on the voters' list and is issued
> with coupons for mouldy bread. You haven't a crumb of truth:
> You create citizens by a whirl. Tom is a worthless yokel,
> bleary with booze; you couldn't trust him with a bucket of mash.[11]

Outer personal freedom is here rejected as a slave value, not worthy of the best people. It is clear, however, that this slave value has permeated the whole society, for Persius goes on to argue the Stoic position against the view that the man is free "who is able to spend his life as he chooses." There are masters other than "the one which the rod lifts from your back."[12] These are mainly one's appetites and lusts. Only through the study of Stoic philosophy can the individual discover true freedom, which is "the upstanding life," in which it is possible to tell "the true from the counterfeit" and to be "alert for the false chink of copper beneath the gold."[13] This seems a rather puerile conception of inner freedom. The final lines of the second satire do slightly better, although they also make clear how closely upper-class nostalgia for the old virtues was identified with Stoic freedom:

> a soul where human
> and divine commands are blended, a mind which is pure within,
> a heart steeped in fine old honor. . . . [14]

Even after making allowance for Persius' youth, there remains something excessively precious, and false, about his Stoicism. He has reduced it to an upper-class conceit, wholly incapable of recognizing its most blatant self-contradictions. One finds it hard to understand how Persius, after so extravagantly praising his freedman tutor, could have failed to see the implicit insult in his contemptuous dismissal of the act of manumission. It was possible, after all, to talk about inner freedom without jeering so abusively at its outer version. The contrast with Horace is instructive. Persius obviously had Horace's praise of his freedman father in mind in writing his own eulogy to his tutor; but how different the view of outer freedom! No wonder Horace poked fun at this version of Stoicism. One can just imagine, too, Cornutus wincing at his pupil's view of freedom. It is easy to understand why, after Persius' premature death, he advised the poet's mother to suppress his juvenilia.

William S. Anderson has ably demonstrated how form repeatedly contradicts content in Persius, especially in the fifth satire, where in the poet's very inability to reconcile the two parts of his poem—one devoted to verbal freedom, the other to moral freedom—he betrays "himself a slave to his own manneristic technique."[15] One suspects that a similar contradiction was typical of all aspects of the life of the upper-class Stoic in imperial times: Stoicism was more form and style than substance, a way of distancing oneself from the rabble and the nouveaux riches and from the painful political realities of the present. Yet, in its very hypocrisy, reactionary Stoicism contradicted the essence of the Stoic conception of moral freedom, for it betrayed an unwitting enslavement to the sins of vanity and the selfish denial of human brotherhood.

The second current of Roman Stoicism also had its origin in the republican era, and we may call it reformist Stoicism. While it shared many of the basic philosophical principles of patrician stoicism, it differed in three important respects. First and foremost, its emphasis was on personal freedom and providence. In the inner life, this entailed a greater reliance on reason as the director of the universe. Man is free less because he simply conforms to the divine spirit of the cosmos than because he is himself that spirit. Identity, rather than conformity, with the divine is the essence of living according to nature. Freedom in the sense of almighty power, a power that is derived from and used for good, was clearly advocated by many of the Stoic writers, most notably Chrysippus in his work *On Zeno's Proper Use of Terminology*, where it is stated, "Besides being free the wise are also kings, since kingship is rule that is answerable to no one; and this can occur only among the wise. . . . A ruler must have knowledge of what is good and bad. . . . Only the wise are holders of public offices, judges and orators, whereas no inferior man is."[16] Once one drops the notion of inherited exclusiveness of virtue, one can easily see how such a view of freedom could support, indeed incite, revolutionary politics. For not only does it justify the removal by any means of the fools who control the body politic, but it encourages the action of the radical leader who is prepared to use force and to destroy the traditional system in order to get his way, that is, to promote his power and freedom.

Second, only a very selective reading of Stoicism could deny it its inherently liberal thrust. For while it may be true that all Stoics held that only the wise and virtuous are free and deserve to be citizens of the inner and, by extension, the outer world, it is equally true that most of them believed in the possibility of acquiring virtue through training. The philosophy was, in fact, strongly opposed to the principle of inheritance. As Charlotte Stough has pointed out,

> The view that virtue and vice are permanently fixed traits of character does not harmonize well with Stoic determinism. That doctrine implies that a person's choices and actions *are* influenced by external causes as well as those internal to the agent himself. So determinism clearly does not rule out the possibility of moral improvement in a vicious person who wants to change and makes the appropriate effort to do so.[17]

In any event, the reformism implicit in Stoic ethics had already been made explicit in the radical political treatises of Zeno and Chrysippus, both of whom advocated social and political changes of such extremity—even incest and cannibalism were under certain circumstances acceptable—that later disciples squirmed with embarrassment at them. Indeed, one of Cato's favored Stoic philosophers, Anthenodorus, had to flee to Rome, and Cato's protection, after he had been caught expurgating the radical elements from the works of the founders.[18]

It was also possible, of course, to abandon the extreme dualism of early Stoicism regarding the wise-free and foolish-slave persons, and to adopt a more practical, humane view which saw human vice and virtue in terms of a gradation. Already in Chrysippus we find the idea of gradations of slavery, which clearly implies the possibility of gradations or types of freedom.[19] Many Roman Stoics took just this step in their interpretation of the philosophy.

What all this added up to was a view of Stoicism that formed the intellectual basis of the second current. A precursor of this was evident in the radicalism of the Gracchi. There is a tradition, which cannot be proven, that the Stoic Blossius of Cumae was one of the philosophers whom Cornelia hired to educate her sons, but it is more likely that the relationship with Tiberius did not begin until he was an adult.[20] Donald Dudley cast serious doubt on the view of many scholars before him that Blossius' Stoicism had much to do with his reformist sympathies, claiming instead that "the Campanian democratic tradition made Blossius the natural ally of Ti. Gracchus," in much the same way that "the oligarchic tradition of Rhodes" rather than his brand of Stoicism made Panaetius so congenial to the conservatism of Scipio Aemilianus and his party.[21] As a sociologist, I am only too happy to agree with him that the real source of Blossius' radicalism was his sociopolitical background, but ideas do reflect and reinforce what is learned from experience. In joining ranks with the Asian anti-imperialist struggle of Aristonicus against Rome, Blossius was more than simply a provincial with a grudge against the oligarchy of the metropolis: he was a classic dedicated revolutionary "committed to the cause of the oppressed masses whenever and wherever the call came."[22] And debate over whether the *Heliopolis* of Aristonicus was directly influenced by Stoicism, or wholly the product of Asiatic sun-worship ideology, seems to miss the point. Both the Gracchi reforms and the revolution of Aristonicus appealed to the poor and downtrodden, and particularly to slaves and freedmen. Both were fought so that all men could be free; both shared the dream of the utopian *Heliopolitae*, that all persons would become citizens in a City of the Sun, where everyone was free. (Nor should it be forgotten that almost all the founding figures of Stoicism were of Asiatic ancestry, beginning with the Semitic Zeno. Indeed, we may speculate that with the *Heliopolitae* Stoicism had gone full circle, rediscovering its Semitic religio-ideological roots.)

I am persuaded by those who argue that there was a clear split in the Stoic school at Rome starting about this time, one group supporting the republican conservatives along the lines suggested earlier, the second supporting the more radical tradition of the Gracchi which was to continue in the reformism and special conception of freedom held by the Populares and to culminate in what may be called the imperial version of Stoicism.[23] It must be admitted, however, that this reformist current waned during the last century of the republic. It may have inspired the Populares, but there is little real evidence of this, certainly not among the more prominent of those who outwardly promoted the *libertas* of the masses. Pompey, who probably came from a distinguished literary family and was related to the Stoic Balbi, was never called a Stoic and was not really involved with intellectual affairs, though he liked the image of the stateman-scholar.[24] Caesar, who was genuinely brilliant and had what looked like an intellectual policy, did write two works against Cato, presumably attacking his brand of Stoicism, but there is no evidence that he adhered to Stoicism or even, as some have claimed, to Epicureanism, although the latter might have provided "a decent cover for skepticism in religion."[25]

During the period of the early principate, this second current of Stoicism resurfaced, now in full support of the monarchial principle, with which it was always more compatible: the inner intellectual prop for the outer concord between organic and personal freedom. Thus Stoicism in the empire was the philosophical support for both the enemies and the supporters of the new order. What Augustus frowned upon, and rightly regarded as subversive, was the old, conservative Stoicism, that of the Younger Cato, Brutus, and Cassius.

Gradually this second current of Stoicism ceased to be reformist and became "salubrious and respectable," standing "for order and for monarchy."[26] Augustus had been educated by two Stoics, and it is likely that he saw in the Stoic conception of providence a spiritual and inner representation of his own providential power in the world. Gilbert Charles-Picard offers some stimulating speculations in this direction. He finds significant that it was in the same year, 26 B.C., that the Pythagorean Anaxilas of Larissa was banished that the Senate presented Augustus with a golden shield symbolizing the four cardinal virtues—courage, mercy, justice, and piety.

> By promoting the dedication of the *clipeus virtutis* Augustus was proclaiming in the most solemn manner his adherence to the political creed of the Stoics. For these disciples of Zeno—who were distrustful of democracy, like most of Plato's successors—believed in the human flock being guided by one shepherd, as a delegate of Zeus, provided he was worthy through his virtues and was as much a model to his subjects as he was a leader.

By banishing the leader of the popular Pythagoreans, Augustus sought to rid Rome of the one remaining cult which he had tolerated: "The empire born of the victory at Actium was not to be the realm of Apollo, but of Jupiter incarnated in Augustus."[27]

Be that as it may, we find only selected or qualified traces of Stoicism in the works of the major writers of Augustus' day. Horace's conversion in his later years is unconvincing. Virgil and Ovid seem more serious in their commitment, though in typically Roman fashion, the influence was selective, largely ethical, and thoroughly divorced from its philosophical context; the former was perhaps more a Pythagorean, and the latter was eventually banished, possibly for Bacchic sympathies. Whatever their commitments, the emphasis is more on submission to fate than on the freedom that comes from identity with it. The link between Stoicism and freedom requires real intellectual effort, and none of these men, however great their genius in other respects, seemed willing or able to make the effort.

That intellectual effort really begins only with Seneca, at least among extant writers. Seneca, in fact, straddles both forms of Stoicism, and this may in part account for much that is intellectually unsatisfactory in his work. It also explains why, although he tutored and served his emperor so well, he was in the end banished and then proscribed by him.

Like many of his upper-class old Stoic contemporaries, Seneca found in philosophy a basis for living with tyranny. Writing on the subject of tranquility to Nero's police commissioner after his return from exile, he declared, "All life is bondage. Man must therefore habituate himself to his condition, complain of it as little as possible, and grasp whatever good lies within his reach. No situation is so harsh that a dispassionate mind cannot find some consolation in it."[28] The essay also reflects the eclecticism of Roman Stoicism, even including some hints of Epicureanism. Like his fellow upper-class Stoics, too, Seneca hardly lived up to his own moral creed. Few men were more slave to their vices. Indeed, one sometimes wonders whether Seneca's life-style was not a deliberate, living denial of it.

Nonetheless, in most of Seneca's writings we find the best expression of the reformist, imperial version of Stoicism. Like his predecessors, he was, for all his personal moral failings, genuinely concerned with the welfare of the slaves and the freedman proletariat of Rome. His effort to save the lives of the four hundred slaves condemned to die because one of their number had killed their master,[29] and his letter approving of a friend's kind treatment of his slaves, reflects his better, liberal side. "Remember, if you please, that the man you call slave sprang from the same seed, enjoys the same daylight, breathes like you, likes like you, dies like you. You can as easily conceive him a free man as he can conceive you a slave. . . . The essence of my teaching is this: Treat your inferior as you would wish your superior to treat you.[30] Philosophically, he departed from the conservative school in his greater emphasis on the interior life and the possibility of improvement. As Donald J. Mooney has recently observed, "This attention to the *profectus*, i.e., the one who is making progress toward the attainment of virtue, gives a practical Roman approach to the individual person and softens the older, simplistic Wise Man–Fool Dichotomy of Stoicism."[31] The most profound difference, however, is found in Seneca's conception of inner and outer freedom. Outwardly and inwardly, Seneca fully advocates the complementarity of organic and personal freedom which Augustus had fashioned. There is a perfect parallelism between the cosmic relation of god to people, the interior relation of reason to the body, and the emperor's relation to the mass of his citizens. Throughout his writings, one relation is used as a metaphor for the others, so that in the end none takes precedence; each is, in turn, *signans* and *signatum*. The soul is a reflection as much of the universe as of the Roman commonwealth.[32] Reason directs and is literally godlike in its freedom. Freedom means "not fearing either men or god; it means possessing supreme power over yourself."[33] At the same time, the body is not condemned. Indeed, body and soul are organically united. But it is not a democratic unity. Rather, the body is allowed a kind of freedom, though one inferior and subject to the directing freedom of the soul. The body's freedom is the inner counterpart of personal liberty. It is partly in tension with the intellect, but, in its place, it functions to divert the intellect.

> The mind must have relaxation, and will rise stronger and keener after recreation. Just as fertile fields must not be forced (without fallow periods their richness is soon exhausted), so incessant labor will crush the mind's elan. A little respite and relaxation restores the mind's energy, but unrelieved mental exertion begets dullness and languor.[34]

Sports and amusements, outdoor walks, carriage rides, and even sometimes a little intoxication are some of the liberties permitted the body, because they organically function in invigorating the spirit. Seneca notes, perhaps ruefully, that Bacchus was surnamed *Liber*, "not because of the license wine gives the tongue, but because it liberates the mind from its bondage to care and emancipates it and animates it and gives it greater boldness for any enterprise. But in liberty moderation is wholesome, and so it is in wine."[35]

This takes us naturally to Seneca's view of outer freedoms in the state, and the way it is expressed in terms of god's relation to people. It is hard to find a more perfect expression of the organic, imperial notion of sovereignal freedom in its asymmetrical interdependence with personal liberty than that in Seneca's letter *On Clemency*, addressed to his former pupil Nero, on his eighteenth birthday. "Peace is deep and abundant," he writes, "justice is firmly seated above all injustice, in full view for all to see is the happiest of administrations in which the only limitation upon the completest liberty is the denial of license for self-destruction."[36] These lines could just as easily have been written by a Victorian schoolmaster to his prime minister. Personal liberty is fully tolerated. But there is a higher freedom, one, indeed, which makes possible the lesser personal freedom of the masses. This is the freedom that inheres in the almighty power of the emperor, a freedom directly analogous to god's. Clemency, according to Seneca, is what justifies this "mighty force," which is "comely and glorious only if its power is beneficent." Seneca first compares the relationship between king and people to that between body and soul. "The whole body's service to the soul is analogous," he writes, in that "this enormous populace which is the shell for the soul of one man is regulated by his spirit and guided by his reason; if it were not propped by his intelligence it would bruise itself by its own strength and crumble to fragments."[37]

Seneca then shifts to the third relation: almightily free and powerful king is to personally free subjects as god is to people: "The ideal to which a prince might best mold himself is to deal with his subjects as he would wish the gods to deal with him." The king shares with god the loneliness of total power and an "inability to descend," which is "the bondage of supreme greatness," a view, we need hardly add, which Nero conspicuously did not share. Later he elaborates,

> Men gaze upon their ruler with just such veneration and adoration as we should upon the immortal gods if they gave us the power of looking upon them. Actually, is he not nearest the gods when he comports himself in accordance with the nature of the gods and is beneficent and generous and potent for good? This should be your goal, this your pattern, to be held greatest only if you are at the same time best."[38]

Seneca's facile shifting here between the inner, the spiritual, and the outer worlds illustrates a peculiar feature of Roman thought, one which sets it off most strikingly from that of the Greek elite. Among the Greeks, as we have seen, the inner world was held firmly apart from the outer. When one was used metaphorically to express the other, it was always absolutely clear that the statement should be taken analogically. In the Roman mind, this distinction is blurred. As Harold Mattingly pointed out, the Roman was "acutely aware of the duality of life," but his "imagination roamed freely between the two." There was nothing "vague or shadowy" about the inner world, nor was it necessarily good. "The supernatural was just the other side of the natural, and like it, contained elements of very diverse qualities. They were like the obverse and reverse of the same coin. As regards reality the spiritual world was more real than the material world, in the sense that in it the 'numina,' the acts of the divine will that make the world go round, have their being."[39]

Actually, this view of the duality was consistent with the underlying principles of Stoicism, since the latter held to the unity and material basis of all life and thought. However, the Romans arrived at this conception not from philosophical principles but from the central role of character in their conception of things. A person's character looked both inward and outward, and what a man did was as much a reflection of his inner life as a reaction to outward circumstances. I suspect that this was the reason why Janus was such an important god among the Romans, taking precedence even over Jupiter in important ceremonies. Beneath the overt conception of him as the spirit of the gate or door and its arch, and thus symbolic of beginnings and of looking both ways, was perhaps a covert but more powerful symbol of human character, facing both worlds. This would explain why the gate of the main temple of Janus was kept open during war and closed during peace, and not the other way around, as one would normally expect in a more overt symbolic statement. An open door is like an open character—honest, courageous, fearless, noble, and all that—one in perfect harmony between inner and outer world.

So far, we have considered how men from the literary elite thought in Stoic terms about inner freedom. Ideally, we would like to hear directly from the two extremes of Roman society, say, an emperor who reflected privately in diaries not meant for publication and an ex-slave, preferably one actually born in slavery, the lowliest origin in Roman society, who became a Stoic philosopher. We might even add to this historical wish list some contact between the two: the emperor, for example, read the works of the freedman. In one of her most mysterious acts of generosity, Clio has actually provided us with just such a pair.

The event is so unusual that the two men in question, Marcus Aurelius and Epictetus, have usually been compared to each other, the overwhelming tendency being to bring out what they have in common. That these two Stoic thinkers did indeed share a great deal cannot be denied. P. A. Brunt mentions two important similarities: "Both insist that a citizen of the great city which includes both gods and men must welcome all the dispensations of providence and be active for the good of his fellows. Both derive individuals' specific duties from his place or station or role or calling or function in society."[40] Brunt then points to one of their differences: that Epictetus wrote for all, whereas Marcus wrote only for himself. Brunt quite understandably emphasizes this difference because it is important for his argument; in fact, though, the two men had far more in common with each other and, the point which I want to stress, differed in one critical respect, having nothing to do with their audience.

More important than the two elements mentioned by Brunt is both men's central concern with the experience of freedom. We should not be misled by the fact that Marcus does not use the word *freedom* any-where near as frequently as Epictetus. The *Meditations* of Marcus has a haunting quality about it. One feels oneself in the presence of a man who is desperately yearning for something, grasping constantly for a truth which, tragically, seems just out of his reach. It is not something he has experienced and lost but something he has never had. He is like Keats's man who has never loved, so while he knows that there is something terribly missing in his life, he cannot quite say what it is. He can only intimate. He will mention it from time to time, but there will be an awkwardness, an acute embarrassment of the soul as he does so. That thing, that unexperienced, unexplainable love which haunts the pages of the *Meditations* is freedom. Alas, he never found it, though he kept searching. Near the end of the spiritual diary and, we may, with Brunt, quite reasonably assume, his life, he is still in-quiring about the requirements of survival. He will "follow reason and the god," but he is still struggling with the urge "to follow impulse, to increase and then again to cease." "How," he still wants to know, "does the directing mind treat itself? Everything depends on that."[41] Indeed.

Now, there are two questions at issue here. The first is, Why was it that Marcus never knew the freedom for which he searched? And the second is, What role did his Stoic creed play in his search? My answer to the first question will be the point of departure for a consideration of the Stoic ethics of Epictetus, after which I will return to the second question by means of a detailed analysis of Marcus' spiritual diary.

The answer to the first question was given by Seneca in one of his most perceptive passages. In his treatise *On Clemency*, Seneca empha-sized the awesome isolation and peculiar "bondage of supreme great-ness" among those selected for the imperial purple.[42] Now, the great dramatic irony of this passage is that it was addressed to Nero, who of all emperors went out of his way to break free from the bondage of greatness. Indeed, it may well have been that Nero studied his teach-er's address to him and took it much more to heart than is normally imagined. It is conceivable that the young emperor, appalled by the truth of his teacher's observation, decided to defy the semidivine bondage of his office by descending as deeply as possible into the very squalor of existence. By waylaying and beating up noble Romans in the dark, by his visits to prostitutes, by incest with and murder of his mother, by homosexuality with his eunuch, and, above all, by degrad-ing his office through acting on the stage, Nero was consciously as-serting his freedom from the isolation and bondage to rectitude which his office imposed on him.

Marcus, on the other hand, had been the perfect emperor. Long before he was adopted for succession by Antoninus, the aging emperor Hadrian had taken to calling him Verissimus because of his reputation for truthfulness. He greeted the news of his adoption with weary resignation. He, too, took seriously Seneca's view that the office was a kind of bondage. Like Nero, he sought his freedom from it—not, however, through the outward decadence of the flesh but by the inward freedom offered by Stoicism, which made his complete acceptance of his outward bondage possible.

And it is here that the parallel with Epictetus is strongest. For what is strikingly peculiar about Epictetus' outward life is not so much that he was eventually a freedman—many of the great Roman Stoics were just that—but that, alone among the great thinkers of the ancient world, as far as I can tell, he was born a slave.[43] Now, while this fact is usually mentioned, its importance has simply not been sufficiently recognized. The man who was born a slave, the *verna*, was often in a more privileged situation in urban households than the captive, although his condition did not differ legally from the latter's.[44] The *vernae* sometimes had the opportunity of being trained for either a skill or a profession, Epictetus being a case in point; often they were "inexactly but significantly regarded as Italians."[45] There was no guarantee of good treatment, however, as Epictetus' case also demonstrates.

The most remarkable thing about the *verna* is that he had never experienced freedom, unlike, say, the *captivus*, who had been born and reared a free person. At the same time, the evidence suggests that the *vernae* yearned for freedom as intensely as the *captivi* and may have achieved it at an even higher rate. Thus Epictetus, the *verna*, at the bottom of the social ladder, had an experience directly parallel to that of the emperor, at the very top. *Both yearned for a freedom they had never experienced.* Both thus had to imagine into being, and in this sense independently re-create, the existential condition of freedom. Imperial heir and *verna* had to search in their souls for the source and meaning of the thing they sought. Of course, they could always observe the experience of people around them who claimed to be free. But such an observation may well have been the beginning of anguish for two such sensitive souls as Marcus and Epictetus. For when they looked, what they saw disgusted them. For Marcus, it was the corruption of court life and the decadence of the nobility, the freest of people; for Epictetus, it was the freedman still tied to the patron, still obliged to perform his *operae* and his *obsequium* for the greater glory and *dignitas* of the man who had once enslaved him. What kind of freedom was that?

And yet, they both yearned for it. What kind of yearning was that? Why did they feel deprived of something so manifestly unworthy of their desire? The answers went beyond a mere shifting of the struggle inward and search for a truer freedom. People had been doing this for centuries, and Stoicism was a ready-made creed for anyone who demanded that the thing he or she could not resist longing for be of greater dignity than what outer freedom seemed to offer. The uniqueness of Marcus and Epictetus was in searching not so much for freedom as for the source of the yearning for, and meaning of, freedom. Shifting the terrain from the outer to the inner world was the beginning, not the end, of the struggle. For unlike the manumitted *captivus*, who knew—whether outwardly or spiritually—exactly what he was looking for, enthroned emperor and freed *verna* had still to find the real slavery and the real freedom, and perhaps then the ultimate source and meaning of their wish for freedom. In this quest, something fundamentally new was added to the Western discourse on freedom. A genuine philosophy of freedom—or, to be more precise, the ontology of freedom—began with these two men.

Let me anticipate the outcome of my analysis by stating my opinion that, though they struggled hard, in the end both men failed in their quest. We are enriched by the record they left us of that struggle, but we should not let our admiration obscure the fact that the struggle was ultimately a profound spiritual disappointment. What is more, both men knew that they were not succeeding. The melancholy that runs throughout every line of the *Meditations*, the disquieting uncertainty behind the overt certitudes of Epictetus, the strange, spiritual irascibility behind the outer sweetness of his temper—all point to the sense of profound spiritual failure that both men experienced deep in their hearts. And for that failure late Stoicism deserves a good part of the blame.

At first reading, Epictetus' aim and means of achieving it seem fairly straightforward. Freedom is "the greatest good"; it is a "great and noble thing, and precious."[46] It is, quite simply, what makes people happy. But what is it, this all-important value? Again, the matter seems clear-cut at first sight. Epictetus is almost formal in his definition: "He is free who lives as he wills," the celebrated chapter on freedom opens, "who is subject neither to compulsion, nor hindrance, nor force, whose choices are unhampered, whose desires attain their end, whose aversions do not fall into what they would avoid."[47]

The very formality and neatness of this definition is what immediately arouses our suspicion. It is not in the nature of this intense old Phrygian to talk this way; not about something as all-consuming as this, his master value. It is not long, in fact, before the cracks beneath the glaze begin to show. He repeats the old Stoic dogma that no bad man is free and that only the free are good, but his defense of this statement lacks conviction. No one, he asserts, wishes to live in error, to be "deceived, impetuous, unjust, unrestrained, peevish, abject." Epictetus knew better than that. For he had been the slave of the freedman of the man who had been the very apotheosis of just such a person, Nero himself, a thoroughly evil man who sought, lived, and died in an Apollonian frenzy of freedom. What is more, he was far too honest with himself to engage in facile condemnation of outward freedom while enjoying it, in the manner, say, of Persius. He had been a slave and had yearned for pure physical personal freedom, and when he had his chance to get it, he grasped it. Furthermore, when Domitian had banished all the philosophers from Rome, Epictetus had not stoically defied the order and stayed in the city he clearly loved—fifteen years later he was talking about the great city as if he were still there, making it possible for us to learn a great deal about Rome just from his incidental remarks.[48]

It was, indeed, precisely because Epictetus had desired, and continued to prize, his outward personal freedom even after becoming convinced of its limitations that he had not only shifted his quest inward, along Stoic lines, but had been forced to depart from the Stoic paradigm in searching for the source and meaning of freedom. It is important to understand that this was not a Stoic problem, for the simple reason that the answer had been given much earlier: freedom was the natural desire of all reasoning human beings and was found to be in harmony with the divine reason that infused the universe. What I am saying, at the risk of intellectual heresy, is that Epictetus had a hard time coming to terms with this dogma, that it is possible he really didn't believe it.

The simple, stark truth of the matter is that if a man really knew what slavery was all about from bitter personal experience, as Zeno and Chrysippus and all the great Stoic teachers had not, and if, moreover, a man had been born a slave and had to rediscover freedom himself, as no other Stoic philosopher of note had done, then it was impossible not to love simple, physical negative freedom. And if one was in love with outer, negative freedom, it was hard to come to terms with the Stoic conception of inner freedom. Epictetus' intellectual challenge, then, was to find a way out of this dilemma. It is with this in mind that we should read all four books of Arrian's *Discourses on Epictetus*.

Epictetus was constantly at war with his creed, for the wisdom of experience clashed on almost every key issue with the wisdom of instruction. The interpenetration of the outer and the inner person is striking in Epictetus, and likely to create problems for anyone trying to understand him in terms of the sharp inner-outer dualism of early or even middle Stoa. On outer freedom, he seems to accept the Augustan complementarity between organic and personal freedom. Freedom in his day was nothing more than "the right to live as we wish,"[49] a right made possible by the emperor's organic power. Outwardly, Epictetus does not disagree with this view of freedom; to the contrary, he takes it so seriously that he is dissatisfied with all hints of constraint on his capacity to do as he pleases. It is one of the purest expressions of laissez-faire. And what is more: "This is not mere self-love; such is the nature of the animal man; everything that he does is for himself."[50] It is thus clear that anyone who is at the bidding of another, or is under the command of some strong impulse such as love or hate or desire for wealth, is not wholly free. To be fully free, one must rid oneself of all such masters. This is obviously an impossible task, so Epictetus offers three alternatives. We may use one of his own striking metaphors, employed in the context of his discussion of rhetoric, and see these three alternatives as inns on a journey home toward perfection, the real, true freedom. And in the same way that the inn of rhetoric is not dismissed outright, indeed has some value as long as its inferior place is recognized, so it is that the first two inns on the journey toward freedom's true home have their value, *in their place.*[51]

The first inn, which we may call the pedestrian or third-best solution, amounts to an awkward form of personal relativism. While clinging to the view that all persons do seek the rational, he concedes that "the rational and the irrational are different for different persons, precisely as good and evil, and the profitable and the unprofitable, are different for different persons."[52] Later he adds, "You are the one that knows yourself, how much you are worth in your own eyes and at what price you sell yourself." This is a far cry from old Stoa, but it works in a rough-and-ready sort of way for the ordinary man. Epictetus almost sounds a note of contempt as he gives his parting bit of advice to those who can do no better than this: "Only consider at what price you sell your freedom of will. If you must sell it, man, at least do not sell it cheap."[53]

The next inn, and second-best solution on the journey toward freedom, straddles the inner and outer spheres and focuses on character. The key intellectual distinction here is between the things that are under our control and those that are not. The master faculty, reason—which is the faculty of choice and refusal, of freedom, and which makes use of external impressions—is what we have under our control. The lower faculties, especially those associated with the body, are not under our control. Similarly, we live in a world dominated by more powerful men, and these are not under our control. However, because the most important faculty is fully under our control, we can always will ourselves to be free. "We must make the best of what is under our control, and take the rest as its nature is"; this is god's will. If you must die, there is nothing you can do about being beheaded; but you are free to die nobly. If you are sent into exile, you accept the order, since this is not under your control; what is under your control, however, is the manner in which you accept it. You are free to go cheerfully and serenely.

This is clearly a cop-out, and although Epictetus comes back to this second-best argument from time to time, he is, to his credit, not entirely at ease with it. As one interlocutor exclaims, "If a person subjects me to the fear of death, he compels me." Epictetus responds that it is not what the person is subjected to that compels him but his decision that he prefers to live: "If you will, you are free; if you will, you will not have to blame anyone, or complain against anyone; everything will be in accordance with what is not merely your own will, but at the same time the will of God."[54] Bear and forbear; it is difficulties that both reveal and train true character.[55] Forbearing difficulties is also the path to freedom: "For freedom is not acquired by satisfying yourself with what you desire, but by destroying your desire."[56] Indeed, he goes so far as to suggest that if a man devotes himself to learning and contemplation, he can achieve self-emancipation, in contrast with other forms of apparent freedom which he equates with the freedom of the runaway slave: "If I emancipate myself from my masters, that is, from those things which render masters terrifying, what further trouble do I have, what master any more?"[57] Although Epictetus insists that by means of the inner strength that comes with forbearance it was possible for him "to get greatness of soul and nobility of character,"[58] we must demur, as indeed have most commentators not prone to masochism. This is, in fact, a thoroughly ignoble view, of human nature, of god, and of freedom.

Clearly dissatisfied, although doggedly repetitive of this view, Epictetus sought refuge in a wholly inner conception of freedom, for only in this sphere could he achieve the absolute version of freedom which he desired. Epictetus' problem was that he wanted his extreme version of freedom to be accepted by the powers that be but realized that no ruler or society could accept such a view of freedom. Our interests clash with those of others, and we are obliged to give way to the stronger. This is resolved in the outer and middle inns in two ways. One is the natural composition of human beings, whose "characteristic quality" is fidelity and friendship. Thus it is "the function of nature, to bind together and to harmonize our choice with the conception of what is fitting and helpful."[59] But the disorder inherent in outer freedom defined in extreme terms is also prevented by the ruler who, when he governs wisely, harmonizes part and whole, doing so, however, on the principle that "the whole is more sovereign than the part, and the state more sovereign than the citizen."[60] The only truly free person, it must have seemed to Epictetus, is the emperor; only he does not have to bear and forbear. The wise ruler, in pursuing his will, reconciles the wills of the parts with each other and with his own. In the outer world we are merely parts whose will must be reconciled and controlled. Hence we cannot be wholly free; for even though an emperor may act according to reason and reconcile us with what is good, he does so independently of our choice, and the capacity to exercise our free will is an essential part of being free.

But in the spiritual realm, the home to which we journey through contemplation, it is different. Epictetus sees the inner universe, to a degree, as a direct analogue to the outer universe. As in the outer world so "it goes also in this great city, the world; for here also there is a Lord of the Mansion who assigns each and every thing its place."[61] In this inner city, too, freedom exists as the highest goal. It is also true that we achieve our freedom by submitting to Zeus. Like the citizens of Nicopolis who "are wont to shout: 'Yea, by the fortune of Caesar, we are free men!' "[62] the citizen of the inner city can also shout, "Zeus has set me free." However, here the similarity ends. Submission to Zeus does not involve the need to reconcile my wishes with those of others, not because there are no others whose wishes must be reconciled in the inner city but because in this sphere I am a part of Zeus, one with him in his divine power: here "you are a being of primary importance; you are a fragment of God; you have with you a part of him."[63] In this city "it can no longer be regarded as unsocial for a man to do everything for his own sake" for what I do is god's will.[64]

It is important to understand that in the inner city Epictetus moves between three forms of freedom relating to three kinds of relationship with god. Sometimes he holds to the more classic Stoic view that we are free because we are one with the almighty, all-knowing power of god, the divine administrator. At other times he interprets the relationship more as a kind of power sharing, an inner civic freedom, in which the inner person is a citizen who shares in the running of the divine administration. And there is a third conception in which the inner person and god are seen not as an identity but more like that which prevails in the outer city. God remains separate from the citizens of his city, as Caesar does in the outer world, but with the important difference that, unlike the outer ruler, the inner ruler gives his citizens total freedom, including the freedom to disobey him. Nowhere is this last stated more clearly than in the chapter on providence:

> God has not merely given us these faculties, to enable us to bear all that happens without being degraded or crushed thereby, but—as became a good king and in very truth a father—He has given them to us free from all restraint, compulsion, hindrance; He has put the whole matter under our control without reserving even for Himself any power to prevent or hinder.[65]

Now, throughout the *Discourses* we find Epictetus shifting from one to the other version of inner freedom, and we can avoid much confusion by bearing this in mind. Why did he vacillate between them? It seems to me that the answer is to be found in Epictetus' own life. As W. A. Oldfather acutely observed, Epictetus "had the point of view of a man who had suffered from slavery and abhorred it, but had not been altogether able to escape its influence."[66] What may be called his god- or master-identified view of inner freedom was that of the freedman who desperately wanted personal freedom but had been too conditioned to survival under slavery to escape wholly the almighty power and discipline of the master. So the two were reconciled by the identification with the ex-master. For such a resolution, Epictetus had the perfect model: Epaphroditus, the freedman and administrative secretary of Nero, who was totally one with his master's interests and power, helping him in the end to take his own life.

The citizen-identified version of inner freedom, while mentioned from time to time, is poorly developed, and is often conflated with the god-identified conception. Thus in the same breath he will shift in speaking from the inner person as a "fragment" of god to one who is one with the godhead. What may be called the self-identified version of freedom, absolute inner personal freedom, reflected the passionate yearning of Epictetus, the slave and freedman, for total and complete independence from the former and, indeed, all masters. It is interesting that, in the inner city, freedom is either something given by the good god and master or is the result of sharing power with or identity with god. There is no talk of self-emancipation, of the need to avoid the spirit of the runaway slave, as there is in the discussion of freedom in the outer and middle inns or spheres.

In spite of these shifts, however, a close reading of the *Discourses* strongly suggests that intellectually the god-identified conception of freedom—freedom as complete power to direct the inner administration—is the one which most harmonizes with Epictetus' other views. He "is free for whom all things happen according to his moral purpose, and whom none can restrain."[67] Sometimes Epictetus goes so far as to speak of subordinating "his own will to him who administers the universe," but more often the inner relationship is less disquietingly identical with the outer world. The sovereign quality of all human beings is moral choice, which, by virtue of reason, "keeps everything else subordinate to it, and this moral choice itself free from slavery and subjection."[68] The citizen of the inner world is made not to serve but to rule. And what, asks Epictetus, is the profession of this citizen ruler? His answer involves a totally organic view of the inner city. By doing what is most natural, asserting our will to rule, we achieve the moral purpose.[69]

Let us now return to the philosophy of Marcus and see how he came to terms with the problem of freedom, especially in light of Epictetus' influence on his thinking. On outward freedom, Marcus has no problems and is in no doubt. His views are thoroughly Augustan. From Severus, he tells us, he has learned "to grasp the idea of a Commonwealth with the same laws for all governed on the basis of equality and free speech, also the idea of a monarchy which prizes the liberty of its subjects above all things."[70] His Christian subjects would certainly have held otherwise, but the judgment of history is favorable on Marcus' reign over his outer kingdom.

It is the inner kingdom that gives him trouble. He seeks redemption but keeps putting it off. He can guarantee the liberty of his subjects (that is, personal liberty under the rule of law) but not his own. "Remember how long you have delayed," he scolds himself,

> how often the gods have appointed the day of your redemption and you have let it pass. Now, if ever, you must realize of what kind of ordered universe you are a part, of what kind of governor of that universe you are an emanation, that a time limit has now been set for you and that if you do not use it to come out into the light, it will be lost, and you will be lost, and there will be no further opportunity.[71]

Here is a man speaking as if he were under a sentence of life, outer life, the fetters of his earthly existence, "a little soul carrying a corpse," as he writes, quoting Epictetus. The thing hangs before him like a rope. He has to find a way out of his bondage before his soul dies. In desperation, he keeps telling himself again and again to "perform every action as if it was the last of your life."[72] Great advice, but one gets the feeling that Marcus, like the modern bourgeois existentialist forever exhorting himself and others, "Commit thyself," while remaining thoroughly bourgeois, knows what to do but not quite how to do it. We know enough about his life independently to realize that he, least of all Romans, lived every act as if it were his last. He was an unhappy man, caring and kind in his own way, but in his detachment and self-absorption both utterly unloving and unlovable, forcing his frustrated wife to seek comfort in the arms of other men, and so unaware of her infidelity that when she died he had her deified.

Marcus had a thoroughly organic conception of both the outer and the inner universe. He is most lucid, and sounds most like a professional Stoic philosopher, on this issue. Because, as I shall argue shortly, it was the source of much of his personal problem, I wish to quote his views at some length. Mankind is, in his view, a community of intelligence[73] in which each member, each citizen has an allotted position. By performing your function naturally, "you complete the social system."[74]

> The Intelligence of the Whole has the common good in view. Therefore it has fashioned the inferior for the sake of the higher, and brought the higher into harmony with each other. You see how it has put some below, others beside one another, and given each his due, and brought the ruling ones together to be of one mind.[75]

"Right reason," law, is what holds the whole together: "there is no difference between the right Reason and the Reason embodied in justice."[76] Now, Marcus consciously sees the inner life in much the same way. Like Epictetus, he sometimes disconcertingly shifts his discussion from the inner to the outer as if there were no meaningful distinction between them. This is most conspicuously so in the eleventh book. Its opening passages make it clear that Marcus regards the rational, ordered universe as a free one. "The properties of the rational soul," he reflects, are that "it sees itself, it shapes itself, it makes itself such as it wishes to be, it gathers its own fruit."[77] In the outer world, the organic system ordered by reason is made to function properly through the direction of the king, who, in ruling, is merely playing his own natural part and thereby completing the system. "We were born for each other's sake. . . . I was born to be their protector, as the ram is to his flock and the bull to his herd."[78] Earlier he also told himself that one thing he should be prepared for is "to do only what reason, as embodied in the arts of kingship and legislation, perceives to be the benefit of mankind."[79]

Much the same thing goes on in the inner world, where the outward king is replaced by what Marcus calls the "directing mind." This concept is obviously very important to Marcus, since he returns to it often. It is, basically, the will that wills itself: "The directing mind is that which rouses itself, modifies itself, and makes itself such as it wishes to be, while making all that happens appear to itself such as it wishes to be."[80] It is, in other words, the ultimate condition of freedom, pure self-directed and self-creating activity. This directing mind not only directs itself but is also "the ruler of your soul."[81] It is strange, however, that Marcus insists on confining it "within its own frontier"— strange because at other times he freely moves between inner and outer worlds. It is allowed to perceive the feelings of the body but should remain indifferent, not passing judgment as to whether the "bodily affections are good or bad." The problem here is not so much the confinement of this ruler of the soul to its own sphere but Marcus' reference to a *you* who must ensure its confinement. Who or what is this other *you* who commands the ruler of the soul?

When we ask this question, we get to the heart of Marcus' dilemma. For centuries before Marcus, beginning most pronouncedly with Plato, thinkers had drawn on the analogy of the king in relation to his state in describing the inner kingdom of the soul. Marcus' teachers, in true Stoic fashion, would have done the same. Marcus, however, was unique among thinkers engaged in making this analogy in that he was the only king who wrote or reflected in any depth on the subject. Unlike everyone else before or after him, Marcus alone knew from personal experience what the outer referent of the analogy meant. And this, precisely, is his problem: kingship is not what it is cracked up to be. The king, for all his great power, does not make that much difference. Marcus has a low opinion of "public men, wisely practical as they believe themselves to be." He says they are "like children with running noses." And what does this genuine philosopher-king think of Plato's philosopher-king? "Do not expect Plato's ideal republic," he cautions himself, quite wisely; "be satisfied with the smallest step forward and consider this as no small achievement. Who will change men's convictions? Yet without a change of convictions what else is public life but enslavement of the people who lament and pretend to be persuaded?"[82]

Marcus the real king turned to the directing mind of the inner kingdom for the power and freedom which the world failed to provide him.

But alas, the inner kingdom did not work any better than Marcus' outer realm, for behind the inner emperor of the directing mind lurked a greater, ghostly power, the *you* whom Marcus addressed, the *you* who had to make sure that the inner king stuck to his realm. So, too, the inner emperor was without clothes; he was a mere completer of the inner psychic system. He might be a bull among his own herd, but above and behind the bull was an elusive pen keeper, the *you*, the unknowable, unteachable *you* to whom Marcus spoke in growing desperation, day after day, year after year.

It is this *you*, to whom the meditations are addressed, whom Marcus saw as the real slave master and not, as the conventional Stoic creed he advocated claimed, the body and its impulses. In one of the most penetrating entries in the diary,[83] Marcus begins by recounting, in the rote fashion of the believer, the Stoic doctrine of the relation between the "fiery part" of the whole person and the body. The lowly bodily elements serve the whole when they are forcibly kept in their place up until the moment when the whole decides to dissolve them. One cannot complain about the body when, like a good slave, it knows and keeps its place. This Marcus had succeeded in doing, for he had been a good Stoic, ever alert to any wicked impulse from his servile body, ready with the whip hand of the controlling mind to keep it in check.

Why, then, was there no peace and tranquility in the inner state? That is what confounded and tormented Marcus:

> Is it not a terrible thing that only the intelligent part of you is rebellious and indignant at the place assigned to it? Yet no force is brought to bear on it, only such influences as are in accord with its own nature. . . . Whenever the directing mind is indignant at anything that happens, then also is it leaving the post assigned to it, for it was made for piety and worship of the gods no less than for justice.[84]

Yet, indignant it remained. Why? What was it struggling against? Could it be that the Stoic doctrine that no force was brought to bear on it was wrong? Did the master have a master? Could it be that the bodily impulses were really the equivalent of the *servus vicarius*, the slave of a slave, a figure familiar to Marcus from the imperial household, and that by concentrating on it he had neglected the slave condition of the body's master?

I am convinced that just such an insight plagued Marcus. The Stoic metaphor of emancipation from inner slavery held force, but the doctrine had misled him terribly in identifying the wrong master and the wrong threat. The idea that one could be free outwardly, even be an emperor, yet be a slave to one's impulses was too pat, too clever by half, in the end too facile. The real danger was slavery to one's self. This is what Marcus' struggle was all about. He had to find the elusive pen keeper, the *you* who separated him from harmony with the world soul, the divine principle. Nothing in his studies had prepared him for that; indeed, everything in his Stoic doctrine had obfuscated the problem, had tricked him into a disastrous diversionary campaign to do battle with the wrong enemy. Until he came to terms with the *you*, he would never be able to emancipate himself.

Once we understand this, the many otherwise cryptic passages and quotations in the diary begin to make sense: "You are born a slave, you have no share of reason,"[85] a wholly un-Stoic remark, left cryptically isolated, now makes perfect sense. So does the next passage, which has baffled many readers: "And in my own heart I laughed."[86] The quotation is from the *Odyssey*. The Cyclopes end their assault on Odysseus when Polyphemus tells them that he is being killed by *Nobody*, leading him to laugh. Was this passage a source of the most bitter and complex irony for Marcus, *not* because he, like the Cyclopes, had withdrawn from the struggle with the real foe on being told by his Stoic teachers that he was being killed by nobody, but precisely because they had failed to tell him that he was indeed being killed by the elusive nobody who was himself, the *you* he harangued and scolded each day but could not find? Then again, there is the statement from Epictetus "Only a madman looks for a fig in winter," a not particularly profound observation and hardly worth quoting—until, that is, we appreciate the peculiar nature of Marcus' struggle, his search for something as elusive as "a fig in winter," his contest against a "nobody," a contest that was driving him mad, for as he notes in another otherwise thoroughly mysterious entry, "The contest is not just about a trifling subject, but about madness and sanity."[87]

In the end, Marcus did find a kind of meager solace. He conceded and gave up the search for emancipation. Life, he finally concluded, is a comic drama in which your entry and your exit are determined by a magistrate. The play may have a structure but, deviating sharply from the tidy organicism of his earlier entries, Marcus concludes his journal with the magistrate telling the protesting comic actor that though the play may have five acts, "in your life, at any rate, the three acts are the whole play."[88] This is a sad note on which to leave a man who spent all his life claiming to believe in the divine freedom of reason in its harmony with the soul of the world: a babbling comic being ushered off the stage as arbitrarily as he had been ushered in, finding comfort in the undignified adieu "Depart graciously, for he who dismisses you is also gracious."

In their search for the elusive grail of the most inner freedom, both Marcus and Epictetus turned to Stoicism as many people turn today to religion. The creed took them far, but not far enough. Marcus the emperor ended his reflections convinced that he had been born, and remained, a slave, unable to find in the inner kingdom the emancipation which all his life he had sought.

The other, Epictetus, the slave of a slave, ended his quest in an inner kingdom modeled on his master's mansion and with a conception of freedom based on complete identification with the power of god. He was like the woman who achieves freedom and independence from men by being utterly male identified. Freedom as the pursuit of one's own identity is finally abandoned. But with it goes, too, the possibility of all real dignity, of personal responsibility as person distinct from god, as woman from man, as slave from master. In one of the saddest passages of the *Discourses*, Epictetus summarizes his creed, which he calls "the road which leads to freedom . . . the only surcease of slavery," by quoting once again from the hymn of Cleanthes.[89] He is then challenged by a member of his audience, who is clearly unhappy with the implications of the creed.

What, he is asked, if a tyrant orders you to say something that is unworthy of you? The question is cruelly perceptive, for it gets right to the heart of the moral problem of late Stoicism, its relegation of certain patterns of behavior to the realm of the indifferent, with the possibility that immoral behavior can on occasion be tolerated. Epictetus is initially stumped. He asks for time to think about the question. The interlocutor will have none of it. "Think about it *now*?" he asks, flabbergasted; what in heaven's name has Epictetus been thinking about all his life, if not this? Epictetus comes out badly in the ensuing exchange. Eventually someone asks him point-blank whether he thinks that he, Epictetus, is free, for all his philosophizing. Epictetus confesses that while he wants to be, and prays to be, he is still "not able to look into the face of [his] masters." He illustrates his failure by reference to his concern with his lameness, but since he uses the plural, one strongly suspects that he has in mind, too, his former literal master. In desperation, Epictetus then states that, though he himself is not free, he can point to someone who is. And who is that? Of all people, Diogenes the Cynic, the very apotheosis of self-identified freedom in both the inner and the outer world. This is most revealing, for it suggests clearly that the view of freedom to which his creed had led him was wholly at variance with the conception of freedom which he most desired. But if freedom was getting what he most desired, then Epictetus, in his inability to achieve the freedom he really desired, was condemned to slavery by the very freedom his creed forced him to advocate. The road to freedom, alas, in the end led nowhere.

No creed should so fail its adherents. The problem with late Stoicism for people such as Marcus and Epictetus was not so much that it was a spent force, intellectually, but that they sought from it something which it was inherently incapable of providing: spiritual freedom. It could not, because only religion could do so, and however great the religious *content* of late Stoicism, it remained divorced from religion in one fundamental respect: it employed as a means of achieving truth the method of speculation, of reason, rather than the method of faith. Faith and reason, as means toward spiritual truth, stand not so much opposed to each other but, as Augustine saw clearly, in conflict over which of the two should take precedence. Stoicism, like all intellectualist creeds, held that before one can believe one must first understand. Augustine and the early Christian fathers, like Euripides centuries earlier, knew that this was a perverse inversion of the path to spiritual truth and freedom.

The Christian moment had not merely arrived. It was long overdue.

PART FOUR

Christianity and the Institutionalization of Freedom

CHAPTER 16

Jesus and the Jesus Movement

1. A RELIGION OF SALVATION ON THE PERIPHERY OF EMPIRE

Christianity emerged as an apocalyptic sect of a strange religion on the distant periphery of the Roman Empire, rapidly grew into a cult in the urban centers of the Hellenistic semiperiphery, and matured into a church in the Roman metropolitan center. Thus, in its most critical period of development, Christianity moved through all levels of the Roman imperial system.

Two things about this development immediately strikes us as quite amazing. One is the sheer magnitude of this feat when viewed from the perspective of world history; the second, and more puzzling, is the rapidity of the development. There are many other cases of important religions moving from rural backward areas to urban centers of influence and power, but the speed with which Christianity developed, especially during its first thirty to fifty years, is unprecedented, and indeed remains something of a sociohistorical enigma.

Whatever the main reasons for the extraordinary diffusion and growth of the religion, one of them must surely have been the fact that it met certain fundamental social, psychological, and spiritual needs of the many peoples of the empire. Our previous analyses of the Greek and Roman world have prepared us for an understanding of what these needs might be. For they were, after all, similar to those which the philosophical creeds and the mystery cults of Greece and Rome had been developed to meet.

The fundamental need of the times was that of salvation—the desperate need for relief from physical and mental strain and uncertainty, for inner peace and security. Christianity began as, and remained, one such religion of salvation, the most successful of them. Like the different creeds and cults, Christianity was to offer its own version of salvation, its own solution to the problem of the times. But it was unique in what it offered, and how it offered its solutions.

All religions of salvation were in one way or another involved with the problem of spiritual freedom or liberation. In the cults of Attis and Cybele, for example, the "disciples' trances freed them from the authority of norms and conventions," and, adds Mircea Eliade, "in a certain sense, it was the discovery of freedom."[1] At essence, they focused on a savior (Greek, *sōtēr*) who in the form of god, or semidivine man or prophet, or even king, delivered or saved his followers from the evils and travails of the world.[2] Such religions differed, as Max Weber observed, in terms of "what one wants to be saved from, and what one wants to be saved for."[3] Christianity belongs to that subclass of religions of salvation for which the hope of salvation has the most transformative implications for the lives of its adherents, involving a rebirth of the spirit in a new life *now* in preparation for life in the hereafter.[4] This rebirth, paving the way for salvation in the afterlife, is based on belief in a soteriological myth of a god or incarnate man-god who struggles with the forces of darkness and, by his victory, makes spiritual liberation possible.[5]

The terrors from which people wished to be saved were not necessarily things to which they felt themselves enslaved. Indeed, the typical religion of salvation saw the main terror as fate, more specifically, as bad luck or fortune. What people wanted was not complete removal from fate, but to be placed on its positive side. Put crudely, the savior saved them from bad luck and brought them good luck. As A. D. Nock pointed out in his classic study of ancient religions, when the jailor at Thessalonica asked Paul and Silas, "What must I do to be saved?" (Acts 16:30), he in all likelihood had no notion of religious freedom in mind but really meant, "What am I to do in order to avoid any unpleasant consequences of the situation created by this earthquake?"[6]

Christianity, alone among the religions of salvation, made freedom the doctrinal core of its soteria. There were, to be sure, other religions which were preoccupied with freedom in the true sense of the term, most notably the cult of Dionysus and Mithraism. But the cult of the Bacchae was limited to only one kind of freedom—the pure expression of negative personal freedom in extreme form—and between this limitation and the excesses of its cultic practices, it was bound to be suppressed by the public authorities. Mithraism, as we have seen, had a more developed conception of religious freedom, and it is precisely for this reason that it was the religion which offered the strongest challenge to Christianity for the ultimate pride of place as the religion of the empire. Mithraism, however, was no match for Christianity with respect to the centrality of freedom in its soteria. Its main objective was not the experience of freedom per se but salvation from unfortunate fate in favor of a positive fate, good luck, in this life.

Christianity did not begin as a religion of freedom. In its earliest phase, that of the movement started by Jesus, and even in its broader Palestinian version, Christianity was largely another eschatological sect, sociologically and religiously very similar to its other Jewish counterparts. Even in this early phase, however, and especially in the teaching and religious behavior of Jesus, one may detect the seeds of later developments. But these seeds were only that: possibilities. The movement Jesus initiated could and did move in several directions, and only one of the variants—the one that triumphed—became the full-fledged religion of freedom that conquered the Roman world.

We may distinguish four phases in the development of early Christianity: the prophetic phase of Jesus and the Jesus movement; the primitive Palestinian sect; the Hellenistic phase of Jewish and gentile Christianity; and the culmination of this phase in the religion of Paul.

Jesus began his teaching around A.D. 29; Paul was martyred about A.D. 60. In the intervening thirty years a religion had not only been created but gone through several remarkable transformations and, in spite of seemingly insurmountable obstacles, was well on its way to becoming one of the important cults of the empire. It is even more remarkable that not only had the organizational basis of the religion's successful diffusion throughout the empire already been established but all its most important theological ideas formulated. Paul, indeed, marks the beginning and the high point of creative Christian theology. With the notable exception of the Johannine writings, Christian theology would take a downhill course for the next four hundred years, at best amounting to no more than crude patristic attempts to reformulate the creed in the more intellectually respectable terms of Hellenistic philosophies, at worst a descent into the most vulgar kind of soteriological legalism.

2. THE JESUS MOVEMENT

Jesus was not the founder of Christianity. Nothing he said or did gave the slightest indication that he wished to found a church. Indeed, the very idea of a church, or even a cult, contradicted everything he said. This seemingly startling fact has been "the most fundamental, delicate and controversial problem" in the study of the early history of the religion.[7] Actually, from the viewpoint of the sociology of religion, church historians have made too much of this problem. It is in the nature of prophets not to found churches but to proclaim some new vision, or to reinterpret an old vision in profoundly new ways. Between the prophet and those who, following him, found a church in his name, there is a simple sociological dialectic. The prophet reveals a new truth about the relationship between mankind and God. His followers translate that truth in terms that are sociologically meaningful. Weber called this the process of routinization.

But with Christianity the matter is not that simple. In the first place, at the heart of Jesus' teaching was the proclamation of the kingdom of God. Some sayings clearly indicate that the kingdom had already arrived; others, apparently less authentic, suggest that it was still to come. Maurice Goguel has reconciled the two by arguing that Jesus saw the coming of the kingdom of God in dynamic rather than instantaneous terms. That is, the apocalypse had already begun with his coming and would be completed very shortly, certainly within his lifetime or soon thereafter. It was still an eschatological message, and, in light of the behavior of his immediate disciples—those constituting the core of the Jesus movement—it was most emphatically an apocalyptic one.[8]

Jesus was a Jew preaching to Jews in terms very similar to those of other apocalyptic preachers of his time. His mission began with the baptism by the leader of one such sect, John the Baptist, some of whose followers resented his imitation of their leader. Furthermore, Jesus explicitly forbade his disciples to preach to the Gentiles, a ban that caused some embarrassment for later gentile converts to the creed. He and his immediate followers were peripatetic charismatics—homeless wanderers who disdained earthly possessions and depended on those to whom they preached for their sustenance. They were of rural, working-class origins—carpenters, fishermen, and the like—and preached in the rural areas around the villages and minor urban centers of Galilee.[9]

Like that of many saviors and divine heroes of the Hellenistic world, Jesus' personal origin was itself ambiguous. The question of the legitimacy of his birth deserves to be taken more seriously.[10] The celebration of homelessness is one thing; his aloofness to his mother, quite another. Jesus' background was marginal in another important respect. He grew up in Galilee, which had a large gentile population (the term *Galilee* literally means "circle of Gentiles") that had remained basically semipagan. While Jesus was certainly a Jew, he may have been a minority member of his own hometown, Nazareth, even though belonging to the majority group in his country. One can only speculate on the effects of this sociologically marginal background. I rather suspect that it may have had something to do with his ambivalence toward Gentiles: on the one hand, fraternizing with them to a degree that scandalized his fellow Jews; on the other hand, forbidding his disciples to preach his message to the Gentiles.

There was a marked hostility to the prosperous people and the urban culture of Palestine. The movement was not, however, in the least bit political, even though its appeal was rooted in the sociopolitical realities of the time. Rather, it gave religious expression to the enormous tensions that had been building up in Palestine from the end of the Maccabean dynasty.[11] The conflicts between the urban elite and the rural poor, between Jews and Gentiles, between marginal colonials and Roman conquerors, between obeyers of the Jewish law and transgressors, had all been vented in the apocalyptic proclamations of numerous Jewish sects. A few of these, such as the Zealots, had been avowedly political and anti-imperialist, and their activism led to the destruction of Jerusalem a few decades after Jesus' crucifixion, marking the end of the Jesus movement in its original form. Most, however, were either apolitical or antipolitical. Apocalypticism makes politics irrelevant.[12]

Like the leaders of many sects of the times, both in and outside of Judaism, Jesus relied more on what he did than on what he said to get his message across. What he did mainly was to work miracles. He was an exorcist who healed the sick, especially the insane, by driving demons out of them. The working of miracles was central to the mission, and success, of both Jesus and early Christianity.[13] Miracles served a twofold purpose in Jesus' ministry. They demonstrated his divine powers and were obviously the main means by which followers were attracted. However, the miracles were also taken as signs of the present, and coming, kingdom of God. The best-authenticated sayings of Jesus—those of the Q community—clearly show that he interpreted his miracles in this way. "If it is by the finger of God that I cast out demons," he said, "then the kingdom of god has come upon you."[14]

In brief, Jesus' religious teaching amounted to a proclamation of the kingdom of God, a call for preparedness and watchfulness, and an implicit statement that he himself, by his miracle workings, was the sign of the beginning of the apocalypse which would soon come to fruition.[15] Sinners, especially those estranged from God in their hearts, regardless of their outward obedience to the law, were called to repentance and were assured a positive response from a merciful God.

Only the bold claim that the kingdom of God had already dawned was original in light of the teachings of other, similar sects of the time. Nor was his ethical teaching, in its general outline, any more original. It may be wondered why an eschatological prophet would want to propound an ethical teaching at all, especially one who claimed that the kingdom of God had already dawned. Surely, it was too late for anyone to change. Christian theologians have exercised great ingenuity in explaining this problem, but there is no need for us to get further into it.[16] While logically contradictory, such ethical preaching appeared religiously consistent to many apocalyptic groups in Jesus' time, the Qumran community, with its strict obedience to law, being a prime case in point.

Whether authentically his or redactions by the evangelists, most of the more celebrated sayings associated with Jesus are actually familiar Jewish sayings of the time; for example, the golden rule—"As you wish that men would do to you, do so to them"[17]—was preached by the liberal reformist Pharisee Hillel. However, the injunctions "Love your enemies and pray for those who persecute you"[18] and "To him who strikes you on the cheek, offer the other also"[19] have no parallel in traditional Judaism. They are sociologically unrealistic as an ethic for normal living, but make a great deal of sense if one believes that the kingdom of God has already dawned and the end is near at hand. More important, they are consistent with what was most radically innovative in the implicit, social doctrine of the Jesus movement, as we will see later.

It is when we explore further those aspects of Jesus' teachings and behavior that were uniquely his own that we begin to detect precursors of the Christian preoccupation with freedom. Jesus' spiritual ministry was new less in the content of what he preached than in his religious behavior and attitude toward God and the law. There is a markedly existential quality in Jesus' approach to religion. He revealed his message in the quality of his relationship with his disciples and followers, and in the unusual method of addressing God. His most striking peculiarity was his attitude toward ritual purity. He ate what his more orthodox fellow Jews considered unclean food, and enjoyed drinking wine to a degree that was offensive to any rabbi. Worse, he associated with riffraff and deviants of all sorts—prostitutes, publicans, and imperial tax collectors. His public informality with children and women was a great scandal to his fellow Jewish contemporaries. Indeed, several of the Gnostic gospels recently discovered at Nag Hammadi suggest that there was among the male disciples some jealousy toward Jesus' favorite, Mary Magdalene. The Gospel of Thomas, composed about the same time as the synoptics, and based on sources similar to the "Q" saying source used by Matthew and Luke, ends with Jesus rejecting the sexist request of Simon Peter to remove Mary from their midst because "women are not worthy of Life."[20]

Jesus' behavior reflected an even more fundamental difference from that of other Jewish apocalyptic leaders: his critical attitude toward Jewish law. It was this, of course, which got him into such trouble with the Jewish leaders, culminating in his condemnation by the Sanhedrin.[21] Even more deplorable was the authoritative manner he assumed when discussing how the law should be interpreted: "You have heard it said . . . but *I* say unto you." The same manner is found in Jesus' peculiar use of the term *Amen* (Truly), not at the end of a prayer, as in traditional Judaism, but at the beginning: "Verily, I say unto you . . ."

Jesus' use of the term *Abba*, in addressing God, was also radically new and offensive to his fellow Jews. This is the intimate and familiar form of the Aramaic word for father, and no Jew of Jesus' time dared address God on such terms. Edward Schillebeeckx finds in Jesus' *abba* address of God "the unique quality of Jesus' religious life,"[22] and it is also his point of departure for the claim that Jesus' mission was essentially a gift of liberation. Jesus, on the one hand, freely established fellowship with an unusually wide range of people, sinners of all sorts, including the very dregs of society. At the same time, he claimed equal intimacy with God. In this way, an important message was expressed, not verbally but through praxis. There was hope and forgiveness for all.[23] His relationships with people "liberate them and make them glad." What he liberated them from was not just a casuistic and rigid view of the law but a constricting view of God.[24] The law and good works had come between God and people; a renewed empathy with God was advocated. Piety was not enough. Disposition, what lurked within the heart, was what mattered in relations with God: "in freeing the individual person he gives him back to himself in a joyful commitment to the living God."[25] While I agree with this interpretation, I am uneasy with the use of the language of liberation to describe Jesus' achievement. In Jesus' view, people had not been fettered to the law; his fellow Jews, as he obviously knew, felt no such constraint. It is therefore anachronistic and culturally inappropriate to speak of Jesus' liberating people from Jewish law; this is to identify Jesus and his world too closely with Paul and his quite distinct social environment. Rather, Jesus felt that the *approach* of his fellow Jews to God—with which they were all too happy—was wrong and in need of redefinition. This is not to liberate; it is to clarify and rectify. As we will see shortly, people were not made *free* by Jesus to love God; they were commanded to do so.

Clearly, a powerful, charismatic personality drew people to him and persuaded them to this new approach to the divine. There is general agreement among historians of the early church that prophecy was its central hallmark.[26] Jesus taught mainly how to be religious the way he was. As a preacher of new ideas, he was not successful: the content of his message, outside of its existential context, was, to repeat, not original; and the throngs who came to see his miracles just as quickly turned against him at his trial. Furthermore, the main outward point of his teaching, that the kingdom of God had already dawned and was soon to materialize, was obviously a failure. It didn't happen.

But while he failed as a preacher and eschatological prophet, he succeeded mightily as a trainer of other prophets. He produced a large number of devoted imitators, a veritable school of charismatics who learned from fellowship and through praxis with him. The result was not only the Jesus movement but the rapid diffusion all over Palestine of his message and, even more, his existential mode of religious-being-in-the-world. His actual message was simply too radical, its failure to change the world too embarrassingly obvious, for them to follow. Instead, his followers imitated him in what he had done best: proclaim the kingdom of God through healing, driving out of demons, and close fellowship with God through loving, intense fellowship with their own disciples.

While not explicitly concerned with freedom, two aspects of Jesus' mission may have paved the way for the later thrust toward the ethic of liberation in post-Palestinian Christianity. Rudolf Bultmann has emphasized that Jesus both denationalized and "dehistoricized" the apocalyptic message of the Jewish prophets. The dawning and coming kingdom of God did not entail a final phase in the history of the Jewish nation and of all nations culminating in a new and glorious Davidic kingdom but was directed at individuals: "The judgement is coming not on nations but on individuals who must give account of themselves before God; and it is individuals whom coming salvation will bless."[27] This dehistoricization of the apocalypse had the paradoxical result of radically shifting the focus of religion onto the personal history of each individual: "precisely that God, who stands aloof from the history of nations, meets each man in his own little history, his everyday life with its daily gift and demand; de-historicized man (i.e. naked of his supposed security within his historical group) is guided into his concrete encounter with his neighbor, in which he finds his true history."[28]

Closely related to this is another peculiarity of the Jesus movement: alone among Jewish prophetic movements of the time, it did not use the exodus "as a model of liberation from foreign rule."[29] Indeed, it was explicitly opposed to all forms of national or political resistance. This unusual emphasis pointed implicitly outward toward "a readiness for reconciliation which transcends frontiers and culminates in the requirement to love one's enemy."[30] But Jesus' explicit muting of this implication presents some awkwardness for those who would like to trace the later universalism of the early church back to its Messiah.

Jesus remained thoroughly Jewish, indeed Near Eastern, in his refusal to interpret human relations with God in terms of the language or metaphor of freedom. Jesus' God is un-Hebraic in his immediacy and emphasis on conscience, but he is very Jewish in his concern with righteousness and in his *demand* for what *he* wants. For Jesus, as for all his fellow Jews, only God is free in his essentially asymmetric relations with people.

In the final analysis, Jesus' originality inheres in precisely this combination of a traditionally Judaic God who demands with a new conception of what is demanded—not legalistic piety or social purity but complete inward purity of heart which, for him, constituted less a rejection of the law than a renewed and better realization of it. On this I find Bultmann thoroughly persuasive. Jesus' God will not be satisfied with a mere observance of the law which leaves people free to do as they please in those areas where the law is silent. There is no such freedom. To the contrary:

> *God demands the whole will of man* and knows no abatement in His demand. . . . Man, upon whose whole self God's demand is made, has no freedom toward God; he is accountable for his life as a whole—as the parable of the talents teaches. . . . *He may not, must not, cannot raise any claim before God,* but is like the slave who only has his duty to do and can do no more.[31]

It is most interesting that Jesus uses a parable about slaves to make one of his most important religious pronouncements. God is equated with the slave master who orders his slave to prepare his supper and expects the slave to wait on him, then have his own supper afterward. The slave receives no thanks for doing what he was commanded and can expect no reward for his service; in like manner, human beings in their relation with God should see themselves as doing what is commanded. They can expect no reward: "We are unworthy servants [slaves]; we have only done what was our duty."[32] What is interesting about Jesus' use of the slave metaphor here (and in other passages) is not that he takes the relation so wholly for granted, or even that he can compare God to a slave master—that also happened in the Hellenistic and Roman worlds—but that he in no way conceives of the relation as one that generates freedom. There is no such ideal in the consciousness of Jesus or among his fellow Palestinian Jews. Like Antigonus of Socho, one of the fathers of the synagogue who lived some two hundred years before Christ and was the originator of Jesus' maxim, Jesus taught that what was demanded was complete obedience to the will of God, a surrender made bearable by complete confidence in him.[33]

But another aspect of the point being made comes closest to what may be called Jesus' dominant or master value. Not freedom, not escape from one's duty, not a free will, but love. What, in Jesus' view, is the will of God? asks Bultmann. "The demand for love," he answers, and there is no doubt that the call to love God and one's neighbors is expressed in the imperative.[34] Here again, Jesus' vision is distinctive even as it draws on contemporary Judaism. Jesus grew up in a highly honorific culture, and the honorific complex of values provided the source metaphor for the Judaic conception of God, as it did for all the ancient Near Eastern peoples.[35] Jesus keeps the honorific idea of an almighty God who demands obedience from his followers, but he departs from it in proclaiming that what he demands to be obeyed most is his command to love.[36] Jesus also departs from the honorific metaphor in his intimacy with the father. His God, while still demanding to be obeyed, is no longer so frighteningly aloof that one cannot even utter his name. He becomes "Daddy." Implicit in this is a third departure from the honorific model: if the all-powerful *Abba* can demand so soft a thing as love, clearly the same holds for all his children; and what is more, *the commandment to love is a commandment to personal equality*. This Jesus demonstrated in his social relations with the dregs of humanity. The hierarchical basis of the honorific system is completely undermined.

This analysis makes it possible to recognize what was truly original in Jesus' most important sermon, that on the mount. Taken out of context, every one of these sayings can be traced back to contemporary reformist Judaism. The poor turning to God for justice was a hallmark of traditional Judaism, as was its tradition of almsgiving. But the traditional context was wholly honorific and hierarchical. No Orthodox Jew would have claimed this to be God's major concern, not only because it would have been inconsistent with his or her sociological view of things but because it was blasphemy to claim to know what God intends for mankind. In breaking out of the honorific mold, while keeping the notion of the commanding God, Jesus arrives at the startlingly new conception of the traditional pieties. He proclaims love to be God's greatest demand but also teaches, as Schillebeeckx has pointed out, that "showing mercy is, despite everything, the deepest purpose that God intends to fulfil in history."[37] Hence we arrive at the real subtext of the beatitudes. They amount to a complete reversal of values:

> What they quite unmistakably enshrine is a spiritual affirmation of the ultimate power of powerlessness—of a belief that however much improving the world by our human resources is necessary . . . at the deepest level there is a suffering, an impotence which no human being can remove and from which we can be liberated only by virtue of the fact that "God will rule" for the final good of all men. There is a human impotence which God alone can relieve. That was the basis on which Jesus himself proceeded.[38]

We arrive, then, with a deeper understanding of the real social meaning of Jesus' ministry and its relation to his spiritual project. There is no conception of spiritual freedom. We surrender totally to God, as a perfect slave does to his master. In our surrender we are relieved of our slavelike spiritual impotence. However, the God to which we surrender warmly commands us to love. In that command is a stunningly radical implication for our outer, social world: we express our love of God by loving our fellow human beings and by recognizing their complete equality with us. This is not the valuation of freedom. It is the insistence on, the celebration of, a value infinitely more challenging, more humane, and more divine. Put simply: Love thy neighbor as thyself.

The world was then neither ready nor willing to live by such an ideal. It is still not ready. Instead of embracing his message, his followers eventually constructed a religion that made not the message but the messenger the object of their devotion. In so doing, they paved the way for the creation of a religion, in his name, which this poor, radically egalitarian country Jew would barely have recognized, a religion that made not equality but freedom its central dogma. Let us now see how it was done.

CHAPTER 17

Between Jesus and Paul

Jesus' ignominious execution on the cross created a monumental crisis for his followers. The trauma was resolved through the dogma of his resurrection and his second coming, which was near at hand, and for which they continued to prepare themselves through repentance and righteous living. And, in imitation of Jesus, they would continue to prophesy, not only through preaching but through the working of miracles. Instead of using the symbol "kingdom of God," as Jesus had done, indicating God's direct intervention, they shifted to the symbol of "Jesus coming as Son of Man," that is, God acting through an intermediary. This, as Norman Perrin and Dennis Duling have argued, is the critical link between Jesus and primitive Christianity.[1]

The kerygma of the resurrection was followed closely by the announcement that Jesus was himself the Messiah for whom the Jews had been waiting: "the proclaimer became the proclaimed."[2] The Palestinian congregation, however, while it made his messiahship central, was careful not to declare Jesus divine. That would have been the decisive breaking point with Judaism; by not doing so, most of the Palestinian congregation could remain, however tenuously, a sect within Judaism.[3]

But Jesus' followers were a laughingstock and a scandal to their fellow Jews. The kerygma of the resurrection and Jesus' messiahship created as many problems as it solved. The idea of bodily resurrection was viewed with derision; a messiah who could work miracles yet not save himself from the cross was an absurdity. The response of the apostolic congregation to this problem—what Bultmann calls "the scandal of the cross"—was to identify the Messiah with the suffering lamb of Isaiah, the anointed one. The idea of a messiah as an expiatory and sacrificial figure was outrageously new in Judaism. It exposed Jesus' followers to greater ridicule, but it offered a meaningful symbolic solution to a painful spiritual dilemma.[4]

This solution was not, however, without its problems. The first was the awkward fact that Jesus had made no explicit claim that he was the Messiah. The second and more problematic was that Jesus at no time in his own ministry anticipated, much less gave, any such interpretation of his death as the early church did. Considering the enormous importance that the early church soon placed on his death, making it more important than his life, it was a profound embarrassment to find no reference to it in the life of the Messiah himself. Nonetheless, with the Easter faith, as Maurice Goguel observed, we have passed from the history of Jesus and the Jesus movement to that of the believing church.[5]

Differences, however, emerged among the believers not long after Jesus' execution.[6] There was a rural group of wandering charismatics which kept close to the areas where Jesus had preached and to this methods and prophecy. A second group, settled in Jerusalem, was led by James, Jesus' conservative brother. This group developed the Easter faith and established the young congregation as a grudgingly recognized sect within Judaism, an essential requirement of which was the prohibition of any claim that Jesus was divine. The other demand was respect for Jewish law, the Torah, and acceptance of temple worship. The price of survival was re-Judaization.

The third group to emerge in Palestine was the band of Greek-speaking Jews in Jerusalem centered on Stephen. When Stephen was stoned to death by his Jewish persecutors, the circle around him fled back to their Hellenistic diaspora bases, taking the religion with them. That flight was the decisive movement in the history of Christianity. Forming the nucleus of what Perrin and Duling have called Hellenistic Jewish Mission Christianity, they proselytized mainly among fellow Greek-speaking Jews of the diaspora and, more successfully, among the gentile "god-fearers" and converts to Judaism, especially in those areas of the Hellenistic world with large Jewish populations.[7] This group reinterpreted primitive Christianity in Hellenistic terms, fusing Hellenic, Jewish, and primitive Christian elements. Jewish Scriptures in Greek, the Septuagint, were reinterpreted as prophecies of Jesus' life and death, and Jewish liturgy and synagogue worship were adapted to the cultic needs of the new religion. The movement's most critical innovation was the use of the Hellenistic title "Lord" (*kyrios*, in Greek) as the most common honorific title for Jesus. This had two effects. It shifted the focus from Jesus the redeemer, the Judaic Christ who would return to judge, to Jesus the glorified Lord. The name Christ (Greek *Christos*, Messiah) became almost what today we could call a surname to the forename Jesus, instead of its literal Palestinian meaning, "Jesus, the Redeemer."

As Christianity spread through the Jewish communities of the Hellenistic world and as more and more Gentiles were converted, it increasingly took on the aspects of a mystery cult. Like the other mystery cults, Christianity also had "its myth of the hero, the gospel story of Jesus; its initiation rite, baptism; its sacred meal."[8] Gentile Hellenistic Christianity took the Christological idea three critical steps further. First, it fully proclaimed Jesus a divine figure, in so doing breaking irrevocably with Judaism. The unintelligible term "Son of Man" was now abandoned in favor of the titles "Son of God" and "Lord." Second, the group reinterpreted Jesus' life and death in the familiar mystery-cult terms of the redeemer or divine lord who descends to earth as an act of saving grace, then ascends back to heaven. This was already implicit in the simple Easter faith of the apostles, and in the more elaborated form of the Jewish missionary group. But it was now fully fused with, and expressed in terms of, the hero myth of the Hellenistic mystery cults. Third, the early gentile Christians moved away from the primitive conception of Jesus' death as a sacrificial act of expiation to the more comprehensible conception of the resurrection as an act of glorification. This got around the embarrassment of Jesus' ignominious death. Not the suffering lamb but the glorified Lord was emphasized: and the promise to believers was that they would, within their lifetime, share in his glorification.

A serious problem with this broad outline is that it fails to explain the rapidity with which the new cult spread.[9] One is astonished to discover, upon closer scrutiny, that Paul's conversion took place no more than six, and quite possibly only two, years after Jesus' execution, in ca. 30. Stephen was martyred a couple years after Jesus' death, and his group began to spread out to the Hellenistic diaspora a year or so later—in other words, almost contemporaneously with Paul's conversion. By the second half of the thirties, there was already a well-established group in Antioch, so distinctive and well known that people began to call its members by a common name: Christians. We have here a real sociological mystery. Cults, it is true, do have a tendency to develop rapidly. But rarely this fast, and, what is more problematic, almost never do such rapid doctrinal changes and "traditions" develop within a period of less than a decade.

Though this question is fascinating, an answer to it would take us too far afield. We may briefly mention only two of the more intriguing recent suggestions. One is that of Martin Hengel, who argues that Jesus had *independently* formulated much of what would appeal to the Hellenistic world and that "the real bridge between Jesus and Paul" was the circle of Hellenistic Jews around Stephen in Jerusalem. Downplaying Gnostic and Hellenistic religious influences, he proposes that "the decisive factor is the spirit-inspired interpretation of *the message of Jesus in the new medium of the Greek language.*"[10] However suggestive, this explanation does not fully account for the rapidity of the cult's diffusion.

An alternative conjecture, powerfully argued by Morton Smith, is that the Jesus movement began its meteoric penetration of the Hellenistic world *before Jesus' death.*[11] This hypothesis rejects the view that Jesus was a mere country hick and the traditional tendency to overemphasize the isolation of rural Palestine. Not only was Palestine far more involved with the wider Hellenistic world than has normally been thought,[12] but, being a small state that emphasized temple worship, it had links between city and country that were far stronger than has normally been supposed. Smith suggests that Jesus may have been a far more traveled prophet than has generally been allowed, and may well have been influenced by alien ideas in his religious thinking and miracle working. The Jesus movement must have been exceptionally popular because of its leader's skill as a miracle worker and his appeal to the poor, for only this can explain why he was executed, and why the movement spread so rapidly after his death: "the course of events presupposes a popular following, the following accords with the miracle stories, both stories and following authenticate the sayings promising salvation for the poor, and these contradict the threat of general damnation."[13] In light of his unusually friendly attitude toward Gentiles and renegades such as the tax collectors Matthew and Thomas, it is reasonable to assume that he prohibited his disciples from preaching to the Gentiles precisely because of their success in so doing, especially if they had begun to do so in his name without his permission, a not uncommon problem faced by most successful prophets at that time.[14]

One of the most effective ways of propagating a message, especially a complex one, is to impart it in two stages—the first priming the targeted audience for what is to come later, the second then completing and reinforcing the message. Something like this took place in early

Christianity. Jesus' fame had broken out of the rural Jewish regions of Palestine and had been spread by imitators and by his wider circle of disciples, the seventy (or seventy-two) whom Jesus "appointed" and sent ahead of him "two-by-two," and who later "returned with joy, saying, 'Lord, even the demons are subject to us in your name!' "[15] Over such a crowd of disciples, Jesus, the very antithesis of organization man, would have had no control; indeed, he shunned full control even over the intimate twelve around him, as Judas' betrayal demonstrates. Almost certainly this group took the news of his miracles and eschatological message to the pagans and Greek-speaking Jews all over Palestine and Syria as far north as Antioch, a region which, as Hengel has noted, "was limited both sociologically and geographically."[16]

Then came the dramatic news of his death, resurrection, and ascension in glory to heaven, brought mainly by the circle around Stephen who had fled Jerusalem. This double-staged propagandistic thrust would have had a tremendous impact on the populations of the region, especially the God fearers and proselytes to Judaism who, we know, were among the earliest converts to Christianity. The "spirit-filled" Stephen group would have found a ready audience for their heralding, ready not just because of the more general psychosocial needs created by the strains and insecurities of the Roman-Hellenistic world but because of the priming of the first wave of "good news" about Jesus.

The heralders would have reinforced their impact by doing what Jesus had taught them: working miracles, especially healing the sick and casting out demons. To all those "marginal people, alienated from the authority structure and deeply conscious of their deprivation of power," as Howard C. Kee describes them,[17] miracles not only offered direct psychosomatic and spiritual aid but were also proof that God acted on behalf of his people, signs of defeat of evil powers and confirmation of the earlier message that Jesus of Nazareth was an agent of divine triumph.

We can fully agree with Morton Smith, then, that the modern tendency to make a rigid distinction between the Jesus of faith and the Jesus of history is in need of revision, that "whatever else Jesus may or may not have done, he unquestionably started the process that became Christianity."[18] To the above must be added two other features of primitive Christianity which accounted for its remarkably rapid diffusion among the poor and lower-middle classes of the Hellenistic world. One was the fact that, unlike the other mystery cults, which demanded of initiates that they first purify themselves before they could partake of the mysteries, primitive Christianity called the wretched and impure of the world to its mysteries and offered them purification as a reward for conversion. From the very beginning it was egalitarian, as Jesus had been, and universalist in its approach.[19]

Primitive Christianity's other appeal was something it shared with proselytizing Judaism: although open to all, it "demanded renunciation and a new start . . . not merely acceptance of a rite, but the adhesion of the will to a theology, in a word faith, a new life in a new people." The idea of faith, in this special sense, was indeed the peculiar contribution of Christianity to religious thought.[20]

To sum up: the news of Jesus' own message, his miracle working, and his existential being-in-the-world as a way of being with God, transmitted during his lifetime; the kerygma of the Easter faith reinforcing this earlier proclamation; the imitative ardor and demonstrative miracle working of those who heralded the faith; and the transformation of both in the social, philosophical, and religious hothouse of the urban Hellenistic populations, alienated and desperate for something new, but something very special to their peculiar set of needs—these factors, taken together, explain the rapid early rise of Christianity.

The next critical phase in the diffusion of Christianity was its movement into the large, overwhelmingly gentile cities of the Roman-Hellenistic world, including Rome itself. Antioch and Jerusalem were the springboards for this third wave. Apart from the predominance of pagan Gentiles among converts, the most fundamental social fact to understand about the settings of this new wave of Christianity is that they were all large-scale urban slave societies. We are now fully immersed in Greco-Roman urban civilization. It is an utterly alien world; yet one which Christianity would conquer within two and a half centuries. Its rate of growth during this period was as phenomenal as that of its first, primitive burst out of rural Palestine into the cities of Palestine and Syria.

We will return to the question of the social factors accounting for Christianity's success in this, Paul's world, in the next chapter. What we want to emphasize now is the importance of the new doctrine itself in explaining its early success in this most civilized part of Europe and the Near East. For while it is no doubt true that the new creed, especially in its reliance on miracles and the driving out of demons, directly appealed to "the unsophisticated and uneducated, and . . . people of low standing in the community,"[21] it is equally well attested that it had an unusual appeal to a significant minority of sophisticated people, and that this group was critical for its success as a religion.[22]

It is the symbolic vitality and adaptability of the kerygma worked out by the Hellenistic Jews, especially in Antioch, that accounts for its appeal to the more enlightened in the advanced Greco-Roman world. This intellectual adaptability has its roots in the doctrinal tension at the heart of the new creed: the tension between the Easter faith, with its focus on Jesus' life as a divine intervention and his death as a saving sacrifice for mankind, on the one hand, and, on the other, the actual message of Jesus with its eschatological promise preliminarily fulfilled in the ecstatic love of God experienced through free, unburdened, and loving fellowship with other people.

Implicit in this tension was the possibility of moving in several doctrinal directions. As Schillebeeckx has pointed out, from a credal core, held by all, which accepted the salvific meaning of Jesus' life and death, a variety of "kerygmatic projects" was possible.[23] Three are of special importance. First, it was possible to emphasize Jesus the proclaimer, focusing on his own special message of hope, love, and equality. This was exactly the appeal of the doctrine to the marginal and the weak in Hellenistic society, especially to women, adolescents, a scattering of slaves, and the free poor. It was also the basis of legitimation for one important group of early Christian missionaries. In other words, Jesus' message continued to appeal to exactly the same kind of people after his death as it had appealed to during his lifetime. To the male leaders of the church, this was both good news and bad news. Good news, in that it provided the doctrinal basis for mass conversion. Bad news, in that Jesus' message could easily get out of hand and become a dangerous and subversive movement not only against church leadership but, even worse, against established authority, getting the young church into serious political trouble. There is very strong evidence from Paul's letters that this was precisely the doctrinal direction taken by the many women who were among the first adherents to Christianity.[24] As Wayne A. Meeks has pointed out, there was considerable ambiguity regarding the status of women in the Corinthian church, several of whom had broken "through the normal expectations of female roles," creating tensions within the congregation which Paul was unable to eliminate.[25]

Equally important, the original message and manner of Jesus became the model and basis of legitimation for one of the two main types of itinerant missionaries who spread the gospel of Christianity throughout the wider Hellenistic world. The charismatic itinerants were distinctive in their commitment to a life of poverty, depending on the charity of those to whom they preached; in contrast, Paul and the community organizers emphasized their economic independence. The itinerants considered themselves the "real apostles" and may have been the group sarcastically referred to by Paul as the "super apostles." By renouncing home, possessions, and stable community life, the itinerants, like Jesus and his disciples, "preached and lived a freedom from basic social responsibilities of a sort which could be put into practice only by those who had removed themselves from the stabilizing and domesticating effects of a continuing life of work—not by virtue of the privilege of possessions, but by means of the ascetic poverty of an insecure marginal existence comparable to the life of the itinerant Cynic philosopher."[26]

Freedom was the main reward of salvation and living the Christian life. Paul, ironically (for reasons we will discuss in the next chapter), was accused by the charismatics of lacking this freedom. We deduce it from his defensive outburst "Am I not free? Am I not an apostle?"[27] Gerd Theissen has argued that there was a direct parallel between this experience of freedom through imitation of Christ and the freedom of the Cynic itinerants. Like them, the Christian itinerant was both "free" and "sent."[28] I suspect that it is this group of early Christians that Schillebeeckx has in mind when discussing what he calls the "*Theios Aner*" kerygma, in which Jesus is "a divine miracle man demonstrating his divine character by acts of power"[29] and who calls his followers to work miracles and live in imitation of him. It was a version of the kerygma that was quickly rejected by the more influential thinkers of the young church, most notably Paul, John, and Luke, who refused to interpret Jesus "after the flesh." Though failing to become canonical, the tradition continued for a long time as an undercurrent in Christianity.

The second doctrinal direction toward which the creative tension at the heart of the Hellenistic Jewish kerygma moved was a strong emphasis on the Easter faith, at the expense of Jesus' actual message and life model. This, of course, was the path of the Easter Christologies. The crucial issue here is not simply that of Jesus the proclaimed over Jesus the proclaimer, since this holds true for all the post-Easter kerygmas, including that of the itinerant charismatics discussed above. Rather, it was the shifting of the focus to Jesus' death: "The most profoundly human thing about man—the matter of his suffering and death—is here made the starting point for a Christological project."[30] However, this second, Christological interpretation of the kerygma was itself capable of moving in several subdirections, depending partly on those elements of the actual message of Jesus which were isolated and fused as secondary motifs with the core of the Easter faith, and also on what elements of Hellenistic religious thought informed the syncretic process.

Clearly there were many possibilities here, but only two were of major significance in early Christianity: one was pure Christology, with almost no reference to Jesus' message and life, the exclusive focus being on his death and its symbolic elaboration. This was the path taken most conspicuously by Paul and the Pauline school, to be discussed in the next two chapters. The second subdirection was one which isolated Jesus' eschatological message as the critical element in his mission and fused it with the Easter faith, using some elements of Greek thought to weld the whole together theologically. This was the path taken by John and the Johannine school.

Finally, the third main direction indicated by the doctrinal tension at the heart of pristine Christianity was an attempt to bring both elements of the doctrine together, giving each equal importance, a theological alchemy made possible by the sheer ingenuity of Greek philosophical and religious thought. This was the path taken by Gnosticism.

Before going further, we should emphasize the common element in all these lines of development from the primitive Hellenistic Jewish-Christian kerygma. All of them saw Jesus, in one way or another, as the decisive figure in the salvation process. All were concerned with the achievement of redemption and, as such, with spiritual freedom, although the meaning of that freedom—the spiritual state from which people were freed, and the condition into which liberation led the believer—varied from one school to the next.

Leaving aside the itinerant charismatics and concentrating on the other groups, we see not only that they all shared a strongly Christological bias but also that the different schools of Christology influenced each other far more than is usually admitted. New Testament scholars seem particularly allergic to any demonstration of the influence of Gnosticism on the other Christologies. In this regard, one of the most significant results of the Nag Hammadi discovery of Gnostic scriptures must surely be a reversal of this entrenched bias. As Kurt Rudolph has recently observed, following his detailed demonstration of the close relationship between Gnosticism and the other Christological schools,

It is not surprising if there is between Gnostic and Christian Christology no such deep gulf as has been repeatedly asserted—especially in more recent theological research. Paul already reckons only with the "risen," i.e. the heavenly pre-existent Christ who has returned to God; the earthly Jesus has for him no longer any significance. The Johannine view of Christ stands still closer to the gnostic: it is not his earthly appearance which is decisive but his heavenly and otherworldly origin which only faith can perceive.[31]

As I remarked above, the differences begin to emerge only when we get into the details of what Jesus' saving act liberated mankind from, and for what his divine intervention redeemed people. According to Gnosticism, human beings are trapped in self-ignorance. The self, which is one with the divine spark, God, the light and the truth, desires liberation from the dark tomb of the body. Jesus' act of liberation is essentially the provision of enlightenment or self-knowledge, and by means of this self-knowledge the soul is able once again to "attain to light." Salvation is possible now: a wholly inward process which spurns the idea of bodily resurrection as "the faith of fools." It was Gnosticism, more than any other branch of Christianity, which reinterpreted the primitive Easter faith notion of the resurrection in the light of the familiar Hellenistic religious theme of the descending and ascending god-man, a conception which hardly changes in Paul or John.[32]

The Gnostic view of liberation reminds one very much of the Stoic conception of freedom, and it is remarkable, and important to bear in mind, that this influence began almost with the beginning of Christology. As Jacques E. Menard has observed, "Man is so much the bearer of a divine spark, he belongs so much to a heavenly cosmology, he is so much a God, that God himself is man."[33] This extreme stance leaves little room for the intervention of an outside messiah, and was therefore unacceptable to Christianity, but the Stoic influence could also have a pronounced effect even on those who condemned Gnosticism. Whether Paul got his views from the Gnostics whom he criticized or directly from his debates with Stoic philosophers, as Luke-Acts suggests, certain phrases and modes of conceptualization of Paul came straight out of Stoicism, as Bultmann showed long ago, especially his use of terms such as "according to" and "contrary to" the will or nature of God.[34]

We do not have the space in this work to pursue all the different ways in which the spiritual notion of freedom was expressed through the central Christian doctrine of salvation. It is not necessary to do so, because most of these different modes of expression of freedom were either condemned or overwhelmed by what later became the orthodox church, as with Montanism and Gnosticism, or became minor doctrinal variants. Elaine Pagels concludes her excellent study of Gnosticism with the remark that the Nag Hammadi texts "suggest that Christianity might have developed in very different directions."[35] This may be so, but what I find equally significant about the Nag Hammadi texts is that they make it perfectly clear that, had Christianity gone in the direction of Gnosticism, it would still have maintained the idea of spiritual freedom at the very center of its soteria. Consider the following:

> Light spoke through his mouth and his voice gave birth to life. He gave them thought and understanding and mercy and salvation and the powerful spirit from the infiniteness and the gentleness of the Father. He made punishments and tortures cease, for it was they which were leading astray from his face some who were in need of mercy, in error and in bonds; and with power he destroyed them and confounded them with knowledge. He became a way for those who were lost and knowledge for those who were ignorant, a discovery for those who were searching, and a support for those who were wavering, immaculateness for those who were defiled.[36]

In *The Odes of Solomon* the theme of freedom is made explicit: "I have been freed from vanities, and I am not condemned. My chains were cut off by His hands; I received the face and likeness of a new person, and I walked in Him and was saved."[37]

Pagels's explanation of the early church's decision to define literal resurrection of the body as the orthodox creed and to condemn Gnosticism as a heresy is persuasive as far as it goes. The doctrine "legitimizes the authority of certain men who claim to exercise exclusive leadership over the churches as the successors of the apostle Peter,"[38] an authority which was severely threatened by the "Know thyself" doctrine of Gnosticism, which by placing the burden of salvation on the individual obviated the need for priestly authority and church organization. We should also take seriously Irenaeus' social criticism of the Gnostics, that they disturbed the peace of the church and were potential subversives and radicals who could draw the wrong kind of attention from the political authorities.[39] The problem with the Gnostics was that, paradoxically, in rejecting the fleshly Christ in favor of inner salvation, they ended up with a way of life disturbingly close to the I-come-with-a-sword social and spiritual radicalism practiced by the human Jesus.

This was certainly a critical factor, but it is not sufficient to explain the forceful rejection of the sect. Nor can doctrinal differences alone explain the rejection, although, as George W. Macrae has shown, these too were important factors, especially the Docetism and chronic dualism of the sect.[40] It may well have been that the early church did not reject Gnosticism—orthodoxy, after all, evolved only over a long period, with many doctrinal flowers blooming and contending for the prize of dominance throughout the first century[41]—but that Gnosticism

failed to make its case long before it was officially condemned by Irenaeus. And the reason it failed was that its doctrine did not resonate
with what was most vital in the real-life situations of its potential converts. It is in the interface of doctrine and social existence that we must
search not so much for the failure of Gnosticism as for the success of
its main competitor.

That competition, of course, was the Pauline version of pure Christology. While all the different versions of early Christianity were, in
one way or another, concerned with the value of freedom, none of
them related the religious expression of freedom so closely, so completely, to the actual experience of freedom as the release from slavery.
In the Christian soteriology that triumphed, freedom in the literal sense
of redemption became the central religious goal, and it was expressed
in terms completely isomorphic with the sociological experience, and
dominant intellectual expression, of the value.

This was the decisive factor in its doctrinal success. It was a stroke
of pure theological, and practical sociological, genius. And it was the
achievement of one man: Paul of Tarsus.

CHAPTER 18

Paul and His World:
A Community of
Urban Freedmen

1. THE SECOND FOUNDER

Few writers of antiquity, secular or religious, have received more attention than Paul. He is the most important and the most complex thinker in the Christian tradition, at times almost impossible to fathom, not only because of the intricacy and originality of his ideas but because of the notorious vitality and obscurity of his style. It is understandable, then, that opinions on Paul, today as in antiquity, vary considerably. To the Ebionites of antiquity, as to Nietzsche and G. B. Shaw, he was Satan incarnate, the root of every perversion in the Western mind. To the Marcionites he was the only true apostle, almost on a par with Jesus; the writings of Augustine and Luther trace their creative sources to him; and it is no exaggeration to say that a great part of modern New Testament theology is nothing more than an extended exegesis on his thoughts.

Whatever one's opinion of Paul, no one would deny that Christianity was not only fundamentally shaped by his views but almost completely determined by them. In remaking Christianity in his own intellectual vision, Paul paved the way for the remaking of the Western consciousness. In this remaking, what the historical Paul actually said was frequently radically reinterpreted, and nowhere more so than in the use of his ideas in the forging of what Krister Stendahl has called "the introspective conscience of the West," a psychological "plague" to which Paul most conspicuously did not fall victim.[1]

It must be noted at once, however, that what Paul's ideas made possible, including its distortions and exaggerations, must be considered at least in part Paul's heritage. In the historical sociology of thought and values, it is obviously vital that we get as clear a picture as we can of what an author, especially one as monumentally generative as Paul, actually said and meant in the context of his times. And this we plan to do.

But it is possible to take strict constructionism too far, in law as in the history of values. It may indeed be true, as Stendahl warns, that Paul's influence was very limited during his lifetime, and for a good period afterward, and that he would have been pleasantly surprised to discover that he had indeed become the apostle of the Gentiles that he so famously assumed himself to be.[2] The rapidity, and extensiveness, of Paul's canonization is at least as important as the actual content of his thought. Stendahl speaks insightfully of a "translation" and a "chain reaction" in referring to this process of reinterpretation, a process which in the end becomes the Christian Pauline tradition, which is as much as saying, the Christian tradition.[3] We wholly concur with his advice to "take a fresh look at the original and make our own translation"—that indeed is the main point of this and the next chapter—but his otherwise suggestive use of the metaphor of translation misses an important dimension of that primary dialectic between text and context that sets in motion the temporal dialectic between the original and the tradition. It is a dimension brought to light if we use another metaphor, that of biological selection. It is precisely that doctrinal "diversity" and "elasticity" of the early church, remarked on by Stendahl and others, which commends this analogy. Paul's thought was one of many equally viable contenders for eventual catholicization, but in the end we are left with one brutal fact of history: Paul's ideas won out, to the nearly total exclusion of others. They did so, clearly, because something in Paul's ideas met not a niche (that is a tautology, in biological as in social systems) or a need (that is reductionism, which is worse than tautology) but the exigencies of that social dialectic whereby thought and human action mutually select and re-create each other in the dynamic process we retrospectively come to call a living tradition. We detect this evolutionary dialectic, in its temporal aspect, as early as Paul's life itself. As William Wrede pointed out long ago, "It was not in Paul's original intention to set Christianity free from Judaism; it was the evolution of the work of his life which of itself forced him to such a step."[4]

Paul's achievement is all the more remarkable when it is considered that he knew exactly what he was doing. This was no Mendel quietly and unknowingly revolutionizing the "science" of the soul on which he wrote. He was a driven, self-confessed "boaster" who knew he was a religious genius,[5] who self-consciously set about the task of constructing a sophisticated theology out of the primitive creed he took over, and who only twice in his copious writings referred to the man who initiated the religion he was remaking, in both cases imperiously refusing to acknowledge his source, in striking contrast with his rabbinical meticulousness in citing the Old Testament prophets. This "truly perceptive intellectual among the Apostles," as Stendahl has remarked, "was not a sympathetic sort of fellow; he was certainly arrogant. But he was great!"[6]

His monumental arrogance did not go unnoticed by the Jerusalem core of the early church, which considered itself its authoritative source, with none other than the brother of the Messiah himself in charge. They warned and rebuked him; for many years they tactfully kept him at bay by sending him on a hopeless and dangerous mission to the outback; in the end they ordered him to headquarters in Jerusalem for a conference—one of the most important in the history of the West—in which he was made to give an account of his strange views.[7] But James and the Jerusalem brethren were out of their depth. Paul knew it, and they knew it. It must have been galling in the extreme for James to witness this strange former persecutor of his brother's followers not only assuming the mantle of Jesus but actually declaring himself the reincarnation of the Messiah and, as such, capable of speaking with *his* authority.[8]

The Danish scholar Johannes Munck, in his classic study of Paul, writes that Paul regarded "himself as one on whom the arrival of the Messianic age depends."[9] I am mystified by his comment that Paul's view of himself was "not as remarkable as it at first seems," for as Munck himself later sums up,

> Paul, as the apostle to the Gentiles, becomes the central figure in the story of salvation. . . . The fullness of the Gentiles, which is Paul's aim, is the decisive turning-point in redemptive history. With that there begins the salvation of Israel and the coming of Antichrist, and through it the coming of Christ for judgement and salvation, and so the end of the world."[10]

By remaking the primitive apocalyptic creed of early Christianity into a gospel of freedom, Paul single-handedly forged in the spiritual consciousness of the West what half a millennium of secular history and thought had done for the secular mind. "Freedom and release from fears, taboos, and restraints was the immediate result of his teaching," as W. H. C. Frend has pointed out.[11] But this, while important, was only the initial and most superficial form of freedom in his message, a precursor of the real spiritual freedom which was the secret of the civilizational impact of his doctrine.

Now, we have already pointed out that, beyond the obvious fact that some notion of freedom is implicit in any religion of salvation, others, most notably the Gnostics, had already begun to develop within early Christianity an explicit focus on freedom. Paul's originality resides not so much in the fact that "his doctrine of salvation is very clearly and consciously formulated as a doctrine of freedom," as the distinguished Pauline scholar Hans Dieter Betz correctly observes, but then promptly misinterprets,[12] as in the way in which he develops the doctrine, the intellectual character of the concept, and its complete centrality in his thought. In Paul, as Wrede observed, "religion is nothing else but an appropriated and experienced redemption."[13]

2. THE SOCIAL CONTEXT OF PAUL'S THEOLOGY OF FREEDOM

It has been estimated that Paul traveled some ten thousand miles during the course of his ministry, always keeping close to the major trade routes and cities of the empire.[14] Any understanding of Paul must begin with an awareness of the world in which he lived and worked *and* of the people to whom he took his ministry.

Let us begin with Paul's social world, because here there is less room for controversy. It is generally agreed that Paul operated in the most urbanized and Hellenized—and in the case of Corinth and Antioch, Latinized—parts of the empire. What is often not stated, or emphasized, is that most of these cities, including the one in which he grew up, Tarsus, had large-scale slave systems[15] and that this fundamental structural similarity with Rome overrides all other sociological differences.[16] Their urban-industrial and commercial structures were based on the work of slaves and, in Corinth, the trade in slaves; and the fundamental social division within them was that between persons of free and slave status. Let it be remembered at this point that all who live in a large-scale slave society are in one way or another influenced by it, be they monarch or beggar, slave or free, rich or poor, male or female. In a large-scale slave society, the slave relation, like a cancer in the blood, pervades all, pollutes all, degrades all, and magnifies in all the overwhelming goodness and desirability of freedom.

This fundamental fact is now beyond dispute, although many New

Testament scholars still seem not to recognize it or appreciate its significance. Slavery was most pronounced in precisely the regions in
which Paul preached, especially Ephesus and Corinth. Indeed Corinth,
the area of Paul's greatest success, had a level of large-scale slavery
which rivaled and possibly surpassed Rome's, as S. Scott Bartchy has
definitively established.[17] The slave population of Corinth during Paul's
time was conservatively estimated at a third of the urban population,
not counting the slaves who were being traded in vast numbers each
day to other parts of the empire. Even more important, another third
of the population was freedmen. Hence, "life as a slave was, or had
been, the experience of as many as two-thirds of the Corinthian population in the first century A.D."[18] Slaves were among the earliest converts to Christianity and were always a not-insignificant segment of
the early Christian congregation.[19]

The legal and socioeconomic framework of slavery in Corinth during
Paul's time, however, was not Greek but Roman. All slaves yearned
for freedom, and most had a realistic expectation of being manumitted
within their lifetime. As in Rome, manumission usually resulted in a
new form of social and economic dependence on the ex-master; and
slaves who were manumitted by Roman citizens automatically received
Roman citizenship.[20] This dependence, however, did not stand "in the
way of social and civil ascent."[21] Frustrated slaves who felt that the
promise of manumission had been delayed too long were prepared to
take the desperate action of running away, in spite of the harsh penalties meted out to those who were caught and to those who helped
them in any way. An entire letter of Paul's, to Philemon, concerning
the runaway slave Onesimus, was devoted to just this problem. Just
why this private letter, of minor doctrinal import,[22] was canonized by
the church fathers has mystified both ancient and modern writers.[23]
The mystery vanishes, however, if the problem was an acute one in
the early church. As Meeks has correctly commented, "The request
which Paul makes of Philemon may not be quite so private a matter as
it appears at first sight."[24] The high rate of manumission, and the realistic anticipation of freedom, considerably eased the tension which
inevitably plagues a large-scale slave system.

Paul was not only fully informed about all aspects of slavery in his
time, and may even have worked alongside slaves in Corinth and Ephesus, but was very knowledgeable about the Roman law of slavery and
manumission.[25] The circumstantial evidence alone would have made
this obvious. In Roman times, ignorance of the laws and mores of the
institution could actually be dangerous: the unlikely hypothetical free
person who innocently harbored a runaway slave could find himself

either legally lynched or reduced to slavery himself. One peculiar feature of Roman Corinth strongly suggests that, if anything, it was perhaps the purest of all slave cultures of antiquity. After having been completely destroyed by Mummius in 146 B.C., it was refounded by Caesar in 44 B.C. The remarkable thing about this event is that its refounding was entirely the work of freedmen, the only such instance of ex-slaves' founding a colony in antiquity. Thus from its very inception Roman Corinth was infused with the ethos and values of the freedman population of antiquity, a social monument to their aspirations and industry. And by now we know what value was absolutely preeminent in the worldview of the successful freedman. This is the world in which Paul had his greatest success. And, as will be demonstrated below, it is precisely among the freedmen class that early Christianity thrived.

At this point it is necessary to clear up one gross misconception concerning attitudes to slavery and freedom in Paul's world. The fact that people considered freedom the most important thing in life is in no way inconsistent with a tolerance for the institution of slavery or, what amounts to the same thing, with a lack of interest in promoting a policy of manumission. Freedmen, we have seen, were among the largest slaveholders in the ancient world. Indeed, the phenomenon of slaves holding slaves, the *servus vicarius* forming part of another slave's peculium, was not uncommon.[26] With the exception of a few fringe groups such as the Essenes and the occasional eccentric Stoic, no individual and no group of people ever questioned the institution of slavery. It is not simply that to have done so would have been considered highly subversive by the authorities,[27] but that slavery was a fact of life, a terrifying part of the human condition like warfare and piracy and plague and death. It is trite, then, to conclude that because Paul or his more prosperous followers, or the later church, fully accepted slavery, they were being hypocritical or, more to our point, did not highly value freedom. It is in the nature of human beings to tolerate, to completely accept in others what would utterly horrify if it applied to them—or, to put it another way, to be utterly neglectful of the absence in others of the things we value most. Examples abound today. The average middle-class American would view with horror the prospect of his daughter's becoming a whore or his son a homeless, alcoholic hobo. Yet the average American walks by just such people every day with complete equanimity.

It is a serious anachronism to marvel at the ancient church's lack of interest in the abolition of slavery or the lateness of its interest in promoting manumission.[28] The real problem in the history of Christianity is not why the church did not take a stand against slavery in ancient times but, as David Brion Davis, with profound sociohistorical insight, was the first to ask and to answer, why it was that the church, after remaining unbothered (like the rest of the world) by the issue for eighteen hundred years, suddenly in the eighteenth century came to consider slavery not only a problem but the greatest evil. But that, as he brilliantly shows, was a peculiarly modern question with a distinctly modern answer.[29]

Having established that Paul and the early Christians lived in large-scale societies where slavery and the values it generates were taken for granted, it may now be asked, Just what segments or classes of these slave societies were most attracted to the new religion? This takes us close to the most vexing question in the historical sociology of the early church, though, happily, it will not be necessary for us to get involved. Whether the church was mainly proletarian,[30] its teachings "offered most often to the unsophisticated and uneducated, and by people of low standing in the community,"[31] amounting as late as the third century to nothing more than "an army of the disinherited,"[32] or is to be regarded "not as a proletarian mass movement but as a relatively small cluster of more or less intense groups, largely middle class in origin,"[33] are matters which, however important in themselves, need not unduly detain us.

We are inclined to agree with Theissen that, with respect to Corinth, both sides are "probably correct," because the Corinthian Christian population was internally stratified, reflecting the wider social structure: "the majority of the members, who come from the lower classes, stand in contrast to a few influential members who come from the upper classes."[34] Meeks seems to share this view, but adds an interesting sociological insight of his own. He observes, "The 'typical' Christian . . . the one who most often signals his presence in the letters by one or another small cue, is a *free artisan or small trader*."[35] But he notes, further, that those who composed Paul's circle of leaders were "people of high status inconsistency": "They are upwardly mobile; their achieved status is higher than their attributed status."[36]

It does not seem to me that the problem of the exact class location of the different segment of the Pauline congregation can ever be settled: the data are simply not there. Abundant evidence, and something approaching general agreement, exists, however, on one crucial sociological matter: that nearly all the leaders of the Pauline congregations were, like Paul himself, artisans or traders, and that the great majority of the early church's members were of this occupation. The real controversy, which we can now comfortably skirt, concerns their level of prosperity: that is, were they the Trimalchios and Echions mocked by Petronius,[37] the wealthy shoemakers and barbers marveled at by Martial[38] and Juvenal,[39] and the freedmen of Caesar's household whose greetings Paul passed on to the Philippians,[40] or were they the ordinary members of these and related occupations, the vast majority of whom were barely able to make ends meet?

No matter. What we do know, with near certainty, is the one matter of great relevance to our subsequent argument: to agree that the vast majority of the members of the Pauline congregations were artisans, as all the experts do, amounts to an agreement that the Pauline church was composed mainly of freedmen, or of slaves with a high expectation of gaining freedom. On this the circumstantial evidence is incontrovertible, as we have already demonstrated in our discussion of the freedmen of Rome. But there is also an abundance of direct evidence, recently reviewed by Dimitris J. Kyrtatas. He concludes from his analysis of New Testament names, and other evidence, that most of them were in all likelihood freedmen and "that Christianity was particularly successful among" this class.[41] He agrees with A. H. M. Jones's impression that the control of city councils by wealthy freedmen Christians may have played an important role in propagating the creed.[42] What is more, an extraordinary number of the imperial slaves and freedmen—the *familia Caesaris*—were converts to the new religion, and it is reasonably suggested that this group may well have been a decisive factor in the rapid rise of Christianity:

> They played an important role in the reorganization of the Christian community in the city of Rome and went on to extend their influence to other communities, such as Corinth and Alexandria. . . . The Christians' success was guaranteed by their superior organization; by their considerable wealth, used to support those in need at Rome and elsewhere; and by their connections throughout the empire.[43]

We may conclude with the following sociological generalizations about Paul and the early Christian congregants to whom he preached: first, that they lived in large-scale slave societies, sharing the secular ethos, values, ideals, and social assumptions of such societies; second, that the great majority of the most important leaders were freedmen or their children; and, third, that perhaps the majority of them were persons who had already experienced, or were expecting soon, the death of the social death of their enslavement and their rebirth—literally, their redemption—into the cherished status of free persons.

We will now show how Paul's theology miraculously transposed this secular experience of slavery-into-freedom, or the intense expectation of a rebirth into social life, into a doctrine of spiritual freedom from which the Western mind would never be released.

CHAPTER 19

Paul and the
Freedom of Mankind

PAUL'S THEOLOGY OF FREEDOM

1. Reading Paul

The first thing that strikes the reader of Paul's letters is that his point of view and important ideas seem to change significantly from one letter to the next, especially between the two great letters, those to the Galatians and the Romans. These differences may be explained in three ways. One is that he was very inconsistent, and later attempted to correct earlier excesses[1] or, more likely, that he was simply confused on the subject of Jewish law.[2] I will be arguing that Paul significantly shifted his emphasis, but not his point of view or any of his basic ideas. Nonetheless, these works are useful correctives to the chronic tendency among theologians toward "simplistic harmonization" of Paul's letters.[3]

The second explanation is that the letters were written over a period of time and reflect inevitable changes and developments in his thinking. It is hard to take this position seriously, for the simple reason that the period of time between Galatians, written about A.D. 54, and Romans, circa A.D. 57, is a mere three or four years, and certainly less than a decade.[4] The third explanation is that Paul shifted his point of view or emphasis, depending on the nature of his addressees, and we have it on Paul's own authority that he did so: his famous comment that he was "all things to all men."[5] This is not an admission of duplicity but, rather, the acknowledgment of an essential missionary tactic.

Paul's style of writing was very unusual, and it does present something of a problem for the nonexpert reader. His letters were mainly spoken and emotionally charged; they were full of interruptions, extended digressions, interpolations, personal confessions, rabbinical exegesis, and paradoxes.[6] One's only recourse is to place oneself at the mercy of the best commentators.[7]

2. Method

In a reading of Paul's theology of salvation, the natural place to begin is with the two related questions that are at the heart of his interrogative framework, that is, the basic set of questions his theology sets out to answer: From what are we saved? Into what are we redeemed? These two questions determine what may be called the fundamental categories of redemption in Paul's thought, to be explained shortly. The believer is saved from one condition and placed into another, its antithesis, through certain *processes of redemption*, all closely linked, constituting Paul's second set of questions. But these processes must be set in motion by some form of divine intervention. Hence Paul's third major concern—the one that critically defines the Christian path of redemption—that of divine agency or *the means of redemption*. For the more sophisticated believers, however—and Paul also had these very much in mind—the answer to the agency question generates another: *How* exactly do the means of redemption operate? This last question determines what may be called *the dynamics of redemption*. Paul is the greatest figure in the history of Western religious and social thought not only because he was the first to pose these questions but because the answers he gave have determined all subsequent reflections on them.

Before we go on to see how Paul answered these questions, we should note an important omission in his interrogative framework. There is no theodicy.[8] Christianity is unusual for its conspicuous disregard for this question; and its lack of interest goes back to Paul. Suffering is a problem not of people in relation to God but of people in relation to their own evil past (original sin) and their future: the conquest of death in the salvation process.[9] The absence may have been due to his apocalypticism, but his views on the subject are difficult to fathom, since they are phrased in highly metaphoric terms, laden with Gnostic imagery, which are at variance with the rest of his symbolic style.[10]

The second preliminary point takes us to Bultmann's observation that Paul's theology makes no attempt to define the nature of God or of mankind and the cosmos. He is concerned only with God "as He is significant for man, for man's responsibility and man's salvation"[11] and with humankind and the cosmos in their relation to God. "For this reason," Bultmann argues, somewhat more controversially, "Paul's theology is, at the same time, anthropology." The same goes for his Christology. Paul, in great contrast to the church fathers immediately succeeding him, is not interested in the *nature* of Christ and offers no speculation about his relation with God. He speaks of Christ "as the one through whom God is working for the salvation of the world and man. Thus, every assertion about Christ is also an assertion about man and vice versa; and Paul's christology is simultaneously soteriology."[12]

3. The Fundamental Categories

What are we saved from? The answer is clear and repeatedly given: we are saved from the spiritual slavery of sin. But to whom or what are we enslaved? Paul is vague on the subject, speaking of "elemental spirts of the universe" with possibly Gnostic allusions.[13] Of more interest is what Paul did not say, but so easily could have said: namely, that we are enslaved to Satan. Paul avoided this vulgar theological sink, which was to plague the medieval mind for centuries. The second point to note is that in Romans Paul speaks not of being enslaved in sin *to* some other force but of being "enslaved *to sin*" and of being "freed *from* sin,"[14] in this way obviating the problem by making sin both condition and master.

We are redeemed, that is to say, bought out of spiritual slavery into its antithesis, spiritual freedom. Freedom is an inherently joyful and prized state. It is the essence of being in Christ: "the Lord is the Spirit, and where the Spirit of the Lord is, there is freedom."[15] Paul repeatedly strikes this note when speaking of the subject: "For freedom Christ has set us free; stand fast therefore, and do not submit again to a yoke of slavery."[16] He is sometimes even a little paranoid about the subject, complaining of unnamed "false brethren secretly brought in, who slipped in to spy out our freedom which we have in Christ Jesus, that they might bring us into bondage."[17] To the dismay of the more conservative Jewish converts, he tells the Corinthians that they are free to eat with unbelievers without being bothered by the squeamishness of others: "For why should my liberty be determined by another man's scruples?"[18]

Running parallel with the root categorical antithesis, slavery-freedom, was a set of other antitheses: law-grace; death-life; sin-reconciliation. By and large, these can be seen as correspondences to the root antithesis. They express the same idea in different ways and are therefore on the same level of importance as slavery and freedom. As he speaks of being enslaved to sin, so Paul sometimes speaks of being enslaved to the law, at other times as being under the law, law here meaning simply slavery. On one level, Paul's attack on law was a revolt against casuistry and excessive preoccupation with outer works. As Francis C. Burkitt noted long ago, when "he says 'All things are allowable,' he really means it," within some broad limits, of course.[19] But there is a second, and wholly Christological, sense in which Paul speaks of the concept of law, namely, that "Christ redeemed us from the curse of the law."[20] Before Christ came, "we were confined under the law . . . until faith should be revealed." The law was actually a good thing, our custodian. We were justified by doing good works and following its precepts. It was all we knew, and it was not all that bad. Paul remained proud of his Jewish heritage. He had not rejected Judaism, but had been drawn by faith to Christ, whose living presence and promise fulfilled the greatest promise of the Jewish religion. Through Jesus' salvific act he had become a free Jew, along with the rest of mankind who believed. In the following passage, one of the most celebrated in the Pauline canon, Paul makes clear the universality of freedom through Christ:

> So that the law was our custodian until Christ came, that we might be justified by faith. But now that faith has come, we are no longer under a custodian; for in Christ Jesus you are all sons of God, through faith. For as many of you as were baptized into Christ have put on Christ. There is neither Jew nor Greek, there is neither slave nor free, there is neither male nor female; for you are all one in Christ Jesus. And if you are Christ's, then you are Abraham's offspring, heirs according to promise.[21]

The antithesis of law is the state of grace, which is simply that condition of purity of heart in the face of God, freely given in the act of redemption, in which Gentiles are "justified" not simply as "honorary Jews," as Stendahl suggests,[22] but as honorary Jews *who are the only free Jews*, along, of course, with those original Jews who accept the faith. In this state of grace the individual instinctively knows the good, and there is no longer any need for law. There is no necessary threat to human morality in this idea. If we have been truly saved, Paul is saying, we can choose only what is good.[23]

The death-life antithesis is another important correspondence for slavery and freedom. I have shown elsewhere that slavery is universally considered a form of social death.[24] It was therefore no surprise to discover that Paul is preoccupied with both physical and spiritual death. He often uses the term in the literal sense, for he shares the distinctive Christian belief in the resurrection of the body and in the ultimate ending of death: "The last enemy to be destroyed is death."[25] It should be noted, however, that Paul did not conceive of the body in purely material terms. A confirmed holist, he saw the body as a totality of perishable and imperishable parts, and only the imperishable or nonmaterial would be resurrected.[26] The second aspect of Paul's treatment of death is his view that "in Adam all die,"[27] the crux of his peculiar notion of original sin, which will be discussed below.

It is in the third aspect of his treatment of the theme of death that Paul most unambiguously reveals his dialectical approach to slavery and freedom. If slavery is spiritual death, then freedom must be the death of death, death negating itself in order to generate the renewal of life which is freedom. Once we understand this, the obscurity and seeming mysticism of all his statements involving death and spiritual freedom quickly dissolve. Before Jesus, death was a mere stagnant thing with no possibility of motion. Jesus' death, and faith in him, inserts in death the motion that leads to death's destroying itself in order to create life and freedom. Hence the believer, through faith, is "always carrying in the body the death of Jesus, so that the life of Jesus may be manifested in our bodies. . . . So death is at work in us, but life in you."[28] The key text on Paul's dialectics on the symbolism of death is the following:

> For if we have been united with him in a death like his, we shall certainly be united with him in a resurrection like his. We know that our old self was crucified with him so that the sinful body [literally, "body of sin"][29] might be destroyed, and we might no longer be enslaved to sin. For he who has died is freed from sin. But if we have died with Christ, we believe that we shall also live with him. For we know that Christ being raised from the dead will never die again; death no longer has dominion over him. The death he died he died to sin, once for all, but the life he lives he lives to God. So you must also consider yourselves dead to sin and alive to God in Christ Jesus.[30]

The meaning of this extraordinary passage, though one of the richest and most pregnant pericopes in any symbolic language, is nonetheless crystal clear.

Finally, there is the sin-reconciliation antithesis. By sin, Paul did not mean the condition of fleshly depravity that modern Christianity has given the term and retroactively imposed on Paul. What most Christians today call sin belongs to the domain that Paul called weakness, but, as Stendahl has pointed out, Paul did not regard such weakness in "the introspective, self-centered, anthropological vision to which we have become accustomed."[31] Sin, rather, is "the enslaving force"[32] which leads us to estrangement from God. The freedom that comes with the negation of slavery, the death of spiritual death, entails a rebirth into reconciliation with God. In the same way that on the secular level the freedman becomes a new creation—manumission according to Buckland being always "the making of a *civis*"[33]—so on the spiritual level, if anyone has been saved through faith in Christ, he is "a new creation."[34]

Paul leaves us in no doubt that he uses these four sets of antitheses as correspondences for each other, with the slavery-freedom antithesis, of course, always being the root term in the entire symbolic statement. Thus he can say of himself, "I through the law died to the law, that I might live to Christ."[35] Meeks, like many other commentators, finds the phrase puzzling: "How did Paul conceive of the law as the means by which the Christian dies to the law?"[36] The puzzle vanishes once we keep the metaphoric source of secular Roman slavery firmly in mind. We have seen not only that slavery generates the discovery and valorization of freedom through the death of its social death but that manumission also becomes a necessity for the survival of any complex system of urban slavery. This is exactly what Paul has in mind when, on the spiritual level, he speaks of dying to the law through the law: the slave becomes a freedman—dies to the law of slavery—through the laws of manumission, an essential part of the law of slavery. The same argument is given, in more complex form, in Romans where Paul argues that it was through the law that we had come to know sin. He was once free (alive apart from the law), but when the law or commandment came he died spiritually, and he adds, significantly, "the very commandment which promised life proved to be death to me."[37] The key to understanding this otherwise perplexing passage is the slavery-freedom dialetric: the very law or commandment of slavery which promised life and freedom—the negation or death of spiritual death—is the same law of slavery which sanctioned our spiritual death. Paul cherishes the freedom he has discovered under the law of slavery so much that he can even declare the law, with a little exaggeration, "holy and just and good," in the same way that a Roman freedman, or an eighteenth-century Jamaican manumittee, freed under the law of slavery, would have joyfully praised the goodness of the law as he contemplated his certificate of freedom.

The three secondary antitheses are used not only as correspondences but as subcategories of the primary slavery-freedom antithesis, and they are direct analogues to the three constitutive elements of real slavery, which have been shown to be powerlessness, social degradation or dishonor, and natal alienation.[38] Thus the spiritual slave is completely powerless under law, is at the mercy of the law, whereas in freedom he has the power of grace. Second, the spiritual slave is utterly degraded, without honor before God or fellow men, a mere surrogate of "elemental spirits," whereas with freedom he or she is alive again, has spiritual recognition as a soul in the community of God. "It is sown in dishonor, it is raised in glory. It is sown in weakness, it is raised in power."[39]

In discussing the third constituent element of slavery, the spiritual counterpart to natal alienation (and it is remarkable that, as he does with secular slavery, Paul emphasizes this as the critical component of the condition of spiritual slavery), Paul draws heavily on the Roman experience of slavery and redemption. Specifically, he has in mind that special feature of the Roman law of slavery known as *postliminium*. Under the law, a Roman citizen who had been captured and enslaved by the enemy lost his rights as a citizen, but if he managed to escape from slavery, by whatever means, and returned to Roman soil, he was immediately restored to his former free status. However, this right of *postliminium* was suspended "if the captive was redeemed for money, till the redeemer's lien is paid off."[40] If we bear this law in mind, one of Paul's seemingly most abstruse comments on the nature of spiritual reconciliation immediately becomes clear:

> But God showed his love for us in that while we were yet sinners Christ died for us. Since, therefore, we are now justified by his blood, much more shall we be saved by him from the wrath of God. For if while we were enemies we were reconciled to God by the death of his Son, much more, now that we are reconciled, shall we be saved by his life. Not only so, but we also rejoice in God through our Lord Jesus Christ, through whom we have now received our reconciliation.[41]

This passage is at first sight very confusing, especially the crucial, third sentence, which appears not only redundant but incoherent: if we are already reconciled through Jesus' death, why is there any need to be reconciled again through his life? Only when we keep in mind the Roman law of *postliminium*, and the experience to which it refers, does the passage make sense. The sinner enslaved in the enemy kingdom of sin is, like his real-life counterpart, enslaved by the enemy of the state, treated like the enemy. He is estranged from God's kingdom and from his mercy and protection. Jesus' death is the first reconciliation. It brings the sinner back to the kingdom of God, the native land of his soul, but the reconciliation is not complete. Exactly as in real life, the sinner's right to *postliminium* is suspended till the redeemer's lien or ransom is paid off. The notion of Jesus' death being a ransom was a common one in the early church, and Paul obviously has this idea in mind here.[42] Jesus, in his kindness and mercy, however, will not leave the believer alone to bear the burden of paying the lien he owes him. The believer, having died to the death of slavery through Christ's blood, can now expect to be fully reconciled to his former status as a free spirit in God's kingdom with the return of the resurrected Christ, this being the promise of the parousia.

4. The Processes of Redemption

Paul, ever the symbolic dialectician, thinks not only in terms of the static antithetical categories but also in terms of the active process of getting from one state to another. That process involves struggle, a continuous exercise of spiritual will. The believer is not some passive thing gratuitously saved by Christ. Once he or she accepts, through faith, the freely given freedom of Christ, he or she initiates the sublation by active choice and keeps it going through internal interaction with God, which is present in the person of Christ infused in the believer's own being, an interaction that imitates the *Abba* intimacy of the redeemer, and through external communion with fellow believers through fellowship, ritual, and love. This redemption is a wholly individual act. All traces of the Judaic conception of collective deliverance are absent. In this active process of living one's emancipation, constantly renewing it, "each man will have to bear his own load" and "not be deceived."[43] It is simply not possible to conceive of a more activist theology: "work out your own salvation with fear and trembling," he advises the Philippians.[44]

Emancipation as an active principle, then, is the root sublation. Corresponding to it are the sublation of the other three antitheses: faith, rebirth, and justification. Thus faith is the active process though which grace sublates law.[45] The sublation of death by life, the next correspondence, is achieved in the act of rebirth or resurrection. The believer dies with Christ and is resurrected with him. Again, rebirth is not a once-and-for-all affair; it is an ongoing process, continuously renewing the believer. Paul appeals to the Corinthians not to lose heart, adding, "Though our outer nature is wasting away, our inner nature is being renewed every day. For this slight momentary affliction is preparing for us an eternal weight of glory beyond all comparison."[46] Finally, there is the process of justification. This term is to be distinguished from the word *reconciliation*.[47] Paul tends to use the term *justified* to mean the process whereby the sinner, and spiritual exile, is reconciled. Reconciliation is the end state, the result of disalienation, which is the action that brings it about. It is possible to be going though the process of disalienation or justification without yet being reconciled. The patient losing his anxieties through psychoanalysis is not yet well—and may never be, though he may be getting there. Paul wrote that "a man is not justified by works of the law but through faith in Jesus Christ."[48]

Faith is obviously the key factor in all three processes of redemption. It is very important in Paul's theology, but from what has already been shown, it should be obvious that reinterpreting it as the all-important factor is a distortion.

5. The Means of Redemption

The third part of Paul's framework can be stated simply: Jesus' crucifixion, suffering, and resurrection together constitute the only means of salvation; and all that is required to become a Christian is to acknowledge this simple but cosmic truth. It is the central message of Paul, the essence of his Christology and his soteriology. To the Corinthians he wrote that it was of "first importance" in his belief "that Christ died for our sins in accordance with the scriptures, that he was buried, that he was raised on the third day in accordance with the scriptures, and that he appeared to Cephas, then to the twelve."[49]

For many, this is also the most disturbing feature of his theology, largely because of its nearly complete disregard for the life and message of the historical Jesus.[50] The point about Jesus, the only point about him, is that he was crucified, suffered, and rose again and, by so doing, ensured the freedom of mankind. And for the sinner the way to take advantage of the means of redemption is awesomely simple: "if you confess with your lips that Jesus is Lord and believe in your heart that God raised him from the dead, you will be saved. For man believes with his heart and so is justified, and he confesses with his lips and so is saved."[51] That is all we need to know. Quarreling with Paul for not saying more about the historical Jesus is like criticizing an author for the book he did not write.

6. The Dynamics of Redemption

But once a person has accepted the faith, how exactly does salvation work? The issues here are complex and, given the nature of our source, there are bound to be loose ends. In Paul's theology, redemption operates on two dimensions, one temporal and the other structural. The temporal dimension concerns the location and significance of Christ's salvific death in cosmic time. Two questions arise here. How did mankind fall into spiritual slavery necessitating Jesus' intervention and redemptive act? And, second, how exactly did Jesus' death save mankind?

6A. Salvation in Cosmic Time   In answering the first question, Paul came up with an explanation that was entirely new in the history of religion. If he did not invent the notion of original sin, he was certainly the person who burdened Christianity with it. There is no trace of such an idea in Judaism. Paul Ricoeur has pointed out that Adam is not an important figure in the Old Testament and that Jesus himself never refers to the myth. "It was St. Paul who roused the Adamic theme from its lethargy; by means of the contrast between the 'old man' and the 'new man,' he set up the figure of Adam as the inverse of Christ, called the second Adam."[52]

Adam, the first man, was wholly physical, and because of his weakness and transgression he fell into the slavery of sin. This resulted in death's coming into the world, both physically and spiritually. Adam thus becomes the prototype of fallen or enslaved mankind. Jesus, the second Adam, is also both a figure in cosmic time and a prototype or, more properly, a counterprototype, for Jesus' Adamic nature is derived from the fact that he is the very antithesis of Adam and intervenes in history to undo the cosmic injury wrought by Adam— enslavement in sin with its harvest of spiritual and physical death.[53] Whereas Adam's sin brought physical death upon his descendants, as well as the possibility of spiritual death, it was not until the coming of Moses, and the law, that a new epoch began. The law made the knowledge of sin, and hence spiritual death, realizable, the direct counterpart of the knowledge that led to Adam's downfall and physical death.[54]

The next decisive event in cosmic history is, of course, Christ's life

and salvific death and resurrection. Then comes the period of waiting
for his return and the end of days:

> For as in Adam all die, so also in Christ shall all be made alive. But each
> in his own order: Christ the first fruits, then at his coming those who
> belong to Christ. Then comes the end, when he delivers the kingdom to
> God the Father after destroying every rule and every authority and power.
> For he must reign until he has put all his enemies under his feet. The last
> enemy to be destroyed is death.[55]

At this point it must be asked: Just how does Christ's suffering and
death save mankind? Exactly how does the cross function in the salvation process? Paul seems to suggest three distinct symbolic functions
of the cross. These are expiation, primal restitution, and dramaturgical
exemplification.

First, Jesus' suffering and death on the cross is an expiatory act which
atones for the sins of mankind. "Christ, our paschal lamb, has been
sacrificed," Paul writes to the Corinthians; and in Romans he stresses
that Jesus' act of expiation was for all.[56] As Charles Scott comments,
"That death was for Paul a necessary link in the process whereby God
wrought the Salvation of men in all its forms and implications."[57] To
whom was the sacrifice made? In keeping with Judaic religious thought,
the sacrifice was obviously offered to God; indeed, it was ordained by
God himself.[58] It is typical of Paul's nontheodicic theology that he is
not bothered by the question of just why God would want such a
seemingly horrible act of self-sacrifice from his only son.

The cross, second, was an act of primal restitution. Adam had been
conquered and enslaved by the flesh, entombed in the body and its
corruption. Jesus' death can therefore be seen as a reenactment of that
primal event, wherein Jesus, like the warrior who has fallen after a
long fight, courageously chooses death, on mankind's behalf, over the
degradation of spiritual enslavement, which the first Adam had chosen. The fight, and the choice of death, however, was not an easy one,
even for Jesus. Paul, in fact, presents a complex account of the reenactment of this primal struggle. The struggle took place over the entire
course of Jesus' life, culminating only in his death. Paul gives his account in the first half of the Christological hymn in Philippians.[59]

> Jesus,
> who, though he was in the form of God,
> did not count equality with God
> a thing to be grasped,[60]

> but emptied himself,
> taking the form of a slave,[61]
> being born in the likeness of men.
> And being found in human form
> he humbled himself
> And became obedient unto death,
> even death on a cross.

The descent into human slavery and suffering, then, culminates in the cross and the first victory over death: "Christ redeemed us from the curse of the law, having become a curse for us—for it is written, 'Cursed be every one who hangs on a tree.' "[62]

Finally, the cross functions in the salvation process as a form of cosmic drama, an exemplification of the sublatory process by which comfort comes out of suffering, good out of evil, life out of death, light out of darkness, power out of powerlessness, freedom out of slavery, and, if one wishes to follow Anders Nygren, love—the new way of fellowship with God and others—out of suffering.[63]

6B. Redemption in Structural, Human Terms   The dynamics of redemption also operate structurally. Here Paul is concerned with the role of the cross as an ongoing process in the life of the believer, a process which begins with acceptance of the faith, expressed ritually in baptism, in which the convert dies to the death of sin.[64] In other words, the structural mechanisms of redemption bring the cross down from the heady heights of cosmic time to human time. In the initiatory ritual of baptism, in the regular ritual of the sacrament, and in the less ritualistic, but no less important, daily act of worship and Christian fellowship, the believer shares the suffering of Christ on the cross and enjoys the freedom and joy that it brings. By following Jesus' example, believers preach as "slaves for Jesus' sake,"[65] through their own suffering ensuring the comfort of others.[66] Like the historical Jesus, Paul sees salvation in terms of now and then. "Behold, now is the acceptable time; behold, now is the day of salvation," he writes.[67]

Finally, there is the ritual of the eucharist. It is most important to note that this ritual, which was to become the single most important symbolic act in Christianity, was not a sacrificial act in Paul's theology, in spite of the importance of the cross for his theology of redemption. Paul remained too much a Jew to have even conceived of the symbolic idea of eating the body, and drinking the blood, of Christ in the eucharist. Communal eating and drinking was, of course, a common ritual not only in Judaism but in nearly all the mystery religions of the times. Paul offered little that was new here. The sacrament was an act of remembrance, like the Passover meal, except that it was a new covenant proclaiming Jesus' death until he returned.[68] Far more important to Paul was the spirit of love, fellowship, and spiritual equality engendered by the communal meal of remembrance.[69] For the first three hundred years of its existence, the church held to this conception of the sacrament, going no further than the notion of a "pure offering." Later, as Richard Hanson has shown,[70] the idea of a pure heart was supplemented by first-fruit offerings, which, still later, became sacrificial offerings of first fruits. It was not until the time of Cyprian that the startling idea first appeared that Christ was being offered up as a sacrifice.

FROM ROME TO ROMANS: PAUL'S TWO FREEDOMS

Once we understand how Paul's theology of freedom is closely modeled on the Roman conception of secular freedom, it will become clear that there was no radical inconsistency or metamorphosis in his thinking. It will be recalled that, with the collapse of the Roman Republic, civic freedom died as a reality for all Romans but was replaced by the absolute sovereignal freedom of the semidivine emperor which organically embraced, and guaranteed, the personal freedom of the freedman proletariat and middle classes. The masses, on the other hand, promoted his divine *dignitas* and celebrated his glory not only because it guaranteed their own personal freedom but because the greater the honor and glory of their emperor, the greater the collective honor and glory of all Roman citizens, since the emperor and his private household—managed by freedmen—both figuratively and, for the masses, literally embodied the imperial state.

Now, Paul held exactly this dual conception of organically related freedoms embodied in a single person. Christ made the church one, was its body, spirit, and head.[71] Although he does not draw the analogy himself, what Maurice Goguel says of the relation between Christ and his followers exactly parallels the relation between emperor and Roman state: "The relationship between Christ and the Church is twofold. Christ is the cause and ground of the existence of the Church which is inconceivable without him. But the Church is also necessary to Christ in order that there may be a subject for his kingship."[72] More recently, Robert Grant has shown how devoted to the monarchial ideal were the early church leaders and to what degree church organization "took on the shape of the state."[73] What has not been recognized, however, is Paul's use of the secular conceptions of freedom within the framework of his own theology of freedom.

There is indeed an important difference between Galatians and Romans. The difference involves a shift in emphasis from personal freedom in Galatians to sovereignal freedom in Romans. In Galatians, Paul was in fighting mood. Other missionaries had invaded his missionary turf and had challenged his apostolic legitimacy. At issue was a matter central to his conception of his mission as apostle to the Gentiles. He had, on the authority of his own unusual conversion,[74] preached that Jewish law, especially that of circumcision, was not a precondition for membership in the Christian faith, that Jesus' divine intervention had indeed meant the end of the law. The Judaizers, whoever they might have been, had declared otherwise. And, as Meeks has rightly commented, "whatever their precise ideology, Paul regarded it as a kind of spiritual slavery against which he spelled out for the first time his conviction that the essential mark of Christianity is freedom."[75] Krister Stendahl has reminded us that the defense of this freedom of the Gentiles was indeed Paul's central concern and that to shift the focus of Paul's interrogative framework by suggesting that his central question was "On what grounds are we to be saved?" as modern reformation scholars, following Luther, have done, is hopelessly to misplace and distort Paul's main purpose.[76]

Given the context, it is understandable that Paul wrote his letter to the Galatians emphasizing personal freedom, the negation of spiritual slavery, as the major reward of faith in Jesus Christ. This is demonstrated by the features of freedom on which Paul focused, and especially in the secular model of manumission which he used in this letter. First, there is the emphasis on equality in freedom. This directly parallels the secular Roman *ideal* of personal freedom: equality before the law. In the freedom guaranteed by faith in Jesus, "there is neither Jew nor Greek, there is neither slave nor free; there is neither male nor female." We can surmise from Corinthians that at least some of those whom he taught interpreted his views as a sanction for gender equality and sexual permissiveness. It is one of the great ironies of Christianity that Paul has been used as the sanction for puritanism, since, as Frend has noted, the "strongly individualist, libertine tradition in early Christianity may be traced back to the Pauline mission, but not beyond."[77] Second, Paul greatly emphasizes personal responsibility in this letter: "each man will have to bear his own load."

But it is in the models of manumission that Paul uses in Galatians that we see how great was his emphasis on personal spiritual freedom as a universal value. He draws on two models metaphorically: adoption and *restitutus*. Manumission by means of adoption was rare in the empire during Paul's time, though later restored by Justinian,[78] and in all likelihood Paul looked to the more common Jewish practice.[79] It entailed the most complete emancipation of the slave, making him fully equal with other heirs of the master: "So through God you are no longer a slave but a son, and if a son then an heir."[80]

Paul's second model of manumission is conveyed through the extremely complicated "allegory" of Abraham's two sons—one by a slave woman, the other by his initially barren wife[81]—an allegory which most commentators have found, at best, "limping."[82] In addition to Old Testament tradition, Paul may have had in mind the popular Roman motif of the wrongfully enslaved free person who was restored to full freedom,[83] especially the case of those penal slaves (*servi poenae*) who, by the imperial edict of *restitutus*, had the effect of their enslavement completely annulled.[84] Christians are like the heirs of the freeborn son of Abraham who had been illegally enslaved by the fraudulently free sons but are eventually fully justified.[85]

The unconditional restoration of full freedom is what these two models of manumission have in common. But equally fascinating is the way they differ. Indeed, in one critical respect they seem to contradict each other: "Cast out the slave and her son, for the son of the slave shall not inherit with the son of the free woman," which Paul quotes approvingly at the end of the tale about Abraham and Hagar, flatly contradicts the message of the earlier, approvingly cited mode of adoptive manumission. The two stories follow each other closely, so Paul is obviously telling us something not only in the unusual choice of manumission models, and in their symbolic similarities, but also in his juxtaposition of their *differences*. It is, in fact, a cunning attack on the principle of inheritance by birth and of membership through descent, laying the foundation for Christian universalism and anti-ethnicity. The non-native, gentile slave is freed and adopted; and the natural children, in the second metaphor, are shown to be the real aliens and slaves and are cast out by the son of the barren woman, who bears him only by means of faith. The stranger becomes the native and inherits his tradition, as the Gentile, through faith in Christ, inherits the promise of Israel. Need we add that this directly transposes to the spiritual level what was the single most important sociological transformation of Paul's time—the freedmen's appropriation of the native Roman, and Corinthian, political, demographic, and social heritage?

What does this freedom bring? And how is it prevented from descending into selfishness and chaos? Paul's answer is remarkably similar to Epictetus': true personal freedom brings its own rewards in joyful love and fellowship, and its own self-control—not control from others but self-discipline. Flesh and spirit are opposed to each other. The person who is free in the spirit can do no wrong, for the fruit of the spirit "is love, joy, peace, patience, kindness, goodness, faithfulness, gentleness, self-control; against such there is no law."[86]

When we move to the letter to the Romans, we seem at first sight to be in a different moral universe, but it is merely the shifting of emphasis to sovereignal freedom, seen from the viewpoint of the master class held by the conservative Roman church dominated by imperial and other wealthy freedmen. Note, first, what is most strikingly present in Romans: freedom as a gift. It is the master's view of things. No ex-slave who had worked his heart out to earn his peculium and pay for his freedom, or had some relative bail him out of slavery, was likely to view the matter that way. *There is not a single reference to freedom as a free gift in Galatians.* Not so in Romans. On whatever level—master, emperor, God—freedom always comes as something given, an act of grace. *Nearly every reference to freedom in Romans is qualified as something freely given.*

The second heavily emphasized theme in Romans follows from this first. If freedom is a free gift bestowed by the master, then clearly it could not have been something earned by the ex-slave, much less something bought. The grace of freedom is bestowed, not earned. Erwin R. Goodenough goes so far as to suggest that in Romans Paul argues that we are made righteous not because of our faith in Christ but because of Christ's faith in God:

> This faith of Christ is simply his trusting that the cross would not be the end, and that God would save him from death because God is *pistos* (trustworthy, reliable or trusting) God is the righteous one who is absolutely supreme in that he is beyond life and death. As we identify with Christ, become one with him, we ourselves are given the faith *of* Christ. It is not our faith, it is no goodness of ours; it is a free gift. By this faith of Christ transferred to us, we may hope for immortality ourselves.[87]

Mankind plays no role in initiating or even in exercising its freedom. The idea of free will is put aside: "it depends not upon man's will or exertion, but upon God's mercy."[88]

Third, there is a clear shift in Romans from the model of freedom as complete and unconditional manumission to the more common model found in real Roman slave society, namely, manumission as a highly conditioned status. The free gift of freedom places the believer under

a strong obligation to God, his righteous master. The faith of the believer, as Bultmann has pointed out, is now understood as obedience,[89]
so Paul can speak of "the obedience of faith."[90] Paul goes so far as to
take over the Hellenistic-cum-Roman idea that true freedom exists only
in enslavement to God. This, surely, is what Paul had in mind when
he argued that Christians, "having been set free from sin, have become slaves of righteousness":

> When you were slaves of sin, you were free in regard to righteousness.
> But then what return did you get from the things of which you are now
> ashamed? The end of those things is death. But now that you have been
> set free from sin and have become *slaves of God*, the return you get is
> sanctification and its end, eternal life. For the wages of sin is death, but
> the free gift of God is eternal life in Christ Jesus our Lord.[91]

There is no need to be unduly upset by this statement, as many commentators have been. Personal freedom is not necessarily threatened
by enslavement to this almighty freedom. It exists on an altogether
different level. Paul is in Romans inviting the believer to share in the
superior freedom of God himself.

The essence of that freedom is righteousness, power, and glory, and
mankind can experience this only by means of enslavement to God,
that is, by becoming exactly what a slave is to his master: a living
surrogate, so completely at one with him that he has no separate identity. It may well have been that medieval and later Christianity morally
sanctioned servitude, but this charge cannot be laid on Paul.[92] It is
degrading to so identify with ordinary mortals, but not with a semidivine emperor, and certainly not with God almighty. Paul repeatedly
speaks of God's sovereignal freedom in terms that may be called the
power language of the imperial ruling elite. Whereas in Galatians the
term *righteous* occurs only four times, in Romans the words *righteousness* and *un-righteousness* appear fifty-one times; the term *power* itself is
never used in Galatians; but occurs fifteen times in Romans; *honor*,
another distinctive Roman power term, never appears in Galatians but
is used nine times in Romans; the expression *wrath* of God appears
eleven times in Romans but only once in Galatians, referring not to
God but to simple human suffering; in the same way that the imperial
might is tempered with *clementia*, so is God's wrath and power tempered in Romans with *mercy*, a term used eleven times there, almost
always in reference to God, in stark contrast with Galatians, where
there is no reference to God's *mercy* and only one use of the term, as
part of the final salutation. Paul goes so far as to argue that "God has

consigned all men to disobedience, that he may have mercy upon all."[93] To give a final example, the Galatians are twice encouraged to obey truth, while in Romans obedience, as we have seen, is repeatedly identified with faith itself. It is no accident that Paul, in describing the nature of God's justice, draws on a passage from the Old Testament in which God is at his most imperious, using the mighty pharaoh as the mere henchman of his will.[94]

Two other areas of the Roman terminology of sovereignal freedom were taken over by Paul. One is his extraordinary appropriation of the Roman ruling class's Stoic emphasis on suffering and endurance as builders of character. Through Christ "we have obtained access to this grace in which we stand." And like a courtier in Caesar's palace, mankind can "rejoice in our hope of sharing the glory of God."[95] Paul boldly turns the contemptuous Roman view of the Christians on its head, arguing that in their endurance and suffering they build just the kind of character which the elite Roman idealized: "we rejoice in our sufferings, knowing that suffering produces endurance, and endurance produces character, and character produces hope. . . . "[96] Gone, it seems, is the radical emphasis on the reversal of status, the sublation of powerlessness into power, which we find in the sermon on the mount and in Galatians.

Finally, there is Paul's elaborate use of the organic metaphor in which all Christians, though united in "one body in Christ," perform different functions according to their gifts. "For as in one body we have many members, and all the members do not have the same function, so we, though many, are one body in Christ, and individually members one of another. Having gifts that differ according to the grace given to us, let us use them. . . . "[97] This, almost word for word, is exactly how a Roman imperialist would view the Roman state and the sovereignal, integrative role of the emperor, whose grace and excellence had brought peace and glory, and was "acclaimed on all hands as an earthly providence."[98]

In spite of these differences—indeed, because of them—it should now be obvious why we find no inconsistency between Galatians and Romans. Paul's theology of freedom, modeled on the Roman secular experience and organic theory of freedom, regards the personal freedom emphasized in Galatians and the sovereignal freedom of Romans as necessary and complementary elements in a composite, chordal value which expresses the organic unity of mankind and God in a single body, a unified spiritual state. Note, too, that Paul, faithful to his secular metaphoric source, has no conception of participative freedom.

The idea of the church as a civic community would come much later, under Greek influence.[99]

The personal spiritual freedom celebrated in Galatians is the freedom of mankind, waiting for God; the sovereignal freedom celebrated in Romans is the freedom of God, waiting for mankind. It is a superior freedom in which mankind can hope to share at the right and proper time. However, Christ's redemption comes in two parts. We are first reconciled to the country of God, given "access" to the grace of his presence, but we have yet to meet him, though the believer has a guarantee that he will at the parousia. At such a time there will be complete identity with God: as perfect slave to perfect master, we will become extensions of the one God, basking in his essence. In this perfect slavery, slavery destroys itself, as master and slave become one. Death, the last enemy to die, goes down with its social and spiritual expressions. It is this higher freedom of total identity that we would really want, if only we knew it, but as long as we remain trapped in the flesh, we are condemned to self-contradiction: "I do not do what I want, but I do the very thing I hate. . . . I can will what is right, but I cannot do it. For I do not do the good I want, but the evil I do not want is what I do. Now if I do what I do not want, it is no longer I that do it, but sin which dwells within me."[100]

Until the end of days, then, mankind must constantly struggle, fight an inward battle. What mankind has discovered, upon its partial reconciliation, its *postliminium* suspended, is the startling truth that the home it seeks, the God in identity with whom it hopes to find perfect peace and freedom, resides within the innermost self. Enslavement in sin, it now turns out, is self-estrangement, which is the same thing as God estrangement. At last we can answer the question with which we began our analysis of the fundamental categories. For now we know to whom Jesus really paid a ransom with his life—to mankind itself, so hopelessly, so absurdly lost in self-enslavement that it demanded a price for its own release, from its own redeemer! ". . . I am carnal, sold under sin. I do not understand my own actions."[101]

In that struggle, during that wait, the lesser personal freedom of the ex-slave who still awaits complete redemption, always running the risk of reenslavement, is nonetheless essential. It is an inferior freedom, to be sure, for it understands only the spiritual language of the slave, is mere negation, and, as such, requires that same loathsome slavery, that same slave law, that flesh, to make itself meaningful and real. Still, it is a comfort while we wait, and it brings mankind to an awareness of that higher freedom—the sovereignal freedom of God which is both near and far in time and being. It can hardly be grasped yet, but it is possible to delight in the mere knowledge of its existence and its nearness: ''For I delight in the law of God, in my inmost self, but I see in my members another law at war with the law of my mind and making me captive to the law of sin which dwells in my members.''[102] Till the final deliverance, then, upon the second coming, mankind must settle for the lesser freedom of the Galatians, using it both as a rallying flag in the continuing struggle against reenslavement and as a spur to the obedience of a superior faith which is hope for the higher freedom that has been guaranteed and that will bring, when it comes, not surrender but perfect union with God.

PART FIVE

The Medieval Reconstruction of Freedom

CHAPTER 20

Freedom and Servitude in the Middle Ages

Rome did not fall. It withered on the vine. External assaults from the barbarian environment were only the proximal, and partial, causes of its decline. Its deeper causes were to be found in the internal contradictions of the slave-based imperial state, contradictions that were already pronounced around the middle of the third century. Nor did the vine that bore the rotting organism of late imperial Rome wither with it. For onto that infrastructure were grafted the rough formations of the Germanic hordes, a structure that remained rooted in the relentless exploitation of the rural masses.[1]

The slave latifundists needed the strong centralized state, because without it they were at the mercy of their slaves. But rural slavery irrevocably led to the localization of power. That, I feel confident in claiming, is a virtual law of large-scale slave society. Absolute power, which is what the latifundist had on his slave villa, did not necessarily corrupt the individual absolutely, as Lord Acton so famously imagined.[2] What absolute power on the local and individual level did corrupt absolutely was the state and any sense of loyalty to it.[3] As the slave latifundia became their own private world, the rich retired in ever greater numbers from the affairs and burdens of state, and from the social squalor of the capital, leaving it increasingly to the military. Private greed and declining civic pride led to the growing separation of those who produced wealth from those who protected it. Deprived originally of the manpower necessary to protect its borders by the latifundists whose farms had depopulated the land of the soldier-farmers who had fought to create the empire and the slave system, the rulers of Rome, of necessity, became dependent on the barbarian forces to defend, and often to lead, the state against its enemies. Without access to the vast internal wealth it protected, the leadership of the state had to seek its support externally in plunder and tribute. But the very peoples it taxed were those to whom it turned increasingly for manpower and leadership.

With few exceptions, the barbarians whose intrusions finished off the imperial state did not come as conquerors. Some were pushed by the Huns and other, still unknown forces. Others were invited. Most, astonishingly, moved in as part of deliberate imperial policy. All of them, as E. A. Thompson has pointed out, envied and were in awe of Rome, and dependent on its trade.[4] Further, the settlement of the barbarians was the deliberate policy of the Romans and in no respect a compromise with them. It was, indeed, a brilliant diplomatic stroke, the perfect policy of co-optation and divide and rule, which may well have prolonged the life of the empire.[5]

In the third century B.C., this process of co-optation led to the rise of an empire; in the changed circumstances of the fourth and fifth centuries A.D., it prolonged the empire in the short run but eventually led to the demise of the centralized state and the rise of the warlord and localized foci of power. The strategy failed in the long run precisely because a vast slave system already existed. The co-opted barbarian leaders soon discovered that the power and wealth of Rome resided not at the center but at the periphery, in control of the latifundia. They therefore either replaced or joined ranks with the slave latifundists, in the process sometimes even enslaving or reducing to colonial status their own people.

So emerged the basic socioeconomic pattern of early medieval Europe. The fundamental process at the base of this pattern was the nearly complete ruralization and increasing enserfment of the population. Before we consider the nature and development of serfdom, however, we must put to rest one cherished historiographical myth: the view that slavery on a significant scale disappeared from Europe not long after the end of the empire. Although few specialists in the history of old Europe now take this view, the subject remains obscure because the problem of "the transition from classical slavery to medieval serfdom," as R. H. Loyn has recently remarked, is "one of the strangely neglected problems in modern historiography."[6] The more scholarly view is that slavery declined throughout the course of the Middle Ages. While, in broad terms, this was true, it is likely to be misleading, for, on the one hand, the institution increased in significance in important areas of Europe, sometimes after an initial decline (in Iberia and Italy), and, on the other hand, even where the decline was most marked (in Germany) slavery remained socially significant throughout the early and later Middle Ages.[7] Apart from one period around 700, large-scale slavery persisted throughout most of France and Italy right down to the start of the feudal age in the early eleventh century.

Although the church never advocated the abolition of slavery, mass conversion to its ranks during the late seventh century did undermine one of the major ideological bases of the system of slavery. Its insistence on the spiritual equality of all persons before God made meaningless the main symbolic difference between slaves and nonslaves. This, in conjunction with the sharp decline in population resulting from the plagues of the seventh century, created a major crisis for the entire system of slavery which, according to Pierre Bonnassie, was on "the edge of bankruptcy" by the year 700. Renewed barbarian invasions, however, soon revitalized large-scale slavery which flourished again throughout the eighth century.

Outside of southern France and northern Italy, slavery either persisted on a modest scale, or was revived on a large scale, or played a secondary but critical role in the economy of the medieval West right down to the dawn of modern history. Visigothic Spain had a large-scale slave system, perhaps more advanced than that which existed under Roman rule. With the Muslim conquest of Spain, slavery surged among both the Islamic invaders and the retreating Europeans as both sides took prisoners in huge numbers from each other. During the latter half of the thirteenth and the first half of the fourteenth century, slavery, after declining in the preceding centuries, made a major comeback in Christian Spain, penetrating to all areas of rural and urban life. Large-scale slavery reemerged in the Mediterranean, especially the islands dominated by Venice, and in urban Portugal; indeed, the slave-based plantations of these powers formed the original prototype of the plantation system that later emerged in the New World.[8]

No more tenable is the still-ingrained historiographic myth that slavery was of minor significance in England and northwestern Europe. If anything, slavery was of more importance in certain of these regions, and for a longer period of time, than in the old imperial heartland of Europe. Recent scholarship on Scandinavia reveals the critical role of slavery in the rural economy, especially that of Norway and Iceland.[9] Slavery played an important socioeconomic role in the early Irish colonization of western Britain and in Anglo-Saxon and post-Norman England. Nine percent of the *counted* population of England consisted of slaves in the late eleventh century, and in several of the western coun-

ties, such as Cornwall and Gloucestershire, the slave population ex-
ceeded 20 percent, larger than the percentage found in several of the
slave states of the antebellum South![10] These were not idle household
servants. The Domesday census shows the typical slave on the demesne to be a plowman or oxherd. It is highly probable, however,
that the Domesday census grossly undercounted the number of slaves
in England. As Rodney Hilton has pointed out, the Domesday com-
missioners were more interested in the demesnes than in the tenant
holdings, but in England, as on the Continent, numerous slaves would
have been hutted as enslaved tenants or *servi casati*. This process continued after the conquest, and by this means the slave population was
slowly assimilated to the generality of unfree tenants. What Hilton has
to say on this development is critical:

> There must have been, therefore, a substantial number of the descendants
> of Anglo-Saxon slaves, *theows*, among the unfree peasants of thirteenth-
> century England. These could in theory be the *nativi* who are bracketed
> with the *villani* in many descriptions of estates *well into the fifteenth cen-*
> *tury*, or the *nativi de sanguine* who appear in the fifteenth century court
> rolls. But this verbal distinction between neifty and villeinage did not
> amount to very much because the pressure of landowner demand for
> extra revenue (including extra labor service) from the manorial population
> resulted in the total confusion of the two, to the disadvantage, naturally,
> of the villein or customary tenant.[11]

"The whole of western Europe practiced slavery" for critical economic
reasons, Georges Duby wrote of the ninth and early feudal centuries.[12]
Aristocratic families depended heavily on slaves to provide the direct
labor they needed to farm their demesne lands and to run the villa
which formed the nodal point of their vast estates. Thus while the serfs
worked the land alienated from them, and paid a substantial part of
their surplus to the lord, either in kind or in dues or in service, or in
a combination of all three, slaves, always a more flexible labor force,
provided the kind of labor which was the medieval counterpart to hired
labor. Slaves were sufficiently numerous that even farmers of modest
means could own two or three. They were concentrated, however, in
"the houses of the nobles and the headquarters of the *villae* [where]
there were of course hordes of them." Duby only slightly exaggerated
in asserting that "agricultural production everywhere depended primarily on them."[13]

Loyn found it puzzling and seemingly paradoxical that the periods
of highest growth in enslavement associated with the colonization

movements in Scandinavia, Germany, and England during the eleventh and twelfth centuries were also times in which the granting of free status mushroomed. He offers a "resolution" in terms of a complicated argument having to do with the growth in use of the currency. We now know that there is really no paradox at all, and therefore nothing to explain. Freedom was in the air in twelfth-century England and Germania precisely because slavery was everywhere on the increase.[14]

Let us now turn to the problem of the emergence and types of serfdom. It was an exceedingly complex and drawn-out process, which came relatively late to some parts of Europe, such as England, or not at all to others, such as Scandinavia. The prevailing view is that the slave population and formerly free peasants were increasingly enserfed. "It is a question of preponderance," as has Loyn said, and after the eighth century serfs were heavily preponderant.[15] Nonetheless, it is best to think of the two institutions as coexisting and mutually reinforcing processes. Slavery and serfdom existed precursorily, and concurrently, in the fabric of emerging Europe like peat and coal in an Irish bog. European serfdom was, in effect, recombinant slavery. What we see developing at certain key junctures during the Middle Ages is a sociological recombination of two of the three elements of slavery into the different forms of serfdom. By coexisting with serfdom, it not only provided models for the reformulation of the other institution but at the same time made possible a public recognition and acknowledgment of its difference from serfdom.

By the late Middle Ages, as slavery waned to insignificance all over Europe, the horror that had once been associated with it was now fully transferred to the mode of oppression that had been reconstructed from it and that replaced it. "The desire for freedom emerges clearly," writes Hilton, "and is continuously present in peasant movements" of Europe,[16] but it was most pronounced during the late Middle Ages, when the desire to escape the degradation of serfdom was most intense. And as in the ancient system of slavery, the master class tried to turn freedom to its own benefit, offering free status as an incentive for the colonization of virgin land. But that drive for emancipation was as much the product of struggle from below as it was the self-serving profferment from above. As Hilton further observes,

> . . . it should not be imagined that freedom proffered from above was the only freedom to be had in the twelfth and thirteenth centuries. It was also demanded, and fought for, and won or bought, by peasant communities consciously organizing themselves to this end, and their organ-

izational effort is as significant for the history of the medieval peasants as such later and better known episodes as the French Jacquerie or the English rising of 1381.[17]

There were three kinds of serfdom, each typical of one of the three main periods in the making of old Europe: *convergent* serfdom, which lasted from the late fourth to the late tenth century; *feudal* serfdom, from the early eleventh to the fourteenth century; and *proprietary* serfdom, from the fourteenth to the nineteenth century. My argument, simply, is that each kind of serfdom, like the other servile conditions (which we will not consider), was defined in relation to slavery, which, as De Ste. Croix has insisted, was "the archetypal form of unfree labor throughout Greco-Roman antiquity" and the Middle Ages. "Slavery," he writes, "*continued to play a central role in the psychology of the propertied class* and of all humble free men."[18] In each period, a different combination of the three constitutive elements of slavery—powerlessness natal alienation, and dishonor or degradation —distinguished by the *absence* of one of these elements in the serf condition, and the positive emphasis of one of those present in both, determined the nature of serfdom. Slavery, as always, continued to remain distinctive in being the only relation of domination with all three of these constitutive elements, but an added factor developed in late antiquity and the Middle Ages: one of the three elements was given special emphasis, in defining slavery itself, in order better to underline the significance of its absence from the serf configuration. The argument is summarized in the diagram on page 353.

THE RECOMBINANT PROCESS IN EUROPEAN SLAVERY AND SERFDOM, A.D. 375–1861

Recombinant Forms and Periods	Servile Types	Constitutive Elements of Servile Types			Direction of Change
		Power-less-ness	Natal Alien-ation	Dis-honor	
Convergent 375–975	Slavery	+	+	+*	
	Serfdom	+*	+	−	
Feudal 1025–1325	Slavery	+	+*	+	
	Serfdom	+	−	+*	
Proprietary West: 1350–1789	Slavery	+	+	+*	
East: 1400–1789	Serfdom	+*	−	+	West East
East: 1790–1861	Serfdom	+*	+	−	

Legend: + = Present
− = Absent
* = Emphasized element

Direction of change is over the period specified in the first column. *Relative* importance of slavery and serfdom is roughly indicated by the vertical axis of cells in the last column.

CONVERGENT SERFDOM

The broad pattern during this period was the socially minor, but sub-jectively meaningful, ascent of the slave into the status of a tenant attached to the land, and the descent of the once-free tenants to the same condition, to being what Theodosius called, in an order issued between 392 and 395, "slaves of the land."[19] Free small farmers con-tinued to exist, along with genuine slaves, whose numbers were even on the rise again during the chaotic times of the fifth century; a declin-ing number of tenant farmers and other forms of dependent labor also survived. Nonetheless, the irrevocable trend was toward this conver-gence into serf status.

In the conversion of slaves (and, later, barbarian captives) to en-serfed tenants, they were sometimes manumitted, at other times not. Freedman status was so circumscribed, and the continued dependency on the ex-master, now patron, so similar, that there was little objective socioeconomic difference between the freed tenant and the domiciled slave. But so despised was the slave condition that the different defi-nition was socially and psychologically meaningful. There may also have been significant change in legal condition. For example, the at-tached tenant could no longer be sold away from his or her family. Masters came to prefer the situation, not only because it reduced management costs but because it was the most effective way of sta-bilizing the slave family and increasing the size of the dependent population.[20]

Likewise, the reduction of formerly free tenants to domiciled-tenant status came about in a variety of ways. Many were reduced to this status as a result of debt. Some free farmers were first enslaved (mainly by the invaders) and then manumitted into serfdom or simply made so de facto. Some, in exchange for protection, voluntarily gave up their land and commended themselves to a lord, continuing to produce on the land from whose ownership they were now alienated. Others, in true mafioso fashion, were made offers of protection they were in no position to refuse. And still others, especially the Germanic lower class that came in with the invaders, saw a subtle but important change in what was already a colonial status: ties of kinship and/or clientship, which, in the manner of advanced tribal systems, muted the absolute power of the Germanic lord, evaporated in the new context and were replaced by the direct, unmediated power of the local big man or pa-tron.[21]

Throughout this period the prototypical relationship between pa-tron, or protector, and bondsman was that of manumitter and manumitted slave, whatever his origin may have been. There were three reasons for this. First, as we mentioned earlier, the slave relation was the archetypal servile relation on which all others were modeled. Second, there already existed, in Roman law, a well-developed legal idiom which nicely defined the relationship. Third, it made good sense sociologically, since the relationship which emerged from the convergence of subjected categories of persons most resembled that of the hutted ex-slave of late imperial times.

The history of the word for serf itself illuminates this development.[22] During the unstable and confused centuries of the late empire and the early Middle Ages, a vast variety of words were used to explain the emerging condition. At first, careful distinctions were drawn between slaves and others, those others also distinguished according to their social origins. Then slowly the old Latin word for slave, *servus*, came to be used to describe the emerging serf, accurately reflecting the fact that the emerging status was most like the condition of the hutted slave. As language closed in on the still desperately held conceit that there was a meaningful difference between serf and slave, it was found necessary to emphasize some ideological difference. The urgency for precision did not come primarily from any desire to spare the feelings of the serfs: nonslave downtrodden persons of the *mansus* were taxed; when Justinian, on the sociologically reasonable grounds that the status of *adscripticius* (the late Roman term for the domiciled tenant) and that of the slave were virtually identical, declared that under the ancient rule of the law of slavery the children of free women and *adscripticii* were to be free, the outcry came so loud and clear from the *ruling* class that he had to make hasty qualifications[23]; nor were the ruling elites unmindful of the fact that the distinction intensified divisiveness among the oppressed.

What is important, in reference to what we have summarized in the first row of the above table, is that the term the persons who were "emancipated" out of slavery most preferred during the long transition up to the early barbarian period was *colliberti*, which harked back to the ancient Roman practice whereby persons manumitted by the same master established a bond "at once juridical and sentimental."[24] They were, of course, no longer free in the classic early imperial sense, being strongly "placed under the *obsequium* of a seigneur"—the disappearance of the term *libertus* reflects this—and confined to the land, but if they were not free, neither were they despised slaves. Their strong sense of confraternity, encouraged by the master, emphasized their sense of pride in this difference. Christianity added a further moral reinforcement of the difference: they were "brothers in Christ," coenfranchised in the real world, as they had been enfranchised by Christ in the spiritual world, a remarkable reversal of the symbolic transposition by which Christianity had developed its own notion of Christian freedom from notions of slavery and freedom in the material world.

To summarize: the overwhelming tendency of this period was to reduce as many of the oppressed as possible to the status of semislaves. The element of slavery that in ancient times had been most constitutive of the relation, natal alienation, was increasingly shared with the bonded person. The main reason for this was the reality that a growing number of serfs, certainly the majority by the sixth century when large-scale slavery reached its widest diffusion in Europe, were of foreign ancestry: not only all those slaves who had been "elevated" to serf or semislave status; but the waves of new recruits to the serf condition brought in by the barbarian invaders, including many of their own, formerly free *coloni*, who were reduced to this status by their leaders. The only real difference between serfs and slaves pertained to the element of honor, of which slaves had none and serfs some, however small. While an honor price was assigned the slave, injuries against him or her were paid to the master. That the serf had an honor price, payable to him or his kinsmen, was not without some legal significance. As serfs they carried no longer the mark of degradation; they shared the honor of having been manumitted. It was about all they had, but for the oppressed the sociological narcissism of small differences is extreme, a tragic truth which late imperial big men, like their counterparts in the U.S. South, knew only too well.

FEUDAL SERFDOM

The Carolingian period, basically most of the ninth century, was one of transition, and saw a resurgence of status confusion. With the reemergence of centralized authority, the large-scale slave latifundia rapidly reappeared during this period.[25] Upon the collapse of this empire, there were mass manumissions leading to what Pierre Dockès has called the second and final ending of latifundic slavery in Europe,[26] a transition completed in France and Italy by the early tenth century. This time, however, a profound shift in the nature and meaning of serfdom was set in motion. Before the Carolingian period, power over the serf had come to be based largely on might and ownership of land. By its end the domination of the serf had become wholly personal. The person was in serfdom, not the land. Now the greater part of a lord's wealth was "not derived from landlordship but from power over men and women."[27] A man remained enserfed to his lord wherever he might be. This process was complete by the early eleventh century and was the socioeconomic foundation of that brutal transformation which Duby calls "the feudal revolution."

We have seen that during the period of convergent serfdom the serf had no natal rights: he had no claims on the communal land and was wholly excluded from any participation in the civic community. The serf was now relieved of the stigma and incapacity of natal alienation, in sharp contrast with the slave, for whom this became the most important of his three constitutive incapacities. Many serfs now owned their own land during the feudal age, and many landless persons were not serfs, most notably, the *colliberti*.

Vassalage, as is well known, became the model of all relations among the free, from the greatest lord in relation to the king, down to the meanest freeman.[28] Hence the old classic notion that all forms of dependence smacked of slavery had to be purged from men's minds. The sensibilities of everyone except the king required some clarity on the matter. Feudal society solved this delicate and vital definitional problem in two ways. First, a new word and a subtle shift in emphasis emerged in the designation and social definition of the slave. The ambiguity in the word *serf* was removed once and for all by the introduction and rapid spread of a new word for slave, throughout Europe, this being the word all the European languages now use—the root term *Slav*, originating in the fact that the Slavic peoples were the main sources of slaves at this time. Closely associated with this was the emergence of the word *Franc* (the origin of the English *frank*) to mean a free man, not only legally but possessed of the character of this group. Primacy returned to natal alienation as the quintessential quality of the slave: the *Slav* being the archetypal stranger, who did not belong. Was this remarkably new and rapidly diffused pan-European identification of the natally alienated slave with a specific ethnic group—something that had never happened during the millennium of large-scale classical slavery—the genesis of Europe's most loathsome heritage of racism? This, it should be remembered, was the real beginning of Europe as a meaningful civilizational entity. Racism, the one indelible scourge of this great collective enterprise that is the civilization of Europe, was present at the creation. Alas.

The serf, by contrast, was no longer natally alienated. Once again he belonged, a member of the community with natal rights that the ruling class was prepared to respect. He even went to war with his lord, presumably to defend the common native land. But he had paid a heavy price for this, because in gaining his natal rights he lost his personal power. Like the slave, he was now owned, body and soul. He could, in fact, be bought and sold, since there was no presumption of attachment to the land. His attachment to his lord was physical, carnal. "The serf's flesh belonged only to the one to whom he was attached by a quasi-physical bond."[29] It was because of this that, though not a slave, he was also most definitely not free.[30]

Having distinguished all nonslave persons from the slave, and given new meaning to serfdom by the emphasis on natal alienation, the free relation of vassalage was at the same time distinguished from the un-free relation of serfdom by the attribution of three powerful new symbolic disabilities to the serf, all heavily focused on his degradation. He alone paid the *chevage*, a modest head tax which by the thirteenth century served only as a symbol of degradation; he alone was subject to *formariage*, a stiff wedding tax which not only ensured manorial endogamy but imposed on the serf the stigma of a hereditary servile class; and only he was subject to the *mainmorte*, which deprived him of inheritance and testamentary rights. In addition, the serf was prevented from giving evidence against free persons. The church reinforced this degradation process by refusing to ordinate him. Serfdom had become a stain, a badge of degradation, identified with a hereditary class which, though it very much belonged, was one into which no free person would dream of marrying. Then came the ultimate social degradation: by the twelfth century it was a punishable slander to call any free man, however poor, a serf. While there were regional variations in these rituals of degradation, and while some countries, such as England, developed the pattern somewhat later than others, what is striking is the commonalities in these developments found all over central and western Europe.[31]

The ancient classic notion of freedom as nonslavery was replaced by the idea of freedom as nonserfdom, and its essence was the fusion of power and honor. Honor we know to be one of the central values of the classical feudal age. Fused with power, it became part of the essence of freedom. The foundation of both was the capacity to bear arms: "a fundamental social dividing line was henceforth drawn according to a new criterion, the bearing of arms. Thereby distinguished from the 'people' were not merely the 'potentates' but also the helmed lieutenants of their power: the horsemen, the knights."[32] At first, these knights were nothing more than "savage agents of seigniorial exploitation" and were so regarded by church and people alike. However, their status changed from the late eleventh century in France, and the twelfth in England, and with this went devolution of jurisdictional power over the serfs from the upper down to the lower elements of the aristocracy. The notion of "hereditary aptitude . . . to command, an inward charisma of power," was diffused downward to the knights. In France, for example, the castle keep, "which was thought of as the symbol of sovereign power and military and jurisdictional dominance," was avidly imitated by the knights, while the peculiar virtue of the knights, the *milites*—courage, military efficiency, and loyalty— was diffused upward to the higher aristocracy.[33] All over western Europe, then, "an equation of free with noble status" crystallized during this period."[34]

In this fusion of power and honor, we find the final triumph of the sovereignal conception of freedom, similar in many respects to its ancient counterpart, but with distinctive medieval accretions. Intimately tied to this generalized conception of sovereignal power was "a new notion of freedom, hereafter conceived of as a privilege." Most of those who did not belong to the lordly orders were considered by those in these orders to be unfree. As Duby has further explained, "It combined on a single farm men whose ancestors were free-born with the descendants of slaves. It gathered up one and all into a homogeneous class, liable to identical services. In this class the characteristics of erstwhile slavery were quickly assimilated."[35] The serf, in other words, while not a slave (in not being natally alienated), was characterized by the two slavelike attributes of degradation and powerlessness and, moreover, was now the quintessential unfree person, especially so where real slavery declined to insignificance. To be free was negatively defined as not being a serf; but it was also positively defined as a highly relative condition. Duby, in the passage just cited, exaggerates to make his point or, rather, gives the situation from the viewpoint of the elite. Wherever freedom is positively and relatively defined, men are bound to struggle over the markers that define its highly fluid boundaries. The bitter dispute that broke out at the start of the thirteenth century in Gonesse concerning what was and was not compatible with "the dignity of a free man," requiring the adjudication of the king, was not uncommon.[36] It is tempting to see this relativism as the distinctive contribution of the Middle Ages. But this would be an error, for sovereignal freedom, as we have seen, was always relative: people who held to this note of the chord of freedom had always believed that men were more or less honorable or powerful. What was distinctive about the Middle Ages was the emergence of sovereignal freedom as the *dominant* note of the chord of freedom, the strongly corporatist nature of its expression, and certain peculiar legal and social criteria for defining degrees of honor and power. What these were will be discussed below.

PROPRIETARY SERFDOM

Between the thirteenth century and the fifteenth, major demographic and economic changes shifted the balance of power in favor of the rural masses. There was not only massive population decline but an increase in the availability of land by various means. The initial effect of these changes was a decline in rents and a general improvement in the condition of the lower classes, reflected in mass manumissions from serfdom in many parts of Europe. However, a reaction set in among the elites, and new techniques of repression and exploitation developed. This reaction was led by the crown on behalf of the magnates of the noble classes. What emerged over the next three centuries was consolidated aristocratic rule facilitated by a more centralized state focused on the monarchy, the political responses to a general crisis of production and control of the producers.

Control of the lower classes was strengthened by restrictions on their freedom of movement. It was during this period that the serf for the first time was forcefully attached to the land. This attachment differs from the first serfdom in that, unlike the former, it was not a by-product of instability and monopolization of landownership. Rather, it was a legally enforced condition of subjection, now made possible by the greatly extended reach and integrative powers of the state. Later still, serfdom was extended to vast new areas of central and eastern Europe, accompanied by the formal abolition of slavery, first in response to centralizing forces similar to those of western Europe and later in response to production for the world market, a transformation facilitated by the fact that serfdom was always imperceptibly close to slavery in these regions.[37] The serf's legal attachment to the land can be seen as the bottom end and microlevel aspect of macrosociological change in the higher levels of European society, namely, the strengthening of regional and corporate attachments.

Out of these economic and political developments the absolutist state emerged. Perhaps the major impetus was the shared concern of monarch and aristocrats to reinforce the oppression of the rural masses. In addition to the direct levy of the lords, the state now imposed a permanent levy in taxation. As Guy Bois observed:

> There was nothing revolutionary in this. The two basic classes of society remained face to face. Only the method by which one exploited the other had changed. The power of the prince henceforth protected that of the lord, extracting from peasant production whatever was needed to maintain the ruling class. Coexistence between the two forms of levy had be-

come necessary, but it was difficult. The more powerful monarchial administration was better qualified to play its role, while the seigneurial administration was crumbling. The way was thus open for greater centralization of the levy, combined with a proliferation of the machinery of the state, with absolutism on the horizon.[38]

It was only with the collapse of absolutism in the French Revolution that serfdom finally came to an end in France; and a far more brutal version of the institution was to flourish in Russia, where, as Richard Hellie has noted, "serfdom was slavery's most important legacy" right up to the 1860s.[39] But we have gone well beyond the confines of this work; to these matters we will return in the next volume of this series of works.

For now, let us close our discussion of serfdom by noting what was distinctive about this last proprietary form of the institution. We have to distinguish three zones of Europe during this period. In Iberia and Italy slavery not only persisted but went through a revival between the fourteenth century and the sixteenth. Here the pattern described for the feudal era persisted, that is, natal alienation remained the critical element differentiating serf from slave. Slavic and other slaves from Asia Minor, as well as a sprinkling of Europeans, became "the domestic enemy", household slaves, in Renaissance Italy[40], as did Africans in Iberia.[41] In northwestern and central Europe slavery faded away, early and rapidly in Scandinavia,[42] more with a grumble in England,[43] more with a whimper in western Europe. Where the serf remained, he acquired nearly all the trappings of the slave: powerless, dishonored, and excluded from the emerging centralized state or its local corporate communities, serfs were bought and sold all over western Europe where they were to be found. They were slaves in all but name. The name, however, remained important, especially for the ruling elites, who, while willing and anxious to keep what remained of serfdom in their midst, were ideologically squeamish about the idea of slavery's persisting in their states. Not everyone shared these sensibilities; there are numerous instances of serfs being referred to as slaves by persons more inclined to call a spade a spade. Let it not be forgotten that there were still over a million serfs in France on the eve of the French Revolution and that, in many respects, the only really positive achievement of that hyped plaything of European historiography was the abolition of serfdom.

In Germany east of the Elbe, and all over eastern Europe, where the formerly free peasant population was rapidly reduced to serfdom on a grand scale, the proprietary pattern persisted until well into the eighteenth century, serfs being distinguished from slaves mainly by virtue of their natality. The extraordinary vitality of the Russian mir, at precisely the time when Russian peasants were being reduced to a harsh form of serfdom, nicely illustrates the point.[44] Toward the end of the eighteenth century, however, especially after slavery had been formally abolished in many of these areas, even this element began to lose its distinguishing significance as the landowner class intensified its exploitation of the serfs in response to the growing world market for their grain. The same commercial forces which led to the growth of capitalistic slavery in the U.S. South also tended to reduce the eastern European serf to the level of the slave. Proprietary serfdom changed to convergent serfdom and was rapidly on the way to becoming pure slavery once again.[45] The recombinant process of enserfment had gone full cycle, ending with a regression to its prototype: large-scale latifundic slavery.

While all this was taking place, the increasingly "free"—that is, non-serf—population was acquiring more and more rights in a broadening conception of sovereignal freedom, associated with the broadening and deepening of the west European state. It is no exaggeration to say that in late medieval western Europe, sovereignal freedom had been remarkably democratized, partly under the impact of revolts by *free* peasants, and urban freeman, wanting more of the individual and corporate liberties and immunities which had emerged as the distinctive pattern of medieval freedom. The time has come, therefore, for us to take a closer look at the nature of sovereignal freedom and its relation to the other two notes of the chord during the Middle Ages.

CHAPTER 21

Medieval Renditions of the Chord of Freedom

The vulgar view that freedom was not a value of any importance in the Middle Ages has been sustained by two misconceptions. One is the tendency of modern historians of ideas to identify freedom with the elements of the value that triumphed in the modern world—namely, personal and civic freedom. Since sovereignal freedom was the version that dominated the medieval consciousness, historians have tended either to downplay or to deny the importance of freedom during these centuries of European history. There should no longer be any need for us to argue the case against this hopeless anachronism.

The second reason for the failure to recognize the importance of freedom is the fact that historians have dismissed as irrelevant the widespread concern with free status in the Middle Ages. The argument has been that a concern with free status must not be confused with a preference for freedom as an ideology. This is a grotesque distortion of historical realities. Freedom as value, we now know, was made possible and generated by the value placed on free status. Only a historiography which hopelessly reifies human values and ideas could fail to recognize both in the serf's yearning and frequent struggle for free status, and in the lord's identification of his free status with honor and virtue, the obvious valorization and idealization of freedom in medieval society.

FREEDOM IN MEDIEVAL LAW

Georges Duby has pointed out that if we are "to lift the ideological veil" and truly understand what was important in "the tangible aspects of existence" it is to the charters and deeds of traditional legal agreements that we must turn. These documents constitue a "retrospective sociography" by means of which we are able to observe what people really valued and "what was going on in village, castle and family."[1] Regarding the subject of freedom this is exactly what Alan Harding has done for us in his brilliant explosion of the myth that political liberty was unimportant during this period.[2] Like others familiar with the legal history of the period, he points out that liberty "is everywhere in medieval charters and legal records," but unlike them, he correctly reinterprets these records to show that, in the vast majority of cases, they do indeed refer to a political conception of freedom. Medieval legal charters clearly demonstrate a conception of freedom as "the power to act in the affairs of the community and to exert influence on one's fellows, free from the interference of the sovereign government,"[3] in other words, what we are calling sovereignal freedom. Freedom was a privilege, a power, granted to persons, normally landowners.

Freedom had three closely related meanings in the charters: territorial immunity, the earliest and most fundamental meaning; tenurial franchise; and the so-called free customs. Liberty meant immunity from royal interference in the possession of a given territory—in short, unencumbered landownership. This, as we have seen, soon developed into a second privilege or power, the *liberalis potestas*, or the free exercise of power over all who resided on the lands owned by the immunist. And developing partly out of this, and partly from the notion of collective rights of conquest among the members of the conquering group, was the "positive right to govern" in one's domain, free of royal interference. This third aspect of sovereignal freedom was the more positive right to exercise juridical and governmental functions in the immunist's territory. It was more commonly called "free custom," rule according to the "custom of the country." It is mainly in this third respect that freedom was transformed from a mere passive status to an active, positive right to rule. In England the lords were granted "sake and soke" by charter, the right to hold court and judge and punish in one's lordly domain—in other words, the rights of state. Magna Carta, the charter which old-fashioned British historians like to cite as the ultimate repository of British freedom, was merely an extension, and extreme legal enactment, as this aspect of sovereignal freedom. This version of freedom as political power was both relative and concentric. It varied in strength from the *liberalis potestas* of the ordinary freeman, through the *libertas notabilis* of the noble lord, up to the *imperialis libertas* or *franchise roiale* of the king.[4] Harding suggests that this pattern was unusually developed in England, but Reynolds's comparative study indicates that this pattern of layered authority was European-wide.[5]

The contents of the plea rolls give us a direct view of how the lords and magnates interpreted these freedoms. Harding found that one of the most common pleas was complaint against another lord's or king's bailiff's infringement of the liberty of a person to keep his own prison and hang whomever he pleased, that is, his "liberty of gallows"![6] To a modern reader, identifying liberty with the power summarily to lynch a fellow human being must seem like a grim joke. But it was no joke in the Middle Ages. And it flows with perfect logic from the age-old idea of freedom as the power to do as one pleases with others. To be sure, this might seem to be a rather steep moral descent from the Platonic, Augustan, and Christian refinements of sovereignal freedom, especially in its organic sense. But it is one of the central arguments of this work that all three elements of freedom, derived as they are from the archetypal relation of slavery, have the potential of being either refined upward into a civilized ideal or backward to the primal domination of slavery at its most elementary state: the savage right that inheres in one man's power of life and death over another. In the political theology of the Middle Ages, which we shall examine in the next chapter, and in the chivalric and honorific code of knights, priests, and ladies, we find sovereignal freedom at its most refined and elevated; in the liberty of gallows we find it stripped back to its primitive roots. Both possibilities existed and were fully realized during the Middle Ages.

The inner dynamic of feudal society was found in the tension between these two versions of sovereignal freedom. In Thomas Bisson's probing analysis of the crisis of the Catalonian franchises during the second half of the twelfth century, we get a fascinating sociological glimpse of this tension, and its implications for king, lord, and peasant at a crucial point in the unfolding of feudal society. Franchisal communities with ancient freedoms had been assaulted by lords brutally on the make: "one of the most terrible, most frequent, and least visible occurrences in medieval history."[7] From their protests and the ensuing response, we learn that there were two ideals of lordship closely modeled on reality. There was bad or afflictive lordship, which in essence was simply the exercise of freedom as absolute power over others solely in the interest of the lord; these lords openly spoke of their bullying exploitation as a part of their immunity. One strongly suspects that the behavior detailed in these cases may have been not atypical of the more familiar banal lordship found all over Europe.[8] And Duby has correctly identified this kind of lordship as ''the tenacious residue of slavery.''[9] But in the appeals and protests from the franchises to their count king, we get a counterpoised ''image of an older order in which the count's benign protectorate had fostered freedoms and moral cohesion that were now being threatened or destroyed,'' an image, Bisson adds, that was not wholly tendentious.[10]

The freedom granted in the charters had two other distinctive attributes: they were privileges granted by a higher authority; and, apart from the lordly immunist, they were often granted less to individuals than to communities. Thus they were granted to fraternities and guilds. These were organized as much for conviviality and defense against the encroachments of others on their limited liberties as for the monopolization of occupations.[11] They were always viewed with suspicion by the clergy and had a well-dressed reputation for ''independence and uncontrollability.'' Guilds collectively shared the medieval goal of sovereignal freedom, both in the limited immunities they had and in their power over against those who were denied the right to practice the crafts they monopolized. They also exhibited some aspect of civic freedom in their strong bond of solidarity, modeled on the family and monastic community, and in ''the collective jurisdiction over their members.'' It is tempting to say that they showed little sense of personal freedom, because of the sometimes coercive nature of their control over their members, especially junior ones. But this would be a gross oversimplification. Guild members were also other things: townsmen, villagers, subversives, and sometimes outright rebels. Besides, we should be careful not to judge the medieval guildsman by a standard higher than the one we apply to advocates of personal freedom in ancient or modern times. It is possible to cherish both personal freedom and an almost authoritarian conformism, as a visit to any number of American suburban or working-class communities by a racially mixed or gay couple will readily attest.

At the parish and village levels, we also find elements of proto-civic freedom embedded within the broader framework of sovereignal freedom.[12] Primarily members of ecclesiastical units which began to emerge all over western Europe in the early ninth century, parishioners performed secular tasks as well, such as road repairs and draining of swamps. It is remarkable that peasants often bought charters of liberties for the right to elect their own clergy. The parish unit overlapped with the village units, and both, separately or together, were the main focus of the lives of the vast majority of the population: the peasants and the serfs. Medieval history, far from being the idyllic pastoral scene of traditional textbooks, was an endless struggle on the part of peasants to secure minimal "customs" and privileges or liberties. These "more or less defined rents, dues and rights of inheritance; exemptions from more burdensome legal procedures; and sometimes the right to elect their own officials."[13] They paid dearly for these liberties; indeed, such payments formed one major source of revenues for the lordly classes. From the perspective of the history of freedom, it is important to understand that these "good customs" were always perceived as freedom by the peasants. Being able to share them collectively was often precisely the mark of free status. We must be careful, however, not to generalize too much, either historically or geographically, about the extent of such rural franchises in medieval Europe. Bisson's study of Catalonia shows that by the thirteenth century, "franchisal communities were like clearings in a thickening jungle of seigneurial violence and exploitation," and that when a community did receive a charter the peasants "were hardly more than interested spectators of a struggle between the count-prince and the lay magnates."[14]

Thanks to the classic works of Henri Pirenne, we have long been familiar with that bastion of medieval freedom—the urban communities. Their charters of liberties, secured within the framework of lordly sovereignal freedom, were the institutional bases of the burghers, the free citizens of the towns. Pirenne's explanation of the origins of these towns—long-distance trade and the wandering merchants—has long been contested and need not concern us, but most of his basic insights have stood the test of time.[15]

> Freedom became the legal status of the bourgeoisie, so much so that it was no longer a personal privilege only, but a territorial one, inherent in urban soil just as serfdom was in manorial soil. In order to obtain it, it was enough to have resided for a year and a day within the walls of the town. "City air makes a man free" . . . , says the German proverb.[16]

Pirenne also clearly recognized the limits of these urban freedoms, especially the fact that the magnates of the cities conceived of them largely in sovereignal terms:

> Without liberty, that is to say, without the power to come and go, to do business, to sell goods, a power not enjoyed by serfdom, trade would be

impossible. Thus they claimed it, simply for the advantages which it conferred, *and nothing was further from the mind of the bourgeoisie than any idea
of freedom as a natural right; in their eyes it was merely a useful one.*[17]

The degree of city autonomy secured, and the spread of these freedoms in the general city population, as well as the surrounding countryside, varied considerably over Europe. At one extreme were the free
cities of Italy and Germany which eventually became autonomous
states. We are most familiar with late medieval and Renaissance Florence, for there the celebrated "rebirth" of European civilization—which
is a historiographic conceit of nineteenth-century Romanticism that we
do not have the space to argue with here—is supposed to have taken
place. Freedom certainly first reemerged as a supreme political value
in Florence, especially after 1343. It was the "fountain-head of freedom," according to Giovanni da Prato; and already in the early fifteenth century, Leonardo Bruni was sounding for all the world like a
twentieth-century American Republican politician at a party convention: "One of the democratic characteristics of our constitution is that
we worship freedom more than anything else, as the end and goal of
our commonwealth."[18] Much the same was true of Venice, whatever
Jacob Burckhardt might have thought; as William Bouwsma has shown,
from very early on, "her subjects enjoyed a high degree of personal
liberty."[19]

Many of the German towns and villages were not far behind. Frag-
mentation and chronic competition among the lords of late medieval
Germany had created a power vacuum which the peasants had rushed
in to fill, creating village and valley communities and judicial and
mountain communes with a strong sense of corporate identity, self-
government, and collective and individual freedom. It was the ruthless
attempt on the part of the lords of the early sixteenth century to de-
prive the peasants of these liberties that was the main cause of the
revolution of the German peasants of 1525; and it *was* a revolution, as
Peter Blickle has persuasively demonstrated.[20]

Elsewhere, the amount of self-governing powers was far less, most
notably in England and Scotland where the "plantation" of new towns
was largely the work of the lords and kings.[21] Three points need emphasis about this growth of urban freedoms. One is that the elites of
these towns often tried to monopolize the rights granted and, what is
even worse, to apply these powers against the mass of townsfolk in
the worst tradition of sovereignal power, especially during the hard
times of the later Middle Ages. In the chronic tendency toward judicial
corruption and outright fiscal exploitation by the town magnates, we

find a nearly perfect counterpart to the banal or bad lordship of the rural areas.[22]

Second, while the degree of freedom achieved varied, the charters leave us in no doubt that what the town provided, above all, was personal liberty. As Beresford shows from his detailed analysis of the content of these charters, what was uppermost in the minds of all urban dwellers was escape from the oppression of the manor and the slavish duties and status of the villein. A change of status, he concludes, "an increase in personal liberty and human dignity" and "the minimum freedom to organise one's life as an urban specialist" were the rewards of burgage tenure.[23]

Finally, we come to the highest level of communal organization in medieval society: that of the entire kingdom, the community of the realm. It is on this level that most historians of medieval constitutional history concentrate. This has left us with a highly distorted and elitist view of the era, and nowhere more so than in the history of freedom. We can best bring the issues into focus by concentrating on the case of England. Ever since the seventeenth century, a cozy nationalist myth has dominated English historical thought on the history of the relationship between the English crown and its higher aristocracy. Briefly, it is the view that the English Parliament as an effective, representative body dates as far back as the thirteenth century and that the liberties wrung from the crown by the aristocrats on behalf of the people of England, and guaranteed in the Great Charter of 1215, which obliged the king to call and consult Parliament before levying scutage or other taxes, constituted the starting point of the history of parliamentary democracy not only for England but for the entire English-speaking world. As G. O. Sayles has bluntly put it, this is pure British, nationalist "propaganda," one given academic respectability in the first part of this century by the nearly canonized work of William Stubbs.[24]

The liberties won during the thirteenth century constituted the sovereignal freedom of the aristocracy: that is, a recognition, in principle, by the king to consult before imposing new taxes on them; and immunity from the restraining hand of the king in the exercise of sovereignal power over their domains. For most of the late Middle Ages, Parliament was nothing more than a court of the king which he summoned when he pleased, usually not to obtain advice but to communicate his demand for new taxes and to ensure that these taxes were effectively collected and that the charters he had granted were being fairly applied. There was always during this period another, more important court, the Great Council, in which the king and the great magnates met. The knights who attended Parliament represented less their communities, more their own personal and peer interests, and they all eagerly sought to please the aristocrats, whom they worshiped and aped. The king was absolutely free to do as he pleased—he was the most sovereignly free person in the system of hierarchical freedoms that constituted the organically layered feudal system—and could "flout the sanctity of custom" with impunity. Parliament was, in essence, merely a convenience of government—an occasionally convenient means of administering the realm—which he was under no obligation to call. Sayles thought that this situation began to change only in the fifteenth century when the peerage "committed suicide and left the monarchy free to become a Tudor absolutism."[25] Even so, it was not until the revolutionary Parliament of the seventeenth century that genuine communal representativeness emerged in England. And it should be added that that was a short-lived episode. Aristocratic rule reemerged with a vengeance after the Englishly misnamed Glorious Revolution, so by the end of the first quarter of the eighteenth century the electorates had either vanished or been hopelessly corrupted by the oligarchy.[26]

More recent studies have largely confirmed the basic findings of Sayles and H. G. Richardson. It has been shown that there was no "aura of inevitability" in the development of parliamentary democracy[27]—that, to put the matter crudely, the English simply lucked out, more than once, in the development of their parliamentary democracy. Parliament's main role for most of the later Middle Ages was one of communication and effective administration, a means by which the king could get some feedback "on how a liberty or privilege, once conceded, was working."[28] The English Parliament, although it shared many features with its continental counterparts, as Sayles and, more recently, Reynolds have emphasized, was nonetheless distinctive in its strongly bicameral nature and in the range of governmental activities that were increasingly assigned to it. It was precisely in the growth of these administrative functions—originally purely a convenience for the king and a burden rather than an honor for the representatives[29]—that we find the source of Parliament's eventual supremacy, and not in the selfish, essentially grasping, and exploitative assertion of liberties by the aristocracy. As J. C. Holt has very nicely put it, "In time, administrative convenience won."[30]

For the magnates and knights, "the preservation and defence of liberty" was, of course, the exploitation and degradation of the masses. We have seen that the little people also used the traditional means of the charters to buy some limited freedoms for themselves, their relation to their lords directly paralleling the lords' relation to either higher magnates or the king. In most cases, however, they either could not afford to buy these freedoms or the lords were unwilling or unable to sell them. When the situation became unbearable, one final form of collective action was open to the serfs and peasants of Europe— rebellion. The more historians shift their gaze to the poor and underclass, or what David Herlihy has called the "medieval underground," the more it is becoming evident that the "golden age" idyll of previous generations of scholars was pure mythology.[31] Indeed, chronic conflict was not confined to the underground: "rural social relationships in the middle ages," writes another eminent scholar of the period, "were characterized by conflict rather than harmony of lord and peasant interests."[32] Whatever the specific secondary goals of these revolts, one objective stood out above all others, that "the search for freedom" was "one of the most burning issues of medieval peasant movements."[33] And as with the main objective sought through the legal means of the charters, the freedom in question was personal liberty, pure and simple: not being under the oppressive constraint of another. To be sure, there was always a strong communal component in these demands, but that is precisely what one would expect in a rural society where nearly all aspects of life had a communal component. If personal, individual freedom was to be secured for a single serf or downtrodden peasant, it was always to his or her advantage to have these rights secured by others in the village or parish. For there was not only strength in numbers but prudence in not being singled out and making oneself the target of envy from one's fellows.

There is evidence of peasant revolts from as early as the late ninth and tenth centuries, most prompted either by attempts by the lords to extend servile demands from rents to labor obligations or by disputes over access to common land.[34] Most of these early rebellions were led by more prosperous free peasants who saw their freedom threatened.

The situation changed drastically beginning in the early thirteenth century. From then, right up to the German peasant war of 1525, the last and possibly greatest peasant war in European history, European society was racked by a continuous wave of mass movements coming from all segments of the lower classes. This was, in most general terms, a response to the so-called agrarian crisis of the period and the attempts of the lords to squeeze more out of them, the increase in the price of urban manufactured goods, the ravages of the frequent and increasingly bloody wars, and acute anxieties over famine and plague. But, as F. Graus has noted, they were also due to their growing awareness that "their servile status was not, as their forebears tended to believe, the result of 'divine will' "; a radical interpretation of Christianity which rejected the Augustinian organic model, and replaced it with a conception of humanity as equal and free, provided the ideological source of nearly all these movements.[35]

Guy Fourquin has provided an excellent typology of these rebellions and revolts.[36] There were *messianic* movements, which were the only ones that called into question the whole foundation of the social order, inspired by primitive Christian doctrine: the popular crusades; the flagellant movements; the great English peasant rebellion of 1381, in its millenarian aspect; and the Taborite uprising in early-fifteenth-century Bohemia are among the best-known cases. Norman Cohn has persuasively shown that it was not the rooted peasant but the marginal and alienated who always formed the leadership of these movements.[37] We will return to aspects of these movements in the next chapter, because while they always had a strong secular component, the search for freedom, where it was a factor, was more often spiritual than secular.

A second category of rebellions were those caused by frustrated *mobility aspirations.* These were the more familiar bourgeois revolts of the burghers wishing to join the seignorial elite, of middle-class guildsmen wanting to join the ranks of the ruling urban patriarchs, and of lower elements of the nobility rising against the major magnates. The masses were drawn into these movements mainly as "tactical forces." On the whole, these were conservative rebellions, as far as the mass of the people were concerned; the rights of the urban communes, once won, were almost always immediately used as a further means of exploiting the poorer members of the urban communities. Finally, there were rebellions directly caused by social and economic *crises.* These were mass "peasant terrors" such as the revolt in maritime Flanders in the early fourteenth century, the jacquerie of mid-fourteenth-century France, and the English peasant revolt of 1381 in its secular aspects.

Two conclusions, important for our argument, can be drawn from our review of the literature. One, already noted, is that in all the peasant revolts one of the main demands was the abolition of serfdom, regardless of the composition of the leadership or followers. In other words, even where the rebels were already free and serfs played a minor role, it was still considered a vital matter to end serfdom. What this clearly demonstrates is the salience of the institution for all working persons. Personal liberty was more than simply the attainment of a status: it was a matter of principle, which those already free were prepared to die for. An equally important conclusion is that the ground for this principle of personal liberty was a radical reading of Christianity as the religion of freedom. In the English peasant revolt of 1381, "the demand for freedom from serfdom . . . was the one most persistently presented when the rebels were directly negotiating with the king and his advisers,"[38] although the leadership of the revolt was almost entirely from the more prosperous ranks of the peasantry.

The point, however, is most poignantly made in the third of the twelve articles of the German peasant rebels of 1525: "Third, it has until now been the custom for the lords to own us as their property. This is deplorable, for Christ redeemed and bought us all with his precious blood, the lowliest shepherd as well as the greatest lord, with no exceptions. Thus the Bible proves that we are free and want to be free."[39] What to the lord was immunity from restraint from his own overlord in the exercise of sovereignal freedom or power over his dependents was to the common man simple immunity from oppression, or personal liberty.

At the same time, all the peasant rebels had a positive conception of what that freedom meant. This was expressed not only in such purely material matters as the reduction of dues and access to common land but in a well-developed notion of common welfare and brotherly love; politically, we find the most sophisticated expression of this positive conception of freedom in the remarkable ideology of a cooperative associate social order offered by the peasants of Germany as an alternative to the feudal system.[40]

It seems, however, that the peasant leadership also held to a version of the idea of freedom as sovereignal power, but with this important difference: that power should be "enjoyed proportionately by all men"; at least that was the demand of Tyler, one of the leaders of the English peasant revolt of 1381, who made an exception for the king, whose power should remain intact.[41] It is interesting that the peasants of Germany had not demanded the abolition of all authority: they were willing to "obey our elected and rightful ruler, set over us by God, in all proper and Christian matters."[42]

This brings us to our final observation. The notion of civic freedom was alive and well among all classes of medieval society. We have already seen that the peasant leaders and burghers, in their purchase of charters of freedom, gave high priority to the right to elect their own secular and spiritual leaders. The same objective comes out in the demands of nearly all the peasant rebels. Participating in the most meaningful civic community, and the one that performed most governmental functions—namely, that of the village, parish, and towns—was a highly valued ideal among all classes. As I have already noted, it would be anachronistic to assert that this was not democracy, because it does not relate to something that resembles the large nation-state. Democracy means participating in the election and running of the unit of political authority that most affects one's daily life. Since that political authority was located at the parish and urban levels throughout the Middle Ages, it makes perfect sense to call these societies democracies. Nor is there any need to qualify the claim by calling it "village democracy," for that too betrays anachronistic biases.

Thus all three notes of the chord of freedom were played throughout the Middle Ages, although different classes and groups tended to emphasize one or another note. There can be no doubt, however, that the dominant note of the cultural chord was sovereignal freedom. The peculiar medieval elaboration of the note into immunist and positive liberties easily allowed for its complementarity with the other two notes. That is to say, immunity, stripped of its lordly connotation of immunity from restraint on powers of exploitation, becomes simple, negative personal freedom, not different from its ancient and modern counterpart. And it is essentially this attenuation which we find among the peasants. Similarly, that other component of lordly sovereignal freedom—the assertion of positive liberties or powers within one's domain—was easily interpreted as civic freedom within one's city or village: the freedom to elect one's leaders, to attend and participate in one's assembly, and so on.

Nonetheless, I do not wish to suggest that there were no distinctively medieval aspects of the chord of freedom. The lords' way of conceiving of freedom in terms of immunities and powers or liberties is one case in point. A second peculiarly medieval conception was that of the divisibility of liberties. To be sure, there were precursors of this in the ancient world's conception of a continuum between pure slavery and pure liberty,[43] but this is not quite the same thing. In the Middle Ages it is not just the space between freedom and unfreedom which is divisible but freedom itself. Third, there is the peculiarly medieval view that these divisible liberties could be bought and sold. The traffic in liberties constituted no small part of the aristocratic class's income throughout the high and late Middle Ages. At its crudest, this was simply a medieval version of the modern Mafia's protection racket, and it goes back to the violent period of late antiquity. The peasants were made offers of liberties by banal lords which they never knew they needed but did not dare refuse to buy. However, in their more refined form, these bartered liberties did constitute the transfer of genuine rights or freedoms, legally expressed in the charters. Finally, there was the communal, and later corporatist, dimension to the purchase of or demand for freedom throughout the Middle Ages. This in no way contradicts the fact that all forms of freedom were also seen in individual terms. Nonetheless, for all classes, the granting of liberties was regarded as something shared by a given group of peers. One could almost define class during the Middle Ages as that group of persons sharing a given bundle of personal, civic, and sovereignal freedoms. At the bottom of the system were those persons having no freedoms at all. At the top was the king, who in theory had complete freedom but in practice had sold or given, or even rented off a part of it.

The day would come, however, when the kings of Europe decided that they wanted their freedom back—from everybody, because they had a divine right to rule, were the *patres patriae* of their people, and alone were free—a freedom which they would use for the good of the body politic, as they and they only were qualified to do, being not only "God's lieutenants upon earth . . . but even by God they are called gods."[44] And this, as James I of England reminded his subjects, was the only "Trew Law of Free Monarchies."[45] That audacious attenuation of the Western ideal of freedom did not occur in the Middle Ages; it was an obsessive conceit of late antiquity[46] that was reborn with modern Europe.

CHAPTER 22

Freedom in the Religious and Secular Thought of the Middle Ages

1. THE HEGEMONY OF SOVEREIGNAL FREEDOM

Emerging Europe never lost its ancient heritage, for as Europe emerged, so did Christianity; indeed, the idea and reality of Europe was as much a Christian undertaking as a sociopolitical one. "As the ancient world collapsed," Judith Herrin has recently observed, "faith rather than imperial rule became the feature that identified the universe, what Christians called the *oikoumene*, and Muslims, *Dar al Islam*. Religion had fused the political, social, and cultural into self-contained systems, separated by their differences of faith."[1]

Out of the cultural chrysalides of Christendom emerged, centuries later, the civilizational unity that would grow into Europe. Because the church was always there, the ideas of the ancient world, encoded in its theology, were present from the moment of creation. In Christianity, Europe had a cultural memory bank of ancient knowledge which was located not only in deep monastic storage—to be retrieved centuries later in the various renaissances of Europe—but in active Christian memory, giving meaning, shape, and hope to societies that for centuries hovered on the brink of dissolution, caught in the vise of external barbaric assaults and internal chaos.[2] Christianity did not just preserve the memory of ancient ideas but, in its own social organization, also presented to the savages that had overtaken the West the only model of advanced organizational behavior, the only practical sociological vision of sociation beyond the blood ties of kindred and clan.

The influence of the church on secular thought and practice persisted regardless of the nature of the relationship between them. Up to the end of the ninth century, when there was complete interpenetration of church and state, all thought was Christian thought. But the same remained true even after the Gregorian reforms and the ensuing tensions between church and state. Critics of papal absolutism used the language and intellectual paradigms of Christianity in their attack on the church's claim to papal plenitude of power. Heretics remained Christian in their language; indeed, they claimed to be pursuing a purer Christianity. And when strictly secular thought, concerned with wholly secular matters, emerged, it also employed the language and thought patterns of Christianity. European political thought remained "Crypto-theological" right down to the seventeenth century.[3] Beginning as pure political theology "hedged in by the general framework of liturgical language and theological thought," European political thought in its later secular phase still borrowed heavily from the metaphors and intellectual concepts of the church. Political theology was replaced by a theocratic theory of politics.

Indeed, as Ernst Kantorowicz has shown, it is one of the more wonderful ironies of late medieval and early modern Europe that the more independent and absolutist the European state became, the more it acquired the trappings and thought processes of the church it sought to separate from and to dominate. And at the same time, the more the church came to look like an absolutist state.[4] To this cultural and structural cross-fertilization must be added the purely sociological effects of the conflict between church and state. Joseph R. Strayer has forcefully argued that the very idea of the modern European state, not to mention its distinctive attributes, has its origins in that generative civilizational conflict.[5]

Intimately tied up with all this was the history of the conception of freedom throughout the Middle Ages and early modern Europe. Since Christian doctrine was quintessentially a doctrine of freedom, it would have been extraordinary if the church's all-pervasive influence had not resulted in the perpetuation of the centrality of freedom. Medieval and early modern thought was simply a continuous reinterpretation and, later, secularization of the thought of Paul, filtered through the paradigmatic and synthetic genius of Augustine, the last great ancient thinker who "provided the medieval consciousness, amid an entirely different sociological and political reality, with its foundation and spiritual weapons." Karl Jaspers exaggerated, but was not far wrong when he added, "No philosopher before Augustine had concerned himself with the uncertainty of freedom, the ground of its possibility or the

question of its actual meaning. But Augustine, thanks to his understanding of St. Paul, considered these matters with an enduring force
of conviction."[6] Not that the Christian fathers before Augustine had
not been preoccupied with the problem of freedom. The most casual
review of their writings immediately reveals the centrality of this value
in their thoughts. As Etienne Gilson observed half a century ago,
"What first claims our attention is the emphatic way in which the
Fathers of the Church insisted on the importance of the concept of
freedom, and the very special nature of the terms in which they did
it."[7] How and why they did so has recently been explored in a fascinating study by Elaine Pagels, who argues that during the four centuries between Paul and Augustine Christians interpreted the Adam
and Eve story as a symbol of freedom in all the ways that mattered to
particular schools of thought, "including free will, freedom from demonic powers, freedom from social and sexual obligations, freedom
from tyrannical government and from fate; and self-mastery as the
source of freedom."[8] All of these interpretations had long preceded
the Christian era, especially in Cynicism, Stoicism, and Platonism. Indeed, it strikes me that the Adam and Eve myth was merely being
adapted, for most in a highly adventitious way, to the socioreligious
circumstances and massive intellectual heritage of Greece which the
fathers eagerly assimilated as a means of making the creed respectable
to the educated classes they hoped to convert. Thus while it is true
that Clement of Alexandria interpreted Genesis 1–3 in terms of moral
freedom, he did so in the course of his criticism of Christian ascetics
who were using the myth to defend their position. The myth itself was
not otherwise of great concern to Clement, merely a point of departure
for his gospel of Christ's salvific act, Christ who is, significantly, "the
Word of truth."[9] What *was* central to his thought, as Werner Jaeger
showed several decades ago, was the fusion of Greek *paideia*, "the
ideals of the political philosophy of the ancient Greek city-state," with
Christian doctrine.[10] The same was true of nearly all the other church
fathers, whatever their particular point of view. No matter how they
may have explained their doctrines, the important fact, as Pagels makes
clear, is that they were all united in the attempt to interpret their views
as the ultimate form of freedom—a predisposition which, as we have
already seen, was wholly Greek by the end of the fifth century B.C.

With Augustine, however, all this was to change. And here Pagels
is right on target in her argument that the Adam and Eve myth is
important not only for his thought but for his special interpretation of
freedom as absolute obedience, slavery, to God, with profound implications for his conception of outer, political freedom.[11] Not that Au-

gustine was not also profoundly influenced by Greek thought; but he used and misused the Greek intellectual tradition with a disdain for their original meaning which his more respectful predecessors would never have dared attempt, if only because more people were familiar with the Greek authors in earlier times.[12] With this intellectual background he ventured on a reading of Paul that was to form the intellectual and theological foundations of Christendom for the next millennium.

Paul's influence on Augustine is so profound that it is dangerously easy to neglect the important differences between them. What Augustine tried to do was to reinterpret the Pauline doctrine of salvation in the light of the Neoplatonic conception of freedom and God. What he actually ended up with was a distinctive vision which distorted and transformed both. In our discussion of Paul we showed that, in the letter to the Romans, he did not really reject the spiritual version of personal freedom; rather, he incorporated it into a theory of sovereignal freedom in which it had an inferior but essential and protected place. We also saw that Paul was not a dualist but a highly sophisticated holist with respect to the human body and its relation to the spiritual.

Augustine deliberately neglected or misread these subtler complexities of Paul. He imposed on Pauline theology a dualism that was not there, that actually came from Platonism and the Manichaeanism which he never quite discarded. He furthermore took the Pauline doctrine of justification by faith out of context and gave it a significance which it never had in Paul. And both these misreadings served the intellectual purpose of degrading and radically downplaying, if never quite removing, the personal notion of freedom from orthodox Christian doctrine. In doing so, Augustine was very much a man of his times. For by the late fourth century and the early fifth, the early imperial compromise between the two freedoms realized in the Augustan *clementia* had long vanished. All that remained was pure sovereignal freedom, and even that faced disintegration with the assault of the barbarians. Alaric's sack of Rome, though only one assault in a very drawn-out affair, was nonetheless seen as a turning point by all thinking persons of the time, as John H. Smith has reminded us. The old order had been shaken to its foundations, and yet the mortal world went on, ''and the Christian leaders were forced to come to terms with it, evolving for themselves a new dialectic of history which would permit them to take responsibility in the imperfect world while still looking forward to the advent of the perfect.''[13]

Augustine's work emerged as that definitive dialectic. Once we un-

derstand him in context, we can better understand why he had to read
Paul the way he did. Paul wrote when the Augustan compromise
reigned triumphant. Augustine was responding to an environment in
which the problem was not how to reconcile personal with sovereignal
freedom but how to preserve any kind of freedom. For him the only
freedom possible was sovereignal freedom. Any attempt to reconcile
it with any other form of freedom ran the mortal risk of destroying
both. There was only one true freedom, the freedom of the city of God.

It is not that Augustine was unaware of humanity's desire for personal freedom. To the contrary, he was more acutely conscious of this
perverse, for him, desire than any other man of his time, coming as it
did from that other main source of his views: his own life and introspection on it. Peter Brown has observed that in the *Confessions* Augustine came to a new awareness of "the limitations of human
freedom."[14] While this is true, I cannot wholly agree with Brown's
earlier remark that Augustine saw himself as a *slave* never to be free.[15]
Augustine wrote abundantly, and although he sometimes compared
himself to a slave, not yet free and yearning for freedom, this is not
the dominant theme; it is, rather, the emptiness of personal freedom.
Throughout his works Augustine uses, sometimes explicitly, more often implicitly, the metaphor of the disillusioned freedman to describe
himself. He is free to move and to choose, but it has brought him no
peace or joy. He still grasps desperately for some better, higher freedom. Like the successful freedman, he can wander from place to place,
but he is the eternal resident alien. He has been emancipated into the
city of man, a false, alien place. He will be free only when he is reconciled to his true home, become again a citizen in the city of God. In
all this he has borrowed directly from Paul.

His two cities are, in essence, the two versions of freedom made
possible by the negation of death. The freedom of the city of man is
not just false; it is evil. It is the arrogance of self-determination—the
Pelagian heresy. It is impure, antisocial, and destructive of the common good. Goodness is the freedom which God alone gives and man
by the grace of Christ passively receives.[16] As in all theories of sovereignal freedom, in Augustine's thought the idea of freedom as a gift
from the totally free master is a persistent theme. The notion of gift
giving is not only "a key-phrase throughout the *City of God*" but, as
Brown shows, in other works of Augustine as well. Augustine attempts to "unravel the origin and relationship of the two 'cities' precisely in terms of this basic relationship of giver and recipient."[17]

Freedom for Augustine is something we long for, even suffer for,
but never something we achieve on our own. It is something given

gratuitously, as a master gives freedom to a slave whom he adopts. Nowhere is this more evident than in Augustine's view of the role of fear in the attainment of freedom. The sinner serves God "with fear and trembling." He distinguishes, however, between two kinds of fear, the servile fear of the slave and disillusioned ex-slave, who fears without love, and the "chaste fear" of the truly freed freedman, the sinner who has been adopted by his loving, generous master, an adoption, however, that is as gratuitous as it is predestined: "Because He gave, because what thou hast cometh not from thee, thou shalt work with fear and trembling, for if thou fearest Him not, He will take away what He gave."[18]

In the very last chapter of *The City of God*, Augustine offers us his vision of the nature of the heavenly city with its eternal bliss. It can be no accident that it is in this climactic chapter that he discusses the nature of freedom, or that the heavenly city is a thoroughly organic world. It is a world in which glory and honor prevail: "In heaven, all glory will be true glory, since no one could ever err in praising too little or too much. True honor will never be denied where due, never be given where undeserved, and since none but the worthy are permitted there, no one will unworthily ambition glory." This sounds suspiciously like a utopian reconstruction of the Augustan state. In this state of "perfect peace," God reigns as "the very Giver of virtue Himself . . . the source of every satisfaction . . . the object of our unending vision, of our unlessening love, of our unwearying praise."[19] It is remarkable that heavenly society is a hierarchical and organic world with ranks upon ranks of rewarded saints, to be graded, undoubtedly, according to their variously merited honor and glory.

> The less rewarded will be linked in perfect peace with the more highly favored, but lower could not more long for higher than a finger, in the ordered integration of a body, could want an eye. The less endowed will have the high endowment of longing for nothing loftier than their lower gifts.

There will be freedom of the will in the bliss of heaven, but this perfect freedom is immune from the temptation of sin. This, Augustine contrasts with the first, earthly freedom which had been given to Adam, a gift of God which, because it allowed for the possibility of choosing sin, "made merit possible." Mankind squandered this first opportunity for freedom in spectacular fashion, choosing sin, and with it death and living misery. By the greater grace of Christ, mankind will be led back "to that larger liberty which frees us from the power of sin."

Because God is the essence of freedom, we will experience his perfect freedom by sharing in his divine nature. This will be the ultimate gift, one we are so incapable of obtaining on our own that in order to experience it we must be remade and perfected by the great giver.

> The conclusion is that, in the everlasting City, there will remain in each and all of us an inalienable freedom of the will, emancipating us from every evil and filling us with every good . . . unclouded by the memory of any sin or of sanction suffered, yet with no forgetfulness of our redemption nor any loss of gratitude for our Redeemer.[20]

This is the conception of freedom that was to dominate both religious and secular reflection on the subject not only through the Middle Ages but also, even more emphatically, throughout the high Reformation period. Even those who most opposed the power of the church, and condemned the principle of papal supremacy, used this conception of sovereignal freedom, grounded in an organic view of society, in their writings. Only in heretical thought do we find any real challenge to this orthodoxy.

Under the overarching hegemony of Augustine, European thought from the end of the western Roman Empire to the end of the seventeenth century was structured by two major questions, one embedded in the other. The first concerned the proper relationship between the religious and the secular spheres of power and influence; the second addressed the question of the nature of power and the individual's place in the given sphere of existence. It is obviously not possible to examine these two problems in any depth here, since such an examination amounts to a history of medieval and pre-Enlightenment Western social thought. What we will do is briefly sketch the framework of this development in order to highlight the nature of reflection on the conception of freedom.

There were four possible interpretations of the broader problem, that of the relationship between the secular and the spiritual spheres. One was complete interpenetration. The world was seen as a unity, a *societas christiana* in which all Christians formed a single religious and political body, symbolically expressed in the body of Christ. Augustine's two cities were in no way identified with church and state, or even with the mortal and transcendental world. Citizens of the city of God, already elected, lived as resident aliens in this world; not all churchmen could claim to be of this city. Many of the elect were completely engaged in the secular part of the earthly world; and many who were good suffered evil.

Thus although for Augustine all power and virtue ultimately rested in God, and all true justice and freedom was to be found in subjection to God, his view in no way implied the subjection of the secular authorities to those of the church, since it was entirely possible that a king might be among the elect while a pope was destined for hell. What is more, until the final day of judgment, the heavenly city needed the secular world, if only because a good number of its ultimate citizens were in temporary, alien residence there.

> So, too, the earthly city which does not live by faith seeks only an earthly peace, and limits the goal of its peace, of its harmony of authority and obedience among its citizens, to the voluntary and collective attainment of objectives necessary to mortal existence. The heavenly city, meanwhile must use this earthly peace; so long as her life in the earthly city is that of a captive and an alien, she has no hesitation about keeping in step with the civil law which governs matters pertaining to our existence here below.[21]

This view of the world fitted well with the actual interpenetration of church and state that characterized Christian Europe from the end of the Roman Empire until the end of the tenth century, a period during which "kings had been considered semi-religious personages and had extensive influence on church affairs," and at the same time, "leading churchmen . . . played an important role in secular affairs, as advisers to kings, as administrators, as rulers of ecclesiastical principalities."[22]

With the investiture crisis of the eleventh century, this tidy integration was shattered, and its deconstruction made possible the social and intellectual construction of the other three kinds of relationship between church and state. One of these—the second kind of relationship—was that advocated in the Gregorian reforms. Church and state were separate, and because of the superiority of the sacred over the secular or, more specifically, because the pope, as the direct descendant of Peter, ruled with direct divine authority, the pope and the church had authority over the state. The political and intellectual storm which this theory of the papal plenitude of power set off was to have enormous ramifications in the later political and legal history of Europe.[23]

The third interpretation of this relationship was the more moderate view that church and state were separate spheres and that the secular and spiritual authorities were supreme in each of their respective domains. This was the view that was to triumph, after many centuries, in the West. But advocates of it could be found from as early as the eleventh century; indeed, it was adopted by most thinkers, religious and secular, who sought a compromise, most notably the French canonist Ivo of Chartres and the author of the *Liber de unitate ecclesiae conservanda*. Most of the best minds of the twelfth and thirteenth centuries who used the *Decretum* of Gratian (ca. 1140) as their point of departure, the so-called Decretists, sought such a dualistic compromise. The intellectual culmination of this tradition during the Middle Ages was, of course, the synthetic work of Thomas Aquinas, who, by reinterpreting Augustine in the light of the newly rediscovered works of Aristotle, was able to work out a theory of separation of spheres which, in spite of a few nagging ambiguities, was to wield a major, if not dominant, influence on subsequent Catholic doctrine. By the fourteenth century, even writers as radical as William of Ockham held this dualist view.

Finally, there were those who insisted on the supremacy of state over church. A long line of German kings, beginning long before Henry IV, along with their legal supporters, embraced this view. But the thinker during the high Middle Ages who most brilliantly advocated this position was undoubtedly Marsilius of Padua. As Alan Gewirth has pointed out, Marsilius was the true intellectual precursor of the Reformation, both because of his direct influence on the supporters of Henry VIII of England and, more questionably, on Luther, as well as on secular thinkers like Hooker and, presumably, Hobbes and Machiavelli, and because of the more powerful though indirect influence of the intellectual problems which he posed.[24] In light of all this, it is a pity he did not have more of an impact on his contemporaries.

Within this outer debate over the relationship between church and state, however, was coiled another set of problems which had both direct and radical implications for the Western *intellectual* conception of freedom. As Brian Tierney has noted, "One of the most important results of the dispute was to encourage the growth of doctrines justifying resistance by subjects to unjust rulers."[25] It was, in other words, a short step from the question which sphere of power—the spiritual or the secular—should dominate to the deeper question of the nature of power itself and the sources of its authority. Once the Western mind latched on to this problem, it set in train a series of reflections that became, in effect, the modern intellectual history of freedom.

The church, because of its involvement with the world, in the running of its own organization and in its worldly affairs, had a conception of sovereignal freedom which, as one would expect, was largely informed by Augustine's own views on the subject. However, what is even more striking is how closely it conformed to the prevailing view of freedom existentially derived from the political and social realities of medieval society. The power of the church with respect to the secular authorities was usually expressed in terms of its freedom. Indeed, the most potent slogan of the entire reform movement was "the freedom of the church"; its claim to superior power was a claim to superior freedom, and any denial of this claim was considered a threat to its freedom. There was no difference between this and the lordly conception of freedom discussed in the last chapter. Nowhere is this more evident than in the correspondence of Gregory VII himself, who repeatedly speaks of "the immunity and liberty which have been granted . . . by this see."[26]

As Tellenbach, most notably, has shown, earthly freedom to the church was "something indefinite and relative: it is both dignity and humility, possibility and bondage, lordship and dependence." Only the freedom of God had no limitation. Because the church was founded by Christ and was a part of his mystical body, it shared completely his freedom.

> It follows, therefore, that the freedom of the Church in its deepest and most universal sense is thought of in absolute terms like the freedom of God; and furthermore: if the freedom of the Church can be injured by corrupt and avaricious clergy or by infidel and violent laymen, God Himself and Christ are touched thereby, and it no longer appears remarkable that prayers are offered to them to protect the Church's rights.[27]

Ironically, the church's own arguments and rhetoric were used against it by supporters of royal supremacy. Secular thinkers took over not only the church's conception of its claim to secular supremacy but also the more elaborately developed Christocratic liturgical concepts by which it justified its spiritual control of the church, the community of whose believers constituted the mystical body of Christ. Late medieval and absolutist theories of kingship, then, amounted to nothing more than a "royal Christology" in which the king became, by degrees, pope figure, then Christ figure with two bodies, one human and mortal, the other divine and eternal, and finally, in the divine right theories of absolutism, a God figure who was the source of law and justice, exercising absolute power and yet under the absolute limitation of law. The mystical body of the church, at the head of which was Christ, was replaced in the political theology of absolutism by the mystical body of the state, at the head of which was the king. This political theology was most elaborately developed in England, where the idea of the king's two bodies was to have unexpected consequences: there it permitted the possibility of deposing and killing the king's natural body, even while celebrating his eternal *dignitas*; indeed, regicide could be justified for the benefit of the king's own "body politic," which was eternal and identified with Parliament.[28]

Continental theorists were less extravagant in their conceptions of sovereignty, but no less effective. In the writings of one of the greatest of late medieval poets and thinkers, we find not only one of the most forceful defenses of the divine source of kingly authority but also the most explicit statement of the idea that freedom was the supreme value of the West and that the king's absolute sovereignal power was the source of this cherished value. Dante's *On Monarchy*, written about 1312, was at one and the same time thoroughly medieval, in its vain wish for a universal government, and modern as well as Aristotelian, in the secular nature of its imagined leadership.

If mankind is to achieve its intellectual potential, peace is essential, and that is best realized in a monarchy: "For if it is otherwise, not only is the end of the civil life thwarted, but even the city ceases to be what it was." Dante buttresses his argument with an extremely organic and holistic theory of society, in which the goodness of the "totality" exceeds that of the ordering of its parts.

> The human totality therefore is said to be properly related to its whole in the same way that its own parts are properly related to the human totality itself. Its parts are related to it by means of a single principle. . . . The totality itself therefore is properly related, absolutely speaking, to the universe or to its ruler, who is God and the monarch, by means of one principle only, namely, a single ruler. Hence it follows that the monarchy is necessary to the world for its well-being.[29]

Mankind is most perfect when it reflects its likeness with the divine, and it does so when it is most in union with the divine. Similarly, people are most perfect when they share in the majesty of the king by being most unified with him. It is interesting that Dante does not suggest for a moment that he is arguing from analogy, although to a modern reader this is what he appears to be doing. The idea of the king as the divine counterpart on earth is so completely taken for granted that he can use what he considers true of God in relation to the universe as *proof* of what is, and should be, the relationship between king and subjects. In like manner, justice is best served when it is rendered by one who is all-powerful with a will that is free from all greed and full of charity and "right love"—namely, a monarch.

Dante then takes up the subject of freedom, and he begins with an unambiguous insistence on its supremacy: "Furthermore, the human race is at its best above all when it is free." Freedom, he tells us, exists only when our judgment determines, "anticipates," our appetites. The brute is not free, because its choices are determined by its appetite. The will is free only when it exists for its own sake and not for something else: "this freedom . . . is the greatest gift conferred by God on human nature, for through it we are rendered happy here as men, through it we are rendered happy elsewhere as gods." It is only under a monarchy that people exist for their own sake and not for something else. Other forms of government, including democracies and oligarchies, "force the human race into slavery." Kingship alone makes justice and freedom possible. Indeed, it is the object of "just regimes such as these [to] aim at freedom, namely, that men may exist for their own sakes."

One version or another of this conception of sovereignal freedom is what dominated the hegemonic thought of the late Middle Ages as well as of absolutist Europe. It will not be necessary for us to explore these ideas any further; our main concern is to emphasize that the notion of freedom was very closely identified with this exalted view of sovereignal power in medieval and early modern thought.

2. ALTERNATIVE CONCEPTIONS OF FREEDOM

Though sovereignal freedom was clearly the dominant note in the religious expression of freedom, we nonetheless find in religious thought, as in secular life, expressions of commitment to the other two notes of the chord. In secular thought, it was not until the late thirteenth and fourteenth centuries that the inner problem posed by the conflict between church and state—that of the nature of power and the source of authority—was to be directly confronted. The renaissance of the twelfth century may have marked new developments in European thought and attitudes among the small minority who were literate, involving an "unprecedented consciousness of the natural processes of renewal," but this renewal, as Gerhart Ladner has rightly noted, was "very much under the sway of the triune God" and directed toward a rebirth of men as sons of God. It was a renewal that enhanced continuity.[30] There may indeed have emerged, too, "a richer and more precise vocabulary for the discussion of the self" that paved the way for later developments, but one is hardly justified in claiming for the twelfth century any marked increase in individuality or discovery of self, even among the elite: witness the nearly complete absence of individualized portraiture both in painting and in writing.[31] And while there may have been a renewed commitment to corporatism, possibly even a new self-consciousness about it,[32] one is inclined to see this, with Georges Duby, as an aspect of the revival of the old trifunctional ideology of the three orders now placed in the ideological service of the recently ennobled and institutionalized order of knights.[33]

A marked change in intellectual attitude certainly took place in the late thirteenth and fourteenth centuries, partly under the impact of the resurgent dynastic national states and the full flowering of Aristotelian ideas. It was then that the problem of authority, hidden within the wider problem of state-church relations, came to the fore. With Averroism emerged the first fully secular view of society in the Middle Ages. "The most striking effect of the new learning," writes Michael Wilks, "was the growth of a belief in the natural, innate capacity of the human individual to regulate his own affairs in the light of a rationalistic interpretation of life."[34] By Aquinas's time three conceptions of the sources of sovereignty had emerged: one was the omnipotence of divinely constituted rule; the second, held by Aquinas and the great majority of thinkers, was the view that the ruler was at once absolute and limited; the third view, still very much in the minority, but a precursor of things to come, was that the ultimate source of sovereignty was the community, the will of the people. A form of civic freedom, we have already seen, had been vigorously pursued and often achieved at the urban and sometimes even at rural communal levels. Now, for the first time, we find its reappearance in high thought.

But just what, if any, was the relationship between the two? Most historians of ideas simply assume a connection, even a casual one, running from ideas to practice. Almost all social and political historians dismiss such claims. Of the major changes that were taking place in the English Parliament during the late fourteenth and the early fifteenth century, A. L. Brown states categorically, "Political ideas had apparently little influence; ideas and attitudes—and misconceptions—were traditional."[35] In all likelihood, the new ideas were responding to the same set of forces that were bringing about changes in social institutions and in the way lay people in the real world thought and felt. We will be brief.

In the political thought of William of Ockham, we find the intellect most directly in the service of the independent dynastic state.[36] Ockham reversed the traditional medieval view that the office makes the man. The individual should act in spite of, not because of, his position. While he was prepared to take the most radical stand in his attack on papal supremacy, Ockham remained quite conservative with respect to the source of authority in the secular sphere. He greatly valued an elite version of civic freedom but rejected any thought of popular sovereignty; by the consent of the ruled he meant only the aristocracy in relation to the monarch.[37] All this was closely determined by his support for his patron, Ludwig of Bavaria. Ockham was far more original and influential, however, in his defense of personal freedom. For the first time in old Europe, we find a thinker stressing the idea of freedom as freedom from the constraints of government. The best form of government is one which rules people who are free in the sense of enjoying personal autonomy and freedom from control. Ockham buttresses this conception of freedom with a quasi-Pelagian reading of Christian freedom. While denying that he was rejecting papal authority, Ockham nonetheless held that Christian freedom was a form of "concrete liberation" in which "the image of Christ as judge and ruler is largely replaced by the image of a shepherd and liberator."[38]

Whereas Ockham was the first medieval thinker to develop a conception of personal freedom as autonomy and freedom against constituted authority, Marsilius of Padua (1275?–after 1343) developed what would be the most radical theory of civic freedom in Europe before Locke. Marsilius conceives of the state as a body based not on ideal ends but on natural propensities.[39] It is natural for mankind to exercise will and to want the sufficient life. Marsilius gives two arguments for popular sovereignty. One is that only when the people legislate will the laws be made for the common benefit. Bad laws, according to him, lead to "unbearable slavery, oppression, and misery of the citizens" and to the downfall of the state. Here we find the first clear medieval identification of the absence of civic freedom with slavery, an identification that dominated later modern European thought. As Gewirth commented, "The citizens become slaves when the laws under which they live are beyond their control, and this because of both the nature of freedom and the consequence of its loss."[40]

Marsilius, however, uses another argument in defense of civic freedom—namely, that self-legislation is an end in itself. Majoritarian rule is justified not merely on utilitarian grounds but as the expression of an inherent value: the natural urge to exercise one's will, to share in the determination of everything that concerns one. Thus a state is free not only when it has just laws to which the people consent but when it has laws which the people participated in framing, and the latter is to be preferred even if it means less efficient laws: "every citizen must be free and not undergo another's despotism. But this would be the case if one or a few of the citizens by their own authority made the law over the whole body of citizens."[41] It is worth noting that it was precisely during Marsilius' day that we find, in the real world of the struggle for urban and rural self-government, a significant shift toward an appreciation of this chartered freedom as an end in itself rather than simply a means to secure more practical liberties.[42] Even so, Marsilius was way ahead of his time; he was condemned for heresy, and there is no reason to believe that his patron, Louis of Bavaria, took seriously a word he wrote.

For alternative views of freedom which were more in tune with the real world, and sometimes even that of the poor and downtrodden, we must turn, once again, to religion, both within and outside of accepted doctrine. Heresy is the obvious starting point. Most medievalists are now likely to agree with R. I. Moore that "heresy and the disposition towards it are an integral part of the European inheritance, not an optimal extra."[43] It is also the main form of "social opposition" in the Middle Ages.[44]

Now, while it may be true that "heresy means choice" and that the "heretic by definition is a man of conscience,"[45] one who, in the words of a twelfth-century French monk, "will not bow your presumptuous neck to the yoke of human obedience,"[46] it does not necessarily follow that such defiance indicates a love of personal freedom; it merely suggests its possibility. The fanatic may be prepared to defy authority and die for a principle that is its very opposite. Religious fundamentalists of all ages, like totalitarians of past times and Nazis and other supremacists of our own, are not lacking in martyrs. One horrible, chronic feature of the apocalyptic movements which "persisted throughout the Middle Ages" was their genocidal anti-Semitism, especially during and after the first two Crusades.[47] Fourquin hardly exaggerates when he sees these movements as containing the "proto-Nazi" roots of modern European racial fanaticism and collective scapegoating.[48] The views of heretics varied widely, and what many of them wanted was not a new church and a new theology of freedom but a return in spirit and fact to the most orthodox teachings of the church. The heretics of the eleventh and twelfth centuries, in particular, were moved to action by the official call for reform by the church itself: they were demanding in their own, often unlettered ways that the church live up to its own high ideals, including, presumably, its conception of sovereignal freedom.

Nonetheless, some heretics, by their actions and their views, implied a commitment to the values of personal freedom and equality, especially during the late Middle Ages. It is significant that many of the more prominent and successful heretics were either covertly or explicitly Pelagian. Henry of Lausanne, like the Cathars of the following century, rejected infant baptism for exactly the same reasons as Pelagius. The twelfth-century heresiarch Arnold of Brescia "was to unite in his person the two greatest revolutionary forces of his age, religious dissent and the spirit of the commune."[49] In the thirteenth and the fourteenth centuries the many forms of heretical mysticism that flourished advocated, in one form or another, a commitment to personal religious freedom. This was particularly so with the movement that grew out of them, namely, the Free Spirit sect. These women audaciously advocated a state of perfection in which the individual could no longer sin and hence could associate freely and equally with men: "They did not need to fast or pray since they had obtained such control over their senses that they could afford to them complete freedom, and that they were no subject to obedience, because 'where the spirit of the Lord is, there is liberty.' "[50] Although religious thought and secular thought were closely intertwined during the Middle Ages and although some heretics held radical social and political views, perhaps only a minority did so.[51] A case in point was the fourteenth-century Oxford religious radical Wyclif, who came close to a doctrine of the priesthood of all believers, translated the Bible and distributed it directly to believers, and "became a near anarchist" in religious matters, yet in secular politics remained so "profoundly conservative" that he condemned the peasants' revolt in the most extreme terms.[52]

However, not all alternatives to the dominant sovereignal conception of freedom were heretical. Within the church itself were to be found many new orders which advanced conceptions of the world—and, implicitly, of freedom—quite similar to those expressed by individuals condemned as heretics. Within the fold of the church were movements such as the Humiliati, the Beguines, and, most notably, the Franciscans and Dominicans, as well as new conceptions of, and metaphors for expressing, the divine which marked a strong and approved departure from the old, pre-Gregorian ways of orthodoxy. What is more, the stimulus for these new developments came as much from the changing social and economic realities of Europe as from the Gregorian reforms. Indeed, as is true of so much of the Middle Ages, the secular and the religious, both in thought and in practice, were inextricably intertwined.

This interrelationship has been recently explored in a highly provocative analysis of the connection between religious poverty and the profit economy.[53] At first sight, the new mendicant orders may seem to have marked a retreat from the world. However, by their emphasis on itinerant preaching and apostolic poverty, they not only addressed the concerns of the newly emerging urban artisanal and merchant classes but provided a justification for the accumulation of wealth (philanthropy and provision for one's family), demythologized money by distinguishing between its function as a medium of exchange (acceptable) and a store of value (unacceptable if purely usurial), and, along with the scholastic tradition of thought they promoted, developed a new "ethical justification for urban society."[54]

These new mendicant orders both were determined by and in turn influenced the new urban classes as they "persisted in the linguistic and formal mode of the money-makers, while avoiding the spiritually harmful aspects of such people's work."[55] However, the mendicants bore a striking resemblance to a group we have already discussed at length, the Cynics of the ancient world. We have seen how the Cynics' deep commitment to the ideal of personal freedom led them to a complete rejection of the material world and a turning inward in their search for true personal freedom. Many contemporaries noted similarities between Cynic preachers and Christian itinerants in the Roman world, Aelius Aristides in the second century and the emperor Julian in the fourth century A.D. being the most noteworthy.[56] The link between Christianity and Cynicism went well beyond mere resemblance. The outlandish martyr Peregrinus [Proteus] (d. 165), Justin Martyr (ca. 100–165), the leader of the Encratite Christian sect, Tatian (flourished 160–80), and the notorious Christian bishop of Constantinople, Maximus, were all Cynics.[57] As Dudley has observed, "The influence of the Cynics on the monastic orders and on the Egyptian eremites was probably considerable, though it is hard to trace; and the Church's toleration of Cynicism is seen not only from Augustine but from the fact that there were Cynics in Byzantium."[58]

No direct connection between the mendicant orders of the later Middle Ages and Cynicism can be claimed. But their social and philosophical similarities have long impressed scholars. The important point about the Dominicans' pun on their own name, when they called themselves *Domini canes*, is not that they were referring to Diogenes (for in all likelihood they were not) but that the lives of the itinerant Dominicans and Franciscans "wandering through the world, voluntarily living at subsistence level, getting money for their needs by toil in the fields or by begging, and everywhere preaching to the people, invite comparison with Epictetus' idea of Cynicism as a special service in an emergency."[59]

But the similarities suggest something else—namely, that this kind of itinerant asceticism, wherever and whenever it manifests itself, implies by its very nature a commitment to personal, spiritual freedom. As Ramsay MacMullen has rightly observed, the Cynics "were to the ancient world what palmers and Friars were to the medieval, a familiar sight everywhere, both suspect and sacred."[60] Mendicant individualism was merely a more visible expression of an ideal that had always been embraced and cultivated by the Christian monasteries. As Troeltsch pointed out long ago, "the early ideal of the Gospel, the anarchy of the faith which is responsible to God alone, of the infinite worth of the free soul, and of the 'shedding abroad' of the Love of God in the love of the bretheren," had not died, but rather had found sanctuary in monasticism.[61]

Hence we should not be surprised to learn that one of the most powerful defenses of personal freedom as a real value, as opposed to the mere bookish speculation of the philosophers and theologians, comes from the greatest mendicant of the Middle Ages, Francis of Assisi, recognized by the church itself as the *alter Christus*, the man whose life came closest to an imitation of Christ.[62] For Francis, the Gospel was the only rule of the friars, and it was they who should decide how to interpret and obey it. When he was asked, in 1222, to adopt one of the long-established monastic rules, he replied to the assembled brothers,

> My brothers, my brothers, God has called me by the way of simplicity
> and of humility, and He has pointed out this way as being the true way,
> both for me and for those who wish to believe me and imitate me. So
> don't talk to me about some rule or other, neither that of St. Benedict nor
> of St. Augustine nor of St. Bernard, nor about any life or way of living
> other than that which the Lord has mercifully shown and given to me.[63]

Francis spoke here in the true spirit of both Cynic and primitive Christian freedom. It is remarkable that such a view could not only have received the official blessing of the church but been uttered by a saint whom all of Christendom thereafter came to regard as the person whose life and thought most replicated those of the Christ they worshiped. Although one would never have arrived at this realization from the formal, hegemonic thought of the times, it is clear from the mere sociological presence and vitality of the mendicant orders that personal liberty, of the most pristine, ancient sort—the liberty of Galatians realized in the surrender advocated in Romans—thrived in the religious mind, as it did in the secular thought of those who resisted.

We should be careful, however, not to get too carried away by this fact. The mendicants, though accepted and admired as holy imitators of Christ, were, like their ancient counterparts, viewed with great suspicion. Their existence makes clear the salience and vitality of the nonsovereignal notes of freedom in the medieval cultural chord. But we should still inquire whether this commitment went beyond these groups. How pervasive were their values? Were people prepared to admire religious freedom as applied to the mendicants but not to themselves? Were the mendicants like the Communist party in Great Britain today, viewed by the church as a kind of socioreligious inoculation, their views accepted as an institutionally astute way of upholding the hegemonic view of spiritual freedom? It is important that we keep in mind a critical distinction: that between the celebration of poverty and a compassion for real poor people. The mendicants were held in suspicion not only by those to their left who questioned their prosperity but also, more seriously, by divines to their right who were always uncomfortable with the radicalism inherent in a too literal celebration of poverty. A strict construction of the vow of poverty could generate hostility to all form of property and a return to the original position of Christ that perfection and the road to heaven required a rejection of wealth. This celebration of real poverty had radical implications both for secular society and for the church which the leaders of both were quick to see. Indeed, after Francis's death one group of his followers did insist on just such a radical interpretation. The Spirituals called for a new "spiritual church" and denounced the church for its wealth and compromises with the secular world.[64] In political thought this interpretation was later to be used by Louis of Bavaria in his struggle with the pope. Both of these radical developments were condemned by the church. In the end, it was the more conservative followers of Francis, the Conventuals, who were legitimized by the church. And in the works of their most famous intellectual leader, Bonaventure, "the second founder of the Friars Minor," the distinction between poverty as a religious ideal and real poverty was carefully and fatefully drawn. It is a distinction that reminds us of another, reported recently by Caroline Bynum: that which late medieval men made between the feminized Jesus of the Mary cult and real women.[65]

The same blend of the institutional and the innovative is found in the remarkable shift toward the reconception of Jesus as mother, most dramatically reflected in the rise of the Mary cult and accompanied by the increase not only of female religious movements but of female saints. In this "rise of affective piety and the feminization of religious imagery," we certainly find a new conception of God as being more nurturing and more loving and suffering and as having power that is more creative. The powerful, glorious, kinglike God of the early Middle Ages is slowly replaced by a Jesus who suffers and cries for his flock as a woman suffers and mourns for her sons.[66] Christ's passion now occupies center stage in European Christian ceremony for the first time. It would be easy to see this feminization of religious imagery not only as indicative of a new release from internal constraints, a new free spirit—as indeed the women of the Free Spirit movement did—but as symptomatic of a sociological change in attitude toward women. Were this the case, we would indeed have found powerful evidence for a wellspring of support for personal freedom in orthodox religion, for no sociological trend more decisively correlates with the growth of commitment to the value of freedom than men's willingness to accept the equality of women.

But, as Bynum has shown, things were rather more complex, and far less radical. There is no evidence that this extraordinary feminization of men's view of their God in any way correlated with growing respect for women. Indeed, as the Cistercian experience and writings amply demonstrate, it was precisely those men most committed to the feminized view of God who had most removed themselves from women and family. Religious piety meant, above all, sexual piety, and the man too alert to the evils of sex is invariably the man hostile to the temptations of women.[67] Female imagery and a feminized conception of God did not replace "authority figures qua rulers or fathers" but rather buttressed that authority by adding a new dimension, one involving "nurturing, affectivity, and accessibility" between men and men, and between men and *their* God.[68]

A recent study by Michael P. Carroll emphasizes that any explanation of the cult of Mary must focus on men: the Virgin Mary is a male invention, an argument reinforced by the peculiar insistence on her *in partu* virginity, in flat contradiction of the New Testament. It suggests that the thing men most identify with women, childbearing, cannot be sacred and pure when achieved naturally. It also suggests, though less emphatically, that women as natural mothers are impure and that the loss of virginity involves a loss of what is most respected in a woman. The worship of the Virgin, if anything, places women in the ultimate double bind. Carroll offers a highly Freudian explanation for the Mary cult, strongly suggested by the high correlation he finds between the cult and the equally popular flagellant movement and emphasis on Christ's passion.[69]

While one is inclined to be skeptical of wholly psychological explanations, it is interesting that one of the leading students of medieval society explains the chronic tradition of heresy and other forms of social alienation, including the cult of courtly love, in term of a strong hostility to the family, marriage, and the church. Intergenerational conflicts rigidly enforced primogeniture among the wealthy, and the problem of unmarriageable women were the main sources of rebellion among men.[70] Not repressed desire for the mother, it seems, but plain ambivalence and downright hostility to women characterize the attitude of many men, and especially male rebels, during the Middle Ages: "Like Mary and like Eve, she was both handmaid and rebel, queen and outcast among them."[71] At the same time, as Eileen Power argued many years ago, in spite of the self-contradictory ideology of female inferiority and divinity of the times, late medieval civilization "comes out well" when judged by the actual realities of women's lives. At all class levels women performed nearly all the usual male tasks, if for no other reason than that their men were so often away. They managed large households and businesses in country and city; and in the nunneries, they worked at crafts; they even fought.[72]

The concurrence of changing demographic, familial, and economic conditions, along with the cult of chastity, created an unanticipated opening for women in high and late medieval Europe. Women found that they could refuse men's control over their bodies and realize an intensely personal freedom by simply taking to its logical conclusion the very virtue which had been excessively idealized in the unrelenting male effort to dominate them. All they had to do was to take vows of chastity and piously insist on becoming brides of Christ rather than brides of men. This, after all, had long been one of the favorite metaphors of the church itself in describing its relationship to God: negatively, from the eleventh century simony had been condemned as a form of spiritual rape; and on the positive side, there was the deification of the Virgin Mary. In many cases, of course, men with too many unendowable women on their hands not only concurred with but encouraged and even pressured women to join the nunneries. But often men found themselves being hoisted by their own petard; severe conflicts developed when an attractive daughter for whom a good marriage had been arranged refused to comply by willfully, and often secretly, taking vows of chastity. Such conflicts became acute when these resisting women decided not to enter nunneries, where at least they could still be controlled, but to lead the eremitic or mendicant life. A revealing case in point is that of Christina of Markyate in England who rejected her family's marital plans for her and became an eremite. Her *Vita* reveals that such a life was by no means solitary, for Christina, a beautiful and passionate woman who unwittingly drove at least one cleric to flashing, had two intense relationships with her male supporters. Her letters to her "most intimate one," the requiting Abbot Geoffery, spoke the language of earthly love, although, to use a distinction that Milton has taught us, a love that was sensuous rather than sensual; free, female, and unphallic.[73]

The rapid spread of the Beguines, a movement dominated by urban middle- and upper-class women, was one of the most remarkable religious and social developments of the Middle Ages. Although never condemned as heretics, these lay sisterhoods were always viewed with great suspicion by more conservative churchmen. The wonder is that they were allowed to exist and flourish at all, for even today such a movement of middle-class women would be considered a scandal in most Western societies, especially America. Can it have been an accident that this movement flourished in the Low Countries? Was the celebration of this altruistic and spiritual form of personal freedom by women an anticipation of the revalorization of the hard personal freedom that came with the invention of capitalism and the drowning cell by the men of this very area of Europe? What were the women who became mothers rather than Beguines up to? What were they nurturing? What misbegotten dreams were these mothers of change displacing in the hearts and minds of the sons they reared?

These are mere speculations. What we can say with near certainty, however, is that the Beguine movement marks one of the high points, perhaps the very highest, in women's experience of freedom. C. H. Lawrence is surely correct in asserting that, "in a genuine sense, the Beguines represented a movement of women's liberation."[74] And yet, this was the period in which one finds some of the most virulent expressions of misogyny in both secular and clerical writings.

Does this extraordinary ambivalence toward women—at once worshiped and reviled, central to the religious and secular life of the culture, yet shunned and unwanted as mates—remind one of another culture? Indeed it does. At this waning moment of medieval civilization, with Europe poised to take off into modernity and later world hegemony, we are taken right back to the very beginnings of European civilization, to the waning decades of the ancient Greek archaic state in the seventh century B.C., before the beginnings of the century of Athens' transformation to its classic era of glory, empire, and the Periclean fusion of the notes of freedom. The cult of the Virgin Mary was the late medieval counterpart to the cult of Hera. The systematic exclusion of women from the most important institution of the civilization, even as the church feminized its God and deified a woman, finds its most striking counterpart in the systematic exclusion of women from the all-important democratic institutions of Athens, even as it celebrated the powerful images of women in its communal drama. The

ambivalence toward women in the cult of courtly love, with its parody
of vassalage and Christian mysticism,[75] and in the worship of the Virgin was the late medieval way of participating in a drama no less tragic,
and sociologically transcending, than that of preclassical mythology
and its later refiguration in classical drama.

And as in ancient Greek myth and drama and in late preclassical
Greek life and culture, women in late medieval society were the quintessential symbol of heresy, the distinctively medieval expression of
personal freedom. One of the most famous medievalists has written
that women appear ''in the history of heresy . . . as in no other
manifestation of [medieval life].''[76]

In the early part of this work, we found that women were the creators of Western freedom because it was they who first socially constructed personal freedom as value, and this was the first note of the
chord to be valorized as an ideal. We found, however, that ancient
women were never satisfied with a purely negative view of personal
freedom, not only because they recognized its potential nihilism and
moral vacuousness but because they could all too clearly see how a
masculated negative liberty easily sublated into liberty as power over
others. Freedom for ancient women was always closely associated with
natural justice, and with being true to self and significant others, even
at the risk of open defiance. Men could not help finding some virtue
in this; but they were also hostile to the idea. Female freedom threatened order (to men then, as to men in modern times)[77] not only because of the possibility of descent into *female* license—uncontrolled
female bodies and emotions, the ultimate male disorder of nature—but
also because a love of the natural was felt to be an implicit assault on
what men most cherished, the created universe, the unnatural order
they had fashioned and imposed on nature, the state being its finest
product. There is no glory in nature, unfashioned; no pleasure in love,
unconquered; no gain in freedom without the promise of power. Men
could cherish negative freedom, pure and simple, precisely because
men cherished positive freedom as power over others. There is real
pleasure to be had in denying another the pleasure of being free over
you. All you need is a competitive spirit. All the better in a zero-sum
world.

The medieval mendicants and lay sisterhoods strongly rejected such
conceptions of personal freedom. The liberation from coercion was certainly prized as a value in its own right, by both men and women. St.
Francis, we are told, abhorred the name of ''master'': ''For the name
'master' is appropriate only for the Blessed Christ, all of whose acts
are perfect,'' and since no mortal man is perfect, ''he commanded that

no one on earth should presume to be called 'Master.' ''[78] It is when we examine just what the liberation from brute constraint, masterhood, entailed that we begin to find differences emerging, especially between men and women mendicants. For many women, and for some male mendicants, especially the early ones, personal freedom meant the inner peace that came from being in touch with one's most inward self. Like the Cynics of ancient times, they rediscovered poverty as ''that heavenly virtue by which all earthly and transitory things are trodden under foot, and by which every obstacle is removed from the soul so that it may freely enter into union with the eternal Lord God.''[79] But they also rediscovered something else, a truth that had been celebrated more by the Epicureans than by the Cynics: that even if we are free in ourselves it is not possible to give full expression to this freedom if others are not likewise free. John MacMurray, the late Scottish philosopher, is the only modern thinker to make this the centerpiece of his theory of freedom, and what he says on the subject perfectly describes the mendicants' view, even though he seems to think that the idea was originally his own: ''Human freedom demands not merely free people, but the relationship of free people. Its final basis lies in real friendship. All reality, that is to say, all significance converges upon friendship, upon the real relationship of one person with another independently real person.''[80] A view of human relationships similar to this explains the emphasis not only on poverty, but on charity, the charity which, as Marguerite Porete so beautifully expressed it, ''has no shame, no dread'' and ''obeys nothing created except by love.''[81]

Beyond this point, a severe breach emerges between those mendicants who remained within the fold of the church and those who were later to be condemned as heretics, especially the women of the Free Spirit movement. In the Free Spirit movement of the late Middle Ages, we find another of those all too rare moments in the history of Western culture when the original creators of the value of personal freedom rise above the surface of history's mannish stream. It is instructive to contrast the feminized God of the male-made Mary cult with the God of real female divines during this very period. Whereas men sought to soften the awesome image of the God they worshiped and to find in Mary an intercessor, a mediatrix between them and the sovereignal almighty, or else to flog themselves senseless in the face of their utter worthlessness and obeisance before God, women mystics sought the ultimate expression of freedom not only through direct communication with God but—the Free Spirit heresy—through actual identity with him.

The Free Spirit movement began in the early thirteenth century and lasted for some five centuries, its adherents spreading from their stronghold in Cologne over a vast area of Europe during its height of influence in the late thirteenth and fourteenth centuries.[82] The movement has many resemblances to Gnosticism, as Cohn notes, and in its purest form was indeed "an affirmation of freedom so reckless and unqualified that it amounted to a total denial of every kind of restraint and limitation."[83] There were strong tendencies toward antinomianism among some circles, especially among those Beghards who practiced nudity. But most versions of the movement were more restrained. From very early on, women occupied an unusually prominent role. This, plus the fact that their conception of inner salvation rendered church, rituals, and priests unnecessary, made them the object of special persecution on the part of the church hierarchy, one German bishop describing them as "vagabonds who refused obedience to men under the pretext that God was best served in freedom."[84] What all versions had in common was the belief that perfect freedom was possible by finding the God within oneself and identifying with it, and that the church with its masses, sermons, and prayers were unnecessary to achieve this. This was heresy, as were their beliefs that the soul could save itself without works and could attain a constant experience of the divine in the present life.[85]

All members of the Free Spirit movement had not only a strong valuation of personal freedom per se but an awareness of the need to give the value content in a manner that did not result in one or both of its twin dangers: isolation or domination. That indeed is what would happen with the uncoupling of immunity from protected liberties in the early modern world, when freedom from any restraint by the state meant the free and selfish exercise of power over others through power over property. The ancient female response to the dangers of personal freedom had been to identify it with natural justice. The approach of Marguerite and her Free Spirit sisters and brothers not only was more relevant to her world but pointed the way to the sole satisfactory resolution in the modern world: self-realization. The liberation from constraining powers does indeed inspire the need for a positive expression of one's own power. Not, however, over others, but over oneself. The ultimate freedom is the discovery of the power, the divine, in one's own being, a discovery which, Marguerite was convinced, could only bring love, for oneself and for others. God is love: "the pure love, the noble love and the high love of the free Soul."[86] The *Mirouer des simples ames* is written in the form of a dialogue mainly among the soul, love, and reason.[87] In one of the most exquisite dialogues, Reason asks Lady

Love what she means when she says that her "Soul is in the true freedom of Pure Love when she does nothing which could be against that which her inner peace requires."

> Let me tell you what it means, Love answers. It means that she does nothing, whatever the circumstances, which works against the perfect peace of her spirit. This is the way of he who is truly innocent, says Love, and the being of whom we speak is true innocence. Reason, Love continues, let me give you an example. Consider a child who is purely innocent: does he do anything, does he refrain from doing anything, should it not please him?[88]

Marguerite's dialogue is the most sublime expression of personal freedom as an inner experience. It was also pure heresy. The dialogue was condemned for the first time in 1306. Instead of recanting, she brought out another edition and sent a copy to the local bishop. Like her ancient mythical counterpart, Antigone, Marguerite chose to defy the powers that be precisely because she could not "share in hatred but in love."[89] The book was condemned a second time in early 1309, and Marguerite was arrested soon afterward. Eighteen months of inquisitorial torture did not break her spirit. She never recanted the views she had published in her hymn to freedom. On the first of June, 1310, Marguerite was burned alive by a huddle of priests, solemnly praying for the freedom of her soul.

We do not know what Marguerite thought as the flames consumed her flesh, but we might not be too far wrong in thinking that the last thoughts of this dying Gaul had something to do with what for the church was her most outrageous *scandalum*, but what to her was the essence of her freedom: "A soul which has such love is herself Love, and can to the Virtues say: 'I bid farewell to you.' "[90]

CODA

Understanding the role of slavery in the creation and history of freedom has forced us to face certain disquieting aspects of the relationship between good and evil, as well as the problem of harmony and contradiction in the etiology of those things we most cherish. Our moral universe is a field of values that are in conflict not only with each other but with themselves. I refer not simply to that incommensurability in our values to which Kenneth Arrow and Martha Nussbaum, in their separate ways, have drawn our attention,[1] but to something far more disturbing. The history of freedom and its handmaiden, slavery, has bruited in the open what we cannot stand to hear, that inhering in the good which we defend with our lives is often the very evil we most abhor. In becoming the central value of its secular and religious life, freedom constituted the tragic, generative core of Western culture, the germ of its genius and all its grandeur, and the source of much of its perfidy and its crimes against humanity. On both the secular and religious levels, its separate elements remained yoked in continuous, creative tension within themselves, and with each other, each at once good and evil, bearing the dread mark of its birth and the glow of its possibilities.

At its best, the valorization of personal liberty is the noblest achievement of Western civilization. That people are free to do as they please within limits set only by the personal freedom of others; that legally all persons are equal before the law; that philosophically the individual's separate existence is inviolable; that psychologically the ultimate human condition is to be liberated from all internal and external constraints in one's desire to realize one's self; and that spiritually the son of God made himself incarnate, then gave his life in order to redeem mankind from spiritual thralldom and to make people free and equal before God—all add up to a value complex that not only is unparalleled in any other culture but, in its profundity and power, is superior to any other single complex of values conceived by mankind. Individually liberating, socially energizing, and culturally generative, freedom is undeniably the source of Western intellectual mastery, the engine of its extraordinary creativity, and the open secret of the triumph of Western culture, in one form or another, over the other cultures of mankind. The facts that, today, almost all peoples embrace the ideal of personal freedom, whatever their actual practice, and that many have come to define the value as instinctively human in order to deny its quintessentially Western origins are telling testimony to its overpowering appeal and inherent goodness.

But personal freedom has had no shortage of critics, both outside the West, from the Islamic world to China and Japan, and within its own borders. At its worst, no value has been more evil and socially corrosive in its consequences, inducing selfishness, alienation, the celebration of greed, and the dehumanizing disregard for the "losers," the little people who fail to make it. Plato, whatever his reactionary intentions, was right in drawing attention to these dangers. They were all too evident in his own day, and they have plagued the course of Western history, precisely at those times when the good version of this note of freedom has been the moral and sociological source of great material and cultural change. This contradiction has been even more marked in the modern world, as the grandeur and horrors of industrial Europe and America make clear. Fundamentalist Muslim leaders who have taken a hard look at this value and decided to spurn it cannot be dismissed as irrational fanatics. Try as we might—and Western philosophers and moralists have tried mightily—the brute historical fact remains that we have been unable to transcend the evils that come with the blessings of personal freedom.

Sovereignal freedom, too, ranges between good and evil, although today we are so inclined to see its evil side that we would like to deny the historical fact that it is, and always has been, an essential note of the chord of freedom. The organic version of sovereignal freedom— the idea that we are most free when we find our rightful place in, and wholly identify with, a hierarchical, purposeful order that is freer and more powerful than its members—is not some shibboleth we can conveniently write out of the conceptual field of freedom by philosophical mandate. As we have seen, it has been the dominant conception of freedom for most of Western history, on both the spiritual and material levels of being. It has not only sustained the West, it has been good for the West. Men with unrestrained freedom of power in both personal and political life were free to change their fellow men, to organize as never before, to create and transform their worlds, to define the good, and to impose the means by which those over whom they exercised their absolute freedom lived, unrestrained by the inertial weight of tradition. But, of course, they were also free to brutalize, to plunder and lay waste and call it peace, to rape and humiliate, to invade, conquer, uproot, and degrade. And on the spiritual level, we have seen that the religious doctrine of God as perfect, sovereignal freedom can entail either the most empowering conception of the relation with the divine, or the most debased, depending on how one defines the nature of one's identification with that absolute divine freedom. The West escaped neither extreme of sovereignal freedom. Indeed, on all levels, the West is, in good part, the peculiar product of both extremes of the sovereignal note of the chord.

This tradition, though no longer hegemonic, is still very much with us and, as the world discovered a mere fifty years ago, is still capable of erupting into a holocaust of evil. However painful the admission, Nazi Germany was, for Germans, a free state, the freest and most powerful collective experience of any Western people up to that time. In their identity with the powerfully free Third Reich, the Germans experienced a freedom that was liberating, ecstatic, and empowering. They correctly called what they experienced "freedom." Moralists and philosophers may rail with outrage at this seeming libel of the ideal we cherish, and write learned treatises "proving" why the Nazis had no right to identify their experience with freedom. But the bleak sociohistorical truth remains that in their claim that what they felt was freedom, the Nazis had the whole long history of the Western tradition of sovereignal freedom on their side, a tradition that goes right back to the greatest mind in the history of the civilization, Plato himself.

The same moral contradiction marks the note of civic freedom. The virtues of a democratic system of government need no defense; it is safe to say that it is the best form of government, and its invention and history, however episodic and bloody, are among the greatest achievements of Western civilization. But there is something evil at the very core of this great system of governance. Plato and the other conservative thinkers of classical Greece also had deep misgivings about the earliest democracy in which they lived, but failed to note its gravest moral failing, no doubt because they took it so much for granted: the fact that the principle of participative politics and of extension of the franchise were invigorated by the exclusion and domination of others. When Robert Michels wrote that "democracy leads to oligarchy, and necessarily contains an oligarchical nucleus,"[2] he was historically correct, though with this important qualification: the oligarchic clique he feared could be, and often was, a majority of free men, sometimes even a moral majority.[3] It is no accident that the first and greatest mass democracies of the ancient and modern worlds—Athens and the United States—share this evil in common: they were both conceived in, and fashioned by, the degradation of slaves and their descendants and the exclusion of women. The chronic, identical evils of Athenian xenophobia and misogyny, and antebellum American racism, nativism, and sexism, served a common purpose and nourished a common good: the profound commitment of both cultures to the inspired principle of participative politics. We, the citizens, the people, the free—those whom we "hold dear," those whom we marry, kith, kin, "not in bondage, noble, glad, illustrious," "beloved"[4]—we the politically free body of men, always, it would seem, tragically require the *them* who do not belong: the ignoble, the nonkith, the nonkin, the people we do not marry, the alien within—the serf, the Jew, the Slav, the slave, the Negro, the people who cannot vote—who demarcate what *we* are, the domestic enemy who defines whom *we* love.

If this history of the West's most important value has taught us anything, then, it is not mainly the "fragility of goodness," as Nussbaum rightly but rather too gently conceives it, and certainly not, to take the opposite, brutalist extreme of Robert Michels, that there are iron sociological laws of freedom that go "beyond good and evil." There are no such iron laws in human culture, and nothing goes beyond good and evil. What we have learned, rather, is the tragic interdependence of good and evil. To its great credit, Western culture has never tried to conceal this terrible truth, although it is one our present era is all too eager to shun. From its secular Greek roots, the West learned the lesson of the tragic dramatists that the only wisdom worthy of remembrance comes from struggle and unfathomable suffering; freedom is the gift of "the wisdom won from pain." From its Judeo-Christian religion, forged in the sickening horror of Roman slave society, the West learned the reinforcing spiritual truth that "out of evil cometh good." The vision of Israel emerged from the bondage of Egypt. Redemption—spiritual freedom—was not simply liberation from slavery to sin, but as Paul saw with his fearsome vision, the suffering of sin made necessary the coming of the Christ and the promise of the cross—that central and most protean civilizational symbol of death and rebirth, estrangement and reconciliation, slavery and salvation. Less obviously, but for that very reason, more subliminally potent, in the image of the nailed, dying God, we see the permanent horror of constraint; in the image of the wooden cross—the vertical crossroad, the Pythagorean "Y"—we see the ultimate veneration of choice.[5] Whether we chose to believe this or not, it is this strange, terrifying vision, at once mortal and divine, that has fashioned the culture and genius of the West.

All who have come up from the abyss of slavery and serfdom—the children of slaves as well as the children of slave mongers—must be humbled by this truth each time we celebrate our freedom.

NOTES

INTRODUCTION

1. Crocker, *Positive Liberty* (The Hague: Marrtinus Nijhoff, 1980), 1.
2. M. I. Finley, *Economy and Society in Ancient Greece*, ed. Brent Shaw and Richard Saller (Hammondsworth: Penguin Books, 1983), 77. For a skeptical view of one of the most celebrated attempts to define liberty in wholly conceptual terms, see John Gray, "Hayek on Liberty, Rights, and Justice," *Ethics* 92 (Oct. 1981): 73–84.
3. Krieger, "Stages in the History of Political Freedom," in Carl J. Friedrich, ed., *Liberty* (New York: Atherton Press, 1962), 3.
4. MacIver, "The Meaning of Liberty and Its Perversions," in Ruth Anshen, ed., *Freedom: Its Meaning* (New York: Harcourt, Brace, 1940), 280.
5. M. I. Finley, *Politics in the Ancient World* (Cambridge: Cambridge Univ. Press, 1983), 73.
6. See, for example, Vilhjalmur Stefansson, "Was Liberty Invented?" in Anshen, ed., *Freedom*, 384–411.
7. Berlin, *Four Essays on Liberty* (Chicago: Univ. of Chicago Press, 1960). A vast literature has emerged around the positive/negative distinction first posed by Berlin. See J. H. Loenen, "The Concept of Freedom in Berlin and Others," *The Journal of Value Inquiry*, 10 (Winter, 1976): 279–285; Gary F. Reed, "Berlin and the Division of Liberty," *Political Theory* 8 (Aug. 1980): 365–80; W. E. Draughon, "Liberty: A Proposed Analysis," *Social Theory and Practice* 5 (Fall 1978): 29–44.
8. Russell, "Freedom and Government," in Anshen, ed., *Freedom*, 249–64.
9. Ibid., 259.

CHAPTER 1

1. Bosanquet, "Personal Freedom through the State," in Robert E. Dewey and James A. Gould, eds., *Freedom: Its History, Nature, and Varieties* (New York: Macmillan, 1970), 191.

2. Orlando Patterson, *Slavery and Social Death* (Cambridge: Harvard Univ. Press, 1982), introd.

3. Aristotle, *Politics*, trans. Ernest Barker, 1254a. (London: Oxford Univ. Press, 1958).

4. Patterson, *Slavery and Social Death*.

5. Thomas Hobbes, *Leviathan*, (London: J. M. Dent, 1914), chap. 21.

6. John Locke, *The Second Treatise of Government*, ed. P. Laslett (Cambridge: Cambridge Univ. Press 1970), 4.9–13.

7. Mann, *The Sources of Social Power* (Cambridge: Cambridge Univ. Press, 1986), 1:53.

8. See Patterson, *Slavery and Social Death*, appendix 2, for data and references.

9. Perdue, *Slavery and the Evolution of Cherokee Society, 1540–1866* (Knoxville: Univ. of Tennessee Press, 1979), chap. 1.

10. For this discussion of the Tupinamba, I have drawn mainly on the following works: A. Métraux, *La civilisation matérielle des tribus Tupi-Guarani* (Paris: Paul Geuthner, 1928); Métraux, "The Tupinamba," in Julian H. Steward, ed., *Handbook of South American Indians*, Bureau of Ethnology Bulletin no. 143 (Washington, D.C.: GPO, 1948), 3:95–133; F. Fernandes, "La guerre et le sacrifice humain chez les Tupinamba," *Journal de la Société des Américanistes de Paris* n.s. Vol. 41 (1952): 139–220; A. Thevet, "Histoire d'André Thevet Angoumoisin, cosmographe du Roy de deux voyages par luy fait aux Indes Australes et Occidentales," reprinted in A. Métraux, *La religion des Tupinamba et ses rapports avec celle des autres tribus Tupi-Guarani*, Bibliothèque de l'école des hautes études, sciences religieuses, vol. 45 (Paris: E. Leroux, 1928), 239–52; Father Evreux, *Voyage dans le nord de Brésil, durant les années 1613 & 1614*, ed. F. Denis (Paris: A. Frank, 1864).

11. Sahlins, *Stone Age Economics* (Chicago: Aldine, 1972), Chapter 1.

12. Métraux, "Tupinamba," 113.

13. Ibid., 112.

14. Ibid., 120.

15. Evreux, *Voyage*, 53.

16. Métraux, "Tupinamba," 114–15.

17. On the anthropology of honor, see J. D. Peristiany, *Honor and Shame: The Values of Mediterranean Society* (London: Weidenfeld and Nicolson, 1965). On honor and its relation to slavery, see Patterson, *Slavery and Social Death*, chap. 3.

18. Fernandes, "La guerre chez les Tupinamba."

19. Mann, *Sources of Social Power*, 39.

CHAPTER 2

1. Orlando Patterson, *Slavery and Social Death* (Cambridge: Harvard Univ. Press, 1982).

2. On China, see H. G. Creel, *The Birth of China* (New York: Frederick Ungar, 1937), 204–16; on Carthage and on many ancient European societies, see Mars M. Westington, *Atrocities in Roman Warfare to 133 B.C.* (Chicago: Univ. of Chicago Libraries, 1938), 12–13, 118–19; on Greece, in particular, see Pierre Ducrey, *Le traitement des prisonniers de guerre dans la Grèce antique* (Paris: E. De Boccard, 1968), 204–6.

3. Bernard Bosanquet, "Personal Freedom through the State," in Robert E. Dewey and James A. Gould, eds., *Freedom: Its History, Nature, and Varieties* (New York: Macmillan, 1970), 192.

4. I. J. Gelb, "Prisoners of War in Early Mesopotamia," *Journal of Near Eastern Studies* 32 (1973): 88.

5. N. Adriani and A. C. Kruyt *De Bare'e Sprekende Toradjas van Midden-Celebes*, (Amsterdam: Noord-Hollandsche Uitgeuers Maatschappij, 1950), Vol. I, 141.

6. Miers and Kopytoff, eds., *Slavery in Africa* (Madison: Univ. of Wisconsin Press, 1977), 17.

7. Ibid.

8. Miller, "Imbangala Lineage Slavery," in Miers and Kopytoff, eds., *Slavery in Africa*, 230.

9. Ibid., 229.

10. Ibid., 208.

11. Ibid., 217.

12. Ibid., 218.

13. For this discussion I draw on the classic ethnographic source on the group, Adriani and Kruyt, *De Bare'e sprekende Toradjas van Midden-Celebes* (The Bare'e-speaking Toradja of Central Celebes), Vol. I.

14. Ibid., 113.

15. Ibid., 2:139.

16. Ibid., 117.

17. Ibid., 143.

18. Ibid., 145 (emphasis added).

19. Ibid., 146.

20. Ibid., 147.

21. Ibid., 141.

22. Mann, *The Sources of Social Power* (Cambridge: Cambridge University Press, 1986), 68.

23. For a discussion of this historiography, see Orlando Patterson, "Slavery," *Annual Review of Sociology* 3 (1977): 410–13.

24. Gelb, "Prisoners of War in Early Mesopotamia," *Journal of Near Eastern Studies* 32 (1973): 70–98; I. M. D'iakanov, "The Commune in the Ancient East as Treated in the Works of Soviet Researchers," in S. P. Dunn and

E. Dunn, eds., *Introduction to Soviet Ethnography* (London: Highgate Rd. Social Science Research Station, 1974), 519–48.

25. See 'Abd al-Muhsin Bakīr, *Slavery in Pharaonic Egypt* (Cairo: L'Institut français d'archéologie orientale, 1952), chap. 2. For related societies, see Bernard J. Siegel, *Slavery during the Third Dynasty of Ur*, Memoirs of the American Anthropological Association, no. 66 ([Menasha, Wis.]: AAA, 1947); Isaac Mendelsohn, *Slavery in the Ancient Near East* (Oxford: Oxford Univ. Press, 1949).

26. See the excellent discussion of this terminology, and of the early period of Israelite history generally, by A. Malamut in H. H. Ben-Sasson, ed., *A History of the Jewish People* (Cambridge: Harvard Univ. Press, 1976), 28–46, esp. 40–43.

27. I. Mendelsohn, "State Slavery in Ancient Palestine," *Bulletin of the American Schools of Oriental Research* 85 (1942): 14–17; Mendelsohn, "On Corvée Labor in Ancient Canaan and Israel," ibid., no. 167 (1962): 31–35.

28. Whitehead, *Adventures of Ideas* (New York: Free Press, 1967), 50.

29. Exodus 23:9.

30. I. J. Gelb, "From Freedom to Slavery," Bayerische Akademie der Wissenschaften: Gesellschaftsklassen im Alten Zweistromland und in den angrenzenden Gebieten-XVIII, (Munich: 1972), 92.

31. Mendelsohn, *Slavery in the Ancient Near East*, 80–81 (emphasis added).

32. Ibid., 74–75.

33. Ibid., 83.

34. Siegel, *Slavery during the Third Dynasty of Ur*, 42.

35. Max Weber, *The Agrarian Sociology of Ancient Civilizations* (London: New Left Books, 1976), 110–11.

36. T. G. H. James, *Pharaoh's People: Scenes from Life in Imperial Egypt* (London: Bodley Head, 1984), chap. 3.

37. Cruz-Uribe, "On the Meaning of Urk.1,122,6–8," in Leonard H. Lesko, ed., *Egypotolgocal Studies of Richard A. Parker* (Hanover: Published for Brown Univ. Press by Univ. Press of New England, 1986), 23–25.

38. Bakir, *Slavery in Pharaonic Egypt*, 48–52; on emancipation by adoption, see 87–88.

39. Jacobson, "Primitive Democracy in Ancient Mesopotamia," in Jacobson, *Toward the Image of Tammuz and Other Essays on Mesopotamian History and Culture*, ed. William L. Moran (Cambridge: Harvard Univ. Press, 1970), 158.

40. Weber, *Agrarian Sociology of Ancient Civilizations*, 109.

41. Frankfort, *Ancient Egyptian Religion* (New York: Harper Torchbooks, 1961), 42.

42. Ibid., 59.

43. Ibid., 58.

44. Ibid., 55.

45. J. H. Breasted, *History of Egypt* (New York: Scribners 1905), chap. 18.

46. For an excellent account of the Akhenaton legend and its origin in

nineteenth-century historiography, see F. J. Giles, *Ikhnaton: Legend and History* (Rutherford, N.J.: Fairleigh Dickinson Univ. Press, 1972), pt. 1.

47. Ibid., pt. 4.

48. Ibid., 113.

49. Redford, *Akhenaten: The Heretic King* (Princeton: Princeton Univ. Press, 1984), 235.

50. Ibid., 235.

51. Whitehead, *Adventures of Ideas*, 49.

52. Redford, *Akhenaten*, 175.

53. Wilson, *The Culture of Ancient Egypt* (Chicago: Univ. of Chicago Press, 1951), 142.

54. Ibid., 178.

55. Ibid., 179.

56. David, *The Pyramid Builders of Ancient Egypt* (London: Routledge & Kegan Paul, 1986), 60.

57. On this see Wilson, *Culture of Ancient Egypt*, 224–29.

58. Cited ibid., 143.

59. James B. Pritchard, ed., *The Ancient Near East: An Anthology of Texts and Pictures* (Princeton: Princeton Univ. Press, 1958), 275–76.

60. Jean-Paul Sartre, *Critique of Dialectical Reason* (London: Verso, 1976) 345–404.

61. Mann, *Sources of Social Power*, 68.

62. Marshal Sahlins, *Social Stratification in Polynesia* (Seattle: Univ. of Washington Press, 1958), 151.

63. Bruce G. Trigger, "Egypt and the Comparative Study of Early Civilizations," in Kent R. Weeks, ed., *Egyptology and the Social Sciences* (Cairo: American Univ. in Cairo Press, 1979), 41.

64. Weber, *Agrarian Sociology of Ancient Civilizations*, 120.

65. Jacobsen, "Mesopotamia," in Henri Frankfort et al., *The Intellectual Adventure of Ancient Man* (Chicago: Univ. of Chicago Press, 1946), 202.

CHAPTER 3

1. For Mycenaean Greece in general I have drawn mainly on the following surveys: M. I. Finley, *Early Greece: The Bronze and Archaic Ages* (New York: W. W. Norton, 1970); J. T. Hooker, *Mycenaean Greece* (London: Routledge and Kegan Paul, 1976); John Chadwick, *The Mycenaean World* (Cambridge: Cambridge Univ. Press, 1976), and Emily Vermeule, *Greece in the Bronze Age* (Chicago: Univ. of Chicago Press, 1964).

2. Yvon Garlan, *Slavery in Ancient Greece*, trans. Janet Lloyd (Ithaca: Cornell Univ. Press, 1988), 27–28. On the relevant texts, see M. Lejeune, "Textes mycéniens relatifs aux esclaves," in *Historia* 8 (1959): 129–44.

3. For what is now the generally accepted view, see M. I. Finley, "Homer and Mycenae: Property and Tenure," *Historia* 6, (1957): 153–69. Finley,

however, may have underestimated the degree of continuity between Athens and the Mycenaean era.

4. Vernant, *The Origins of Greek Thought* (Ithaca: Cornell Univ. Press, 1982), chaps. 3–4. On the problem of evidence, see Oswyn Murray, *Early Greece* (Stanford: Stanford Univ. Press, 1980), 13–37.

5. Vernant, *The Origins of Greek Thought*, 54. In addition to more specialized works cited below, I have drawn mainly on the following general works and source collections: M. I. Finley, *The World of Odysseus* (London: Penguin, 1971); A. Snodgrass, *The Dark Ages of Greece: An Archeological Survey of the 11th to 8th Centuries B.C.* (Edinburgh: Univ. of Edinburgh Press, 1971); M. M. Austin and P. Vidal-Naquet, eds., *Economic and Social History of Ancient Greece* (Berkeley: Univ. of California Press, 1977), chaps. 2–3; C. G. Starr, *The Origins of Greek Civilization, 1100–650 B.C.* (New York: Knopf, 1961); V. A. Desborough, *Greece in the Dark Ages* (London: Benn, 1972); Murray, *Early Greece.*

6. Snodgrass, *Dark Age of Greece*, 387.

7. Desborough, *Greece in the Dark Ages*, 311–12.

8. Snodgrass, *Dark Ages in Greece*, 394.

9. Ibid., 379.

10. Boardman, *The Greeks Overseas* (London: Penguin Books, 1964); Claude Mossé, *La colonisation dans l'antiquité* (Paris: F. Nathan, 1970); and Snodgrass, *Archaic Greece*, 38.

11. Heichelheim, *An Ancient Economic History* (New York: Humanities Press, 1964), 1:274–75.

12. Finley, *World of Odysseus*, 61. See also, Garlan, *Slavery in Ancient Greece*, 29–37. I have also drawn on J. A. Lencmann, *Die Sklaverei im mykenischen und homerischen Griechenland* (Wiesbaden: Franz Steiner, 1966).

13. Vernant, *Origins of Greek Thought*, chap. 30.

14. Homer, *Odyssey* trans. Richmond Lattimore, 17:323–24.

15. Homer, *Iliad* trans. Richmond Lattimore, 14.259.

16. Hesiod, *Theogony*, trans. A. N. Athanassakis, 211–25.

17. Ibid., 123–24.

18. Homer, *Iliad*, 20.190–94.

19. Ibid., 16.830–36.

20. Ibid., 6.454–58.

21. Nagy, *The Best of the Achaeans: Concepts of the Hero in Archaic Greek Poetry* (Baltimore: Johns Hopkins Univ. Press, 1979), 184 and, more generally, chaps. 10, 11, and 12.

22. Garlan, *Slavery in Ancient Greece*, 45.

23. Raaflaub, *Die Entdeckung der Freiheit: Zur historischen Semantik und Gesellschaftsgeschichte eines politischen Grundbegriffs der Griechen* (Munich: C. H. Beck, 1985), 40–41.

24. Homer, *Iliad*, 6.526–29.

25. Garnsey, *Famine and Food Supply in the Graeco-Roman World* (Cambridge: Cambridge Univ. Press, 1989), 57; see also Murray, *Early Greece*, chap. 4.

26. Murray, *Early Greece*, 223–26.
27. Austin and Vidal-Naquet, *Economic and Social History of Ancient Greece*, 56–58.
28. Finley, *Economy and Society in Ancient Greece*, eds., B. D. Shaw and R. P. Saller (New York: Penguin Books, 1981), 156.
29. Murray, *Early Greece*, chaps. 8–10. For a revisionist view which downplays the sociohistorical impotance of the hoplite reform, see Snodgrass, "The Hoplite Reform and History," *Journal of Hellenic Studies* 85 (1965): 110–22.
30. Hesiod, *Works and Days*, trans. A. N. Athanassakis, 33–35.
31. Ibid., 270–73.
32. Starr, *Origins of Greek Civilization*, 303.
33. Hesiod, *Works and Days*, 290.
34. Ibid., 256–57.
35. Vernant, *Origins of Greek Thought*, 62.
36. While agreeing with Eva Cantarella that there are no grounds for earlier idealistic interpretations which found "traces of matriarchial organization" in the Homer epics, I do not share her judgment that the "roots of Western misogyny go back to" these poems. See her, *Pandora's Daughters*, trans. Maureen B. Fant (Baltimore: John Hopkins Univ. Press, 1987), 32–33. For contrasting views with respect to Greece, see reference to Arthur cited in note 41 below. For more comparative assessments, see Katherine M. Rogers, *The Troublesome Helpmate: A History of Misogyny in Literature* (Seattle: Univ. of Washington Press, 1966), esp. chap. 1.
37. Hesiod, *Works and Days*, 65–69; *Theogony*, 570–93.
38. Hesiod, *Works and Days*, 373–75; 700–01.
39. Linda S. Sussman, "Workers and Drones: Labor, Idleness, and Gender Definition in Hesiod's Beehive," in J. Peradotto and J. P. Sullivan, eds., *Women in the Ancient World: The Arethusa Papers* (Albany: State Univ. of New York Press, 1984), 79.
40. Ibid., 89.
41. Arthur, "Early Greece: The Origins of the Western Attitude toward Women," in Peradotto and Sullivan, eds., *Women in the Ancient World*, 23–25.
42. Hesiod, *Works and Days*, 730–32.
43. He may have gotten it from lore about the Egyptians. Herodotus, 2.35.3, informs us that Egyptian men of his day urinated while squatting, their women while standing, the opposite of Greek practice. Of course, we have no reason to believe this improbable account of Egyptian behavior.
44. Archilochus, P. Colon. 7511, trans. Mary R. Lefkowitz, in Lefkowitz and Maureen B. Fant, eds., *Women's Life in Greece and Rome: A Source Book in Translation* (Baltimore: Johns Hopkins Univ. Press, 1982), 99.
45. Lefkowitz and Fant, eds., *Women's Life in Greece and Rome*, 12–16.
46. W. K. Lacey, *The Family in Classical Greece* (Ithaca: Cornell Univ. Press, 1968), 68.

47. Haynes, *Greek Art and the Idea of Freedom* (London: Thames and Hudson, 1981), chap. 1.
48. Ibid., 31.
49. Frag. 68, in Lefkowitz and Fant, eds., *Women's Life in Greece and Rome*, 16.

CHAPTER 4

1. De Ste. Croix, *The Class Struggle in the Ancient Greek World* (Ithaca: Cornell Univ. Press, 1981), 279. However, the dangers of relying too heavily on these poems should always be borne in mind. On Theognis, see now T. J. Figueira and Gregory Nagy eds., *Theognis of Megara: Poetry and the Polis* (Baltimore: Johns Hopkins Univ. Press, 1985), esp. chaps. 1, 2, and appendix. See M. M. Austin and P. Vidal-Naquet, *Economic and Social History of Ancient Greece* (Berkeley: Univ. of California Press, 1977), 206–7.
2. The remark of Demades came much later. Plutarch, "Solon," in *The Rise and Fall of Athens: Nine Greek Lives*, trans. Ian Scott-Kilvert (New York: Penguin Books, 1960), 59.
3. J.-P. Vernant, *The Origins of Greek Thought* (Ithaca: Univ. of Cornell Press, 1982), 51.
4. Ibid.
5. Ibid., 54. On ancient literacy generally, see Williams V. Harris, *Ancient Literacy* (Cambridge: Harvard Univ. Press, 1989.)
6. Plutarch, "Solon," 57.
7. Ibid., 56–59. On the fragments of Solon and useful commentary see Austin and Vidal-Naquet, *Economic and Social History*, 59–60; 210–17.
8. Heichelheim, *An Ancient Economic History* (New York: Humanities Press, 1964), 2:33. See also, Oswyn Murray, *Early Greece* (Stanford: Stanford Univ. Press, 1980), 190–91.
9. Mondolfo, "The Greek Attitude to Manual Labor," *Past and Present*, no. 2 (1952), 5.
10. Finley, *Economy and Society in Ancient Greece*, eds., B. D. Shaw and R. P. Saller (New York: Penguin Books, 1981), chap. 7.
11. For a good discussion of attitudes toward work in antiquity generally, see Claude Mossé, *The Ancient World at Work* (New York: W. W. Norton, 1969), 25–30.
12. The parallels with the postemancipation West Indies are striking. Like their counterparts in ancient Greece, British plantation owners solved their sudden labor crisis by turning to the large-scale importation of indentured Asian labor. And, like the emancipated Greek farmers, West Indians, though prepared to work as hard as any other group of small farmers on their desperately small plots of land, developed a chronic distaste for any form of labor for others.
13. M. I. Finley, *Ancient Slavery and Modern Ideology* (New York: Penguin Books, 1980), 88.

14. Toutain, *The Economic Life of the Ancient World* (New York: Barnes and Noble, 1968), 33. Cf. Garnsey, *Famine and Food Supply in the Graeco Roman World* (Cambridge: Cambridge Univ. Press, 1988), 107–19. For what is still the standard view, see Austin and Vidal-Naquet, *Economic and Social History of Ancient Greece*, 69. See, more recently, Russell Meiggs, *Trees and Timber in the Ancient Mediterranean World* (Oxford: Clarendon Press, 1982).

15. This basic assumption underlies the argument of Michael H. Jameson's "Agriculture and Slavery in Classical Athens," *Classical Journal* 73 (1977): 122–41. The assumption unnecessarily exposes an otherwise brilliant analysis to criticism, on which see Ellen M. Wood, *Peasant-Citizen and Slave*, (London: Verso, 1988), 51–63. See also, Garnsey, *Famine and Food Supply*, 113–17.

16. Orlando Patterson, "The Structural Origins of Slavery: A Critique of the Nieboer-Domar Hypothesis from a Comparative Perspective," in Vera Rubin and Arthur Tuden, eds., *Comparative Perspectives on Slavery in New World Plantation Societies* (New York: New York Academy of Sciences, 1977), 12–34.

17. See Meiggs, *Trees and Timber*; for comparison with ancient Rome and the Mediterranean generally, see K. D. White, *Roman Farming* (London: Thames and Hudson, 1970), 225–27.

18. De Ste. Croix, *Class Struggle*, 40. On slavery more generally, see 133–74 and appendix 2.

19. Yvon Garlan, *Slavery in Ancient Greece*, trans. Janet Lloyd (Ithaca: Cornell Univ. Press, 1988), 40.

20. On agricultural methods in antiquity, see Mossé, *Ancient World at Work*, 31–38; and on Greek smallholder agriculture in particular, see 49–57. Mossé, it should be noted, believes (p.55) that slaves were a supplementary work force among the smallholders.

21. Orlando Patterson, "Slavery and Slave Formations," *New Left Review* 117 (1979): 31–67.

22. Wood, *Peasant-Citizen and Slave*, 42–46; Starr, "An Overdose of Slavery," *Journal of Economic History* 18 (1958): 17–32; Jones, *Athenian Democracy* (Baltimore: Johns Hopkins Univ. Press, 1977), 10–20.

23. Degler, "Starr on Slavery," *Journal of Economic History* 19 (1959): 271–77.

24. For an excellent, well-balanced recent survey of the economic uses of slaves, and their treatment, see Garlan, *Slavery in Ancient Greece*, 60–73, 138–55.

25. Jameson, "Agriculture and Slavery in Classical Athens," 122–45.

26. Garnsey, *Famine and Food Supply*, chap. 4; De Ste. Croix, *Class Struggle*, chap. 4. De Ste. Croix suggests that there was a rise in the standard of living of all sectors of the Athenian population over the course of the 6th and 5th centuries, but cites no evidence to support this claim. In light of the experience of the modern Third World peasants, it is safer to speculate that ancient "modernization" did little to improve the condition of the masses, even the politically free masses of Athens.

27. For a recent review of these estimates, see Garlan, *Slavery in Ancient Greece*, 57–60.

28. Degler, "Starr on Slavery," 271.

29. James H. Oliver, *Demokratia, the Gods, and the Free World* (Baltimore: Johns Hopkins Univ. Press, 1960), 117.

30. Plutarch, "Solon," 74. See also Murray, *Early Greece*, 226–31.

31. Victor Ehrenberg, *From Solon to Socrates* (New York: Methuen, 1968), 84–86.

32. Walter Burkert, *Greek Religion* (Cambridge: Harvard Univ. Press, 1985), 141.

33. Ehrenberg, *From Solon to Socrates*, 87.

34. For a good analysis see D. M. Lewis, "Cleisthenes and Attica," *Historia* 12 (1963): 22–40. See also Murray, *Early Greece*, 254–59.

35. For the classic statement on this, see R. H. Lowie, *Origin of the State* (New York: Harcourt Brace, 1927), chap. 4.

36. Osborne, *Demos: The Discovery of Classical Attika* (New York: Cambridge Univ. Press, 1985), 74.

37. Ibid., 42–46, 69–70. See also J. K. Davies, *Athenian Propertied Families 600–300 B.C.*, (Oxford: Clarendon Press, 1971).

38. Osborne, *Demos: The Discovery of Classical Attika* chaps. 3 and 4, and p. 142.

39. Ibid., 92.

40. Ostwald, *From Popular Sovereignty to the Sovereignty of Law: Law, Society and Politics in Fifth-Century Athens* (Berkeley: Univ. of California Press, 1986), p. 50 and, more generally, chap. 1. See also W. G. Forrest, *The Emergence of Greek Democracy: The Character of Greek Politics 800–400 B.C.* (London: Weidenfeld & Nicholson, 1966), esp. chaps. 8–9.

41. Ostwald, *From Popular Sovereignty to the Sovereignty of Law*, 49, 82.

42. For excellent analyses of the system, its critics, and its actual workings, see Jones, *Athenian Democracy*, chaps. 3 and 5. For the sources and a brief discussion see M. Crawford and D. Whitehead, eds., *Archaic and Classical Greece: A Selection of Ancient Sources in Translation* (Cambridge: Cambridge Univ. Press, 1983), 235–64.

43. Wood, *Peasant-Citizen and Slave*, 81–82.

44. See H. D. F. Kitto, *The Greeks* (Harmondsworth: Pelican Books, 1960), 243–52; L. Pearson, "Popular Ethics in the World of Thucydides," *Classical Philology* 52 (1957): 228–44; Alvin W. Gouldner, *The Hellenic World: A Sociological Analysis* (New York: Harper Torchbooks, 1965).

45. Whitehead, *The Ideology of the Athenian Metic* (Cambridge: Cambridge Philosophical Society, 1977), 121.

46. Vidal-Naquet, *The Black Hunter* (Baltimore: Johns Hopkins Univ. Press, 1986), 206.

47. Pohlenz, *Freedom in Greek Life and Thought: The History of an Ideal* trans. Carl Rofmark (Dordrecht: D. Reidel, 1966).

48. Raaflaub, *Die Entdeckung der Freiheit* (Munich: C. H. Beck, 1985). This is a

more formal and systematically arranged version of an earlier work, *Zum Freiheitsbegriff der Griechen* (Berlin: Akademie-Verlag, 1981).

49. Pohlenz, *Freedom in Greek Life and Thought*, 4–5; Raaflaub, *Entdeckung der Freiheit*, 29–54.
50. Raaflaub, *Entdeckung der Freiheit*, 54–70.
51. See Ellen Meiksins Wood's discussion of the "myth of the idle (Greek) mob" in European historiography, in her *Peasant-Citizen and Slave*, chap. 1. I know of no serious living scholar who takes this "myth" seriously, as Wood's review itself makes clear, so I am a bit puzzled by the attention she devotes to it.
52. Andrews, *The Greek Tyrants* (London: Hutchinson, 1956). Andrews's argument has been criticized by A. M. Snodgrass in "The Hoplite Reform and History," *Journal of Hellenic Studies* 85 (1965): 110–22. However, it has recently been strongly supported by G. E. M. De Ste. Croix, who claims that it "is now sufficiently established." See his *Class Struggle*, 282 and, more generally, 278–83.
53. Pohlenz, *Freedom in Greek Life and Thought*, 9. And for a detailed discussion of the philological evidence, see Raaflaub, *Entdeckung der Freiheit*, 108–25.
54. Herodotus, *The Histories*, trans. Aubrey De Selincourt (New York: Penguin Books, 1973), 364–65.

CHAPTER 5

1. Pohlenz, *Freedom in Greek Life and Thought: The History of an Ideal*, trans. Carl Rofmark (Dordrecht: D. Reidel, 1966), 9.
2. Simon Hornblower, *The Greek World*, 479–323 B.C. (London: Methuen, 1983), 12–13.
3. Victor Ehrenberg, *From Solon to Socrates* (London: Methuen, 1967), 174–75. On the influence of Persia during the sixth century, see Oswyn Murray, *Early Greece* (Stanford: Stanford Univ. Press, 1980), chap. 14.
4. Pohlenz, *Freedom in Greek Life and Thought*, 10–17.
5. Kurt Raaflaub, *Zum Freiheitsbegriff der Griechen* (Berlin: Akademie-Verlag, 1981), 245; for a more systematic treatment of the same subject, see his *Die Entdeckung der Freiheit* (Munich: C. H. Beck, 1985), 71–108 and pt. 4.
6. Herodotus, *The Histories*, trans. Aubrey De Selincourt (New York: Penguin Books, 1973), 427–28.
7. See, for example, ibid., 595.
8. W. R. Paton, ed. and trans., *The Greek Anthology* (London: Heinemann, 1917), vol. 2, 279.
9. Ehrenberg, *From Solon to Socrates* 177–179.
10. Paton, *The Greek Anthology*, vol. 2, 141.
11. Ibid., vol. 2, 243.
12. Pindar, "Olympian," 2.61–68, in *The Odes of Pindar*, trans. C. M. Bowra (New York: Penguin Books, 1969), 80–83.

13. Pindar, "Pythian," 2.56–58, ibid., 148.
14. Pindar, "Isthmian," 8.16–17, ibid., 51–52.
15. James H. Oliver, *Demokratia, the Gods, and the Free World* (Baltimore: Johns Hopkins Univ. Press, 1960).
16. Ibid., chap. 4 and plate 1.
17. Ibid., 127.
18. Ibid., 133.
19. Pohlenz, *Freedom in Greek Life and Thought*, 11. For an exhaustive discussion, see Raaflaub, *Entdeckung der Freiheit*, 125–47. But compare Oliver, *Demokratia*, chap. 5.
20. Herington, *Aeschylus* (New Haven: Yale Univ. Press, 1986), 70–71. For an excellent recent analysis of what he calls "the sociology of Aeschylus' imagined Persia," see Pericles Georges, "The Human Fabric of the *Persae*" ms.
21. Quoted in, and translated by, Charles Rowan Beye, in his *Ancient Greek Literature and Society* (Ithaca: Cornell Univ. Press, 1987), 78.
22. Ibid., 79.
23. Herington, *Aeschylus*, 62.
24. Aeschylus, *The Persians*, trans. Seth G. Benardete (Chicago: Univ. of Chicago Press, 1956), 400–405.
25. Ibid., 591–93.
26. Ibid., 821–29.
27. See Herington, *Aeschylus*, 75.
28. Aeschylus, *The Suppliant Maidens* (trans. Seth G. Benardete), (Chicago: Univ. of Chicago Press, 1986), 368, 398–401.
29. Ibid., 948.
30. See David Whitehead, *The Ideology of the Athenian Metic* (Cambridge: Cambridge Philosophical Society, 1977), 89–97. Pericles' citizenship law, requiring both parents to be citizens in order for the child to inherit citizenship status, was initiated in 451–50.
31. Aeschylus, *The Suppliant Maidens*, 991–94.
32. Ostwald, *From Popular Sovereignty to the Sovereignty of Law* (Berkeley: Univ. of California Press, 1986), 141–45.
33. Hornblower, *Greek World*, 44–45.
34. J. K. Davies, *Democracy and Classical Greece* (Stanford: Stanford Univ. Press, 1983), 73.
35. Ibid., 73–75.
36. Aeschylus, *The Eumenides* 690–98.
37. E. R. Dodds, "Notes on the *Oresteia*," *Classical Quarterly*, n.s., 3 (1953): 20, cited in James C. Hogan, *A Commentary on the Complete Greek Tragedies: Aeschylus* (Chicago: Univ. of Chicago Press, 1984), 174.
38. See, for example, Aeschylus, *Agamemnon* (trans., 1636–42).
39. Yvon Garlan, *Slavery in Ancient Greece* (Ithaca: Cornell Univ. Press, 1988), 68.
40. Herodotus, *Histories*, 475.

41. Ibid., 477.

42. On the peculiar growth of freedom, equality and mass oppression in Sparta, see Oliver, *Demokratia*, especially chaps. 2, 3, and 5 and Murray, *Early Greece* ch. 10. We know too little about other Greek states to make any meaningful sociological comparisons. See Michael Grant, *The Rise of the Greeks* (New York: Collier Books, 1987), esp. chaps. 4–8; and for the tantalizing case of Chios with its large-scale slave system and "respect for the rights of free citizens," 137–49.

CHAPTER 6

1. Siegfried Lauffer, *Die Bergwerkssklaven von Laureion* (Wiesbaden: Akademie der Wissenschaften und der Literatur, Mainz, 1956), 171.

2. Ibid., 204–5.

3. Ibid., 214–26. Lauffer correctly refrains from calling this mass escape a revolt. Indeed, the operation of the mines continued throughout the war. Actual revolts did not take place until the second century, contemporaneously with the great Sicilian slave revolts against Rome on which see pp. 227–48.

4. Fine, *The Ancient Greeks: A Critical History* (Cambridge: Harvard Univ. Press, 1983), 383.

5. Finley, "The Athenian Empire: A Balance Sheet," in M. I. Finley, *Economy and Society in Ancient Greece*, ed. B. D. Shaw and R. P. Saller (London: Penguin Books, 1983), chap. 3; De Ste. Croix, *The Class Struggle in the Ancient Greek World* (Ithaca: Cornell Univ. Press, 1981), 290–92. The disagreements between these two scholars on this subject are minor and need not concern us.

6. De Ste. Croix, *Class Struggle*, 290.

7. Finley, "Athenian Empire," 59.

8. De Ste. Croix, *Class Struggle*, 290.

9. Thucydides 1.76.2, cited in and translated by Finley, *Economy and Society in Ancient Greece*, 61.

10. De Ste. Croix, *Class Struggle*, 291.

11. Oliver, *Demokratia, the Gods, and the Free World* (Baltimore: Johns Hopkins Univ. Press, 1960), 106–14.

12. A good case in point is Wood's argument that "there are strict limits to the explanatory power of the Athenian empire." There are indeed. What is not clear is who the people are who have failed to recognize these limits. See Ellen M. Wood, *Peasant-Citizen and Slave* (London: Verso, 1988), 123.

13. Ostwald, *From Popular Sovereignty to the Sovereignty of Law* (Berkeley: Univ. of California Press, 1986), 78, and, more generally, 77–83.

14. Finley, *Economy and Society in Ancient Greece*, 83.

15. Ibid.

16. Ibid., 91–92.

17. Finley, "Was Greek Civilization Based on Slave Labor?" in Finley, *Economy and Society in Ancient Greece*, 115.
18. There is a vast literature on both. On Pericles the two primary sources are also the most accessible: Thucydides, *The Peloponnesian War* (trans. Rex Warner), esp. 2.34–65; and Plutarch, *The Rise and Fall of Athens*, trans. Ian Scott-Kilvert (New York: Penguin Books, 1960), chap. 6. On both men, see Victor Ehrenberg, *Sophocles and Pericles* (Oxford: Oxford Univ. Press, 1954).
19. Thucydides, *Peloponnesian War* 2.36.
20. Ibid., 2.37.
21. Ibid.
22. Ibid., 2.41.
23. Locke, *The Second Treatise of Government*, ed. Peter Laslett (Cambridge: Cambridge Univ. Press, 1970), 5.27. Locke, of course, drew radically different conclusions from this premise in developing his theory of property. The premise, however, that we are personally free in the antislaveness of our personal ownership of ourselves is identical.
24. Plutarch, "Pericles," in *Rise and Fall of Athens*, 169.
25. Thucydides, *Peloponnesian War*, 2.39.
26. Ibid.
27. Ibid., 2.40.
28. Ibid., 2.42.
29. Ibid.
30. Ibid.
31. Ibid., 2.43.
32. Ibid., 2.44.
33. Aeschylus, *Agamemnon* trans. Richmond Lattimore (Chicago: Univ. of Chicago Press, 1953), 1303.
34. Herodotus, *The Histories*, trans. Aubrey De Selincourt (New York: Penguin Books, 1973), 6.11.
35. Thucydides, *Peloponnesian War*, 2.65. As Plutarch, commenting on this passage, pointed out, it was Pericles who started the practice of allotting the land of subject states to poor Athenians and of granting allowances for the performance of civic duties. Plutarch, "Pericles," in *Rise and Fall of Athens*, 173–74.
36. J. K. Davies, *Democracy and Classical Greece* (Stanford: Stanford Univ. Press, 1978), 37.
37. Nicole Loraux, *The Invention of Athens: The Funeral Oration in the Classical City* (Cambridge: Harvard Univ. Press, 1986), 52.
38. Ibid., 104.
39. Ibid., 199.
40. Ibid., 172–220.
41. Thucydides, *Peloponnesian War*, 2.43.
42. Ibid., 2.46 (emphasis added).

CHAPTER 7

1. W. K. Lacey, *The Family in Classical Greece* (Ithaca: Cornell Univ. Press, 1968), 151. See in particular Roger Just, *Women in Athenian Law and Life* (London: Routledge and Kegan Paul, 1989) chap. 1.

2. Marilyn B. Arthur, "Early Greece: The Origins of the Western Attitude toward Women," in John Peradotto and J. P. Sullivan, eds., *Women in the Ancient World* (Albany: State Univ. of New York Press, 1984), 34; Raphael Sealey, *Women and Law in Classical Greece* (Chapel Hill: Univ. of North Carolina Press, 1990), 36–40; Just, *Women in Athenian Law and Life*, ch. 5.

3. Lacey, *Family in Classical Greece*, 105.

4. Victor Ehrenberg, *The People of Aristophanes: A Sociology of Old Attic Comedy* (New York: Schocken Books, 1962), 196; Sarah B. Pomeroy, *Goddesses, Whores, Wives, and Slaves*, 87. However, cf. Just, *Women in Athenian Law and Life* 68–70.

5. See K. J. Dover, "Classical Greek Attitudes to Sexual Behavior," in Peradotto and Sullivan, eds., *Women in the Ancient World*, 145–51. See also Eva Cantarrela, *Pandora's Daughter* (Baltimore: Johns Hopkins Univ. Press), 38–51.

6. Pomeroy, *Goddesses, Whores, Wives, and Slaves*, 69, Cantarella, *Pandora's Daughter* 43–44.

7. Pomeroy, *Goddesses, Whores, Wives, and Slaves*, 56. On the few exceptions that proved the rule see Cantarella, *Pandora's Daughter*, 71–75.

8. Pomeroy, *Goddesses, Whores, Wives, and Slaves*, 88. On the implications of the reforms of Solon relating to women, see Arthur, "Origins of the Western Attitude toward Women," 28–37.

9. Ehrenberg, *People of Aristophanes*, 205; Pomeroy, *Goddesses, Whores, Wives, and Slaves*, 71–73, 88–92; On the role of class in determining different attitudes to women, see Arthur, "Origins of the Western Attutude toward Women." For a balanced recent review of the evidence see Just, *Women in Athenian Law and Life*, chs. 6–7.

10. Ehrenberg, *People of Aristophanes*, 203.

11. On this I am in complete agreement with Philip Slater, though I do not necessarily go along with his Freudian interpretations. See his *The Glory of Hera* (Boston: Beacon Press, 1968). Cf Just, *Women in Athenian Law and Life*, chap. 7 esp. 134–35.

12. Arthur, "Origins of the Western Attitude toward Women," 50. On male attitudes to women and the relation of such attitudes to slavery and disorder, see Just, *Women in Athenian Law and Life*, ch. 8.

13. Kitto, *The Greeks* (London: Penguin Books, 1962), 228–29 and, more generally, 219–36. Apart from disagreements with his interpretation of the evidence, we must seriously question any male interpretation of the condition of women which begins with the facetious remark (p. 219) "Most men are interested in women, and most women in themselves." For an example of the classic misuse of tragic drama as data for the social condi-

tion of women, see A. W. Gomme, "The Position of Women in Athens in the Fifth and Fourth Century B.C.," in his *Essays in Greek History and Literature* (Oxford: Basil Blackwell, 1937), 89–115.

14. Taplin, "Emotion and Meaning in Greek Tragedy," in Erich Segal, ed., *Greek Tragedy: Modern Essays in Criticism* (New York: Harper & Row, 1983), 12.
15. Ibid., 10–12.
16. Martha C. Nussbaum, *The Fragility of Goodness: Luck and Ethics in Greek Tragedy and Philosophy* (New York: Cambridge Univ. Press, 1986), 9–13.
17. Froma I. Zeitlin, "The Dynamics of Misogyny: Myth and Mythmaking in the Oresteia," in Peradotto and Sullivan, eds., *Women in the Ancient World*, 159.
18. Goldhill, *Reading Greek Tragedy* (Cambridge: Cambridge Univ. Press, 1986), 77–78.
19. See, generally, H. Lloyd-Jones, *The Justice of Zeus* (Berkeley: Univ. of California Press, 1971); for a good recent discussion of the semantic field covered by the Greek term *dikē*, see Goldhill, *Reading Greek Tragedy*, chap. 2. On the symbolic roles of women as agents of continuity and of disorder, irrationality and sexual freedom see Just, *Women in Athenian Law and Life*, chaps. 9–10.
20. Aeschylus, *Seven against Thebes*, 321–39.
21. Pierre Vidal-Naquet, *The Black Hunter* (Baltimore: Johns Hopkins Univ. Press, 1986), 211. See also Just, *Women in Athenian Law and Life*, 172–77; 187–88; 191–97. In emphasizing the elite male conception of freedom as personal control, Just neglects the reality of personal freedom as liberation from outer and inner control, and the ambivalence of many, including Euripides toward this female-slave freedom.
22. Euripides, *Andromache* trans. J. F. Nims, 186–91.
23. Ibid., 459–60.
24. Aeschylus, *Suppliant Maidens* trans. Seth Benardete, 527–28.
25. Aeschylus, *The Libation Bearers* trans. R. Lattimore, 132–35.
26. Ibid., 915.
27. Ibid., 11.
28. Ibid., 24–31.
29. Ibid., 76–85. Emphasis added. The last phrase is literally translated as "chilled with hidden secret grief."
30. Ibid., 101–4.
31. Ibid., 110–11. Emphasis added.
32. Ibid., 112.
33. Ibid., 114.
34. Ibid., 160–63.
35. Ibid., 599.
36. Ibid., 830.
37. Ibid., 599–602.
38. Ibid., 807–10.

39. Hogan, *A Commentary on the Complete Greek Tragedies: Aeschylus* (Chicago: Univ. of Chicago Press, 1984), 135.

40. Aeschylus, *Libation Bearers*, 819–25.

41. Ibid., 863–65.

42. Ibid., 942–45. It should be noted that the word translated as "free" in this passage is not the more usual *"eleuther"*, but, literally the word for "escape."

43. Ibid., 1046.

44. Ibid., 1063.

45. Ibid., 1073–74.

46. Sophocles, *Electra* trans. David Grene, 1241.

47. Ibid., 1509–10.

48. Euripides, *Electra*, 866–69.

49. Ibid., 1049–50. Professor Valerie Warrior in a personal communication suggests caution with the translation "fight me free." It is better rendered as "speak with *free speech*."

50. Which is literally true, as John Dowling has recently demonstrated in his brilliant treatise *The Retina* (Cambridge: Harvard Univ. Press, 1988).

51. Euripides, *Electra*, 868–69.

52. See Nussbaum, *Fragility of Goodness*, 71–72. Nussbaum sees other meanings in the light imagery of the play, but they are not incompatible with my own. See also Charles Segal, *"Antigone*: Death and Love, Hades and Dionysus," in Segal, ed., *Greek Tragedy*, 176. For a more general discussion, see Goldhill, *Reading Greek Tragedy*, 199–221.

53. Euripides, *Hecuba* trans. William Arrowsmith, 55–57.

54. Ibid., 331–33.

55. Ibid., 415.

56. Ibid., 784.

57. Ibid., 431.

58. Ibid., 480–84.

59. See Goldhill, *Reading Greek Tragedy*, 219–20.

60. Euripides, *Hecuba*, 1259–73.

61. Nussbaum, *Fragility of Goodness*, 414. In a vicious satire Semonides (sixth century B.C.) compares the mind of women to animals: M. Lefkowitz and M. Fant, eds. *Women's Life in Greece and Rome* (Baltimore: Johns Hopkins Univ. Press, 1982), 14–16.

62. Vermeule, *Aspects of Death in Early Greek Art and Poetry* (Berkeley: Univ. of California Press, 1979), p. 180 and chap. 6.

63. Ibid., 181.

64. Ibid., 183–84.

65. G. M. A. Grube, *The Drama of Euripides* (New York: Barnes and Noble, 1961), 400.

66. Euripides, *Hecuba*, 1267.

67. On the image of the "city-ship," see Nussbaum, *Fragility of Goodness*, 59.

68. Vermeule, *Death in Early Greek Art and Poetry*, 183.

69. Euripides, *Hecuba*, 434-37.
70. Ehrenberg, *Sophocles and Pericles* (Oxford: Basil Blackwell, 1954), 1.
71. Ibid., 38-43.
72. Ibid., 33.
73. For an excellent history of interpretations of the play in a range of disciplines, see George Steiner, *Antigones: How the Antigone Legend Has Endured in Western Literature, Art, and Thought* (Oxford: Clarendon Press, 1986).
74. See, most recently, Martin Ostwald, *From Popular Sovereignty to the Sovereignty of Law* (Berkeley: Univ. of California Press, 1986), 148-61.
75. Ibid., 161.
76. Goldhill, *Reading Greek Tragedy*, chap. 1, has many wise things to say on all this. See also the profound comments in chap. 8.
77. Sophocles, *Antigone* trans. Elizabeth Wyckoff, 781-800.
78. Charles Segal, "Antigone," 167-71.
79. Sophocles, *Antigone*, 1258-60.
80. Ibid., 1271-72.
81. Ibid., 1319.
82. This is my main reservation regarding Ehrenberg's otherwise intriguing comparison of Creon, Oedipus, and Pericles in his *Sophocles and Pericles*, chap. 2.
83. Sophocles, *Antigone*, 362-74.
84. Ibid., 1264.
85. Goldhill, *Reading Greek Tragedy*, 106. But see Ehrenberg's commentary on Ion's famous description of Sophocles as a worthy Athenian who "was in political matters neither clever nor active": *Sophocles and Pericles*, 138-40.
86. Plutarch, "Pericles," in *The Rise and Fall of Athens* (New York: Penguin Books, 1960), 173.
87. Sophocles, *Oedipus at Colonus* trans. Robert Fitzgerald, 538, 548.
88. Ibid., 1705, 1720.
89. Segal, "The Menace of Dionysus: Sex Roles and Reversals in Euripides' Bacchae," in Peradotto and Sullivan, eds., *Women in the Ancient World*, 196.
90. This classification is an elaboration of E. Topitsch's threefold distinction between biomorphic, sociomorphic, and technomorphic symbols seen from the semantic perspective. See his *Vom Ursprung und Ende der Metaphysik* (Vienna: 1958).
91. Sophocles, *Antigone*, 1167.
92. Charles Segal, "Antigone," 166-76.
93. Sophocles, *Antigone*, 451.
94. Turner, *The Forest of Symbols* (Ithaca: Cornell Univ. Press, 1967), 30-32, and chap. 4 generally.
95. Sophocles, *Antigone*, 61-64; 381-82.
96. Ibid., 480-85.
97. Ibid., 648-61.

98. Ibid., 559–60. See Nicole Loraux, *Tragic Ways of Killing a Woman*, trans. Anthony Forster (Cambridge: Harvard University Press, 1987), 37–42.

99. For further explicit references to the gender opposition, see ibid., 741, 756, 290. For commentary supporting this, see Steiner, *Antigones*, 185f.; Froma Zeitlin, "Thebes: Theater of Self and Society in Athenian Drama," in J. Peter Euben, ed., *Greek Tragedy and Political Theory* (Berkeley: Univ. of California Press, 1986), 123f.; Charles Segal, "Antigone," 171f.; Warren J. Lane and Ann M. Lane, "The Politics of Antigone," in Euben, ed., *Greek Tragedy and Political Theory*, 162–82; and see, more generally, Pierre Vidal-Naquet, "Slavery and the Rule of Women in Tradition, Myth and Utopia," in his *Black Hunter*, 205–23.

100. Charles Segal, "Antigone," 171.

101. Sophocles, *Antigone*, 677–80.

102. Segal, "Antigone," 171–172.

103. Sophocles, *Antigone*, 90–91.

104. Ibid., 93–97.

105. Ibid., 480–85.

106. Ibid., 506–9.

107. Ibid., 633–74.

108. Lane and Lane, "Politics of Antigone," 179.

109. Ibid., 171.

110. Nussbaum, *Fragility of Goodness*, 79–82.

111. Sophocles, *Antigone*, 63.

112. Sophocles, *Electra*, 1508–10.

113. Sophocles, *Antigone*, 446–525, esp. 450–70.

114. Steiner, *Antigones*, 247.

115. Ibid., 247–48.

116. Ibid., 248.

117. Orlando Patterson, *Slavery and Social Death* (Cambridge: Harvard Univ. Press, 1982), 60.

118. Sophocles, *Antigone*, 882.

119. Ibid., 841–51.

120. On these beliefs and practices see, on Jamaica, Orlando Patterson, *The Sociology of Slavery: Jamaica, 1655–1838* (London: McGibbon & Kee, 1967); on the nearly universal tendency of Barbadian slaves to bury their dead with the head of the corpse facing the African homeland, see Jerome Handler and Frederick W. Lange, *Plantation Slavery in Barbados: An Archeological and Historical Investigation* (Cambridge: Harvard Univ. Press, 1978).

121. Steiner, *Antigones*, 264.

122. Sophocles, *Antigone*, 875.

123. This is the meaning glossed by Seth Benardete from the literal meaning, "generated in place of another," cited in Zeitlin, "Theater of Self and Society in Athenian Drama," 126. See also Goldhill, *Reading Greek Tragedy*, 102.

124. Sophocles, *Antigone*, 852–55.
125. Ibid., 832–36.

CHAPTER 8

1. On the war and its consequences, and on the fourth century generally, I have drawn on G. E. M. De Ste. Croix, *The Origins of the Peloponnesian War* (Ithaca: Cornell Univ. Press, 1972); De Ste. Croix, *The Class Struggle in the Ancient Greek World* (Ithaca: Cornell Univ. Press, 1981), 291–326; Simon Hornblower, *The Greek World, 479–323* (London: Methuen, 1983), chaps. 12–15; M. M. Austin and Pierre Vidal-Naquet, *Economic and Social History of Ancient Greece* (Berkeley: Univ. of California Press, 1977), 131–55, 334–83; and John V. A. Fine, *The Ancient Greeks: A Critical History* (Cambridge: Harvard Univ. Press, 1983), chaps. 11 and 12; and J. K. Davies, *Democracy and Classical Greece* (Stanford: Stanford Univ. Press, 1983) chaps. 7–12.
2. R. J. Hopper, *Trade and Industry in Classical Greece* (London: Thames and Hudson, 1979), chaps. 3, 4, and 7.
3. Yvon Garlan, *Slavery in Ancient Greece*, trans. Janet Lloyd (Ithaca: Cornell Univ. Press, 1988), 73–84. W. L. Westermann, *The Slave Systems of Greek and Roman Antiquity* (Philadelphia: American Philosophical Society, 1955), 25. On the Delphic manumissions during the second and first centuries B.C., see Keith Hopkins, *Conquerors and Slaves* (Cambridge: Cambridge Univ. Press, 1978), chap. 3.
4. Victor Ehrenberg, *The People of Aristophanes* (New York: Schocken Books, 1962), chap. 7.
5. Whitehead, *The Ideology of the Athenian Metic* (Cambridge: Cambridge Philosophical Society, 1977), 16–17, 115–16.
6. Ibid., 57.
7. Ibid., 121.
8. "Hyperides," in *Minor Attic Orators, vol. 2*, trans. J. O. Burtt, (Cambridge: Harvard Univ. Press, Loeb Classical Library, 1954), 364–65.
9. Lycurgus, "Against Leocrates," 40–41, in *Minor Attic Orators*, 45.
10. Whitehead, *Ideology of the Athenian Metic*, 58.
11. Aristophanes, *Assemblywomen*, trans. David Barrett, (Harmondsworth: Penguin, 1977), 722.
12. Aristophanes, *Lysistrata*, trans. Alan Sommerstein, (Harmondsworth: Penguin, 1973), 375, 463.
13. Isaeus, *Oration*, trans. E. S. Forster, (Cambridge: Harvard Univ. Press, Loeb Classical Library, 1927), 8.12.
14. Aristophanes, *The Clouds*, trans. Alan Sommerstein, (Harmondsworth: Penguin, 1973), 1414.
15. Aristophanes, *The Wasps*, trans. David Barrett, (Harmondsworth: Penguin, 1964), 517, 602, 653.

16. See, for example, Aristophanes, *The Birds*, trans. David Barrett, (Harmondsworth: Penguin, 1977), 523.

17. Pseudo-Xenophon, *The Constitution of Athens*, trans. G. W. Bowersock, (Cambridge: Harvard Univ. Press, Loeb Classical Library, 1953) 1, 7–9.

18. Ibid., 1.11.

19. G. M. A. Grube, *The Drama of Euripides* (New York: Barnes and Noble, 1961), 35.

20. For this and the following quotations: Euripides, *Electra*, trans. Emily Vermeule, (Chicago: Univ. of Chicago Press, 1959), 367–78.

21. Ibid., 383–90.

22. Arnheim, *Aristocracy in Greek Society* (London: Thames and Hudson, 1977), 171.

23. R. B. Appleton, *Euripides the Idealist* (London: J. M. Dent, 1927), 74.

24. Euripides, *Iphigenia at Aulis*, trans. Philip Vellacott (Harmondsworth: Penguin, 1972), 450–53.

25. Ibid., 1271–75.

26. J. A. O. Larsen, "Freedom and Its Obstacles in Ancient Greece," *Classical Philology* Vol. 57 (1962) 232. See Thucydides, *The Peloponnesian War*, trans. Rex Warner 1.76.2; 3.45.6. For a fuller treatment of Thucydides' biases and realism see Leo Strauss, *The City and Man* (Chicago: Rand McNally, 1964), chap. 3.

27. Larsen, "Freedom and Its Obstacles," 230.

28. Peter Garnsey, *Famine and Food Supply in the Graeco-Roman World* (Cambridge: Cambridge Univ. Press, 1988) chaps. 9–10. Still useful is M. Rostovtzeff, *The Social and Economic History of the Hellenistic World* (Oxford: Clarendon Press, 1941), Vol. 1.90–125.

29. Demosthenes, *Against Aristocrates*, trans. J. H. Vince, (Cambridge: Harvard Univ. Press, Loeb Classical Library, 1935), 206–9.

30. Demosthenes, *Liberty of the Rhodians*, trans. J. H. Vince, (Cambridge: Harvard Univ. Press, Loeb Classical Library, 1930), 18.

31. Ibid., 28–29.

32. Isocrates, *To Philip*, trans. George Norlin, (Cambridge: Harvard Univ. Press, Loeb Classical Library, 1928), 104.

33. Rostovtzeff, *Social and Economic History* Vol. 1: 189–247.

34. John Briscoe, "Rome and the Class Struggle in the Greek States, 200–146 B.C.," in M. I. Finley, ed., *Studies in Ancient Society* (London: Routledge and Kegan Paul, 1974), 53.

35. Gruen, *The Hellenistic World and the Coming of Rome* (Berkeley: Univ. of California Press, 1984), 133–142.

36. Rostovtzeff, *Social and Economic History*, Vol. 1, Ch. 4.2; Moses Hadas, *Hellenistic Culture: Fusion and Diffusion* (New York: W. W. Norton, 1959); F. W. Walbank, *The Hellenistic World* (Cambridge: Harvard Univ. Press), 1982.

37. Badian, "Alexander the Great and the Unity of Mankind," in G. T. Griffith, ed., *Alexander the Great: The Main Problems* (Cambridge: Heffer, 1966),

287–306. For the more conventional view of Alexander's cultural mission see W. W. Tarn, "Alexander the Great and the Unity of Mankind," ibid., 243–86; C. A. Robinson, "The Extraordinary Ideas of Alexander the Great," ibid., 53–72. Also A.H.M. Jones, *The Greek City from Alexander to Justinian* (Oxford: Clarendon Press, 1940) chaps. 1–2.

38. Rostovtzeff, *Social and Economic History*, vol. 1 esp. 381–422, 530–42. See also Max Pohlenz, *Freedom in Greek Life and Thought* (Dordrecht: D. Reidel, 1966), 106–15. Jones, *Greek City*, chap. 2, is still useful although now badly dated by its chauvinistic tone and misconceptions of the level of civilization of the non-European peoples conquered by Alexander. Cf. Martin Bernal, *Black Athena: The Aftroasiatic Roots of Classical Civilization* (New Brunswick, 1987: Rutgers Univ. Press), esp. chaps. 4–9.

39. See, for example, Iza Biezunska-Malowist, *L'esclavage dans l'Egypte graéco-romaine: Période ptolémaïque*, vol. 1 (Warsaw: Polskiej Akademi Nauk, 1974), chaps. 2 and 4.

40. Briscoe, "Rome and the Class Struggle," 73. For a fuller treatment of this subject, see Gruen, *Hellenistic World*, 143–57.

CHAPTER 9

1. K. J. Dover, *Greek Popular Morality in the Time of Plato and Aristotle* (Berkeley: Univ. of California Press, 1974), 5. See, in particular, chaps. 3 and 6.

2. E. R. Dodds, *The Greeks and the Irrational* (Berkeley: Univ. of California Press, 1951), chap. 6.

3. Lionel Pearson emphasizes this point in his *Popular Ethics in Ancient Greece* (Stanford: Stanford Univ. Press, 1962), esp. p. 2 and chap. 1. However, one must be careful not to assume that the popular interest in drama and epic poetry carried over into purely intellectual speculation.

4. G. E. M De Ste. Croix, *The Class Struggle in the Ancient Greek World* (Ithaca: Cornell Univ. Press, 1981), 449.

5. Dodds, *Greeks and the Irrational*, 192–95.

6. Still the best treatment of the subject is Max Pohlenz, *Freedom in Greek Life and Thought* (Dordrecht: D. Reidel, 1966), 46–105, for the classical age, and 106–60, for the Hellenistic period. Kurt Raaflaub, in his most recent work, confines his discussion to the classical period and concentrates, perhaps too heavily, on the ideological ramifications of what I am calling sovereignal freedom. See his *Die Entdeckung der Freiheit* (Munich: C. H. Beck, 1985), pts. 5 and 6. In the appendix to his earlier *Zum Freiheitsbegriff der Griechen* (Berlin: Akademie-Verlag, 1981), 295–316, Raaflaub did survey the subject of inner freedom, although in a nonanalytic manner.

7. Havelock, *The Liberal Temper in Greek Politics* (London: Jonathan Cape, 1957), 400.

8. Plato, *Protagoras*, trans. W.K.C. Guthrie in Edith Hamilton Cairns, ed.,

The Collected Dialogues (Princeton: Princeton Univ. Press), 1961. On the distortion of the Sophists, see W. K. C. Guthrie, *The Sophists* (Cambridge: Cambridge Univ. Press, 1971), 51–54. Havelock, *Liberal Temper*, chaps. 7 and 11.

9. The literature on this subject is vast. I have relied mainly on the following, both for their interpretations and to guide me through my own readings of the relevant texts: Guthrie, *Sophists*; Havelock, *The Liberal Temper*; E. R. Dodds, *The Ancient Concept of Progress and Other Essays on Greek Literature and Belief* (Oxford: Clarendon Press, 1985), esp. Chaps. 6 and 7; Victor Ehrenberg, *From Solon to Socrates* (London: Methuen, 1967), Chap. 8; Farrar, *The Origins of Democratic Thinking* (Cambridge: Cambridge Univ. Press, 1988).

10. Guthrie, *Sophists*, chap. 2; Ehrenberg, *From Solon to Socrates*, 338–51; Farrar, *Origins of Democratic Thinking*, 38–43. The translation of the fragment of Protagoras is from Kathleen Freeman, ed. and trans., *Ancilla to the Pre-Socratic Philosophers* (Cambridge: Harvard Univ. Press, 1948), 125.

11. Guthrie, *Sophists*, chaps. 4 and 7.

12. Martin Ostwald, *From Popular Sovereignty to the Sovereignty of Law* (Berkeley: Univ. of California Press, 1986), 93. Guthrie makes the same point, although he gives it less emphasis, in his *Sophists*, esp. 19–20.

13. As Dodds has wisely warned, following Gilbert Murray, one set of changes never entirely replaces another: agglomeration rather than substitution was the norm, though there were striking exceptions. Dodds, *Greeks and the Irrational*, 179.

14. Ibid., 130.

15. Dover, *Greek Popular Morality*, 133–60.

16. Guthrie, *Sophists*, 21.

17. Martin Bernal, *Black Athena: The Afroasiatic Roots of Classical Civilization*, vol. 1 (New Brunswick: Rutgers Univ. Press, 1987), introd. and chap. 1. Although very sympathetic with Bernal's basic argument, I should note that the acknowledgment of influences, even strong ones, does not necessarily imply a downplaying of the originality of a given movement of ideas or cultural revolution. To take a modern example which should appeal to Bernal, the revolutionary originality of jazz as a musical genre created by black Americans is in no way undermined by the evidently strong influence of Western popular and classical music on its development. Nonetheless, the deliberate refusal by many classicists to recognize non-European influences on the development of Greek civilization is indeed an intellectual scandal, as racist in temper as are the works of musicologists who overemphasize the European origins of the jazz aesthetic.

18. Guthrie, *Sophists*, 21; also Havelock, *The Liberal Temper* esp. 11–35; 156–7; 378.

19. Dodds, *Ancient Concept of Progress*, 99.

20. Farrar, *Origins of Democratic Thinking*, 77 and, more generally, 77–98. On

Plato's denigration of Protagoras and the problem of deciphering the true content of his doctrine see Havelock, *The Liberal Temper* 157–90; see also 191–231.

21. Guthrie, *Sophists*, chap. 10.

22. Plato, *Protagoras*, 323e.

23. Havelock, *The Liberal Temper* 190. See also, Ehrenberg, *From Solon to Socrates*, 348–49.

24. Plato, *Protagoras* 319a, 327e–328a.

25. Farrar, *The Origins of Democratic Thinking* 47.

26. Ibid., 192–93, and more generally 192–278.

27. Ibid., 241. But see Havelock, *The Liberal Temper* chap. 6.

28. Freeman, *Ancilla to the Pre-Socratic Philosophers*, 162.

29. Farrar, *Origins of Democratic Thinking*, 95–96.

30. Plato, *Protagoras* 337c–d.

31. Dodds, *Ancient Concept of Progress*, 101.

32. Guthrie, *Sophists*, 155–60.

33. Havelock, *The Liberal Temper*, chap. 10. For the fragments see Freeman, *Ancilla* 144–53.

34. Dodds, *Ancient Concept of Progress*, 101–2.

35. Farrar, *Origins of Democratic Thinking*, 97.

36. Plato, *Gorgias*, trans. W. D. Woodhead, in Hamilton and Cairns, eds., *Collected Dialogues*, 452d–e.

37. Ibid., 452e.

38. Ibid., 483b–c.

39. Ibid., 483c–e.

40. Ehrenberg, *From Solon to Socrates*, 350.

41. Plato, *Crito* trans. Hugh Tredennick, 52d. On Socrates generally see Guthrie, *History* vol. 3 chaps. 8–9. On the "Socratic problem" of identifying what was distinctively the thought of Socrates see Guthrie, *History* vol. 3: 323–377. Cf the fascinating recent reconstruction of Socratism by Eric A. Havelock in his, "The Socratic Problem: Some Second Thoughts", in John P. Anton and A. Preus, eds. *Essays in Ancient Greek Philosophy* vol. 2 (Albany: State Univ. of New York Press, 1983), 147–85.

42. R. H. S. Crossman, *Plato Today* (London: George Allen & Unwin, 1959), 92. Plato, it should be noted, has had his defenders, for example, R. B. Levinson, *In Defense of Plato* (Cambridge: Harvard Univ. Press, 1953). See also Guthrie, *History*, vol. 4: esp. 312–321; 560–561.

43. Karl Popper, *The Open Society and Its Enemies*, vol. 1 (London: Routledge and Kegan Paul, 1962), 87.

44. On the chronology and periodization of Plato's works, see Guthrie, *History* vol. 4, chap. 3.

45. Plato, *Republic*, trans. Paul Shorey, in Hamilton and Cairns, eds., *Collected Dialogues*, 368e–369a.

46. Ibid., 389b.

47. Ibid., 547c–550b; 555b–565d.

48. Ibid., 562c. The frequent use of the Greek word *eleutheria* (freedom/liberty) in this part of the *Republic* is striking.

49. Ibid., 561d. Trans. H. D. P. Lee (Harmondsworth: Penguin, 1955).

50. Plato, *Statesman*, trans. J. B. Skemp, in Hamilton and Cairns, eds., *Collected Dialogues*, 294a. See Guthrie, *History*, vol. 4: 171.

51. Plato, *Statesman*, 309d.

52. Plato, *Laws*, trans. A. E. Taylor, in Hamilton and Cairns, eds., *Collected Dialogues*, 4.716c. For commentary see Guthrie, *History*, vol. 5:329–82.

53. Plato, *Laws*, 693b.

54. Ibid., 693e.

55. Ibid., 701b.

56. Ibid., 963–66.

57. Ibid., 942.

58. Ibid., 942c.

59. Aristotle, *Politics* trans. Ernest Barker, (Oxford: Oxford Univ. Press, 1958), 1310a.

60. Note that what I am calling "civic freedom" in this work is what Aristotle calls "political," and that my "personal freedom" he calls "civil": Ibid., 1317b. See also footnotes 1 and 2 by Barker, ed. *Politics* p. 234.

61. Aristotle, *Politics*, 1310a.

62. Ibid., 1319b.

63. Ibid., 1317b (emphasis added). See Havelock's ingenious derivation of the liberal norm from Aristotle's biased account in his *Liberal Temper* chaps. 11 and 12.

64. See Aristotle, *Politics*, 1319b, 1330a.

65. Ibid., 1255b. See Havelock, *The Liberal Temper* 323; 351–53. While in general agreement with Havelock's commentary on Aristotle's treatment of slavery, I consider Aristotle a much better sociologist of the institution than Havelock is prepared to give him credit for.

66. See, in particular, Aristotle, *Politics*, 1325a.

67. Ibid., 1277b.

68. See Aristotle, *Magna Moralia*, trans. G. Cyril Armstrong, (Cambridge: Harvard Universtiy Press, 1979) 1.ii–iii.

69. Aristotle, *Politics*, 1295a. It should be noted that the word translated here as "freedom" is the Greek *anempodiston* meaning, literally, 'unencumbered'.

70. Ibid., 1295b.

71. Ibid., 1296a.

CHAPTER 10

1. See E. R. Dodds, *The Greeks and the Irrational* (Berkeley: Univ. of California Press, 1951), esp. chap. 6 and, with respect to Plato, chap. 7. See also his "Euripides the Irrationalist" in his *The Ancient Concept of Progress* (Oxford: Clarendon Press, 1985), 78–91.

2. To question it, but never to replace or even seriously to erode it in the popular mind. See K. J. Dover, *Greek Popular Morality in the Time of Plato and Aristotle* (Berkeley: Univ. of California Press, 1974), 133–44; 246–68.

3. Martin Ostwald, *From Popular Sovereignty to the Sovereignty of Law* (Berkeley: Univ. of California Press, 1986), 130.

4. David Grene, "Introduction to *Prometheus Bound,*" in his *Aeschylus II* (Chicago: Univ. of Chicago Press, 1956), 134; John Herington, *Aeschylus* (New Haven: Yale Univ. Press, 1986), 175–76.

5. Aeschylus, *Prometheus Bound*, trans. David Grene, 180–82.

6. Ibid., 953–70.

7. Ibid., 535–45. Emphasis added. In a personal communication Professor Valerie Warrior warns that the emphasized text might be too freely translated. The Greek literally reads: "not fearing Zeus in your own (private) mind."

8. Ibid., 907–8.

9. "Anaxagoras of Clazomenae," Fragment 12, in Kathleen Freeman, ed., *Ancilla to the Pre-Socratic Philosophers* (Cambridge: Harvard Univ. Press, 1983), 84. For useful critical histories and commentaries on the Presocratics see Jonathan Barnes, *The Presocratic Philosophers* (Boston: Routledge & Kegan Paul, 1982; W. K. C. Guthrie, *A History of Greek Philosophy* (Cambridge: Cambridge Univ. Press, 1971), vol. 1. Alternate translations of the fragments, essential in light of their obscurity, are to be found in G. S. Kirk, J. E. Raven, and M. Schofield, eds. *The Presocratic Philosophers* (New York: Cambridge Univ. Press, 1983) and Jonathan Barnes ed., *Early Greek Philosophy* (Harmondsworth: Penguin, 1987).

10. Herington, *Aeschylus*, 175–76.

11. Sophocles, *Oedipus at Colonus* trans. Robert Fitzgerald, (Chicago: Univ. of Chicago Press, 1954), 548.

12. Ibid., 656–60.

13. Aeschylus, *Prometheus*, 513, 520.

14. Sophocles, *Oedipus at Colonus*, 1705.

15. Ibid., 576–79.

16. Euripides, *Iphigenia at Aulis*, trans. Philip Vellacott, (Harmondsworth: Penguin, 1972), 1400–1. The Greek text reads literally: "it is right that Greeks rule barbarians."

17. Ibid., 1383–84.

18. Ibid., 1330–31. Vellacott's translation of this passage might be too free. E. B. England proposed the following: "When men search out their fate

they are sure to find that it is a hard one," in *The Iphigenia at Aulis of Euripides* (New York: Arno Press, 1891, 1979), 133.

19. Euripides, *Iphigenia at Aulis*, 567–74.

20. See Gilbert Murray *Euripides & His Age* (Westport: Greenwood Press, 1918, 1979), 97–99. Gregory Vlastos explores this notion of equality and justice in early Greek cosmologies, though not in reference to Euripides. See his "Equality and Justice in Early Greek Cosmologies," in David Furley and R. E. Allen, *Studies in Presocratic Philosophy* vol. 1 (London: Routledge and Kegan Paul, 1970), 56–91.

21. Euripides, *The Bacchae* trans. William Arrowsmith, (Chicago: Univ. of Chicago Press, 1959), 775–78. On the Dionysiac religion and its place in the play, see E. R. Dodds, *Euripides Bacchae* (Oxford: Clarendon Press, 1960), Intro: parts 143; See also Dodds, *The Ancient Concept of Progress & Other Essays* (Oxford: Clarendon Press, 1985), chap. 5; Murray, *Euripides*, 91–9. See also Simon Goldhill, *Reading Greek Tragedy* (Cambridge: Cambridge Univ. Press, 1980), chap. 11.

22. Euripides, *The Bacchae*, 396–400.

23. Ibid., 424–33. For commentary on this disputed passage see E. R. Dodds, *Euripides Bacchae*, 128–30.

24. Euripides, *The Bacchae*, 902–05. On the meaning of these "deceptively simple lines" as Dodds calls them, see his *Euripides Bacchae*, 190–1.

25. Euripides *The Bacchae*, 918–20.

26. Ibid., 895–96. See Dodd *Euripides Bacchae*, 189–90.

27. J. C. Field, *The Philosophy of Plato* (London: Oxford University Press, 1969), 42; cf. E. R. Dodds, *The Greeks and the Irrational*, chap. 7.

28. Plato, *Phaedo* trans. Hugh Tredennick, Edith Hamilton & H. Cairns, eds., *The Collected Dialogues of Plato* (Princeton: Princeton Univ. Press, 1963), 79e–80a. On the problem of the interrelation of body and soul and the further question of *harmonia* and immortality in the *Phaedo* see C. C. Taylor, "The Arguments in the *Phaedo* Concerning the Thesis That the Soul Is a *Harmonia*," in J. Anton and A. Preus, eds., *Essays in Ancient Greek Philosophy* (Albany: State Univ. of New York Press, 1983), 217–31.

29. Plato, *Republic*, trans. H. D. P. Lee, (Harmondsworth: Penguin, 1955), 443c–e.

30. Ibid., 577d.

31. Ibid., 586d–e.

32. Gregory Vlastos, "Slavery in Plato's Thought," in M. I. Finley, ed., *Slavery in Classical Antiquity* (Cambridge: W. Heffer, 1960), 133.

33. Ibid., 139.

34. Ibid., 145.

35. Aeschylus, *The Eumenides* trans. Richmond Lattimore, (Chicago: Univ. of Chicago Press, 1953), 697–99; See also James C. Hogan's commentary in his *A Commentary on the Complete Greek Tragedies: Aeschylus* (Chicago: Univ. of Chicago Press, 1984), 174, n.698f.

36. Rosenmeyer, "Tragedy & Religion: The *Bacchae*" in Erich Segal, ed., *Greek Tragedy: Modern Essays in Criticism* (New York: Harper & Row, 1983), 371.

37. Kroner, *Speculation in Pre-Christian Philosophy* (London: Longmans, 1957), 18.

38. Boas, *Rationalism in Greek Philosophy* (Baltimore: Johns Hopkins Univ. Press, 1961), 133.

39. Ibid., 161.

40. This and the next sentence draw on William Sale, *Existentialism & Euripides* (Berwick: Aureal Publications, 1977), 80–123. However, I am not in full agreement with Sale's conclusions to his work: see 124–25.

41. Guthrie, *The Sophists*, 6.

42. Euripides, *The Bacchae*, 894–96. This translation captures more the poetry and sense rather than the literal meaning of what is a difficult passage. cf. Geoffrey S. Kirk trans., *The Bacchae* (Englewood Cliffs: Prentice-Hall, 1970), 888–96.

43. Walter Burkert, *Greek Religion* (Cambridge: Harvard Univ. Press, 1985), 162.

44. Ibid., 167.

CHAPTER 11

1. M. I. Finley, *The Ancient Greeks* (New York: Viking Press, 1964), 113–14.

2. Plato, *Phaedo*, trans. Hugh Tredennick, in Edith Hamilton and H. Cairns, eds. (Princeton: Princeton Univ. Press, 1963), 80c–e, 81.

3. Xenophon, *Memorabilia* trans. E. C. Marchant, 4.5.6–8. On Socrates' conception of the soul, see W. K. C. Guthrie, *A History of Greek Philosophy*, vol. 3 (Cambridge: Cambridge Univ. Press, 1969), 467–84.

4. Aristotle's distinction between two kinds of ethical values—those of morality, which are deeply rooted in our emotions, though emotions disciplined by reason, and those of speculation, which are exclusively the concern of reason—is a direct elaboration of the ethical theory of Socrates when we rid it of Platonic mysticism and "puritanism." See Aristotle, *Nicomachean Ethics* trans. J. E. C. Welldon, 10.1–7.

5. On the origins of puritanism in Greek thought, see E. R. Dodds, *The Greeks and the Irrational* (Berkeley: Univ. of California Press, 1951), 139–56.

6. Dudley, *A History of Cynicism* (New York: Gordon Press, 1974), chaps. 2 and 3.

7. Diogenes Laërtius, *Lives*, trans. R. D. Hicks, 6.2.

8. Dudley, *History of Cynicism*, 13–14, 27.

9. Dodds, *Greeks and the Irrational*, chap. 2.

10. Aristotle, *Nicomachean Ethics*, 1.3, 3.7.

11. Ibid., 3.9.

12. Diogenes Laërtius, *Lives*, 6.38.

13. Ibid., 6.45.13.

14. Dudley, *History of Cynicism*, 13.

15. Walter Burkert, *Greek Religion* (Cambridge: Harvard Univ. Press, 1985), 210.

16. Diogenes Laërtius, *Lives*, 6.40.

17. Dudley, *History of Cynicism*, 99.

18. Pohlenz, *Freedom in Greek Life and Thought* (Dordrecht: D. Reidel, 1966), 120.

19. Lucretius, "The Nature of the Universe" in A. A. Long and D. N. Sedley, eds., *The Hellenistic Philosophers*, vol. 1, *Translations of the Principle Sources with Philosophical Commentary* (Cambridge: Cambridge Univ. Press, 1987), 66–67.

20. Epicurus, "Letter to Menoeceus," 127, in Long and Sedley, eds., *Hellenistic Philosophers*, 113. Professor Valerie Warrior, in a personal communication, points out that while the term "freedom" may reasonably be inferred from the use of the Greek word *anankaiai* (necessary) in the passage, nowhere in fact does the *eleuthero* root for "freedom" occur in this letter.

21. J. S. Mill, *Utilitarianism* (London: J. M. Dent, 1910), 5 and chap. 2.

22. Epicurus, "Letter to Menoeceus," in Long and Sedley, eds., *Hellenistic Philosophers*, 113–14.

23. Compare, however, Cynthia Farrar, *The Origins of Democratic Thinking* (Cambridge: Cambridge Univ. Press, 1988), chap. 6, where it is suggested that Democritus *assumes* a configuration of secondary properties "which serve as causes of the configuration's corporate behavior" (p. 204).

24. Epicurus, "Letter to Menoeceus," 134, in Long and Sedley, eds., *Hellenistic Philosophers*, 102.

25. For further discussion of the metaphysical basis of Epicurus' doctrine of freedom, especially the celebrated notion of the atomic "swerve," see A. A. Long, *Hellenistic Philosophy* (Berkeley: Univ. of California Press, 1974), 25–41; and the commentary in Long and Sedley, eds., *Hellenistic Philosophers*, 52, 107–12.

26. Epicurus, Vatican Sayings 40, in Long and Sedley, eds., *Hellenistic Philosophers*, 104.

27. Epicurus, *On Nature*, 34.26–30, in Long and Sedley, eds., *Hellenistic Philosophers*, 103.

28. Epicurus, Vatican Sayings 58 and 70, in Long and Sedley, eds., *Hellenistic Philosophers*, 126.

29. Diogenes Laërtius, in Long and Sedley, eds., *Hellenistic Philosophers*, 133.

30. Rist, *Stoic Philosophy* (Cambridge: Cambridge Univ. Press, 1969), chap. 4. See also A. A. Long, *Hellenistic Philosophy* (Berkeley: Univ. of California Press, 1986), 108, and more generally chap. 4.

31. Todd, "Monism and Immanence: The Foundations of Stoic Physics," in John M. Rist, ed., *The Stoics* (Berkeley: Univ. of California Press, 1978), 137–60.

32. Diogenes Laërtius, *Lives*, 7.83.

33. Ibid.

34. G. B. Kerferd, "What Does the Wise Man Know?" in Rist, ed., *Stoics*, 134.

35. Todd, "Monism and Immanence," in Rist, ed., *Stoics*, 159.

36. Diogenes Laërtius, *Lives*, 7.122. For further sources and commentary on the zeno's view of freedom see Long and Sedley, eds., *Hellenistic Philosophers*, 432–37.

37. Diogenes Laërtius, *Lives*, 7.23.

38. Ibid., 7.109. Cf. Plato, *The Republic*, 443d–44a, and see Guthrie, *History of Greek Philosophy*, vol. 1, 21; vol. 4, 478–79.

39. Cicero, *On Fate*, 30, in Long and Sedley, eds., *Hellenistic Philosophers*, 339.

40. On the development of this final phase of civic freedom, emphasizing the rule of written law in Athens, see Martin Ostwald, *From Popular Sovereignty to the Sovereignty of Law* (Berkeley: Univ. of California Press, 1986), chap. 10.

41. Marcian 1, in Long and Sedley, eds., *The Hellenistic Philosophers*, 432.

42. See, in particular, Alexander, *On Fate*, in Long and Sedley, eds., *Hellenistic Philosophers*, 389–90.

43. See Long and Sedley, eds., *Hellenistic Philosophers*, 320–21 with accompanying texts, espeically 65G and 65T.

44. Stobaeus, 1.79, 1–12, in Long and Sedley, eds., *Hellenistic Philosophers*, 337.

45. Rist, *Stoic Philosophy*, 214.

46. Stough, "Stoic Determinism and Moral Responsibility," in Rist, ed., *Stoics*, 224.

47. Ibid.

48. Philo, *Every Good Man Is Free*, trans. F. H. Colson, 17–18.

49. Ibid., 60.

50. Ibid., 45.

51. Ibid., 20.

52. Ibid., 141. The lines from Euripides' *Auge* which so moved the audience were: "The name of freedom is worth all the world; if one has little, let him think that much."

53. Epictetus, *The Discourses as Reported by Arrian*, trans. W. A. Oldfather, (Cambridge: Harvard Univ. Press, 1925), bk. 1, chap. 17:28–29.

54. Ibid., bk. 4.

CHAPTER 12

1. I draw on the following general works, in addition to more specialist studies cited later: A. N. Sherwin-White, *The Roman Citizenship* (Oxford: Clarendon Press, 1973); E. Badian, *Foreign Clientelae* (Oxford: Clarendon Press, 1958); Kurt A. Raaflaub ed. *Social Struggles in Archaic Rome: New Perspectives on the Conflict of the Orders* (Berkeley: Univ. of California Press, 1986); Géza Alföldy, *The Social History of Rome* trans. D. Braund and F. Pollock (Baltimore: Johns Hopkins Univ. Press, 1986); Karl Christ, *The Romans* (Berkeley: Univ. of California Press, 1984); Arnold Toynbee, *Hannibal's Legacy*, 2

vols. (London: Oxford Univ. Press, 1965); E. T. Salmon, *The Making of Roman Italy* (Ithaca: Cornell Univ. Press, 1983), and the source collections, Tenney Frank et al., eds., *Rome and Italy of the Republic*, vol. 1 (Baltimore: Johns Hopkins Univ. Press, 1933), and A. H. M. Jones, *A History of Rome through the Fifth Century*, vol. 1 (New York: Walker and Co., 1968).

2. The historiography of early republican Rome is very controversial and will remain so in view of the paucity of the sources, on which see Raaflaub's Preface and methodological contribution (chapter 1) to his *Social Struggles*. A few scholars even question the very idea of a political-economic conflict, for example, R. E. Mitchell, and to a lesser extent M. Toher, in Raaflaub, *Social Struggles* chaps. 5 and 10, respectively.

3. Raaflaub, "From Protection and Defense to Offense and Participation: Stages in the Conflict of the Orders," in Raaflaub ed. *Social Struggles*, 216.

4. On the origins the of conflicts see, Jean-Claude Richard, "Patricians and Plebeians: The Origins of a Social Dichotomy," in Raaflaub, ed., *Social Struggles*, esp. 125–29. On parallels with early Greece and the thornier problem of direct Greek influence see Raaflaub, "The Conflict of the Orders in Archaic Rome: A Comprehensive and Comparative Approach," in his *Social Struggles*, esp. 29–46.

5. Richard, "Patricians and Plebeians," 127. See also De Ste. Croix, *The Class Struggle in the Ancient Greek World* (Ithaca: Cornell Univ. Press, 1981), 335.

6. Toynbee, *Hannibal's Legacy*, 1:321.

7. Raaflaub, "From Protection to Defense," 199; see also 219–20.

8. For details see Sherwin-White, *Roman Citizenship*, chap. 2; also Salmon, *The Making of Roman Italy*, chaps. 2 and 3; and William V. Harris, *War and Imperialism in Republican Rome 327–70 B.C.* (Oxford: Clarendon Press, 1979), 58–68.

9. Salmon, *The Making of Roman Italy*, 66.

10. Badian, *Foreign Clientelae*, chap. 1 (for the early period).

11. Christ, *Romans*, 21.

12. Garnsey and Saller, *The Roman Empire* (Berkeley: Univ. of California Press, 1987), 33.

13. Alföldy, *Social History*, 27. The evolution of this process was complicated. See Sherwin-White's comments in his *Roman Citizenship*, esp. 57–58.

14. For an excellent review of recent archaeological work pertaining to slavery and economic change in Roman Italy, see D. W. Rathbone, "The Slave Mode of Production," *Journal of Roman Studies* 73 (1983): 160–68.

15. M. I. Finley, *Ancient Slavery and Modern Ideology* (New York: Penguin Books, 1980), 83–84. But compare Keith Hopkins, *Conquerors and Slaves* (Cambridge: Cambridge Univ. Press, 1978), 24. On the Twelve Tables, see Alan Watson, *Roman Slave Law* (Baltimore: John's Hopkins Univ. Press, 1987), 16, 24f, 35f, 68f, 76f.

16. Richard, "Patricians and Plebeians," 125–26; Raaflaub, "From Protection and Defense," 213–14, 237.

17. See Livy's colorful account, translated in Frank, ed., *Economic Survey of Ancient Rome*, 1:32.

18. Eva Cantarella, *Pandora's Daughters* (Baltimore: Johns Hopkins Univ. Press), 126.

19. Hallett, *Fathers and Daughters in Roman Society: Women and the Elite Family* (Princeton: Princeton Univ. Press, 1984), esp. chaps. 1–3.

20. J. P. Balsdon, *Roman Women* (London: Bodley Head, 1962) 33–43.

21. Frank, ed., *Economic Survey of Ancient Rome*, 1:10.

22. On the allotment system and its demographic consequences, see P. A. Brunt, *Italian Manpower 225B.C.–A.D.14*, (Oxford: Oxford Univ. Press, 1971), 28.

23. Badian, *Foreign Clientelae*, 153.

24. De Ste. Croix, *The Class Struggle*, 336.

25. Harris, *War and Imperialism*, 184–85. The literature on this period is vast. In addition to the general works mentioned above, I have relied on the following, and on more specialist works cited where appropriate: P. A. Brunt, *Social Conflicts in the Roman Republic* (New York: W. W. Norton, 1971); P. A. Brunt, *Italian Manpower*; Ronald Syme, *Roman Revolution* (Oxford: Oxford Univ. Press, 1960); Toynbee, *Hannibal's Legacy*, vol. 2; E. Badian, *Publicans and Sinners* (Ithaca: Cornell Univ. Press, 1972); Garnsey and Seller, *Roman Empire*; Mary Beard and Michael Crawford, *Rome in the Late Republic* (London: Duckworth, 1985); Claude Nicolet, *The World of the Citizen* (Berkeley: Univ. of California Press, 1988); and idem, *L'Ordre equestre à l'époque républicaine (312–43 av. J-C)* (Paris: E. de Boccard, 1974).

26. No scholar doubts the enormous impact of the wars, but opinions differ about how great the devastation was. Brunt paints a less gloomy picture than Toynbee, arguing that slaves, women, and children kept production going during the war. He nonetheless agrees that there was a serious overall decline in production, and total devastation in regions such as Campania, which was not worked again until after 211 B.C. Brunt, *Italian Manpower*, 67, and, for more detail, 270–77. Compare Toynbee, *Hannibal's Legacy*, vol. 2. On the Roman attitude to war see Harris, *War and Imperialism*, esp. 47–53, and on the economic aspects of warfare, see chap. 2.

27. Brunt, *Italian Manpower*, 282.

28. Brunt, *Social Conflicts in the Roman Republic*, 14.

29. Brunt, *Italian Manpower*, 281–84. On the role of war in the development of the slave system, and on the Roman economy and society generally, see Hopkins *Conquerors and Slaves*, chap. 1. I am in broad agreement with Hopkins's analysis, but differ in some important points of detail, indicated below. I am also inclined to accept Finley's position (supported by Brunt's work) that an important kind of slave society existed before the Hannibalic wars, although this does not necessarily contradict Hopkins; there are different kinds of slave societies. See E. Badian's important review of Hopkins in *Journal of Roman Studies* (1982) 72:164–69.

30. Garnsey, "Non-Slave Labor in the Roman World," in Garnsey, ed., *Non-*

Slave Labour in the Greco-Roman World (Cambridge: Cambridge Philological Society, 1980), 34–47. For an excellent collection of the relevant ancient sources see Thomas Wiedemann, ed., *Greek and Roman Slavery* (Baltimore: Johns Hopkins Univ. Press, 1981), esp. parts 7–9.

31. Boren, "The Urban Side of the Gracchan Economic Crisis," in Robin Seager, ed., *The Crisis of the Roman Republic* (Cambridge: Heffer, 1969), 54–66.

32. Brunt, *Italian Manpower*, 81, 297–343.

33. On the use of slavery as a means of recruiting skilled labor in antiquity, see Alison Burford, *Craftsmen in Greek and Roman Society* (Ithaca: Cornell Univ. Press, 1972), 58. The standard work on freedmen in the late Republic remains S. M. Treggiari, *Roman Freedmen during the Late Republic* (Oxford: Oxford Univ. Press, 1969); see also Hopkins, *Conquerors and Slaves*, 115–32; and for a collection of relevant sources, see Wiedemann, ed., *Greek and Roman Slavery*. part 3.

34. See Badian, *Publicans and Sinners*, chaps. 1–3.

35. On the relative size and proportion of the free and slave populations, see Brunt, *Italian Manpower*, 121ff.

36. Ibid., chap. 3.

37. Kirschenbaum, *Sons, Slaves and Freedmen in Roman Commerce* (Jerusalem: Magnes Press, 1987), esp. Intro. and chaps. 1–2.

38. Brunt, *Social Conflicts in the Late Republic*, 27; for the bases of these calculations, see Brunt, *Italian Manpower* 121ff.

39. P. A. Brunt, *Social Conflicts in the Later Republic*, 40. On the slave revolts see now, Keith R. Bradley, *Slavery and Rebellion in the Roman World 140 B.C.–70 B.C.* (Bloomington: Indiana Univ. Press, 1989), esp., 128–32. For a good short history of structural crisis and resistance in the second century B.C. see Alföldy, *Social History*, 42–64.

40. P. A. Brunt, "The Equites in the Late Republic," in Seager, ed., *Crisis of the Roman Republic*. However, see Badian's important qualification regarding the greater lust for economic power in this class, in his *Publicans and Sinners*, footnote 157, p. 156.

41. Beard and Crawford, *Rome in the Late Republic*, esp. chaps. 1, 4, and 5.

42. Nicolet, *World of the Citizen*, esp. 383–98. On the New Men see T. P. Wiseman, *New Men in the Roman Senate 139 B.C.–A.D. 14* (Oxford: Oxford Univ. Press, 1971).

43. Syme, *Roman Revolution*, chap. 11.

44. Earl, *The Moral and Political Tradition of Rome* (Ithaca: Cornell Univ. Press, 1967), 11–12.

45. Bleicken, *Staatliche Ordnung und Freiheit in der römischen Republik*, (Kallmünz: M. Lassleben, 1972), chaps. 1–2.

46. Ch. Wirszubski, *Libertas as a Political Idea at Rome During the Late Republic and Early Principate* (Cambridge: Cambridge Univ. Press, 1950).

47. Buckland, *The Roman Law of Slavery* (1908; reprint, Cambridge: Cambridge Univ. Press, 1970), 437.

48. Ibid., 2.
49. Earl, *Moral and Political Tradition of Rome*, 31–33. See also De Ste. Croix, *Class Struggle*, 330–31.
50. Clare, *The Roman Mind* (New York: W. W. Norton, 1968), 15.
51. See esp., Keith Hopkins, "Elite Mobility in the Roman Empire," in M. I. Finley, ed., *Studies in Ancient Society* (London: Routledge and Kegan Paul, 1974), 103–10. See also Badian, *Publicans and Sinners*, 49 and chap. 3.
52. Earl, *Moral and Political Tradition of Rome*, 13.
53. On the origins, nature, and limitations of the voting system, see Nicolet, *World of the Citizen*, 226–315.
54. M. I. Finley, *Politics in the Ancient World* (Cambridge: Cambridge Univ. Press, 1983), 85.
55. Nicolet, *World of the Citizen*, 214. De Ste. Croix strongly emphasizes the "insidious forms of the institution of patronage and clientship" in *The Class Struggle*, 341–43.
56. Syme, *Roman Revolution*, 152–61. Erich S. Gruen, *The Last Generation of the Roman Republic* (Berkeley: Univ. of California Press, 1974) esp. chap. 2; Lily Ross Taylor, *Party Politics in the Age of Caesar* (Berkeley: Univ. of California Press, 1949) chaps. 1, 2, 5.
57. It should be emphasized that Caesar, like Pompey, published no political platform, and we can only infer their political positions from their behavior. On Caesar, see Matthias Gelzer, *Caesar: Politician and Statesman*, trans. Peter Needham (Cambridge: Harvard Univ. Press, 1968); Caesar's political, as well as his social and economic measures, are carefully assessed in Zwi Yavetz, *Julius Caesar and His Public Image* (Ithaca: Cornell Univ. Press, 1983) chaps. 2 and 4; see also Syme, *Roman Revolution*, chaps. 4–6; on Pompey, see Robin Seager, *Pompey: A Political Biography* (Berkeley: Univ. of California Press, 1979), esp. 187–88.
58. Cicero, *In Catilinam* trans. M. Macdonald, 4.16–17. On Cicero's background, friends, and his essentially conservative equestrian sympathies, see Elizabeth Rawson, *Cicero: A Portrait* (London: Allen Lane, 1975), esp. 1–11, 141–45, and chap. 12. For his political leadership and views, see chaps. 5 and 9; See also W. K. Lacey, *Cicero and the End of the Roman Republic* (London: Hodder & Stoughton, 1978), esp. chaps. 2, 3, and 5. Of the many comparisons of Cicero and Caesar, as well as the other prominent Populares, see R. E. Smith, *Cicero the Statesman* (Cambridge: Cambridge Univ. Press, 1966), esp. 212–35, and Gruen, *The Last Generation*, 292–310; For Cicero's own views on law and politics, see the selections translated by W. K. Lacey and B. W. Wilson, *Res Publica: Roman Politics and Society according to Cicero* (Bristol: Bristol Classical Press, 1978).
59. Wirszubski, *Libertas as a Political Idea*, 13.
60. Ibid., chap. 5. Note, however, that it was this very right that Cicero violated in his prosecution and execution of the Catiline co-conspirators. In his speeches against Cataline we find Cicero at his best and worst, esp. *In Catilinam* 4.

61. Wirszubski, *Libertas as a Political Idea*, 29.

62. Ibid., 17.

63. Ibid., 83.

64. Garnsey, *Social Status and Legal Privilege in the Roman Empire* (Oxford: Oxford Univ. Press, 1970).

65. Earl, *Moral and Political Tradition of Rome*, 60.

66. Nicolet, *World of the Citizen*, 394.

67. Syme, *Roman Revolution*, 155.

68. Nicolet, *World of the Citizen*, 398.

CHAPTER 13

1. G. E. M. De Ste Croix in *The Class Struggle in the Ancient World* (Ithaca: Cornell Univ. Press, 1981), 340–42, emphasizes the patron-client system in his answer to this question. We agree that this was an important factor but find others of equal or greater importance.

2. For an early critique of Mommsen and the later bourgeois "modernist" scholars, see R. J. Wipper, *Beiträge zur Geschichte des römischen Imperiums* (Berlin: 1923); a more recent statement of the classic Marxist position is found in S. L. Uttschenko, *Der weltanschauhlich-politische Kampf in Rom am Vorabend des Sturzes der Republik* (Berlin: Akademie Verlag, 1956), 6–26.

3. Joseph Vogt, "The Structure of Ancient Slave Wars," in his *Ancient Slavery and the Ideal of Man* (Cambridge: Harvard Univ. Press, 1975), 50, 54, 84–85. It is not being suggested that there was any large-scale desertion to the camp on the part of the free lower-class Romans, and the extremist Marxist claim that these revolts constituted some kind of ancient international class struggle with socialistic objectives is sheer fantasy. See, for example, Karl Bücher, *Die Aufstände der unfreien Arbeiter, 143–129 v. Chr.* (Frankfurt: J. D. Sauerländer, 1874). The role of free persons is played down by Keith R. Bradley in his *Slavery and Rebellion in the Roman World,* (Bloomington: Indiana Univ. Press, 1989), 99.

4. Vogt, "Structure of Ancient Slave Wars," 49.

5. Claude Nicolet, *The World of the Citizen in Republican Rome* (Berkeley: Univ. of California Press, 1988), 291–97.

6. Ibid., 297–310.

7. M. I. Finley, *Politics in the Ancient World* (Cambridge: Cambridge Univ. Press, 1983), 85, 90–91.

8. Tacitus, *Annals,* trans. Michael Grant, 13.27.

9. P. A. Brunt, *Social Conflicts in the Roman Republic* (New York: W. W. Norton, 1971), 9.

10. On the use of this strategy for the unification of Italy, see A. N. Sherwin-White, *The Roman Citizenship* (Oxford: Clarendon Press, 1980), chap. 6; on its use in imperial expansion, see esp. chaps. 10 and 13; and on the un-

usual system of citizenship by manumission, "a vastly more numerous group than the enfranchised externs of free birth," see 322–34.

11. Harold Mattingly, *The Man in the Roman Street* (New York: W. W. Norton, 1966), 109.

12. Karl Christ, *The Romans* (Berkeley: Univ. of California Press, 1984), 47.

13. Ibid., 74.

14. Mattingly, *Man in the Roman Street*, 111.

15. Nicolet, *World of the Citizen*, 398.

16. MacMullen, *Enemies of the Roman Order: Treason, Unrest, and Alienation in the Empire* (Cambridge: Harvard Univ. Press, 1967), 179.

17. Ibid., chap. 5.

18. P. A. Brunt, "The Roman Mob," *Past & Present*, no. 34 (1966): 18.

19. Plutarch, *Cicero*, trans. Rex Warner, 24. When all is said and done though, it must be conceded, especially by the historical sociologist, that Cicero was a great source.

20. Ibid. For a lively account of this sordid period, see F. R. Cowell, *Cicero and the Roman Republic* (London: Penguin Books, 1973), 232–46.

21. Yavetz *Plebs and Princeps* (Oxford: Clarendon Press, 1969).

22. Ibid., 54.

23. Ibid., 136.

24. Ibid., 105.

25. W. W. Buckland, *The Roman Law of Slavery*, (1908; reprint, Cambridge: Cambridge Univ. Press, 1970), 1.

26. It is the one generalization in comparative historical sociology I am prepared to declare, unequivocally, a social law. See Orlando Patterson, *Slavery and Social Death: A Comparative Study* (Cambridge: Harvard Univ. Press, 1982), chap. 10.

27. See K. R. Bradley, *Slaves and Masters in the Roman Empire: A Study in Social Control* (New York: Oxford Univ. Press, 1984), 83.

28. Hopkins, *Conquerors and Slaves* (Cambridge: Cambridge Univ. Press, 1978), 115–31.

29. Wiedemann, "The Regularity of Manumission at Rome," *Classical Quarterly*, n. s., 35, no. 1 (1985): 168.

30. Frank, *An Economic History of Rome* (Baltimore: Johns Hopkins Univ. Press, 1927), 213.

31. Rawson, "Family Life among the Lower Classes at Rome in the First Two Centuries of the Empire," *Classical Philology* 61 (April 1966): 82. See also Marion Park, "The Plebs in Cicero's Day: A Study of Their Provenance and of Their Employment" (Ph. D. diss., Bryn Mawr College, 1918), in Park and M. Maxey, *Two Studies on the Roman Lower Classes* (New York: Arno Press, 1975), 5–90. See also P. A. Brunt, *Italian Manpower, 225 B.C.–A.D. 14* (Oxford: Oxford Univ. Press, 1971), 121f.

32. Rawson, "Family Life among the Lower Classes," 82. Note that even scholars skeptical of the use of the inscriptions for quantitative purposes, such as Treggiari, agree that "the population of the urbs was mainly lib-

ertine.'' Susan Treggiari, *Roman Freedmen During the Late Republic* (Oxford: Oxford Univ. Press, 1969), 166.

33. A. M. Duff, *Freedmen in the Early Roman Empire* (Oxford: Oxford Univ. Press, 1928), 70–71.

34. Petronius, *Satyricon*, trans. Michael Haseltine, 57. See, however, the freer but much jollier translation by William Arrowsmith, *The Satyricon of Petronius* (Ann Arbor: The Univ. of Michigan Press, 1959).

35. Treggiari, *Roman Freedmen*, 167–69. See the letter attributed to Quintus Tullius Cicero in Jo-Ann Shelton, *As the Romans Did: A Source Book in Roman Social History* (New York: Oxford Univ. Press), 220–24.

36. The best treatment of the subject is still Peter Spranger, *Historische Untersuchungen zu den Sklavenfiguren des Plautus und Terenz* (Wiesbaden: Akademie der Wissenschaften und der Literatur, Mainz, 1960). On the historical accuracy of these plays, see pp. 52f. On the problem of Romanization, and for a useful categorization of the slave types treated in Plautus, see C. Stace, ''The Slaves of Plautus,'' *Greece and Rome*, 2d ser., 15 (April 1968): 64–77.

37. Bonner, *Education in Ancient Rome* (Berkeley: Univ. of California Press, 1977), 46.

38. Michael Grant, *Roman Myths*, (Harmondsworth: Penguin Books, 1973), 91.

39. See, in particular, Robert E. A. Palmer, *Roman Religion and Roman Empire: Five Essays* (Philadelphia: Univ. of Pennsylvania Press, 1974), 115–17; also H. H. Scullard, *Festivals and Ceremonies of the Roman Republic* (Ithaca: Cornell Univ. Press, 1981), 58–60, 117–18.

40. Palmer, *Roman Religion and Roman Empire*, 117.

41. Keith Hopkins, *Conquerors and Slaves*, 212.

42. This was not the case, however, outside of Rome, where almost the opposite trend developed, that is, slaves displaced freedmen from the Lares cult, in some cities even becoming *magistri*. See Franz Bömer, *Untersuchungen über die Religion der Sklaven in Griechenland und Rom, vol. 1: Die wichtigsten Kulte und Religionen in Rom und im lateinischen Westen* (Wiesbaden: Akademie der Wissenschaften und der Literatur, Mainz, 1958), 46–47.

43. Ibid., 52–53; Treggiari, *Roman Freedmen*, 203–04.

44. Treggiari, *Roman Freedmen*, 212.

45. Cited in Hopkins, *Conquerors and Slaves*, 217.

46. Ibid., 222.

47. Treggiari, *Roman Freedmen*, 203.

48. Bömer, *Religion der Sklaven*, 1:78–86.

49. Peter Garnsey and Richard Saller, *The Roman Empire* (Berkeley: Univ. of California Press, 1987), 170.

50. R. L. Gordon, ''Mithraism and Roman Society,'' *Religion* 2 (Spring 1972): 92–121.

51. Arnold Toynbee, *Hannibal's Legacy*, 2:368.

52. Treggiari, *Roman Freedmen*, 204–7. The entire episode is reported in Livy 39.8–18.

53. Toynbee, *Hannibal's Legacy*, 2:392.

54. Bömer, *Religion der Sklaven*, 110–33; Scullard, *Festivals and Ceremonies*, 91–92.

55. Bömer, *Religion der Sklaven*, 143–59.

56. Gordon, "Mithraism and Roman Society," 101.

57. Bömer, *Religion der Sklaven*, 172–74.

58. Gordon, "Mithraism and Roman Society," 101.

59. See Ethel Hampson Brewster, *Roman Craftsmen and Tradesmen of the Early Empire* (New York: Burt Franklin, 1971). On the despised tanners, cobblers, and barbers who were typical of this group, see pp. 18–19, 54–60, 87–93.

60. Bömer, *Religion der Sklaven*, 160.

61. See, for example, Duff, *Freedmen in the Early Roman Empire*. Less typical are his remarks (p.207) on the ruination of Rome and the dilution of the original Roman stock by the freedmen; they are not only silly but almost racist. For an excellent collection of ancient sources on Roman attitudes toward freedmen see Shelton, *As the Romans Did*, 195–205.

62. Ramsay MacMullen, *Roman Social Relations, 50 B.C. to A.D. 284* (New Haven: Yale Univ. Press, 1974), 117 and chap. 4. One should be equally careful, however, not to be too self-righteous about the venality of the Roman plutocracy, for reasons Badian has made clear in his, *Publicans and Sinners* (Ithaca: Cornell Univ. Press, 1983), esp. chaps. 4 and 5.

63. Petronius, *Satyricon*, 29.

64. N. Rudd, *The Satires of Horace* (Cambridge: Cambridge Univ. Press, 1966); Oscar E. Nybakken, *An Analytical Study of Horace's Ideas*, Iowa Studies in Classical Philology, no. 5 (Scottsdale, Pa., 1937).

65. Horace, *Satires*, ed. and trans. Charles E. Passage, *The Complete Works of Horace* (New York: F. Ungar, 1983), 1.89–99.

66. Finley, "The Silent Women of Rome," in his *Aspects of Antiquity* (New York: Viking Press, 1969), 131.

67. Beryl Rawson, "Children in the Roman *Familia*," in Rawson, ed., *The Family in Ancient Rome: New Perspectives* (Ithaca: Cornell Univ. Press, 1986), 197.

68. On the Caribbean see Orlando Patterson, *The Sociology of Slavery: Jamaica, 1655–1838* (London: Mcgibbon and Kee, 1967), 167–70; and on the comparative data generally see idem, *Slavery and Social Death* (Cambridge: Harvard Univ. Press, 1982), 263–264.

69. W. W. Buckland, *The Roman Law of Slavery* (Cambridge: University Press, 1908), 397–8.

70. *Corpus Inscriptionum Latinarum* 1.2.1837, trans. and cited in Jo-Ann Shelton, ed., *As the Romans Did: A Source Book in Roman Social History* (New York: Oxford Univ. Press, 1988), 205.

71. Alan Watson, *Roman Slave Law* (Baltimore: Johns Hopkins Univ. Press,

1987), 13–14. On the sex ratio and its possible consequences see K.R. Bradley, *Slaves and Masters in the Roman Empire* (New York: Oxford Univ. Press, 1987), 73–74.

72. Keith Bradley, "Wet-nursing at Rome: A Study in Social Relations," in Rawson, ed., *The Family in Ancient Rome*, 203.

73. Ibid, 220–22.

74. *Tusculanae disputationes* 3.1–2, cited in, and trans. by Bradley, "Wet-nursing at Rome," 201.

75. Susan Treggiari, "The Freedmen of Cicero," *Greece and Rome*, vol. 16 (Oct. 1969), 201.

76. Ibid. 196.

77. Pliny, *Letters*, 6.3. Trans. and cited in Thomas Weidemann, ed., *Greek and Roman Slavery* (Baltimore: Johns Hopkins Univ. Press, 1981), 129–30.

78. Finley, "The Silent Women of Rome," 131.

79. Shelton, *As the Romans Did*, 290.

80. For more on which see, J.A. Crook, "Women in Roman Succession", and his "Feminine Inadequacy and the *Senatusconsultum Velleianum*," in Rawson, ed., *The Family in Ancient Rome*, 58–82; 83–92; see also W.K.Lacey, "*Patria Potestas*," idem, 121–44.

81. Schulz, *Classical Roman Law* (Oxford: Clarendon Press, 1951), 103.

82. Ibid, 116.

83. Cantarella, *Pandora's Daughters* (Baltimore: Johns Hopkins Univ. Press, 1987), 135–137.

84. Ibid 137–139. See also Beryl Rawson, "The Roman Family," in her *Family in Ancient Rome*, 19–20. For more on the classical law of *dos* see Schulz, *Classical Roman Law*, 120, 122–129.

85. Cantarella, *Pandora's Daughters*, 140–141.

86. Rawson, *The Family in Ancient Rome*, 33–37.

87. Suetonius, *Tiberius*, trans. J.C.Rolfe, 35. It should be noted that they were joined in these protests by young elite men who "voluntarily incurred degradation from their rank" to avoid the law. See also, Tacitus, *Annals*, 2.85, trans. C.H.Moore and J. Jackson.

88. See in particular, Juvenal, *Satires*, 6, trans. G.G.Ramsay. On this literature generally see Cantarella, *Pandora's Daughters*, 141–148.

89. Hallett, "The Role of Women in Roman Elegy: Counter-Cultural Feminism," in John Peradotto and J.P. Sullivan, eds., *Women in the Ancient World: The Arethusa Papers* (Albany: State Univ. of New York Press, 1984), 241–262. Professor Hallett shifted her tone noticeably in another work, to be discussed below; see note 90.

90. Hallett, *Fathers and Daughters in Roman Society: Women in the Elite Family* (Princeton: Princeton Univ. Press, 1984), 218–243. Note that Hallett's view is directly opposed to that of Beryl Rawson's who argues that the small size of the Roman upper class family led to a strong emphasis on the conjugal tie, in "The Roman Family," 15. Rawson, however, seems to be extrapolating from the modern nuclear family.

91. Hallett, *Fathers and Daughters*, 102–108.
92. Ibid, 65. Hallett draws from the rich anthropological literature on the "matrifocal" family in the Caribbean in developing her concept of filiafocality. I am very intrigued by this, given my own work on the subject. It seems to me, however, that this literature creates more theoretical problems than it solves for Hallett, but I reserve judgment at this time and will return to the subject in a future publication. See R.T. Smith, *The Negro Family in British Guiana* (London: Routledge and Kegan Paul, 1956). See also Orlando Patterson, "Persistence, Continuity and Change in the Jamaican Working Class Family," *Journal of Family Studies*, 7, no. 2 (1982): 135–61.
93. Hallett, *Fathers and Daughters in Roman Society*, 67.
94. Schultz, *Classical Roman Law*, 150.
95. W.K. Lacey, "Patria Potestas," in Rawson, *The Family in Ancient Rome*, 140.
96. Kirschenbaum, *Sons, Slaves and Freedmen*, 59.
97. Ibid, ,42–43. For more on this see G. Micolier, *Pecule et Capacite patrimoniale* (Lyon: Bosc Freres, M. et L. Riou, 1932), 501, 510.
98. Kirschenbaum, *Sons, Slaves and Freedmen*, 127.
99. Ibid, 140, 196.
100. Ibid, 163–196.
101. Marcel Mauss, *The Gift*, trans. Ian Cullison (New York: W.W.Norton, 1967).
102. Cicero, *De officiis*, 1.7.22. trans. Walter Miller.
103. On Cicero's and other elite fathers' attitudes see Hallett, *Fathers and Daughters*, 336–343.
104. Cicero, *De officiis*, 1.15.47–48. See the commentary by Kirschenbaum on these passages in *Sons, Slaves and Freedmen*, 168–169.
105. Patterson, *Slavery and Social Death*, 211–214.
106. See, for example, Finley, *Aspects of Antiquity*, 131.
107. On the naming of women see Hallett, *Fathers and Daughters*, 77–83.
108. Ibid, 82.
109. Ibid, 80.
110. Ibid, 79.
111. Sallust, *Bellum Catilinae*, trans. J.C.Rolfe, 24.3–25.5. Discussed in Hallett, *Fathers and Daughters*, chap. 1 and 35–36.
112. Syme, *The Augustan Aristocracy* (Oxford: Clarendon Press, 1986), 185.
113. Tacitus, *Annals*, trans. A. F. Church and W. J. Brodribb, 12.7; see also 6.25.
114. Suetonius, *The Deified Augustus*, trans. J. C. Rolfe, 40.3.
115. For a good discussion of this historiography, see K. R. Bradley, *Slaves and Masters in the Roman Empire*, 145–9.
116. Atkinson, "The Purpose of the Manumission Laws of Augustus", *The Irish Jurist*, n.s. (1966), 356–374.
117. Ibid, 371. See also, Bradley, *Slaves and Masters in the Roman Empire*, 86–95.

CHAPTER 14

1. Augustus, *Res gestae divi Augusti* trans. P.A.Brunt and J.M.Moore, 1.1.
2. Grant, *From Imperium to Auctoritas* (Cambridge: Cambridge Univ. Press, 1946), 408–53. However, for a recent departure from this see Zvi Yavetz, "The Res gestae" and "Augustus Public Image" in Fergus Miller and Erich Segal eds., *Caesar Augustus: Seven Aspects* (Oxford: Clarendon Press, 1984), 9–10.
3. Grant, *From Imperium to Auctoritas*, 412.
4. Ibid., p. 443. See also the Introduction of Brunt and Moore to the *Res gestae*, 8–16.
5. Syme, *The Roman Revolution*, (Oxford: Oxford Univ. Press, 1960), 322. See also G. E. M. De Ste. Croix, *Class Struggle in the Ancient Greek World* (Ithaca: Cornell Univ. Press, 1981), 362.
6. Augustus, *Res gestae*, 5, 15, 22. On the tradition of gift exchange between emperor and people, see Fergus Miller, *The Emperor in the Roman World* (Ithaca: Cornell Univ. Press, 1977), chap. 4.
7. Hammond, "Res olim dissociabiles: Principatus ac Libertas—Liberty under the Early Roman Empire," *Harvard Studies in Classical Philology* (1963), vol. 67: 93.
8. Ibid., 99.
9. Ibid., 101.
10. Ibid., 102.
11. Earl, *The Age of Augustus*, 71.
12. Augustus, *Res gestae*, 34–35. On the vexed question of whether or not Augustus addressed himself mainly to the plebeians of Rome, see the comments and qualification of his former views by Yavetz in his "Res gestae and Augustus' Public Image," 8–20.
13. Charlesworth, "The Virtues of the Roman Emperor," *Proceedings of the British Academy*, (1937), 127.
14. Syme, *Roman Revolution*, 520.
15. Yavetz, *Res gestae*, 26.
16. De Ste. Croix, *Class Struggle*, 366–67. The passage commented on is in Tacitus, *Annals*, 1.75.1–2.
17. Charlesworth, "Virtues of the Roman Emperor," 111.
18. Ibid., 127.

CHAPTER 15

1. A. A. Long, *Hellenistic Philosophy* (Berkeley: Univ. of California Press, 1974), 132–233.
2. See, for example, Cicero, *De Republica*, trans. C.W.Keyes, 1.1–2, 1.34.
3. Diogenes, Laërtius, *Lives* trans. A.A.Long and D.N.Sedley, 7.32–33.
4. Cicero, *De Republica*, 1.34.51.

5. Sallust, *Bellum Catilinae* trans. J.C. Rolfe 2–3. Classicists have endlessly debated the origins and nature of Sallust's ideas, on which see Ronald Syme, *Sallust* (Berkeley: Univ. of California Press, 1964), chaps. 5 and 14. In contrast with Syme, who calls Sallust an Epicurean, Rudolph P. Hock has recently strongly argued that he was the typical early Roman Stoic in, " 'Servile Behavior' in Sallust's *Bellum Catilinae*," *Classical World* 82, no. 1 (1988): 1–24.

6. Ramsay MacMullen, *Enemies of the Roman Order* (Cambridge: Harvard Univ. Press, 1966), 53.

7. Ibid.; see also Long, *Hellenistic Philosophy*, 234–35.

8. Arnold, *Roman Stoicism* (London: Routledge and Kegan Paul, 1958), 397. There are shades of the British empire in Arnold's account, but that is precisely why his bias might just be the right one here.

9. Ibid., 392.

10. Persius, *Satires*, trans. Nial Rudd, 3.63.

11. Ibid., 5.73–77.

12. Ibid., 5.125.

13. Ibid., 5.105–6.

14. Ibid., 2.72–74.

15. Anderson, "Part vs. Whole in Persius Fifth Satire," *Philological Quarterly* 39 (1960): 81.

16. Diogenes Laërtius, *Lives*, 7.1321–22.

17. Charlotte Stough, "Stoic Determinism and Moral Responsibility," in John M. Rist., ed., *The Stoics* (Berkeley: Univ. of California Press, 1978), 213.

18. Rawson, *Intellectual Life in Late Republican Rome* (Baltimore: Johns Hopkins Univ. Press, 1985), 82.

19. Diogenes Laërtius, *Lives*, 7.121–22.

20. Alvin H. Bernstein, *Tiberius Sempronius Gracchus: Tradition and Apostacy* (Ithaca: Cornell Univ. Press, 1978) 46.

21. D. R. Dudley, "Blossius of Cumae," *Journal of Roman Studies* 31 (1941): 97.

22. Bernstein, *Tiberius Sempronius Gracchus*, 46.

23. See James B. Becker, "The Influence of Roman Stoicism upon the Gracchi's Economic Land Reforms," *La Parola del Passato* 19 (1964): 125–34.

24. Rawson, "Intellectual Life," 104–9.

25. Ibid., 109.

26. Ronald Syme, *The Roman Revolution*, (Oxford: Oxford Univ. Press, 1960), 461.

27. Charles-Picard, *Augustus and Nero: The Secret of Empire*, trans. Len Ortzen (New York: T.Y. Crowell Co., 1966), 59.

28. Seneca, *On Tranquility*, trans. Moses Hadas, 10.

29. Tacitus; Annals, 14: 42–45; trans. John Jackson.

30. *Seneca*, Epistle 47. trans. Moses Hadas.

31. Mooney, "The Rational Psychology of Lucius Annaeus Seneca" (Ph.D. diss., State University of New York, Albany, 1980), 7.

32. Seneca, *On Providence*, trans. Moses Hadas, 5.

33. Seneca, *Epistles*, 75.18.
34. Seneca, *On Tranquility*, trans. Moses Hadas, 17.
35. Ibid.
36. Seneca, *On Clemency*, trans. Moses Hadas, 1.
37. Ibid., 3.
38. Ibid., 19.
39. Mattingly, "The Emperor and His Clients," in A. J. Dunston, ed., *Essays on Roman Culture: The Todd Memorial Lectures* (Toronto: Stevens, 1976), 181.
40. Brunt, "Marcus Aurelius in His Meditations," *Journal of Roman Studies* 54 (1974): 6.
41. Marcus, *Meditations*, trans G.M.A. Grube, 12.33.
42. Seneca, *On Clemency*, 8.
43. We know, however, of many *vernae* prominent in other pursuits. See Susan Treggiari, *Roman Freedmen during the Late Republic* (Oxford: Oxford Univ. Press, 1969), appendix 1, p. 248.
44. On the legal aspects of *verna* status, see W. W. Buckland, *The Roman Law of Slavery* (1908; reprint, Cambridge: Cambridge Univ. Press, 1970), 9, 397–401.
45. Treggiari, *Roman Freedmen*, 11.
46. Epictetus, *Discourses*, trans. W.A. Oldfather, 4.1.52.
47. Ibid., 4.1.1.
48. See Fergus Millar, "Epictetus and the Imperial Court," *Journal of Roman Studies* 55 (1965): 141–48.
49. Epictetus, *Discourses*, 2.1.23.
50. Ibid., 1.19.11.
51. Ibid., 2.23, esp. 36–41.
52. Ibid., 1.2.5.
53. Ibid., 1.2.34.
54. Ibid., 1.17.28–29.
55. Ibid., 1.23.
56. Ibid., 4.1.175–76.
57. Ibid., 1.29.63.
58. Ibid., 1.9.32.
59. Epictetus, *Fragments*, trans. W.A. Oldfather, 6.
60. Epictetus, *Discourses*, 2.10.5.
61. Ibid., 3.22.4–5.
62. Ibid., 4.1.13–14.
63. Ibid., 2.8.11–12.
64. Ibid., 1.14.15.
65. Ibid., 1.6.40–41.
66. W.A. Oldfather, introduction to *Epictetus* (Cambridge: Harvard Univ. Press, Loeb Classical Library, 1979), 1:xvi.
67. Epictetus, *Discourses*, 1.12.19. Oldfather's translation of the Greek *proairesis* as "purpose" is better rendered here as "choice."
68. Ibid., 2.10.1.

69. Ibid., 2.10.4–30.
70. Marcus, *Meditations*, 1.14.
71. Ibid., 2.4.
72. Ibid., 2.5.
73. Ibid., 12.26.
74. Ibid., 9, 23.
75. Ibid., 5.30.
76. Ibid., 11.1.
77. Ibid., 11.1.
78. Ibid., 11.18. An allusion to Epictetus.
79. Ibid., 4.12.
80. Ibid., 6.8.
81. Ibid., 5.16.
82. Ibid., 9.29.
83. Ibid., 11.20.
84. Ibid.
85. Ibid., 11.30.
86. Ibid., 11.31. See Homer *Odyssey* 9.413.
87. Marcus, *Meditations*, 11.38.
88. Ibid., 12.36.
89. Epictetus, *Discourses*, 4.1.128–31.

CHAPTER 16

1. Eliade, *A History of Religious Ideas*, trans. W. R. Trask (Chicago: Univ. of Chicago Press, 1982), 2: 289.
2. On *soter* and its different shades of meanings, see Arthur D. Nock, "*Soter* and Euergetes*," in his *Essays on Religion and the Ancient World*, Ed. Zeph Steward (Oxford: Clarendon Press, 1972), 720–735.
3. Weber, *The Sociology of Religion* (Boston: Beacon Press, 1963), 147.
4. Ibid., 150.
5. Ibid., chap. 12.
6. A.D. Nock, *Conversion* (Oxford: Clarendon Press, 1933), 91.
7. Maurice Goguel, *The Primitive Church* (London: George Allen & Unwin, 1964), 28–29.
8. Ibid., 29.
9. Gerd Theissen, *Sociology of Early Palestinian Christianity* (Philadelphia: Fortress Press, 1978), chaps. 2–3.
10. Morton Smith, *Jesus the Magician* (San Francisco: Harper & Row, 1978), 26–27, makes one of the strongest cases for such a reconsideration.
11. Theissen, *Sociology of Early Palestinian Christianity*, chap. 7. Joseph Blenkinsopp traces the origins of these movements to a much earlier period. See his "Interpretation and the Tendency to Sectarianism: An Aspect of

Second Temple History," in E. P. Sanders, ed., *Jewish and Christian Self-Definition*, 2 vols. (Philadelphia: Fortress Press, 1980–81), 2:1–26.

12. For an interesting recent interpretation of the interplay of politics and religion in Palestine during this period, see Alan F. Segal, *Rebecca's Children: Judaism and Christianity in the Roman World* (Cambridge: Harvard Univ. Press, 1986), esp. chaps. 1–3.

13. See Nock, *Conversion*, 89; and, more recently, Howard C. Klee, *Miracle in the Early Christian World* (New Haven: Yale Univ. Press, 1983), esp. chap. 5.

14. Luke 11:20; see also Luke 10:17.

15. Edward Schillebeeckx, *Jesus: An Experiment in Christology* (New York: Vintage Books, 1981), 140.

16. See, for example, Rudolf Bultmann, *Theology of the New Testament* (New York: Scribner's, 1951), 1:20–21.

17. Luke 6:31; Matt. 7:12.

18. Matt. 5:44.

19. Luke 6:29.

20. Gospel of Thomas, 114. Note, however, that Jesus' way of resolving the tension—promising to turn Mary into a man—offers little comfort to a modern feminist. For what it is worth, see also the much later Gospel of Philip, 63.32–64.5.

21. Gunther Bornkamm, *Jesus of Nazareth*, trans. Irene and Fraser McLuckey (New York: Harper, 1960), 105; Bultmann, *Theology of the New Testament*, 11.

22. Schillebeeckx, *Jesus*, 267.

23. Ibid., 213.

24. Ibid., 256.

25. Ibid., 200.

26. See, in particular, Norman Perrin and Dennis C. Duling, *The New Testament* (New York: Harcourt Brace Jovanovich, 1982), 76–77.

27. Bultmann, *Theology of the New Testament*, 25.

28. Ibid., 25–26.

29. Theissen, *Sociology of Early Palestinian Christianity*, 64.

30. Ibid.

31. Bultmann, *Theology of the New Testament*, 13–14. (emphasis in original).

32. Luke 17:10. While the word 'servant' may be an accurate translation of the Koiné, Jesus in all likelihood used the term 'slave' since this is the word used in the popular of maxim of Antigonus. See n.33 below.

33. Elias J. Bickerman, "The Maxim of Antigonus of Socho," *Harvard Theological Review*, 44 (Oct. 1951): 153–65; see esp. 163–64 For the correct translation of the maxim which shows that the word 'slave' and not 'servant' was used in Jesus' time see references cited in n.1.

34. See Mark 12:28–34; Luke 19:29–37.

35. Bruce J. Malina, *The New Testament World: Insights from Cultural Anthropology* (Atlanta: John Knox Press, 1981), esp. chaps. 2 and 3.

36. In this, however, he was not original. Bickerman notes that "the casuistic distinction between 'loving' and 'fearing' God [was] hotly debated in Jesus' time between the schools of Shammai and of Hillel." See "Maxim of Antigonus of Socho," 164.

37. Schillebeeckx, *Jesus*, 177.

38. Ibid., 177–78.

CHAPTER 17

1. Perrin and Duling, *The New Testament* (New York: Harcourt Brace Jovanovich, 1982), 76 n. 11.

2. Rudolf Bultmann, *Theology of the New Testament*, vol. 1 (New York: Scribner's, 1951), 33.

3. On Judaism's tolerance for sects and the factors accounting for the final break with Christianity, see Lawrence H. Schiffman, "At the Crossroads: Tannaitic Perspectives on the Jewish-Christian Schism," in E. P. Sanders, ed., *Jewish and Christian Self-Definition* (Philadelphia: Fortress Press, 1980–81), 2:115–56.

4. Bultmann, *Theology of the New Testament*, 1:45–46.

5. Goguel, *The Primitive Church* (London: George Allen & Unwin, 1964), 86.

6. Perrin and Duling, *New Testament*, 73–79; Goguel, *Primitive Church*, chap. 1.

7. Perrin and Duling, *New Testament*, 79–81.

8. Ibid., 82.

9. On this, see esp. Martin Hengel, *Between Jesus and Paul* (London: SCM Press, 1983), chap. 1.

10. Ibid., 24 (emphasis in original).

11. Morton Smith, *Jesus the Magician* (San Francisco: Harper & Row, 1978).

12. Ibid., 68–69.

13. Ibid., 24.

14. Ibid., 35, 137.

15. Luke 10:1–17.

16. Hengel, *Between Jesus and Paul*, 40.

17. Kee, *Miracle in the Early Christian World* (New Haven: Yale Univ. Press, 1983), p. 147 and, more generally, chap. 5.

18. Smith, *Jesus the Magician*, 5.

19. A. D. Nock, *Conversion* (Oxford: Clarendon Press, 1933), 206.

20. Ibid., 14.

21. Ramsey MacMullen, *Christianizing the Roman Empire*, A.D. 100–400 (New Haven: Yale Univ. Press, 1984), 37.

22. See Dimitris J. Kyrtatas, *The Social Structure of the Early Christian Communities* (London: Verso, 1987), esp. chap. 6.

23. Edward Schillebeeckx, *Jesus: An Experiment in Christology* (New York: Vintage Books, 1981), pt. 3, esp. sect. 1.

24. 1 Cor. 7.13, 11:2–16, 14:33–36.
25. Meeks, *The First Urban Christians* (New Haven: Yale Univ. Press, 1983), 70–71).
26. Gerd Theissen, *The Social Setting of Pauline Christianity* (Philadelphia: Fortress Press, 1982), 27.
27. 1 Cor. 9:1.
28. Theissen, *Social Setting of Pauline Christianity*, 44.
29. Schillebeeckx, *Jesus*, 425.
30. Ibid., 435.
31. Kurt Rudolph, *Gnosis: The Nature and History of Gnosticism* (San Francisco: Harper & Row, 1987), 159.
32. Ibid., esp. 113–71.
33. Menard, "Normative Self-Definition in Gnosticism," in Sanders, ed., *Jewish and Christian Self-Definition*, 1:149.
34. Bultmann, *Theology of the New Testament*, 1:71.
35. Pagels, *The Gnostic Gospels* (New York: Random House, 1979), 170.
36. *Gospel of Truth*, 31.14–35, trans. G. W. MacRae, in James M. Robinson, ed., *The Nag Hammadi Library* (San Francisco: Harper & Row, 1978).
37. *The Odes of Solomon*. trans. J. H. Charlesworth, (Oxford: Oxford Univ. Press, 1973), 74f.
38. Pagels, *Gnostic Gospels*, 7.
39. For an excellent discussion, see Gerard Vallee, "Theological and Non-Theological Motives in Irenaeus's Refutation of the Gnostics," in Sanders, ed., *Jewish and Christian Self-Definition*, 1:174–85, esp. 183.
40. Macrae, "Why the Church Rejected Gnosticism," in Sanders, ed., *Jewish and Christian Self-Definition*, 1:126–33.
41. For the classic statement of this thesis, see Walter Bauer, *Orthodoxy and Heresy in Earliest Christianity*, ed. R. Kraft and G. Krodel (Philadelphia: Fortress Press, 1971).

CHAPTER 18

1. Krister Stendahl, "The Apostle Paul and the Introspective Conscience of the West," in his *Paul among Jews and Gentiles and Other Essays* (Philadelphia: Fortress Press, 1976), 78–96; see also 16–17.
2. Ibid., 69.
3. Ibid., 72.
4. Wrede, "Paul's Importance in the History of the World," in Thomas S. Kepler, ed., *Contemporary Thinking about Paul* (New York: Abingdon-Cokesbury Press, 1950), 390.
5. On Paul's boasting, see E. A. Judge, "Paul's Boasting in Relation to Contemporary Professional Practice," *Australian Biblical Review* 16 (1966): 37–50.
6. Stendahl, *Paul among Jews and Gentiles* 52, 39.

7. Norman Perrin and Dennis C. Duling, *The New Testament* (New York: Harcourt Brace Jovanovich, 1982), 77–78, 86–87, 296–97. Gerd Theissen, *The Social Setting of Pauline Christianity* (Philadelphia: Fortress Press, 1982), 45–46; but, in contrast, see Johannes Munck, *Paul and the Salvation of Mankind*, trans. F. Clarke (Richmond: John Knox Press, 1959), chap. 10.

8. W. H. C. Frend, *The Rise of Christianity* (Philadelphia: Fortress Press, 1984), 93.

9. Munck, *Paul and the Salvation of Mankind*, 42.

10. Ibid., 49.

11. Frend, *Rise of Christianity*, 105.

12. Betz, *Paul's Concept of Freedom in the Context of Hellenistic Discussions about the Possibilities of Human Freedom*, (Berkeley: The Center, 1977), 6.

13. Wrede, "Paul's Importance," 391.

14. Wayne A. Meeks, *The First Urban Christians* (New Haven: Yale Univ. Press, 1983), 16.

15. T. R. Glover, "Tarsus," in Kepler, ed., *Contemporary Thinking about Paul*, 84.

16. This is not to deny that there were important differences, as Edwin Judge points out in his "St. Paul and Classical Society," *Jahrbuch für Antike und: Christentum* 15 (1980): 19–36.

17. F. Scott Bartchy, "Mallon Chresai: First Century Slavery and the Interpretation of 1 Corinthians 7:21" (Ph.D. diss., Harvard Univ., 1971).

18. Ibid., 96.

19. Ibid., 97–99.

20. It is worth noting that a tradition, going back to Jerome, claims that Paul's family had been taken as prisoners of war from Galilee to Tarsus, and that his father had acquired Roman citizenship after being manumitted from slavery by his Roman master. See Jerome, *De viris illustribus*, 5.

21. Bartchy, "Mallon Chresai," 130.

22. David Daube has valiantly squeezed out what little theological significance can be found. See his "Onesimus," in George W. Nickelsburg and George W. MacRae, eds., *Christians among Jews and Gentiles: Essays in Honor of Krister Stendahl* (Philadelphia: Fortress Press, 1986), 409–43.

23. See P. R. Coleman-Norton, "Paul and the Roman Law of Slavery," in Coleman-Norton, ed., *Studies in Roman Economic and Social History in Honor of Allan Chester Johnson* (Princeton: Princeton Univ. Press, 1951), 166–72.

24. Wayne A. Meeks, ed., *The Writings of St. Paul* (New York: W. W. Norton, 1972), 192.

25. Bartchy, "Mallon Chresai," 81–95.

26. See W. W. Buckland, *The Roman Law of Slavery* (1908; reprint, Cambridge: Cambridge Univ. Press, 1970), 239–49.

27. Frend, *Rise of Christianity*, 133.

28. For a sensible discussion of the issue see Dimitris J. Kyrtatas, *The Social Structure of the Early Christian Communities* (London: Verso, 1987), 29–36, 63–71.

29. Davis, *The Problem of Slavery in Western Culture* (Ithaca: Cornell Univ. Press, 1966). We will consider Davis's argument and the issues it addresses in the second volume of this work.

30. Gustav Adolf Deissmann, *Paul: A Study in Social and Religious History*, trans. W. E. Wilson (New York: Harper & Row, 1957). Of the more prominent modern scholars on this side of the debate, see John Gager, who insists that "Christian communities of the first two centuries derived their adherents from the lower classes of the Roman empire—slaves, freedmen, freeborn Romans of low rank, and non-Romans (peregrini) of various nationalities." See his "Religion and Social Class in the Early Empire," in Stephen Benko and John J. O'Rourke, eds., *The Catacombs and the Colosseum: The Roman Empire as the Setting of Primitive Christianity* (Valley Forge: Judson Press, 1971), 99.

31. Ramsay MacMullen, *Christianizing the Roman Empire, A.D. 100–400* (New Haven: Yale Univ. Press, 1984), 37–39.

32. E. R. Dodds, *Pagan and Christian in an Age of Anxiety* (Cambridge: Cambridge Univ. Press, 1965), 134.

33. Robert M. Grant, *Early Christianity and Society* (New York: Harper & Row, 1977), 7.

34. Theissen, *Social Setting of Pauline Christianity*, 69.

35. Meeks, *First Urban Christians*, 73 (emphasis added).

36. Ibid., 73. Elsewhere, however, Meeks speaks of persons of "relatively high wealth," leading at least one of his reviewers to complain of inconsistency: H. W. Pleket, in *Vigiliae Christianae* 39 (1985): 192–96, esp. 193–94. However, the more recent work of Kyrtatas, reported below, strongly indicates that Meeks is not necessarily inconsistent.

37. Petronius, *Satyricon*, trans. William Arrowsmith, 46.

38. Martial, *Twelve Books*, trans. J. Pott and F. Wright, 3.59, 7.64.

39. Juvenal, *Works*, trans. G. G. Ramsay, 1.24.

40. Philippians 4:22.

41. Kyrtatas, *Social Structure of the Early Christian Communities*, 71–74.

42. Ibid., 127–28. See Jones, *The Greek City: From Alexander to Justinian* (Oxford: Clarendon Press, 1940), 298.

43. Ibid., 85.

CHAPTER 19

1. The most extreme modern proponent of this disjunctive view is Hans Hubner, *Law in Paul's Thought*, trans. James C. Gerig (Edinburgh: T. & T. Clark, 1984).

2. See H. Raisanen, "Paul's Theological Difficulties with the Law," *Studia Biblica* 3 (1980): 301–20; but see Roy Yates's comment in his "St. Paul and the Law of Galatians," *Irish Theological Quarterly* 51 (1958): 121–22.

3. This point is made forcefully by M. Barclay, in his highly favorable review

of Hubner's *Law in Paul's Thought* in *Journal of Theological Studies* 37 (April 1986): 185.

4. I follow Meeks's dating here, but, as he himself points out, the issue remains a controversial one among New Testament scholars. See Wayne A. Meeks, ed., *The Writings of St. Paul* (New York: W. W. Norton, 1972), 10, 66.

5. 1 Cor. 9:19–23.

6. See Martin Dibelius, "Paul as a Letter Writer," in Thomas S. Kepler, ed., *Contemporary Thinking about Paul* (New York: Abingdon-Cokesbury Press, 1950), 177–81; and A. D. Nock, "The Style and Thought of Paul," ibid., 182–86.

7. My main guides are Meeks, ed., *Writings of St. Paul,* and the Revised Standard Version of *The Oxford Annotated Bible;* for the structure and style of the letters, I have relied on Norman Perrin and Dennis C. Duling, *The New Testament* (New York: Harcourt Brace Jovanovich, 1982), 127–97. I have also, naturally, learned a great deal from the comments on these matters by the many specialist works of interpretation on Paul that I have read, as well as older commentaries such as those of Martin Luther and John Locke, read, admittedly, more for insight into the thought of the interpreters than into that of the interpreted.

8. For the classic sociological treatment of theodicy, see Max Weber, *The Sociology of Religion* (Boston: Beacon Press, 1963), chap. 9.

9. See Rudolf Bultmann, *Theology of the New Testament* (New York: Scribner's, 1951), 1:349, 2:146.

10. 2 Cor. 4:16–18, 5:1–5. Compare the even more symbolically discordant 1 Cor. 15:35–57, with its clumsy mixed metaphors and alien pastoral imagery. The overall impression is that Paul, normally so sure of himself, is winging it.

11. Bultmann, *Theology of the New Testament,* 1:191.

12. Ibid. This interpretation has been strongly contested, most notably by Krister Stendahl, *Paul among Jews and Gentiles* (Philadelphia: Fortress Press, 1976), esp. 24–25. It is precisely on this point, however, that I find Stendahl too much of a literalist. Our concern is with Paul's religion, the thing he created in fervent *dialogue* with his audience. Paradoxically, we risk distorting Paul the Christian by too eagerly searching for Paul the man.

13. Gal. 4:1–9.

14. Rom. 6:6–7.

15. 2 Cor. 3:17.

16. Gal. 5:1.

17. Gal. 2:4.

18. 1 Cor. 10.28–29.

19. Francis C. Burkitt, "An Ethical Anarchist," in Kepler, ed., *Contemporary Thinking about Paul,* 310.

20. Gal. 3.13.

21. Gal. 3:23–29.

22. Stendahl, *Paul among Jews and Gentiles*, 5.
23. See the introduction and selections in pt. 4 of Meeks, ed., *Writings of St. Paul*, 215–72.
24. Orlando Patterson, *Slavery and Social Death* (Cambridge: Harvard Univ. Press, 1982).
25. 1 Cor. 15:26.
26. 1 Cor. 15:50.
27. 1 Cor. 15:22.
28. 2 Cor. 4:10–12.
29. See Meeks, ed., *Writings of St. Paul*, 77 n. 3.
30. Rom. 6:5–11.
31. Stendahl, *Paul among Jews and Gentiles*, 51.
32. C. Harold Dodd, "The Ancient Wrong," in Kepler, ed., *Contemporary Thinking about Paul*, 263. See also Bultmann, *Theology of the New Testament*, 1:239–53.
33. W. W. Buckland, *The Roman Law of Slavery* (1908; reprint, Cambridge: Cambridge Univ. Press, 1970), 439.
34. Gal. 6:15.
35. Gal. 2:19.
36. Meeks, ed., *Writings of St. Paul*, 16 n. 9.
37. Rom. 7:10.
38. See Patterson, *Slavery and Social Death*, introd.
39. 1 Cor. 15:43.
40. Buckland, *Roman Law of Slavery*, 304. Ernst Levy has argued that this rule went into effect only during the latter half of the second century A.D., but he is the only person to do so, and relies on questionable literary and circumstantial evidence. See his "Captivus Redemptus," *Classical Philology* 38 (July 1943): 159–76.
41. Rom. 5:8–11.
42. The term is used in the disputed First Letter to Timothy 2:6; see also Mark 10:45.
43. Gal. 6:5–10.
44. Phil. 2:12.
45. Gal. 2:20–21.
46. 2 Cor. 4:16–18.
47. Here I reluctantly disagree with Meeks, who, along with most other commentators, suggests that the terms are used synonymously in Paul's theology. Meeks, ed., *Writings of St. Paul*, 76 n. 5.
48. Gal. 2:15.
49. 1 Cor. 15:3–5.
50. Wilhelm Heitmuller, "Hellenistic Christianity before Paul," in Meeks, ed. *Writings of St. Paul*, 308–19. Compare, however, Harris Franklin Rall, "How Paul Thought of Christ," in Kepler, ed., *Contemporary Thinking about Paul*, 280–82.
51. Rom. 10:9–10.

52. Ricoeur, *The Symbolism of Evil*, trans. E. Buchanan (New York: Harper & Row, 1967), 238.

53. 1 Cor. 15:45–48.

54. Rom. 5:12–14.

55. 1 Cor. 15:22–26.

56. Rom. 3:22–25; see the pseudo-Pauline Eph. 1:1, which asserts that "we have redemption through his blood."

57. Charles A. Anderson Scott, "The Death of Christ as a Sacrifice," in Kepler, ed., *Contemporary Thinking about Paul*, 327.

58. Gal. 1:3–5.

59. Phil. 2:6–8.

60. Quite possibly an allusion to the Adamic myth: see Meeks, ed., *Writings of St. Paul*, 87 n. 6.

61. Deliberately mistranslated as "servant" in the King James and most modern editions. Paul is not suggesting here that Jesus actually succumbs to the powers of enslavement. Rather, he voluntarily becomes a slave both as a necessary condition for his sacrificial act of emancipation and as a supreme act of cosmic empathy: Jesus takes on the shape of humankind to know from the inside what it is like to suffer the degradation of fleshly, incarnate slavery. The idea of the god descending in order to rise again was a common theme in the Hellenistic religions, as we have already noted. But here it is joined to the wholly new theme of the God becoming enslaved in human flesh and degradation.

62. Gal. 3:13.

63. Nygren, "The Agape of the Cross," in Kepler, ed., *Contemporary Thinking about Paul*, 333–41.

64. Rom. 6:2–4.

65. 2 Cor. 4:5.

66. See esp. 2 Cor. 1:3–7; 2 Cor. 6:4–10.

67. 2 Cor. 6:1–2. It is remarkable that Paul does not seize the opportunity to quote the saying source of Jesus here; instead, he cites a passage from Isaiah.

68. See 1 Cor. 11:23–29.

69. 1 Cor. 12:13.

70. Richard P. C. Hanson, "Eucharistic Offering in the Pre-Nicene Fathers," in his *Studies in Christian Antiquity* (Edinburgh: T. & T. Clark, 1985), 83–112.

71. Eph. 4:3–6.

72. Goguel, *The Primitive Church* (London: George Allen & Unwin, 1964), 58.

73. Grant, *Early Christianity and Society* (New York: Harper & Row, 1977), chap. 2.

74. Stendahl insists on describing Paul's experience as a "call" rather than a "conversion," but I think he goes too far here in his otherwise brilliant attempt to reinterpret Paul as an outer-directed sort of person; or, to be

outrageously sociological, to Scandinavianize a too thoroughly German-
ized, inner-directed, guilt-ridden Paul. Stendahl, *Paul among Jews and Gentiles,* 7–23.

75. Meeks, ed., *Writings of St. Paul,* 12.

76. Stendahl, *Paul among Jews and Gentiles,* esp. 1–7.

77. W. H. C. Frend, *The Rise of Christianity* (Philadelphia: Fortress Press, 1984)
106.

78. Alan Watson, *Roman Slave Law,* (Baltimore: Johns Hopkins Univ. Press,
1987) 27–28.

79. F. Scott Bartchy, "Mallon Chresai" (Ph. D. diss., Harvard Univ., 1971),
92–93. See also Jacob J. Rabinowitz, "Manumission in Roman Law and
Oriental Law," *Journal of Near Eastern Studies,* 19 (Jan. 1960): 42–45.

80. Gal. 4:5–7.

81. Gal. 4:22–27.

82. Meeks, ed., *Writings of St. Paul,* 19 n. 7.

83. It was also one of the most popular motifs in Roman comedy. See Peter
Spranger, *Historische Untersuchungen zu den Sklavenfiguren des Plautus und
Terenz* (Wiesbaden: Akademie der Wissenschaften und der Literatur,
Mainz, 1960), 70–72.

84. Buckland, *Roman Law of Slavery,* 410–11.

85. David Brion Davis correctly argues that "the concept of slavery is further
widened" by this allegory. But so, even more, was the concept of freedom in the Western consciousness. See the seminal discussion in his *The
Problem of Slavery in Western Culture* (Ithaca: Cornell Univ. Press, 1966),
esp. 83–90.

86. Gal. 5:22–24.

87. Erwin R. Goodenough with A. T. Kraabel, "Paul and the Hellenization
of Christianity," in Jacob Neusner, ed., *Religions in Antiquity,* (Leiden:
E. J. Brill, 1968) 45.

88. Rom. 9:16.

89. Bultmann, *Theology of the New Testament,* 1:314–17. Bultmann, it should
be noted, fully recognizes Paul's metaphoric use of his sociological experience: see, on this point, 1:218–19.

90. Rom. 1:5.

91. Rom. 6:20–23.

92. See Davis's discussion of this problem, in his *Problem of Slavery in Western
Culture,* 85–86.

93. Rom. 11:32.

94. Rom. 9:17–18.

95. Rom. 5:1–2.

96. Rom. 5:3–5.

97. Rom. 12:4–8.

98. Charles Norris Cochrane, *Christianity and Classical Culture* (New York: Oxford Univ. Press, Galaxy, 1957), p. 110 and chap. 3.

99. And even then, it would be participative citizenship in what was a highly organic religious community. Greek influence, especially after Clement of Rome, if anything, strengthened the organic metaphor in the conception of an *ordo Christianus*. See Werner Jaeger, *Early Christianity and Greek Paideia*, (Oxford: Oxford Univ. Press, 1961), esp. 17–26.
100. Rom. 7:15–20.
101. Rom. 7:14–15.
102. Rom. 7:22–23.

CHAPTER 20

1. On the ending of the Western empire I have found the following most useful: E. A. Thompson, *Romans and Barbarians: The Decline of the Western Empire* (Madison: Univ. of Wisconsin Press, 1982); Peter Brown, *The World of Late Antiquity* (London: Thames and Hudson, 1971); A. H. M. Jones, *The Later Roman Empire, 284–602*, 3 vols. (Oxford: Blackwell, 1964); Jones, *The Roman Economy*, ed. P. A. Brunt (Oxford: Basil Blackwell, 1974); G. E. M. De Ste. Croix, *The Class Struggle in the Ancient Greek World* (Ithaca: Cornell Univ. Press, 1981), pt. 8; F. W. Walbank, *The Awful Revolution: the Decline of the Roman Empire in the West* (Liverpool: Liverpool Univ. Press, 1969). More specialist works are cited below.
2. As the case of the pious Melania and her husband, owners of thousands of slaves, indicates. Cited in M. I. Finley, *Ancient Slavery and Modern Ideology* (New York: Penguin Books, 1980), 123.
3. This is strongly emphasized by De Ste. Croix, in *Class Struggle*, 497–503; Pierre Dockès, *Medieval Slavery and Liberation* (Chicago: Univ. of Chicago Press, 1982), 84; and Walbank, *Awful Revolution*, 91–95.
4. Thompson, *Romans and Barbarians*, 17, 38.
5. Ibid., 25–37.
6. Loyn, "Currency and Freedom: Some Problems in the Social History of the Early Middle Ages," in H. Mayr-Harting and R. I. Moore, eds., *Studies in Medieval History: Presented to R. H. C. Davis* (London: Hambledon Press, 1985), 14. Could the neglect be due, one wonders, to a fear of what might be discovered—that slavery persisted throughout Europe—or, even more disturbingly, that it and its sister institution, serfdom, were the real sustaining sources of Europe's most cherished ideal?
7. The standard study is still Charles Verlinden, *L'esclavage dans l'Europe médiévale*, vol. 1, *Péninsule ibérique, France*; (Bruges: De Tempel, 1955), vol. 2, *Italie, colonies italiennes du Levant, Levant latin, Empire byzantin* (Ghent: Rijksuniversiteit, 1977). A major recent synthesis which differs in important respects is Pierre Bonassie, "Survie et extinction du regime esclavagiste dans l'Occident du haut moyen age (IV–XI s.)," *Cahiers de Civilisation medievale* vol. 28 (1985): 307–343. See also Georges Duby, *The Early Growth of the European Economy* (Ithaca: Cornell Univ. Press, 1974) E. A. Thompson,

The Goths in Spain (Oxford: Clarendon Press, 1969); P. D. King, *Law and Society in the Visigothic Kingdom* (Cambridge: Cambridge Univ. Press, 1972), esp. chap. 6; Dockes, *Medieval Slavery and Liberation;* but compare C. R. Whittaker, ''Circe's Pigs: From Slavery to Serfdom in the Later Roman World,'' *Slavery and Abolition* 8 (1987): 88–122, which disputes Dockes's claim that slavery was extensive in northern France. For an overview see Anderson, *Passages from Antiquity to Feudalism*, vol. 2, chaps. 2–3. For estimates of the relative sizes of the slave populations of medieval Europe, see Orlando Patterson, *Slavery and Social Death* (Cambridge: Harvard Univ. Press, 1982), appendix C, p. 354.

8. Charles Verlinden, *The Beginnings of Modern Colonization* (Ithaca: Cornell Univ. Press, 1970). The continuity thesis is intriguing, but we must distinguish between structural and cultural factors before accepting it. For a good study of late medieval Mediterranean slavery, see Jacques Heers, *Esclaves et domestiques au Moyen-Age* (Paris: Fayard, 1981); see also D. Phillips, *Slavery from Roman Times to the Early Transatlantic Trade* (Minneapolis: Univ. of Minnesota Press, 1985), chap. 6.

9. Peter Foote and David M. Wilson, *The Viking Achievement* (London: Sidgwick and Jackson, 1970), 52–53. See the fascinating debate surrounding the genetic history of Iceland, where, it has recently been shown, less than 20 percent of the population is of Norwegian ancestry, in stunning contradiction to the universally accepted view. It has been strongly suggested by some that the mainly Celtic peoples (read ''Irish'') who were mixed in were of slave ancestry: see Lettin Fegersten Saugstad, ''The Settlement of Iceland,'' *N.A.R.* 10, 1–2 (1977): 60–65. Of the commentators see, in particular, Sveinbjorn Rafnsson, ''Comments on the Settlement of Iceland,'' ibid., 70–72. See also Saugstad's ''Reply to Comments on the Settlement of Iceland,'' ibid., esp. 80.

10. F. W. Maitland, *Domesday Book and Beyond* (1897; reprint, Cambridge: Cambridge Univ. Press, 1960). On the little studied but very important system of slave trading and slavery among the Irish between the fifth and the seventh centuries, see N. W. Patterson, ''Archeological Aspects of Early Irish Slavery,'' Paper read at the Colloquium on Celtic Studies, Dept. of Celtic Languages and Literature, Harvard University, Spring 1990.

11. Hilton, *The Decline of Serfdom in Medieval England* (London: Macmillian, 1983) 14–15 (emphasis added).

12. Duby, *Rural Economy and Country Life in the Medieval West*, trans. Cynthia Postan (Columbia: Univ. of South Carolina Press, 1976), 37.

13. Ibid., 37–39.

14. This is not to say that the association with the growth of the currency, mentioned in Loyn, ''Currency and Freedom,'' 14, is not correct. No causal relationship is shown, however; and none, we now know, is needed.

15. Loyn, ''Currency and Freedom,'' 15.

16. Hilton, *Bond Men Made Free: Medieval Peasant Movements and the English Rising of 1381* (New York: Viking Press, 1973), 72.

17. Ibid., 74. The same point is made for the earlier period of emancipations by Bonassie in "Survie et extinction," 335.

18. De Ste. Croix, *Class Struggle*, 259 (emphasis added).

19. A. H. M. Jones, "The Roman Colonate," in his *Roman Economy*, 293–307, esp. 297. See also Finley, *Ancient Slavery and Modern Ideology*, 123–49.

20. De Ste. Croix, *Class Struggle*, 147–48 and, more generally on the entire process of enserfment, 147–62, 226–69. De Ste. Croix argues that the promotion of slave families reduced the surplus accruing to the slaveholders, who sought to make it up by further squeezing the free, especially the free tenant, population. That may have been so, but the reduced management and supervisory costs may have more than compensated for time lost in child rearing; and the gratitude of the *colonus*, who was no longer a despised slave, even if not yet a free man, may also have enhanced motivation.

21. Dockes, *Medieval Slavery and Liberation*, pp. 77–84 and chap. 4.

22. Finley, *Ancient Slavery and Modern Ideology*, 124–26, 146–48; Jones, "Roman Colonate," 303–6.

23. Jones, "Roman Colonate," 305–6.

24. For a detailed discussion of the history of the term, see Marc Bloch, *Slavery and Serfdom in the Middle Ages* (Berkeley: Univ. of California Press, 1975), 124–28.

25. Georges Duby, *The Early Growth of the European Economy* (Ithaca: Cornell Univ. Press, 1974), chap. 4; Dockes, *Medieval Slavery and Liberation*, 101–5, 233–38.

26. Dockès, *Medieval Slavery and Liberation*, 104–5.

27. Duby, *Early Growth of the European Economy*, 227–32.

28. For the classic account, see Marc Bloch, *Feudal Society* (London: Routledge and Kegan Paul, 1962), vol. 1, pt. 4; for the most widely accepted modern interpretations see Duby, *Early Growth of the European Economy*, chaps. 6 and 8; Rodney Hilton, *Class Conflict and the Crisis of Feudalism* (London: Hambleton Press, 1985), chap. 18; and Guy Fourquin, *Lordship and Feudalism in the Middle Ages* (London: George Allen & Unwin, 1976), 115–62.

29. Bloch, *Slavery and Serfdom*, 61.

30. Ibid., 77.

31. Hilton, *Bond Men Made Free*, 55–62. On England, see J. Hatcher, "English Serfdom and Villeinage," *Past & Present*, no. 90 (1981): 1–39. For France see Duby, *The Three Orders* 159–60.

32. Duby, *The Three Orders*, 154.

33. Georges Duby, *The Chivalrous Society* (Berkeley: Univ. of California Press, 1977), 85, 135–48.

34. Hilton, *Bond Men Made Free*, 55.

35. Duby, *Early Growth of the European Economy*, 172.

36. Bloch, *Slavery and Serfdom*, 86.

37. Jerome Blum, *The End of the Old Order in Rural Europe* (Princeton: Princeton Univ. Press, 1978), 38–44. On the far more complex case of Russia, see

Richard Hellie, *Enserfment and Military Change in Muscovy* (Chicago: Univ. of Chicago Press, 1971), esp. Chap. 7; and Hellie, *Slavery in Russia, 1450–1725* (Chicago: Univ. of Chicago Press, 1982), chaps. 1, 2, 10, and 18. In spite of Hellie's nearly exhaustive treatment of these subjects, I have still not been able to grasp just how the two institutions differed in law or social practice during this period. The ambiguity may have originated in the "paradoxical" attitude to the peasants' freedom of movement in the earlier century, discussed in Jerome Blum, *Lord and Peasant in Russia: From the Ninth to the Nineteenth Century* (Princeton: Princeton Univ. Press, 1961), 106–13.

38. Bois, *The Crisis of Feudalism: Economy and Society in Eastern Normandy c.1300–1550* (Cambridge: Cambridge Univ. Press, 1984), 407. See also Hilton, *Class Conflict and the Crisis of Feudalism*, chaps. 19 and 23; compare Anderson, *Lineages of the Absolutist State* (London: Verso, 1974), esp. chap. 1.

39. Hellie, *Slavery in Russia*, 710. On that legacy see Blum, *End of the Old Order*, pt. 3; and for an interesting comparison of it with U.S. slavery which I do not always agree with, see Peter Kolchin, *Unfree Labor: American Slavery and Russian Serfdom* (Cambridge: Harvard Univ. Press, 1987).

40. For a brilliant analysis see Iris Origo, "The Domestic Enemy: The Eastern Slaves in Tuscany in the Fourteenth and Fifteenth Centuries," *Speculum* 30 (July 1955): 321–66. See also C. Klapisch-Zuber, "Women Servants in Florence during the Fourteenth and Fifteenth Centuries," in Barbara Hanawalt, ed., *Women and Work in Preindustrial Europe* (Bloomington: Indiana Univ. Press, 1986), 56–80; and Susan M. Stuard, "To Town to Serve: Urban Domestic Slavery in Medieval Ragusa," ibid., 39–55. On the more advanced slave systems of late medieval Italy, see Charles Verlinden, *L'esclavage dans l'Europe médiévale*, vol. 2., and Heers, *Esclaves et domestiques*, chaps. 4–5.

41. On Spain between the thirteenth and fifteenth centuries, see Verlinden, *L'esclavage dans l'Europe médiévale*, 1:300–531; on sixteenth-century Seville see Ruth Pike, "Sevillian Society in the Sixteenth Century: Slaves and Freedmen," *Hispanic American Historical Review* 47 (1967): 344–59.

42. Joan Dyste Lind, "The Ending of Slavery in Sweden," *Scandinavian Studies* 50 (1978): 57–71.

43. Hilton, *Decline of Serfdom in Medieval England*.

44. Kolchin, *Unfree Labor*, 201–6 and esp. 331–33.

45. Ibid., esp. chaps. 1 and 2 and pp. 359–75.

CHAPTER 21

1. Duby, *The Three Orders: Feudal Society Imagined* (Chicago: Univ. of Chicago Press, 1980), 147. See also Susan Reynolds, *Kingdoms and Communities in Western Europe* (Oxford: Clarendon Press, 1984), 1–11. Reynolds' discus-

sion of the tradition of associative experience in terms of different levels of organization—guilds, parishes, villages, towns, provinces, and the broadest association of realm or kingdom—is useful. However, she greatly underestimates the role of individual agency, especially that of lordship, in medieval society.

2. Harding, "Political Liberty in the Middle Ages," *Speculum* 55 (July 1980): 423–43.

3. Ibid., 423.

4. Ibid., 431. For a more detailed discussion of the hierarchy of powers, see Guy Fourquin, *Lordship and Feudalism in the Middle Ages* (London: George Allen & Unwin, 1976), 51–54; and, on the identification of nobility with *libertas* all over Europe, see 82–83.

5. Reynolds, *Kingdoms and Communities*, 221–22, 331.

6. Harding, "Political Liberty in the Middle Ages," 434–35.

7. Bisson, "The Crisis of the Catalonian Franchises (1150–1200)," in Jaume Portella i Comas, ed., *La formació i expansió del feudalisme Català* (Barcelona: Collegi Universitari de Girona, 1986), 163.

8. See Fourquin, *Lordship and Feudalism in the Middle Ages*, 95–96, 170–73.

9. Georges Duby, *The Early Growth of the European Economy* (Ithaca: Cornell Univ. Press, 1974), 175.

10. Bisson, "Crisis of the Catalonian Franchises," 171.

11. Reynolds, *Kingdoms and Communities*, chap. 3.

12. Ibid., chaps. 4 and 5.

13. Ibid., 131–132. This was much less the case in England; see R. H. Hilton, *The English Peasantry in the Later Middle Ages* (Oxford: Clarendon Press, 1975), 91–94.

14. Bisson, "Crisis of the Catalonian Franchises," 168, 172.

15. For evaluations of Pirenne's thesis in the light of more recent work see David M. Nicholas, "Medieval Urban Origins in Northern Continental Europe: State of Research and Some Tentative Conclusions," *Studies in Medieval and Renaissance History* 6 (1969): 107–14.

16. Pirenne, *Economic and Social History of Medieval Europe*, trans. I. E. Cleg (New York: Harcourt Brace/Harvest Book, 1937), 51. The argument is explored at much greater length for the Low Countries in his *Early Democracy in the Low Countries: Urban Society and Political Conflict in the Middle Ages and the Renaissance*, trans. J. V. Saunders (New York: Harper & Row, 1963).

17. Pirenne, *Economic and Social History of Medieval Europe*, 50 (emphasis added).

18. Cited in N. Rubinstein, "Florence and the Despots: Some Aspects of Florentine Diplomacy in the Fourteenth Century," *Transactions of the Royal Historical Society*, 5th ser., 2 (1952): 21–22.

19. Bouwsma, *Venice and the Defense of Republican Liberty* (Berkeley: Univ. of California Press, 1968), p. 93 and chap. 2.

20. Blickle, *The Revolution of 1525: The German Peasant War from a New Perspective* (Baltimore: Johns Hopkins Univ. Press, 1981), esp. chap. 4.

21. On England and Wales see, Maurice Beresford, *New Towns of the Middle Ages* (Gloucester: Alan Sutton, 1988), esp. chap. 7.

22. See Stephen Rigby, "Urban 'Oligarchy' in Late Medieval England," in John A. Thomson, ed. *Towns and Townspeople in the Fifteenth Century* (Gloucester: Alan Sutton, 1988): 62–86.

23. Beresford, *New Towns of the Middle Ages*, 212–220.

24. Stubbs, *The Constitutional History of England* (Oxford, 1896–98). For a cogent criticism of this historiography, see G. O. Sayles, *The King's Parliament of England* (New York: W. W. Norton, 1974), 1–20. See also the collection of papers by H. G. Richardson and G. O. Sayles, *The English Parliament in the Middle Ages* (London: Hambledon Press, 1981), esp. nos. 1, 2, 4, and 26.

25. Sayles, *King's Parliament of England*, 128.

26. See J. H. Plumb, *The Origins of Political Stability: England, 1675–1725* (Boston: Houghton Mifflin, 1967), chap. 3.

27. Holt, "The Prehistory of Parliament," in R. G. Davies and J. H. Denton, eds., *The English Parliament in the Middle Ages* (Manchester: Manchester Univ. Press, 1981), 3.

28. Ibid., 24.

29. J. R. Maddicott, "Parliament and the Constituencies, 1272–1377," in Davies and Denton, eds., *English Parliament in the Middle Ages*, 73.

30. Holt, "Prehistory of Parliament," 28. The ways in which this happened are lucidly and thoroughly discussed in the other papers of this volume.

31. David Herlihy, "Alienation in Medieval Culture and Society," in Frank Johnson, ed., *Alienation: Concept, Term and Meanings* (New York: Seminar Press, 1971) 127.

32. Rodney Hilton, *Bond Men Made Free* (New York: Viking Press, 1973), 234.

33. Ibid., 54.

34. Ibid., chap. 2.

35. F. Graus, "From Resistance to Revolt: The Late Medieval Peasant Wars in the Context of Social Crisis," in Janos Bak, ed., *The German Peasant War of 1525* (London: Frank Cass, 1976), 2.

36. Fourquin, *The Anatomy of Popular Rebellion in the Middle Ages* (Amsterdam: North-Holland, 1978), 2.

37. Cohn, *The Pursuit of the Millennium* (London: Temple Smith, 1970), 53–70.

38. Hilton, *Bond Men Made Free*, 224.

39. "The Twelve Articles," in Blickle, *Revolution of 1525*, appendix 1, p. 197.

40. Blickle, *Revolution of 1525*, chap. 8 and pp. 187–93.

41. Hilton, *Bond Men Made Free*, 225.

42. Blickle, *Revolution of 1525*, 198.

43. See M. I. Finley, "Between Slavery and Freedom" and "The Servile Statuses of Ancient Greece," in his *Economy and Society in Ancient Greece*, ed. B. D. Shaw and R. P. Saller (New York: Penguin Books, 1981), 116–49.

44. James VI and I, "A Speech to the Lords and Commons of Parliament at

White-Hall'' (1610), in David Wootton, ed., *Divine Right and Democracy* (London: Penguin Books, 1986), 107.

45. James VI and I, *The Trew Law of Free Monarchies* (1598), reprinted in Wootton, ed., *Divine Right and Democracy*, 99–106.

46. On the identification of power with intimacy and ''friendship'' with God among the great men of late antiquity, see Peter Brown, *The Making of Late Antiquity* (Cambridge: Harvard Univ. Press, 1978), esp. chap. 3.

CHAPTER 22

1. Herrin, *The Formation of Christendom* (Princeton: Princeton Univ. Press, 1987). Ernst Troeltsch's discussion of the church's role in the medieval unity of civilization is still valuable. See, *The Social Teaching of the Christian Churches* (New York: Macmillan, 1931), vol. 1, 201–254. See now, Michael Seidlmayer, *Currents of Medieval Thought With Special Reference to Germany*, trans. D.Barker (Oxford:Basil Blackwell, 1960), chap.1.

2. Ernst H. Kantorowicz, *The King's Two Bodies: A Study in Medieval Political Theology* (Princeton: Princeton Univ. Press, 1957), 235. See also Pierre Courcelle, *Late Latin Writers and their Greek Sources*, trans. Harry Wedeck (Cambridge: Harvard Univ. Press, 1969).

3. Kantorowicz, *The King's Two Bodies*, 16.

4. Ibid., 193–94.

5. Strayer, *The Medieval Origins of the State* (Princeton: Princeton Univ. Press, 1970). This point, however, was long anticipated by Troeltsch in *The Social Teaching of the Christian Churches*, 1: 325.

6. Karl Jaspers, *Plato and Augustine* (New York: Harcourt Brace/Harvest Book, 1962) 95.

7. Etienne Gilson, *The Spirit of Medieval Philosophy*, trans A. H. Downes (New York: Scribner, 1936), 304.

8. Pagels, *Adam, Eve and the Serpent* (New York: Random House, 1988), xxv.

9. Clement of Alexandria, ''Exhortation to the Greeks,'' in *Clement of Alexandria*, trans. and ed. G. W. Butterworth (Cambridge: Harvard Univ. Press, Loeb Classical Library, 1919, 1982), 251. See also chap. 11.

10. Jaeger, *Early Christianity and Greek Paideia* (Oxford: Oxford Univ. Press, 1961), 38, 45–46, 72–73.

11. Pagels, *Adam, Eve and the Serpent*, p. 120 and chap. 5 generally.

12. On Augustine's misreading of Plotinus' ideas on the freedom of the will, see John H. Smith, *The Death of Classical Paganism* (New York: Scribner, 1976), 221; on his use or misuse of Stoic themes, gained mainly second-hand from the Neoplatonists, see Alvin J. Holloway, ''The Transformation of Stoic Themes in St. Augustine'' (Ph.D. diss., Fordham Univ., 1966), esp. chap. 5, which has an insightful comparison of Augustinian and Stoic treatments of the problem of evil.

13. Smith, *Death of Classical Paganism*, 218.

14. Brown, *Augustine of Hippo* (Berkeley: Univ. of California Press, 1967), 172–73.

15. Ibid., 156.

16. Augustine, *The City of God*, trans. Gerald Walsh et al., 14.28.

17. Brown, *Augustine of Hippo*, 325–26.

18. *Ps.* 103, *Serm.* 4.16, in Erich Przywara, *An Augustine Synthesis* (New York: Harper Torchbooks, 1958), 412.

19. Augustine, *City of God*, 22.30.

20. Ibid.

21. Ibid., 19.17.

22. Strayer, *Medieval Origins of the State*, 21–22. On the development of royal theocracy and the proprietary churches see Gerd Tellenbach, *Church, State and Christian Society at the Time of the Investiture Conflict*, trans. R. F. Bennett (New Jersey: Humanities Press, 1979), chap. 3.

23. For a good short history of the conflict see Uta-Renate Blumenthal, *The Investiture Controversy* (Philadelphia: Univ. of Pennsylvania Press, 1988), esp. chaps. 3–5; and on the polemical literature of the contest see I. S. Robinson, *Authority and Resistance in the Investiture Contest* (Manchester: Manchester Univ. Press, 1978). Strayer makes a case for the political impact of the conflict. Harold J. Berman argues that the reforms had even stronger legal, and as a result, economic and social consequences. See his *Law and Revolution* (Cambridge: Harvard Univ. Press, 1983).

24. Gewirth, *Marsilius of Padua: The Defender of the Peace* (New York: Columbia Univ. Press, 1951), chap. 8. The problem of church-state relations is discussed by Marsilius in the second "discourse" of his *The Defensor Pacis*, trans. Alan Gewirth (New York: Columbia Univ. Press, 1951).

25. Tierney, *The Crisis of Church and State, 1050–1300* (Englewood Cliffs: Prentice-Hall, 1964), 86. See also Robinson, *Authority and Resistance*, esp. 114–135.

26. See, for example, "Allocation in Praise of Cluny," in H. E. J. Cowdrey, ed. and trans., *The Epistolae Vagantes of Pope Gregory*, 99. See also Gregory to Ruldolf, Feb. 1079, ibid., 69.

27. Tellenbach, *Church, State and Christian Society*, 126–127.

28. Kantorowicz, *The King's Two Bodies*, 261f; 399–400.

29. Dante, *On Monarchy*, in Ralph Lerner and Muhsin Mahdi, eds., *Medieval Political Philosophy* (Ithaca: Cornell Univ. Press, 1963), 418–38.

30. Ladner, "Terms and Ideas of Renewal," in Robert L. Benson and Giles Constable, eds., *Renaissance and Renewal in the Twelfth Century* (Cambridge: Harvard Univ. Press, 1982), 1–33.

31. John F. Benton, "Consciousness of Self and Perceptions of Individuality," in Benson and Constable, eds., *Renaissance and Renewal in the Twelfth Century*, 263–95.

32. Caroline W. Bynum, *Jesus as Mother: Studies in the Spirituality of the High Middle Ages* (Berkeley: Univ. of California Press, 1982), 83.

33. Duby, *The Three Orders: Feudal Society Imagined*, trans. Arthur Goldhammer (Chicago: Univ. of Chicago Press, 1980), chaps. 21–25.

34. Wilks, *The Problem of Sovereignty in the Later Middle Ages* (Cambridge: Cambridge Univ. Press, 1964), iii.

35. A. L. Brown, "Parliament, c. 1733–1422," in R. G. Davies and J. H. Denton, *The English Parliament in the Middle Ages* (Manchester: Manchester Univ. Press, 1981), 140. On Europe generally, see Reynolds, *Kingdoms and Communities*, 319–23.

36. See Arthur Stephen McGrade, *The Political Thought of William of Ockham* (Cambridge: Cambridge Univ. Press, 1974).

37. Ibid., 106–7.

38. Ibid. 148.

39. Marsilius of Padua, *The Defensor Pacis*, 1. chaps. 4–5. See Gewirth's commentary in his *Marsilius of Padua*, 55.

40. Gewirth, *Marsilius of Padua*, 223.

41. Marsilius of Padua, *The Defensor Pacis*, 1.12.

42. Reynolds, *Kingdom and Communities*, 183.

43. Moore, *The Birth of Popular Heresy* (London: Edward Arnold, 1977), 7.

44. David Herlihy, "Women in Medieval Society" (Smith History Lecture, University of St. Thomas, Houston, 1971), 10. See also his "Alienation in Medieval Culture and Society," in Frank Johnson, ed., *Alienation: Concept, Term and Meaning* (New York: Seminar Press, 1971), 125–40. On this see also Duby, *The Three Orders*, 130–134.

45. Moore, *Birth of Popular Heresy*, vii; Moore, *The Origins of European Dissent* (New York: St. Martin's Press, 1977), 44.

46. Moore, *Origins of European Dissent*, 101.

47. Norman Cohn, *The Pursuit of the Millennium* (London: Temple Smith, 1970), 37, 68–88.

48. Guy Fourquin, *The Anatomy of Popular Rebellion in the Middle Ages* (Amsterdam: North-Holland, 1978), 94–95.

49. Moore, *Origins of European Dissent*, 136.

50. M. D. Lambert, *Medieval Heresy* (London: Edward Arnold, 1977), 178. See also Georges Duby, *The Knight, the Lady, and the Priest: The Making of Modern Marriage in Medieval France*, trans. Barbara Bray (New York: Pantheon Books, 1983), 107–110. Duby argues that one reason heresy failed "was that it was seen by its contemporaries, and represented to them by its enemies, as a kind of feminist movement."

51. Moore, *Origins of European Dissent*, 268, criticizes earlier scholars for too readily assuming such an association.

52. Lambert, *Medieval Heresy*, 229.

53. Lester K. Little, *Religious Poverty and the Profit Economy in Medieval Europe* (Ithaca: Cornell Univ. Press, 1978).

54. Ibid., 173.

55. Ibid., 201–2.

56. On Julian's distaste for monasticism, and his view that monks were the

Cynics of the Christian world, see Charles Norris Cochrane, *Christianity and Classical Culture* (New York: Oxford Univ. Press, 1957), 269-70.

57. See Donald R. Dudley, *A History of Cynicism* (New York: Gordon Press, 1974), 172-82, 204-8.

58. Ibid., 174.

59. Ibid., 211.

60. Ramsay MacMullen, *Enemies of the Roman Order* (Cambridge: Harvard Univ. Press, 1967), 60.

61. Troeltsch, *Social Teaching of the Christian Churches*, vol. 1, 161-162. For the classic statement on monastic individualism see Herbert B. Workman, *The Evolution of the Monastic Ideal* (London: Epworth Press, 1913), 22-37. See also Tellenbach, *Church, State and Christian Society*, 77-88.

62. Jaroslav Pelikan, *Jesus through the Centuries: His Place in the History of Culture* (New Haven: Yale Univ. Press, 1985), 133.

63. Cited in Little, *Religious Poverty and the Profit Economy*, 166.

64. Pelikan, *Jesus through the Centuries*, 140-41.

65. Bynum, *Jesus as Mother*, 135-146.

66. Ibid., esp. chap. 4.

67. Ibid., 146-69. On clerical misogyny see Duby, *The Knight, the Lady, and the Priest*, 145-146, 212-218.

68. Bynum, *Jesus as Mother*, 154.

69. Carroll, *The Cult of the Virgin Mary* (Princeton: Princeton Univ. Press, 1986).

70. Herlihy, "Alienation in Medieval Culture and Society." See also Duby, *The Knight, the Lady, and the Priest*, 110, 145-47.

71. Herlihy, "Women in Medieval Society," 12. See also Duby, *The Knight, the Lady, and the Priest*, 106, 218.

72. Eileen Power, "The Position of Women," in Susan G. Bell, ed., *Women: From the Greeks to the French Revolution* (Stanford: Stanford Univ. Press, 1973), 159-80.

73. Sharon K. Elkins, *Holy Women of Twelfth Century England* (Chapel Hill: Univ. of North Carolina Press, 1988), 27-38.

74. Lawrence, *Medieval Monasticism* (London: Longman, 1984), 190.

75. Herlihy, "Alienation in Medieval Culture and Society," 131-32.

76. G. Volpe, *Movimenti religiosi* (Florence, 1922), 17, cited in Herlihy, "Women in Medieval Society," 10.

77. See Carole Pateman, *The Disorder of Women* (Stanford: Stanford Univ. Press, 1989), chap. 1. Ironically, modern male thinkers such as Rousseau and Freud were convinced of women's incapacity to develop a sense of justice. But they share with the ancients the view that women, by their very nature, are antithetical to the state.

78. Ugolino de Monte Santa, *The Little Flowers of St. Francis*, trans. Raphael Brown (New York: Doubleday/Image Books, 1958), 293.

79. Ibid., 69.

80. John MacMurray, *Freedom in the Modern World* (New York: Appleton-Century, 1934), 169.

81. Porete, *Le mirouer des simples ames*, ed. Romana Guarnieri, in *Corpus Christianorum: Continuatio mediaevlis*, vol. 69 (Turnhout: Brepols, 1968), 4.4.

82. The best account in English is still Cohn, *Pursuit of the Millennium*, 148–86.

83. Ibid., 148.

84. Ibid., 161.

85. On the heresies of Marguerite Porete, see Edmund Colledge and Romana Guarniero, "The Glosses by 'M. N.' and Richard Methley to 'The Mirror of Simple Souls,' " *Archivo Italiano Per La Storia Della Pieta* 5 (1968): 357–82, esp. 372–73.

86. Porete, *Mirouer des simples ames*, 1.8–9.

87. One of the best interpretations in English of the *Mirouer* is still Evelyn Underhill's "The Mirror of Simple Souls," *Fortnightly Review* 95, (1911): 345–54.

88. Porete, *Mirouer des simples ames*, 29.1–14.

89. Sophocles, *Antigone* 523, trans. Elizabeth Wyckoff,

90. Porete, *Mirouer des simples armes*, 6.1–5. See the comment on this by Colledge and Guarnieri, "The Glosses by 'M.N' and Richard Methley," 380–381.

CODA

1. Arrow, *The Limits of Organization* (New York: W. W. Norton, 1974), 15–29; Nussbaum, *The Fragility of Goodness* (Cambridge: Cambridge Univ. Press, 1986), 78.

2. Michels, *Political Parties*, trans. Eden and Cedar Paul (New York: Collier Books, 1962), 6.

3. A point not missed by Kant. See his "Perpetual Peace: A Philosophical Sketch," trans. H. B. Nisbet, in Hans Reiss, ed., *Kant's Political Writings* (Cambridge: Cambridge Univ. Press, 1970), 101.

4. See "free" in *The Oxford English Dictionary*; for more on the etymology of the words "free" and "liberty," see Calvert Watkins, *The American Heritage Dictionary of Indo-European Roots* (Boston: Houghton Mifflin, 1985), 53; and Ernest Klein, *Comprehensive Etymological Dictionary of the English Language* (Amsterdam: Elsevier, 1971).

5. "Y" signified crossroad, the symbol of choice among the Pythagoreans, a Hellenistic Orphic cult which may have influenced the primitive Christians. The crossroad was the symbol of choice among many peoples, including the Romans, especially in the Lares cult. See Werner Jaeger, *Early Christianity and Greek Paideia* (Oxford: Oxford Univ. Press, 1961), 8–9. Cf. *James*, 3.6.

INDEX

Abba, Jesus' use of term, 299, 302

Abika, 24–28, 26–28

Abraham (Biblical figure), 339

Absolutism, and monarchy, 360–361, 385–386

Acton, Lord, 347

Adam and Eve myth, 378–379

Adam (Biblical figure), 334, 381

Adriani, N., 29, 30

Adserto (term), 260

Aeschylus, 170; civic freedom and, 114; *The Eumenides*, 177; *Libation Bearers*, 54, 111–115; *Oresteia* trilogy, 92; *The Persians*, 87, 88–89; personal freedom in, 114; *Prometheus Bound*, 166–168, 168, 169; *Seven against Thebes*, 110; *The Suppliant Maidens*, 88, 89–92

Africa, precolonial, 23–28

Agriculture: in Middle Ages, 350; Roman farmer-settlers and, 207, 210; Roman slave labor and, 212–213; and slavery, 68–70

Akhnaton, 44. *See* Amenhotep IV

Alaric, 379

Alcidamas, 151, 152–153

Alexander the Great, 143, 144, 147

Alföldy, Géza, 207

Amenhotep IV (Akhnaton), 38–41

Anaxagoras, 168, 170

Anaxilas of Larissa, 271

Anderson, William S., 268

Andrews, Anthony, 80

Anouilh, Jean, *Antigone*, 121

Anthenodorus, 269

Antigone, 401

Antigonus of Socho, 302

Antiochus of Ascalon, 264

Antiphon, 151, 153

Anti-Semitism, 390

Antisthenes, 119, 184

Apiru, 33

Apocalypse, dehistoricization of, 300–301

Apocalyptic movements, in Middle Ages, 390

Appleton, R. B., 140

Aquinas, Thomas, 384, 388

Archilochus, 88

Archinus, 136

Arete, 84, 87, 88, 101, 103–104, 165

Aristides, Aelius, 392

Aristocratic freedom. *See* Sovereignal freedom, in Pericles

Aristonicus, 270

Aristophanes, 134, 136; *The Clouds*, 137; *Lysistrata*, 137; *The Wasps*, 137

Aristotle, 10, 76, 135, 137, 147, 149, 156, 161–164, 181, 384; Diogenes and, 185; ethical values and, 434n4; *Politics*, 162; theory of ethics, 183

Arnheim, M. T. W., 139

Arnold, Edward, 266

Arnold of Brescia, 391

Arrian, *Discourses on Epictetus*, 279

Arrow, Kenneth, 402

Art, and slavery, 62–63

Arthur, Marylin B., 61

Asceticism, Christian mendicants and, 392–394, 399

Athens, exclusion of women in, 397

Atkinson, Kathleen, 256

Auctoritas, 220, 222, 223, 259, 261; concept of, 258

Augustine, 316, 377–383, 384, 392; *Confessions*, 380; Greek intellecutal tradition and, 379, 466n12; Paul's influence on, 379–380; theory of freedom, 190

Augustus, 230, 233, 380, 381; civic freedom and, 219, 233, 256, 258–260; concept of freedom for, 231, 258–263; expansion of personal freedom and, 256–257; feminist opposition and, 251; freedom in Rome under, 337; Lares cult and, 238–239; plebeians and, 233; Stoicism and, 266, 271

Authority: popular sovereignty and, 389; problem of, 388

Autocracy, 159

Averroism, 388

Bacchus *Liber*, 273

Badian, Ernst, 144, 206, 210, 214, 215

Balbi, 270

Barbarians, Roman slave latifundia and, 347–348

Bartchy, S. Scott, 320

Basanquet, Bernard, 9, 22

Beard, Mary, 217

Beguines movement, 391, 397

Beresford, 369

Berlin, Isaiah, *xii*, 3, 220

Bernal, Martin, 150, 429n17

Betz, Hans Dieter, 319

Biological selection, Pauline tradition and, 317

Bion of Borysthenes, 184

Bisson, Thomas, xvii, 365

Bleicken, Jochen, 219–220

Blickle, Peter, 368

Blossius of Cumae, 269–270

Boas, George, 178, 179

Bois, Guy, 360

Bömer, Franz, 240, 242, 243

Bonaventure, Saint, 394

Bonnassie, Pierre, 349

Bonner, Stanley F., 237

Boren, Henry, 214

Bouleutai, 75

Bouwsma, William, 368

Bradley, Keith, 249

Breasted, J. H., 38

Briscoe, John, 144

Brother, as religious term, 242

Brown, A. L., 388

Brown, Peter, 380

Bruni, Leonardo, 368

Bruno, Giordano, 190

Brunt, P. A., 215–216, 229, 231, 232, 233, 275

Brutality, and slavery, 213

Brutus, M. Junius, 264

Buckland, W. W., 220, 330

Bultmann, Rudolf, 300, 301–302, 304, 313, 327, 341

Burckhardt, Jacob, 368

Bureaucracy, in Rome, 218

Burkert, Walter, 73, 180

Burkitt, Francis C., 328

Bynum, Caroline, 394, 395

Caesar, Gaius Julius, 224–225, 233; Augustus and, 259; concept of liberty and, 223, 224–225; Stoicism and, 270

Caligula, 233

Callicles, 155, 156, 158

Callimachus, 85

Cannibalism, 14, 15–16, 269

Cantarella, Eva, 209, 250, 413n36

Carolingian period, 356

Carroll, Michael P., 395

Cassandra, 103

Catiline, 232

Cato, M. Porcius, 264, 266, 269, 270

Character, Epictetus and, 280–281

Charles-Picard, Gilbert, 271

Charlesworth, M. P., 263

Chastity, medieval cult of, 396

Cherokees, 12

Christ, Jesus. See Jesus of Nazareth

Christ, Karl, 207, 230

Christian Church: freedom from secular authority, 384–385; relation between Christ and, 337; views of slavery, 349

Christianity, 240, 242, 263; development of, 293–295; difference between slave and serf and, 355–356; early appeal of, 308–310; early doctrinal trends in, 310–312; Gnosticism and, 312–315; influence of Paul on, 295, 316; influence of secular thought in Middle Ages and, 376–382; and the inner life, 182; introduction of, 240; Jesus movement and, 295, 296–303; link between Jesus and, 304; medieval peasant rebellion and, 371–373; mendicant orders in, 391–394; name "Christ" applied to Jesus and, 306; other religions of salvation and, 294–295; phases in the development of, 295; rapid rise of, 323; rapid spread of, 306–309; Roman-Hellenistic world and, 309–310; and Stoicism, 187; types

of early missionaries in, 310–311; views on slavery in history of, 321–322; Western commitment to freedom and, xvi. See also Heresy; Jesus movement

Christian theology, 295

Christina of Markyate, 396

Chrysippus, 192, 193–195, 269, 279; On Law, 194; On Zeno's Proper Use of Terminology, 268

Church-state relations: as interpenetration, 382–383; in Middle Ages, 377, 382–384; separation of spheres and, 383–384; supremacy of church in, 383; supremacy of state and, 384. See also Power, nature of

Cicero, 223–224, 232–233, 249, 254, 264; concept of freedom, 223–224, 232–233; Roman plebs and, 232–233

Circus (Roman), 230, 231

Citizenship, Roman, 207, 229, 235, 236

Civic freedom: absence of, and slavery, 389; in Aeschylus, 89, 114; in Athens, 89, 97, 135–137, 194, 436n40; in Athens vs. Rome, 209–211; conception of, among Roman elites, 210, 221–226, 265, 266; decline of, in Greek world, 145; defined, 4–5; in Demosthenes, 142; and ethnic Greeks, 144; and Euripides, 140, 171; and gender, 77; and Greek drama, 90–91; Hortensian law of 287 and, 204, 223; and the Imbangala, 27–28; internalization of, 196; and logos, 196; in medieval society, 366, 373–374; moral contradictions of, 404; Ockham and, 389; in Pericles, 100, 103, 104; in Plato, 158; popular sovereignty and, 388–390; and Protagoras, 151, 152; size of Roman Republic and, 228; and slavery, 25, 77–78; and Socrates, 156; and the Sophists, 142; in Sparta, 143; and the Tupinamba, 18. See also Democracy

Clare, M. L., 221
Class: and Aristotle, 163–164; conflict
    and, in Rome, 211, 216; early
    Christian Church and, 322–324; in
    Greece, 48–52, 57; and slavery,
    135–145. *See also* Struggle of the
    Orders
Claudius, 244
Cleisthenean democratic revolution,
    166; Sophists and, 149–150
Cleisthenes, 74, 76, 81, 97
Clemency, 273–274, 341
Clement of Alexandria, 378
Clement (pope), 460n99
Cleon, 96
Clientela system, 206, 215, 216–218,
    225; Augustus and, 259–260; Ro-
    man slave system and, 216–217
Clodius, 232, 233
Cohn, Norman, 372, 400
Collective solidarity, and slavery, 73–
    74, 80–81
Colliberti, 355, 357
Community: communal structure in
    Rome, 227–228; freedom granted
    in charters and, 366–369; solidarity
    among local Roman elites, 206–
    207; as source of sovereignty, 388–
    390
Comprador system, 206
Constitution of Athens (Old Oligarch),
    138
Conventuals (followers of St. Fran-
    cis), 394
Convergent serfdom, 352, 353, 354–
    356, 362
Corinth, 319–321, 322–323
Cornutus, 267, 268
Courtly love, 395, 398
Crates (Cynic), 191
Crawford, Michael, 217
Crocker, Lawrence, 1
Cross, symbolism of, 304–305, 335–
    336, 405–406, 470n5
Crossman, R. H. S., 156
Cruz-Uribe, Eugene, 36
Cult of Bacchae. *See* Dionysus, cult of

Cults: Roman freedmen and, 237–
    244; world affirming, 242–244;
    world denying, 241–242
Cultural freedom, 185
Cynicism, 184–187, 191–192, 392
Cyprian, Saint, 337

Dante Alighieri, *On Monarchy*, 387,
    386
David, A. R., 40
Davies, J. K., 91
Davis, David Brion, *xiii*, 322,
    459n85
Death: and freedom, 131; social,
    slavery as, 9–10, 21–22; symbolism
    of, in Greek tragedy, 125, 126–127,
    130–132; theme of, in Paul's theol-
    ogy, 329–330, 331, 332–333
Death-life antithesis, in Paul's theol-
    ogy, 329–330, 331, 332–333
Debt bondage, 57–58, 66–67, 70, 204,
    208–209
Decretists, 384
Degler, Carl, 71
Demades, 65
Deme, 74–76, 91
Democracy, 76, 97; and aristocratic
    rule, 98–99; and Aristotle, 161–
    164; doubts about, in classical
    Greece, 404; Greece and, 74–77;
    and imperialism, 95–97; and liter-
    acy, 65–66; in medieval society,
    373–374; and Plato, 158–160, 175;
    reasons for failure of, in Rome,
    227–229; Roman civic freedom
    and, 218, 221–222, 223; among Ro-
    man elites, 229; and slavery, 96,
    97–98; and slave society, 72, 74–
    77; as threat to Roman plebeians,
    231; and women, 129. *See also*
    Civic freedom
Democritus, 152, 188
Demos, 50
Demosthenes, 142–143
Desborough, V. A., 49

De Ste. Croix, G. E. M., 64, 69–70, 96, 97, 148, 211, 262, 352, 415n26, 462n20
Determinism, Epicurus and, 188–190
Dignitas, imperial, 261
Diogenes Laërtius, 185, 193
Diogenes of Sinope, 119, 184–187, 197, 289
Dionysus, cult of, 241, 294–295
Dishonor, serfdom and, 353, 356
Divine tragedy, 122–123, 125
Divorce, in Rome, 250–251, 252
Dockès, Pierre, 356
Dodds, E. R., 92, 147, 151, 153, 156
Domesday census, 350
Dotal laws, 250–251, 253
Dover, K. J., 147, 149
Draco, 65
Dualism, in Roman thought, 274–275
Duby, Georges, 350, 357, 359, 364, 366, 388
Dudley, Donald R., 186–187, 269, 392
Duling, Dennis, 304, 305

Earl, Donald, 219, 221, 225, 260
Easter faith, 305, 306, 309, 310, 311–312, 313
Eastern Europe, serfdom in, 361–362
Ebionites, 316
Economic crisis, and peasant rebellion, 372
Ehrenberg, Victor, 74, 120, 121, 156
Electra myth, 115–117, 139–140
Eliade, Mircea, 294
England. *See* Great Britain
England, E. B., 432n18
English Parliament, 369–370, 388
English peasant revolt of 1381, 372–373
Entertainments, and distraction of underclass, 230
Epathroditus, 283
Ephialtes, 72, 76, 97, 98

Epictetus, 198–199, 340, 392; *Discourses*, 278–284, 289; parallels with Marcus Aurelius, 275–278, 285, 289
Epicureanism, 187–190
Epicurus, 187–190
Equality: gender, 248–249, 395; political, in Rome, 221, 223–224
Ethical teachings, of Jesus, 298
Ethnicity, identification of slavery with, 357
Euripides, 116, 119, 121, 139, 140, 141, 161, 169–173; *The Bacchae*, 110, 119, 141, 171–173, 178–180; Electra myth, 115–117, 139–140; *Hecuba*, 117–20; *Iphigenia in Aulis*, 140–141, 170; Plato and, 178–180
Exploitation: in feudal England, 370–371; of rural Roman masses, 347–348

Faith, in Paul's theology, 332–333
Familia, 215
Farrar, Cynthia, 152, 154
Fate, in Chrysippus, 193–194
Father-daughter relation, and elite Roman women, 252-256
Feminism: heresy and, 468n50; among Roman elites, 251
Fernandes, Florestan, 15
"Filiafocality," 252, 446n92
Fine, John V. A., 96
Finley, Moses I., xiv, 50, 56, 67, 68, 96, 97, 98, 181, 208, 222, 228, 247, 249
Flagellant movement, 395
Florence, Italy, 368
Florentinus, 220
Fortuna cult, 240, 242
Fourquin, Guy, 372, 390
France, 361, 461n7
Francis of Assisi, 393–394
Frank, Tenney, 208, 209–210, 235
Frankfort, Henri, 37
Fraternities, in Middle Ages, 366
Free customs, 364, 366–369

Free will, 188–190

Freedmen: in African culture, 24–28; and convergent serfdom, 354; in Greece, 71, 79, 134–135; in Near Eastern culture, 34–36; in South Pacific culture, 31–32. *See also* Roman freedmen

Freedom, 187; and *arete*, 101, 103–104; aristocratic conception of, 84–87, 93, 97; Aristotle's view of, 161–164; and assent, 194; in Christian doctrine, 294–295, 303; in Christian kerygma, 313–314; in classical Greece, 2; continuity of, *xii–xiii*; and death, 131; defined, 3–4; among elite males, 422*n*21; as enslavement to God, 378–379; and friendship, 190; and gender, 4, 53–55, 59, 62, 104–105; as gift, 340, 380–381, 387; Gnostic view of, 313–314, 319; good and evil as inherent in, 402–406; in Greece vs. Rome, 220; and Greek drama, 88–90, 121, 126, 127–129; influence of Christian doctrine and, 376–382; intrinsically positive, 192; Jesus' religious behavior and, 298–300; Jesus' religious pronouncements and, 301–302; in Middle Ages, 372–373, 374; negative view of, 358–359; in Paul's doctrine, 318, 319, 338–339; and Plato, 176–178; Plato's view of, 156–161; and power, 178; as power, 154–155, 168, 169, 171–172, 183; search for meaning of, 277–278; as total power, 36–38, 39–41; traffic in, in Middle Ages, 374–375; and virtue, 195. *See also* Civic freedom; Inner freedom; Inner vs. outer freedom; *Libertas*; Personal freedom; Sovereignal freedom

Freeman, among Tupinamba, 27–28

Free Spirit movement, 385, 391, 399–401

Fee status, value placed on, and freedom as value, 363

French Revolution, 361

Frend, W. H. C., 319, 338

Freud, Sigmund, 469*n*77

Friendship, 190, 399

Galba, Servius Sulpicius, 260

Garlan, Yvon, 55, 70

Garnsey, Peter, 68, 207, 213, 224, 240

Gelb, Ignatious, 22, 33, 34

Gender, and freedom, 4, 53–55, 59, 62, 104–105

Gender equality: and religion, 395; under slavery, 248–249. *See also* Women

Gentiles: early Christianity and, 306, 317; views of Jesus toward, 296–297. *See also* Paul of Tarsus

Geoffery, Abbot, 396

Germanicus, 233

Germany: medieval towns in, 368; peasant revolution of 1525 in, 368, 371, 373; serfdom in, 361–362

Gewirth, Alan, 384, 389

Gift exchange, among Romans, 254

Giles, F. J., 38

Gilson, Etienne, 378

Giovanni da Prato, 368

Gnostic gospels, 299, 312

Gnosticism, 312–315

God(s): Epictetus and, 282–283, 284; female view of, 399; freedom as identity with, 386–387, 399–401; freedom as submission to, 282, 340–342, 343–344, 378–379; freedom of, 341, 385; Jesus' approach to, 301–302; man's relation to, in Pauline theology, 326–327

Goguel, Maurice, 296, 305, 337

Goldhill, Simon, 109, 124

Goodenough, Erwin R., 340

Gordon, R. L., 241, 243, 244

Gorgias, 151, 155

Gospel of Thomas, 299

Gracchan reforms, 215, 222, 270

Gracchi, the, 214, 224, 233, 269–270; Stoicism and, 269

Gracchus, Tiberius, 214, 269–270

Grant, Michael, 259, 261

Grant, Robert, 337

Graus, F., 371

Great Britain: in history of freedom, 369–371; medieval peasant rebellion in, 371–373; slavery in, 349–350, 461n10; urban freedoms in, 368

Greece: ancient, and slavery, 42; aristocratic resurgence, 55–63; class structure in, 57; decentralized tribalism and, 49–50; and democratization, 74–77, 91; importance of intellectuals in, 147–148; Metics in, 90–91, 133–138; misogyny in, 60, 61; Mycenae, 48–49; and resident aliens, 92; and Roman conquest, 144–145; rudimentary state formation and, 50–55; and slave society, 70–72; status of rural masses in, 415n26

Greek tragedy: as cultural evidence, 108–109; and dog imagery, 118–119; and hair imagery, 171; and light imagery, 117–118, 423n52; Persian wars and, 87–89; symbolic antitheses in, 125–126; and women, 109–120, 127–132; women in, 397–398

Gregorian reforms, 383, 391

Gregory VII (pope), 385

Grene, David, 166–167

Gruen, Erich S., 143–144

Guilds, in Middle Ages, 366–367

Guthrie, W. K. C., 150, 179

Hadrian, 277

Hallett, Judith P., 209, 251, 252, 253, 255–256, 445n90

Hammond, Mason, 260

Hannibalic wars. See Punic Wars

Hanson, Richard, 337

Harding, Alan, 364, 365

Harris, William V., 211

Havelock, Erik A., 148, 152, 153

Haynes, Denys, 62

Hegel, Georg, 185

Heichelheim, F. M., 50, 67

Heliopolitae, 270

Hellenistic Jewish Mission Christianity, 305–306

Hellie, Richard, 361

Hengel, Martin, 307, 308

Henry IV (German king), 384

Henry of Lausanne, 390–391

Henry VII (king of England), 384

Hera, cult of, 397

Heracles, 186

Heresy, 390–401, 468n50. See also Pelagian heresy

Herington, John, 87, 88, 168

Herlihy, David, 371

Herodotus, 81, 84, 93, 103, 413n43

Herrin, Judith, 376

Hesiod, 56–63, 64–66

Hillel (Pharisee), 298

Hilton, Rodney, 350, 351

Hippias, 151, 152

Hobbes, Thomas, 10, 384

Hogan, 114

Holt, J. C., 370

Homer, 50, 51–55, 60, 84, 85; Odyssey, 288

Honor, fusion with power, in feudal period, 358–359. See also Dishonor

Honor price, 356

Hooker, Richard, 384

Hopkins, Keith, 235

Hoplite revolution, 65

Horace, 229, 245–247, 268, 271

Hornblower, Simon, 91

Hortensian Law of 287 B.C., 204, 210, 223

Humanistic individualism, of the Sophists, 149

Human sacrifice, 21

Humiliati movement, 391

Hyperides, 136

Iamblichus, 152
Iliad, 52–53, 54
Imbangala, 24–28
Imperator, 259
Incest, 269
Indirect rule, Roman, 206–207. *See also* Self-government, in medieval towns
Individuals: Christian redemption and, 332–333; Jesus movement and, 300–301; in Roman republic, 223–225; Sophists and, 149; in twelfth century, 387–388. *See also* Personal freedom
Inner freedom, 165–180, 183, 185, 193, 195, 196, 198; absolute freedom and, 281–283, 284; and Antisthenes, 184; asceticism and, 392–394, 399; and Christianity, 169; citizen-identified version of, 283; and Cynicism, 186; and Epicurus, 187; and Euripides, 178; Gnosticism and, 313; god-identified view of, 283, 284; in Greek tragedy, 167–173; in Pauline theology, 327–331; and Plato, 177; Roman vs. Greek views of, 274; and women, 171
Inner vs. outer freedom, 146–147, 193; Epictetus and, 278, 279–284; Epicurus and, 187–190; Marcus Aurelius and, 278 284–289; organic view of, 285; Stoics and, 265–268, 269, 272–273, 277
Intellectuals, 147–148
Irenaeus, 314, 315
Isaeus, 137
Isocrates, 143
Israelites, 33–34
Italy: expansion of Rome into, 204, 205–207; impact of Punic Wars on, 212; medieval towns in, 368; persistence of slavery in, 361
Ivo of Chartres, 384

Jacobsen, Thorkild, 36, 44
Jamaica, 77
James, T. G. H., 36
James (brother of Jesus), 305, 318
James I (king of England), 375
Jameson, Michael, 71
Janus, 275
Jaspers, Karl, 377
Jaeger, Werner, 378
Jesus movement, 296–303; differences within, 305–306; Hellenistic world and, 306–307; social doctrine of, 298, 301–303
Jesus of Nazareth, 295, 378, 381, 382, 385, 394; as charismatic, 300; death and resurrection of, 334–336; as incarnate slave, 458n61; originality of, 301; Paul and, 333–336; peculiarities of, 298–300; role in Jesus movement, 307; sermon on the mount, 302–303; slave metaphor and, 302; symbolism of the cross and, 304–305, 335–336, 405–406, 470n5; teachings of, 296–303; titles applied to, 306; use of term *Abba*, 299, 302
Jewish law, 338; Easter faith and, 305; freedom from, in Paul's teachings, 328–329; human relationships with God and, 299–300; Jesus' attitude toward, 299; Paul's knowledge of, 325
Jewish sects, 297
Jews: Jesus as Messiah and, 304–305; Jesus movement and, 296, 300; Pauline Christianity, 327–328
Jimbanza, 26–28
John the Baptist, 296
Jones, A. H. M., 71, 323
Julian, 392
Justification by faith: Augustine and, 379; in Paul's theology, 333
Justinian, 220, 355
Juvenal, 251, 323

Kabosenja, 29
Kantorowicz, Ernst, 377
Kasanje, 25–26
Keats, John, 276
Kee, Howard C., 308
Kingdom of God, in Jesus' teaching, 296, 297–298, 300
Kirschenbaum, Aaron, 215, 254
Kitto, H. D. F., 108, 421*n*13
Knights, 358–359, 388
Kopytoff, Igor, 23, 24
Krieger, Leonard, 1
Kroner, Richard, 178
Kruyt, Albert C., 29, 30
Kyrtatas, Dimitris J., 323

Lacey, W. K., 62
Ladner, Gerhart, 387
Lane, Ann, 129
Lane, Warren, 129
Lares cult, 237–240, 443*n*42
Large-scale slavery: freedom of lower-class women and, 247–248; impact in Greece vs. Rome, 227; Paul's theology of freedom and, 319–324; persistence of, into feudal age, 348–351; plagues of seventh century and, 349; timing of, in Athens vs. Rome, 210–211. *See also* Slave society
Larsen, J. A. O., 142
Law: Augustus' concept of freedom and, 260, 262; freedom of Roman women and, 250–251; majoritarian rule and, 389; political equality in Rome and, 223–224; Roman concept of freedom and, 220. *See also* Jewish law; Medieval law; Roman law
Law-grace antithesis, in Paul's theology, 328–329, 331, 332
Lawrence, C. H., 397
Lay sisterhoods, 397, 398
Leocrates, 136
Levitas popularis, 234
Levy, Ernst, 457*n*40

Lex Poetelia Papiria de nexis (326 B.C.), 208, 210
Liberalis potestas, 364, 365
Libertas: Caesarean vs. Ciceronian view of, 223–224; in early Rome, 210; as economic security, 230; elitist conception of, in Rome, 219, 221–222, 223, 225–226, 233–234; in late Roman republic, 219–226; literary sources on, 219–220; in middle and late Roman Republic, 211–219; as term, 219–221
Lincoln, Abraham, 1
Literacy, and democracy, 65–66
Locke, John, 10, 92, 101, 389, 420*n*23
Loraux, Nicole, 103–104
Louis of Bavaria, 390, 394
Love: in Christian teachings, 302, 337, 340; freedom as, 129; Free Spirit movement and, 400–401
Loyn, R. H., 348, 350, 351
Lucan, 266
Lucretius, 187
Ludwig of Bavaria, 389
Luther, Martin, 316, 338, 384
Lycurgus, 136
Lysias, 135, 137

Machiavelli, Niccolò, 384
MacIver, Robert, 2
MacMullen, Ramsay, 231, 266, 392
MacMurray, John, 399
Macrae, George W., 314
Magna Carta, 364
Magna Mater, cult of, 241
Majoritarian rule, 389
Mann, Michael, 11, 12, 32, 43
Manumission: in African culture, 24–28; Augustus and, 256–257; Delphic, 426*n*3; in Greece, 95, 134–135, 162; Lares cult and, 237–238; in Paul's writings, 338–341; in preliterate cultures, 21–24; serfdom and, 354–355, 360; of women, in Rome, 248–249

Manumission rate: for ethnic Greeks, 144; expectations of slaves and, 320; in urban vs. rural system, 214–215, 235

Marcionites, 316

Marcus Aurelius: *Meditations*, 276, 278, 284–289; parallels with Epictetus, 275–278, 285, 289

Marius, 216

Marriage, and Roman law, 250, 257

Marsilius of Padua, 384, 389–390

Martial, 323

Martyr, Justin, 392

Marx, Groucho, 218

Marxist interpretation, of ancient Rome, 227, 441n3

Mary cult, 394–396, 397, 399

Mary Magdalene, 299

Masses. *See* Roman freedmen; Roman plebians

Materialism, 187, 244

Mattingly, Harold, 230, 274

Mauss, Marcel, 254

Mavala, 26–28

Maximus, 392

Medieval law, 364–375

Meeks, Wayne A., 310, 320, 322, 330, 338

Men, and slavery, 78–79, 83

Menard, Jacques E., 313

Mendelsohn, Isaac, 35

Mendicants, 391–394, 398–401

Menippus of Gadara, 184

Mens Bona cult, 240

Mesopotamia, 22, 34, 36

Messianic movements, 372

Metics, 90–91, 92, 133–138, 162

Métraux, Alfred, 14

Michels, Robert, 405

Middle Ages: freedom in cities during, 367–369; guilds, 366–367; medieval charters, 364–366; medieval law, 364–375; persistence of slavery in, 348–351

Miers, Suzanne, 23, 24

Miller, Joseph C., 24, 25–28

Miltiades, 84–85

Milton, John, 397

Miracles, 297, 300, 304, 308, 309

Misogynistic literature, 251

Misogyny: in Athenian and American democracy, 405; in Greece, 60–61; in Middle Ages, 397

Mithraism, 242–244, 294, 295

Mommsen, Theodor, 227

Monarchy: absolutism and, 385–386; proprietary serfdom and, 360–361

Mondolfo, Rudolph, 67

Mooney, Donald J., 272

Moore, R. I., 390

Moral introspection, 182

Mummius, 321

Munck, Johannes, 318

Muslim fundamentalists, 403

Mystery cults, 240–244; Christianity and, 306

Nag Hammadi texts, 313–314

Nagy, Gregory, 54

Naming practice, in Rome, 254–255

Natal alienation: Antigone and, 128–129; serfdom and, 128–129, 352, 356, 361–362

Naturalistic functionalism, in the *Republic,* 157

Naturalistic introspection, 184

Natural justice, 110, 116, 130, 398, 400

Nature, vs. convention in Greek tragedy, 166, 172, 179

Nazi Germany, 404

Near East, 33–41

Nefertiti, (queen), 39

Nero, 233, 276, 279, 283

Nerva, 262

Ngundu, 25

Nicolet, Claude, 217, 222, 225, 228, 231

Nietzsche, Friedrich, 156, 316

Nike (goddess of victory), 85–86

Nock, A. D., 294

Non-Western cultures: concept of freedom in, *x*; critics of freedom and, 403; sovereignal freedom and, 43, 44

North American Indians, and slavery, 12

Numismatics, 259

Nunneries, 396

Nussbaum, Martha, 109, 118, 129, 402, 405

Nygren, Anders, 336

Obsequium, 255, 261

Odyssey, 51–52

Oldfather, W. A., 283

Old Oligarch, 138, 142

Oligarchy: democracy and, 405; power of Roman emperors and, 262; in eighteenth-century England, 370

Oliver, James H., 72–73, 85, 86, 87

Oppian Law of 195 B.C., 209

Optimates, 222–225, 237

Organic freedom, 157; in Athens, 135–137; Augustus and, 231, 258–263; as dominant conception of, in West, 403-404; inner man and, 285; in Mithraism, 243–244; and personal freedom, 244, 273–274; in Plato, 160–161; Roman plebeians and, 231; Roman populares and, 224–226; in thought of Middle Ages, 382. *See also* Sovereignal freedom

Original sin, notion of, 334

Osborne, Robin, 74–76

Ostwald, Martin, 76, 91, 98, 99, 121, 149, 150

Outer freedom, 165–180, 166, 185; and Cynicism, 186; in Greek tragedy, 167–173; organic view, 165; in Plato, 159, 177; and women, 170, 171. *See also* Inner freedom; Inner vs. outer freedom

Ovid, 271

Pagels, Elaine, 313–314, 378

Panaetius of Rhodes, 195–196, 264

Parliamentary democracy, 370

Pastoralism: in ancient Italy, 212–213

Patria potestas, 250, 252–253

Paul of Tarsus, 315, 377–380, 454*n*20; charismatics and, 310–311; conversion of, 306, 458*n*74; doctrine of freedom and, 311, 318–319; inconsistencies in writings of, 325–326; as the second founder of Christianity, 316–319; social context of theology of, 319–324; theology of freedom of, 325–337; two freedoms of, 337–344

Peculium, 134, 138, 215, 253, 340. *See also* Gift exchange

Peisistratids, 72–73, 74

Peisistratus, 73

Pelagian heresy, 380, 390

Peloponnesian War, and slavery, 133–134

Perdue, Theda, 12

Peregrinus, (Proteus), 392

Pericles, 76, 96, 99–105, 120, 168, 420*n*35; and civic freedom, 100, 103, 104; and personal freedom, 100–101, 104

Perrin, Norman, 304, 305

Persian wars, 83, 87–89

Persius, 266, 267–268

Personal freedom, 23, 196; in Aeschylus, 114; in Aristotle, 161–162; in Athens, 79, 135–137, 142; in Augustinian doctrine, 379–380; critics of, 403; and Cynics, 184, 185; defined, 3, 4; in early Greece, 53, 54; economic insecurity and, 208–209; of elite Roman women, 249–256; in Euripides, 116, 119, 141; good and evil aspects of, 402–403; in Hellenistic world, 144; heresy and, 390–391; and the Imbangala, 24–25; individual rights in Rome and, 223–226; inner vs. outer freedom and, 279–284; in medieval period, 366, 369, 371,

Personal freedom (*cont.*)
372–373, 396–401; Near Eastern
cultures and, 34–36; negative
(non-slavery), 3, 141, 162, 198,
220; non-Western world and, 42,
43; Ockham and, 389; organic
freedom and, 244, 272–274; in
Paul's theology, 337–344, 379; in
Pericles, 100–101, 104; in Plato,
158, 160, 183; as recent concept,
xii–xiii; religion as support for,
395; Roman concept of, 220; Roman freedwomen and, 247–249;
Roman plebeians and, 231, 233,
234–236; under rule of law, 284;
and slavery, 17, 22; and Sophists,
153, 154; in Sophocles, 131–132;
sovereignl freedom and, 256,
273–274, 337–344, 379; and Stoicism, 197; Stoic view of, 267; as
value, *xv*, 398, 399, 400; and
women, *xv*, 54, 78, 109–120, 137,
170–171, 398, 399, 400. *See also* Inner freedom
Peter (apostle), 383
Petronius, 236, 323; *Satyricon*, 245
Philemon, Paul's letter to, 320
Philip V of Macedon, 143, 229
Philo, 197–198
Pindar, 85, 89, 101
Pirenne, Henri, 367–368
Plantation system, 213, 349
Plato, 10, 119, 149, 156, 161, 170,
181, 286, 403, 404; Euripides and,
178–180; *Laws*, 159–161, 176; meta-
phor of slavery and, 163; *Phaedo*,
174; *Republic*, 157–159, 174–175;
Statesman, 176; theory of the soul,
173–178
Plea rolls, 365–366
Pleasure, 188
Pliny the Younger, 249
Plutarch, 67, 73, 190, 232
Pohlenz, Max, *xiv–xv*, 79–81, 82, 84,
148, 187
Polus, 155
Pompey, 233, 270

Popper, Karl, 156, 157
Populares, 222–225, 230, 270
Porcia (daughter of Cato), 264
Porete, Marguerite, 399, 400, 401
Portugal, slavery in, 349
Posidonius, 195–196, 264
Postliminium, 331–332, 343
Power: elite Roman women and,
255–256; of emperor, and Roman
people, 260–262; freedom and,
178; fusion with honor in feudal
period, 358–359; localization of,
and large-scale slavery, 347–348;
nature of, in European thought,
382, 384–387; negative freedom
and, 398; over others, in Middle
Ages, 364–366; of rural masses, in
Middle Ages, 360
Power, Eileen, 396
Praxagora, 137
Princeps, 266
Private enterprise, 215
Propaganda: early spread of Christi-
anity and, 307–308; on liberty in
Britain, 369; on liberty in Rome,
225–226
Proprietary serfdom, 352, 353, 360–362
Protagoras, 149, 151–152, 154
Punic Wars, 211–213; socioeconomic
impact of, 211–213, 438n26
Pythagoras, 173
Pythagoreans, 271

Qumran community, 297, 298

Raaflaub, Kurt, *xiv–xv*, 55, 79–81, 84,
204, 428n6
Racism: American, 405; European
civilization and, 357
Rawson, Beryl, 236, 445n90
Rebirth: Christianity and, 294, 387;
Mithraism and, 244; in Paul's the-
ology, 332–333

Redemption, in Paul's theology: in cosmic time, 334–336; dynamics of, 326, 334–337; fundamental categories of, 327–332; means of, 326, 333–334; processes of, 326, 332–333; in structural terms, 336–337

Redford, Donald, 38, 39, 40

Relativism, 150–151, 280

Religion: Christianity and, 293–295; emergence of Europe and, 376–377; feminization of images in, 394–395, 399; intellectuals and, 148; Jesus' approach to, as existential, 298–299; Roman freedmen and, 237–244; salvation and, 294; and slavery, 30, 73–74; sovereignal freedom and, 404. See also Christianity; Church-state relation; Cults; Heresy; Jesus movement; Mystery cults; Stoicism

Religions of salvation, 240–244, 293–295. See also Christianity

Resident aliens, in Greece. See Metics

Resurrection of Jesus, 304–305, 306, 313, 334–336. See also Cross, symbolism of

Reynolds, Susan, 370, 463n1

Richard, Jean-Claude, 204

Richardson, H. G., 370

Ricoeur, Paul, 334

Rights: of medieval English peasants, 371; of serfs, 358. See also Civic freedom; Individuals; Voting

Rist, John M., 191, 196

Ritual, in Christianity, 336–337, 400

Roman economy: and debt bondage, 208–209; expropriated land and, 205, 207; Hannibalic wars and, 212; rural, 211–213, 217; urban, 214–216, 235

Roman elegists, and women, 251–252

Roman emperor: bondage of, 276–277, 278, 286; masses' view of ideal leader and, 234

Roman freedmen: appeal of early Christianity and, 231, 322–324; economic status of, 208–209, 243–244; elite attitudes toward, 229, 444n61; influence on religious life, 237–244; master-identified freedom of, 283; naming practice and, 254; political influence of, 236–237; predominance of descendents of, 235; secular values and, 244–247; Stoic view of freedom and, 267–268; in urban Rome, 215

Roman law: marriage and, 250, 257; postliminium in, 331–332, 335; slave relation and, 355

Roman plebeians: co-optation of, 204–205, 206–207; as corrupted class, 230–231; expropriated land and, 205; personal freedom of, 225–226; political behavior of, 229–230, 231–234; ruling elite and, 233–234; slave ancestry of, 229, 235–236

Roman women: elite, personal freedom of, 249–256; freeborn, 209; lower class, personal freedom of, 247–249; sexual freedom and, 241; sublation of personal to sovereignal power, 256

Rome: civic culture in, 218; co-optation of barbarian leaders and, 348; co-optation of plebeian leaders in, 204–205, 206–207; defeated peoples and, 205–206; elite conception of freedom in, 210, 221–226, 265, 266; exploitation of the rural masses and, 347–348; female formidability in, 209; imperial expansion and, 205–207; indirect rule and, 206–207; intra-elite conflict in, 205–206, 211; literary sources on, 219; Marxist interpretation of, 227, 441n3; nature of slavery in, 207; as a patriarchal society, 209; political system in, in late Republic, 216–219; rise of Christianity and, xvi; slave ancestry of

Rome (*cont.*)
  population in, 229, 235–236,
  245–247; struggle of the orders in,
  203–211
Rosenmeyer, Thomas G., 178
Rostovtzeff, M., 143
Rousseau, Jean-Jacques, 469n77
Routinization, process of, 296
Rudolph, Kurt, 312
Ruling elites: in early Christian
  church, 323; early spread of Christianity and, 309–310; in medieval
  towns, 368–369; proprietary serfdom and, 360, 361; in Rome, and
  adscripticius status, 355; in Rome,
  and class co-optation, 204–205,
  206–207
Rural masses. *See also* Serfdom
Russell, Bertrand, 3, 4
Russia, serfdom in, 361–362, 463n37

Sahlins, Marshal, 13, 43
Saller, Richard, 207, 240
Sallust, 256, 264, 266, 448n5
Salvation: Christian notion of free-
  dom and, 311–314, 315; Paul's the-
  ology of, 326
Sartre, Jean-Paul, 42
Sayles, G. O., 369, 370
Scandinavia, 349, 461n9
Schillebeeckx, Edward, 299, 303, 310,
  311
Schultz, Fritz, 250
Scipio Aemilianus, 270
Scott, Charles, 335
Secessio (political strike), 204
Segal, Charles, 125, 127, 128
Siegel, Bernard J., 35
Self-government, in medieval towns,
  367–369. *See also* Indirect rule
Self-knowledge, 313–314
Self-realization, 400
Seneca, 272–274; *On Clemency*, 273–
  274, 276
Serf, vs. slave, 355

Serfdom, 353, 356–359; coexistence
  of slavery with, in middle ages,
  351; degradation of, 358; drive for
  emacipation under, 351–353; legal
  attachment to the land and, 360;
  types of, 352
Serf (term), 355
Servile types, constitutive elements
  of, 9–10; serfdom and, 353;
  women and, 78
Severus, Alexander, 262–284
Shamelessness: and the Cynics, 185;
  and Diogenes, 186; and Zeno, 191
Shaw, George Bernard, 316
Shelton, Jo-Ann, 249
Silvanus cult, 240
Simonides, 85
Sin: enslavement to, 327–328, 330,
  343; freedom from temptation of,
  381–382; as weakness, in Paul's
  theology, 330
Sin-reconciliation antithesis, in
  Paul's theology, 330, 331
Slave, as term, 357
Slavery: acceptance of institution of,
  in ancient world, 321; and agriculture, 68–70; in ancient Greece, 42;
  in Aristotle, 162–163; and art, 62–
  63; in Athenian and American democracy, 405; and cannibalism,
  14, 15–16; and Cherokees, 12; and
  class, 135–145; coexistence of serfdom with, in Middle Ages, 351–
  353; and collective solidarity, 73–
  74, 80–81; communal structure in
  Roman Republic and, 227–228;
  constitutive elements of, 352; cultural conceptions of, 10; and Cynicism, 184; and debt bondage, 57–
  58, 66–67, 70; defined, 9–10; and
  hired labor, 71; and human sacrifice, 21; and the Imbangala, 24–28;
  and the Israelites, 33–34; and Kasanje, 25–26; as liberating, in
  Rome, 244–247, 248–249, 252–256;
  and manual labor, 67–68, 70; and
  men, 78–79, 83; in Mesopotamia,

Slavery (*cont.*)
22, 34, 36; in the Near East, 33–41;
and North American Indians, 12;
Persia and, 83–84; and Plato, 174–
176; in precolonial Africa, 23–28;
release from, 23, 26, 31, 34–35, 42,
95, 134–135; and religion, 30, 73–
74; Roman law on, 331–332; and
skilled labor, 439*n*33; as social
death, 9–10, 21–22; in the South
Pacific, 28–33; threat of, and debt
bondage in Rome, 208; and the
Toradja, 22, 28–33; and Tupinamba, 13–19, 22; and United
States, 71; and value of freedom,
16–17, 19, 20, 41–42, 55; and
women, 21, 31, 50–52, 53–54, 58–
59, 60, 78, 128; in Zeno, 193. *See
also* Large-scale slavery
Slavery-freedom antithesis, in Paul's
theology, 327–328, 330–332
Slave society: appeal of Christianity
in, 309; defined, 72; and democracy, 72, 74–77; and Greece, 70–
72; localization of power and, 347–
348
Slave system: *clientela* system and,
216–217; in rural Italy, 212–214,
228; in urban Rome, 214–215, 235.
See also Large-scale slavery
Slavic peoples, 357
Smith, John H., 379
Smith, Morton, 307–308
Snodgrass, A. M., 49
Social conflict, in medieval England,
371
Social War (91–89 B.C.), 206, 216
Socrates, 151, 155, 156, 165, 181,
182–183, 434*n*4
Soldiers, Roman, 216
Solon, 64, 66–68, 69, 72–73, 74, 76,
79
Sophists, 148–155, 158, 165, 166;
civic freedom and, 142; humanistic
individualism of, 149; and relativ-
ism, 150–151, 153; and slavery,
162

Sophocles, 120, 170; *Antigone*, 99,
117, 121–132; Electra myth, 115–
117; *Oedipus at Colonus*, 168–169
South Pacific, 28–33
Sovereignal freedom, 3–4, 17, 25, 26,
28, 32–33, 37, 39–40, 43, 44, 94;
Akhnaton and, 39–40; and the
Pharaoh, 37; aristocratic rule in
England and, 369–371; in Athens,
94; of Augustus, 231, 258; Christian mendicants and, 393–394; defined, 3–4; in Demosthenes, 142;
dominance of, in Middle Ages,
359, 363, 373–374, 376–387; in Euripides, 141; in feudal society,
365–366; good and evil aspects
of, 403–404; and Gorgias, 155;
Homeric notion of, 82; and the
Imbangala, 25, 26, 28; and
imperialism, 96; intellectual recon-
structionism of, 154; nature of, in
Middle Ages, 362; non-Western
world and, 43, 44; organic form
of, 164, 193, 231, 258, 273–274,
382; in Paul's writings, 337–344; in
Pericles, 101–102, 103, 104; personal freedom and, 256, 273–274,
337–344, 379; and Plato, 157, 160–
161; as power over others, 4, 43,
364–366; as privilege, 359; religious thought in Middle Ages
and, 376–387; Roman concept of,
220–221; Roman conquest and,
144; in Sophocles, 128, 130; and
Sparta, 93; and the Toridja, 32–33;
and the Tupinamba, 17; in Zeno,
193. *See also* Organic freedom
Spain, 349
Sparta, 92–93, 143
Spiritual freedom, 145; defined, 180.
See also Inner freedom.
Spirituals (followers of St. Francis),
394
Starr, Chester G., 58, 71
Steiner, George, 130, 131
Stendahl, Krister, 316, 317, 318, 328,
330, 338, 456*n*12, 458*n*74

Stephen (follower of Jesus), 305, 306, 307, 308
Stoicism, 191–199, 264–290; appeal of, to Roman elites, 265–266; and Cynicism, 187; differences between reformist and reactionary, 268–269; dominance of, 263; Epictetus and, 275–284, 289; Gnostic views and, 313; imperial version of, 270, 271; Marcus Aurelius and, 275–278, 284–289; reactionary form of, 266; reformist form of, 268–275; search for meaning of freedom and, 289–290; Seneca and, 272–274
Stough, Charlotte, 196–197, 269
Strayer, Joseph R., 377
Struggle of the Orders, in Rome, 203–205; absence of large-scale slavery during, 211; effects, 221; impact on development of freedom, 207–211
Stubbs, William, 369
Suetonius, 256
Suffering, in Paul's theology, 342
Sulla, 217
Sussman, Linda S., 61
Symbolic antitheses, categories of, 125–126
Symbolic interactionism, 151–152
Syme, Ronald, 226, 256, 259

Tacitus, 228, 256, 261, 262
Taplin, Oliver, 108
Tatian, 392
Tellenbach, Gerd, 385
Tenant farmers, in Europe, 354
Tenurial franchise, 364, 365–366
Territorial immunity, 364–365, 374
Theissen, Gerd, 311, 322
Theodosius, 354
Theognis of Megara, 64, 65
Theophrastus, 73
Thetai, 50
Third World, 214

Thompson, E. A., 348
Thrasybulus, 135
Thucydides, 103, 142
Tiberius, 233, 262
Tierney, Brian, 384
Timocracy, 158
Tiro, 249, 254
Todd, Robert B., 191, 192
Topitsch, E., 424
Toradja, 22, 28–33, 116
Toutain, Jules, 68
Toynbee, Arnold, 204, 211
Treggiari, Susan, 240, 245
Tribunate, 223, 233
Tribunicia potestas, 233–34, 259, 261
Troeltsch, Ernst, 393, 466n1
Turner, Victor, 127
Tyler, Wat, 373
Tyrtaeus, 85

U.S. South, 71, 213, 356, 362
Universalism: Paul's theology and, 339; of primitive Christianity, 308–309
Urban economy, slavery and, 214
Utilitarianism, 188, 190

Values: freedom and, for Epictetus, 278; influence of Roman freedmen and, 244–247; in Jesus' teachings, 298; in Roman republic, 221, 222
Varro, M. Terentius, 264
Vassalage, 357–358
Venice, Italy, 349, 368
Vermeule, Emily, 118
Verna, 277–278
Vernant, Jean-Pierre, 49, 51, 65
Vespasian, 260
Vidal-Naquet, Pierre, 79
Virgil, 271
Virtue: for Diogenes, 191; European nobility and, 359; and Roman masses, 234; Roman values and,

Virtue (*cont.*)
221, 222, 234, 260; Stoicism and, 266, 267, 268, 269
Virtus. See Virtue
Vlastos, Gregory, 175–176
Voting: in Roman Republic, 222, 228

War: *clientela* system and, 216; development of slave system and, 438n29; Roman social orders based on, 211. *See also specific wars*
Warrior, Valerie, *xvii*, 423n29, 435n20
Wealth: *clientela* system and, 216–217; slave system and, 212
Weber, Max, 35, 36, 37, 44, 294, 296
Welfare, in Rome, 230, 231
Western civilization: moral contradictions of freedom in, 402–406; racism at beginnings of, 357
Western Europe, slavery in, 349–351
West Indies, 414n12
Whitehead, Alfred North, 34, 40, 177
Whitehead, David, 79, 135, 137
Wiedmann, Thomas, 235
Wilks, Michael, 388
William of Ockham, 384, 388–389
Wilson, John A., 40
Wirszubski, C., 219, 220, 224
Women: ambivalence toward, in Middle Ages, 396–398; in Athenian and American democracy, 405; early Christianity and, 310; empathy with slaves, 78; exclusion of, in Athens, 129; in Greek drama, 100–120, 127–132, 397–398; heretical mysticism and, 391, 395, 398–401; natural justice and, 110, 116, 398, 400; *patria potestas* and, 252–253; personal freedom and, *xv*, 54, 78, 137, 170–171, 398, 399, 400; Roman elegists and, 251; and slavery, 137; social conditions of, in Greece, 106–108; Mary cult and, 394–395; as without sense of justice, 469n77. *See also* Roman women
Wood, Ellen Meiksins, 70, 77, 419n12
Wrede, William, 317, 319
Wycliff, John, 391

Xenophon, *Memorabilia*, 183

Yavetz, Z., 233, 262

Zealots, 297
Zeno, 191–194, 195, 265, 269, 270, 279
Zeus Eleutherios, cult of, 241–242